This is the first literary study of the career of Richard Rolle (d. 1349), a Yorkshire hermit and mystic who was one of the most widely read English writers of the late Middle Ages. Nicholas Watson proposes a new chronology of Rolle's writings, and offers the first literary analysis of a number of his works. He shows how Rolle, as a writer of passionate religious works in Latin and later in English, has as his principal focus the establishment of his own spiritual authority.

The book also addresses wider issues, suggesting a new way of looking at mystical writing in general, and challenging the prevailing view of the relationship between medieval and Renaissance attitudes to authors and authority.

CAMBRIDGE STUDIES IN MEDIEVAL LITERATURE 13

Richard Rolle and the Invention of Authority

CAMBRIDGE STUDIES IN MEDIEVAL LITERATURE 13

General Editor: Professor Alastair Minnis, Professor of Medieval Literature, University of York

Editorial Board
Professor Piero Boitani (Professor of English, Rome)
Professor Patrick Boyde, FBA (Serena Professor of Italian, Cambridge)
Professor John Burrow, FBA (Winterstoke Professor of English, Bristol)
Professor Alan Deyermond, FBA (Professor of Hispanic Studies, London)
Professor Peter Dronke, FBA (Professor of Medieval Latin Literature, Cambridge)
Tony Hunt (St Peter's College, Oxford)
Dr Nigel Palmer (Lecturer in Medieval German, Oxford)
Professor Winthrop Wetherbee (Professor of English, Cornell)

This series of critical books seeks to cover the whole area of literature written in the major medieval languages – the main European vernaculars, and medieval Latin and Greek – during the period *c.* 1100–*c.* 1500. Its chief aim is to publish and stimulate fresh scholarship and criticism on medieval literature, special emphasis being placed on understanding major works of poetry, prose and drama in relation to the contemporary culture and learning which fostered them.

Titles published
Dante's Inferno: *Difficulty and dead poetry*, by Robin Kirkpatrick
Dante and Difference: Writing in the Commedia, by Jeremy Tambling
Troubadours and Irony, by Simon Gaunt
Piers Plowman *and the New Anticlericalism*, by Wendy Scase
The Cantar de mio Cid: *Poetic creation in its economic and social contexts*, by Joseph Duggan
The Medieval Greek Romance, by Roderick Beaton
Reformist Apocalypticism and Piers Plowman, by Kathryn Kerby-Fulton
Dante and the Medieval Other World, by Alison Morgan
The Theatre of Medieval Europe: New research in early drama, edited by Eckehard Simon
The Book of Memory: A study of memory in medieval culture, by Mary J. Carruthers
Rhetoric, Hermeneutics and Translation in the Middle Ages: Academic traditions and vernacular texts, by Rita Copeland
The Arthurian Romances of Chrétien de Troyes: Once and future fictions, by Donald Maddox
Richard Rolle and the Invention of Authority, by Nicholas Watson

Richard Rolle and the Invention of Authority

NICHOLAS WATSON

Department of English,
University of Western Ontario

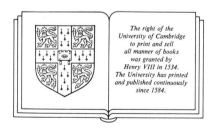

*The right of the
University of Cambridge
to print and sell
all manner of books
was granted by
Henry VIII in 1534.
The University has printed
and published continuously
since 1584.*

CAMBRIDGE UNIVERSITY PRESS

Cambridge
New York   Port Chester   Melbourne   Sydney

Published by the Press Syndicate of the University of Cambridge
The Pitt Building, Trumpington Street, Cambridge CB2 1RP
40 West 20th Street, New York, NY 10011-4211, USA
10 Stamford Road, Oakleigh, Victoria 3166, Australia

First published 1991

Printed in Great Britain at the University Press, Cambridge

*A catalogue record for this book is
available from the British Library*

Library of Congress cataloguing in publication data
Watson, Nicholas.
Richard Rolle and the invention of authority / Nicholas Watson.
p.   cm. – (Cambridge studies in medieval literature: 13)
Includes bibliographical references and index.
ISBN 0–521–39017–6
1. Rolle, Richard, of Hampole, 1290?–1349 – Authorship.
2. Devotional literature, English (Middle) – History and criticism.
3. Christian literature, Latin (Medieval and modern) – England –
History and criticism.
4. Authorship – Religious aspects – Christianity.
5. Authority in literature.
6. Mysticism – England.
I. Title.   II. Series.
PR2136.W38   1992   91–12812   CIP
821'.1–dc20

ISBN 0 521 39017 6   hardback

CE

Fortunately, to arrest these incoherencies, or rather, to vary them, a haggard, inspired-looking man now approached – a crazy beggar, asking alms under the form of peddling a rhapsodical tract, composed by himself, and setting forth his claim to some rhapsodical apostleship.

(Herman Melville, *The Confidence Man*, chapter 36)

Contents

Preface

The following chapters constitute a study both of Rolle's writing career as a whole and of most of his individual works. No literary study of Rolle has ever been written, and no general assessment of his career has been made in the sixty-odd years since the publication of Hope Emily Allen's *Writings Ascribed to Richard Rolle*; moreover, except in the field of editing, Rolle scholarship has advanced with disappointing sluggishness in this period. Under these circumstances, two approaches to writing a literary-critical analysis offered themselves. One was to present Rolle's works so far as possible in terms of their literary relations, investigating sources and analogues of particular passages, concepts, and stylistic peculiarities, with a view to placing them squarely within the relevant literary and devotional traditions. Given our growing knowledge of the history of Anglo-Latin literature and of English devotion such an approach would be profitable, and is increasingly becoming a scholarly *desideratum*. The other approach, the one I decided to take, was to focus less on Rolle's affiliations with tradition than on his idiosyncrasies, and to try to account for these in terms of the internal logic of his works and career. In adopting this approach, I have of course had to introduce a good deal of background material into the introduction, the notes, and certain parts of the text, if only in order to be able to distinguish 'tradition' from 'idiosyncrasy'. But so far as I can, I have told the highly particular story of Rolle's literary development as a self-coherent narrative in its own right. Only a detailed internal examination of Rolle's works, it seems to me, can hope to account for their bewildering and alien workings, and to prepare a way for a more fully contextualized appreciation of his place in English literary and religious history.

My assumptions about the character of Rolle's writings and my overall argument as to what accounts for their eccentricities become clearer as the study proceeds. Broadly I argue that his career as a writer, and the themes he developed throughout that career, are manifestations of an overriding concern with his own spiritual status, and that the force behind most of his works is the determination to establish and exercise a form of eremitic and mystical authority. In pursuing this theme, I am naturally concerned with more general issues, especially with the chronology of Rolle's writing career (the subject of an excursus on which my entire argument is based), with how his works are structured, and with the evangelistic or pastoral concerns they show for their readers. However, I do not give equal prominence to all areas of his literary activity. I have not conducted a formal study of his style, remarkable though that often is, and only touch on a number of his works, particularly the more conventional biblical commentaries; one long work, the *Latin Psalter*, presents so many problems in establishing a reliable text and determining its place in the chronology of Rolle's career that I have thought it better not to discuss it individually at all.

Although all Rolle's known works (except for *Super Magnificat* and *Super Mulierem Fortem*) have been edited or printed at one time or another, and have in many cases been translated, he is not an accessible writer. Two important works, *Super Psalmum Vicesimum* and *Super Canticum Canticorum*, still have to be read in thesis editions, and many others have not been printed since the sixteenth or seventeenth century; most of the translations are unsatisfactory. One of my preoccupations has hence had to be with conveying the tone and content of the works under discussion. I have consequently quoted widely and at length, translating the Latin quotations in a way which is meant both to render them correctly and to give a sense of Rolle's heterogeneous writing styles. For quotations I have used both sixteenth-century and modern editions, but have imposed a number of my own typographical conventions and readings on them. In Latin quotations (but not Middle English), *u* and *v* have their modern signification, long *i* (*j*) is represented by *i*, but spelling is not otherwise necessarily consistent. All biblical citations are quoted and translated in Rolle's sometimes distinctive versions, and are placed in italics; translations are again my own. I have not attempted in any sense to re-edit quoted passages – while this would in many cases have been a useful exercise, it would also have taken years. I have, however, checked editions against a reliable manuscript whenever I considered there to be serious uncertainties, and have repunctuated (silently) where I felt this was desirable. In translating and referring to passages in Latin, I have assumed that Rolle is mainly addressing male readers, often on the subject of himself or themselves, and have accordingly felt free to use masculine forms even where the Latin is able to avoid gender-specificity; on a similar principle, I refer to the readers of Rolle's English works with feminine pronouns.

This study grew out of interests in religious language and mysticism that were first aroused at school by Paul Bates and the late Trevor Park, and were developed in undergraduate studies at Cambridge with John Stevens and Helen Houghton. At Oxford I benefited enormously from the care lavished on the M.Phil. in medieval English studies by Pamela Gradon, Anne Hudson and Douglas Gray, and particularly from Vincent Gillespie's generous and imaginative supervision of my thesis, 'Argument and Audience in the *Incendium Amoris* of Richard Rolle' (1984), in which I first worked out my view of Rolle; Vincent also read an earlier draft of this book, and made a number of suggestions which had a major impact on how I set about revising it. This book acquired its present title and took something approaching its present form as a Ph.D. thesis at the University of Toronto (1987), where I

Preface

had help from several more people. The late Denton Fox was a tolerant and conscientious supervisor and helped me to maintain an all-important sense of humour about theses and mystics; I shall always be grateful to him for his encouragement, unfailing interest and eminently practical kindness. George Rigg suggested Cambridge University Press as a possible publisher, gave essential advice over many problems relating to the Latin texts and how they should be translated, and read the whole thesis at least twice with long-suffering enthusiasm; I would have taken much longer and written much less well without his support. Both during the writing of the thesis and the long process of altering and expanding it into a book, Claire Fanger has been my most faithful reader, making hundreds of comments, corrections and suggestions, most of which I have acted on; she insisted I take the art of writing with proper seriousness, introduced me to hagiography, corrected my translations, and was the best sounding-board I could have had. I would like to thank all these people for their help. The incisive (and invariably justified) comments and criticisms of Alastair Minnis, my general editor, precipitated the final revision of my manuscript, and for this – at least now it is done – I am also most grateful. Finally, I have enjoyed the continuing support of several universities and foundations, without which I could never have completed my research. In Toronto I was the recipient of one of the Connaught Foundation's far-sighted fellowships for non-Canadian students (1984–1986), and latterly of a fellowship from the Social Sciences, Humanities and Research Council of Canada (1986–1987). S.S.H.R.C. have also financed three years of postdoctoral research, two at The Memorial University of Newfoundland, the third at McMaster University, who helped fund my year as a Canada Research Fellow. It is a great pleasure to be able to thank all these institutions for their help, and to record my gratitude to them.

This book is dedicated to two people without whom it would not have been written at all. The first is my wife, Anne Savage, who persuaded me to embark on a Ph.D. and has had to live with the consequences ever since. My conception of Rolle's career owes much to her passionate attention to language and to her awareness of the ways in which words both mask and reveal intention; if the picture which emerges from this book is psychologically plausible, this is largely thanks to her. The second is the great scholar of medieval English religiosity Hope Emily Allen, without whom we might still know hardly anything about Rolle, and whose *Writings Ascribed to Richard Rolle* has been my constant, immeasurably helpful, companion. She is often wrong, occasionally wildly so, but her bemused fascination with her subject is enlivening and (under the circumstances) marvellously benign. She has prevented my own fascination with Rolle from hardening into the dislike which, faced with so intolerant and sometimes so dislikeable a subject, we seem both to have found a temptation, and for this I owe her more than a merely scholarly gratitude.

Department of English   1 July 1990
University of Western Ontario

xiii

Abbreviations

Allen	Allen, Hope Emily *Writings Ascribed to Richard Rolle, Hermit of Hampole, and Materials for his Biography.* MLA Monograph Series 3. New York, Heath and Co. (1927)
BL	British Library, London
Bodley	Bodleian Library, Oxford
CUL	Cambridge University Library
EETS (os)	Early English Text Society, original series
English Writings	Allen, Hope Emily, ed. *English Writings of Richard Rolle, Hermit of Hampole.* Oxford, Clarendon Press (1931)
MED	*Middle English Dictionary*
PL	*Patrologia Latina*, ed. J.-P. Migne (Paris, 1844–1864)

INTRODUCTION

Contexts: three preliminary essays

I: READING MYSTICAL WRITING

Mystical writers have long been in a special category for the Christian Church. In their role as reporters of direct contact with the divine, they have necessarily been highly regarded, in so far as they help to validate the central mysteries of the faith. Yet they are also often seen as challenging the proper understanding of those mysteries, hence as constituting a threat to the theology and political structure of the Church. Since the Church is a hierarchic institution which as such has a vested and conservative interest in its own continuity, this negative view is inevitable and in a sense valid. Mystical writing fuses subjective experience and expression with absolute declarations as to the nature of truth; however submissive it may be in fact, it is thus heady and potentially uncontrollable, always in a position to lay powerful claims to an authority which lies outside and above ecclesiastical institutions, even to deny the authority which inheres in those institutions. Mystical writing – an individual's report of a moment or moments of mediation between heaven and earth – is also by its nature complex; it has always been difficult even for those ecclesiastics who are well disposed to mysticism to determine what is being said, and then to decide whether it is consistent with orthodoxy. Thus it is not surprising that while there are many examples of successful relationships between visionaries and the ecclesiastical establishments of their time (St Catherine of Siena, St Bridget of Sweden), there are also cases in which the relationship has been difficult (John Ruusbroec, Meister Eckhart), or disastrous (Marguerite Porete). For the more daring of these writers, difficulties tend to persist; Eckhart's confident 'liberty of spirit' still alarms as many readers as it excites, and for many of the same reasons that it alarmed some of his contemporaries.

Mystics are also in a special category for literary critics. Since most of the modes of literature that critics traditionally encounter are considered forms of fiction, the manner in which mystical writing fuses two categories which it insists we treat as *fact*, the personal and the transcendent, renders it especially problematic and interesting. On the verbal 'surface' of the text, the extreme difficulty of describing experience of the divine in human language challenges the mystical writer to adopt complex metaphoric and expository strategies. These in turn challenge the critic, who has the task of elucidating an

I

encounter between an inevitably limited and formal religious language and an experience which is at once of the utmost spontaneity (whatever the preparation that precedes it) and of absolute significance. It is quite as hard to analyse the literary ramifications of this encounter as it is to gauge its orthodoxy. For example, there are no literary criteria with which to assess the claims many mystics make that their depictions of eternal felicity are wholly inadequate. To take these claims seriously is to become involved with theological questions of the relationship between language and divine truth. But to fail to take them seriously – to call them 'inexpressibility *topoi*' and leave it at that – is to resign any possibility of writing a real account of the text.

Much of the literary criticism that has been devoted to mystical writing starts from some such attitude of resignation, approaching the verbal surface of a text with a mixture of aesthetic and religious awe, and employing its own tropes of inexpressibility to avoid having to look any further: 'We must leave these questions to practising mystics', or worse, 'What Mother Julian meant we cannot know in this life.' More usefully, other commentators focus on the didactic structures of mystical texts and the responses they were intended to evoke, challenging the assumption, deeply embedded in the modern resurgence of interest in mysticism, that mystics are like Romantic poets obsessed with the desire to express their experience for its own sake. But the problem with any simple rejection of this anachronistic reading is that it is partly valid; mystics sometimes *are* rather like Romantic poets, and approaches that ignore this fact also ignore a vital feature of their writing: the highly charged relationship they have with what they write. Certainly we cannot account for all the processes through which mystics translate their experience into language, since their experience is ineffable. But the psychological events which lie behind any work of literature are ineffable, inasmuch as they must be expressed in the formal medium of language and can never be recovered by readers. Even where the nature of those events is important to our understanding of a literary work, or is one of its major themes (as in some of the poetry of Wordsworth), we can do no more than to indicate the ways in which experience is formalized and deflected by language. As literary critics, then, we can engage as seriously with mystical as we can with any other kind of writing – and do so (as I hope to show) on our own ground, without adopting the reductionism of either of the approaches I have mentioned. A theological reading of a mystical work may assess (for example) what doctrinal assertions the work makes and how these relate or contribute to Christian orthodoxy; sensitive theological readers like Edmund Colledge or David Knowles are preoccupied with the balance of doctrinal positions taken by mystical writers. The literary-critical equivalent of such a reading will focus instead on what we can call a mystical writer's 'predicament' in formulating doctrinal positions, articulating an appropriately didactic discourse and describing mystical experience; it will look at the specifically *mundane* pressures that beset a mystical text, impelling it towards complex and ambiguous claims for its own status as an embodiment of truth.

The ambiguities of these claims derive in part from factors intrinsic to a mystic's experience, in part from the difficult relationship such experience creates between a mystic and the ecclesiastical establishment. This last term must be understood broadly, as including (1) the ecclesiastical reader whose interests are those of the political hierarchy of the Church, (2) the tradition of Christian teaching expressed through the writings the Church accepts as authoritative and (3) (most important if also somewhat intangible) the psychic structure of the mystic's own inner commitment to the Church as authority and comforter. Mystical experience itself may be more or less planned, or be a bolt from the blue. Either way, unmediated contact with the divine must affect all areas of a mystic's life, for such contact both annihilates the pretensions of everything less than the divine and confers a special status on whoever has experienced it. The mystic's inherited view of her or his relationship with the ecclesiastical establishment is hence threatened. That establishment must retain its role if the mystic is to remain committed to an orthodox stance; to abandon such a stance is to risk a loss of spiritual balance and a fall into spiritual anarchy, as well as the tangible perils that can result from falling foul of the ecclesiastical authorities. Thus the import of the experience may have to be defined forcibly in terms of Christian orthodoxy. Yet conversely, and in spite of the risks, the authority of tradition and establishment will also have to be redefined in relation to the authority that the experience and its recipient now have. For a mystic to allow such redefinitions to occur is to allow the very fabric of her or his intellectual and emotional constitution to be challenged: perhaps a painful, certainly a dislocating, process. The decision to proclaim mystical experience in a written form makes this process explicit, and thus even more problematic. The difficulty of mystical texts is not only a product of the ineffability of experience; it reflects the fact that, by writing, the mystic is making a bid to articulate and institutionalize a new self-understanding and a recreated attitude to the earthly Church in terms of mystical experience – and is doing so in front of an audience that always in principle includes the whole Church, earthly and heavenly. A host of inner doubts, political and spiritual fears, and anticipations of criticism flood in.

Not surprisingly, therefore, some mystical writers do not project a clear or consistent view of the status of their experience. They may still be in doubt not only as to their own status and that of the language in which they are proclaiming their experience of the divine, but also as to the kind of deference they owe to Christian orthodoxy. For example, can the recipient of mystical experience claim to be a soul chosen by God for perfection? Are the mystic's words divinely inspired, or do they partake of the fallibility of all human discourse? Can the content of the revelations which the mystic is proclaiming be reconciled with the norms of Christian orthodoxy? The difficulties raised by such questions are intensified by the gulf between mystical experience and the mystic's understanding, and made even more acute by the implied presence of a reader. The reader may be a disciple, in which case she or he must be protected and edified. Or the implied reader may be a critic; anxiety as to the reaction of ecclesiastical authorities to what is said (or, as perhaps with Porete's *Mirouer des simples ames*, a desire to mislead such authority) is a major cause of the ambiguity of mystical texts. Yet the most critical reader of all is likely to be the mystical writer, for whom every statement must be assessed in relation to its orthodoxy and usefulness, its confirmity to the inner truth of the revelations, and its effect on the writer's own spiritual balance. To write a mystical work is to be placed in the demanding and vulnerable role of the prophet.

All these complexities are evident in a work like Julian of Norwich's *Revelation of Love*. Although it took well over twenty years to write, this work is still almost overwhelmed by the inexpressibility of the visions on which it is based. Julian overcomes her problems of expression only by giving readers the sense that the circumlocutions and repetitions which result from her difficulties are the most effective possible image of the distance between God and her own human understanding. But her predicament has other dimensions, too, for she is anxiously unclear as to the status of her visions, of her role as a visionary, and of her book, and has a lively sense of the dangers (which she regards as closely related) of succumbing to pride and succumbing to unorthodox statement. These things further deflect her intentions and modify the direction of the work that she writes – as is strikingly shown in the first version of her book, which suppresses all mention of what the second version sees as the most profound of her visions. Although she emphasizes the supreme importance of the experience she has been granted, she is anxious to avoid asserting her own importance; the showings, she thus insists, were sent to all, not merely to her. Yet this act of humility paradoxically places great emphasis on her own role as a writer. Only through her book can others apprehend the revelations for themselves; if God intended them for all, her book must be regarded as an authoritative vehicle for them. Thus her written Revelation assumes the transcendent authority of the one she received from God, and its author is thrown unwittingly into the very forefront of her work.

Such is one of several essentially circular processes that give Julian's work a tension which coexists with her much admired serenity, and that show how difficulties and dangers persist in the articulation of her experience in spite of that serenity. Once one has recognized the existence of this tension, in the work of Julian or of another mystic, it becomes impossible to regard the mystic's written utterance as the straightforward, if imperfect declaration of transcendent experience it is often thought to be. Mystical writing becomes (*inter alia*) the expression of an intricate predicament of an essentially 'this worldly' kind. Harold Bloom has made fashionable a Freudian view of the Romantic artist's relationship with a literary 'parent' as governed by an 'anxiety of influence': a need to emphasize originality by concealing the artist's deep affinities with one or more previous writers (Bloom 1973). Julian's predicament would seem to be the inverse of this: an anxiety of originality or authority. Some such anxiety is fundamental to much mystical writing – and it is certainly so to the career of Richard Rolle.

Rolle wrote copiously in several different genres, the bulk of his work consisting of biblical commentary and didactic instruction, his preferred literary modes including apocalypse and satire. Yet all his writings are in important ways centred around his experiences as a solitary and as a mystic, even where these are not his overt subjects – for these experiences validate the rest of his life, as they validate his writing, and his belief in his own authority. He is a scriptural commentator because his union with God causes his interpretations to be inspired; he is a guide to the contemplative life because his own experience of it is exemplary and should thus be regarded as normative; he prophesies the end of all things, exhorts sinners to repentance and announces the love between God and humanity that can be attained on earth, because having attained such love himself he is of all humanity the one with authority to do these things. One could not easily find a mystical writer who generalizes from his particular experience to a greater extent, or with greater satisfaction, than does Rolle.

This process of generalization is so complete as to seem at first almost automatic and devoid of any sense of difficulty: as if Rolle, that most extroverted of mystics, merely declares the significance of his experience, with an apparent disregard for the constraints of authority. Of course this is not so, and could never be so for any medieval Christian, whether orthodox or heretical. In practice most of what Rolle wrote (at least in Latin) is permeated by his consciousness of real or potential opposition, by the need to balance assertions of authority with deference to others and by an acute, often shrill, vulnerability. Both as a result of this consciousness and of Rolle's fundamental beliefs, his interpretation of his experiences is already shaped by Christian orthodoxy, as it is by his interpretations of the Bible and by the exemplary models he adopts. Throughout his work he presents himself in terms of existing personae: the Desert Fathers, the saintly king and psalmist David, the Apostle; the repentant sinner, the nightingale, the perfect soul, the solitary contemplative. These figures are intended to define his relation to the earthly and heavenly Church in such a way as to deflect criticism. On one level their deployment is thus a response to the difficulties he shares with other mystical writers; while their use is often didactic they form an important part of his assertion of his high status in the earthly Church – for such an assertion is necessary if his writings are to be accorded the authority he believes they merit.

But although Rolle's overt claim to high status and enjoyment of his own spiritual importance distinguish him radically from Julian as a personality, they do not enable him to escape the ambiguities that beset her. In much of his writing similar ambiguities emerge as literary problems which reflect what are clearly personal uncertainties. These problems include an inconsistent view of the status of his words which parallels Julian's uncertainty – except that in Rolle's case, characteristically, the centre of greatest difficulty is not so much in how he views himself, but in how he thinks others will view him. How, for example, can he act to convince readers of his sanctity (the quality that is to mark him out as possessing true authority), when a deep and self-abnegatory humility is traditionally thought of as basic to the saintly personality? The sense of incoherence that problems like this create in the modern reader of Rolle has led some to regard him as self-obsessed to a point just this side of sanity; like Margery Kempe he has been subjected to a pseudo-psychoanalysis that attempts to label the ways in which he was 'abnormal' rather than to comprehend the nature of his difficulties. While he never comes to seem anything other than idiosyncratic, on closer inspection such difficulties turn out to be manifestations of a literary and personal predicament as complex, and perhaps as unavoidable, as Julian's.

Yet part of that predicament, for Rolle as not for Julian, is precisely his own unconsciousness of its details. In some of his most important works he seems imperfectly aware of the tense relationship between his assertiveness and his need to convince others of his humility, and fails to recognize the incongruity in the juxtaposition of his need to establish that his writings are authoritative with his necessary insistence that his authority does not require establishment, since it already exists. Such a lack of self-awareness suggests that it is almost as important to him that he should avoid thinking of his own writing in these strategic terms as that he should convince others of his straightforwardness. Many of his works thus have to manœuvre their way towards a solution to his literary predicament without even their writer allowing himself to become conscious of what he is doing. Such works become clearer when we notice how Rolle's necessary unconsciousness of contradictions in his writing does not emerge merely negatively, in bald manifestations of his naivety; it operates positively and strategically, diverting both reader and writer from a naked perception of the latter's problematic position.

On this level of unarticulated intentions, Rolle is an unconsciously subtle writer – an oxymoron vital to reading him successfully – and here, if anywhere, he justifies the dislike that many of his readers feel for him. Yet here he is also, from a critical viewpoint, at his most interesting; for his works (which are overtly didactic and evangelistic) show a successive, and, in his own terms, successful, working out of difficulties such as those mentioned. This process involves a gradual comprehension, articulation and reconciliation of contradictions and difficulties, and the realizing of a literary persona that is largely in control of all of these difficulties, and finally even of the process of their articulation. This persona is the final stage in Rolle's prolonged attempt to manifest his authority; it justifies the whole enterprise of his life and writing, and proves, in the terms he has set up for himself, that his view of his own importance as a contemplative is correct. The argument here is as far as it could be from reiterating the prevailing view that after a period of instability Rolle 'settled down', for the mature works in which this persona is most loudly manifested, *Melos Amoris* and *Super Lectiones Mor-*

tuorum, are even more assertive than the less integrated works; indeed, in these works assertion becomes a basic literary device.

This study involves a reappraisal of the shape of Rolle's career through analysis of the structures of his works, and of his intentions – evangelistic, pastoral, apologetic – in writing them. As with all mystical writers, Rolle touches from time to time on the inexpressibility of his experience, evolving his own rhetorical music to overcome his difficulty of expression. As with all mystical writers, he is concerned with enhancing the spiritual lives of his readers, arguing a highly particular case as to what such enhancement involves. However, the thesis maintained here is that the most important organizing principle in Rolle's works is his attempt to develop an assertive yet exemplary persona, in response to a complex predicament at the heart of which is the problem of the mystical writer's authority.

To this point, my account of the relationship between mystic, establishment and the idea of authority has posed as ahistorical. While its examples have been taken from the fourteenth century, and the term 'mystic' has been used to describe a Christian operating within a broadly Catholic milieu, I have allowed the implication to stand that a similar structure of tensions and oppositions could be found in any period or religious context. To a limited extent this is probably true. Yet it is of course also true that the details of the predicaments of mystical writers vary fundamentally from century to century, place to place and even individual to individual, according to the ways in which the Church, religious authority, mysticism and writing itself are regarded. The rest of this introduction is accordingly concerned with a more historically contextualized approach to some of the matters already raised in general terms – authority, the nature of mystical experience, the relationship between authority and experience – which attempts to delineate parts of the scene on which Rolle's particular drama was played out.

II: THE STRUCTURE OF THE PERFECT LIFE

By the early fourteenth century, a number of large developments in late medieval religiosity had come to maturity, several of which are of particular relevance for contemporary concepts of religious authority. These can mostly be seen as outgrowths of what Brian Stock depicts as the increasing dominance of texts and textuality in the eleventh and twelfth centuries: the period in which 'oral discourse effectively began to function within a universe of communications governed by texts . . . [which] thereby emerged as a reference system both for everyday activities and for giving shape to larger vehicles of explanation' (1983, p. 3). The first and most general of these developments can be called the 'bureaucratization' of religion: the enormous extension of the Church's power and articulation of its structure from the eleventh century on – encompassing (*inter alia*) the growth of a more centralized and powerful papal government, and the formation of new monastic and fraternal orders in the twelfth and thirteenth centuries, as well as the drive to reform the secular clergy and laity initiated by the fourth Lateran Council in 1215. This process was responsible for the production of a huge and ever-increasing quantity of writing; indeed, the ecclesiastical structure that emerged was so complex that it could only have been sustained by writing. In principle, however flexible the situation was in practice, the late-medieval Church defined the position of each one of its members, and the relationships that existed between them; thus it claimed political, legal and social authority. It also aimed to define the boundaries of thought, to distinguish between a realm of orthodoxy and one of heterodoxy; increasingly, by attempting to formalize and refine its own canonization procedures, it tried to reserve to itself the right to decide which individuals lived such holy lives that they were worthy of veneration (Vauchez 1981); it safeguarded its own future, by bestowing more authority on the voices of some of its members than others, and by placing great emphasis on the moral worth of an attitude of obedience to its dictates. Thus it attempted to enter the minds of its members in a more intimate way than before, in order to realize, as fully as possible, its responsibilities as the body of Christ on earth. Hence in the late Middle Ages a religious issue was also an 'ecclesiastical' one, almost inevitably impinged upon by some part of the vast network of assumptions, arguments and definitions that constituted the weightily textual presence of the Church.

Even if he had been more isolated, intellectually and physically, than he was, Rolle could not have embarked on any part of his project without being conscious of this network, and without trying to accommodate it. It provided a structure, a discourse, in which his sense of his identity could be developed and through which he could communicate it to others. It is true that his writings often express indifference to the earthly Church, as though he located himself outside its forms. But these gestures do not stand up to examination; indeed, they provide good instances of the way in which, far from being aloof from the late-medieval Church, Rolle's entire career is an attempt to claim his place *within* the network of ecclesiastical relationships. For example, *Incendium Amoris* (caps. 31–32) claims that although Rolle is still alive, he is a participant in the songs of the angels in heaven, and can therefore take little part in the earthly song of liturgical worship; he continues to attend Mass when he must, but does not necessarily participate in the chanting of plainsong, and will not – in spite, one gathers, of having a fine singing voice – join the choir. (The passage is quoted and discussed in detail on pp. 136–137.) On the face of it, these chapters look like an assertion of freedom from the constraints of ecclesiastical norms by an anti-establishment mystic absorbed in an untrammelled communion with heavenly reality. But the gesture of refusal they make depends on Rolle's awareness of a pressure of obligation, which he here asserts he can and should sidestep. Such pressure is a sign of his continuing involvement with the very structure he claims to have transcended. For he does not simply engage in angelic communion: he writes about it, in order to explain why it is better than liturgical communion, and, by writing, reaffirms his engagement with the Visible Church on a new level, the level of discourse. His apologia places the Church's liturgical worship and his experience of song in opposition to one another, as mutually exclusive ideals (the sound of one blots out the other); at the same time, a cross-current of remarks in these chapters cautiously notes that he continues to fulfil his ecclesiastical obligations of attendance at Mass. More important, the structure of opposition he employs is itself part of a reassuringly learned tradition of argument by contraries. Thus the reader is confronted not with an expression of anti-establishment mystical experience, but with a hierarchy of rules and ideals, which occupy far more of the foreground of these chapters than the harmonious pleasures of angelic communion. Rolle's engagement in the affairs of the Church, which the text pretends is a thing of the past, immediately re-enters by a back door. What he claims is an experiential relationship with religious truths, which can only occur outside the ecclesiastically appointed means for communion with God, proves to be permeated by a characteristic awareness of texts and normative structures.

Many of these 'normative structures' are invoked in the following chapters, as Rolle's life and writing touches on them, or reflects a sense of their presence; for example, part of Chapter 1 assesses his career in relation to hagiographic models of behaviour, while several chapters take note of his sense of the boundaries of orthodoxy. But one such set of structures is of sufficient importance and complexity to merit preliminary attention: those that have to do with the definition of the highest form of the religious life. Medieval thinkers produced several models for determining what constituted, in an essential rather than an individual sense, a better, or 'more perfect', form of life than any other. Although these models are always constructed on formal and idealistic principles, the life they eventually uphold as the highest tends to be that represented by the section of the Church from which they emanate; thus Dominicans stress preaching, Carthusians contemplation, Benedictines a secluded but communal existence, and all these mutually contradictory models exist side by side, often scarcely affecting each other. Rolle in turn upholds his way of life, and it is vital to his programme to show that hermits of his own type are the most perfect of all. But the development of his model does not take place without reference to its rivals; on the contrary, much of this study bears witness to how hard he works to incorporate as many of them as he can into his own structure of thought.[1]

The oldest and most important model for deciding on the best form of human life originated in patristic commentaries on Luke 10.38–42, the story in which Christ commends Mary's rapt attention to his words more highly than Martha's conscientious concern for domestic details. Drawing on a broad distinction between one sort of lifestyle and another that goes back as far as Pythagoras, Origen and almost all later commentators treated Martha as a representative of the 'active' life, Mary of the 'contemplative'.[2] It followed from this analysis that Christ was praising a way of life that was centred on attention to himself as the 'pars optima' (see Luke 10.42), the best way to live. The manner in which such attention might best be bestowed was at first open to discussion. Christians in late antiquity naturally identified this life with the *otium liberale* of the scholar, and with any period of prayer and reading, as well as with the more extreme retirement of the Desert Fathers. As a result, the contemplative life was not initially identified as the property of any particular group within the Church; all Christians could contemplate, and all – as was stressed by both Augustine and Gregory – ought to be prepared to leave contemplation from time to time for the life of service to others.[3] However, in time the term 'contemplative life' came to be used more and more as a professional designation for monks, nuns, anchorites and hermits who had the leisure (*otium* again) to give their whole attention to God. Those who did not – lay Christians and the secular priests who ministered to them – were thought of as living the active life, and the two kinds of life, as distinct professions, were regarded as for the most part mutually exclusive.[4] The practice of the corporal works of mercy, obedience to moral and divine law, and, in the case of priests, the exercise of the office of preaching defined the limits of the active life; the life of prayer and continuous devotion to God was the preserve of the contemplative. Coenobites and solitaries were thus assumed to be essentially superior to others in their way of life. Such a conclusion suited the earlier medieval Church, which was dominated by monks, and was still accepted by many until the end of the Middle Ages and beyond. The late fourteenth-century *Cloud of Unknowing*, for example, is confident that the path to perfection leads through the 'common' or lay life, to the 'special' life of the monk, to the 'singular' one of the solitary, and thence to the practice of the highest forms of contemplation (cap. 1).[5]

The continuing dominance of this model of thought in some circles can be seen in a group of *quaestiones* which build another model upon it, by asking: 'Is the solitary life more perfect than the life lived in community?'[6] The question is important only because those who ask it assume that the eremitic and the coenobitic life are the two forms of the 'pars optima', the better of which can be considered the best life of all. While some disagreed with the conclusions of these *quaestiones* – a scribe even wrote at the end of one, 'Explicit de reclusis exemplar falsum et incorrectum' (Oliger 1934, p. 259) – the answer given was always that the solitary life was highest. Benedict had ruled that a monk could not leave his monastery for the world, but could to become a hermit; Cuthbert would not have become an anchorite after living as a monk had the solitary life not been superior (p. 256). To become perfect, the coenobitic life is best; to practice a perfection achieved, the solitary life – which, according to Augustine, is also the most beneficial to others (p. 247) – is superior. This is the conclusion assumed by the *Cloud* author, and widely accepted in principle. In the eleventh and twelfth centuries, Peter Damian, his hero Romualdus, and many others struggled to cut themselves off from the world in this belief; a certain glamour still attached to the eremitic life generations later. It seems likely that, had he wished to, Rolle could have operated entirely within the assumptions of these two models: that the contemplative life is better than the active; that the solitary life is a higher form of the contemplative life than the coenobitic; and thus that the solitary life is the most perfect of all the modes of Christian existence.

However, by the fourteenth century, other models were in existence, which regarded at least some of the traditional features of the active life, notably preaching, as integral parts of what it meant to live perfectly. Speaking generally, these models returned to the roots of the traditional active-contemplative dichotomy, in order to challenge some of the ways in which it had ossified, and to emphasize matters which it ignored. Augustine and Gregory, who regarded the active and contemplative lives as states which no Christian should neglect, sometimes mentioned a third state, which combined both lives and was better than either; this was the life of the preacher, sometimes known in the late Middle Ages as the 'mixed' life.[7] For Gregory, the ideal preacher is a holy man, advanced in contemplation, who 'imparts to others in the active life what he has received in the contemplative' (Steele 1979, p. 141). A contemplative pastor does wrong if he neglects to take preaching seriously (Butler 1927, p. 257, citing *Regula Pastoralis* II.7). Preaching is in its way a nobler office than contemplation alone: 'Preachers do not only restrain themselves from vices, but also inhibit others from sin, lead them to faith and instruct them in good behaviour' (*Homilia in Ezechiel* II.iv.6, quoted in Steele 1979, p. 45). Even though the origins of the two approaches are the same, this kind of language encourages interpretations of the perfect life that differ markedly from the model in which the professional contemplative Mary is by definition superior to the secular Martha.[8]

Such a treatment of the perfect life was bound to appeal to at least two groups in the late Middle Ages. The friars practised a way of life which could not be confined by stereotyped portraits of the contemplative, since they moved about (thus attracting charges from conservatives that they were *girovagi*, wandering monks), preached and performed works of mercy. Secular priests were also preachers, and were made increasingly conscious of the dignity of this office by the mass of thirteenth- and fourteenth-century pastoral material which stresses its importance, defining who it is that can preach, and the characteristics they must possess.[9] Pastoral and preaching manuals often point out that only priests who have the cure of souls, and others with a legitimate licence, are allowed to preach; Rolle's contemporary, Robert of Basevorn, follows canon law when he writes in his *Forma Praedicandi* (1322) that nobody, lay or religious, may preach unless permitted to do so by a bishop or the Pope (pp. 241–242). Manuals also elevate the office of preaching by stressing that it is to be distinguished from teaching (Gillespie 1980 explores this distinction in detail). Thus the first chapter of the early fifteenth-century *Speculum Christiani* states:

Richard Rolle and the invention of authority

A Grete differens es be-twene prechynge and techynge. Prechynge es in a place where es clepynge to-gedyr or foluynge of pepyl in holy dayes in chyrches or other certeyn places and tymes ordeyned ther-to. And it longeth to hem that been ordeynede ther-to, the whych haue iurediccion and auctorite, and to noon othyr. Techynge es that eche body may enforme and teche hys brothyr in euery place and in conable tyme, os he sees that it be spedful. For this es a gostly almes-dede, to whych euery man es bounde that hath cunnynge.

(2.5–13)[10]

Teaching was an office which anyone competent could and should practise in private when appropriate and necessary; according to Henry of Ghent's late thirteenth-century *Summa Quaestionum*, 'even' women, though barred from any kind of preaching, could teach other women in private (cited in Minnis 1986, p. 90). Teaching was a spiritual work of mercy, which might on occasion save souls. Preaching, on the other hand, was a public and officially sanctioned office, the specific and constant aim of which was the salvation of the souls of its hearers. In the thirteenth-century discussions of the *magisterium* of the preacher (see Leclerq 1946), preaching, as Minnis states, 'was described in the most fulsome of terms. According to [the Dominican] Humbert of Romans . . . the office of preaching is apostolic, angelic and divine; its foundation, which is Holy Scripture, excels all other sciences' (Minnis 1986, p. 89, citing similar statements in preaching manuals by Alan of Lisle, John Bromyard and pseudo-Aquinas). Accounts of the rewards of the blessed sometimes claim that preachers will be given a special aureole (golden crown), similar to that to be given to virgins (who include religious and secular priests) and martyrs. Book VII of Hugh of Strasbourg's *Compendium Theologicae Veritatis* (caps. 29–30), a work well known to Rolle, states that as martyrs overcome the world and virgins the flesh, so preachers overcome the devil, 'whom they expel not only from themselves but from the hearts of others'. This aureole is not reserved exclusively for preachers, but it is closely associated with them.[11]

With the office of preaching restricted to professionals and praised in these terms, it is not surprising that high expectations should be had of its practitioners, and high claims made on their behalf. In the context of the pragmatic discussions of the *officium praedicatoris* analysed by Leclerq and Minnis, these were often tempered by a clear sense of the gap between the lives of many actual preachers and the dignity of the office they filled. Yet the first chapter of *Speculum Christiani* is uncompromising in demanding from its priestly readers sufficient religious knowledge, purity of life, and con-scientiousness in teaching the articles of faith; those who fail to measure up are said (in words taken from Gregory) to be worthy of damnation. And in the more theoretical contexts of discussions of the states of life, the office of the preacher is sometimes outrightly treated as the highest of religious callings, combining, as it does in Gregory's writings, the best features of active and contemplative states. In his tortuous treatise on the states of life (*Summa Theologica* II.ii, qq. 179–189), Thomas Aquinas moves close to this view, stating that prelates are more perfect than religious, since they are in the position of perfecters, rather than seekers after perfection (q. 184, art. 7, referring specifically to preaching). This claim depends on an earlier argument (q. 182, arts. 1–3) that the prelate combines active and contemplative lives, and that both can be practised without mutual hindrance; the life of the prelate is thus 'mixed'.[12] Again, Steele (p. 242) quotes a remark by Jacob de Voragine (from the *Sermones de Sanctis*) which sums up a standard position: 'There is active life, which is the "good part", contemplative life, which is the "better part", and a life composed of both, which is the "best part".' This is the life which *Piers Plowman* (at least in the A text) calls 'Dobest':

> Dobest is a-boue bothe [Dowel and Dobet] and bereth a bisschopes crosse,
> Is hoket atte ende to holden hem in good lyf.
> A pyk is in that potent to punge a-doun the wikkede,
> That wayten eny wikkednesse Dowel to teone. (A IX.86–89)

Although questions still remain, there is little doubt that, as Langland originally conceived them, Dowel, Dobet and Dobest were meant as equivalents of active, contemplative and 'mixed' lives; that he saw the last of these, in which action and contemplation are combined, as the highest form of the spiritual life; and that, like Aquinas, he associated it with the life of bishops.[13] Finally, Richard of St Victor's *De Quattuor Gradibus Violentae Caritatis* describes what seems to be a version of 'mixed' life as the highest degree of love, in which the soul is so insatiable for God, and so aware that she cannot have him wholly in this life, that she 'descends beneath herself' (177.11–12), and 'humbles herself' (173.5–6) by serving others. After her espousal, marriage and union with Christ, in this fourth stage she undergoes confinement (*puerperium*), and delivers her offspring (153.20–29). Preaching is not mentioned as central to this fourth stage, but *puerperium* is clearly a metaphor for evangelism: the fourth degree of love seems to be an affective version of the 'pars optima' of 'mixed' life (Pankhurst 1976, p. 207).

If 'mixed' life had been as well defined as the active and contemplative states, the model of perfection in which it represents the highest ideal might well have ossified in the same way the straightforward Martha–Mary model did; in that case, preachers would have been enshrined at the top of one hierarchy of the states of life, as solitaries were at the top of another. As should by now be evident, there are signs that some such process did take place. But in practice 'mixed' life, which had no firm biblical basis for existence, and was defined merely as a combination of features of the other two lives, was too fluid and vague a concept to take a firm hold in any one form. Indeed, it is far from clear how widespread or specific medieval knowledge of the concept was. For all their interest in the dignity of preachers, preaching and pastoral manuals show so little interest in the Gregorian notion of the preacher as contemplative, or in the active-contemplative model in general, that it is doubtful that most preachers thought of themselves as practising the 'mixed' life. The term itself is relatively rare – to the extent that its Middle English equivalent, 'medled lyf' may not have been used until it was popularized, at the end of the fourteenth century, by Walter Hilton (Steele 1979, pp. 218–219, borne out by MED's article on 'medled'). It is true, on the other hand, that contemplatives sometimes describe themselves as blending contemplation with action (as we shall see shortly). But it is not always clear whether they are thinking explicitly in terms of a triadic model of active, contemplative and 'mixed' lives, or whether we are in the presence of some other model. For example, writings about contemplation often refer generally to its *utilitas* to humanity. In the *quaestio* about monks and solitaries by Aquinas mentioned earlier, Augustine is quoted as stating that hermits greatly benefit humanity by their example and their prayers (Oliger 1934, p. 247; see Augustine's *De Moribus Ecclesiae* 1.31). In *The Cloud of Unknowing* we find the same claim made (with doubt-defying vagueness) for the spiritual exercise the author is enjoining on his eremitic disciple: 'Alle men leuyng in erþe ben wonderfuli holpen of þis werk, þou wost not how' (9.22–23). It is easy enough to discern a general relationship between this *topos* and the idea of 'mixed' life, but it would require extensive research to determine precisely what that relationship is. 'Mixed' life is only a single strand in a varied tradition of thinking about spiritual *utilitas*.

Given this fact, it is not surprising to find discussions of 'mixed' life which (for all Gregory's praise) do not regard it as the highest form of the spiritual life. A good example is to be found in the brilliant variations which Hilton performs on 'medled lyf' in his English epistle *Mixed Life*, drawing widely on the literature of the lives (as Clark 1979 shows) for the unusual purpose of persuading a layman, who wished to leave his home and his dependents in order to live as a contemplative, to stay where he was.[14] Just as 'prelates and oþire curates', he says, divide their time, 'sumtyme [to] vsen werkes of actif lif, in help and sustenaunce of hem silf and of here suggetis . . . and sumtyme for to leuen al manere bisynesse outeward, and ʒeue hem vnto praieres and meditacions' (145–152), so some 'temporal men' must do the same, whatever their inclinations. Those who follow this 'medled lyf' do as Christ did (177–195), and follow the 'ordre of charite' (166). But while it is necessary for some, 'mixed' life is of less absolute value than the contemplative (223–237), just as labour at Christ's feet is of less ultimate value than labour at his head (273–310). The relatively low status Hilton accords the activity of priests and 'temporal men' is of special significance in this epistle, where he is trying to praise their state as highly as he can, in order to give his correspondent some outlet for his spiritual ambitions. We find essentially the same view expressed in the Carthusian Nicholas Love's translation of pseudo-Bonaventure's *Meditationes Vitae Christi*, the *Mirrour of the Blessyd Lyf of Jesu Christ*; here preaching is described as merely the higher part of the active life (p. 159, cited in Steele, pp. 138ff.). In spite of their sensitivity to the needs of those in the world, the long-standing monastic ideal of the contemplative life was still potent for these writers.

There is, then, no clear definition of the 'mixed' life, and no single answer to the question of whether it corresponds to the 'perfect' life. Steele (1979) finds so many different applications of the concept that he sensibly comes to no general conclusion about its status, suggesting that it remains, on the whole, the designation of a professional activity: 'An acceptable summary of the evidence might suggest that "medled lyf" was thought to be not, indeed, the exclusive, but the special preserve of those officially charged with the spiritual care of the faithful' (p. 224). This is my general conclusion also. Yet counter-examples present themselves in response even to this cautious formulation. The *Consuetudines* of Guigo, which lay down the rule of life of the Carthusian order, places great emphasis on copying books: 'So that, since we cannot do so with our mouths, we may preach the word of God with our hands' (cap. 28.3, discussed in Gillespie 1980). Here the most secluded of the contemplative orders lays claim to a special kind of preaching role, acknowledging a duty to engage in activities of more tangible spiritual *utilitas* than their daily round of prayer and ascesis. It seems that 'mixed' life was a concept of such plasticity that almost all could regard themselves as sharing in its rather uncertain prestige.

This sketch of medieval models of the perfect life, and of the prestige attached to various forms of the religious life, has had to raise many issues and invoke a substantial body of religious literature. It is interesting, then, that while it is often hard to map his precise position on this multi-dimensional graph, Rolle's writings should manifest an abiding preoccupation with the whole range of subjects mentioned here: definitions of perfection, positions as to the legality and ideology of preaching, and questions about its status in relation to action and contemplation. Indeed, he addresses many of these issues explicitly, and in formal, semi-scholastic language.

His discussion of the active and contemplative lives in *Incendium Amoris*, cap. 21 is a case in point, for without being strictly a *quaestio*, it is a serious discussion of its subject, sharing many of the procedures, and some of the terminology, of Aquinas's treatment of the lives in *Summa Theologica* (II.ii, q. 182). The relative status of the two lives is introduced as a matter of doubt: 'Dubitatur autem a quibusdam que sit magis meritoria et nobilior, scilicet, contemplativa vita an activa' (204.20–21: 'But some are in doubt which is nobler and of greater merit, the contemplative life or the active'). As in a *quaestio*, the wrong answer is considered first: some think that good works and preaching give active life the edge. But this is quickly denied (Rolle never expounds in detail any case he opposes): those who think it are ignorant of the contemplative life.[15] Active life can boast works of mercy and preaching, but these 'pertain to an accidental reward, which is joy of created good' (205.12–13: 'Talia opera pertinent ad premium accidentale, quod est gaudium de bono creato'); contemplative life is superior because its reward is a 'premium essenciale' (204.29), the joy of uncreated good: again, the language can be paralleled in Aquinas (II.ii, q. 182, art. 2, reply obj. 1). Rolle's analysis of the two lives goes on to discuss the fact that contemplative angels (seraphim) are higher than active ones (archangels), and to insist that to live is better than to preach – the major emphasis of the second half of the chapter is, indeed, on the status of preaching. We are told, in concessionary style, that there are several ways to please God, one (in an interesting echo of Guido's *Consuetudines*) being to manifest one's preaching by writing (206.20–21). Lastly it is reiterated that combining active and contemplative lives is almost impossible; Christ and Mary did so, but ordinary mortals can combine preaching only with the lower forms of contemplation. Here Rolle is in disagreement with Aquinas, who claims that contemplative and active lives can be combined (*Summa Theologica* II.ii, q. 182, art. 3). Steele's analysis of this chapter (1979, pp. 214–216) suggests that its use of Christ and the Virgin is polemical, since both were usually taken as models of 'mixed' life. If this is so, this chapter displays a firm grasp of the principles and *topoi* of treatments of the lives, while pursuing a thoroughly conservative line of opposition to 'mixed' life.

Rolle is also interested in and knowledgeable about the question of whether the coenobitic or the solitary life is to be preferred – agreeing, of course, with the traditional answer, and arguing his case several times and with some vehemence. Emile Arnould has shown that one such argument, in *Melos Amoris*, cap. 47, again follows much the form of the *quaestio* (1937a); the same is true when the issue is raised in *Super Canticum Canticorum* (pp. 20–29), and to an extent in the discussion of solitude in *Incendium Amoris*, caps. 13–14. In *Melos Amoris*, Rolle proceeds by argument and counter-argument, quoting an authority against his position (Anselm), refuting him out of Matthew's gospel (11.11), and showing that Augustine's words about monks do not imply that he thought them superior to solitaries; here he brings all the apparatus of scholastic debate to bear on the issue. The passage in *Incendium Amoris* is looser, but many of the authorities mentioned also occur in *quaestiones* on the solitary life. Cap. 13 opens by quoting Ecclesiastes 4.10, '*Woe to one who is alone*', and glossing the phrase in words Margaret Deanesley suggests (note on 180.2–3) are adapted from Hugh of St Victor: '*Ille enim solus est cum quo Deus non est*' (180.2–3: 'For someone is alone only when God is not with him'); verse and gloss occur in one of the *quaestiones* printed by Oliger (1934, p. 250). Two of these same *quaestiones* use the career of St Cuthbert, who was bishop, monk and finally hermit, as an *exemplum* to prove their case (pp. 253, 256); Rolle also writes of the saint leaving his bishopric for an anchoritic life as proof of the superiority of the latter (181.11–12: '*Beatus Cuthbert ab episcopatu ad anachoriticam vitam transivit*'). Such points of contact suggest that he knew *quaestiones* on the subject of solitaries and monks, and wanted to indicate that he was working within a previously defined tradition.[16]

Rolle's position on the contemplative life is therefore traditional, indeed old-fashioned; 'mixed' and monastic lives get short shrift when set against the eremitic life, which is the highest form of the spiritual life. *Super Canticum Canticorum* sums his whole case up in a long sentence:

Cum ergo constat vitam contemplativam digniorem esse et magis meritoriam quam activa vita, et omnes viros contemplacionis solitudinem amantes et precipue in amore divino ferventes, liquet profecto quod, non monachi vel alii, quicumque ad congregacionem collecti, summi sunt, aut maxime Deum diligunt, set solitarii, contemplacione sublimati, qui, pro magno eterni amoris gaudio quod senciunt, in solitudine sedere incessanter concupiscunt. (26.26–27.7)

[Thus, since it is established that the contemplative life is worthier and of greater merit than the active life, and that all contemplative men love solitude and burn preeminently in the divine love, it is surely clear that neither monks nor any others who are gathered together as a congregation are the highest, or love God the most; rather, it is solitaries, lifted up into contemplation: who, for the great joy in eternal love that they feel, desire to sit unceasingly in solitude.]

Since Rolle was a hermit, this is the position we would expect him to adopt. However, he also displays less predictable interests and attitudes. For example, while cap. 21 of *Incendium Amoris* gives preaching a relatively low status, some of his other works show a special interest in preaching. *Judica Me*, a work he wrote for a secular priest, contains two model sermons, and indicates his awareness of the laws and responsibilities governing the *magisterium* of a preacher. Thus he states that a secular priest must have 'bona vita, scientia recta, predicacio discreta' (*Judica Me* 20.8–9: 'A good life, correct knowledge, proper preaching'), a list of qualities typical of those expected of the preacher (as outlined in cap. 1 of *Speculum Christiani*; see also Minnis 1986, pp. 89–91); and he is aware, indeed regretfully so, that as a hermit who is not in religious orders he is not allowed to preach but must confine himself to teaching (*Judica Me* 18.18–20). In *Melos Amoris* he complains that people are being licensed to preach who do not possess the requisite knowledge: 'Sed errant nunc undique miseros mittentes qui oracula ignorant clause Scripture ... ac prohibent precipuos proferre sermonem' (*Melos Amoris* 152.17–19: 'But now [bishops] err, sending everywhere wretches who are ignorant of the secrets of the Scriptures; they prohibit the pre-eminent ones from proferring sermons'). Again the note of regret is clear. His interest in preaching also causes him to mention, both in *Melos Amoris* and *Emendatio Vitae*, the aureole that the preacher will receive in heaven. *Melos Amoris* declares: 'Predicator perfectus pueros parturit ad pacem portandam, et capiet coronas quia captivos convertit coram Cunctipotente' (152.12–14: 'Perfected as a preacher, he brings forth boys to bear peace and will capture crowns in the presence of the Omnipotent for converting captives'); here the 'coronas' are aureoles, while the phrase 'pueros parturit' is a reminiscence of Richard of St Victor's use of the term *puerperium* to describe the fourth degree of passionate love. *Emendatio Vitae* states that contemplatives who continue to preach will merit an aureole (f. 142r. 4–5: 'caeteris operibus aureolam propter suam praedicationem merentur'). As we shall see, both works display a far more sympathetic attitude to the 'mixed' life than we found in *Incendium Amoris* – and in both, we again find Rolle well up on a complicated subject.

Rolle's eremitic career was thus enacted within his awareness of a series of conflicting views of the best way to live, and he thought of his life, and the lives of those for whom he wrote, in terms of these views. But the formal question of his status as a hermit was not the only thing affecting his claim to authority. As a mystical writer whose *materia* was his own experience, he was also deeply aware of contemporary notions about the relationship between such experience, the attainment of sanctity, and the wielding of spiritual and literary authority; indeed, throughout his life he was even more concerned to extol his own experience than to assert the supremacy of the eremitic life. By way of rounding off this contextualization of Rolle's career, it will thus be useful to sketch some of the issues associated with those key late medieval terms, *auctoritas* and *experientia*, after first looking at the genealogy of the particular kinds of religious experience Rolle spent his life celebrating.

III: AFFECTIVE EXPERIENCE AND SPIRITUAL AUTHORITY

If one tendency of late medieval religious culture was, as I stated, an increasing institutionalization, another current of equal importance ran in a different direction: towards a greater emphasis on affective experience. Signs of this are omnipresent, but among the earliest and most significant was a radical shift in the way Christ was depicted, described and addressed. From the late eleventh century on, the old image of a victorious warrior God who was to be feared and rendered loyal homage began to be replaced by that of a humanized crucified Saviour, whose death should evoke violent feelings of grief, compassion and love. Such feelings were cultivated in what may have been a new practice, Passion meditation, an individual and often exclusively affective exercise in imagining, and imaginatively responding to, the events of Christ's death in the minutest and most painful detail. By the end of the fourteenth century, written meditations and longer affective biographies of Christ were established genres of Middle English literature. But the Latin sources of this literature are older: portions of Anselm's *Orationes sive Meditationes* (c. 1100), or of meditations that came to be attached to Anselm's (such as those of John of Fécamp and Aelred); dozens of passages lovingly culled from the works of Bernard (d. 1153) and various 'Bernardine' writers; and several remarkable thirteenth- and early fourteenth-century works, such as the *Stimulus Amoris* (by James of Milan) and the *Meditationes Vitae Christi* (probably by John of Caulibus), both of which were attributed to Bonaventure. Rolle knew most or all of these writings, and shared their assumptions about the vital role of affective experience as an agent of spiritual regeneration. He was probably the author of the most elaborate and arguably the best of the English Passion meditations (*Meditation B*), and his recommendation of the practice of meditating on Christ's life and death at various phases of the spiritual life may have had a significant impact on the development of Middle English devotional literature, and assuredly did on the spiritual lives of thousands of medieval readers. He was also a celebrated exponent of a related but more abstract devotion to the humanity of Christ, the 'devotion to the Holy Name of Jesus', and wrote copiously in Latin and English in praise of that name (as oil poured out, medicine for the soul, honey for the mouth and music in the ears), in terms which show him both fully engaged on a personal level and well aware of the sources of this devotion: passages of Bernard's *Sermones super Cantica Canticorum* (especially number 15), the great Bernardine hymn, *Dulcis Ihesu Memoria* (c. 1200), and an elaborate thirteenth-century poem by John of Hoveden, the *Philomena*. Rolle drew on these works because they spoke to his experience; Christ was evidently in some sense present to him, and the experience of intimacy with Christ was of great significance to his spiritual life, as it is to many of his writings.[17]

However, as we shall see in more detail in Chapter 2, Rolle's experiential spirituality was not in fact centred around the humanity of Christ, but around his own sensations of passionate love for God, which he took as manifestations of the presence of the Holy Spirit in his soul, and (it seems, though he is not clear on this point) of his union with God. It will become clear that there is much in his depictions of the symptoms and effects of divine love that is untraditional. But in general terms his discussions of love themselves belong to well-defined literary and mystical traditions, which developed alongside the devotion to the humanity of Christ (often overlapping with it) but are distinct from it. Rolle held that the soul's ascent to God takes place through the ordering of the faculty of love, the *affectus*, so that it turns its back on its former, secular, objects, and pours itself out in a measureless desire for God, a desire which is equivalent to mystical union. The theological positions underlying this general type of mysticism were fully articulated in the thirteenth century by Bonaventure, whose affective psychology, as Gillespie shows (1982), can be a useful tool in analysing Rolle's didactic procedures. Yet Rolle himself may not have been more than dimly aware of Bonaventure's thought (see Moyes 1988, vol. 1, pp. 2–4). The discussions of love and its role in uniting the soul with God on which he most clearly draws are from the twelfth century, and share with his own writing an elaborately rhetorical approach to their subject that, coupled with a daring sense of theological possibilities, makes for reading which is in itself (as it is clearly meant to be) an affective experience. Two of the discussions I am alluding to, the account of the four degrees of love in Bernard's *De Diligendo Deo* and the whole of Richard of St Victor's *De Quattuor Gradibus Violentae Caritatis*, follow much the same pattern, being descriptions of the way the soul ascends to God by successive transformations of the affective faculty. Bernard's version of these transformations is precise: first we love ourselves for our own sake; next we come to love God, but still for our own sake; then we ascend to love God for the sake of his innate attributes; and in the fourth and final stage, unattainable in this life except in brief moments of mystical union, we love ourselves only for the sake of God. Richard takes elements of this pattern from Bernard, but his degrees of 'violent' love (*insuperabilis, insepa-*

rabilis, singularis and *insatiabilis*) are described in a variety of ways which do not amount to precise definitions, instead constituting alternative metaphorical routes to the summit of mystical union (which again lies beyond the reach of the present life). Rolle, who studied these accounts closely and who borrows three of Richard's degrees of love in several of his works (see, e.g., Chapter 8, n. 18) disagrees importantly with both writers, especially over the topic of mystical union (see Chapter 6, nn. 14–20). Yet many of his assumptions, ideas and images can be traced back to them (or to some of the other works of Bernard, notably the *Sermones super Cantica Canticorum*). In particular, he seems to have learnt from them the rhetorical and conceptual possibilities of the paradox which surrounds the idea of 'ordered' love, and is latent in the verse from which the term 'ordered' is derived (*'The king has brought me into the wine-cellar, and he has ordered the love in me'*, Song of Songs 2.4): that this process of ordering is directed towards a love which is infinite and violent, which breaks down all barriers and never rests content with any settled order. Bernard sums up this paradox at the opening of the *De Diligendo Deo*, which states simply that 'Causa diligendi Deum, Deus est; modus sine modo diligere.' Richard's treatise demonstrates ordered, measureless love in its very form (four orders which are continually changing), and in its elaborately patterned but violently excited language. The same paradox is celebrated in many places in Rolle's writings, sometimes with explicit reference to love 'sine modo', and is encapsulated in his mystical experience of spiritual song, which is by its nature ordered but at the same time rhapsodic, and which for Rolle marks the soul's arrival at the highest attainable degree of love.

The other twelfth-century discussion of love on which I think Rolle drew (see Chapter 6, n. 27) is Hugh of St Victor's brief work *De Laude Caritatis*, most of which is a highly affective address to a personified *Caritas* in praise of her ability to reunite heaven and earth and bring about the salvation of humanity. Hugh develops his address from biblical passages about love, notably from the letters of Paul and John, and in the style of Paul's encomium in 1 Corinthians 13 applies strings of epithets to love, forming her portrait piece by piece, like a mosaic: 'Tu es plenitudo justitiae, perfectio legis, consummatio virtutis, agnitio veritatis. Via igitur es, o Charitas. Qualis via? Superexcellens, suscipiens, dirigens et perducens. Cujus via? Via hominis ad Deum, et via Dei ad homines' (PL 176, col. 974). The *De Laude Caritatis* is theologically precise and gives some solidity to the figure of *Caritas* by showing her in action at the Incarnation, where she is herself incarnate in the incarnate Christ. Nonetheless, the form of the work has the tendency to draw our attention away from the drama of salvation in which love's crucial role is played out, and to focus it on love as an object of praise and desire in her own right, less of a *via* or a *mediatrix* than a goal in herself. This tendency is present in a different way in the *De Quattuor Gradibus Violentae Caritatis* (probably influenced by the *De Laude Caritatis*), where love is not personified but is described as an experience so rich and all-encompassing that what it is that love loves is often almost forgotten. In some of the works inspired by Richard, like the anonymous *Tractatus ad Severinum de Gradibus Caritatis* or Gerald of Liège's *Quinque Incitamenta ad Deum Amandum Ardenter*, the emphasis on love as an experience in and of itself is even more marked, and the line of thought is constantly being interrupted by affective exclamations or carefully wrought tropes of inexpressibility. I have found no evidence that Rolle knew these later works, but like them he often seems to think of love as an experience in its own right, and like them his writing lacks the underlying theological clarity of Hugh and Richard. His own passages in praise of love, somewhat in the style of Hugh, are often very fine, but are oddly detached from any sense of the larger place love occupies in the Christian universe. When he writes of his mystical experiences of heat, sweetness and song, he has the habit of treating them essentially as inner sensations which, while they have considerable metaphysical implications and are often said to have been sent *by* God, can be described with only cursory reference to the fact that the sole purpose and condition of their existence is to be directed back *to* God. In theological and conceptual terms, this is no doubt a bad thing, and may well account for much of the modern criticism that has been directed at Rolle by theological scholars (see, e.g., Knowles's influential critique in *The English Mystical Tradition* (1961), chapter 4). But in affective and rhetorical terms it is, if anything, an advantage, for it enables Rolle to communicate a remarkably tangible sense of his experience, making it manifest to us in a way which leaves Hugh's account of love (though hardly Richard's) seeming cold by comparison. Besides, if we see this aspect of Rolle's works as situated within a late-medieval tradition of writing about passionate love for God, it becomes clear that he is doing little more than exploiting affective possibilities latent within an existing literary mode which almost from the start had tended to be more celebratory than analytic.[18]

When Rolle writes of his highly original experiences of mystical love he does so with at least the general sanction of earlier writers such as Bernard and the Victorines, and hence within a set of assumptions he could have expected much of his audience to share, or at least recognize. This is important to bear in mind when confronting the experiences themselves and the fact that they seem to have no significant predecessors in mystical tradition, for it implies that Rolle's early readers may have been less startled by (and less suspicious of) the experiences than we might expect them to be, or indeed be ourselves. In practice, the complexities of his predicament as a writer seem to have little to do with the originality of his mystical subject-matter in itself; they reside, rather, in his continuing determination to argue that his experiences can legitimately be seen as normative, and thus as possessing authority, both over the reader and in the context of an affective mystical tradition some of whose tenets they challenge. Rolle writes explicitly in order to change the way people think about and engage in affective mysticism, and does so on the basis of his interpretation of a particular set of events in his own life. Yet it is not the events themselves, but the claims they make on his readers – and indeed on the Church as a whole – that (as we shall see) set alarm-bells ringing in work after work.

That such claims, however problematic they are, are even possible, has to do with a complicated late-medieval sense of the ways in which contemporary personal experience interacts with the normative structures handed down by tradition, within both religious and secular cultures. The idea of authority has been seen in various lights as I have sketched different contexts for Rolle's career during the course of this introduction. It has appeared as the Church; as a formal attribute of the office of the preacher; as an implied attribute of the most perfect state of human life (whatever that is taken to be); and, in the first part of this final essay, as something inherent in a spiritual or literary tradition, especially in the writers who are considered its founding *auctores* or *auctoritates*. In the present context, authority is something quite different: it is a potential attribute of human experience itself, if such experience is (or can be described in such a way as to make it seem) genuine, powerful, meaningful and important enough to merit serious consideration. It would be unwise to underestimate the weight of significance accorded certain forms of personal experience during any part of the Middle Ages (as the perpetual vitality of the hagiographic tradition forcibly reminds us). But in the fourteenth century, this sense of significance was reserved especially for private and affective experiences, which, under the proper conditions, could come to be regarded as having importance for everyone, and thus as contributing to (perhaps even modifying) the tradition from which they sprang. Some of the clearest examples of this process at work are provided by late-medieval visionaries. As we saw, Julian of Norwich wrote her book on the understanding that her revelation was not in a true sense 'private' at all, but was sent by God to the whole Church. Thus not only was it incumbent on her to publicize it, it could be used as a yardstick with which to conduct a re-examination of the whole of Christian doctrine as it pertains to the nature of God. At one point, worrying over apparent discrepancies between her revelation and received Christian doctrine, she even distinguishes the two as respectively 'the hygher dome [that] God shewed hym selfe in the same tyme [of the revelation]' and 'the lower dome [that] was lernyd me before tyme in holy chyrche' (p. 488, 45.23–25). In a different vein, *The Book of Margery Kempe* provides numerous examples of an uneducated laywoman struggling to show that her intimacy with God makes her a figure of spiritual authority, both during her life and throughout the momentous process of the composition of her autobiographical saint's life itself (Lochrie 1986). What is notable is how often she succeeds in gaining respectful notice, whether from other women or from many of the ecclesiastics she or her book encountered, from Archbishop Arundel himself, to the priest who acted as her amanuensis, to the Carthusians who respectfully annotated their copy of her work, to whoever it was who persuaded Wynkyn de Worde to print portions of it. Caroline Walker Bynum's fine study of the spirituality of medieval women, *Holy Feast and Holy Fast* (1987), shows that the positive attention Kempe at least sometimes attracted was itself a dim reflection of the greater power wielded by her Continental predecessors, whose intimacy with the reality of God made them objects of veneration in their own lifetimes. For their admirers (to adapt the opening of *The Wife of Bath's Prologue*) it seemed as if these women knew truth by 'Experience, though noon auctoritee were in this world' – hence as if they were themselves authoritative embodiments of the truth. And though this view was contestable in particular instances – as her book testifies, many people (lay and cleric) regarded Kempe's somewhat lurid manifestations of her religious *experientia* as evidence that she was deluded, possessed, or mad, rather than divinely inspired – the principles underlying such deference to *experientia* were widely accepted. An immediate predecessor of Julian and Margery Kempe, St Bridget of Sweden, is a good example of what was possible, for her revelations were treated as genuine during her own lifetime, were translated into Latin (albeit in an edited form), duly publicized (see Colledge 1956), and as a result were able to make a real impact on the way late-medieval people thought of heaven, hell and purgatory. In the career of St Bridget, we see experiential knowledge formally recognized and brought within the structure of institutional truth.

The increased prestige of personal experience of this kind is, of course, part and parcel of the rise of an affective and personally oriented devotion outlined above. One of the theoretical bases of this devotion, which forms an invaluable coordinate in plotting the somewhat shadowy notion of the authority of experience, can be traced in a distinction made by late-medieval thinkers between two kinds of knowledge: intellective knowledge (*scientia*, or in some contexts *scientia ut scientia*) and affective knowledge (*sapientia*, or *scientia ut sapientia*). A.J. Minnis's *Medieval Theory of Authorship* (1984, chapter 4) shows how this distinction was refined by and helped to structure discussions of the difference between human science, whose end is the acquisition of knowledge, and the divine science revealed in the Scriptures, the purpose of which is to convert the will to God. According to some theologians (notably Franciscan ones), the Scriptures are written in a variety of affective literary modes, because readers experience these more immediately and intimately than they do rational arguments. As Bonaventure says in the prologue to the *Breviloquium* (cap. 5), 'the *affectus* is moved more by examples than by arguments, more by promises than by reasons, more by devotions than by definitions' (see Minnis 1984, p. 127). Thus Scripture itself aims to give its readers *experientia* of the truths it articulates, and rewards those who look at it for wisdom rather than merely for knowledge. This way of thinking about the Scriptures both relies on and supports a number of assumptions about human psychology (in medieval terms, the structure of the soul), and about mystical theology (or in what form, and with which of its faculties, the soul is to be united with God). As a result, the distinction between *scientia* and *sapientia* easily came to be applied not only to literary modes but to the kinds of understanding possessed by individual Christians.

So much is clear from the following passage, taken from a fourteenth-century translation (one of several) of Friar Lorens d'Orléans's *Somme le Roi* (itself dated 1279):

> þe ȝifte of wisdom, þat clerkes clepen sapience . . . is non oþer þing þan a sauerous knowynge, þat is a good sauour and a grete delite in þe herte. For oþer-wise knoweþ he þe wyn þat seeþ it in a faire pece or verre, and oþer-wise he þat tasteþ it, drynkeþ it, and sauoureþ it. Many philosophres knewen God bi þe creatures, as bi a myrour wher þei loked as bi resoun and bi vnderstondyng . . . but þei ne feled neuere no þing bi taste of riȝt loue ne bi deuocion. Also þer be many cristene, clerkes and lewede, þat knowen hym wel bi bileue and bi þe bokes; but for þei han þe sauour mysordeyned bi synne, þei mowe no þing fele, no more þan a seke man may fynde sauour in good mete.
>
> (*The Book of Vices and Virtues*, 272.6–273.2)

Here, *sapientia* is the salvific knowledge of God that comes through personal *experientia* of his good wine, which pagan philosophers and learned sinners lack; the distinction between the two modes of knowing is close to being treated as antonymous. It is not far from such language to an attitude which is suspicious of learning itself, and which exalts the ignorant for their intuitive love and understanding of God: an attitude which Rolle exemplifies in his dedication of *Incendium Amoris* to the 'rudibus et indoctis' (who prefer to love God than to seek presumptuously to understand him, like the 'magnis theologicis infinitis quescionibus implicatis', 147.10–11); which is evident in certain parts of *The Book of Margery Kempe*; and which we find embodied most consciously (if also somewhat ambiguously) in the figure of Piers Plowman, the rustic who knows Truth 'as kyndely as clerke doth hise bokes' (B v.545). The pivotal role Langland gives to Piers in the development of his great didactic poem is a remarkable example of the authority that could be accorded experiential knowledge, even when it was unsupported by any large measure of *scientia*. For although it is Reason who (in passus v) preaches to the people, dressed as a bishop, it is Piers who then directs their activities and wins them Truth's pardon, just as it is Piers who later 'impugns' Clergy and sets 'alle sciencies at a sope save loue one' (XIII.124), who gives Will (here an embodiment of the human *affectus*) his long tasting of the 'apple' of the Redemption (XVI–XVIII), and who becomes identified (XVIII.22–25) with the human nature of Christ. If Mary Davlin (1981) is right in claiming that the 'kynde knowing' which Will seeks during the course of *Piers Plowman* is Langland's translation of the term *sapientia*, then Piers himself, as the poem's richest and most moving embodiment of what such knowing involves, should be seen as a different kind of translation of the same concept.

Piers has authority within the dream world of *Piers Plowman* because he has personal experience of the truth. In an analogous way, the poem itself has a claim to didactic authority because its author can write of his personal experience of the series of events ordered and made meaningful by Piers. It was no doubt largely in order to make this chain of authority-through-experience clear that Langland framed his poem as a series of dream-visions interspersed with waking episodes in which the narrator reflects on what he

Introduction: Contexts

has seen and heard. The third of these episodes (at the end of B VII), which occurs after Piers has torn the pardon he received from Truth and squabbled with the priest, acknowledges the poet's dependence on Piers with especial force by implying that the latter's incomprehensible and apparently misguided actions undercut Langland's entire project, the elucidation of Will's dreams. When the narrator quotes from the *Disticha Catonis* (II.31), 'Sompnia ne cures' (alluding to the whole distich: 'Take no account of dreams, for while asleep the human mind sees what it hopes and wishes for') he is introducing the threatening possibility that the poem should not after all be regarded as an account of a true vision, but of a lesser kind of dream, a mere phantasm – and thus that the poem should be seen as no more than an entertainment, whose author is laying claim to a far greater degree of authority than is proper (VII.150, see also XII.23). While the episode as a whole seems to stand behind Piers (if a little doubtfully), it is not surprising that in the waking episode in passus VIII the poem veers off to consider the *scientia* Piers has challenged, abandoning its hero for five whole passus (to XIII.123) and betraying a degree of nervousness and anxiety which is surely authorial as well as narratorial. Only after Langland has investigated and in a certain sense exposed the pretensions of *scientia* in the third vision can he return the poem by degrees to a world in which the radical figure of Piers is again seen as possessing unchallengeable authority.

As a literary visionary who is writing a poem with theological pretensions, Langland is in much the same situation as that of any mystical visionary, in that formally the authority he would like his work to possess is dependent on the authenticity of literary material which coincides (whether fictionally or not) with his own experience. Yet this situation is by no means unusual among late-medieval poets, any more than it is among the mystics. It can be paralleled in the work of the other great medieval poet-theologian, Dante, especially in the *Commedia* itself, the authority of which at least ostensibly depends on our acceptance of a fictional premise: that Dante really went where he said he went. In a more general sense, it is analogous to the situations of all the writers, both religious and secular, who as the Middle Ages drew to a close found themselves more and more aware of the importance of their imaginative *experientia*, and of the awkward relationship between their own status as *moderni* and the weighty authority of the writers of the past, the 'ancients'. Here it is useful to refer back to Minnis's *Medieval Theory of Authorship*, which traces the evolution of attitudes to authors and authority between the twelfth and fourteenth centuries, taking as its overarching theme the ways in which two related processes contributed to the self-consciousness which was integral to the situation of the late-medieval author. (In both processes we can glimpse the omnipresent influence of affective spirituality.) The first was that whereby '*auctoritas* moved from the divine realm to the human' (1988 edition, p. viii), as biblical commentators increasingly focussed on the multiplicity of the ways in which the Holy Spirit speaks to humanity through the Bible – hence on the distinctive characteristics of each individual book, and eventually on those of the human author or authors through whom the Spirit chose to communicate the truths contained in each book. Thus David, Solomon, Paul and John came to be treated more as individuals, less as mere mouthpieces of divine truth (and in their wake, increasing interest was also shown in the personal traits of secular authors such as Aristotle, Cicero or Ovid). The second concomitant process was that whereby *auctoritas* shifted 'in some measure from the past to the present' (ibid.), as modern writers laid progressively more confident claim to an authority in some sense equivalent to that of the ancients, sometimes appropriating the terminology and the methodology of biblical commentary to achieve their ends. Thus in the *Vita Nuova* and the *Convivio* Dante writes commentaries on his own poetry; in *The Life of Dante* Boccaccio treats a modern writer as an *auctor* whose status is equivalent to that of the ancients (just as Dante enrols himself among the great writers of Greece and Rome in *Inferno* IV); and in his 'familiar letter' to Cicero, Petrarch addresses a great *auctor* as a colleague of whom it is possible to make a respectful but critical appraisal (ibid., pp. viii–xiii, 211–217). In the late twelfth century Walter Map grumbled that in the eyes of his contemporaries 'the only good *auctor* was a dead one' (p. 12, Minnis's paraphrase). By the end of the fourteenth century, this kind of attitude, though still alive, was in slow retreat. Yet the extraordinary alternations of ambition and self-doubt discernible in Langland's poem, like the more poised ambiguities of Chaucer's narrative persona, are a measure of the complicated situation in which educated writers found themselves not long after the death of Rolle: impelled to take themselves and their own experience as fourteenth-century moderns seriously, yet anxiously aware of the limits of their own authority and the ways in which it might be challenged. Rolle is far from being alone in having to 'invent' his own authority. While there are enormous differences of tone and context, the puzzled musings over what is to be his *matere* that afflict the Chaucerian poet-dreamer in *The Parliament of Fowls* and *The House of Fame* nonetheless have a real relationship with Rolle's ostentatiously confident declaration, at the opening of *Melos Amoris*, that his subject-matter is the holiness of the moderns and how it equals that of the saints of long ago. In practice neither writer can assume the mantle of *auctoritas* untroubled by their awareness that their own experience has far less immediate weight than the continuing presence, in their respective traditions, of their great predecessors.

In this sketch of the problematic idea of the authority of experience, we have in a sense returned to the starting-point of this introduction, the difficult relationship that tends to exist between the inspired individual and the establishment. What is new is that in this specifically late-medieval context the 'inspired individual' need not necessarily be a mystic, and the 'establishment' need not correspond to the ecclesiastical institution; the model proves also to apply to the relationship between poets and their authoritative literary forebears, and may have other analogues as well. We will come back to this point in the epilogue to this study, where I argue that an understanding of Rolle's career has implications for the way we read many late-medieval writers, not only the mystics. For the present, however, it is time to begin our examination of that career, and of the laborious process whereby Rolle discovers, develops and elevates an interpretation of his own experiences and a self-conception based on those experiences.

PART I

I

Interpreting Rolle's life

The surviving works of the fourteenth-century English hermit and mystic Richard Rolle are voluminous. His two complete psalm commentaries, with his commentaries on the Lord's Prayer, the Creeds, Lamentations, and Revelation (*English Psalter*, *Latin Psalter*, *Super Orationem Dominicam*, *Super Symbolum Apostolorum*, *Super Symbolum S. Athanasii*, *Super Threnos*, *Super Apocalypsim* – the last is incomplete) would themselves take up a good thousand columns of a hypothetical continuation of the *Patrologia Latina*. Yet even in terms of length, these works account for no more than half his output. He also wrote five more discursive biblical expositions, *Super Canticum Canticorum* (on the first verses of the Song of Songs), *Super Lectiones Mortuorum* (on parts of Job), *Super Psalmum Vicesimum*, *Super Mulierem Fortem* (on a text in Proverbs) and *Super Magnificat*; three works we can loosely call treatises, *Incendium Amoris*, *Contra Amatores Mundi* and *Melos Amoris*; several epistles or works of instruction in Latin (*Judica Me*, *Emendatio Vitae*) and English (*Ego Dormio*, *The Commandment*, *The Form of Living*); a Latin poem to the Virgin (*Canticum Amoris*), probably two English Passion meditations, and a handful of short English prose pieces and lyrics. Of this second group of substantially original works, the English works have become famous as early masterpieces of prose or poetry, while the Latin works deserve an equal reputation not only for their oddity but for their rhetorical skill and sometimes beauty. Rolle was among the most stylish, as well as the most prolific, writers of late-medieval England.

The authorship of these works is well attested by Rolle's distinctiveness of style and thought and by numerous manuscript ascriptions,[1] and generally the manuscripts of the works do not present major textual difficulties. It is true that his editors have had to distinguish the genuine forms of his works from many adaptations, translations and false ascriptions.[2] Yet the problem here is not too little information but too much. During the fifteenth century he was one of the most widely read of English writers, whose works survive in nearly four hundred English (or American) and at least seventy Continental manuscripts, almost all written between 1390 and 1500 (as well as in ten sixteenth- and seventeenth-century printed editions).[3] We must have almost a complete record of his output.

Unfortunately, our knowledge of the background to Rolle's writing career is much sparser. Neither the order of most of his works nor the occasion of their composition has been established. *Judica Me* (a kind of pastoral manual) addresses a member of the secular clergy who is said to have asked him to write the work (18.1–2). Manuscript rubrics link some of his later works with specified individuals: in MS Dd.v.64 *Ego Dormio* is said to have been written for a nun of Yedingham (near Pickering), *The Commandment* for a nun of Hampole, and *The Form of Living* for the anchoress Margaret (ff. 29r., 34r., 1r.), called 'Margareta de Kyrkby' in MS Longleat 29 (f. 30r.), for whom the *English Psalter* (according to MS Laud Misc. 286, f. 1r.–v.) was also made; elsewhere *Emendatio Vitae* is associated with a 'William' (Allen, pp. 518–520). But all background to the composition of most of Rolle's works is irrecoverable – as we should expect of a writer who lived outside the centres of learning and seems often not to have written for a specific occasion or audience. Even the investigation of Rolle's sources is hampered by uncertainty as to what books were available to him, and by his practice of not citing such authorities as he uses.

The information we do have concerning his life reflects not modern academic priorities but medieval hagiographic ones, for after his death Rolle was widely regarded as a saint. Although no *vita* seems to have been written, and no canonization procedure properly initiated (Vauchez 1981, pp. 294–300), our major source of information concerning Rolle's life, an *Officium et Miracula*, was compiled in the hope of – and perhaps partly to further – his canonization; it probably dates from the 1380s (Allen, p. 51). The nine *lectiones* of the *Officium* mostly consist of stories of Rolle's early life, supported by convincingly specific details, but too reminiscent of anecdotes in a work like the *Fioretti* to be wholly trusted.[4] Indeed the work bathes the life and personality of its protagonist in a charm redolent of St Francis himself. Of simple facts, the *Officium* tells us only this: Rolle was born at Thornton, near Pickering in Yorkshire, son of William Rolle. He studied in Oxford under the sponsorship of Thomas de Neville, archdeacon of Durham, but left without a degree in his nineteenth year, desiring to pursue a holy life. Later he fled from home and became a hermit for the same reason, and lived on the estate of a John de Dalton, one of his father's neighbours (see Allen, pp. 444–466 and Arnould 1937b for Dalton's identity). Dalton's interest in Rolle was aroused by his wife's finding him at prayer in their chapel, by the discovery that his sons had known him at Oxford, and by the quality of his spontaneous sermon; the interest seems to have been sustained by the women of Dalton's household, including his wife. Eventually Rolle left Dalton, 'ex divina providencia' (*lectio viija*), and went elsewhere (his writings imply that he moved around for a period). He had a distinctive form of mystical experience consisting of sensations of *fervor*, *dulcor* and *canor* (heat, sweetness, song), and was able to talk and write at the same time. He died near the Cistercian nunnery at Hampole in Yorkshire – having presumably had an association with the place for some time, since he acted as a spiritual guide to one of its nuns, Margaret Kirkeby, after her enclosure as an anchoress at East Layton, in Richmondshire.

Apart from his writings, the other sources for Rolle's life ought to be the manuscripts of his works; but in practice these add little except for the date of his death – 1349. It is odd that this is so, since these same manuscripts betray a greater degree of interest in his life than any of the other 'English Mystics' evoked; numbers of his scribes and readers succumbed to the charm that the *Officium* recreates. Their captivation is apparent in biographical notes in MS Vienna 4483, interesting for the seriousness of their attempts to reach back through his writings to his personality (Allen, pp. 39–45); in drawings and scrawls of Rolle, and annotations of his works which refer fondly to 'Ricardus';[5] and in the compilation *Oleum Effusum*, which partly consists of autobiographical passages from two of his works.[6] Later devotional writers also discuss the dangers of an excessively literal imitation of Rolle's mystical practices, in a way that suggests the imaginative appeal his spiritual life must have had for his readers.[7] The fact that little of this biographical material is very informative (Rolle after all did not write merely 'in wulgari anglico' as MS Vienna 4483, f. 137r. says he did), is perhaps due to his limited popularity during his lifetime. The history of his early reputation is not clear, but there is little evidence that he was at once accorded the outstanding position that he acquired in the fifteenth century. For us he survives almost entirely as an author, the evidence for whose human individuality is bound up in the complex textures of his works.

Having said as much, these writings are in many ways very informative about Rolle's life. He has none of Julian of Norwich's reticence in telling us about himself, and often alludes to incidents in his past. Indeed his teachings about the contemplative life are based overtly on his experiences, which he recounts for their exemplary importance, often with artful charm. Without introducing even a discontinuity of tone into their narrative, the compilers of the *Officium* were able to make heavy use of quotations from his works (especially *Incendium Amoris*) for their hagiographic account of his life. But while the biographical information to be gleaned from Rolle's works is invaluable, its significance is far from unambiguous, in relation either to the actual events of his life or to the nature of his personality. His early years seem well chronicled; he often mentions his conversion, and we gather from *Incendium Amoris* (cap. 15) that within five years of this event he had experienced all the spiritual sensations around which his mystical life was formed, *fervor, dulcor* and *canor*. These experiences made him a prophet of joy, an exultant praiser of God who believed that penitence is for spiritual beginners. We know little of the rest of his life, except that all his works stress the joy he feels in the love of God; but this in itself seems to justify the somewhat honeyed view of him common in the fifteenth century. Yet other features create a less pleasant impression. There is a defensiveness to much of his writing, which sits oddly with his elevation of joy and vaunted indifference to the world's approval. He portrays himself as having enemies who

33

criticize him for his way of life, and condemns these in passages of general but vituperative satire. He writes as often about the damnation of the wicked, or his enemies, as he does about the love of God. Worst, it comes to seem suspect that a figure the *Officium* treats as a saint should devote so much energy to telling us that he is one.

The experience of reading Rolle is thus more likely to make us conscious of encountering a striking personality than to inform us of how it truly operated, or of the events which engaged it. At the same time, a reading of his works gives urgency to the quest for understanding his life, for they are at once fascinating and incomprehensible, operating on principles that continually elude the reader. It seems likely from their subjectivity and vehemence that his own experience is the key to their confusions. However unpromising the subject, an analysis of Rolle's works must begin by appraising the sketchy evidence we have for the nature of his life.

II

Such appraisals have not been in short supply during the last ninety years, which has seen the development of a substantial body of biographical writings about Rolle.[8] Nineteenth-century studies of his work were mostly stylistic and philological (Allen, pp. 19–21 provides a list) and were often based on *The Prick of Conscience* – until in 1910 Hope Emily Allen showed that this poem was not his. But the 1890s saw the publication of Carl Horstmann's two massive volumes of English devotional writing, under the provocative title *Richard Rolle of Hampole, an English Father of the Church* (1895–1896); this provided a generation of readers with works that could be attributed to him by default (Horstmann's policy being to include any devotional work that he considered 'northern', or that otherwise took his fancy). Its second volume also contains a detailed biographical portrait of Rolle with quotations from his Latin works (pp. v–xliii), a wonderfully imaginative fantasia on the *Officium* which provided the basis for many others (especially Clay 1914 and Porter 1929) and was the formative (largely unacknowledged) source for Allen's understanding of him. Here originated the persistent image of Rolle as a sturdy, anti-establishment figure, moving about through Yorkshire with his hermit's rucksack and his message of joy. The sudden growth in the popularity of mysticism, stemming from a number of important early twentieth-century studies of the subject – William James's *The Varieties of Religious Experience* (1902), Baron von Hügel's *The Mystical Element in Religion* (1908) and Evelyn Underhill's *Mysticism* (1911) – naturally seized on Rolle, and focussed on the nature of his life and religious experience.[9] By 1930 he had been the subject of two book-length biographical studies (G. Hodgson 1926, Comper 1928), some articles (Moorman 1914, Watts 1916, Noetinger 1926, Patch 1928, *et al.*), an enterprisingly cross-cultural saint's life (Verier Elwin's *Richard Rolle, Christian Sannyase*, 1930), and a disappointing novel (R.H. Benson's *Richard Raynal, Solitary*,

1906).[10] Even Allen's vast book (1927), which established the canon of Rolle's works, to the discomfiture of devotees of Horstmann's version of the hermit (as Geraldine Hodgson's injured rearguard action, *Rolle and 'Our Daily Work'* (1929b), makes painfully clear), and which is now usually treated as a manuscript study, is called *Writings Ascribed to Richard Rolle, Hermit of Hampole, and Materials for His Biography*. Biographical conjecture occupies at least as much space in this book as the description of works and manuscripts (see Excursus 1 for an account of Allen's presentation of Rolle).

The widespread interest in Rolle subsided after the early 1930s, and has not fully returned in spite of the attention that has recently been accorded the *Cloud* author, Walter Hilton, Julian of Norwich and Margery Kempe. However, there has been a steady trickle of work on Rolle, much of it textual or editorial, and hence essential for a study such as this; literary studies, especially of the Latin works, are still few in number. Lives of the hermit have remained a *topos* of editions and theses concerned with him, such as Nicole Marzac's *Richard Rolle de Hampole (1300–1349): Vie et œuvres suivies du tractatus super Apocalypsim* (1968), Elizabeth Murray's edition of *Super Canticum Canticorum* (1958), E.J. Arnould's edition of *Melos Amoris* (1957) and Gabriel Liegey's study of the rhetoric of that work (1954). Other studies have analysed some of his works with a view to making discoveries about his religious life. These have discussed Rolle's 'authenticity' as a mystic, and have tried to discern whether his writings show signs of his having achieved union with God or whether his claims to be spiritually 'advanced' were unwarranted.[11]

These biographical studies range from the popular to the scholarly and differ significantly in detail and emphasis. There are accounts of Rolle's life which represent it as having been conducted in harmony with the norms of post-Tridentine Catholic orthodoxy (Noetinger 1926) or the conventions of hagiography (Arnould 1937a, 1960). There are Wordsworthian views of his life (as in the foreword to Comper's biography). Horstmann (introducing his first volume) sees him as a symbol of Teutonic individualism, endemic in the English personality in spite of the Frankish effeminacy mingled with our Anglo-Saxon stock. He has been subjected to psychoanalytic readings that cast doubt on his mental stability (Allen); he has been chosen to symbolize the spiritual balance that typifies a mystic (in G. Hodgson's 1926 book, *The Sanity of Mysticism: A Study of Richard Rolle*). He has been portrayed as individualistic Yorkshireman (Heseltine 1932a), proto-Protestant (Porter 1929), anti-scholastic (Hardwick 1916), moderate Englishman (S.B. James 1941), robust independent (S.B. James 1949), and 'maverick' saint (Russell 1978).

Taken as a whole, these studies are of great interest, as a testimony to the fascination Rolle's life, both 'outer' and 'inner', has aroused. Like their medieval predecessors, most of these readers seem to have responded to Rolle as a saintly personality; they have accordingly recreated him in whatever image they thought best captured their own ideals of sainthood. (Even

Allen's psychoanalytic account of Rolle's career fashions it into a paradigm of self-discovery.) Yet in scholarly terms the emphasis on his biography rather than his works has done more harm than good. While I have stated that we must come to decisions about his life in order to understand his writings, almost all the studies mentioned, both popular and scholarly, seem preoccupied with biography to the exclusion of any interest in those writings. Those scholars who do approach them do so with assumptions about his personality and life already formed, and so distort what they interpret. Since we can know little of his life, but have all too much evidence of his writing career, such a procedure is perverse. Indeed, it has given rise to a situation in which, for all the hundred or so critical works listed in the most recent bibliographies (Sawyer 1978, Lagorio and Bradley 1981, Alford 1984), an analytic appraisal of Rolle as a writer can hardly be said to have begun.

III

The distortions that result from misreading Rolle's life and personality are evident even in the work of the two most sensitive and informed of his biographers, Maurice Noetinger and Emile Arnould. These French Catholic scholars were anxious to dispute the imputations of two non-Catholics (Horstmann and Allen) that Rolle was a nonconformist and rebel against the ecclesiastical establishment, perhaps with heretical leanings. Both thus interpret his life as saintly in a traditional way – as having been lived in humble obedience to the Church. Although in doing so they uncover much that is of use for understanding Rolle, their findings are undermined by the presuppositions which shape the portraits they draw of him.

Noetinger's article, 'The biography of Richard Rolle' (published in *The Month*, 1926), announces documentary evidence that Rolle studied at the Sorbonne and reinterprets the account of his life given in the *Officium* in the light of this evidence.[12] Noetinger claims that the *Officium*'s account of the young Rolle throwing on his rudely fashioned hermit's garb and fleeing his father's house is no more than a pious fiction. Arguing that his stay at the Sorbonne must have occurred before he became a hermit, Noetinger draws a new picture of his conversion; it becomes the decision of a *magister* of mature years and in priestly orders to give up his temporal ambitions and follow God. Seeing him as a learned priest makes explicable several incongruities in his life: his preaching a sermon, his direction of the nuns of Hampole, his writing career. If he had been a layman, such activities would have been unusual, even irregular.

This presentation of Rolle occasioned some controversy in the late 1920s and 1930s, after Noetinger's death.[13] In spite of its documentary basis, the motive force of the argument is Noetinger's dislike of the hermit of the *Officium* and of Horstmann's biography, and his desire to see in him a kind of sanctity more to his taste. Thus he is an astute commentator on the *Officium*'s status as a work of piety rather than of history, while being extremely naive

36

about the accuracy of Rolle's own biographical statements. He uses passages from *Incendium Amoris* in which Rolle bewails his unclean youth to contradict the *Officium*'s uniformly saintly view of the hermit, and thereby to argue that for some time he must have been 'in the world'; this becomes a specific argument, from seventeenth-century manuscript evidence, that he was at the Sorbonne. But Noetinger ignores the didactic purposes of Rolle's autobiographical writing and the tradition of humility *topoi* they evoke. The conclusion of his article, which returns to the story of Rolle's conversion, itself succumbs to the formalizing conventions of hagiography:

[Assuming that he was indeed at the Sorbonne], it will easily be seen that it not only makes Rolle's life more intelligible but that it also improves the character of his holiness. Perhaps his conversion appears now less marvellous; but instead of the impulsive deed of a self-sufficient boy, we have the generous resolution of a man who deliberately gives up the honours and worldly fame to which he was entitled; instead of a haughty scorn for a degree of learning which he has never reached, we have the deep humility of a scholar who conceals what he knows. It seems to us that Rolle does not lose by the change. (Noetinger 1926, p. 30)

Here the saintly virtues of resolution and humility are conjured out of Rolle's failure to claim distinctions he never possessed – for it is clear that Noetinger's argument that he was a learned priest is erroneous. Although Allen (1932a) may place too much emphasis on two manuscripts which state that he was not a priest, the fact that neither the *Officium* nor his own writings claim he was in orders is powerful negative evidence. A writer so given to self-explanation would surely mention his authoritative position as a priest if he were in orders, and Allen must be right in reading his remark in *Super Lectiones Mortuorum*, 'I am no bishop, prelate, nor rector of the Church', as proof of his lay status (see 196.2–3, and Allen 1932a). We would expect the *Officium* to be as eager as Noetinger to explain that in preaching Rolle was merely doing his priestly duty; to present him as an institutional figure would increase the chances of his canonization. Moreover, Arnould destroyed the basis of Noetinger's argument when he showed the evidence of Rolle's attendance at the Sorbonne to be spurious (1939, corroborated by Sargent 1988). There is every reason to assume that he was not in orders.

Since Noetinger's facts are apparently wrong, it may seem that the picture he draws of Rolle is unimportant. Yet the spirit of his account remains influential, especially in the work of Arnould. Arnould's introduction to his edition of *Melos Amoris*, widely praised as the best account of Rolle's life and thought available, nevertheless contains just the presuppositions as to his conventionality that we observed in Noetinger. On the face of it, Arnould's account is not open to objections; for example, he is duly suspicious of the biographical concerns of his scholarly forebears (as his 1939 demolition of Noetinger's argument, reprinted in an appendix to his edition, also shows). On closer inspection, however, this account reveals serious weaknesses. Early in his introduction (pp. v–xi), Arnould criticizes two predecessors, Horstmann and Allen, who read a passage in *Melos Amoris* as describing

37

Rolle's quarrel with a contemporary bishop. Arnould recalls that he showed (in a 1937 article) that the passage is a debate not with the ecclesiastical authorities of Rolle's day but with an earlier bishop, Anselm – hence that the passage does not indicate that Rolle was an object of official distrust. However, this piece of close reading fails to prove all that Arnould wishes it to. He uses it as a warrant to be dismissive of Horstmann and Allen's entire presentation of Rolle, and to draw sweeping conclusions in the rest of his introduction: 'Others, led astray by passages taken without their context, or understood too literally ... have sought to make him a rebel against ecclesiastical authority. It can be confidently asserted that not one line in any of Rolle's extant writings justifies such a view' (p. lii). Yet Arnould does nothing to justify this assertion. While Rolle was no proto-Protestant as Horstmann thought, nor the rebel presented by Allen, we shall see that he does not acknowledge a duty of obedience to any ecclesiastical authority, asserting a high view of his own status in the Church. The energy of his individualism requires some explanation.

Arnould does not confront this side of Rolle's personality and writing, managing to tidy and moderate the many instances of assertive individualism to be found in *Melos Amoris*. His introduction to this work largely consists of an account of Rolle's life and doctrine, which intersperses quotations from *Melos Amoris* with his own summarizing statements; these combine to form a coherent doctrinal and biographical narrative. The end product is indeed an orthodox and systematic exposition of a mystic's progress, but to create this, Arnould has to extract passages from all over the long and rambling treatise, and to organize them into a framework of his own devising, the coherence of which is provided by himself. While it has initial cogency, this is not the fair-minded method he implies it is. Further, his attempt to normalize Rolle relies heavily on his paraphrases of passages, rather than on the text of *Melos Amoris* itself, and these former are often more palatable than the passages which they represent. Rolle does not 'admit', for example, that the triumph of the elect 'is not free from a sense of vindication or even the satisfaction of revenge' (p. li, see 48.20, 191.20), he exultantly asserts it. Nor does the remark, 'ecclesiastical authorities ought to verify the competence of those they appoint to that office of preaching' (p. liv), catch the spirit of the original: 'Sed errant nunc undique miseros mittentes qui oracula ignorant clause Scripture' (152.17: 'But now they err, sending wretches everywhere who are ignorant of the secrets of the Scriptures').

Arnould's generalization seems based on a predisposition, essentially similar to Noetinger's, to think of Rolle as exemplary. He thus accepts Rolle's autobiographical statements, which are carefully designed to be as exemplary as possible, at their face value. The disruptive statements in Rolle's writing are interpreted in the light of this self-portrait, and discovered to be less unusual than had been supposed; where the writer asserts equality with or superiority to the saints, this now exemplifies 'the simplicity of the truly humble' (p. xxx). Step by step, Rolle is recreated as an institutionalized holy man, an integrated member of the Church Militant whose vehemence proceeds purely from the depth of his love for God and the purity of his concern for the Church. While Arnould rightly accuses Allen and Horstmann of 'bias . . . blemishes . . . distortions' (p. vii), his own normalization of Rolle invites the same criticisms.

In spite of their faults, the work of Noetinger and Arnould is not to be dismissed. They are among the few scholars who have read most of what Rolle wrote and they base their accounts on the appraisal of evidence as well as on personal predilections. Even their anxiety as to his relations with the ecclesiastical establishment of his day points us usefully towards that issue. Less whimsical than Horstmann or Allen, less sentimental than Comper or Hodgson, their recreations of his life are at least based on hagiographic models that can properly be applied to the Middle Ages. After a fashion their rejection of Horstmann and Allen is even proper; Rolle's life, as told by himself and by the *Officium*, does have to be understood in terms of exemplary norms, and cannot be regarded too readily as wayward.

This point has been made most clearly by John Alford, who has shown the extent to which the exemplary models which influence the account of his life given by the *Officium* are also evident in Rolle's presentation of himself. Alford's 1973 study of biblical *imitatio* in Rolle's works points to several such models, alludes to 'Rolle's tendency to describe his personal condition in terms of biblical language and personalities', and warns that 'we should be doubly cautious in approaching his autobiographical comments' (p. 10). An article of 1976 applies this caution to the *Officium*'s description of Rolle's conversion. Rather than seeing the story of his flight into the wilderness as depicting a piece of adolescent foolishness, Alford argues that its details are symbolic, recalling biblical or other models; formally invested with his hermit's garb, Rolle retires like Christ into the wilderness. Not only were the compilers of the *Officium* aware of these models; Rolle must have been himself. Indeed, 'his whole life seems to have been a series of such calculated gestures' (p. 22), in which he enacted the life of Christ, the patience of Job, or the persecuted persona of the psalmist (p. 24).

Alford's brief accounts of Rolle's use of models are important mainly because of the sophisticated way they link the question of the nature of his personality with his practices as a writer. Rolle's personal acts of *imitatio* can also be perceived in the moment-by-moment adoptions, adaptations and developments of biblical language performed throughout his written work, and identified by Alford (1973) as a fundamental characteristic of his style. His grander gestures can be assessed through study of these smaller ones. However, as it stands, this depiction of Rolle as imitator can be taken in more than one direction. We could use it to blaze a trail back to a view of Rolle as an exemplary figure of the kind Noetinger and Arnould describe, in this vein: 'If Rolle's life was lived according to biblical models, it should be regarded as saintly; if he is so regarded, and his writings also imitate biblical models, they should be accorded the respect due to the works of a saint, and can not very well be seen as rebellious or as assertively individualistic.' Or, in less naive style, we can focus on the 'calculated' nature of Rolle's gestures, and look at his relationship to the personae he evoked and to his contemporaries. To present oneself as exemplary is not necessarily to be perceived as such. Noetinger and Arnould would both seem to assume that a Rolle who is in some sort exemplary must intrinsically be in a proper – that is, a humble and obedient – relation to the hierarchy of the Church, and must also have an essentially unproblematic relationship with those around him. In the rest of this chapter, I wish to question these assumptions by analysing the *Officium* narrative and Rolle's works in order to see what sorts of relations he may have had with the ecclesiastical establishment and with his contemporaries, especially his patrons. By arguing that these relations were in some respects unusual and difficult, I hope in effect to drive a wedge between the exemplary Rolle, whose life re-enacts the lives of the saints, and the man who manipulates these re-enactments. Bearing Alford's warnings in mind, the discussion is not principally concerned to explore the 'personality' of this latter figure, or to determine the presence or absence of a quality of 'holiness' within this personality; such concepts need to be fleshed out with more biographical information than we have. Its aim is mainly to locate potential sources of tension in Rolle's life – especially between his way of life and the norms by which the eremitic life was usually lived – and to show that his works respond to such tension in ways it is hard to call exemplary. Rolle's difficulties on this score seem to me fundamental to the complex inter-relationship of his life and his works.

IV

Alford's analysis of Rolle's conversion only touches on the models to which the *Officium*'s narrative alludes; here, they can usefully be discussed in the context of a similar narrative, that of the conversion of St Francis in Bonaventure's *Legenda S. Francisci*. Rolle flees his father's house (*lectio prima*) in much the spirit that St Francis strips himself of all his clothes to settle his earthly debt to his own father (cap. 2). Both narratives portray exemplary acts of obedience to a text that remained important to Rolle, Luke 14.26: '*If one comes to me and does not hate his father and mother . . . he can not be my disciple*' (see, e.g., *Judica Me* 15.16–21); many incidents in saints' lives (to the pattern of which Francis and Rolle are also conforming) present the same model.[14] In both, conversion consists of abandoning an old way of life out of fear, disgust with self or world, and devotion. Such a view of conversion is pervasive in medieval religious writing, as in many passages of Rolle's works. While the *Officium* is as concerned with the presentation of exemplary behaviour as is Bonaventure, this is a case in which we might expect exemplary narrative to coincide with reality: Rolle abandoning the career chosen for him to pursue a spiritual career as a hermit.

Both the *Officium* and the *Legenda* equate conversion with a change of clothing as well as the abandonment of home. In ordination and baptism rites a change of garments always symbolizes a changed life: putting off the old, putting on the new (Ephesians 4.22–24); being clothed with the longed-for garments of heaven (2 Corinthians 5.1–4). In both narratives the change of garments is both solemn and funny; Francis strips naked in Assisi's main piazza, while Rolle's efforts as a tailor (his first habit is made by himself from two of his sister's dresses and his father's hood) produces only a 'confusam similitudinem heremite', and convinces his sister he is insane. Bringing out the exemplary nature of Rolle's actions, the response following the *lectio prima* of the *Officium* then opens 'the saint has fled to solitude', while the *lectio secunda* begins with him arriving at the home of a neighbour, who later reclothes him. This narrative pattern follows the *Legenda* so closely that the latter might even be a source of the *Officium* here.[15]

However inchoate the feelings from which it sprang, Rolle's conversion was therefore not atypical, coinciding with a recognizable pattern of exemplary Christian behaviour. By refusing to agree to the plans his secular superiors have for him, he bows to the more authoritative demands of his spiritual destiny. But this is not the whole story; however fitting Rolle's conversion is from a hagiographic perspective, in institutional terms the same actions run counter to the expected norms. A hermit was required to receive authorization for his way of life, from his abbot if he was a monk, from his bishop if he was a secular priest or layman; this was the situation in canon law (in civil law, too, after 1388), and often in practice (Clay 1914, pp. 85–90). Such authorization took the form of a service of profession and benediction, like the late example printed by Clay from a Lydda pontifical (pp. 199–202).[16] In this ceremony, the hermit, who is described as 'converted from worldly vanity', approaches the bishop or his representative carrying his new habit, is questioned about his intentions, makes a profession, and then strips off his old clothes, and puts on his habit. Much of the ceremony is concerned with the habit itself (described as 'vestimenta professioni heremitice conveniencia'), which is the symbol and proof of the hermit's profession. A fourteenth-century *Regula Heremitarum* also emphasizes the importance of the hermit's receiving his habit from the proper ecclesiastical source: 'Let him have such clothes as the bishop in whose diocese he lives ordains for him, or his patron if he is a church prelate' (Oliger 1928, p. 305). After the ceremony, the hermit is questioned again before retiring to his cell, to make sure that he understands his obligations and intends to live according to a rule. Yet the *Officium* presents its protagonist as turning himself into a hermit, performing an act of quasi-sacramental and legal significance, without the authority to do so; converted from the world, he too strips naked and dons the habit, with his sister for congregation, before retiring into the desert. The *Officium*'s account of this keeps as close as it can to ecclesiastical ceremonies of benediction. For all his comic spontaneity, Rolle is portrayed as fussily concerned for the details of his clothing (Alford 1976, pp. 21–22): after ordering his sister, a day in advance, to produce a white and a grey dress, as well as a hood, he cuts the sleeves off the grey one, puts the white one on next to his skin and the grey one on top, before swathing his head in the hood. Thus he follows an injunction in the *Regula Heremitarum* (pp. 305–306) that a hermit's outer garment should be a penitential grey or black, and that his habit as a whole should not be the same as that of any particular religious order. As soon as he reaches the Daltons his habit is nonetheless changed, to conform with the other requirement mentioned in the *Regula* (and noticeably flouted by his first costume), that a hermit's clothing not be 'nimium curiosa' (p. 316); his new clothes are described as 'vestibus convenientibus heremite' (*lectio iiija*). In the versicle which follows the account of his profession in *lectio prima*, we are also told that in the 'desert' to which he flees he keeps a 'perfectam regulam' of holy love, with love directing ('abbas amor dat morum formulam / sancte vite'). Clearly, the compilers of the *Officium* were aware that their protagonist should have made a profession and been instructed in a rule of life. Equally clearly, there was in fact no formal ecclesiastical involvement at this stage of his eremitic career; even his second habit is given him by a lay patron, rather than a prelate. Since the *Officium* shows Rolle thus disregarding his legal responsibilities, it seems likely that he was never licensed as a hermit, and that his position, formally speaking, was anomalous. Here we seem to have located a possible source of tension between Rolle and the ecclesiastical authorities.[17]

Yet in fact it is difficult to show that his lack of a formal profession need have mattered much; indeed, in spite of the legislation concerning the licensing of hermits, there is no evidence that Rolle's position as a self-made hermit would necessarily have attracted any adverse official attention. The *Dictionnaire de Droit Canonique* (vol. 5, col. 417) points out how vaguely defined the status of hermits was as late as the seventeenth century; even the question of whether they were to be regarded as laymen or have the legal privileges of ecclesiastical status was in doubt. Bonaventure (*In Librum Quartum Sententiarum*, dist. 227, dub. 3) assumes them to be genuine religious who have an obligation to practise chastity, although they are not bound by a vow of obedience; but he has nothing to say about who is to enforce that obligation. Legislation on the status of hermits both before and after the Council of Trent assumed that not all would seek permission for practising their way of life. The informality of the institution in England is borne out by the lives of some of Rolle's most distinguished eremitical forebears – Christina of Markyate, Wulfric of Hazlebury (twelfth century) and Robert of Knaresborough (thirteenth) – none of whom went through episcopal ceremonies to become hermits. Rolle evidently did not regard himself as under a vow of obedience to anyone other than God, and called his decision to become a hermit a 'singulare propositum' to differentiate it from the vows taken by 'obedienciarii'. This seems to be a conventional, not an idiosyncratic, stance.[18] Since hermits were not bound by vows and, unlike anchorites, did not need organized financial backing, it is easy to see why regulations requiring them to submit to ecclesiastical direction might be ignored, perhaps especially in the enormous diocese of York. Indeed, there are few signs that the ecclesiastical authorities were preoccupied with hermits to anything like the same extent that they were with anchorites.[19]

We should thus not assume that Rolle's formally anomalous position would in itself have caused official difficulty. Indeed, in spite of Horstmann and Allen's efforts to make him a conscious rebel, there are no indications that he was ever actually in official difficulty. When he writes of being criticized, it is from monks, patrons, and others; his worst detractors, he states, were those whom he first thought of as close friends (*Incendium Amoris* 188.17–18: 'Nam eos pessimos detractores habui, quos prius amicos fidos putavi'). Perhaps he is referring here to the patrons who provided his board and lodging, since a passage shortly after this (196.31–197.26) makes much of the relationship between patron and *pauper* as a friendship; as will become clear, many of his problems do seem to have involved his relationships with patrons. But even if Rolle's difficulties with secular patrons were serious, they would probably not have given rise to an official challenge to his way of life. It seems most unlikely that such a challenge – one that might have made overt the oddity of his self-defined relationship with the Church, and pushed him into extremism or conformity – occurred.

But why did Rolle incur these criticisms, and why did they matter? I suggest that there are two main reasons, the first of which is simply that he emerges from his works as an abrasive personality, with a highly developed sense of his own rightness and importance in the scheme of things. One tactic his works employ for persuading readers is to imply that those who disagree face damnation; the daily equivalent of so emphatic a stance might naturally make as many enemies as disciples, however charming its propounder. Such a stance seems the product of a mind inclined to vehement categorization, and dependent on a belief in opposition for its own sense of coherence: a mind that almost creates enemies. To say this is to claim no more than that, like Margery Kempe, Rolle cultivated the idea of persecution, and that the distinctive tone of his writings had some relation to his personal tone.

The second, much more elaborate, reason is that even if Rolle's career was not of the kind that was likely to create official difficulty, his life as a hermit was still sufficiently unusual to cause suspicion, give opponents room for criticism, and put him on the defensive. This is hard to demonstrate, partly because much basic research on English eremitism remains to be done, but even more because the term 'hermit' covers such a wide range of late medieval English types. There are the uneducated hermits of the sort praised and satirized in *Piers Plowman*: bridgebuilders, roadmenders and vagabonds, laymen in habits who begged alms and tilled the soil, for whom the simple Rule of St Paul the Hermit was written (V. Davis 1985). At the other end of the scale, there are hermits of the Carthusian and other eremitic orders, some of whom were highly educated, and the few religious writers who were hermits: the 'Monk of Farne' who was a Durham Benedictine; the author of *The Cloud of Unknowing*, of whom we know little, but who was probably a university graduate turned hermit, anchorite, or perhaps Carthusian; and Walter Hilton, who was a hermit for a dissatisfied period between being at university and entering an Augustinian canonry.[20] Given this range, it is difficult to theorize with confidence about what behaviour might have been considered usual, or unusual, in a hermit like Rolle. However, one fourteenth-century work does go some way towards setting up a standard of eremitic behaviour, against which his can be measured: the *Regula Heremitarum*, a work which was at one stage wrongly ascribed to Rolle himself. This work concentrates on the external features of the eremitic life – which are our concern here – with a flexibility that made it useful for many kinds of practitioners. It also quotes widely from recognized authorities on eremitism, especially Aelred's *De Institutis Inclusarum*. The influence of this work was strongly felt in fourteenth-century Yorkshire, as it was elsewhere (Moyes 1988, vol. 1, pp. 33–53 *passim*). Thus it seems likely that many English hermits followed precepts similar to those laid down in the *Regula*. Here I shall assume that this work crystallizes the behaviour that Rolle's contemporaries would have recognized as proper in a hermit.[21]

Like most treatments of the eremitic life (e.g. *Piers Plowman*, C VIII.187–202, XVII.6–71), and in spite of the fact that in practice many of them lived in towns (as the Oxford MS states, p. 314), the *Regula* describes hermits as those who renounce the world for the desert (*heremus*). The life of the desert is one of austerity. Hermits are *pauperes* living in humble cells, and should not even devote attention to repairing them. They are not to eat too much, or too richly (pp. 299–300); the Oxford MS enjoins three days of fasting a week (p. 316), and the Cambridge MS quotes Aelred against using the ideal of *discretio* as an excuse for indulgence, 'for true discretion is to put the soul before the body' (p. 304). They must keep silence when possible (p. 303). In order to avoid idleness, and in imitation of the Desert Fathers (pp. 306–307, 311), they are to sustain themselves by hard manual labour; if they are incapable of this, they may beg, or find a patron to look after them (p. 302). When not working, they are to spend their time in prayer; in the Oxford MS, this includes the canonical Hours, the accompanying Hours of the Virgin, and daily Mass (p. 320). They should prefer to learn than to teach (p. 303). While they owe formal obedience to nobody, their bishop, or a clerical patron or priest, should take note ('notificare') of how they are living, and correct them if need be; or else, with the bishop's permission, they may find a wise old monk or priest to whom they may occasionally confess (pp. 304–305). They should cherish chastity, and avoid at all costs the company of women – this point is made vehemently, with the help of some pithy anti-feminist comments out of Jerome (pp. 303, 307–308). But the matter on which the *Regula* expends most energetic attention is that of stability.[22] Hermits are desert dwellers ('demorantes', p. 300) and should not move around: 'Heremita igitur discurrere non presumat' (p. 301). They may have to leave their cells to find means to live (Oxford MS, pp. 314, 316–317), but they must always return, and must not change their place of abode. Those who do not maintain eremitic stability the *Regula* calls *girovagi*, quoting the *Benedictine Rule* (cap. 1) against these false hermits. It thereby alludes to a long tradition of satire against wandering hermits, who are characterized by writers from Peter Damian in the eleventh century to Langland in the fourteenth as lazy, lecherous, greedy men whose version of the contemplative life has nothing to do with abandoning the world, and who threaten to undermine the very basis of the Church, the principal of order.[23] *Girovagi* are the antithesis of the life depicted by the *Regula*: a life which is less regulated than the other religious professions, with a degree of independence, but which is also austere and disciplined, and contains its own system of checks and balances; a life which, like that of anchorites, is essentially penitential in character.

In a few respects, Rolle's life fits well into this general model. He regarded himself as a *pauper*, and a desert-dweller in the tradition of the Desert Fathers (*Judica Me* 15.22–16.17). He needed silence in order to further his experience of *canor* (*Incendium Amoris*, cap. 33); silence was, indeed, something of an obsession, constantly searched for ('Solebam profecto quietam querere', *Incendium Amoris* 188.6). He often writes against idleness (e.g. in *The Bee*, and in *Super Canticum Canticorum* 8.9–9.8). Yet if we gather together all the *Officium* and Rolle himself imply about his way of life, the picture that emerges differs greatly from that found in the *Regula Heremitarum*. It may not have been unusual that his departure into the desert should in practice have meant merely removal to a neighbour's shed (*Officium*, *lectio iija*). But having established himself as a hermit, there are signs that Rolle did not always practise the expected austerities:

Verum ex quo quis illud acciperit, nunquam deinceps ab illo plene recedit, quin semper maneat fervor, canor, aut dulcor, si omnia ista non assint; omnia autem simul manente nisi cum nimia infirmitate [capitis] vel pectoris seu lateris reprimitur, aut nimia fame vel siti quibus caro frangitur, vel nimis frigore, calore vel itinere impediatur. Oportet ergo ipsum qui in divino amore vult canere vel canendo iubilare et ardere in solitudine existere, et in nimia abstinencia non vivere nec superfluitati se aliquatenus exhibere. Melius tamen esset pro se si in modico nesciens excederet mensuram, dummodo bona intencione ad sustentandum naturam illud agat, quam si nimis ieiunio deficere inceperet, et pre imbecilitate corporis canere non valeret . . . Comedi ergo et bibi de hiis que meliora videbantur; non quia delicias amavi sed ut natura sustentaretur in servicio Dei et in iubilo Ihesu Christi, conformans me illis cum quibus morabar bono modo propter Christum, et ne sanctitatem fingerem ubi nulla est, et ne homines me nimis lauderent ubi minus essem laudabilis. Recessi eciam a plerisque, non quia me communiter et duriori modo paverunt, sed quia non concordavimus in moribus, vel propter aliam racionabilem causam. Audeo tamen dicere cum beato Iob: *Stulti despiciebant me, et cum recessissem ab eis detrahabant mihi* [Job 19.18]. Verumtamen erubescent cum me viderint qui dixerunt me nullicubi velle morari, nisi ubi delicate possem pasci. (*Incendium Amoris* 174.27–175.31)

[Certainly, ⟨this experience⟩ never completely leaves the person who has received it. Instead, either heat, sweetness, or song always remains, when all of them are not present. And, indeed, all remain at once – unless ⟨the contemplative⟩ is held back by too great an infirmity of the head, or the breast, or the sides; or the flesh is weakened

45

by too much hunger or thirst; or too much cold, or heat, or travelling, gets in the way. So the one who wants to sing in divine love, or by singing to rejoice and burn, must dwell in solitude, and not live in too much abstinence, nor manifest any kind of indulgence. However, it would be better for him if, unknowingly, he went a little beyond measure – since he would do so with the good intention of sustaining nature – than if he should begin to fade through too much fasting and be unable to sing through physical weakness. Thus I have eaten and drunk things which seemed lavish: not because I loved delicacies, but so that I could sustain nature in the service of God and in rejoicing in Jesus Christ; conforming myself, in a good sense, to those with whom I was living – for the sake of Christ, and so that I should not invent holiness where none was, and so that people should not praise me too much where I was less praiseworthy. I also left several people, not because they fed me communally and coarsely, but because we did not agree in our ways of life or for some other reasonable cause. But I dare say with the blessed Job: *Fools despised me, and when I left them they disparaged me.* Still, those who said that I would not stay anywhere I could not dine well would blush when they saw me.]

It seems, from this account and others (e.g. *Incendium Amoris* 146.15–147.8; 271.20–23), that asceticism interfered with Rolle's experience of *fervor*, *dulcor* and *canor*, which required him to be relaxed, not too tired from manual work or travel, not too hot or cold, and fairly well fed. As a contemplative whose stance was explicitly anti-penitential (see *Incendium Amoris* 270.11–16), he had no spiritual reason for the harsh austerities that Aelred enjoins; on the contrary, as he states here, he had practical reasons for avoiding them. His argument is not altogether untraditional: Walter Hilton, for example, writes in a similar vein about the need to avoid excessive fasting as much as excessive eating (*The Scale of Perfection* 1, caps. 72–76; see also Chapter 2, n. 11). Nonetheless, it is clear that he was criticized for his eating habits, and this can only be because it was thought he should live more austerely than he did. Moreover, although he denies the charge of gluttony with conviction, he is still defensive: his claim that he conforms deliberately to those around him comes uneasily from one who has left the world, and real anxiety breaks out when he calls his critics *stulti*.[24] To the extent that he succeeded in avoiding the cold, fatigue and physical labour which interrupted his joyful union with God, it seems likely that he would have attracted other criticisms: for preferring a comfortable cell to the tumbledown shed that the *Regula* recommends (p. 300); for not keeping long vigils or fasts; for not supporting himself by manual labour.[25] Again, cap. 31 of *Incendium Amoris* speaks of *canor* and liturgical song as mutually exclusive. Although Rolle assures us that he attends Mass, he also states that his appearances on feast-days (when Mass is sung, not said) are against his will, made merely for the purpose of avoiding scandal (233.27: 'propter obliquos morsus populorum'). Such remarks (as well as the conspicuous absence of references to the divine office even in his pastoral writings) give us cause to doubt that he attended Mass, and said the other services, with the regularity that was expected. Here again he may have provided his opponents with grounds for attack.

There is worse to come, for, far from avoiding the company of women, Rolle was evidently much lionized by them, and had more than one important female friendship. The *Officium* has one scene in which the lady of the house and her friends come to be instructed by him (*lectio sexta*), another in which he helps fend off demons who are attacking a dying patroness (*lectio viija*). *Incendium Amoris* speaks of the dangers of friendship with women, but also states that such friendship is possible – an unusual emphasis in the medieval literature of *amicitia*, which suggests that Rolle was aware of idiosyncrasy in this regard (see pp. 224–225). No doubt the *Regula*'s injunction to avoid women was often ignored for good reasons, and without causing any comment. But several passages in Rolle's works suggest that his female friendships gave rise to sexual scandal. Cap. 12 of *Incendium Amoris* recounts several anecdotes, all involving female patrons (179.14–17), in which he was too familiar with women (praising the size of one's breasts, touching another), or they were with him – as with the woman who praised his lovely looks and voice, but scorned him as a eunuch (178.31–179.12, quoted below, pp. 129–130). When *Judica Me* cryptically refuses to explain 'to anyone alive' the whole reason why Rolle left his cell (2.17–18: 'non totum dico quare recessi nec alicui viventi indicare volo'), it is hard, in the light of these other incidents, to avoid presuming that here again he is concealing some sexual embarrassment. His way with female patrons evidently had its disadvantages.

Yet the most serious way in which Rolle was felt to diverge from the proper conduct of the eremitic life was in the fact that he moved from one cell to another. We know this from several references in his works and one in the *Officium*, all of them highly defensive. The *Officium* (*lectio viia*) states that after some time (spent probably with the Daltons), 'the saint went elsewhere, doubtless in order to assist in the salvation of many by living in many places'. This implies that he moved more than once; indeed the phrase 'crebra loci mutacio' ('frequent change of place') is used. His action is defended from the calumnious by being compared to accounts in the *Vitae Patrum*, where some of the holiest of the Desert Fathers are said to have changed their cells, and is then justified in canon law. Rolle's own justifications are similar. *Incendium Amoris*, cap. 15 claims that the Desert Fathers changed cells in search of quiet and were criticized by the wicked on that account (188.6–23); another passage, quoted above, says vaguely that he moved 'quia non concordavimus in moribus, vel propter aliam racionabilem causam'. Both passages bear out the *Officium*'s suggestion that his moves were numerous, at least at some stage of his career. Both also treat the people whom Rolle left (his patrons) as culprits and critics – while implying that they may have not been the only critics – and deal with them bitterly: they are 'fools [who] despised me'; like a stirred-up cesspit, they give off nothing but stench (188.13: 'De latrina amoto operculo, non exalat nisi fetor'). Another passage, this time from *Judica Me*, gives a detailed and ingenuous account of what was presumably Rolle's first move, away from the Daltons. Here his defence is more legalistic;

he writes of his formal obligations towards his patron, and his rights as a hermit. But again, bitterness is mostly directed against his erstwhile patron:

Si heremita dicerer cuius nomine indigne vocor, non erit nec merito esse poterit scandalum audientibus si corporalem habitacionem mutarem aliquando, vel ab una cella ad aliam transirem, cum non sum obligatus magis in uno heremo quam in alio moram meam stabilire. Unde non inutile arbitrandum est si in iuventute mea plura loca viderim, ut de melioribus statui meo conveniencius unum eligere possem. Nam vos scitis et a me sepius audistis me ibi velle morari, et certe de hoc mentitus sum nequaquam, quia statim ut Deus scit et vos cogniscitis mutati fuerunt quantum ad me qui ministrare assueverunt. Propter quod mihi gravius fuit. Moram meam ut putabam antequam ibi venirem habere potui propter fructus colligentes. Quorum causa ita locum abhorrui ut in illo loco numquam a festo Pentecosten usque ad festum Sancti Martini manere cogitavi. Et quid proderit mihi in hyeme locum tenere et in estate propter incommoda compelli recedere? Melius puto ibi sedere in hyeme ubi etiam quiete valeam in estate esse. Verumptamen non totum dico quare recessi nec alicui viventi indicare volo. Porro, ut mihi videbitur, parvum vel nichil de me curavit. Adquirat ergo sibi alium quem amplius amare disposuit. In omnibus enim dictis et promissis meis condiciones subintelligo generales huiuscemodi, videlicet: si vixero; si potero; si hoc melius pro me visum fuerit; et super omnia si Deus sic voluerit. Si condiciones ergo sint mutate, in quo culpandus sum si non persisterem in ea qui prius voluntate?   (*Judica Me* 2.2–3.1)

[If I be spoken of as a hermit – and I am called by such a name, though unworthily – it will not be, nor rightly could it be, a scandal to those who listen if I should sometime change my bodily home, or if I should move from one cell to another – since I am not obliged to establish my dwelling in one hermitage more than in another. Thus it ought not to be judged as useless if I inspected several places in my youth, so that I could choose from the best that one most suitable for my condition. For you know and often heard from me of my intention to remain there, and I certainly did not lie at all in this, since, as God knows and you also are aware, those who used to minister to me were suddenly very much altered towards me. So I suffered all the worse. I could not have the dwelling that I had thought I could before I went there, because of those gathering the harvest. For this reason I hated that place, so that I thought I could never live there from the feast of Pentecost right until the feast of St Martin. And what good is it to me to keep the place in winter and be forced to leave in summer because of its disadvantages? I think it better to sit in winter where I will also be able to live quietly in summer. Yet I do not tell the whole reason that I left, nor wish to reveal it to anyone alive. Besides, as it seemed to me, he ⟨*or she*⟩ cared little or nothing about me. So let him ⟨*or her*⟩ get himself ⟨*or herself*⟩ another one whom he ⟨*or she*⟩ has decided to love more. For in all my remarks and promises I assume these kinds of general conditions – namely, if I live, if I can, if it seems the best thing for me; and, above all, if God wants it that way. Thus if the conditions should change, how should I be to blame if I do not persist in the plan I first intended?]

This passage is remarkable for the rawness of its emotion and the naivety of its defence. Rolle has left a cell – having undertaken to stay there – because it is too noisy, because his patrons have changed their attitude to him, and for a further, undisclosable reason. In protest against his departure, it emerges, a patron has written a letter laying charges against him, to which he declines any reply (3.4: 'Ad ea que improperavit mihi in littera sua non respondeo');

this might have been written to Rolle himself, to a new patron, or to the priest to whom *Judica Me* is addressed. It is clear that on this occasion feeling against Rolle spread out from his difficulties over his cell, to make him a 'scandalum audientibus', to touch in some way the priestly recipient of *Judica Me*, and to lead others, as *Judica B1* says, to deny Rolle the status of hermit altogether (18.7–9: 'Nonnulli nempe cum heremiticam vitam considerant, me etiam heremitam non esse inpudenter affirmare non formidant'). This is as close as we can get to a detailed account of any of the occasions on which Rolle was subjected to criticism.

In contrast with the stand the *Regula Heremitarum* takes on the stability required of hermits, both the *Officium* and Rolle himself insist that there are justifications for moving one's cell – the former citing canon law, the latter denying that hermits are in any way obliged to stay where they are. Both positions are defensible (although I have not been able to find statutes of the kind to which the *Officium* claims to be referring). Anchorites were occasionally given permission to change their cells for several reasons, including noise and inconvenience (Warren 1985, pp. 70, 77–78, 212–213), the very causes Rolle cites. Hermits, who are not under a vow to remain where they are (or indeed to do anything else), could likewise change cells quite legally, for the same or for different reasons, and without permission. Although Rolle is defending himself in terms of a somewhat narrow and unidealistic concept of obligation, his change of abode was probably not unusual. Yet Rolle's innocence in terms of canon law seems not to have helped him to avoid or ignore his critics. Indeed, the storm in a teapot which is the opening of *Judica Me* was evidently in some sense a serious matter. It had considerable impact on Rolle's subsequent writings, while the fact that the compilers of the *Officium* needed, perhaps half a century after the event, to draw attention to his changes of cell in order to defend them, suggests that they continued to be notorious.

I can think of two reasons why a squabble like this might have come to seem of real importance. One is that the kind of eremitic life Rolle wanted to live made special demands on his relationships with his patrons, who seem to have been expected to provide him with food, clothing, comfortable but secluded shelter, perhaps writing materials, while still acknowledging their inferiority to him, as recipients of his far greater gifts of counsel (*Officium*, *lectio sexta*) and prayer (*Incendium Amoris* 197.6–14). Such an arrangement, unsupported by institutional authorization and attention as it was, seems peculiarly liable to overheat, as evidently it did at least once. The other reason is that once Rolle had asserted his independence from one or another patron, and gone elsewhere in search of quiet, it could be claimed, unfairly but cogently, that this joyous anti-ascetic, who did not perform manual work, and who seems to have been suspiciously charming and handsome, was in reality greedy, indulgent, lecherous, idle and unstable, a false hermit who lived under no rule – in other words, that he was a typical *girovagus*. This would be a serious accusation to make against someone with Rolle's pretentions to holiness and exemplarity, one that could not avoid having personal and literary repercussions. Having none of the sophisticated self-doubt that marks Langland's presentation of Will in these terms (see nn. 20 and 23) he could only see such an accusation as posing a fundamental threat to his whole view of himself, as a member of the most perfect order of the Church. But it is easy for us to see, in the light of the differences between Rolle's version of eremitism and the way it is described in the *Regula Heremitarum*, how the accusation might be credible among those who had reason to resent Rolle, or who knew nothing else about him. For here was an educated man, a prolific and talented writer, who preferred a life of reasonable comfort to one of asceticism and penitential self-deprivation; who was notoriously popular with women; who moved from place to place, and did not (it would therefore seem) submit for any prolonged period to the spiritual direction of an older priest or monk, as the *Regula* advises; who patronized whichever patron he pleased; and who, in short, apparently lived a life of much the kind Langland satirizes through the figure of Haukyn:

> Y-habited as an hermite an ordre by hym-selue,
> Religioun sanz reule and resonable obedience . . .
> *(Piers Plowman* B XIII.285–286)

This might indeed be a 'scandalum audientibus'. It would be all the more so if it also became widely known that he lacked ecclesiastical patronage and authorization – that he, like Langland's Will, had 'shope [him] into shroudes' (Prologue, 2), and had no official status as a hermit. Under such circumstances, the comic story of his conversion might have started life not as a saintly tale but as a piece of malicious gossip.[26]

In concluding this attempt to reach back through Rolle's writings to some aspects of his biography, we need to enter several caveats. One is that in noting the major differences between his highly positive and anti-ascetic account of the contemplative life and the largely penitential spirituality of the *Regula Heremitarum*, I have treated his attitudes as if they were more or less unique. In fact, while the next chapter argues that much of his mystical system is indeed so, we have already seen (pp. 18–22) that his basic attitudes and vocabulary of spiritual celebration have their own traditions. While his behaviour as a hermit seems to have been regarded as abnormal by some, it was also susceptible to positive interpretations that I have not had an occasion to explore here. This thought leads to another: that Rolle's life was not as lacking in ecclesiastical connections as his own writings imply. *Incendium Amoris* and *Judica Me*, from which my biographical reconstruction has mostly been derived, are both fairly early works (see Excursus 1) and cannot be taken to testify to the conditions of the whole of his career. Indeed, their autobiographical moments are unlikely to provide a complete picture even of its early stages, for they ignore (or rather assume) the fact that, even while Rolle was defending his way of life so vehemently, he was also building a reputation as a writer and spiritual teacher. We know that *Judica Me* was a commissioned work, written for a secular priest, and that the English works were likewise intended for particular readers. Excursus II of this book argues that most of the rest of his output – with its learned Latin discussions of the contemplative life, some of which borrow from other writers whose works he is not likely to have owned himself – must have been written with an educated audience in mind, and with the patronage of book-owning individuals. Thus the very existence of *Incendium Amoris* suggests a level of clerical approval of Rolle, even though he never writes about receiving such approval. Further, when he writes about the criticisms he has received he does not only present his actions as exemplary; he implies that the fact that he is being criticized has exemplary significance in itself, as a manifestation of the persecution which the elect must always suffer. The theme of persecution has special importance in his works, as the next chapter shows (pp. 63–64), and he seems to have liked to think of himself as a latter-day martyr. Given that he builds this kind of exemplary edifice on his own difficulties with patrons and others, we cannot take what he says entirely on trust. Rather than minimizing the extent and scope of the criticism he has received, for example, he might actually be concerned to exaggerate it. To declare that the hand of every man is against you allows considerable scope for self-dramatization; to report that a few people have complained about your dietary habits does not.

Yet even after taking all these things into account, we are still left with Rolle's defensiveness, with the criticisms to which he says he was subjected, and with the fact that together they comprise a challenge to the whole basis of his life as a contemplative. It is clear, moreover, that this challenge was made, and that Rolle was in fact accused of being a *girovagus*. Near the beginning of *Super Canticum Canticorum*, as he establishes his credentials for expounding the 'kiss of the mouth', he writes of his unappeased longing for God, states that he is but a pilgrim on earth, with no abiding home ('manentem mansionem', 3.1), and compares himself to Cain: 'quemadmodum Caim [sic] vagus et profugus factus fuit pro culpa fratricidii super terram, ita et ego in hoc exilio incerte sedis de loco ad locum transeo' (3.2–4: 'Just as Cain became a wanderer and a fugitive on the earth because of his sin of fratricide, so in this exile I, too, wander from place to place, unsure of a resting-place'). Cain is a stock character in anti-girovagal satire, who is often used in works written against friars, and is named as an *exemplum* of the perils of instability by the *Regula Heremitarum*.[27] Here Rolle is ruefully acknowledging the charge that he is a mere wandering vagabond, and at the same time answering it with skilful indirection: his wandering is a sign of his spirituality and is the 'inconvenient wandering of the elect [which] increases their merit' (3.8–9: 'discursus incommodum electis meritum exaggerat'); it is quite unlike the eager running about of the reprobate, which mirrors their inner instability.[28] In this work of Rolle's middle period (see Excursus I), defensiveness has mostly been woven into large-scale oppositions between running and sitting, noise and quiet, inner and outer; there is little of the direct self-defence we encounter in *Judica Me*. Nonetheless it is apparent that when Rolle set out to write *Super Canticum Canticorum*, he was addressing an audience whom he knew might think of him as a *girovagus* (a 'scandalum heremitarum', as he calls *girovagi* placatingly in *Incendium Amoris* 183.16). When we note that this passage of *Super Canticum Canticorum* reappears in *Melos Amoris* (11.20–12.29; see Excursus I, item 3.3), its defensive gloss on the theme of wandering further elaborated, we have cause to believe that Rolle saw this charge as among the most serious of all the threats to his authority.

A nineteen-year old Richard Rolle could perhaps have become a hermit with the naivety implied by the *Officium*, unconscious of the strangeness of his action, following a series of saintly models with simple fervour. But in the light of the above, he could not have maintained this unselfconsciousness; he would have been brought face to face with his own oddity the first time he was criticized for his way of life. In effect a choice must have been present to him: to regularize his position, by joining a religious order or by living his hermit's life as conventionally and discreetly as possible; or to claim that his position was regular as it stood. The fact that his writings insist uncompromisingly on his rightness suggests that his version of the eremitic life must have been of great importance to him. It also suggests that he was not the uncomplicated saintly figure Noetinger and Arnould attempt to make him. If he became a saintly figure, in his own eyes and in those of posterity, it was by dint of a strategic relation to the hagiographic models that Alford has pointed to in his work; these models, and the works in which they appear, thus had a self-justificatory purpose.

In his writings Rolle has decided that he is right to live the solitary life in the way that he does, and is concerned to prove it. A detailed consideration of the evolved view of the eremitic life that justifies such a decision must be delayed until the next chapter, but a brief statement can be made here. For Rolle, the uninstitutionalized nature of the eremitic life must have constituted its attraction. It is this that distinguishes that life from the coenobitic and anchoritic versions of the religious vocation, and this that he emphasizes in his assessments of the relative merits of the coenobitic and eremitic vocations: coenobites are always 'obedienciarii', while his own vocation is a 'singulare propositum', a decision made in relation to God, not a vow made to an ecclesiastical superior. This emphasis on his own independence is important to his conviction that he has no ecclesiastical superiors: that the solitary life is the highest of all vocations. Indeed, Rolle interprets his mystical experiences as placing him 'above' the earthly Church, for he claims his experience of *canor* to be a participation in the song of the saved. Only an eremitic life lived outside the constraints of vows of obedience – only the uninstitutionalized institution of eremiticism – could have sustained the development of so ambitious a self-definition.

Rolle was no conventional saintly or devout figure. The information we have about his life does not enable us to do more than guess at most of the particularities of his day-to-day existence, or at the personal forces that motivated his actions and decisions. Yet it does seem to create a satisfactory context for some of the major elements in his works, from his ideas as to the status of the solitary life to his remarkable defensiveness over his practice of it. Treated on their own, Rolle's works appear confusing and confused. However little we know of his life, an understanding of the personal tension that manifests itself in his works is essential if we are to perceive the nature of their underlying unity.

2

The structure of Rolle's thought

Much of the previous chapter tries to explain why Rolle was so vulnerable to criticism, by indicating ways in which his eremitic life might have seemed anomalous to his contemporaries. This chapter examines the major themes of his writing, through which he articulates his audacious argument as to the status of the solitary mystic in the Church, and points to ways in which these, too, are idiosyncratic. In theory I am here concerned merely with a broad exposition of ideas and make no assessment of the purpose they are made to serve. Yet in practice the assessment tends to make itself. Since the structure of Rolle's thought is explicitly built around a particular view of his own status, even this introductory account of his exposition of the perfect life cannot avoid conveying that he is deeply concerned with the matter. Thus, in spite of itself, this survey anticipates the findings of my overall argument by pointing to the conclusion that Rolle's writing is not primarily didactic at all, but apologetic in its fundamental orientation.

I

There would be small point in building a discussion of Rolle's thought around his teachings on the central doctrines of Christianity, as if he were a theologian. He has little to say about Creation and Fall, Redemption and the Trinity, and what he does say is conventional and closely based on a source. His only systematic theological works are *Super Orationem Dominicam*, *Super Symbolum Apostolorum* and *Super Symbolum S. Athanasii*: derivative verse-by-verse expositions of major doctrinal texts, which indicate (as was perhaps intended) no more than that their author is wholly orthodox. Elsewhere he usually assumes that the nature of true belief is self-evident. *Incendium Amoris*, caps. 5–7, one of a very few formal doctrinal expositions in his works, is exceptional in putting his Trinitarian orthodoxy ostentatiously on show; but here again his account is wholly conventional, and his main point is that the Trinity is a mystery on which it is unwise to ponder: 'Let us not examine too closely things we cannot understand in this life' (163.28–29: 'Non nimis investigemus ea que in via comprehendere non possumus'). Regarding doctrinal deliberation as speculative rather than devotional, he seems to have heeded his own warning against it – that 'the harder teachings should be left to academics and learned men with long experience of sacred doctrine' (*Emendatio Vitae*, f. 139v. 15–17: 'Difficiliores vero sententiae disputantibus et ingeniosis viris longo tempore in sancta doctrina exercitatis relinquant'). When he requires doctrinal information himself, he relies on general guides: the *Glossa Ordinaria* for biblical glosses and Hugh of Strasbourg's *Compendium Theologicae Veritatis* for much of the rest. With the help of these and perhaps a small number of other works, he is always adequately informed, even about detailed theological points; but he is seldom concerned to be informative.

Nor does Rolle have much to say about the major Christian doctrines from a devotional point of view. He wrote a good deal about Christ, including lyrics, Passion meditations, and a scattering of devotional passages, one of which acquired fame as the *Enconium Nominis Ihesu*, gaining him a medieval reputation as the foremost exponent of the popular devotion to the Holy Name of Jesus.[1] Malcolm Moyes (1988, chapter 2) has shown that, as a Yorkshire writer, Rolle was heir to a local tradition of Cistercian and Cistercian-inspired spiritual writing, in which affective devotion to Christ played a major part; he can, indeed, himself be regarded as an exponent of this love-centred spirituality, which derives not only from Bernard but from Aelred of Rievaulx, the poet John of Hoveden, and the anonymous author of the hymn *Dulcis Ihesu Memoria* (see pp. 18–22). Rolle was certainly influenced by the affective, celebratory attitude of these writers towards Christ, and could neither have lived nor written as he did without them. Yet it would be a mistake to regard him as mainly a Christocentric writer. His debts to Cistercian spirituality are those of mood and imagery more than of Christology. His Passion lyrics and meditations were written to fulfil a relatively lowly function in the lives of spiritual beginners, while his more sophisticated English and Latin works make fairly few references to the Passion (although see *Melos Amoris*, caps. 29–32), except to say that meditation thereon belongs to the early stages of the spiritual life (see *Emendatio Vitae*, cap. 8). It is true that he associates devotion to the Holy Name with more advanced spiritual states; but his invocations of Jesus are almost devoid of theological content, and their structural importance, as we shall see, is in their connection with his experience of *dulcor*. Christology has none of the complexity and interest in Rolle's thought that it has, for example, in that of Julian of Norwich.

Similar things can be said about the importance of penitential themes in Rolle's writing. While he made notable contributions to the literature of penitence (as Moyes 1988, chapter 3 forcefully points out), especially in *Super Threnos Ieremiae* and *Super Lectiones Mortuorum*, his exercises in this mode seldom impinge upon the usual foci of his writing. He knew several of the classic expositions of the *de contemptu mundi* theme, such as Innocent III's *De Miseria Condicionis Humane*, the *Speculum Peccatoris* and the pseudo-Bernardine *Meditationes Piissimae*. But his interest in this theme is limited to a small number of works and passages in works, mostly written towards the end of his career, and all concerned with the early stages of the spiritual life.

Thus in *Emendatio Vitae*, references to the *de contemptu mundi* theme are confined to the description of conversion in the first two chapters; in the epistle *Ego Dormio*, the penitential lyric 'Al perisshethe and passeth þat we with eigh see' (84–91) illustrates the lowest stage of the spiritual life. In Rolle's view, advanced contemplatives, whose careers form by far the most important subject of his writing, have moved beyond the need to articulate self-abnegatory contempt for the world, just as they have moved beyond the need to focus intensively on the humanity and Passion of Christ.

All in all, Rolle tends to take the main themes of Christian theology and religiosity for granted to such an extent that his writing often gives the impression of being disconnected from the mainstream of Christian thought. Reading him, it frequently seems that we have strayed into an esoteric world in which the principal landmarks are structures distinctive to Rolle himself. It is true that much of this air of eccentricity turns out to be the product of an idiosyncrasy not of thought but of focus, and that (as we saw in the introduction) a certain number of apparent oddities are in fact endemic to a literary tradition in which he is working, of writings extolling and analysing 'violent' love. Yet even when he mirrors pre-existing structures of thought most closely, the literalistic way in which he applies them to his own situation, and his concentration on a few issues to the exclusion of others, makes them assume a new and puzzling aspect.

The only moment of salvation history (and the only corner of Christian doctrine) with which Rolle's thought is almost invariably involved is the Judgement. Almost all his works are concerned with the division of souls that takes place at the end of the world. *Judica Me* contains two accounts of the Day of Judgement; *Super Apocalypsim* and *Super Threnos* are concerned with apocalyptic events prophetically foretold; both Psalter commentaries are incessantly concerned with the division of humanity into the good and the bad; almost half the chapters of *Incendium Amoris* end by anticipating the joys of the elect or the sorrows of the reprobate; the climax of *Melos Amoris* is its account of the coming *gloria sanctorum* and the horrors of damnation. Rolle's imagination is as dominated by the concept of future judgement as if he was after all the author of the *Prick of Conscience*.

His presentation of the Judgement is not, though, as crude as this remark suggests. He is not concerned with the more pictorial kinds of apocalyptic – with its descriptions of the vale of Jehoshaphat and the physical location and structure of hell – and he does not deal in the inflationary *topoi* meant merely to scare the reader into virtue: the Fourteen Torments, the Thousand Tongues of Steel (*Prick of Conscience* 6446). For Rolle the Judgement is rather a moment of moral revelation, when the true nature of the good and the wicked will be made known, and a transcendent order will triumph over the corrupt earthly one; it is a moment of reversal for the wicked and vindication for the elect, but of realization, in different senses, for both. The elect can now experience fully what before they only anticipated:

Exultabunt itaque sancti in gloria pre dotibus anime, que sunt: cognicio, amor et fruicio Creatoris. *Letabuntur in cubilibus suis* [Psalm 149.5] pre dotibus corporis glorificati, que sunt: claritas, impassibilitas, agilitas, subtilitas.

(*Melos Amoris* 181.18–21)[2]

[*The saints will exult in glory* for their spiritual endowments, which are knowledge, love, and enjoyment of the Creator. *They will rejoice in their beds* for the endowments of their glorified bodies, which are clarity, immunity to suffering, agility, keenness.]

The damned have to recognize their earthly blindness to their condition:

Videntes namque reprobi se iusto Dei iudicio ab electorum gloria perhenni excommunicacione sequestratos, inexcogitabili tristicia contabescent . . . Tunc dicent illi miseri in inferno collocati: '*Ve nobis quia peccavimus* [Lamentations 5.16]; obtenebrati erant oculi nostri ut mala nostra videre non poteramus'. (*Judica Me* 8.19–21, 9.12–14)

[For the reprobate will be consumed with unthinkable sadness when they see themselves cut off in eternal excommunication from the glory of the elect by God's just judgement. Then those wretches gathered in hell will say, '*Woe to us, for we sinned*; our eyes were blinded so we could not see our evil'.]

Cut off from the sight of God, they are still granted a kind of insight.[3]

For Rolle, then, one of the most important things about the Judgement will be that the wicked will have to admit that they were wrong and that the elect were right. Hell, as well as heaven, will witness the vindication of the elect. A group of the elect (the *pauperes*), however, will be summoned to the Judgement not to be judged but to judge: 'O ineffabilis gloria pauperum, o inestimabilis laus sanctorum, qui a consiliis et iudiciis deiecti sunt, et cum Christo congregati in eius iudicio sedentes iudicabunt' (*Melos Amoris* 180.36–181.2: 'O unutterable glory of the poor, O inestimable renown of the saints, who were cast out from courts and councils and now will judge, gathered together with Christ, sitting in his court!').[4] After the Judgement the elect will rejoice in the suffering of the damned: 'Et in ultimo iudicio cum viderit mundanum miserum terre quam dilexerat derelictum, non solum non compacietur, sed etiam de morte mali letabitur. Unde Propheta: *Videbunt iusti et super eum ridebunt* [Psalm 51.8][5] (*Judica Me* 6.19–22: 'And at the Last Judgement, when he sees the worldly wretch bereaved of the earth that he loved, not only will he have no compassion, but he will even rejoice at the death of the wicked – as the prophet says: *The just will look on and laugh at him*'). The scorn that the elect will feel for the damned is a saintly equivalent of the contempt that the reprobate feel for the elect now; they will laugh ('ridebunt') because the reprobate derided ('deridebant'): 'Et [reprobi] electos Dei habebunt accusantes, quos bene vivere videbant, nec opera eorum neque exhortaciones imitabantur, sed eos deridebant et despexerant' (*Judica Me* 7.15–17: 'And the reprobate will have God's elect for accusers, whom they saw living virtuously, and followed neither their works nor their exhortations but derided and despised them'). Like Lazarus, the elect are paupers here but will be blessed in the next life; like Dives, the reprobate are rich here, 'tiranni, perversi divites, pauperum oppressores, iniqui principes'

(*Super Psalmum Vicesimum* 22.25–23.1) – and will be judged worthy of damnation.

The positions of elect and reprobate after the Judgement will thus be the exact reverse of their current positions except that they will be immovable. The elect have bought an eternal reward by giving up the temporal world and its pleasures; the reprobate have bargained away eternity to gain the fleeting riches of the temporal: 'Proinde pensemus dum adhuc peccare possimus, prospera mundi fugere, adversa libenter tollerare. Mala namque mens cum gaudet deperit, et seipsam quasi blando veneno, dum in creatura iocunditatem querit, occidit' (*Incendium Amoris* 156.9–12: 'Accordingly, while we are still able to sin, let us decide to flee the world's prosperity and to sustain its adversities willingly. For the evil soul perishes while it rejoices, and kills itself, as with sweet poison, while it searches for pleasure in created things').

As notes 2–5 show, there is nothing of itself unusual in this depiction of the Judgement. What is unusual, at least in so concentrated a form, is the way that these ideas become for Rolle the building-blocks of a narrowly antithetical and symmetrical model of Christian moral history as a whole. For Judgement does not only occupy a crucial place as a future event in his works; the coming division of souls suffuses his thinking about this life to such an extent that it often seems that it has already occurred, and elect and reprobate know their places in advance. Both the title and the content of the *Liber de Amore Dei contra Amatores Mundi* suggests this predestinarian view: 'Habent igitur celestis amor et secularis sectatores suos; sed inter se continue decertant, quis illorum amatum suum amplius diligat, cum alter ad Christum alter ad mundum tanto ambitu suspirat' (3.27–30: 'So both worldly and heavenly love have their followers; but they continually contend with one another as to which of them loves his beloved more, the one sighing after Christ, the other after the world, with such great eagerness'). This depiction of spiritual warfare is deliberately fanciful in imagining the lovers of God and of the world in conscious competition. But while Rolle normally assumes the wicked to be culpably ignorant of their spiritual state, he almost always speaks of *electi* and *reprobi*, and the patterns of behaviour which distinguish each group, as though it is clear who fits into which category. He denies having any knowledge of or interest in the predestined fate of individuals, and denounces those who judge others (*Judica Me* 1); but he still satirizes the wicked as though their obduracy was established, their damnation assured. Just as their eyes are to be forcibly opened on the Day of Wrath, so in this life they are irrecoverably blinded (a favourite image) by their foolishness: 'Excecantur utique oculi secularium tenebris viciorum; sed et sapiencia mundi per quam magnos se esse putant nimirum stultos efficit et a vere sapiencie lumine in obscura ducit' (*Contra Amatores Mundi* 3.41–44: 'You see, worldly eyes are blinded by the darkness of sin. But the world's wisdom, through which they think themselves great, also certainly makes them fools, and leads them from the light of true wisdom into the dark'). The division of souls at the Judgement thus has its counterpart for Rolle in a schematic opposition between the good and the evil in this life. The wicked, though rich and powerful, are already reprobate and can do no right; the good, though poor and despised, are already elect and can, in effect, do no wrong. Instead of viewing the world tropologically, as a vale of soul-making (in the way a pastoral writer like Walter Hilton generally does), Rolle habitually sees it anagogically, as though through the foreseeing eyes of God himself, and in the form in which the Judgement is to fix it forever.

Yet when Rolle speaks of *electi* and *reprobi* he is not generally concerned with the whole of humanity, but with two smaller groups, one good, one evil:

Unde notandum est quod quatuor erunt ordines in iudicio: duo electorum et duo reproborum. Primus ordo electorum erit apostolorum et sequencium eos, scilicet, perfectorum, qui omnia pro Christo perfecte reliquerant et in viam paupertatis Christum secuti sunt. Et isti iudicabunt alios, unde Job ait, *Non salvat impios, et pauperibus iudicium tribuit* [Job 36.6]. Quoniam et hic a tirannis et malis hominibus incaute iudicamur et contempnimur, ibi a nobis tiranni et alii mali discrete iudicabuntur. Secundus ordo electorum erit beatorum Christianorum, qui fidem et dileccionem Christi tenuerunt et opera misericordie ex iuste acquisitis diligenter fecerunt ... Tertius ordo erit falsorum Christianorum, qui fidem Christi habuerunt et illam bonis operibus non impleverunt. Et istis improperabitur quia non pascebant esurientes, nec potabant sicientes ... Quartus ordo erit illorum qui fidem Christi non habuerunt. *(Judica Me 74.5–75.4)*

[Concerning which it is to be noted that there will be four groups in the Judgement, two elect and two reprobate. The first group of elect will be of apostles and their followers, that is the perfect, who left everything perfectly for Christ, and followed Christ in the way of poverty. These will judge others, as Job says: *He does not save the impious, and entrusts judgement to the poor.* For since we are judged and despised foolishly here by tyrannical and wicked people, so there tyrants and the other wicked will be judged discerningly by us. The second group of elect will be of blessed Christians, who held to the faith and to the love of Christ, and who dutifully performed the works of mercy with goods justly acquired. The third group will be of false Christians, who had the Christian faith and did not implement it by good works. These will be reproved for not feeding the hungry, not giving drink to the thirsty. The fourth group will be of those who did not have Christian faith.]

This distinction between groups of saved and damned is common in medieval theology;[6] but in many of his works Rolle uses it in his own way by applying it directly to his picture of the world *before* the Judgement. *Electi*, *pauperes* and *perfecti* are thus distinguished from ordinary Christians (the *pusilli fideles* or *mediocriter boni*)[7] in his accounts of this life; and this distinction regularly corresponds to one he draws between contemplatives or hermits and Christians in active life. The former group are the main concern of almost all his works and (we shall see) are treated as members of an elite club: different criteria apply to them than to ordinary Christians; different rewards will be allotted to them. In dealing with the evil, Rolle always writes of the first of the groups of reprobate:

Reprobi vero, omnino inaniter se habent erga Deum. Audiunt enim verbum Dei cum anxietate, orant sine affeccione, cogitant sine dulcedine. Intrant ecclesiam, implent parietes, tundant pectora, emittunt suspiria, sed ficta plane, quia ad oculos hominum, non ad aures Dei perveniunt.   (*Incendium Amoris* 149.34–150.3)

[But the reprobate conduct themselves with utter futility towards God. For they hear the word of God restlessly, pray without desire, think without sweetness. They go into church, fill it from wall to wall, beat their breasts, gasp out sighs – but all quite falsely, since they reach the eyes of people, not the ears of God.]

For most of the occasions on which he uses the words, *reprobi* refers only to false Christians (not also to pagans), and *electi* to those (especially solitaries) who have attained the summits of perfection (not also to the *mediocriter boni*); indeed much of his writing scarcely acknowledges the existence of anyone who fits into neither category.

Thus in Rolle's account of this world there is for the most part no middle ground on which the evil could repent and reform or the good suffer a fall from grace. Not that he believed that there was no such middle ground: it is clear from his few attempts to write for the *mediocriter boni* (as in most of *Judica Me* and in *Super Lectiones Mortuorum*) that in theory he saw the life of ordinary Christians as a continual and uncertain struggle with sin. But he has little interest in and small ability to write about this struggle; indeed, for all his theoretical knowledge of its existence he often seems to forget about it. His portrayal of evil is so undifferentiated that even when he tries to analyse the process of damnation in the manner of a pastoral writer (as in *Incendium Amoris*, cap. 23), the result shares the harshness and externality of satire. Instead of being analyses of a problem that afflicts everybody, his portrayals of sin seem to anticipate the joy he will have in triumphing over the reprobate at the Judgement, by triumphing over them on earth. Far from inviting them to be converted, his treatments of the wicked consist mainly of reproofs, the objects of which are satirical types whose lot is already determined: corrupt clergy, rulers, lovers of the world, who play out their role of persecuting the elect, while the latter contend with them by going on, heedless of tribulation, to their enormous heavenly reward.

II

The one spiritual process which Rolle does write about is that whereby the *perfecti* achieve their high state. If the reprobate are homogeneous stereotypes in his works, the *electi* are described with great particularity as those whose regeneration has taken place according to a specific model. The way in which this model is applied varies according to the context in which it appears, but nowhere does it diverge substantially from his accounts of his own spiritual experiences. One corollary of this fact is that in spite of the significance of the theme of regeneration in his works, the focus of interest, even in his depictions of the elect, is never the psychological intricacies or moral difficulties of spiritual advance; his own experience of such complexities was evidently so slight that he is naive and indifferent in dealing with them. His interest is rather in the structure of advance and the interpretation of that structure – and 'interpretation' here equals 'elevation'. If Rolle's treatment of the reprobate is concerned more with the *topoi* of blame than with analysis, in discussing the elect he is always somehow concerned with their praise; indeed, those whose progress towards holiness follows the pattern he describes come to be accorded the highest spiritual status. In order to grasp the logic of his position we must look at his version of the ascent to God from its beginning: an enterprise that involves examining the affective and autobiographical accounts found in works like *Incendium Amoris*, in the context of the more structured and distanced pastoral discussions found, pre-eminently, in *Emendatio Vitae*.

The elect are those who set their hearts to love Christ, not the world:

> Noverint universi in hoc erumpnoso exilii habitaculo immorantes, neminem posse amore eternitatis imbui, neque suavitate celica deliniri, nisi ad Deum vere conventantur. Converti quippe ad ipsum oportet, et ab omnibus rebus visibilibus in mente penitus averti, priusquam poterit divini amoris dulcedinem saltem ad modicum experiri. Hec quidem conversio fit per ordinatum amorem, ut diligat diligenda, vel non diligenda non diligat. (*Incendium Amoris* 148.1–7)

> [Everyone lingering in this wretched place of exile should know that they cannot be imbued with the love of eternity nor be anointed with heavenly sweetness unless they are truly converted to God. For a person must be converted to him and totally turned away from everything visible in his mind before he can experience even a little of the sweetness of divine love. This conversion occurs through ordered love, so that what should be loved is loved, while what ought not to be loved is not loved.]

For Rolle, the process of spiritual advance begins not with moral doubt or confusion, but with conversion and the ordering of the affections, so that the will is put in tune with the self-evident moral structure of the world, and so that the individual can say, in the words of the Song of Songs (2.4), '*Ordinavit in me charitatem*'. The opening four chapters of *Emendatio Vitae*, a work which self-consciously mirrors Rolle's model of spiritual ascent in its own structure, are thus respectively entitled *De Conversio*, *De Contemptu Mundi*, *De Paupertate* and *De Institutione Vitae*, the first urging readers to this turning to God, the next three indicating what it is they are to turn from and how the converted life, in its broad outlines, should be organized. Conversion is, of course, initiated by God: 'For if God, in his grace, did not go before those elect whom he has determined to save, he would not find anyone among the sons of men whom he might justify' (*Super Psalmum Vicesimum* 7.13–15: 'Nisi enim Deus electos quos salvare decrevit gratia preveniret, inter filios hominum non inveniretur quem iustificaret').[8] Yet it is also a process which begins at a definitive moment and requires vigorous human activity. Rolle's own spiritual ascent began with his flight into the wilderness, an act of headstrong determination in which he literally turned away from the world. *Emendatio Vitae* exhorts the reader in more abstract terms to do the same thing, citing the brevity of human life, the uncertainty of the hour of death, and other *de contemptu mundi* motifs (f. 130r.). One of the Passion meditations is an aid for readers who wish to convert their affections from the world to Christ in the more positive and forcible way popularized by the *Stimulus Amoris*; by dwelling on the details of Christ's death, and on their own incapacity to respond to that death as emotionally as they should, the readers of these works are meant to wrench their wills away from wordliness and into a proper attitude of faith and feeling:

Now is þe malice of my hert, þat is so wikked, more þan is þy passioun, þat is þy precious deth, þat wroght such wondres and manyfold more, and þe mynd þerof stirreth nat my hert? Bot, swet lord, a drop of þy blode droped vpon my soul in mynd of þy passioun may suple and soft my soule in þy grace, þat is so hard. I wot wel, swet Ihesu, þat my hert is nat worþy þat þou sholdest come þerto and þerin aly3t. I ask hit nat of þe dignite of þy sepulcre. Bot, swete Ihesus, þou ly3ted in to helle to visite þer and ryghtyn; and in þat manere I ask þy comynge in to my soule.

(Meditation B, 507–16)

Here it is Christ who is begged to induce a response in the work's readers, but their own wills (sustained by the affective force of Rolle's prose) are nonetheless assumed to be very much active participants.

Conversion is turning from the world to Christ. It is also a movement from an existence centred on the body to one focussed inwardly: a convert 'has almost let go external perception, is wholly gathered within, is wholly lifted up into Christ' (*Emendatio Vitae*, f. 135v. 1: 'Pene exteriores sensus amittit, totus intus colligitur, totus in Christum elevatur'). Such language is commonplace in itself, but Rolle's application of it is typically extreme. The outside world is given almost no place in his writing. For spiritual and economic reasons, most contemplatives recognize a need to maintain a balance between inner activities and various kinds of structured engagement in the world. Thus *Ancrene Wisse* divides its injunctions for the solitary life into 'outer' and 'inner' rules, including in the latter liturgical prayer, food, clothing and day-to-day conduct; in this it follows Aelred's *De Institutis Inclusarum*, as do many other late-medieval Rules (see Ayto and Barratt 1984, p. xli). Aelred's own ultimate source is the *Benedictine Rule*, which of course places much emphasis on the liturgy, and also directs monks to manual work as a way of avoiding idleness; thus cap. 48 (*De Opere Manuum Cotidiano*) opens 'Otiositas inimica est animae' – 'Idleness is the enemy of the soul'. In obedience to the injunction to manual work, even the Carthusians, who considered themselves an eremitic order of especial rigour, copied books as a physical labour which was meant to balance the strenuous inner life expected of them.[9] Rolle, however, does not prescribe such a balance. He is anxious to avoid the charge of idleness (e.g. 'Non ergo contemplatores celestis iubili ociosi sunt', *Super Canticum Canticorum* 6.9–10), but the labour he enjoins is rather the 'labor ... dulcis, desiderabilis et suavis' of contemplation (6.22–23) than bodily labour, which he thinks of small value ('Parum enim prodest corporalis exercitacio', 6.15) – and the term *contemplatio*, here as always in his work, refers to private not liturgical prayer.[10] His own anchoritic rule, *The Form of Living*, is almost entirely concerned with the inner life, and gives no help as to how a recluse is to pray, structure her day or keep herself in food. Where he does write of the matters comprised in the outer rule it is to urge their unimportance. Although he first experienced *canor* while engaged in a communal recitation of the psalms (*Incendium Amoris*, cap. 15), he ceased to regard even the liturgy as relevant to him (cap. 31). Similarly, as we saw in Chapter 1, asceticism has little value for him, and he recommends conformity with others as a guide to eating habits (*Emendatio Vitae*, f. 137r. 7). He does not envisage a life in which food and shelter is a problem; his own life was economically dependent on patrons, and he did not regard himself as obliged to do anything to support himself. For Rolle, the living of an inwardly gathered life entails a rejection of the concerns of the outer life so total as to require that contemplatives be accorded a wholly special status.[11]

The movement from a sensual outwardly directed existence to an inner and spiritual one has, of course, its difficulties. *Super Canticum Canticorum* contains a famous anecdote of one of Rolle's temptations, in which a devil appears to him as a beautiful woman, but is scared off by his praising the blood of Christ (47.26–48.16). In *Emendatio Vitae* he writes more generally of the 'triple cord' that binds men (*sic*) to the earth: riches, female flattery and youthful beauty (f. 135r. 44–45). But this obviously personal list (compare *Incendium Amoris* 166.22–167.14), like his other accounts of temptations encountered by converts, is of interest mainly for what it omits. Unlike more practical spiritual guides, Rolle dwells almost exclusively on problems caused by the blandishments of world or flesh, and says little about inner dryness, sins of pride and envy, and other spiritual trials.[12] On the few occasions when he alludes to a range of sins and temptations, such as in the last part of *Judica A* (10–15), cap. 4 of *Emendatio Vitae*, and a passage of *The Form of Living* (332–484), his writing is often mechanical. The last of these works merely lists categories of sins and their remedies, borrowing its material directly from the *Compendium Theologicae Veritatis* (as Ogilvie-Thomson's notes show), without regard for relevance; it is unlikely that any of its intended readers can have needed injunctions against drunkenness, gifts to harlots or usury. Moreover, Rolle's discussions of temptations seldom invoke the common-places which regard them as instruments of growth, and so give them a positive role in the structure of spiritual ascent; even his accounts of the early stages of this ascent treat temptation merely as a nuisance to be dealt with as quickly as possible. Lacking an appreciation (and probably much experience) of spiritual struggle, Rolle has little sense that sin is hard for contemplatives to deal with. He often uses the formula 'At the beginning we are sharply stung, but at the middle and end we are delighted by heavenly sweetness' (*Judica Me* 16.2–3: 'In inicio graviter pungimur, sed in medio et in fine celesti suavitate delectamur'); yet he has little use for the idea that the elect, at any stages of their careers, encounter internal obstacles serious enough to threaten them.

The most serious obstacle contemplatives encounter is not a temptation at all but the external trial of persecution. All the elect must expect to suffer opprobrium, scandal-mongering and detraction (*Judica Me* 10.21–22); whoever wishes to rejoice with Christ must first be a partner with him in tribulation (11.2–3). Where *Ancrene Wisse*, like most works in the tradition of penitential spirituality, regards suffering as something which any would-be follower of Christ must deliberately seek (see part VI), Rolle assumes it will be brought about mostly by the external agency of the enemies of the elect. Moreover, he usually identifies it not with bodily pain or temptation but with verbal abuse. Even caps. 5–6 of *Emendatio Vitae* (*De Tribulatione Patienter Sustinenda* and *De Patientia*), which generalize the theme of tribulation in order to appeal to a broad readership, frequently betray the assumption that it is equivalent to persecution. Yet while he often refers to his own enemies, he does not tell elect readers what persecution to expect for themselves, nor how to deal with it. For the most part, his interest in the theme is that it shows those who suffer persecution to be the chosen of God, linking them with the early Christian witnesses and martyrs:

Palam facere, dico, *ea que oportet fieri cito* [Revelation 1.1] ... Animat nos sanctus Iohannes quasi inevitabilia ostendens adversa calumpniarum, improperiorum et magnarum tribulacionum, non solum ab extraneis sed eciam a falsis fratribus, quorum persecucio eo est magis periculosa, quo occulta ... Hos perverse mentis ideo permittit Deus longe lateque discurrere, et malivolas linguas ac venenosas relaxare, ut paciencia electorum exerceatur et gloriosius coronentur ...

(*Super Apocalypsim*, 120.17–32)

[*To make known*, I say, *those things which must soon come to pass.* St John encourages us by showing as virtually inevitable the suffering of calumnies, reproaches, and great tribulations, not only from outsiders but also from false brothers, whose persecution is the more dangerous in that it is secret. For God allows these perverse-minded people to rush about hither and thither and give free rein to their malevolent and poisonous tongues, so the patience of the elect may be tested, and they may be crowned the more gloriously.]

It is true that this emphasis on persecution is typical of eremitic writing from the *Vitae Patrum* on, so that even *Ancrene Wisse* (especially the opening pages of part III) is somewhat improbably preoccupied with the opprobrium the anchoresses must suffer (see also William of St Thierry's *Epistola Aurea* III–VI). But Rolle's handling of this traditional theme is still notable for the narrowness of its focus and the repetitiveness of its treatment.

If Rolle is not very helpful, as a pastoral writer, in his depictions of the difficulties new converts must expect to have to face, he is hardly more so in his positive instructions. Almost the only tool for directing the mind to God he describes in any detail in the generalized Benedictine triad of spiritual exercises, *lectio*, *meditatio* and *oratio*:

Tria vera exercicia cognoscere debemus quibus succendimur in amore Dei, videlicet, sacra leccio, oracio, meditacio. Leccio amantem ... nobis insinuat. Oracio ad amorem Christi nos inflammat. Meditacio in amoris dulcedinem nobis continuacionem subministrat. (*Judica Me* 17.1–5)

[We should recognize three exercises by which we are set alight in the love of God, namely holy reading, prayer, meditation. Reading introduces us to the beloved. Prayer inflames us in the love of Christ. Meditation affords us a continuation in the sweetness of love.]

In the same vein as *Judica Me*, *Emendatio Vitae* recommends contemplatives to move between these three exercises at will, in order to inspire love in themselves (f. 139v. 35–38): a use of the triad that recalls the prologue to Anselm's *Orationes sive Meditationes*, where the reader is encouraged to let her or his thoughts move from reading, to meditation, to prayer, as seems best.[13] *Emendatio Vitae* gives a chapter to each of the three. *Oratio* has pride of place (cap. 7), but the term covers so wide a range (from recitation of the office to the moments before the experience of *canor*) as to render the chapter's advice on the subject of only general relevance. One of the most striking indications of Rolle's indifference to the mundane details of the spiritual life is this lack of clarity about the forms and occasions of prayer. *Canor* is a heightening of a kind of verbal prayer; Rolle's works are full of elaborate and impassioned prayers; yet the most specific advice he gives about prayer is that one should sit, not kneel, to do it. *Lectio* (cap. 9) has special importance for Rolle: reading the affective parts of the Scriptures kindles love ('accendunt nos ad amandum', f. 139v. 19) and teaches us to avoid sin. His biblical commentaries were presumably intended to assist in this process, and indicate how important he thought it to be; but his treatment of the exercise, here and elsewhere, is brief. *Meditatio* receives a fuller treatment than either *lectio* or *oratio* (cap. 8), because Rolle is anxious to warn readers against treating it as more than a means to an end. The practical tone of this chapter derives from its negativity: meditation is easy to practise to excess; it makes no difference what subject is chosen for meditation, since the exercise is of only temporary use. Such advice is conventional (visual meditation was often seen as a mere prologue to contemplation), but gives few indications as to how the exercise is to be performed. Like the other stages of the spiritual life discussed so far, prayer, reading and meditation are mainly significant for Rolle because they lead to something else.[14]

What this 'something else' is the last three chapters of *Emendatio Vitae* sketch in different ways. Cap. 10 (*De Puritate Mentis*) describes the goal of the conversion of the will as inner purity; once this is achieved, love is 'ordered' in the way the opening of *Incendium Amoris* says it must be. Total purity is not possible in this life, because venial sin cannot quite be destroyed. But affective prayer, reading and meditation can destroy the effects of venial sins as soon as they occur, by burning them up in the heat of charity (see Chapter 5, n. 22): 'Quamvis enim aliunde peccet venialiter cito tamen propter suam integram intentionem ad Deum directam deletur; fervor namque charitatis in ipso existens, omnem rubiginem peccatorum consumit' (*Emendatio Vitae*, f. 139v. 42–44: 'For while he may sin venially sometimes, his sin is at once annihilated, because his whole will is turned to God; for the fire of love dwelling in him consumes every speck of sin'). Cap. 11 (*De Amore*) then gives an account of the *fervor caritatis*, which draws on many of Rolle's earlier writings (see Excursus 1, item 2.1–6), as well as on Richard of St Victor's *De Quattuor Gradibus Violentae Caritatis* (see pp. 216–218), and in a general sense on Bernard. Had Rolle's account of the spiritual life stopped at this point, there would still be relatively little to distinguish him from any of the writers of luxuriant prose in celebration of passionate love whom I discussed in the introduction (pp. 18–22). However, it does not stop. As cap. 12 of *Emendatio Vitae* (*De Contemplatio*) implies and many of his other works make very clear, for Rolle 'violent' love cannot constitute the fulfilment of a contemplative's aspirations until it expresses itself in four specific mystical experiences: Sight into Heaven, *fervor*, *dulcor* and the climax of the perfect life, *canor*. With the adumbration of these experiences, he passes beyond the traditional language of affective spirituality on to ground which is increasingly his own, and where his own life is by far his most significant source. Indeed, writing of *fervor* and *canor* near the end of *Incendium Amoris*, Rolle admits that he is himself unable to suggest parallels for them: 'Ob hoc utique evenit huiusmodi amatori quod nequaquam in aliquorum doctorum scriptis inveni aut reperi expressum' (237.21–23: 'Then indeed there happens to this kind of lover something I never discovered in any of the writings of the learned nor heard expounded').[15] Here, accordingly, we must explore in a little more detail.

The final chapter of *Emendatio Vitae* gives a somewhat allusive rendering of Rolle's mystical thought. For a fuller account we must turn to *Incendium Amoris*, which, as well as containing the most famous narrative of his experiences (in cap. 15), provides several shorter third-person summaries:

Cum ergo homo ad Christum perfecte conversus cuncta transitoria despexerit, et se in solo conditoris desiderio immobiliter ut mortalibus pro corrupcione carnis permittitur fixerit: tunc nimirum vires viriliter exercens primo quasi aperto celo supernos cives oculo intellectuali conspicit, et postea calorem suavissimum, quasi ignem ardentem, sentit. Deinde mira suavitate imbuitur, et deinceps in canore iubilo gloriatur. Hec est ergo perfecta caritas, quam *nemo novit nisi qui accipit* [Revelation 2.17], et qui accipit nunquam amittit, dulciter vivit, secure morietur.   (*Incendium Amoris* 202.26–35)

[So when someone perfectly turned to Christ despises all transitory things and unmovingly attaches himself solely in desire for the Creator (so far as fleshly corruption renders this possible for mortals), then truly, exercising his strength manfully, first with intellectual vision he sees the celestial citizens, as though heaven had been opened; then he feels a very sweet heat like fire burning; next he is imbued with wonderful sweetness; and thereafter he glories in joyful song. This then is perfect charity, *which nobody knows unless he receives it*; and he who receives it never lays it down. Sweetly he lives; confidently he will die.]

The images used to describe the four experiences are derived from all five senses: sight (Sight into Heaven), touch (*fervor*), smell or taste (*dulcor*), sound (*canor*). They occur in this order (to be understood as an ascending scale) in most of Rolle's works, and in pastoral as well as autobiographical contexts. *Ego Dormio* tells a nun that she will have these same experiences:

At þe begynnynge, when þou comest thereto, þi goostly egh is taken vp in to þe light of heuyn, and þare enlumyned in grace and kyndlet of þe fyre of Cristes loue, so þat þou shal feel verraily þe brennynge of loue in þi herte, euermore lyftynge þi thoght to God and fillynge þe ful of ioy and swetnesse, so myche þat no sekenesse ne shame ne anguys ne penaunce may gref þe, bot al þi lif shal turne in to ioy. And þan for heynesse of þi hert, þi praiers turneth in to ioyful songe and þi þoghtes to melodi.

(*Ego Dormio* 225–233)

The images may shift their meaning in different contexts, but the structure of Rolle's account, once formulated, is rigid. In his view it constitutes the definitive form in which the elect, while in this life, rejoice in God.

The first experience, Sight into Heaven, is notable as a sign of blessings to come, but is otherwise of obscure significance. It seems to be a temporary state which is made insignificant by the experiences that succeed it – perhaps because it lacks their affective force. *Incendium Amoris* says this about it:

Ab inicio namque alteracionis vite mee et mentis usque ad apercionem hoscii celestis, ut revelata facie oculus cordis superos contempletur, et videret qua via amatum suum quereret, et ad ipsum iugiter anhelaret, effluxerunt tres anni, exceptis tribus vel quattuor mensibus. Manente siquidem hoscio aperto usque ad tempus in quo in corde realiter senciebatur calor eterni amoris, annus unus pene transivit.

(*Incendium Amoris* 188.24–189.6)

[From the beginning of the transformation of my life and mind up until the opening of the heavenly gates – so that the heart's eye could contemplate the supernal with face unveiled, and could see by what way it should seek its beloved and continually desire him – three years less three or four months went by. Nearly a ⟨further⟩ year passed (the heavenly gates staying open) before the time when the heat of eternal love was really felt in the heart.]

Sight is here contrasted with the feeling of love that accompanies *fervor*; its low status is made clear by its presentation as 'seeing the way' rather than as part of that way. But while Rolle's accounts of the ascent to God seldom do more than mention it, he has at least two reasons for retaining it in his exemplary model. One is that he experienced something which he thought of as a sight into heaven, and considered that this fact alone made it important. The other is that without invoking such an experience it would be difficult for him to draw on the visual imagery of contemplation employed by the Fathers: Gregory's description of God as an 'incircumscriptum lumen' (see, e.g., *Super Canticum Canticorum* 1.7–8), or the pseudo-Dionysian image of 'ascent' to God. Such metaphors would be hard for any mystical writer to dispense with, and are important for Rolle as indications that he is describing a genuine and spiritual experience with authoritative precedents, for all his insistence on literal heat and a spiritually audible song.

The source of the image of 'Sight into Heaven' is Revelation 4.1. The comment on this passage in *Super Apocalypsim* implies a good deal about the place of the experience in the overall structure of Rolle's thought:

Et ecce ostium aperto in celo. Cum obscuritas scripturarum in Ecclesia ostenditur, quasi ostium in celo aperitur. Vel sic: dum devota mens perfecte nititur ut a sordibus purgetur, dumque continua meditacione et oracione se sursum erigit . . . subito

67

insolita lux apparet et mentem attonitam rapit, sicque ut contemplativus efficiatur cum oculis cordis iam mundatus ad celestia contemplanda suscipitur, ostium in celo aperitur, non corpori sed spiritui, et deinde dona melliflua descendunt et archana patefiunt.   (156.13–21)

[*And behold, a door open in heaven.* When the darkness of the Scriptures is set forth by the Church, it is as though a door into heaven is opened. Or thus: when the devout soul strives perfectly to be purged from uncleannesses, and when it lifts itself upward by continual meditation and prayer, an unusual light suddenly appears and snatches away the amazed mind. And so, in order that he may become a contemplative, and with his heart's eye now cleansed, he is caught up to the sight of heavenly things, a door is opened in heaven (not corporeally but spiritually) and from it descend mellifluous gifts, and secrets are thrown open.]

Here Rolle gives two interpretations of the same verse, the first derived from his source, a commentary by pseudo-Anselm of Laon, the second his own.[16] The juxtaposition of these readings suggests that he saw this experience as a culmination of *lectio*, in which he suddenly understood the spiritual sense of the Scriptures, without as yet having the affective experience of the divine which *fervor* was to provide. *Emendatio Vitae* describes *lectio* as an intellectual exercise ('Ad lectio pertinet ratio et inquisitio veritatis', f. 141r. 23–24), from which affective meditation and prayer can arise; *Super Apocalypsim* here suggests a reciprocal process in which meditation and prayer lead back to *lectio* at a higher level, where 'secrets are thrown open'.

Rolle's next two experiences can be dealt with quickly. The one to which he gave the name *fervor* was the culmination of a long period of prayer and meditation, in which his soul was suddenly granted the gift of response to and feeling for God, and kindled in love. This sensation evoked *dulcor*, a mixture of longing and fulfilment summed up by the Bride's cry '*Let him kiss me with the kiss of his mouth*' (Song of Songs 1.1). The prologue to *Incendium Amoris* (quoted on pp. 113–115) conveys vividly the excitement these feelings create, and the way they transcend all the contemplative's earlier spiritual exercises. Indeed, *fervor* and *dulcor* stand in the same relation to *meditatio* and *oratio* as Sight into Heaven does to *lectio*. Cap. 15 of *Incendium Amoris* says that Rolle first experienced them while delighting in the sweetness of meditation or prayer (189.7–8: 'Dum suavitate oracionis vel meditacionis multum delectarer'). Cap. 7 (*De Oratione*) of *Emendatio Vitae* likewise says that 'We truly pray when our soul is inflamed by the fire of the Holy Spirit' (f. 138v. 38–40: 'Tunc enim veraciter oramus cum . . . animus noster igne Spiritus Sancti inflammatur'), and later adds that true prayer leads to 'ineffabilis dulcor' (46). Cap. 8 (*De Meditatione*) makes the same claims for the higher forms of meditation, in which love is fervent and sweet (f. 139r. 36: 'Qui utique amor fervor et dulcor est'). More dramatically, at their height both experiences are seen as raising those who undergo them to exalted spiritual conditions. As *Incendium Amoris* says, contemplatives who burn in love are like the burning Seraphim who contemplate God, and after death will take their seat with them (cap. 3):[17]

The structure of Rolle's thought

Amor namque inhabitat cor solitarii . . . Fervet hinc funditus et languet lumini, cum sic sinceriter sapit celescia; et canit mellite sine mesticia, clamorem efferens dilecto nobili sicut seraphycum [*see* Isaiah 6.3], quia conformitur in mente amorosa; dicitur, 'En amans ardeo anhelans avide!' Sic igne uritur inestimabili amantis anima . . . Sanctus quidem solitarius quia pro Salvatore sedere sustinuit in solitudine, sedem accipiet in celestibus auream et excellentem inter ordines angelorum.

(Incendium Amoris 184.5–11, 14–16)

[For love inhabits the heart of the solitary. On this account he burns from his very centre, and languishes for the light, when he thus truly tastes the celestial, and he sings honeyedly without heaviness like the Seraphim, uttering a cry to his noble beloved, which is fashioned in an amorous mind; ⟨and⟩ it says, 'Ah! avidly panting, loving I burn!' So the soul of the lover is consumed in an unthinkable fire. Indeed, since the holy solitary suffered to sit in solitude for his Saviour, he will receive in the heavens a golden and excellent seat among the ranks of the angels.]

Dulcor does not become the basis of any claim so specific as this, but the opening of *Super Canticum Canticorum* suggests, echoing the third of Bernard's *Sermones super Cantica Canticorum*, that only one who has truly experienced the sweetness of heavenly communion with God will dare to ask for the 'kiss of the mouth'. The imagery of *dulcor*, like that of *fervor*, also gives Rolle an automatic link with other exponents of affective mysticism, and ties his experience closely, if implicitly, to that of the Bride in the Song of Songs, of the psalmist (mystically interpreted), or of the contemplative who ascends through the four grades of violent love described by Richard of St Victor.

Yet while *fervor* and *dulcor* are of lasting importance in all of Rolle's writings, even these experiences are significant mainly on account of the culmination to which they point: to the gift of *canor*, the highest earthly goal of the contemplative. Cap. 15 of *Incendium Amoris* tells us that Rolle received *fervor* and *dulcor* while he was praying and meditating in a chapel. The same chapel was the setting for his reception of *canor* nine months later:

Dum enim in eadem capella sederem, et in nocte ante cenam psalmos prout potui decantarem, quasi tinnitum psallencium vel pocius canencium supra me ascultavi. Cumque celestibus eciam orando toto desiderio intenderem, nescio quomodo mox in me concentum canorum sensi, et delectabilissimam armoniam celicus excepi, mecum manentem in mente. Nam cogitacio mea continuo in carmen canorum commutabatur, et quasi odas habui meditando, et eciam oracionibus ipsis et psalmodia eundem sonum edidi. Deinceps usque ad canendum que prius dixeram, pre affluencia suavitatis interne prorupi, occulte quidem, quia tantummodo coram Conditore meo. Non cognitus eram ab hiis qui me cernebant, ne si scivissent me supra modum honorassent, et sic perdidissem partem floris pulcherrime, et decidissem in desolacionem. *(Incendium Amoris* 189.19–190.6)

[While I was sitting in the same chapel and saying the night-psalms before supper as best I could, I heard as it were a ringing of psalmody, or rather of singing, above me. And when I was stretched out in prayer and with all my desire towards heavenly things, I do not know how but I soon felt a symphony of song within myself and caught up from heaven the most delicious harmony, which remained with me in my mind. For my thought was forthwith changed into a tuneful song; and I had as it were

69

melodies in my meditation, and I also gave out the same song in my prayers and psalmody. Finally, because of the abundance of the internal sweetness, I burst forth into singing what before I had spoken – but silently, because only before my Maker. I was not noticed by those who observed me, in case they should have recognized me and honored me immoderately – and so I would have lost part of the loveliest flower and descended into desolation.]

Canor is superficially similar to *fervor*, although affecting a different spiritual sense. Like *fervor* it develops out of the exercises practised by contemplatives during their time of self-preparation, rising out of *cogitacio* (which stands in here for *lectio*) and *meditatio*, but especially out of *oratio* (in this case, the saying of the night-psalms). As *Emendatio Vitae* implies, *oratio* is the exercise that, above all, leads to contemplative experience: 'Ad orationem pertinet laus, hymnus, speculatio, excessus, admiratio; et sic in oratione vita contemplativa consistit vel meditatio' (f. 141r. 19–21: 'To [the exercise of] prayer pertain praise, hymnody, contemplation, rapture, wonder; and thus the contemplative life consists in prayer or meditation'). Moreover, the heavenly source of Rolle's *canor* is itself a 'psallencium', while if *canor* has any non-experiential source, it is to be found in the psalms, with their adjurations to sing, in the general concept of the liturgy, and perhaps in the specific practice of the singing of the *jubilus*, the wordless musical elaborations on the last syllable of the *Alleluia*, at High Mass (Womack 1961, chapter 1). Again like *fervor*, *canor* is a gift from above that at first seems to involve merely an intensification of the recipient's spiritual life, a new dimension of richness. Yet in Rolle's developed account it is of far more importance than this. Whereas *fervor* and *dulcor* are little more than gifts that refresh the pilgrim *in via*, *canor* emerges as in effect the goal of the journey, arrival at the Heavenly City: a final transformation of the soul. In this chapter, I can describe the elaborate structure that Rolle erects around his experience of *canor* only in a preliminary way.

Cap. 15 of *Incendium Amoris* tells us that Rolle was initially silent about his gift of *canor*; in cap. 31 (quoted on pp. 136–137), he describes his first attempt to articulate the significance of the gift, after being goaded by people critical of his way of life, and especially of his refusal to sing in the choir at Mass. His reply to these critics becomes an important theme of his writings. *Canor*, he argues, is incompatible with earthly song and noise. He is a solitary because only in quiet can be experience *canor*. On the other hand, those who criticize him – Christians in the world or in religious communities – are scarcely able to experience or even understand it, since they live amidst noise. It is difficult to tell how literal this argument is meant to be, although in caps. 31–33 of *Incendium Amoris* it is presented in crudely physical terms; the fact that *Emendatio Vitae*, cap. 10 speaks of *canor* as arising directly from a purified mind (f. 140v. 45–52) suggests equations between earthly sound and worldly sin on the one hand and solitude and purity of thought on the other, and may imply that we are dealing here with a sustained metaphor. Yet *Contra Amatores Mundi* also says:

Omnis melodia mundialis, omnisque corporalis musica instrumentis organicis machinata, quantumcumque activis seu secularibus viris negociis implicatis placuerint, contemplativis vero desiderabilia non erunt. Immo fugiunt corporalem audire sonitum, quia in se contemplativi viri iam sonum susceperunt celestem. Activi vero in exterioribus gaudent canticis, nos contemplacione divina succensi *in sono epulantis* [Psalm 41.5] terrena transvolamus . . . Alioquin iam desinimus canere, atque ab illa invisibilis gaudii affluencia cessare, ut dum ab illis corporaliter perstrepentibus non fugimus, veraciter [discamus] quia nemo unquam in amore Dei gaudere potuit, qui prius vana istius mundi solacia non dereliquit. (*Contra Amatores Mundi* 4.102–117)

[All mundane melody, all corporal music contrived by instruments and organs, however much they may satisfy active people and seculars bound up in business, will certainly not be desirable things for holy contemplatives. Indeed they flee from hearing corporeal sound because contemplative people have already received celestial sound in themselves. Actives rejoice in external songs; but we, set alight by divine contemplation, transcend the terrestrial *With the sound of feasting*. Otherwise we fall away from song and lose the richness of that invisible melody; so that while we do not flee from those bodily pandemoniums, we truly learn that nobody can ever rejoice in the love of God unless he first relinquishes the vain solaces of this world.]

It follows from this depiction of *canor* that solitaries like Rolle are more or less beyond the criticism of all those who have not experienced it, since they cannot know the significance of what they are missing. It also follows that those who experience *canor* will wish to take as little part in communal events as possible, including the liturgical worship of the Church, since their inner music will be interrupted; this is why Rolle says he did not want to sing in the choir, and is his most individual reason for insisting on the superiority of the solitary life to all other ways of serving God – that quiet can only be found in solitude. Unlike *fervor* and *dulcor*, *canor* thus radically distinguishes those who receive it from the rest of humanity.

Yet if *canor* is important enough for its recipient to be justified in shunning all but nominal participation in the Church's worship, and if it is impossible to criticize those who have it, the gift must have enormous intrinsic significance. This significance Rolle defines by means of a daring antithesis. Although the *perfecti* no longer profitably participate in the worship of the earthly Church, their practice of *canor* is also an act of participation – in the worship of the heavenly Church. In singing spiritual songs, the perfect are joining, while still on earth, with the chorus of the saved and the angels in heaven; they are enjoying a part of their heavenly reward in advance:

Est enim angelica suavitas quam in animam accipit et eadem oda, etsi non eisdem verbis laudes Deo resonabitur. Qualis angelorum, talis est iscius concentus, etsi non tantus, nec tam perspicuus, propter carnem corruptibilem que adhuc aggravat amantem. Qui hoc experitur eciam angelica cantica expertus est, cum sit eiusdem speciei in via et in patria. (*Incendium Amoris* 237.4–10)

[So it is an angelic sweetness that he takes into his soul, and angelic song, even if he will not resound the praises of God in the same words. For this harmony is like that of the angels, although neither so great nor so clear, because of the corruptible flesh which still weighs down the lover. He who has experienced this ⟨harmony⟩ has also

71

experienced angelic song, since this is of the same sort both on the road and in the Fatherland.]

The transformation brought about in the elect soul by the gift of *canor* is thus fundamental. In effect, the mature contemplative is already *in patria* – already a member of the Church Triumphant, who participates in the felicity to which all the saved will eventually be called, and who is almost disengaged from the world's sin. Indeed, Rolle's contemplatives, while they are still on earth, participate not merely in the common joys of heaven but in the higher forms of ecstasy. Their place on earth is lowest of all, but their place in heaven will be (and already implicitly is) the highest, with the Seraphim who burn in contemplation of God. These *perfectissimi* experience frustration at the barriers their flesh imposes between them and God, and long to die, for their conversion from this world to the next is already so complete that they have nothing to fear, and much to relish, in the prospect of the Judgement – where it will be they who will judge sinful humanity with Christ and his apostles. *Canor*, in short, is the highest gift attainable in this life and an expression of the highest degree of holiness: *Incendium Amoris* calls it (with *fervor* and *dulcor*) 'summa perfeccio christiane religionis' (185.16–17), while in *Melos Amoris* (cap. 1) its existence in today's world is taken as proof that sanctity is still not dead. The gift of *canor* brings the earthly careers of the elect to a joyful standstill, for they can subsequently have nothing further to look forward to and little to fear in this life; the ordering of their affections is already complete.

Canor is the keystone of the simple, even in its way logical, structure that is Rolle's thought, the basis of his high view of the status of the earthly elect, the source of his idiosyncrasy as a mystical writer. Other late medieval writers, from Bernard and Richard of St Victor to Ruusbroec and the Rhineland mystics, express from time to time the view that something approaching complete perfection is possible in this life; works like Ruusbroec's *Spiritual Espousals*, and indeed the *De Quattuor Gradibus Violentae Caritatis*, present as ambitious and extreme a view of the holiness attainable by the contemplative as anything we might find in *Incendium Amoris*. However, we would have to look far – and to writers Rolle could not have known, such as Marguerite Porete, or Hadewijch – to find other structures built so high from such slight and tendentious foundations of personal experience; even in mystical literature it is remarkable for an individual's experience to be the overt basis of so ambitious a position. Richard of St Victor may be allowed the last word, for the peroration of his great work on violent love, which speaks of the boldness love engenders in the soul, applies strikingly well to Rolle – who not only experienced such love, but told the world that he had, and spent a lifetime trying to prove that the form of his experience was definitive: 'Ecce in quantam pie presumptionis audaciam consummatio caritatis solet mentem hominis erigere, ecce quomodo facit hominem ultra hominem presumere!' (177.1–5) – 'See in what boldness of pious presumption the consummation of charity elevates the human mind! See how it makes a human presume beyond the human!'

72

PART II

3

Active life: *Judica Me* as apologetic pastoral

The first part of this study has looked at Rolle's career as a whole from several perspectives, in an attempt to arrive at some working definitions. The following analysis of *Judica Me* initiates a series of chapters which look individually, in more or less detail, at all of his works (except the *Latin Psalter*). Few have been explicated with care, and most are seldom read; these analyses thus have to start from scratch, beginning with generalized descriptions, and supporting findings with frequent quotations. Yet the main purpose of these chapters is not so much with explication as with the development of an overarching account of his writing career: an account which can be subdivided into three closely related themes. The first theme concerns the relationship between apology and didacticism – which must not be thought of as mutually exclusive entities, but rather as literary impulses which may or may not conflict. Apology emerges only gradually out of the didacticism of the early works, but becomes the dominant strain in his middle period before rejoining forces with Rolle's didactic impulses in such late works as *Emendatio Vitae* and *Super Lectiones Mortuorum*. The second theme concerns the progressive articulation of the structure of ideas I described in the previous chapter: a structure which responds well to Rolle's apologetic needs (and is clearly a product of them), but which can also be employed in the generalized pastoral writing characteristic of the late works. The third theme concerns the development of his self-presentation, from the embattled but defiant hermit of *Judica Me*, to the self-aggrandizing saint of *Incendium Amoris*, to the triumphant prophet of *Melos Amoris*, to the sober spiritual guide of *The Form of Living*. The sum of these themes is the argument that Rolle's writing career was deeply self-concerned, and is comprehensible only as a prolonged, and ultimately largely successful, search for spiritual and literary authority.

This account makes two assumptions which should be stated in advance. One is that the works on which it focusses – Rolle's most unusual and independent writings – are better guides to his development than the more conventional ones. The other is that the order in which I discuss his works is broadly that in which they were written. While it is usually agreed that *Judica Me* is an early work, *The Form of Living* a late, there is no such consensus about the place of *Melos Amoris* and *Contra Amatores Mundi*, and I believe I am the first to place *Incendium Amoris* so early. Arguments for this chronology are detailed in Excursus I, but a good reason for thinking that it is right – the coherence it bestows on our picture of Rolle's development – should be clear before then. One assumption I try not to make prematurely is that my argument that apology is central to Rolle's career is correct. From *Incendium Amoris* to *Melos Amoris*, his writings can hardly be discussed except in terms of apologetic, but in the earlier analyses I make laborious efforts to show how far works can nonetheless be seen as didactic entities. This account of *Judica Me* takes the process furthest by offering a double reading, first viewing the work as a persuasive piece of didactic writing, and only after this showing how didacticism is also disrupted by Rolle's apologetic needs.[1]

I

Judica Me is a 12,000-word Latin pastoral manual in the form of an epistle, parts of which are sermon, biblical exposition and self-vindication, and most of which is taken directly from *Oculus Sacerdotis*, a work by a contemporary and fellow-Yorkshireman, William of Pagula.[2] For all its derivative status, the work has an independent and unusual structure, partly explained by the particularity of its intended audience; it seems to have been written at the request of a clergyman (18.1–2) who knew Rolle well (2.8–11), and naturally discusses whatever its author thinks relevant for his reader. Yet the work also manifests a great interest in formal structure on Rolle's part, and a concern to tie its heterogeneous subject-matter into a coherent whole. In spite of this, it has previously been treated as a collection of short works; Allen calls it 'a series of miscellaneous tracts' (p. 93), and others agree (Daly 1984, pp. li–liii, Marzac 1968, pp. 41–43). The work is admittedly divided into four diverse parts: an original opening, which Allen calls *Judica A*, followed by three parts based on different sections of *Oculus Sacerdotis*, which she calls *Judica B1–3*; these divisions are present in the text and discernible in the manuscripts.[3] Yet *Judica Me* remains one of the most carefully constructed of Rolle's works, the problem with which is rather that there are too many structuring principles in operation than too few.

The first part of *Judica Me* is reminiscent of several literary forms. It begins, in the manner of a sermon, with a *thema*: '*Judica me Deus et discerne causam meam de gente non sancta*' (1.1, Psalm 42.1: '*Judge me, God, and divide my cause from the unholy people*').[4] *Judica A* is a homily without the formal structure of a university sermon; however, there is a *prothema*: '*De vultu tuo iudicium meum prodeat; oculi tui*, O bone Jesu, *videant equitates*' (2.1–2, Psalm 16.2: '*May my judgement proceed from your face; may your eyes*, O good Jesus, *look upon equities*').[5] These verses introduce the theme of Judgement central to *Judica Me*, and are the first in a network of similar verses which link the sections of the work. The opening of *Judica B1* quotes several: Psalm 9.19, 17: '*Quoniam non in finem oblivio erit pauperis* et *cognoscetus Dominus iudicia faciens*' (18.11–12: '*For the poor will not be forgotten in the end*, and *the Lord will be shown when he brings about the judgement*'); and John 8.7 (the woman taken in adultery) with Romans 2.1: '*In quo . . . alium iudicas teipsum condempnas; eadem enim agis que iudicas*' (19.8–9: '*Insofar as you judge another, you condemn yourself; for you do the same thing that you judge*'). *B2* urges the penitent to confess with 1 Corinthians 11.31 ('*Si nosipsos iudicaremus non utique iudicaremur*', 30.6–7: '*If we judged ourselves we would certainly not be judged*'), and the verses *B3* quotes are immediately concerned with the Judgement. The interlocking of verbally related biblical texts, which Alford (1973) argues to be crucial to the local structures of Rolle's prose (pp. 11ff.), is here used to hold together a whole work.

More locally, the theme and protheme at the outset of *Judica Me* introduce a kind of epistolary sermon structure, the *exordium* of which, a passionate defense of Rolle's recent activities as a hermit, corresponds to the *captatio benevolentiae* used by preachers to win over their audience (see Robert of Basevorn's *Forma Praedicandi*, cap. 24). The first exemplum of the use and abuse of judgement (to be analysed later, but already quoted and discussed in Chapter 1, pp. 47–49) thus concerns Rolle himself, who pleads that only God has the right to judge him. This apology leads to the conclusion that nobody should judge others (3.9–10), and then to a prophetic account of the great approaching day when God will judge all, which consists of a short passage on the joys of the blessed and a prolonged (1300-word) account of the miseries of the reprobate. Rolle's attempt to imitate the declamatory cadences of a sermon is particularly successful here; the writing has a remarkable forward momentum, is full of exclamatory and antithetical rhetorical figures, and manages to create both an affective response of fear and an intellectual understanding of the processes of damnation. The aim of the passage is stated explicitly at its outset:

Audite iam de iustorum letitia quod delectat, diligenter attendite de peccatorum miseria quod [deterret]. Sed forte dicis quis, 'Fidem habeo, baptizatus sum, unum Deo adoro, simulacra non veneror: quomodo ergo dampnari potero?' Non sis deceptus quicumque es . . . Qui terrenas divicias seu carnales, paupertates celestes post-ponendo, noscuntur diligere – quia dum aliquando mortali peccato se maculant longe ab amore Dei se distare sciant – illi abeunt in regionem longinquam a Deo patre, recedendo non per motum corporis sed per vicia sua male voluntatis. Et dissipant bona sua luxuriose vivendo, hoc est, sensus suos in terrenis rebus acquirendis ponendo. Cum quis namque temporalia inordinate et contra voluntatem Dei appetit, racionis thesaurum et predia quinque sensuum consumenda sordibus scelerum exponit et iniquitatem addens super iniquitatem excecatur, ne intret in iusticiam. Et tot passibus ad infernum properat quot malis actibus obedire non formidat. Et quidem in istis temporibus in quibus deveniunt fines temporum maxime superbi regnant, ypocrite president, homicide dominantur, fornicatores sublimantur, avari divicias et dignitates acquirunt, iracundi et invidi se proponunt – ut iam vix unus invenitur qui dolum non sequitur . . . O dira condicio peccatoris, qui pro peccatis brevis temporis penam patitur eterne dampnacionis! Modico delectatur et incessanter amaricari meretur. Modo eligit inebriari vino terrene dulcedinis, pro quo postea potabitur fetore absinthii infernalis. Iam calore desidorium carnalium infatigabiliter estuat, sed in terrore sempiterni doloris frigefieri vehementer timeat. In dulcore presentis seculi suum parat gaudium in felle fetentis abissi. Non ignoret percipere mercedem. Gaudens cum mundo, non potest regnare cum Christo; dolens pro terrenis, non gaudebit cum celestibus. Si amittit pecuniam nimium constristatur. Et mortaliter peccare letificatur. Paupertatem odit. In rebus mundi deceptoriis spem ponit. Necesse est illum decipi, qui in deficientibus voluit fundari. Omnis enim qui in rebus finiendis sperat, finitis illis impossible est quod sperans non cadet. Quomodo enim stabit, quando illud super quod stetit ad nichilatum fuerit? Crede quod audis. Huiusmodi sunt omnes qui terram magis quam celum diligunt. Qui quia in mundanis finem ponunt, finito mundo, sine fine peribunt. (4.20–6.15)

[Now hear of what delights, the joy of the just; listen carefully to what deters, the woe of the sinful. But perhaps one of you will say, 'I have faith, I am baptized, I worship one God, I do not adore idols: how then can I be damned?' Do not be deceived, whoever you are. Those who are known to love earthly or carnal riches, putting behind them heavenly poverty – for whenever they stain themselves with mortal sin, they should know how they place themselves far from the love of God – these go away into a region far from God the Father, receding not by any bodily movement but through the vices of their evil wills. And they dissipate their goods in luxurious living – directing their senses, that is, to the acquiring of worldly things. For when anyone desires temporal things inordinately and against God's will, he exposes the treasure of the reason and the estates of the five senses to be eaten up by the filth of crimes, and adding sin to sin he is blinded, so that he may not enter into justice. And he rushes to hell with as many paces as there are sins that he fearlessly obeys. And certainly in these times especially, in which the ends of the ages are approaching, the proud are in power, the hypocrites rule, murderers have dominion, fornicators are honoured, misers get riches and high positions, the wrathful and the envious thrust themselves forward – so that there is hardly one to be found who does not follow deceit. O appalling condition of the sinner who for a short-lived sin must suffer the punishment of eternal damnation! He pleases himself for a little while, and reaps eternal bitterness. Now he chooses to be made drunk with the wine of earthly sweetness for which afterwards he will drink the poison of hellish wormwood. Now he burns indefatigably with the heat of fleshly desire; but let him be terribly afraid to be frozen in the horror of everlasting sorrow. In the sweetness of the present world he prepares his joy in the poison of the fetid abyss; let him not be mistaken in perceiving his reward. Joying in the world he cannot reign with Christ; anxious over earthly wealth, he will not rejoice with the angels. If he loses money, he is excessively saddened; and he rejoices in sinning mortally. He hates poverty. In the deceitful things of the world he puts his hope; it is necessary that one should be deceived who wants to build on a spurious foundation. For each one who bases his hope on things that end must needs fall, along with his hope, when those things end. For how will he stand when what he is standing on has become nothing? Believe what you hear. Such are all who love the earth more than heaven. So those who confine their ends to the world will, at the end of the world, perish endlessly.]

This account begins casually, with a speaker who thinks to possess an adequate faith; 'sed forte' seems to introduce a digression, but surprisingly leads straight to the narrative of the reprobate. The slight shock this structure produces encourages repudiation of the speaker's complacency by the reader, and a fearful realization that an externally worthy Christian can still be damned – implicitly that we, too, may be 'deceptus'. Such feelings of identification and repudiation continue to structure our response to the reprobate's progress. 'Deceptus' introduces the important theme of knowledge. Mortal sinners are urged to understand ('sciant') how far they are from God, yet are known ('noscuntur') to prefer carnal to heavenly things. Whoever ignores all warnings is blinded ('excecatur') by wickedness and passes beyond hope of salvation; Rolle hopes to prevent this blindness by helping readers to recognize basic metaphysical truths. Yet such recognition is of course affective as well as cognitive. If the images in the first part of this passage – journey away from God, consumption of the treasure of the reason – are intended to analyse the sinner's progress, the sense of inevitability created by the verbs of motion ('abeunt . . . recedendo . . . properat . . . deviat . . . transit') is also frightening; once the foot of 'male voluntatis' has taken its first step, there seems little hope of escape.

The pressure both to understand and to fear – to repudiate and to identify with the reprobate – is kept up. Rolle laments the evils of the age, dividing sinners into types (hypocrites, homicides, fornicators), whose common evil is manifested by the parallel *membra* in which they are described, and whose number and power is set against 'vix unus' who is righteous. This imbalance will be reversed at the Judgement – as is implied by the *exclamatio* 'O dira condicio peccatoris', and the *contentiones* which contrast a sinner's present with his future: 'modo', 'modico', heat and sweetness, with 'incessanter', 'postea', cold, poison. Parallel sentence-structures and rhyme ('in dulcore presentis . . . in felle fetentis') intensify the contrasts. A *dissolutio*, which recalls the sinner's evil actions, leads to the more distanced tone of 'crede quod audis', and finally to the *traductio* or *conclusio*: 'quia in mundanis *finem* ponunt, *finito* mundo, sine *fine* peribunt'.[6] These figures thus provide a close verbal analogy to the metaphysical structures they depict, and appeal at once to the reason and to the feelings. The reader should also 'non ignoret percipere mercedem', for the evil-doer's position is absurd as well as terrifying; like the house built upon sand, 'Quomodo enim stabit quando illud super quod stetit ad nichilatum fuerit?'

The rest of the account of reprobation is set at the Judgement, and is increasingly distanced from the wicked and preoccupied with the elect's rejoicing at their fall (6.9–7.2). Yet the traditional language used here is frightening enough; *exclamationes* and *membra*, employing *similiter cadens* and *similiter desinens*, convey the implacability of the moment, while *contentiones* again dramatize the transition from joy to sorrow:

Habebunt namque reprobi mundum accusantem quem nimis dilexerant; demones accusantes quibus servierant; carnem accusantem quam castigare noluerunt; et electos Dei habebunt accusantes quos . . . despexerant. Desuper videbunt Christum vindicantem, subtus infernum sensient absorbentem. Quorum gloria vertitur in dolorem, pulcritudo in deformitatem, dulcedo in amaritudinem . . . (7.13–20)[7]

[Reprobates will face the world as accuser, which they loved too much; demons as accusers, whom they served; the flesh as accuser, which they would not castigate; and they will have the elect of God as accusers, whom they . . . despised. Above they will see Christ the avenger, below feel hell the devourer – they whose glory is turned to grief, beauty to deformity, sweetness into bitterness.]

Even the damned finally recognize their situation, and warn the reader: 'Tunc dicent illi miseri in inferno collocati: *"Ve nobis quia peccavimus; obtenebrati erant oculi nostri* [Lamentations 5.16–17] ut mala nostra videre non poteramus"'" (9.12–14: 'Then those wretches gathered in hell will say, *"Woe to us, for we sinned; our eyes were blinded* so we could not see our evil"'"). Rolle in turn warns that merely hearing of damnation is not enough, claiming that proper attention to the passage must turn the reader from sin but showing that he cannot force such attention: 'Ista leguntur, quare non creduntur? Si credantur, quare non timentur? . . . Utique, si recte crederent, valde timerent; et sic timendo saltem a mortalibus peccatis se subtraherent' (9.20–24: 'Such things are read; why are they not believed? Or if they are believed why are they not feared? Truly, if they believed properly they would be much afraid, and in so fearing would draw back at least from mortal sin').

This section, then, combines dramatic and conceptual coherence with the variety of approaches needed to woo readers into a sense of their condition. Rolle contrives his account with a clear sense of how a typical response should work. As we would expect, the rest of *Judica A* is designed to channel this response into virtuous activity. Again, this aim is stated explicitly, in the words of a biblical epistle: *'Hec scribo vobis ut non [peccetis]* [1 John 2.1], ut motibus illicitis viriliter resistatis, ut abstineatis vos a pravis desideriis' (10.11–12: *'I write this to you so that you will not sin*, so that you will manfully withstand illicit inclinations, and abstain from depraved desires'). Consideration of this final section must wait until the second part of this chapter, but it gives advice appropriate for a priestly reader, telling him to be chaste, moderate, devout, humble: 'Omnis namque talis indigne ad altare accedit, qui de aliquo mortali peccato se maculatum sensit. Ve qui nondum Domino reconciliatus, officium reconciliacionis exercet!' (13.14–17: 'For all such, who know themselves to be spotted by any mortal sin, approach the altar unworthily. Woe to him who exercises the office of reconciliation while not yet reconciled himself to God!').

Judica A is a homily written mainly to further the salvation of its immediate reader.[8] Most of the rest of *Judica Me* concerns the office of the priesthood and how the reader is to exercise it for the salvation of others. Its tone, carefully established from the start of *Judica B1*, is modelled on the expository clarity and generality of the pastoral manual:

Cupienti mihi peticioni vestre satisfacere occurrit ex una parte invidencium malicia ex alia caritas divina. Pugnant itaque ista duo in me, sed ut patebit: *Sapientia vincit maliciam, attingens a fine usque ad finem fortiter, et disponens omnia suaviter* [Wisdom 7.30; 8.1]. Unde et vobis habenda est discrecio non modica, ne dum cuicumque hunc libellum indifferenter ostenditis iuventutem meam invidorum dentibus acerbiter corrodendam exponatis. Nonnulli nempe cum heremeticam vitam considerant, me etiam heremitam non esse inpudenter affirmare non formidant.   (18.1–9)

Judica Me *as apologetic pastoral*

[While I was concerned to meet your request, the envy of the malicious rushed at me on one side and on the other divine charity. So these two fight within me, but as it will appear: *Wisdom subdues malice, reaching out mightily from one end even to the other, and sweetly setting all things in order.* Thus you must have no little discretion, in case when you show this little book casually to anyone you expose my immaturity to be savagely gnawed by the teeth of the envious. Indeed, when some examine the eremitic life they do not fear to assert shamelessly that I am not even a hermit.]

This opening recapitulates that of *Judica A*, here using the language of an epistolary prologue, and, formally speaking, reducing all that has gone before to the status of a preamble: a structural oddity that draws a line between the homiletic beginning and the pastoral continuation of the work.[9] Again Rolle links defensiveness to larger didactic structures, for the *discretio* the reader is to use in circulating *Judica Me* is a quality of the judgement *B1* describes as essential to the priest (23.9). Next Rolle points out that his work is a compilation, and – still working within the conventions of the epistolary prologue – modestly ascribes its worth to God and its wisdom to his predecessors:

Verumptamen que vestro statui profutura iam video compilare studui, ut non mihi laus detur sed Deo, a quo quicquid boni habuerimus ab illo procul dubio habemus. Immo, si vobis vel aliis legentibus dignum videatur, sciatis quia de verbis precedencium patrum illud extraxi, et ad utilitatem legencium in quodam brevi compendio redegi, ut quod ego nondum in publico predicando cogor dicere, saltem vobis ostendam scribendo, qui necessitatem habetis salubriter predicare . . .   (18.14–20)

[Still, I have tried to compile those things which I think at the moment will be to the benefit of your condition, so that praise may accrue not to me but to God, from whom there is no doubt that we have whatever is good. Now if it seems worthy to you or to other readers, know that I drew it from the sayings of earlier fathers, and reduced it into a kind of brief compendium for the use of readers, so that I may declare, by writing at least to you, who have a duty to preach wholesomely, that which I do not yet have to utter by preaching in public.]

This passage briefly but self-consciously adopts an academic convention by alluding to the work's *causae*: efficient cause (Rolle, the 'precendencium patrum', and God), material cause ('que vestro statui profutura'), formal cause (the form of *compilatio*) and final cause (praise of God). The disavowal of responsibility for a work is also a *topos* of prologues to compilations.[10] Rolle invokes these conventions in order to distance *Judica Me* from the controversy with which 'nonnulli' have surrounded its author. Even here, then, he is conscious of the problematic nature of his authority, as is clear from the distinction he makes between his function as a writer not obliged (he presumably means 'not allowed') to preach, and the reader's as preacher: a distinction which shelters the work behind its ancillary role as manual, while suggesting a reason for the sermon structure of *Judica A* and *B3*.[11]

The distinction also serves as a characteristically skilful transition to the main subject of *B1* and the first of the things 'que vestro statui profutura iam video', the importance of consistency in a priest:

Sed [necessitatem habetis] et solerter cogitare ut bona, que communi populo predicare intenditis, vosmetipsi secundum quod status vester exigit eadem immo digniora instanter agatis, ut cum alios de suis culpis iuste reprehenditis de vobismetipsis easdem culpas extirpetis.   (18.20–24)

[Yet you have also a duty to consider sagaciously that you must yourself, as your office demands, zealously perform the same good things – or even better ones – that you strive to preach to the common people; so that while you justly reprehend others for their faults, you may extirpate the same faults from your own self.]

In order to preach wholesomely ('salubriter predicare'), the priest must first consider sagaciously ('solerter cogitare') the need to live to at least the standards of holiness about which he is preaching. The rest of *B1* is concerned with the virtue, knowledge and discretion pertinent to the office of the priesthood – 'bona vita, scientia recta, predicacio discreta' (20.8–9) – and borrows about half its material from the beginning of the *Dextera Pars* of *Oculus Sacerdotis*. As the prologue to *B1* and the nature of its source suggest, the emphasis is on the priest as preacher, and the level of discussion is mostly practical and formal, concerned with the functioning of priests as professionals, not with their own salvation or spiritual development. The seamless way in which Rolle's prose elides with what is, in effect, William of Pagula's, shows how well he has assimilated the tone, as well as the material, of the form in which he is working:

Debet utique esse officium sacerdotum: nulli nocere et omnibus prodesse. Quia tot penis digni sunt quot ad subditos exempla male vite prebent ... Nec possunt sacerdotes se excusare propter iuris ignoranciam, cum nulli sacerdotum liceat ignorare, nec quicquam facere quod sanctorum patrum regulis poterit obviare.
                                                     (20.11–21.5)

[So this should be the function of priests, to harm no one and help everyone. For they are worthy of as many punishments as they provided examples of bad living to their flock. Nor can priests excuse themselves on the grounds of not knowing the law since a priest is not allowed not to know it, nor to do anything which might conflict with the rules laid down by the holy fathers.]

Almost every word here is from William, Rolle's abbreviations of his source even increasing its stylistic distance from the richer, more effusive periodic structures of *Judica A*.

Yet in spite of the careful prologue to *B1*, Rolle finds it difficult to write in this aloof way; the ardent tone of *Judica A* keeps intruding. For example, like William, Rolle illustrates the need for learning in priests with a proverb about the blind leading the blind; but he then goes on to show his own learning, concern for Scripture and preaching skill by adding appropriate verses and comments, quickly finding his way back to the good works of the elect, and preaching directly at his reader (23.12–24.14). The ending of *Judica B1* similarly expands the mention in *Dextera Pars* of 1 Timothy 4.13 ('*Listen to reading and teaching*', see 25.4) into an independent conclusion:

Diligenter adhibe curam eis, quibus te preesse contigerit. Agnosce animos et actus singulorum ... Diligenter ergo stude et perscrutare libros in quibus quod ad salutem anime tue et aliorum pertinent poteris invenire. Nam procul dubio, si delectacionem in sacra scriptura niteris querere, etiam in divino amore rapieris iubilare.

(25.5–26.3)

[Diligently devote attention to those whom it falls to you to govern. Know well the thoughts and acts of each one. Thus scrutinize and study carefully the books in which you can find what pertains to the salvation of your soul and of others. For if you strive to seek joy in the Holy Scriptures, you will without doubt also be snatched away to rejoice in divine love itself.]

The passage shifts from the priest's duty to others to his love for God, and from considering the pastoral usefulness of learning to the practice of *lectio divina*; the 'scientia recta' (20.9) required by the priest proves to be affective rather than intellectual in nature. Rolle is not prepared to leave the reader of *B1* with the idea that virtue practised or knowledge acquired merely *ex officio* is sufficient.

In a sense, then, Rolle's didactic intentions in writing *Judica B1* are at odds with the distinction its prologue seems to make between the first two parts of *Judica Me*. The prologue marks a division between a homiletic introduction and a pastoral manual, while the first part of the manual itself seeks to break down that distinction:

Quicumque enim es qui accedis ad iudicandum alios, prius discucias teipsum et iudica ut tu recte in teipso iudicatus etiam alios recte iudicare possis. Quoniam igitur necesse est ut unusquisque ad celestia regna tendens caritate non ficta informaretur, illam vobis, scilicet, caritatem Dei et proximi, pre omnibus et in omnibus habendam commendo, sine qua utique nec quisque salvari poterit et cum qua nec aliquis peribit. Unde et scire debetis quod qui Deum non diligit, proximum amare nescit; nam in amore Dei proximum addiscit diligere, et in dileccione proximi amorem Dei nutrire. Sed si amoris divini dulcedinem sentire cupitis oportet profecto ut totum cor vestrum ad querendum Christum prebeatis ... Distat ergo inter amorem Dei et amorem mundi. Nam in principio amor mundi ad modum suum dulcescit, sed in fine amarissimus est. Amor vero Christi in inicio pro penitencia nos cogit amarescere, sed paulatim in nobis crescens mirabili leticia nos facit habundare. Vos igitur firma fide, certa spe, vera caritate insigniti, secure ad curam animarum accedite, ut recte instructi etiam alios recte instruere valeatis. Ista namque tria sacerdoti pertinent, scilicet, bona vita, scientia recta, predicacio discreta. Nihil tam periculosum est apud Deum, nec tam turpe apud homines, quod quis senciat veritatem et non libere pronunciat illam.

(19.9–20.11)

[Therefore, whoever you are who undertake to judge others, you should first examine yourself; and judge yourself so that you, having been correctly judged in yourself, can correctly judge others. For because it is necessary that each person who is striving for the heavenly kingdom should be imbued with a charity that is not feigned, I commend it – that is, charity to God and to neighbour – to you as worthy to be had before everything and in everything; for neither will anyone be able to be saved without it, nor will anyone who has it perish. And so you should know that he who does not love God does not know how to love his neighbour; for in loving God one learns to love one's neighbour and in the love of one's neighbour the love of God is nurtured. But if you desire to feel the sweetness of divine love, it is necessary that you set your whole heart to seek Christ. Thus there is a great difference between the love of God and the love of the world. For at first worldly love is sweet in its way, but in the end it is very bitter. But the love of Christ constrains us to be bitter through penitence at the beginning, yet, gradually growing in us, makes us abound with a marvellous joy. So you who are marked by firm faith, a certain hope and true charity, undertake the cure of souls securely, so that being rightly instructed you may also be worthy to instruct others rightly. For these three things are appropriate for a priest, namely a good life, correct knowledge and proper preaching. For nothing is so dangerous in relation to God nor so shameful before people as that he who knows the truth should not pronounce it openly.]

This passage plays elaborately with 'judgement', 'love' and their necessary interconnection. While the subject is now the priestly office, Rolle shows that a merely professional rectitude is inadequate; 'caritate non ficta' is necessary, for the love of neighbour that must characterize a priest cannot exist without love of God, arising 'ex amore iusticie'. At times here Rolle engages directly with his reader's soul in the manner of *Judica A*: 'si . . . cupitis', 'in principio amor mundi . . . dulcescit'. Although we return to the subject and tone of a manual, it is as though a protest as to the suitability of that tone has been registered. The apparent irrelevance of the last phrase of the passage (the first statement taken from *Oculus Sacerdotis*) suggests that Rolle is again thinking of his wish to 'pronounce' truth himself. A thread of frustrated self-restraint seems to run through this part of *Judica Me* as it turns from evangelism to less exciting tasks.

The tension between Rolle's desire for affective contact with readers and the manual form of *Judica B* must not be overstated, for the choice of topics from *Oculus Sacerdotis* included in *Judica B* in itself seems calculated to allow for as much of such contact as possible. The work is far from being a complete pastoral guide. It says nothing about Church discipline or the daily details of the Christian life, does not discuss sacramental theology and shows little interest in either the theology or the practicalities of the active life.[12] Rolle is concerned only with the subject in which, as a hermit, he is a specialist: the inner lives of his readers and their charges. This focus gives cohesion to the work, and often allows its author scope for the dramatic engagement he craves.

Rolle wrings drama even out of *Judica B2*, a 5,000-word abridgement of *Pars Oculi* of *Oculus Sacerdotis*, which moves in order through a model confession, taking into account the possibilities for sin and penance as it goes. Here he can only be involved in the souls of others at third hand: '⟨Istis iam dictis ad utilitatem vestram,⟩ videndum est ⟨consequenter⟩ de multis casibus periculosis in confessionibus contingentibus qualiter sit penitencia iniungenda'[13] (27.1–3: 'Now after these things have been said for your own use, the next matter to be dealt with is that of the many difficult cases in the practice of confession concerning the imposition of penance'). This section will be 'ad utilitatem legencium' (18.18) in a different sense from *B1*; the *transitio* is self-consciously proper. For the most part, *B2* abridges its source with few embellishments. Yet there are signs that Rolle desires active involvement in the drama of the encounter between priest and penitent. For example, where the priest in *Pars Oculi* expounds Lamentations 2.19 to encourage the penitent to 'pour out his heart like water', listing ways in which people avoid doing this, Rolle develops this into a short sermon: wine, oil and milk cannot be 'poured out' from a vessel so completely as water can be. Hence each stands for a different variety of incomplete confession: one accompanied by excuses, one in which sins are held back out of shame or fear, one in which the pleasure of sin is not repudiated (32.7–33.10): '*Effunde igitur sicut aqua cor tuum, non excusando sed fortiter accusando, nec aliquod peccatum nec aliquam delectacionem peccati in te morari permittendo, quia non sequitur veniam qui vult unam retinere culpam*' (33.13–16: '*So pour out your heart like water*, not excusing but firmly accusing yourself, not letting any sin nor any pleasure in sin remain in you – for whoever wants to keep back one fault does not obtain pardon'). This addition is clearly aimed at making explicit the dramatic nature of confession, and again this is suggestive of Rolle's desire for direct didactic engagement with his audience.[14]

Judica B3 offers plenty of scope for such engagement since like *A* it is a homily on the Last Judgement, the first half of which is partly derived from a model sermon in *Dextera Pars*. Although Rolle chooses not to circumscribe it by introducing it explicitly as a model sermon – this would reduce its immediate impact – such is also its formal function in *Judica Me*. The section has a homiletic structure, first outlining (as a basis on which a preacher might expand) the theological narrative of the Judgement, then adding a hortatory conclusion with *exempla*. Yet the section is not merely a preaching aid; as the climax of Rolle's attempt to blend the manual form with more direct kinds of instruction, it performs several didactic and structural functions. Lacking a formal explanation of its purpose like those given in *B1* and *B2*, it seems also designed as a piece of direct didacticism, and adds a peroration and instructive conclusion to William of Pagula's sermon-outline in much the hortatory style of *A*:

Respuendum est igitur huius mundi gaudium quia ut ait scriptura: *Risus dolore miscebitur, et extrema gaudii luctus occupat* [Proverbs 14.13] ... ⟨Unde dicit apostolus: *Quod oculus non vidit, nec auris audivit, nec in cor hominis ascendit, que preparavit Deus diligentibus se* [1 Corinthians 2.9] ... Sciendum est quod contra tres hostes iugiter debemus pugnare et eorum maliciam a cordibus nostris procul expellere ut in bono perseverantes Christus Deus noster nos dignetur in suo regno coronare.⟩
(76.9–77.8)

[The joy of this world is thus to be spurned, for as the Scripture says, *Laughter is mixed with grief, and sadness attacks the outposts of joy*. For this reason the apostle says: *God has prepared for his lovers what the eye has not seen, what the ear has not heard, what has not entered man's heart*. We must know that we should fight continually against the three enemies and expel their malice far from our hearts, so that, persevering in good, Christ our God may deign to crown us in his kingdom.]

Richard Rolle and the invention of authority

Other passages seem closer to theological than to pastoral statement:

⟨Erunt igitur sancti in corpore et anima glorificati, impassibiles, immortales, agiles, subtiles, mirabiliter fulgentes, alii aliis splendidiores. Quia qui hic Deum ardencius diligunt, ibi Deo propriores et maiori gloria et lumine perfusiores eternaliter erunt. Omnium etas erit una; statuta vero diversa.⟩ (69.4–9)

[Thus the saints will be glorified in body and soul, immune to suffering, immortal, keen, rare, marvellously shining, some more resplendent than others – because those who here love God more burningly will there be nearer to God, and will be shot through for ever with greater glory and light. The age of each will be the same, but their states different.]

This, like a passage about the quadripartite division of souls at the Judgement (74.5–75.6, quoted on p. 59, and also an addition of Rolle's), suggests that *B3* was designed partly to recapitulate *Judica A* (as a sermon returns to its opening), partly to compensate for the short account of the elect given there by adding a brief account of their destiny.[15]

As well as recalling the reader to the emphases of *Judica A*, especially to the Judgement which overshadows all earthly things, *B3* draws together several of the pastoral themes of *Judica Me*: the need for true contrition, for total restitution, and for the correct motive in doing good. The work ends with three carefully organized *exempla* derived from Caesarius and Peter Damian, in which the recently dead return to explain how they came to be damned (77.20–79.6; for sources see Daly 1984, pp. 119–120, nn. 24–26): an official is punished for failing to restore property embezzled by an ancestor; a rich man tells his wife that his almsgiving was useless, since he acted out of vainglory; a worldly cleric confesses that his absolution was useless because he retained the desire to sin. The stories illustrate the dominant theme of *Judica Me*, the importance of the inner life; thus, like the *exordium* of *A*, they plead for inner purity and attack hypocritical disparities between inner and outer self. The *exempla* are carefully connected; contrition is seen to be incomplete without restitution, and both without purity. One transition, for example, reads:

Ideo karissimi *Effundite cor vestrum tanquam aquam coram Domino* [Lamentations 2.19] ut nec voluntas peccandi nec delectacio nec dulcedo peccati in vobis ultra remaneant; sed et cavete diligenter ne aliena bona rapiatis, quoniam non dimittitur peccatum nisi restituatur ablatum. (78.7–11)

Therefore, beloved, *Pour out your hearts like water before the Lord*, so that neither the will to sin nor the delight and the sweetness of sin remain in you any more. But also be scrupulously careful that you do not take the goods of others, for sin is not forgiven unless stolen goods are restored.]

The *exempla* are appropriate at the close of a model sermon, but Rolle's concern with their appropriateness as an ending to *Judica Me* as a whole shows, yet again, how important structural considerations were to him in writing the work. *B3* makes an impressively well-integrated ending to what we have seen to be a heterogeneous, if thematically coherent, structure.

86

II

The conflation of modes of writing and structures that make up *Judica Me* is thus in many respects satisfying. The most serious tension so far noted is between the work as a pastoral manual and as a didactic epistle: between indirect and direct didactic discourse. However far Rolle's adaptation of the manual form moves it towards dramatic engagement, and however carefully the prologue to *B1* attempts to separate the opening sermon from what follows, no fusion of the two modes occurs; even *B3* juxtaposes without reconciling them. Yet in a sense this tension is purposeful, an intentional subversion of the distanced tone of the pastoral manual, and of the separation between professional and personal behaviour that this tone implies – and as we saw in the introduction (pp. 11–13), there is a substantial body of medieval writing which makes similar demands that the clergy see their lives as requiring uncompromising moral and spiritual standards. Moreover, there is no reason why such a confusion should have mattered to medieval readers, who often had a sophisticated and fluid sense of possible perspectives.[16]

Yet the tension is intriguing, for if Rolle wanted an immediate didactic relationship with his readers it seems odd that he should have written a pastoral manual at all. Presumably a request by his priestly friend and the availability of a manuscript of the newly completed *Oculus Sacerdotis* were factors in his decision to write. However, the circumstances Rolle outlines at the beginning of *Judica A* suggest a more specific explanation: that as a young writer whose status as a true hermit had recently been challenged, he was anxious to avoid making too obvious a claim for his own authority as a teacher (especially of a priest). I have suggested that in the prologue to *B1* he shelters behind the idea that his work is a *compilatio* and a manual, which derives its authority from the Fathers and is no more than an ancillary aid to the clerical life. These claims seem prudent in the circumstances, although it is not surprising either that they are not strictly true, or that Rolle's attempts to make them true create their own frustrations. If my analysis is correct, from this perspective the indirect discourse of *Judica B* acts as a cover for its direct appeals to the reader, and the conflation of modes in *Judica Me* has a specifically defensive function. The second part of my analysis of the work develops a similar argument with respect to *Judica A*, parts of which I will now examine in more detail, in order to show how, as well as being a didactic homily, this part of the work is a concerted, if inchoate, attempt by Rolle to defend his position as a hermit. As soon as we turn from the structure to the actual content of this homily, our attempt to see it as a satisfactory and self-sufficient piece of didactic writing collapses – to be replaced by an uneasy and fragile alliance of writing modes, in which apology, it would seem, is the dominant force.

The opening of *Judica A* is a prayer of imperilled righteousness which appropriates the language of the psalms to fit the speaker into a structure of persecution and faith: a structure which at once denies any possibility that he is in the wrong. This strategy places Rolle above attack, but has the corresponding disadvantage that it also places him above being seen to defend himself. Thus *Judica A* has to build his moral authority indirectly:

Judica me Deus et discerne causam meam de gente non sancta [Psalm 42.1]. *A Deo qui scrutatur cor et renes volo iudicari, non ab homine qui solummodo videt ea que exterius apparent, quoniam qui de alienis cordibus iudicare presumit, indubitanter sciat quod in errorem cadit. Et qui motum corporis de loco ad locum instabilitatem mentis pronunciat absque dubio grave pondus super se posuisse cognoscat. Quamobrem, ut ab invidentibus et maliciosis de me incaute cogitantibus ac loquentibus clemencia Christi me liberet, necesse mihi supervenit clamare cum propheta:* Domine, *libera animam meam a labiis iniquis et a lingua dolosa* [Psalm 119.2]. *Quoniam tu,* Domine, probasti me, et cognovisti me; tu cognovisti sessionem meam et resurrectionem meam, et tu solus intellexisti cogitaciones meas [Psalm 138.1–3].

(1.1–13)[17]

[*Judge me O God, and divide my cause from the unrighteous.* I desire to be judged by God, who inspects the heart and the loins, not by someone who only sees those things that show on the outside. For he who presumes to judge the hearts of others should know for certain that he is falling into error. And he who asserts the movement of the body from place to place to be instability of mind can understand that he is without doubt placing a heavy burden on himself. But in order that the mercy of Christ may free me from the envious and malicious, who think and speak of me recklessly, I am forced by necessity to cry out with the prophet: *Lord deliver my soul from evil lips and from a deceitful tongue.* For you, *Lord, have proved me, and known me; you know my sitting and my rising, and only you have understood my thoughts.*]

Rolle argues that God alone has the right to judge, because people rely on externals in forming opinions; anyone who presumes to judge others is thus wrong by definition. God discerns righteous and unrighteous, and reads hearts ('scrutatur . . . probasti . . . cognovisti . . . intellexisti'), but people who aspire to this omniscience may be sure only that they are in error. This error is a 'grave pondus' attributable only to the 'invidentibus et maliciosis'; Rolle defines his enemies ever more harshly and clearly. Meanwhile he himself gains ground, for the folly of his enemies allows him to pronounce on God's behalf that they should know *without doubt* ('absque dubio') that they are wrong. His enemies confuse the inner self with 'ea que exterius apparent', Rolle's 'motum corporis' with 'instabilitatem mentis'; but the confidence of his prayer shows his heart to be pure.

After depicting his true standing and that of his enemies before God, Rolle can defend his actions, not to his enemies but to his friend: 'Nam vos scitis et a me sepius audistis me ibi velle morari . . . et vos cognoscitis mutati fuerunt quantum ad me qui ministrare assueverunt' (2.8–11: 'For you know and often heard that I intended to stay there; also you know how much those who used to serve me changed in their behaviour towards me'). The friend is identified with the cause of truth and told why Rolle has acted as he has, because like God he knows ('scitis . . . cognoscitis') the hermit's intentions. The trustful tone of this passage is broken by mention of the patron's letter of complaint (3.4; see p. 48, where the entire passage is quoted), but Rolle can now claim to be without animosity towards his enemies, having demonstrated their moral nullity:

Quicquid de me dicant vel faciant non nocet cor meum, quia etsi hic modicum pro Christo sustineam, spero tamen eternam in celo percipere remuneracionem, illud verbum recolens propheticum: *Patiencia pauperum non peribit in finem* [Psalm 9.19]. Hec scribo vobis ut non iudicetis quemquam priusquam iudicaverit eum Christus. Nescitis enim que geruntur in mente quamquam cernitis hominem ambulantem in carne. Unde nec laudes secularium cupio nec illorum maliciam pertimesco. (3.5–12)

[Whatever they say of me or do to me, they cannot hurt my heart, for even if I here sustain a little for Christ, I hope to receive an eternal reward in heaven, recalling the prophetic words: *The patience of the poor will not perish in the end.* I write this to you so that you do not judge anyone before Christ has judged him; for you are ignorant of the thoughts nurtured by the mind, although you see a person walking about in the flesh. As a result, I do not desire the praise of the worldly and am not terrified of their malice.]

The passage transforms criticism into the persecution that is the mark of the elect; since criticism is based only on externals and persecution can hurt only his body, Rolle's heart is untouched ('non nocet cor meum'). The moral, not to judge those still in the flesh, juxtaposes 'carnem' with his 'cor', knowledge ('nescitis') with sense perception ('cernitis'), and refers pointedly to the author's eremitic ambling ('ambulantem'). After this odd interplay of defensive and didactic modes, which both turns the opening into an *exemplum* and gives moral statements a defensive undertone, Rolle's final expression of indifference to the world apparently closes the subject of his persecution. Having established his purity and his right to speak on God's behalf, he can now assume a preacher's role in unveiling the Last Things.

Yet in exercising his moral right to 'preach', he continues to vindicate himself and denigrate his enemies; although he does not refer to himself again until almost the end of *Judica A*, defensive themes run right through his depiction of the Judgement. In writing of the joy of the blessed immediately after the last passage quoted, he describes the reward the persecuted *pauperes* receive for their patience:

Veniet dies, ecce prope est . . . in qua nos omnes non solum de factis et de dictis sed etiam de cogitationibus ante tribunal Christi reddemus rationem. O quam felix qui tunc stare poterit ad videndum Christum, et leto vultu in eum prospicere et nullius adversarii opposiciones formidare. Hic est qui super omnia Deum dilexit et in thesauris terrene pecunie non speravit, sed Christum posuit adiutorem suum quem ita contra malam audicionem habebit adiutorem . . . O melliflua spes refugii veri amatoris Christi qui, dum carnales et mundani ministris infernorum crudeliter agitantur, sub aliis Conditoris sui ab omni formidine malorum mitissime protegitur . . . Qui nunc ne ab illo gaudio illudantur per adversantes sibi, cum Propheta clamant ad Christum: *sub umbra alarum tuarum sperabo donec transeat iniquitas* [Psalm 56.2], scilicet diaboli, carnis et mundi . . . Audite iam de iustorum letitia quod delectat . . .
(3.13–4.10, 20, see 76.14)

[The day will come, behold it is near, on which all of us will give account before the judgement seat of Christ, not only of our deeds and words, but even of our thoughts. O how happy he who will then be able to stand to see Christ, and to look at him with a joyful face, and fear the opposition of no adversary! He will be the one who loved God above everything, and did not trust in the treasury of earthly wealth; instead he placed his trust in Christ, and will therefore have a helper against evil reports. O honeyed hope of refuge for the true lover of Christ who – while the carnal and worldly are cruelly driven by ministers of hell – is protected so gently from all fear of evil, under the wings of his Creator; they who now, in case they should be cheated of any joy by their enemies, cry to Christ in the prophet's words: *I will hope under the shadow of your wings until iniquity* – that is, the world, the flesh and the devil – *passes over*. Hear now of what delights, the joy of the just.]

Since the instruction to read this passage homiletically ('Audite') does not occur until its close (the point at which the narrative turns to the damned) we actually read the passage in relation to the opening, in which Rolle is himself the 'pauper'. Allusions to persecution and to God's searching of the heart only encourage this tendency; even thoughts ('cogitationibus') will be revealed at the Judgement, where the poor's purity will be vindicated (and thus the 'incaute cogitantibus' of the malicious be punished: see 1.7). The elect (the patient poor) need fear no 'opposiciones' and will be shielded from 'malam audicionem' (compare 'audientibus', 2.4); they are sheltered even now under God's wings from their 'adversantes'. These latter are formally identified with 'iniquitas', the triad of world, flesh and devil (for Rolle is aware of his didactic responsibilities), but the passage nevertheless broadcasts a message to potential human opponents: God protects his own even in this life.

The account of the reprobate's progress to damnation underlines the same message from a negative perspective. While Rolle's 'motum corporis de loco ad locum' is not to be identified with 'instabilitatem mentis' (1.5–6), the reprobate go 'into a place far from God the Father, receding not through any bodily movement but through the vices of their evil wills' (5.6–7). They, not Rolle, are the true *girovagi*. Their damnation is a result of deception, blindness and envy (4.24; 5.12, 14, 16), yet they are *knowingly* ('sciant', 5.6) stained with mortal sin. As in the opening of *Judica Me*, words for knowledge and ignorance abound, identifying the speaker's viewpoint with truth and certainty; only in hell will the reprobate's eyes be opened to see their blindness (9.13–14). No more will they envy the good and despise the poor (8.14–15), but will be dismayed to be cut off from those elect they persecuted in life (8.20–21); it will be these who now accuse them of sins (7.13–14: 'electos Dei habebunt accusantes') and rejoice in their downfall (6.20–24). This whole account of the Last Judgement heralds Rolle's coming vindication. He cannot with prudence or consistency threaten his enemies overtly; he can and does associate himself with God's cause and with the *electi* – despised in this life, triumphant in the next – and hence can link those who oppose him with the reprobate.

In the account of the Judgement just re-examined, defensive and didactic modes are mutually dependent; apology shelters behind a homiletic voice which itself depends on the effectiveness of the apology for its success. But in the final part of *Judica A*, to which we now turn, coexistence gives way to competition, as an apologetic presupposing predestination struggles to assert itself in a section of exhortation that must presuppose the freedom of the reader's will to reform. The resulting confusion demonstrates what is to be Rolle's greatest problem with pastoral writing: that it is only applicable in a world not yet irradiated – as his defensive vision of things must be – with the predestined certainties of the Judgement. The direction that this section's exhortations seem to want to take – which we have seen to be the didactic thrust of *Judica Me* as a whole – is to urge his priest friend towards the life of perfection: a topic on which he, as a hermit, is an expert. The problem is that the friend, a secular priest, is in active not contemplative life, and as such is not one of the perfect poor who, as *Judica B3* tells us, will help Christ to judge humanity (74.5–12). Given his need to defend his own position as a poor hermit, Rolle cannot afford to undermine the dignity of these perfect *pauperes*, who must be seen as a kind of closed shop, and so cannot state directly that the priest can follow the life of perfection. Instead he gives a good deal of advice which does not seem directed at the priest at all, in an apparent attempt to suggest simultaneously that the priest can achieve divine love and that this privilege is reserved for hermits.

The kind of exhortation that generally follows a Judgement homily assumes its readers to have been terrified by its evocations of hell, and indicates what must be done if hell is to be avoided. This section begins in much this negative way, by claiming that the homily should at least deter people from mortal sin (9.23–24), and stating explicitly that avoidance of sin is its purpose (10.11): an odd beginning to a call to a perfection which aspires to total purity. But almost at once we have language suggestive of a more advanced spiritual state, for Rolle adjures his reader to let his riches consist in loving Christ and to endure opprobrium (10.20–21), adding:

Non erres, frater. Nemo potest gaudere cum Christo qui prius non fuerit secutus illum in hoc mundo. Si dicis, 'Perfecti sequuntur Christi qui pauperes pro illo fiunt, et sine velle diviciarum nudi transeunt', intellige: qui non est particeps in tribulatione, nec erit in carnis glorificatione.   (10.24–11.3)

[Do not be mistaken, brother. Nobody can rejoice with Christ who has not first been his follower in this world. If you say, 'The perfect follow Christ who become poor for him, and go their way naked without the desire of riches', understand this: he who is not a partner in tribulation will not be one in the glorification of the flesh.]

All at once the topic is the imitation of Christ, not the mere avoidance of hell, while Rolle is working to emphasize (on behalf of his priestly reader who does not live in poverty) that suffering for Christ, not worldly poverty *per se*, is the key to identification with him. Adaptation of the language of perfection to the priest continues with a redefinition of tribulation to include martyrdom by world, flesh and devil (11.8, see 4.10). It seems that anyone who successfully fights with temptation is on the way to perfection, except for 'the insignificant faithful' (11.10, 'pusilli fideles') who perform works of mercy and try to avoid at least mortal sin (11.9–18), but do not follow Christ in tribulation. The distinction between 'pusilli' and 'perfecti' redraws that between active and contemplative (as in 74.5–17), but in such a way as to include a priest in active life among at least the potential perfect; this indeed seems to be its sole purpose.

Rolle now directly urges the priest to become a *perfectus*: 'Si vis etiam per-fectus esse, audi Dominum dicentem, *"Nisi quis renunciaverit"*, inquit, *"omnibus que possidet non potest meus esse discipulus"* [Luke 14.33]' (11.26–12.2: 'If you want also to be perfect, hear the Lord speaking: *"Unless someone will give up all that he possesses he cannot be my disciple"*, he says'). The statement at first seems to revoke the concession made earlier, by insist-ing that total poverty is after all necessary to perfection. But desire for wealth, not wealth as such, quickly emerges as the real enemy, as Rolle acti-vates his favourite distinction between internal and external:

Denique hic omnibus renunciat qui voluntatem habendi temporalia pro Christo relinquit . . . Quia magis volo te divicias habere et illas non diligere quam non habere et illas concupiscere. Non omnes qui apparent pauperes, pauperes sunt. Quia nonnulli qui paupertatem foris ostendunt intus per cupiditatem pauperiem amittunt.   (12.3–16)

[In practice someone renounces everything when he gives up the desire for temporal-ities for the sake of Christ. For I would rather that you have riches and not love them than not have them and desire them. Not all who seem poor are truly poor; for some who display poverty outwardly lose their inner poverty through concupi-scence.]

He then settles to the task of commending the virtues necessary for the perfect life and springing from the root of poverty (12.16–18), in a passage of careful relevance to the priest – who is told to do his duty ('diligenter ordinem tenens', 13.8) and warned against administering the sacrament while in a state of sin (13.12–17), and against overconfidence (12.25, 13.18).

Yet for most of this passage it is difficult to believe that a *via perfectionis* is at issue. Many of the miscellaneous commands which form its bulk (13.5–15.1) would not be out of place in the instructions that common parishioners (the 'mediocriter boni', 11.10) receive from the priest in *Judica B2* – not to be drunk, greedy, wordy, worldly (14.9–18). While the theme of perfection is not abandoned, the priest's status as an active Christian is not forgotten, even at the passage's climax:

Ardore caritatis . . . suffoca parvulos Babilonis, id est iniquas cogitaciones et pravos motus. Mundi et carnis desideria nociva non crescant, sed potius habundancia spirit-ualium gaudiorum subtus quasi interfecta iaceant . . . Consolacionem namque divinam non sentit qui terrenam cupit, nec dulcor eterni amoris in illa anima infundi-tur que in fluxibilibus et instabilibus huius vite presentis delectatur. Mirabilis est dulcedo celestis que non conceditur inherenti rebus terrenis. Recordare itaque quia *arta est via que ducit hominem ad celum* et ideo pauci vadunt per eam, et *lata est via que ducit ad infernum* et *multi* transeunt *per illam* [Matthew 7.14, 13]. Durum et nimis amarum tibi videtur perhenniter cruciari cum diabolo. Ergo dulce tibi videtur modicum in servicio Christi laborare, ut postea sine fine cum Christo possis gaudere.

Judica Me *as apologetic pastoral*

Quia si vis diligere mundum, semper cognosces te esse immundum; et si carnaliter te
vivere non trepidas, certe ad perpetuam mortem velociter currere non cessas.

(14.21–15.13)

[With the fervour of charity, smother the children of Babylon, that is wicked thoughts
and depraved desires. May the poisonous desires of the world and the flesh not grow,
but be cast down as though destroyed by an abundance of spiritual joy. For he who
desires earthly consolation will not experience divine consolation, nor is the sweetness
of eternal love imbued in that soul who delights in the changes and chances of this
present life. Wonderful is the heavenly sweetness, and it is not granted to clingers to
earthly things. Remember then that *narrow is the way that leads people to heaven*, so
that few go by it, and *wide is the road which leads to hell and many go by it*. It would
seem hard and terribly bitter to you to be punished eternally with the devil. So may it
seem sweet to you to toil a little in the service of Christ, so that afterwards you may
rejoice with Christ for ever. So if you wish to love the world, always know yourself to
be impure; and if you do not fear to live after the flesh, certainly you do not cease to
speed quickly to everlasting death.]

Here the priest is told of the sweetness of heaven in one breath and of hell in
the next; the ardour of his love is apparently not enough to release him from
the need for fear, or from the continuing struggle with sin.

After this rather grudging peroration a dislocation occurs, for the singular
address to the priest suddenly gives way to the general 'vos' (15.16), and to an
address applicable specifically to hermits, from which the priest, who cannot
very well flee into the wilderness, is excluded:

Si vos delectat heremus ut in solitudine habitetis, vel saltem si singulare propositum
teneatis iugiter, scitote quod in principio durum laborem habetis; sed paulatim in
amore Christi crescentes, ineffabile gaudium invenietis. Verumptamen propter
asperum introitum nullus sapiens spaciosam et delectabilem derelinquet viam. In
inicio graviter pungimur, sed in medio et in fine celesti suavitate delectamur. O felix
tristicia quam statim sequitur consolatio divina! . . . Letatur enim heremus a pauperibus Christi visitari.

(15.22–16.8)

[If the desert delights you so that you live in solitude, or at least if you keep
continually to your singular intention, know that at first you will have hard work, but
as you grow gradually in the love of Christ you will come to ineffable joy. However,
because of the harshness of the entrance, none of the worldly wise will leave the
spacious and pleasant road. At the beginning we are badly stung, but in the middle and
at the end we rejoice in celestial sweetness. O happy sadness which is at once followed
by divine consolation! For the desert rejoices to be visited by Christ's poor.]

The promises made here recall the last remarks addressed to the priest, but
with important differences. Where the priest is offered joy 'postea', in
heaven, the hermit will attain it 'paulatim', on earth; where 'arta est via'
applies to the whole of the priest's earthly *via*, the hermit's is only hard at the
beginning ('asperum introitum'). Rolle boldly states that solitaries can reach
the sweetness of heavenly joy in this life ('in medio'); he has been more
cautious in relation to the priest. What has been smuggled into the exposition
under cover of these imprecise parallels – and in the context of increasingly
explicit autobiographical statements – is an expression of the superiority of
the solitary life to that of the secular clergy, and implicitly to all others:

93

Tantum namque gaudium sencio sub heremitice habitacionis voluntate ut nec volo nec possum illud inerrare. Absit igitur ut tam crudeliter deviarem quod aliud sinistrum sive demeritum de appetentibus heremum loquerer. Sub cuius nomine diabolum non timeo, terrena contempno, carnem spiritum subiugo. Benedictum sit illud nomen heremeticum et illud singulare propositum in quo amare disco, iubilare consuesco, salvacionem securus expecto. Nullum in ecclesia ordinem reprehendo, sed solitudinem maxime diligo ac laudo. (16.9–16)

[For I feel such joy in my desire for an eremitic habitation that I do not wish to, nor can I, express it. Let me never, then, go so rudely astray that I speak anything evil or offensive about those who seek the desert. As one of their number I do not fear the devil, I despise worldly things, I subdue the flesh to the spirit. Blessed be the name of hermit and the singular plan of life in which I learn to love, become accustomed to sing, wait securely for salvation! I do not find fault with any order in the Church, but I praise and love the solitary one most greatly.]

The apparent concession which ends this passage in fact points up the gulf between other states of life and Rolle's own 'propositum'. Where the priest was warned to fear falling away and was told of the continuing difficulty of the spiritual life, Rolle awaits his salvation securely and has begun his heavenly rejoicing already. Although it may be that this passage is also intended in some way for the priest – for *Judica A* ends with general spiritual advice that uses both second-person singular and first-person plural forms, as though priestly and eremitic audiences are now united – its immediate impact is that of a vaunt, as Rolle celebrates his superiority over his friend.

In the last section of *Judica A*, then, Rolle's apologetic concerns turn an exposition of the *via perfectionis*, as it applies to a secular priest, into a glorification of the solitary life which places that life far beyond what the priest has been told he can aspire to. Even before this point the exposition has betrayed contrary assumptions as to what is appropriate for the priest's spiritual life. The homiletic structure of *Judica A* as a whole, with its careful stirring up of the reader's fear of damnation, suggests a popular sermon too crude for Rolle's priest friend, and the last section of *Judica A* is indeed concerned to treat him as a more spiritually advanced Christian than the *pusilli* who live well through fear of damnation. On the other hand, in this section Rolle is not prepared overtly to hold out the possibility that the priest may achieve the perfection available to the solitary, and continues to offer advice and warnings appropriate for the *pusilli*. To an extent these confusions may be caused simply by lack of experience, or alternatively by Rolle's awareness that his work was to have more than one reader (see n. 8). Yet it is clear that he writes about damnation, perfection, and the solitary life in the ways he does at least partly for apologetic reasons. Edification is not the only function of *Judica A*.

For the most part, this analysis has treated the apologetic theme in *Judica Me* as a reflection of Rolle's immediate desire to establish his credibility as a teacher, in the face of the questions that had arisen as to his integrity as a hermit. However, it becomes evident in the last part of *Judica A* that in practice the theme is not merely subordinated to this goal; for here it actually works against it, undermining the clarity of the work's didacticism, and focussing a dangerous amount of attention on Rolle's high view of his own status. A cautious impersonality would have been more practical; but clearly practicality is not the most important concern of Rolle's apologetic writing. In the next major works that Rolle was to write, this apologetic theme becomes his leitmotif, subsuming all his interests into a single metaphysical model, and creating one of the most distinctive of medieval Latin voices. In *Judica Me* this model is presented only simply, as an apologia linked to an account of the elect and the damned. But even here the theme has the power to be a displacing force and focusses a number of Rolle's deepest concerns: the Judgement, a future event of overwhelming relevance in the present; the radical split between interior and exterior; the superiority of the solitary life to all other forms of the religious life; and, critically, *the establishment of his right to speak*.

All of these concerns can be found in *Judica B* as well as in the apologetic context of *Judica A*; the occasionally tense relationship between impersonal and direct discourse in the former, indeed, seems to parallel that between apologetic and homiletic discourse in the latter. However, the immediate future of these concerns in Rolle's works lies with the topic towards which *Judica A* unexpectedly leads: the praise of the solitary life. The way this topic emerges confusingly, from between the crevices of a work whose supposed subject is quite different, is a revealing sign of the frustrated uncertainty Rolle brought to the writing of *Judica Me*. In his next major work, *Incendium Amoris*, such frustration bears fruit in a remarkable development of his narrative persona, and in a new-found ability to deal directly with apologetic themes. The work is written overtly in praise of the solitary life, and with his own experience as its exemplar; as a result it goes some way towards uniting the didactic and the apologetic modes that are separate in *Judica Me*, and prepares the way importantly for the integrated, albeit eccentric, structures he was to evolve for works like *Contra Amatores Mundi*. Yet we shall find that lack of self-awareness also bears fruit in *Incendium Amoris*, for in attempting to unite the didactic and the defensive in this work, Rolle created difficulties for himself and for the reader beside which the minor incoherencies of *Judica Me* will pale.

4

Contemplative life, 'Seeing into Heaven': commentaries and *Canticum Amoris*

Judica Me is clearly a careful composition by a writer still searching for a suitable subject-matter and a personal voice. Before describing the way that search culminates in *Incendium Amoris*, I want to comment on a group of other works which form part of the compositional background from which his mature writings emerge. From my present perspective these works are not of great individual interest; the brief treatment they receive in this chapter is thus mostly in the context of the more 'important' works discussed elsewhere: how they reflect the youthful preoccupations of *Judica Me*, while anticipating the thematic emphases and literary structures of the later parts of Rolle's career. The group consists of *Super Symbolum Athanasii* (if this is his), *Super Symbolum Apostolorum*, *Super Orationem Dominicam*, *Super Apocalypsim*, *Super Threnos*, *Super Mulierem Fortem*, *Super Magnificat* and (although it belongs in a quite different category) *Canticum Amoris*.[1] All are surely the products of the early part of Rolle's career, written during a period that began before he wrote *Judica Me* and ended about the time he composed *Incendium Amoris*. Almost all of them are commentaries, based on the *Glossa Ordinaria* or other glosses, and sometimes varying no more from their sources than does *Judica B* from the parts of *Oculus Sacerdotis* it uses. As Clark (1986, pp. 196–197) also argues, this derivativeness is one reason for thinking of them as early works. A young writer as concerned to gain acceptance as the author of *Judica Me* would be likely to begin his career with cautious imitation not bold statement, and therefore derive his first works from well-known exemplars. Moreover, these works are also derivative or conventional in other senses. In most of them Rolle presents himself in the subordinate roles of *compilator* (as in *Judica Me*) or *commentator*, not as an *auctor* who takes responsibility for his own declarations. Several of them expound central liturgical texts (Creeds, the *Magnificat*, the Lord's Prayer) and assert the necessity of orthodox belief as if to demonstrate their author's knowledge of orthodox doctrine. They lack many features of Rolle's mature writing, such as its heavy alliteration and emotionalism; they are seldom self-referential; seldom do any of them convey the intimacy of tone characteristic of him. Most important, their mystical content is largely derivative; they tend to avoid explicit discussion of the mystical experiences which Rolle describes in *Incendium Amoris*, and on which he bases his claim to authority in all his later works. There are thus good grounds for regarding them as early

96

essays in a variety of styles, which embody the same search for literary individuality that underlies *Judica Me*. While Rolle's development need not have been a consistent or schematic business, there are also some grounds for supposing that the works in this group to which the above generalizations apply least happily were written later than the more derivative works (see pp. 276–277). In moving from the less to the more individual of these works, my exposition may therefore be approximating a chronological account of his progress.

The commentaries on the Creeds, the Lord's Prayer, Lamentations and Revelation are the works in the group least characteristic of Rolle's later writing. Generally, they closely reflect the language and preoccupations of their sources (in so far as those have been identified).[2] If my argument for their early composition is correct, we can state the same case another way by seeing these works, like *Judica Me*, as parts of a deliberately tentative beginning to Rolle's career. Yet they are not without distinctiveness; in some respects they parallel the more forthright aspects of *Judica Me* and form an important part of Rolle's early definition of his literary and religious ground. For one thing, scriptural commentary was to remain a fundamental part of his literary activity, not only in the two Psalter commentaries, but in more independent works from *Super Lectiones Mortuorum* and *Super Canticum Canticorum* to the *postillae* that make up *Melos Amoris*. Just as in *Judica Me* Rolle stakes a claim, based on his status as a hermit, to be regarded as an expert on the inner life, so, in writing commentaries on Scripture, he implicitly asserts that he is an authority on the revealed truth. The basis for this assertion again has to do with the fact of his being a hermit, since in his view hermits are closer to God and thus occupy a more authoritative position in the Invisible Church than others. But his works also imply a more particular claim for his status as an authoritative, indeed an inspired, interpreter of Scripture (and perhaps the Creeds). In many places in his writings, he refers to the 'mysteries' concealed in Scripture: *Judica B2* describes the task of biblical exposition as requiring 'scienciam et notitiam celestem secretorum' (34.9–10), while *Melos Amoris* complains of the fact that priests 'oracula ignorant clause Scripture . . . nesciunt nimirum nodum nudare, nec ut solvant signacula a spiritu spirantur' (152.17–18, 20–21: 'They are ignorant of the secrets of the Scriptures; they do not know how to lay bare the knot, nor are they inspired by the Spirit to solve the significations'). We saw in Chapter 2 (pp. 67–68 and n. 16) that, in glossing the '*door open in heaven*' in *Super Apocalypsim* (Revelation 4.1, 156.12), Rolle first adapts pseudo-Anselm of Laon, stating that the verse refers to the way that 'When the darkness of the Scriptures is set forth by the Church, it is as though a door into heaven is opened', then goes on to add his own interpretation of the verse in relation to mystical experience. The juxtaposition of these interpretations amounts to a claim that Rolle's experience of 'Seeing into Heaven' enables him to penetrate the Scriptures as never before, through a transcendent and affective version of the exercise of *lectio*. Having had direct experience of the heavenly reality to which Scripture points – at its deepest level, that of anagogy – the mystic is uniquely qualified to plumb the depths and expound them to others. In the same way that an aspiring *magister* at Oxford or Paris began his career by composing another commentary on the *Sententiae* of Peter Lombard, so Rolle as a young contemplative writer might naturally learn his trade by gaining experience in the unlocking of scriptural doors, beginning, cautiously, with the standard gloss as his guide, but gradually aspiring to more and more independence of thought and structure. That Rolle seems to have chosen to write scriptural commentaries so early in his career – perhaps under the initial impact of what he came to regard as merely the first and lowest of his various mystical experiences – thus suggests that he had already begun to formulate a view of himself as a divinely inspired *glossator*. In the light of this train of thought, even the most conventional of these works come to seem implicitly audacious.

It is true that neither in *Super Apocalypsim* nor in the other earlier commentaries does Rolle claim any form of inspiration, or indeed refer to his own activities as a writer at all; in the mature commentaries, his sense of his relation to scriptural truths and to the activity of expounding them was to become much more confident. Yet even in these early works, and even when he is sticking most closely to his sources, he is far from merely going through the motions. This is evident in his choice of texts on which to comment, and in the foci of the commentaries themselves. The attention Rolle was to lavish on the works he regarded as the chief biblical *exempla* of his experience of *canor*, the Psalms and Canticles, is anticipated in *Super Threnos*, which also expounds biblical poetry, 'metrica lege compositi' (f. 123r. 6–7). The theme of Judgement central to *Judica Me* appears not only in *Super Apocalypsim* and *Super Threnos*, but in *Super Orationem Dominicam* and *Super Symbolum Apostolorum*, both of which develop narratives of the Judgement out of short statements in their texts:

Adveniat regnum tuum: regnum Dei semper est; sed *veniat*, id est, manifestetur hominibus quibus ut lux caecis non videtur, quod nullus ignorare poterit cum filius Dei iudicare venerit, in quo regnabunt et sancti, quia ipsis debetur.
(*Super Orationem Dominicam*, f. 146r. 21–23; see *Glossa Ordinaria*,
PL 114, col. 101)

[*Thy kingdom come*. The kingdom of God is eternal. But *let it come*, that is let it be manifested to people by whom it is not seen, like light to the blind, so that no one can be unaware of it, when the son of God comes to judge – in which kingdom the saints will also reign, as is due them.]

The image of blindness and the allusion to the reign of the saints are characteristic of the Rolle who wrote *Judica A*. Similarly, though in a more historical vein than usual for him, the comment on 'He shall come again to judge the living and dead' in *Super Symbolum Apostolorum* is a disquisition on when and how the Judgement will take place according to the New

Testament and the Psalms, while the final clauses of the Apostle's Creed evoke a compendium of biblical and patristic lore on the salvation of the elect which recurs in Rolle's writing as late as *Melos Amoris*.

Thus the subject-matter of these commentaries suggests Rolle's early realization that his main concerns were with the anagogical phase of history and the prophetic portions of Scripture. These concerns are developed in *Super Apocalypsim* and *Super Threnos*, neither of which consistently fore-shadows the later Rolle in a stylistic sense, but both of which provide indications of his major themes. Both works are about Judgement, but the former looks forward to the Last Things in a mood of prophetic excitement, while the latter looks back, comparing the Church of better days with the corrupt modern institution with which God is angry. Since both biblical texts are highly emotional, and since Rolle often comments on them in a similar spirit, both works thus incorporate many of his most characteristic gestures, from elegy to prophetic denunciation to exultation. Indeed, we can see in both commentaries the beginnings of the process by which these gestures are formed from biblical models: a process of osmosis from text to commentary that becomes fundamental to Rolle's later writings (as Alford 1973 shows). His habit of writing on the prophetic and poetic parts of Scripture means that he often has to expound first-person narrative, which in turn requires first-person explication; like most commentaries written to the pattern of the *Glossa Ordinaria* (the pattern 'text – *id est* – gloss'), the nature of the involvement of gloss with text requires the two to be written partly in the same voice. Bonaventure states that the commentator 'annexes' his own words to those written by others for the purpose of clarifying them (see Minnis 1984, p. 94, quoting from the prologue to Bonaventure's commentary on the *Sententiae*). Typically this process demands a mixture of impersonal explication and amplification, in which the text is often worked into the grammatical structure of the commentary. Since he seldom expounds a text dialectically, it is easy for Rolle to use the commentator's fictitious 'I' to involve himself in his text and to identify himself with its narrator, as he seems to have involved himself in the model confession in *Judica B2*.

That he is thus involved cannot be proved at any given point; interaction between Rolle's own experience and the texts on which he comments does not become overt in any of his glosses. Only in works like *Incendium Amoris*, in which he speaks *in propria persona*, can he openly annex biblical phrases and models for his own use. Yet the process by which Rolle identifies with exemplary biblical characters or statements, which is to become so important to his apologetic presentation of himself, is already evident in the way *Super Apocalypsim* depicts its texts as having been written out of a personal predicament much like Rolle's own (as he presents it in *Judica A*). John, like Rolle, is a solitary contemplative suffering tribulation:

Ego, Iohannes, frater vester et particeps in tribulacione, id est paciens easdem angustias quas et vos patimini, et eadem causa: unde, sicut particeps sum gracie et tribulacionis in presenti, ita *et regno* ero particeps, id est in gloria in futuro; *et patiencia in Ihesu*,

99

quasi in nomine Ihesu et ad honorem eius paciens, non pro aliquo temporali commodo, sed respectu eterne remuneracionis. *Fui in insula que appellatur Pathmos, propter verbum Dei et testimonium Ihesu Christi.* Hic est commendacio ex loco; locus enim solitarius aptus est in quo secreta celestia revelentur. Magnam quippe utilitatem affert solitudo pro Deo pure suscepta, et qui vitam solitariam perfecte sectantur, ab immensis periculis se erutos gaudebunt; et si in primis quidem gravibus temptamentis vexentur, postea sine dubio ineffabili suavitate iubilabunt, patebunt archana, atque superna gloria totum cor personabit. Pathmos 'vorago' dicitur, et ipsa sancta conversacio in solitudine cuncta vicia devorat, omnem immundiciam eliminat, et ipsum Dei virum ad celestia contemplanda exaltat.

(Super Apocalypsim 127.30–128.4)

[*I, John, your brother and companion in tribulation*, i.e. one suffering the same anguishes you also suffer, and for the same reason: so that just as I share in grace and tribulation in the present time, I will also be a sharer *in the kingdom*, i.e. in the future glory, *and in the suffering in Jesus*, i.e. suffering in the name of Jesus and for his honour, not for any temporal gain but for the sake of an eternal reward. *I was in the island which is called Patmos, because of the word of God and the testimony of Jesus Christ.* These words recommend what follows on account of the place – for a solitary place is a fitting one in which heavenly secrets may be unveiled. Indeed solitude sustained only for God yields great profit, and those who follow the solitary life perfectly will rejoice to have escaped immense dangers; and if in the beginning they are vexed by difficult temptations, afterwards they will doubtless rejoice in ineffable sweetness, mysteries will lie open to them, and heavenly glory will resound through the whole heart. 'Patmos' means 'abyss', and this same saintly life in solitude 'engulfs' all vices, swallows up all uncleanness and exalts this man of God to heavenly contemplation.]

Most of this passage has the commentator in his role as preacher, as the text's 'commendatio ex loco' is expanded into Rolle's own commendation of the solitary life (which is at least in part self-commendation, an implicit declaration of his credentials) with its typical distinction between 'in primis' and 'postea' (see *Judica Me* 15.25–16.3), and its hint of affective rhetorical structures in the *membra* that begin with 'ineffabili suavitate iubilabunt'. This quasi-sermon grows out of the way the commentary form enables Rolle to identify verbally with the narrator, John. The fact that this identification is pertinent, since Rolle also writes as a solitary to whom 'archana' have been unveiled 'sine dubio', is probably intended to be noticed, and to enhance the authority of the commentary. After establishing John's status as a solitary, Rolle returns to the subject of his suffering. Here the prose is affective as well as explanatory, dramatizing the scene as if the commentator's (not the apostle's) experience is under discussion:

Et posuit dexteram suam super me, id est manum misericordie et auxilii atque proteccionis sue super infirmitatem meam positam sensi, ut possem pati et vellem sufferre tribulaciones ultra quam conferrent vires mee humanitatis; *Dicens noli timere* opprobria et angustias pati. (134.23–27)[3]

[*And Christ placed his right hand upon me*, i.e. I felt the hand of his mercy and help and protection placed on my infirmity, so that I could endure and would be willing to suffer tribulations more severe than my human strength would allow; *Saying, do not be afraid* to suffer opprobrium and anguish.]

John's history seems to mirror Rolle's quite closely. He is a persecuted solitary to whom Christ appears with a gift of supernatural grace, which enables him to prophesy to the Christian Church, exposing its hypocrisy, and to see mysteries through the 'door' of contemplation. Even when pseudo-Anselm treats John's vision as referring not to mystical experience but to an illumined reading of the Scripture, Rolle can implicitly identify himself with the apostle, as he throws new light on the Scripture by adding his own inspired readings to those he finds in his sources. Only the first clause here is derived from pseudo-Anselm:

Et oculi eius velut flamma ignis, id est provisores Ecclesie ad utilitatem aliorum habent dona Spiritus Sancti, eorum corda ad amorem inflammantis; vel pocius oculi Christi sunt viri summi et contemplativi, pre aliis membris corporis Christi lucidi, et in alto positi ad decorem tocius faciei; qui sunt *velut flamma ignis*, scilicet ardentes interius, quia igne eterni amoris mirabiliter succensi sunt, et totum cor suum quasi in igne conversum est: unde se per contemplacionem ad superna rapiunt, et divino gaudio natura eorum transmutata in dulcedine celestis meli, in spiritu liquefiunt. In quibus flamma illa amor est, per quam ita melliflui facti sunt, quod et orando iubilant; de qualibet scriptum est: *Impleatur risu os tuum et labia tua iubilo* [Psalm 125.2].

(132.19–30)

[*And his eyes were like flaming fire*, i.e. the Church's Providers have the gifts of the Holy Spirit which inflames their hearts to love for the benefit of others; or better, Christ's eyes are the greatest men [*sic*] and contemplatives, more luminous than all the members of Christ's body, and placed on high to embellish his whole face – who are *like a flaming fire*, i.e. burning within, because they are wonderfully kindled with the fire of eternal love, and all their heart is as though turned into fire. For which reason they are snatched to heavenly things by contemplation, and once their natures have been transformed into the sweet honey of heaven by divine joy, they melt in the spirit. In these people, love is that flame by which they thus are made mellifluous, so that in praying they rejoice. Of such flame it is written: *Then let your mouth be filled with laughter and your lips with joy.*]

Here, the contemplative already occupies the controversially high position Rolle is to insist is his from *Incendium Amoris* on and, although he is not explicitly a solitary, his experience of God obviously includes what was to be called *fervor*, and alludes apparently deliberately both to *dulcor* and *canor*. Rolle's privileged knowledge of these experiences enables him to add authoritatively to the tradition of commentary on this passage; conversely, the passage is made to validate the experiences themselves. With the imagery of Revelation at his disposal, and with the commentator's justification for expounding it, Rolle is able to be more forthright than in *Judica Me*, and seems poised on the verge of the self-referential directness of *Incendium Amoris*. Indeed, the fact that of all Rolle's extant works *Super Apocalypsim* alone is perhaps unfinished could be suggestive. Just as he was unsatisfied with the ancillary role of the writer of a pastoral manual in *Judica B*, he was perhaps frustrated by the distance the role of the commentator interposed between personal or affective writing and the subject of Revelation.[4]

Although Jeremiah, like John and Rolle, is a 'pauper' and a solitary

(f. 127r. 35; v. 35), the self-referential nature of *Super Threnos* is less overt than in *Super Apocalypsim*. Many moments in the work are reminiscent of the turns of Rolle's mind, but these spring less from his imaginative involvement in Jeremiah's predicament than from the opportunities provided by particular phrases. Yet aspects of that predicament and of the widowed Jerusalem's desolate state do have an implicit personal significance for him:

Ieremias spiritu moeroris plenus, vehementi exclamatione plena dolore et admiratione ait: *Quomodo*, id est, quam subita et inopinate est destructio tam dilectae civitatis, quia *sedet sola civitas*, id est, ecclesia culpis exigentibus Dei praesentiam amittens, olim *plena populo* sanctorum. Et nunc *facta est quasi vidua* pro turpitudine foeditatis, a sponso Iesu Christo relicta, et terrenis operibus sordidata . . . Anima sola sedet, quae suavitate amoris Christi caret. Et quasi vidua plangitur . . . Quia enim in luce virtutis stare noluit, in tenebras peccatorum deiecta ruit . . . Unde et vox plangentis sequitur. *Beth. Plorans ploravit in nocte.* Quae sit quae ploret, Beth litera ostendit, quae domus interpretatur, id est, ecclesia vel fidelis anima, in qua Christus habitare dignatur, si se mundum conservet . . . Plorat sponsa a complexu sponsi remota; plorat pro desiderio coelestis patriae. Plorat in peccatorum suorum et aliorum recordatione. Plorat quippe non in omnibus, sed in his qui mortui sunt mundo, in viris contemplativis, amore Christi ardentibus et mellifluis devotione delicatissima factis.

(*Super Threnos*, f. 123r. 17–v. 10)

[Jeremiah, full of the spirit of mourning, with vehement exclamations full of grief and dismay says: *How*, i.e. how sudden and unexpected is the destruction of so lovely a city; for *the city sits alone*, i.e. the Church loses God's presence by the compulsion of sins, although she was formerly *full of people* – of the saints. And now *it has become like a widow* because of the ugliness of her filth, abandoned by her husband Jesus Christ, and made shabby by earthly works. The soul who lacks Christ's sweet love sits alone, and cries like a widow, for because she would not stand in the light of virtue she fell, cast into the darkness of sins. Thus the voice of the mourner adds this: *Beth. Crying she cried in the night.* The letter 'Beth', which means 'house', shows who it is who cries, i.e. the Church or the faithful soul in whom Christ deigns to dwell if the faithful keeps himself pure. The spouse cries because she is far from the embrace of her husband; she cries out of longing for the heavenly fatherland. She cries for the memory of her sins and those of others. Certainly she does not cry in everyone, but in those who are dead to the world, in contemplative men [*sic*] burning in the love of Christ, and made mellifluous by very pure devotion.]

The problem with the exposition of Lamentations for the purposes of a commentator's identification with biblical models is that the 'widowed city' represents several things at once – the Church deprived of its saints through sin, the repentant Church mourning through its saintly men, a soul who lacks Christ, Christ himself, the faithful soul – while the weeping Jeremiah and the mourning city are movingly identified with one another in Lamentations itself, to the extent that it is unclear for most of the work which of them is speaking. Such a mingling of good and evil and of moral responsibility is uncongenial to Rolle, as his manœuvring in the passage may indicate; throughout *Super Threnos* he tries so far as possible to make Jeremiah's mourning prophetic and denunciatory, distancing the speaker from the sins of Jerusalem or the Church and identifying him with the *pauperes* and the elect. But if the work allowed him only limited freedom to develop towards personal or self-referential discourse, it did provide him with much that was to be useful to him in writing his more moralistic and penitential works. For example, both the vocabulary and many of the exegetical techniques of *Super Threnos* – particularly the subtle analyses of changes of speaker in the biblical text – reappear in the late commentary *Super Lectiones Mortuorum*. Moreover, in that work Rolle again adopts the attitude of the speaker here and presents himself as involved in the Church's delinquencies, a sinner like the rest of humanity; it is easy to see why Faber printed both together in his 1536 edition of several of Rolle's works (see n. 1). Again, parts of *Super Threnos* share the imagery of moral blindness and of futility that make so notable a contribution to Rolle's hellfire sermon in *Judica A* (see, e.g., f. 124r.–v.). The preoccupation of *Judica Me* with the need for priests to have moral purity, sound knowledge and real spiritual aspirations, is also a feature of this work – which reproves the contemporary Church in the succinct image 'sacerdotes virginibus copulant' (f. 124r. 13), and refers to those who do not study the Scripture as heretics (f. 124r. 44–48). Finally, the work focusses on contemplatives, especially hermits, as having a special part to play in the reformation of the Church; this is increasingly true as the work proceeds (especially in the exposition of cap. 4), but even cap. 1 describes contemplatives (with 'good preachers') as the cheeks (*maxilla*) of the Church, wet with tears, and sharing the active labours of Martha (f. 123v. 1–12). This account of the role of contemplatives provides Rolle with a justification for writing *Judica Me*, as his contribution to the Church's daily endeavours to restore its own beauty ('quibus pulchritudinem suam quotidie renovare non cessat', f. 123v. 5–6); it is of considerable importance for Rolle's future development and self-presentation.

Rolle's tendency in *Super Threnos*, *Super Apocalypsim* and the commentaries on the Creeds and Lord's Prayer is already to interpret texts as referring where possible to the elect. This tendency becomes more marked in the other brief commentaries with which this chapter is concerned, *Super Magnificat* and *Super Mulierem Fortem*. These works are much closer to the imagery, tone and manner of Rolle's mature writing, and, unlike the works discussed so far, have no known source. *Super Magnificat* indeed opens by indicating that Rolle intends to interpret the text in an original way: '*Magnificat anima mea Dominum*. Istum psalmum benedicte Virginis dicimus canticum; tamen in persona veri amatoris Christi non incongrue illum pro magna parte possumus exponere' (MS Rawlinson c.397, f. 1r. 3–7: '*My soul doth magnify the Lord*. This psalm is called the song of the blessed Virgin; but for much of its course we can, not unsuitably, expound it in the person of the true lover of Christ'). The decision to make the speaker of the *Magnificat* a lover of Christ turns the whole song into a description of the *electi*, heralding the dominance of this topic in Rolle's mature biblical expositions and treatises. It also gives the exposition of this short text a thematic coherence that the commentaries discussed so far have lacked. Like Rolle's only other systematic exposition of an entire text in this vein, *Super Psalmum Vicesimum*, the work could almost be described as an affective treatise, which attempts a stylistically consistent treatment of a single subject, and has a rhetorical and thematic interest partly separate from that of the text with which it is ostensibly concerned. The work proceeds largely by means of repetitive rhetorical figures (*similiter cadens, gradatio, disjunctio, membrum, commutatio*; see Chapter 3, n. 6), which give it much the air of an incantatory list:

Illa ergo anima Deum magnificat quam perversa cogitacio non aggravat, quam immunda delectacio non maculat, quam nullus peccati consensus devastat; sed, ad seipsam conversa immo et supra se quoque elevata, in Deo Ihesu suo exaltat et iubilat: ut veraciter secundum versum canere posset: *Et exultavit spiritus meus in Deo salutari meo.*
(f. 1r. 7–14)

[For God is magnified by that soul whom evil thought does not burden, whom unclean pleasure does not stain, whom no consenting to sin destroys, but who, converted to herself and indeed also raised above herself, exults and rejoices in Jesus her God, so that she may truly sing the second verse: *And my spirit has rejoiced in God my Saviour.*]

Although the exposition is not in fact organized along the lines this opening suggests, the rhyming clauses here resemble the rhyming divisions of an 'academic' sermon (see Wenzel 1986, pp. 66–75); in this respect, too, the work resembles Rolle's mature writings, which frequently suggest the structures and tones of preaching. Yet what is preached here, in language whose rhythms quickly become monotonous, is only the crudest version of Rolle's mature thought. Devotion to the Holy Name, poverty and love are the goals of the spiritual life, which is described in general terms, in relation to the supreme virtue of humility, which cannot be separated from the practice of true charity (f. 1r. 40–44). But negative injunctions – to avoid sin and flee the world – predominate over positive ones, as they do in *Judica A*, and much of the work merely lists sins. There seem ample grounds for regarding the work as a relatively early experiment.

Super Mulierem Fortem can only loosely be described as a commentary at all. It is a brief exposition of Proverbs 31.10 (occupying two single-column folios of MS Emmanuel 35), which in most manuscripts is titled or subtitled as for a short treatise or sermon: *Hampole de Activa Vita et Contemplativa.* The work develops a single argument and assumes that all the texts it quotes refer specifically to the elect. It asserts the superiority of contemplative over active life, and argues for a specific application of the former term against those who wrongly regard themselves as contemplatives ('Asserunt enim insipidi et indiscreti se contemplativos esse', MS Emmanuel 35, f. 23r. 4–5). The term only applies to solitaries who leave the world and undergo a process of spiritual ascent which *Incendium Amoris* describes as Rolle's own: 'Contemplacio ergo non adquiritur nisi relicta tumultu seculari totum cor ad amandum Deum prebeatur' (f. 23v. 9–10: 'For contemplation is not attained unless, leaving behind all worldly noise, the whole heart is made acceptable for loving God'). After attacking the claims of other 'contemplatives' (who are arrogant usurpers of a title to which they have no right), most of the work describes that ascent, using two other texts to support its case; Song of Songs 3.10 (*'Its columns are of silver'* etc.) proves the necessity of stability and the value of contemplation, then Psalm 41.1–5 (*'As the hart desires a spring of water'* etc.) is used as a paradigm of ascent, culminating in a depiction of exultant feasting which Rolle uses elsewhere to refer explicitly to *canor* (*'In voce exultacionis et confessionis sonus epulantis'*, Psalm 41.5; compare, e.g., *English Psalter*, p. 154). Only at the peroration does Rolle return to the text from Proverbs, at the moment that he begins to apply the third-person descriptions of mystical ascent to himself and the reader:

Hoc denique modo contemplacionem adquirimus, ut in nobis *mulierem fortem* in oculis salvatoris nostri veraciter ostendamus, quia dum cor nostrum in amore Ihesu Christi ardere non desinit, ab omni terrena et carnali concupiscencia penitus refrigescit . . . gaudentes canimus, canendo amamus, amando et ardendo requiescimus, et eterne glorie sedem securius expectamus. (f. 24r. 24–v. 4)

[In fact we attain contemplation in this way, so that we may truly reveal in ourselves *a strong woman* in the sight of our Saviour, because as long as our heart does not cease to burn in the love of Jesus Christ we grow entirely cold to all earthly and carnal desires. Rejoicing we sing, singing we love, loving and burning we rest, and look forward more securely to a seat of eternal glory.]

Unlike *Super Magnificat*, *Super Mulierem Fortem* contains almost all the features of Rolle's mature style, and most of the themes of his developed mystical writing. This peroration, with its first-person plural discourse, reads like a passage from *Incendium Amoris*; furthermore the structure of the work, with its sermon-like *thema* and integration of a number of different texts, anticipates that of Rolle's extended biblical expositions: *Super Psalmum Vicesimum*, and especially *Super Canticum Canticorum*. The only features we expect to find and do not are direct allusions to Rolle's experience, and, more surprisingly, any prominent exhortation to love God and attain *canor*, such as his later expositions and treatises contain; the work describes spiritual ascent, partly in the first-person plural and in highly affective terms, without making readers feel the full impact of that description on their spiritual lives. The lack of an explicitly didactic conclusion is perhaps a sign that Rolle thought he was writing a commentary rather than a sermon, and still distinguished carefully between the two. For all the confident way the work expounds his mysticism, these omissions seem to signal his continuing caution.

The last work glanced at here, the short poem in praise of the Virgin, *Canticum Amoris*, also makes a contribution to the group of major works that begin with *Incendium Amoris* (if it is indeed an early piece). The poem demonstrates Rolle's debt to a poetic tradition he knew through the work of his Yorkshire predecessor John of Hoveden (from whom he borrows directly in *Incendium Amoris*):[5] a tradition of elaborate and ardent devotional writing, in which the narrative of the Passion, the glory and beauty of the Virgin, or whatever grand subject it may be, is treated in a 'high' style of epic elaboration, often at epic length.[6] In relation to other exercises in this mode of writing, the ardent terms in which *Canticum Amoris* praises the Virgin are neither unusual nor, I think, outstandingly fine. But in relation to Rolle's career in particular, the work does suggest interesting developments, for it introduces more forcibly than in *Judica Me* or *Super Apocalypsim* the mystical language of heat, sweetness and song, and presents the poet himself far more than before as a personality. Indeed, much of the poem is concerned not so much with the Virgin herself as with the poet's feelings about her:

Zelo tui langueo,	Virgo speciosa,
Sistens in suspirio,	mens est amorosa.
Diu dare distulit,	diva generosa,
Quod cordis concupiit,	musa non exosa.
Salve, salus miseri	mei et medela,
Arcet amor operi,	cuius tenet tela;
Pectus palam percutit;	clamo cum cautela:
Dilecta me diripit,	privans parentela.
Hec dulcis dilectio	mentem obumbravit;
Gerens iam iudicio,	hanc urens amavit,
Iuvenem ingenue	amor alligavit,
Et astantem strenue	sibi separavit.
Puella pulcherrima	prostravit ludentem,
Fronsque serenissima	facit hunc languentem;
Crines auro similes	carpunt conquerentem;
Gene preamabiles	solantur sedentem . . .
Tantam pulcritudinem	presto sum placare
Mellisque dulcedinem,	vel guttam gustare,
Dignare, dulcissima,	quod dilexi dare:
Est quo ardet anima	amenum amare . . .
Lancea letificat	que mentem transfixit;
Amantem amplificat:	sic dilectrix dicit.
Ludam cum hac leviter,	ut fides se fixit;
Nam sonans suaviter	cithara revixit.
Pulcritudo perforat	claustrum cordis mei
Et amantem roborat	gemma speciei;
Nichil nunc iocundius	restat requiei
Quam si carmen canimus	cantus iubilei.
Eminente langueo	lucentis decore
Et pene deficio;	sic artor amore;
Mors michi medebitur,	levans a languore,
Nec fervor frustrabitur	felix ab honore . . .
Virgo decora pari sine,	vivens pure dilexi,
Squalentis heremi	cupiens et in aruis haberi,
Per citharam sonui	celicam, subiectus amori.
Virgo quam cecini,	animam sublima Ricardi.

(*Canticum Amoris* 1–16, 49–52, 93–104, 155–158)

106

[I languish in eagerness for you, O beautiful Virgin. The mind is lovesick, staying in sighing. For long the noble goddess has put off giving what she has desired of the heart, the ⟨yet-⟩undetested muse. / Hail, salvation and remedy for my wretchedness! Love hinders the work whose tools he holds. He strikes the heart openly; I cry out with care. My beloved tears me open, taking me away from my kin. / This sweet love overshadowed the mind; now carrying it away from the Judgement, burning it loved this mind. Love nobly tied the youth and separated him from himself, though he resisted strongly. / The loveliest of girls bowled over the pleasure-seeker, and the serenest of brows makes him a languisher. Her locks like gold consume the sad one; her wonderfully lovely cheeks console the sitter. / I wait to please such beauty and to taste such honeylike sweetness, even a drop. O sweetest one, deign to give what I love! It is pleasant to love that with which the soul burns. / The spear which transfixed the mind makes it rejoice, it enlarges one who loves: so the loving girl said. May I play with her lightly, since faith has established itself; for the cithara has come alive with sweet sound. / Beauty pierces the cloister of my heart, and invigorates the lover with jewel-like loveliness ⟨or the jewel of beauty strengthens the lover⟩. Nothing more pleasant remains for my leisure than if we sing a song, the joyful chant. / I languish and nearly fail for the outstanding beauty of her light; so I am constricted by love. Death will be a healing for me, lifting me from languor, nor will fervour be thwarted, happy from her honour. / O lovely maiden without equal, I love you cleanly in my life, desiring to inhabit the fields of desert waste. I have sung the heavenly ⟨maiden⟩ with my cithara, pressed down ⟨as I am⟩ beneath love. Virgin whom I celebrate, raise up Richard's soul.][7]

Canticum Amoris manifests imagery, feelings, literary conventions and influences which set it apart from all the works yet discussed. *Judica Me* and the commentaries are by their nature concerned with instructing the reader, so that the personality or emotions of the writer can only properly be introduced as a didactic instrument, and are circumscribed by didactic exigencies. Although *Judica Me* begins with an explicit apologia and *Super Apocalypsim* expounds Revelation with reference to *fervor*, *dulcor* and even *canor*, nowhere in these works can Rolle give voice to his feelings *in propria persona*. *Canticum Amoris*, on the other hand, is explicitly a work of praise, the primary audience for which is not, in principal, an earthly reader but the Virgin; the work thus has few responsibilities to its actual readers, who participate in an experience which concerns them only in so far as they identify with the poet. Freed from his duties as an instructor, Rolle seems also freed from fear of institutional suspicion, for what could be more natural or less dangerous than a young hermit's composition of a work of praise which makes no claim to possess didactic authority?[8] In experimenting with the poetry of praise, he was thus able to develop his literary persona into something like the charming, joyous hermit-saint beloved of medieval readers, and to introduce in relation to the Virgin many of the themes and images which reappear elsewhere in his work applied to Christ, or to love.

Rolle's poetic personality is actually what makes the poem a success, for the narrator's sincerity and emphasis on how the Virgin affects him act as aids to the reader's identification with the language of praise, giving life to the conventional *topoi* by which the Virgin is described. In this rhetorical and undidactic context, success – poetic effectiveness – is self-justifying, while the extravagance of some of the speaker's language is no more than appropriate. Presenting himself as a young pleasure-seeker prostrated by love for a heavenly maiden and inspired to sing her praises, Rolle indeed shows restraint, if we compare his language with the rococoist contortions John of Hoveden and Walter of Wimborne delight to perform. The restraint is possibly a product of the level of Rolle's engagement in this poem, for like *Incendium Amoris*, *Canticum Amoris* recounts parts of his own history: his being torn away from the world and 'parentela', separated 'strenue' in soul from self-love and made to desire life in the 'squalentis heremi'. In spite of the conventionality of much of its cataloguing of the Virgin's perfections, the poem attempts, then, to be a product of Rolle's particular situation: to be a specifically eremitic effusion that ends by describing the poet's situation and by giving his name. The restrained way in which the imagery and *topoi* of praise are never allowed to take on too much or too abstract a life of their own, but remain tied to the spiritually sexual relationship the poem depicts, also ensures that the reader remains aware of, impressed by and identified with the personality of the poet.[9]

In the context of this particular applicability of the poem's situation to its author, some of its imagery and machinery also take on a special interest. The zeal Rolle feels for the Virgin manifests itself in language that in his later career will acquire an explicitly technical significance: he burns in love – 'urens', 'ardet', 'fervens' (58), 'caluit' (63); tastes the Virgin's sweetness – 'mellisque dulcedinem' (and see 69–76, which praise her delicious smell); longs for death – 'mors michi medebitur'; and, most important, in writing the poem, he sings. Like much praise poetry, *Canticum Amoris* is much preoccupied with the processes of its own composition – with the song the poet is singing as he writes. It opens (if we take 'diva' and 'musa' to parallel 'virgo') by invoking the Virgin as muse, and greeting her specifically as one who enables Rolle to call out ('clamo'), albeit warily (unless 'cum cautela' means 'with love-sick desperation'); she gives him the inspiration ('amor') to sing in the same way that she has taken him away from his kin. The poem says often how pleasant it is to sing ('carmen canimus cantus iubilei'), or that the poet is singing ('canticum emitto mansuetus; / Melos mulcet musicum', 81–82: 'I give out a gentle song; a sweet strain soothes the musician'), or comments on the remarkable value of song ('Melos et mirificum, in quo vincor mori', 132: 'A song and a wonderful thing, through which I am brought to death in defeat'). The vocabulary connected with song, and with sweetness, is almost as rich in this tiny work as in *Incendium Amoris*; Rolle's heavy use of alliteration in the poem equally anticipates his later works. Such an emphasis on the singing of the song may be a feature of the tradition of praise in which *Canticum Amoris* was written (and of praise itself, which generally reduces itself to the imperative 'praise!'),[10] but still has an untraditional destiny in Rolle's later works – as we shall see particularly clearly when we come to *Melos Amoris*. In a yet unfocussed way, the poem is moving towards the definition of *canor* as a mystical, not merely a rhetorical, state, and thus towards the singing of praise as a mystical, as well as a rhetorical, exercise – in other words, towards the concern of Rolle's mature works.

In order to investigate this crucial development we must turn now to *Incendium Amoris*: the work in which Rolle wrote his first explicit and systematic accounts of *fervor*, *dulcor* and *canor*, adumbrated for the first time an open claim to spiritual authority, and transformed the discreet commentator's 'I' and the winsome narratorial voice of *Canticum Amoris* into a far more ambitious and authoritative voice – a voice which has the power to charm us with a tale from the work's very opening.

PART III

5

Contemplative life, *Fervor: Incendium Amoris*

I

Except for three brief experiments (*Super Magnificat, Super Mulierem Fortem* and *Canticum Amoris*), all the works considered so far as stages in Rolle's development have derived their form, and a high proportion of their material, from a source. Although only *Judica Me* makes this point directly, most of the *auctoritas* that these works may be deemed to possess is likewise borrowed, a product of the respect their readers feel for words and literary or religious structures which were used by, and are thus still redolent of, the *precedentes patres* (*Judica Me* 18.17). The tone we have seen these works striving, mostly successfully, to achieve is that of a professional, if on occasion warm, impersonality; only *Canticum Amoris*, and one passage at the opening of *Judica Me*, present the writer in a more immediate and individual way, the first in affective phraseology which is itself highly conventional, the second in language whose naive directness is probably inadvertent. As *Incendium Amoris* opens, by announcing as its subject the elucidation of its own passionate, and highly original, description of its author's *experientia*, it is immediately clear that the struggle to find a personal voice and a personal *auctoritas* has begun in earnest – that Rolle's writing career has entered a new, and crucially important, phase:

Admirabar [amplius] quam enuncio quando siquidem sentivi cor meum primitus incalescere, et vere non imaginarie, quasi sensibile igne estuare. Eram equidem attonitus quemadmodum eruperat ardor in animo, et de insolito solacio; propter inexperienciam huius abundancie, sepius pectus meum si forte esset fervor ex aliqua exteriori causa [palpavi]. Cumque cognovissem quod ex interiori solummodo effer-buisset, et non esset a carne illud incendium amoris et concupiscencia, [in quo compertus sum] quod donum esset Conditoris, letabundus liquefactus sum in affectum amplioris dileccionis, et precipue propter influenciam delectacionis suavissime et suavitatis interne que cum ipso caumate spirituali mentem meam medullitus irroravit. Prius enim quam infunderetur in me calor ille consolatorius et in omne devocione dulcifluus, non putavi penitus talem ardorem aliquibus evenire in hoc exilio; nam ita inflammat animam meam ac si ignis elementaris ibi arderet. Nequaquam, ut quidam aiunt, aliquos in amore Christi 'ardentes' quia vident illos cum diligencia et contemptu mundi ad divina servicia mancipatos. Sed sicut si digitus in igne poneretur fervorem indueret sensibilem, sic animus amare quemadmodum predixi succensus, ardorem sentit veracissimum, aliquando minorem intensiorem vel maiorem, aliquando minorem prout carnis fragilitas permittit. Quis enim in corpore mortali estum illum (in suo summo gradu prout hec vita patitur) continue existentem diu tolleraret? Deficere denique oporteret pre dulcedine et magnitudine superfervidi affectus et inestimabilis utique ardoris; et nimirum hoc avide amplecteretur atque ardentissimo exoptaret anhelitu, ut in ipso mentis muneribus mirificis mellite incendio animam exalans, moreretur migrans ex mundo, et captus statim in consorcium canencium laudes creatori.

Sed occurrunt quedam caritati contraria, quia obrepunt sordes carnis et temptant tranquillos. Necessitas quoque corporalis atque affecciones [humanitatus] impresse erumpuosique exilii anguscie ardorem ipsum interpolant, et flammam (quam sub metaphora ignem appellavi, eo quod urit et lucet) mitigant et molestant. (Non utique auferunt quod auferri non poterit, quia cor totum involvit.) Et propter talia, fervor ille felicissimus ad tempus absens apparet; et ego, quasi frigidus remanens donec redeat mihi, videor desolatus, dum sensum illum ignis interni, cui cuncta corporis et spiritus applaudent et in quo secura se scient, non habeo ut solebam ... Istum ergo librum offero intuendum, non philosophis, non mundi sapientibus, non magnis theologicis infinitis quescionibus implicatis, sed rudibus et indoctis, magis Deum diligere quam multa scire conantibus. Non enim disputando sed agendo scietur, et amando. Arbitror autem ea que hic continentur ab istis questionariis (et in omni sciencia summis, sed in amore Christi inferioribus) non posse intelligi. Unde nec eis scribere decrevi, nisi postpositis et oblitis cunctis que ad mundum pertinent, solis Conditoris desideriis inardescant mancipari ... Quo enim sciencoires sunt, eo de iure apciores sint ad amandum, si se vere spernerent et ab aliis sperni gauderent. Proinde quia hic universos excito ad amorem, amorisque superfervidum ac supernaturalem affectum utrumque ostendere conabor, iscius libri titulus Incendium Amoris sorciatur.   (145.1–147.32)

[I was more greatly amazed than I can tell when for the first time I truly felt my heart growing hot, and blazing in a real not an imaginary way, as if with a palpable flame. I was truly astonished by the way burning burst out in my soul, and also by the unusual sense of comfort. Because of my lack of experience of this fullness, I had to pat my chest a lot just in case the heat was the result of some outside agency. And when I knew that it boiled up only from within, and that this kindling of love was not caused by the flesh nor by concupiscence – from which I learned that it was a gift of the Maker – I melted joyfully into an emotion of greater love; and chiefly because of the influx of the sweetest of delights and of inner sweetnesses, which with that same spiritual ignition bedewed my soul to the very marrow. For before that heat was poured in upon me, consolatory and flowing with sweetness in all devotion, I really did not believe that such a burning could happen to anyone in our present exile; for it inflames my soul just as if an elemental fire were burning there – yet not in the way people say that some 'burn' in the love of Christ, because they see them given over to the service of God, with diligence and with contempt for the world. But just as if a finger placed in a flame would be enveloped by a palpable heat, so the soul, inflamed with love in the way I spoke of, feels a quite genuine burning, at different times less or more intense – sometimes less according to what the frailty of the flesh allows. For who in this mortal body could long tolerate the continual existence of that fire in the highest degree which the present life allows? In the end he must needs be extinguished by the sweetness and greatness of super-fervent desire and truly incalculable ardour. Yet doubtless, he would avidly embrace and very ardently, pantingly, long for this: to die, breathing out his soul in that same burning of a mind made honey-sweet by wonderful gifts, departing the world, being at that moment captured into the consort of those who chant praises to their Creator.

But some things occur contrary to charity, for filth of flesh creeps up and tempts the tranquil. Also bodily necessity, and desires imprinted with human weakness, and the anguish of this wretched exile, interrupt that same ardour, and dampen and spoil that blaze which I have called metaphorically a flame, because it consumes and enlightens. (Certainly they do not take away what cannot be taken, since it involves the whole heart.) And because of such things, that happiest of heats seems absent for a while; and I seem desolate, staying as if frozen until it comes back to me, as long as I do not have that sensation of internal fire (to which everything in body and in spirit responds, and in which they know themselves at rest) that I am used to. So I offer this book for the consideration not of philosophers, not of the worldly-wise, not of the great theologians enwrapped in endless *quaestiones*, but of the simple and untaught who strive more to love God than to know many things. For he is not known through disputation but through doing and loving. But I reckon that what is discussed here could not be understood by those intellectuals, who are supreme in all sorts of learning, but inferior when it comes to loving Christ. So I have forborn to write for them unless, putting behind and forgetting everything related to the world, they burn to be subjected to nothing but longing for the Creator alone. For the more knowledgeable they are, the more apt they would be, in principle, for loving, if they readily despised themselves and rejoiced to be despised by others. Consequently, because I here inflame all people to love, and try to manifest both the super-fervent and the supernatural effect of love, the title chosen for this book is The Burning of Love.]

Chapter 4 considered several of Rolle's first works, which were labelled 'early' because in them his major themes are articulated only tentatively. Although *Incendium Amoris* itself marks only a transitional phase in a continuing process of development, this opening makes a strong case for our acclaiming the work 'mature', since here Rolle finds the voice which even now defines him for most of his readers. This is the distinctive voice that praises the Holy Name in *Super Canticum Canticorum*, recounts a fearful experience in *Contra Amatores Mundi*, and appeals to Margaret Kirkeby in *The Form of Living*. His narratorial personality comes in more distant and authoritative guises, but the popularity of *Incendium Amoris* is as clear an indication as the inclusion of this passage in the *Officium* (as part of its *lectio quinta*) that this is how his readers liked to think of him: as passionate, audacious, frank; as sensual, charming, diffident and ingenuous.[1] The odd combination of qualities (like those of a spiritualized practitioner of *fine amour*) form a personality that remains Rolle's most inclusive and durable strategy.[2]

Rolle's presentation of himself as ingenuous in this passage is far from being so. As in *Judica Me*, he adopts an 'artificial' opening for his work: an *exemplum* which illustrates his subject and aims to make us well disposed towards it (*Poetria Nova* 134–154). The *exemplum* seems a deliberate attempt to surprise the reader, engaging his interest at once, but also familiarizing him with the novelty of the work's subject-matter so as to allay suspicion from the start. Thus *Incendium Amoris* begins with the author's own surprise when the fire that gives the work its title first flared up in him. He is so astonished that he jumps to a crudely physical conclusion and starts patting his chest, before noticing that the feeling boils up 'ex interiori'. Laughter at his 'inexperienciam' encourages us to accept his realization ('cognovissem', 'compertus') that his *fervor* is not sinful but is 'donum Conditoris'; 'carne' and 'concupiscencia' are contained here by alliterating words expressing the true significance of *fervor*, while the confidence of the narrator's language ensures that we laugh not at him but at his younger self. Once this self has understood the true nature of his experience, he consents to it, further increasing its intensity ('liquefactus sum'). The language of *dulcor* ('dilectacionis suavissime') and the intensity of the heat implied by 'caumate' and 'medullitus' draw the reader imaginatively into Rolle's sensations.[3] The narrator's glance back to the time when he thought his experience impossible ('non putavi') is thus also a retrospective moment for the sympathetic reader, who has been introduced to *fervor* and *dulcor* and is now ready to accept a distinction between merely metaphorical uses of the terms and the real thing. The fuller discussion of *fervor* that follows goes on emphasizing this specialized manifestation of God's love, accustoming us to accept Rolle's experience as a matter of importance on which he is the principal authority. In part of the passage omitted above, we are given practical examples of his know-how, as he lists things that make *fervor* hard to maintain – all of which point towards the solitary life – and assures us of his expertise in overcoming all such problems. At the end of the quoted passage, he sets his kind of knowledge against intellectual understanding (*sapientia* against *scientia*) by ostentatiously dismissing, only to reinclude, academics as part of his intended audience.

In a sense this introduction to a work, and to a mystical experience with which Rolle knows his readers will be unfamiliar, is audacious. It does not even glance towards an obvious alternative strategy for opening the work: to expound biblical texts concerned with *fervor* and *dulcor*, introducing his experience by way of an example. Such an opening would have stressed the scriptural authority underlying Rolle's interpretation of his experience, and might thus have diverted critics; but his main concern in beginning the work with autobiographical anecdote seems rather to have been to impose his presence on the treatise from the start. Yet in view of the significance Rolle will accord his experience later in the work, its introduction here can also be seen as careful, even diffident, for it focusses to a degree he does nowhere else on mere sensation, and disarms criticism with a personal testimony that as yet makes no metaphysical claims.[4] His only interest at this stage seems to be in convincing the reader that *fervor* exists and that he himself knows about it. Thus the success of this passage in effect depends on the winsomeness of the self-portrait it draws: a portrait that, whatever its relation to the 'real Rolle' was, is a careful and strategic creation.

That the portrait is indeed a success is clear from the fame of the passage, copied, printed and paraphrased scores of times, and still familiar to anyone who knows anything of Rolle. In terms of his literary development the portrait also marks a victory, as a comparison with self-referential passages in his early works will indicate. The language of ecstatic love used in *Canticum Amoris* here takes on a specific meaning; the discussion of mystical experience, which *Super Apocalypsim* conducts only as impersonal scriptural exposition, here becomes personal testimony; the subject-matter of *Judica Me*, which proved to be imperfectly suited to his apologetic needs, is here replaced by the presentation of didactic material in a context which is intrinsically concerned with self-justification. For all the artfulness of this opening, the writing is buoyant and triumphant with self-discovery. However, as I have indicated, the new stage of his literary activity which this passage initiates was also to prove more problematic than anything he had faced earlier. As *Incendium Amoris* develops his ambitious case as to the significance of *fervor*, *dulcor* and *canor*, it creates difficulties with his carefully conceived persona which threaten the work and its author with dislocating confusion. Rolle finds himself asserting his own sanctity, both as a product of his argument that all those who receive *canor* are saints, and in order to guarantee the truth of the daring things he proclaims. Such assertions are at best an embarrassment, at worst a disaster for his self-presentation, threatening his credibility as a saintly persona by undermining the diffidence and meekness which sanctity also demands. The redefinition of assertiveness (and of himself as an individual who can legitimately be assertive) that emerges as his solution, brilliant and significant for the rest of his career as it is, evolves only by degrees, as the work recurrently bumps (with all the clumsiness that word suggests) into aspects of his problem.

II

Formally speaking, the opening of *Incendium Amoris* is a prologue to a series of forty-two sections, which vary in length from between a few hundred and several thousand words each; some manuscripts call this a *tractatus* (Allen, pp. 213–224), but Rolle refers to it as a *liber* ('iscius libri'), like the *Liber de Amore Dei contra Amatores Mundi* and 'Liber de Perfeccione et Gloria Sanctorum' (*Melos Amoris*; see Chapter 7, n. 2). The tradition to which the prologue belongs is that of the dedicatory epistle, beloved of twelfth-century religious writers and evoked by Rolle in *Judica B1* (see Chapter 3, n. 9). There, he uses modesty *topoi* common in such contexts; here, he derives some of his air of modest charm from the courteous authorial personae who introduce many Cistercian treatises (see n. 2), and takes the epistolary form as an excuse for talking about himself. Yet most prologues of this type address only a single reader (as in Bernard's *De Gradibus Humilitatis et Superbiae* and *De Diligendo Deo*, or Aelred's *De Spirituali Amicitia*) or else a well-defined group (as in William of St Thierry's *Epistola Aurea*); this indeed accounts for the warmth and directness characteristic of the genre. What is remarkable about this dedicatory epistle is the way that it does not address any such specific audience, but rather offers the work, in a grandly general gesture, first to the 'simple and untaught', then to any intellectual who will take it seriously, finally to 'all people'. That so carefully intimate a prologue should aspire to introduce a fresh-faced Rollean persona not to a defined audience but to the entire world is a forceful indication both of the scope and of the vagueness of the writer's ambitions at this point in his career.

The prologue indicates that the *liber* it introduces is entitled *Incendium Amoris* because the work aims to 'inflame' everyone to love and to 'manifest' love's fervent nature. These aims are appropriate in a work we might regard as an affective treatise; yet they, too, are vague, suggesting a mixture of didactic and controversial modes, as though Rolle was out to convert the world but also to prove something to it. A careful structuring of the work is called for if he is serious about fulfilling these aims. In none of his longer early works had he attempted to create such a structure independent both of a source and a biblical text. To what extent does he succeed here?

A reader's first impression is likely to be that he does not succeed at all. Both the vagueness of the work's aims and the mixture of its modes are immediately apparent. Cap. 1 opens with a general discussion of the need for all to be converted to the love of God, a topic we would expect to initiate an organized discussion of how this can be achieved (as in *Emendatio Vitae*). But the rest of the chapter is satirical, consisting of a series of withering comparisons between the ways in which lovers of God and lovers of the world behave. Cap. 2 similarly begins with a useful pastoral statement, but almost immediately moves on to exult in the glory of the elect. In these opening chapters, and again and again in the rest of the work, we experience the same dislocation that we encountered in the last part of *Judica A*, when material ostensibly aimed at helping the reader instead proved to be concerned with celebrating the superior virtues of hermits (see pp. 92–94). As *Incendium Amoris* proceeds, it consequently becomes ever harder to think of the work as suggesting any kind of coherent programme for the reader to follow, or as being written to produce any specific didactic impact. Our initial sense of displacement is augmented by the remarkable heterogeneity of kinds of writing and modes of address in the work: autobiography, ecstatic prayer, discussions of active versus contemplative life, pastoral instruction, are juxtaposed apparently at random with theological disquisitions on the Trinity, a short treatise on spiritual friendship, and passages of estates satire (see caps. 15, 16, 21, 20; 5–7, 39, 30); material apparently aimed at beginners is sandwiched with puzzling inconsequentiality between discussions of *canor* apparently written for the *perfecti* (as in caps. 19–28). Worse still, on investigation of the work's manuscripts, even the reassuring apparatus of chapter numbers and headings in Deanesley's edition (taken from MSS Dd.v.64 and Emmanuel 35) turns out to be inauthentic; Rolle's original was apparently divided, most unhelpfully, into distinct, unnumbered sections.[5] At the same time, the work does not seem wholly incoherent, if only because it is so repetitive that it could only have been written under the influence of a single set of ideas and feelings; it is carried along by its vehement elevations of the elect and denunciations of the reprobate, and by the incessant excitement aroused by the topics of *fervor*, *dulcor* and *canor*. A first reading of *Incendium Amoris* is likely to produce an annoyed sense that one ought not to feel so confused as one usually does.

The structures that show Rolle taking his didactic responsibilities most seriously are also, oddly, those that most seriously dislocate any attempt to read *Incendium Amoris* through, disrupting its most organized sections. For example, caps. 5–8 carefully develop several lines of thought. Cap. 5 is a discussion of *scientia* versus *caritas*; cap. 6 is a formal account of the doctrine of the Trinity, aimed at refuting those puffed up by *scientia*; cap. 7 opens with the same topic, before going on to extol the elect for practising *caritas* rather than concerning themselves with *scientia*; cap. 8 deals with the sufferings the elect must undergo. Yet the transitions between these chapters are articulated in a way that seems designed rather to obscure their coherence than otherwise. Each begins abruptly, without reference to its predecessor, as though initiating not continuing a topic, and perorates so decisively that the new chapter is bound to read like a new beginning, even where it continues with the same subject. Cap. 6 ends as follows:

Laudabile ita est, Deum perfecte, scilicet incomprehensibilem esse, cognoscere; cognoscendo, amare; amando, iubilare in eo; iubilando in eo requiescere; et per quietem internam ad requiem pervenire sempiternam. Non moveat te quod dixi Deum perfecte cognoscere, et negavi te Deum posse scire, cum tamen psalmista dicat: *Pretende misericordiam tuam scientibus te* [Psalm 35.11]. Sed sic istam auctoritatem intellige si non vis errare, *scientibus te*: scilicet 'hiis qui sciunt te Deum amandum, laudandum, adorandum, glorificandum, solum omnium rerum Conditorem, super omnia, per omnia, et in omnibus, qui est benedictus in secula seculorum. Amen.'

(162.7–18)

[It is therefore praiseworthy to know God perfectly, that is, to know him to be incomprehensible; and knowing him to love him, loving him to rejoice in him, rejoicing to rest in him, and by inner quiet to arrive at eternal rest. Do not be worried that I have told you to know God perfectly and also denied you can know God, when the psalmist says: *Extend your mercy to those who know you*. But if you are not to go wrong, understand this saying about *those who know you* as follows: as meaning 'those who know that you, God, are to be loved, praised, adored, glorified as the only Creator of everything, above all, through all and in all, who is blessed for ever and ever, Amen'.]

Yet after this affective and contrived climax, the opening of cap. 7 reverts to the academic language used in the earlier parts of cap. 6: 'Sic ideo quidam errantes vellent dicere tres essencias, quia dicunt tres personas, cur eciam non dicerent tres Deos?' (162.19–22: 'So if some bunglers want to say that there are three essences because there are three persons [in the Godhead], why do they not also say that there are three Gods?'). The words 'sic ideo' signal this return to an earlier topic, but the reader's experience is one of displacement, not continuity; in practice the new chapter demands a new reading occasion and a different kind of attention from the end of cap. 6.

Incendium Amoris contains dozens of hiatuses as interruptive as this. Although they create confusion for anyone attempting a systematic reading, their function is structural – they are expressions of didactic priorities, not mere displays of ineptitude. In discussing the Trinity, Rolle is more concerned to make his subject available to the reader's *affectus* than he is to make it intellectually easy to follow; hence he brings his chapter to a stirring peroration. Likewise, in opening a new chapter he is often more concerned to engage the reader's attention than to link a new chapter with its predecessor. These features of *Incendium Amoris* obviously tell against its developing any large-scale argument, or providing readers with a step-by-step guide to the spiritual life. On the other hand, they do act as aids to readers in the immediate sense that they help stir up a fervent love or fear, and thus impel them affectively towards God. From this perspective, *Incendium Amoris* is closer to being a collection of short didactic pieces than a treatise – as though Rolle wrote it as an extroverted fourteenth-century equivalent of a work like Anselm's *Orationes sive Meditationes*.[6]

However, other structural elements of *Incendium Amoris* show Rolle thinking of his work in the opposite way, as a sustained exposition. While chapters function as separate entities they also tend to fall into groups that deal with a topic in detail. Thus although caps. 5–8 are separated by the ending and opening devices I mentioned, they still operate as a single exploration, with a clear relation to the wider issue of who the elect and their enemies are. The same proves to be true of several other groups of chapters, once one disregards the features of their structure that are products of Rolle's determination to have an immediate effect on his reader. Behind the barrages of exhortation and exclamation, caps. 13–15 all define and defend the solitary life, caps. 25–27 are structured round the opposing concepts of pride and humility, and caps. 31–34 form a detailed exposition of *canor*. In this last group Rolle seems especially anxious to give an impression of continuity, since he links the beginnings of a series of chapters with the ends of their predecessors by simple verbal devices; caps. 31–34 respectively begin 'Quoniam *autem*', 'Electus *igitur*', '*Sed* in hoc', '*Revera* non absque racione', the italicized words all gesturing vaguely backwards. Since all these chapters (and a number of others which employ the same device) end with at least as resounding a *peroratio* as the one I quoted from cap. 6, Rolle is here directly working against his tendency to structure his sections independently. This suggests that the reader of *Incendium Amoris* is expected to treat its single sections both as self-sufficient and as parts of a coherent larger structure.

Two other general devices focus attention on this larger structure. One is simply that the work is full of allusions to or reiterations of its title. The imagery and subject of fire is not as pervasive as the prologue suggests, but many chapters open with statements reminding us that the whole work is ostensibly concerned with the *incendium amoris*: 'Contemplativi viri qui excellenter uruntur amore eternitatis' (cap. 3); 'Amoris eterni incendium humana anima non sentit' (cap. 4); 'Ex magno amoris incendio tantus virtutis decor in animo crescit' (cap. 8); 'Incendium amoris in animam veraciter assumptum cuncta vicia expurgat' (cap. 22); 'Divinitatis amor hominem quem perfecte penetrat, et igne Sanctus Spiritus veraciter inflammat' (cap. 40). Through these chapter openings, Rolle conveys the impression that he is writing a series of expatiations on aspects of *fervor*, many of which end (as so many chapters of the work do end) in retailing either the fervent joys of heaven or the tormenting fires of hell – as though the work was no more than an expansion of its title. Yet it is much more than this; by the time he wrote *Incendium Amoris*, Rolle had after all experienced *canor* as well as *fervor*, and regarded it as far the more significant spiritual gift. It is not, then, surprising that at the same time as he is emphasizing *fervor* as the leitmotif of *Incendium Amoris*, he is also working to another, more complex scheme.

The three most important statements about Rolle's mystical experience in *Incendium Amoris* (those made respectively in the prologue, in cap. 15 and in cap. 31) occur at regular intervals, dividing the work into almost equal parts (respectively forty-two, forty-five and forty-six pages of Deanesley's edition). This is deliberate, for an inspection of the way the work uses mystical imagery shows each part to allude in particular to one of Rolle's mystical experiences. The first autobiographical statement tells us how Rolle acquired the gift of *fervor* (with its accompanying *dulcor*), and initiates a series of chapters in which *fervor* and other terms associated with it dominate the discussion. *Canor* and *dulcor* are of course mentioned, but often in ways which imply that they are somehow offshoots of *fervor*, rather than independent experiences.[7] In caps. 13–15, the dominance of *fervor* is challenged, as Rolle elaborately reintroduces it as part of a triad involving *dulcor* and *canor* also, and recounts the stages whereby he received all three gifts. The culmination of cap. 15 is Rolle's account of how he achieved his supreme gift, *canor*, but the next fifteen or so chapters dwell less on spiritual song than they do on the imagery associated with sweetness. The new focus is best seen in the emergence of the *amore langueo* theme in caps. 16–17, and in the increasing use of the language of the Song of Songs, much of which Rolle associated with *dulcor*; cap. 26 consists of an exposition of the first verse of the Song of Songs full of the language of touch and taste.[8] In these chapters there is still much about fire, but little concerning song. An explanation for this absence is provided by cap. 31, which picks up Rolle's remark in cap. 15 that he was at first silent about his gift of *canor* (quoted on pp. 131–132), and describes the way in which he was goaded into speaking of it by attempts to make him sing in the choir at Mass. It seems that *Incendium Amoris* has been imitating this reticence, and that Rolle is signalling his decision to deal directly with *canor*. This, at least, is what he then does: cap. 31 opens the way to a series of chapters which mainly concern song, and are appropriately written in the most elevated and alliterative language found in *Incendium Amoris*; it is obvious even on first reading that this part of the work has a special air of excitement and clarity of focus compared with its predecessors.[9]

In cap. 42, the last chapter of the work, Rolle alludes to his own life a final time, by telling us that early in his converted life he wished to sing sweetly like the nightingale, a desire which *canor* has now fulfilled in a startlingly literal way. The anecdote reaches back in time behind even the account of

Rolle's acquisition of *fervor* given in the prologue, summing up all his experience as a development of his original *singulare propositum* (see 277.5–6). Such an ending implies that *Incendium Amoris* has a circular structure, and perhaps points to the fact that its last section contains a more articulate version of things that Rolle has been saying throughout the work, rather than a series of wholly new insights. But the main impact of the tripartite division of *Incendium Amoris* is to unveil Rolle's message progressively, in terms of increasingly elevated mystical sensations. Many readers experience the work as static, and given its continuing allusions to the *incendium amoris* and the way its sections tend to fall apart into discrete units, this is not surprising. However, it seems that Rolle intended to create a different impression, and to produce the effect of a kind of continuous *crescendo* that subsumes all those units, and the excitement each is supposed to produce in the reader, into an overarching structure.

What kind of structure, then, did Rolle attempt for his first substantial original work? The model I suggested, Anselm's *Orationes sive Meditationes*, accounts for some of its structural features, but to find more precise models we must look for works that like Anselm's are a collection of discrete units, but that also demand an extended reading. Two such models which we know were available to Rolle suggest themselves as having been influential in different ways. One is Bernard's *Sermones super Cantica Canticorum*, a series of self-contained expositions which together form a single account of his mystical theology. As with *Incendium Amoris*, some of the sermons (e.g. 39–45) are independent discussions of particular points, while others (e.g. 1–12, 67–72) fall into groups which are carefully connected by forward and backward references, and by a common topic or set of images. Rolle and Bernard share a concern for the crafting of individual sections and an anxiety for local effects with a general, often informal sense of the whole work. *Incendium Amoris*, moreover, often reads very much like a series of delivered discourses to a group of intimate disciples. For all its distinctively latemedieval atmosphere, *Incendium Amoris* often does not seem too distant in tone or in structure from this twelfth-century Cistercian masterpiece.

The other model *Incendium Amoris* suggests is the Bible, as this was seen through the eyes of theologians such as Alexander of Hales and Bonaventure (see pp. 23, 25–26 and Minnis 1984, pp. 119–145). For these Franciscan thinkers, the Bible is intended chiefly to appeal to the wills of its readers not to their reasons, and from a literary viewpoint can be regarded as a vast and variegated essay in the affective modes of writing. The reason many biblical books and modes (*multiplex modi*) are necessary, explains Bonaventure in the prologue to his *Breviloquium*, is so that if one approach fails to convince and convert the reader, another may succeed, and the intention of the work as a whole, to help humanity attain salvation, will thereby be fulfilled (cited in Minnis 1984, pp. 126–128). *Incendium Amoris* clearly resembles this account of the Scriptures. Its prologue and many other passages (e.g. in caps. 5–7) dismiss the propounders of *quaestiones* in a way which places deliberate stress on the importance of love rather than knowledge. The work as a whole is written in an array of affective literary modes, falling into separate sections the import of which, like that of the Scriptures, adds up to a single message. Alford (1973, pp. 12–16) has shown how richly biblical the work's language is. Most important for my present argument, *Incendium Amoris* imitates the pattern of gradual revelation of truth presented in the Scriptures. From Genesis to Revelation, in contexts as popular as English cycle drama or as abstruse as the historiographic speculations of Joachim da Fiore, medieval writings show how God reveals himself progressively, through the events chronicled in Scripture. The biblical exposition of truth progresses from antitype to type, from Creation to Redemption to Judgement, and gives rise to literary and theological works which reveal their message in similar ways, with evolving clarity and power: *Piers Plowman*, *The Divine Comedy*, Julian's *Revelation of Love*. In expounding Rolle's mysticism at once serially and progressively, *Incendium Amoris*, like these far greater works, must be looking to the Bible as to a source.

It seems that *Incendium Amoris* should be read as trying to do much what its prologue says it will do: to 'excite' all to love, and to demonstrate the 'super-fervent' nature of love, that is, to proclaim not only *fervor* but *dulcor* and *canor* as mystical experiences central to the Christian life at its highest. The work is at once an exercise in affective evangelism and a revelation of previously undeclared truths, structured around narratives of how these were bestowed on Rolle. As an evolving revelation of this kind, the work is thus inherently an apology both for the importance of Rolle's experiences and for him. In the rest of this chapter, I wish to examine the apologetic strategies that shape *Incendium Amoris*.

III

If we think of *Incendium Amoris* as an apologia for its author, its overall strategy can be described by saying that in this work Rolle articulates the full structure of thought outlined in Chapter 2. Humanity is divided into elect and *reprobi*; the elect are identified with solitaries, solitaries with those who experience *canor* and *fervor*, and Rolle is thus clearly identified as one of the elect. *Canor* gives the elect remarkable spiritual authority, for all the persecution they endure on earth. Consequently they should be obeyed by ordinary Christians whose salvation is not assured – and, at the Judgement, they will be able to damn those who refused to listen to them. Rolle thus declares his status as Christian, as hermit, and as spiritual authority to be unassailable. He has not merely a right but a duty to proclaim the truth by writing his book, and the reader has a corresponding duty to obey him. Even if the reader neglects the obligations imposed by the work, they will only be deferred, and final compliance will be an eternal grief not an everlasting joy. Neither God nor Rolle will be mocked.

In writing what was probably the first of his works to revolve around this structure of ideas, Rolle experienced difficulties not from the ideas as such but from their deployment. His argument about *canor* and the elect is extreme and needs delicate handling. More important, it proves deeply problematic for him to articulate the claim that he is one of the elect, and reveal the extent to which his metaphysical structure is built on his own experience. On the one hand, it is vital to the apologetic effectiveness of *Incendium Amoris* that Rolle assert his sanctity as convincingly as possible and stress the exemplary character of his experience; only by doing so can he securely place himself 'within' his own metaphysical structure. At the same time, it is very hard for him to prove such assertions. An external *auctoritas* cannot be brought to bear on a case so concerned with *experientia*, since this case is necessarily based on the uncertain evidence of Rolle's testimony. Thus Rolle has to rely on his own powers of persuasion and self-presentation to convince the reader; he has to be his own investigator and witness in a canonization process, conducted unofficially, with himself as its subject. Yet, on the other hand, in some respects it is equally essential that he should avoid stating his case directly. Saints do not write about their own holiness; at least in the popular mind, they are too humble, too alive to the dangers of spiritual pride, to think of themselves as saintly. For Rolle to assert that he is of the elect is to lay himself open to charges that he is not properly humble, that he is, on the contrary, glutted with spiritual pride, and thus to risk disproving the very case for his sanctity that he is making. Again, writers who wield spiritual authority do not normally make their own status a major theme. Not only is it tautological to write a work in order to prove that the work being written has authority, but religious *auctores* are assumed to have more urgent matters (like the salvation of humanity) to discuss, and to take their own duty to write for granted. For Rolle to give the impression that he is anxious about his own authority and is writing *Incendium Amoris* in order to build it up is to risk his seeming self-seeking, unconcerned with the human predicament, and unfit to be regarded as an authority. While the work must make the reader see Rolle as already enshrined in a high niche of the Church Triumphant, a position from which he has a duty to pronounce on humanity's destinies, it is vital that it appear to be doing something more valuable than intentionally elevating its writer into a saintly *auctor*.

The sum of all these considerations is so complicated that, however neat Rolle's apologetic structure may be, he appears in an almost impossible position for convincing the reader of its viability. It is, perhaps, even surprising that he tries to do so, rather than simply expounding his case for the elect and himself in a way the reader can take or leave; after all, he has inbuilt protection against disapproval, for he can transform it at once into 'persecution', and thus compel it to validate rather than undermine his position. Yet *Incendium Amoris* does take its readers' reactions very seriously, and for several connected reasons. First, Rolle has a real desire to propagate his experiences of passionate love, to engage in what Richard of St

Victor's *De Quattuor Gradibus Violentae Caritatis* calls spiritual 'childbirth' ('puerperium', see pp. 13, 17) the genuine exercise of the responsibilities which are entailed by being one of the saints; so much is clear from the *Officium* and (we shall see) from the shape his whole career takes. Second, in spite of his habit of thinking oppositionally, he has no desire to detach himself from the earthly Church, and indeed has a deep institutional loyalty to it; what he wants is an elevated place within the Church, not separation from it. Third, Rolle is on one level deeply unsure of his own response to the assertive claims he is making. For most of the work, he seems not to be comfortable with the metaphysics he has built around himself, and to fear that if he states his position too assertively he may actually fall prey to spiritual pride. It is as though he observes his own development of a saintly persona with real uncertainty as to its outcome. His sensitivity to the reader's potential criticism is like the sensitivity of an anxious man to some inner voice urging caution. Perhaps a worried conservatism is the most important of the forces that turns *Incendium Amoris* from a simple declaration of its author's status into the tortuous document it is.

As we investigate the evasions and manœuvres of *Incendium Amoris*, it is important to recognize, then, the extent to which they are directed at Rolle himself, in his capacity as an anxious, critical reader. My accounts of the work's structure and of the exigencies he faced in constructing his apologia may have given the impression that he was in full control of his work and his strategies. If this were true, it would be hard to avoid seeing him as manipulative of the reader in a way which invites charges of spiritual pride, even cynicism. Yet it is true only in the sense that *Incendium Amoris* shows Rolle employing strategies on himself, to find ways of avoiding such charges and of progressing beyond them. On one level, the evasions in the work, and its development towards an articulated account of *canor*, reflect an inner, auto-didactic process which seems far from cynical. The fact that the work resolves the problem of its author's self-assertiveness gives it all the appearance of a rite of passage: Rolle's initiation of his reader *and himself* into an explicit acceptance of his spiritual authority.

The first fifteen chapters of *Incendium Amoris* illustrate most of Rolle's basic manœuvres, as well as forming a distinct stage in his strategy. This section of the work builds towards the account of his reception of *canor* in cap. 15, the first all-but-explicit declaration of his high status within the metaphysical structure of the universe. Three distinct things have to happen to alleviate the contradictory pressures this declaration exerts on the work, while allowing it to be as striking as it needs to be. The work must display an appropriate and recognizable spiritual concern for its readers, and thus justify its existence; Rolle's metaphysics must be outlined in a way which is acceptable, and which does not at once reveal too explicit a connection with the writer's experience; yet readers must be brought to trust and honour Rolle himself, and to associate him with the highest spiritual states. Not surprisingly, the tensions between these necessities are often dislocating and render the work incoherent, while Rolle achieves a balance between them largely by sleight of hand. Indeed he often manipulates his readers into agreement by deliberate dislocation. Confused by so many shifts of subject and emphasis but inclined towards tolerance by the enthusiasm he brings to every subject, his readers are in effect decoyed into becoming receptive to a case of which *Incendium Amoris* could not hope to convince them logically.

I have already illustrated the main way in which the work attempts to display a concern for the welfare of its readers, by making its discussions accessible to their affective faculties in order to convert them to the love of God. While all the advice and appeals contained in these discussions tend to be undetailed – for Rolle's real attention is elsewhere – in combination they create a pervasive impression of a didactic voice with a great many urgent things to say at once. The things themselves change in response to a variety of exigencies, but for readers concerned with their edification the message is clear. Rolle is urging them to follow the example of the elect by ascending as near to God as they can in this life; he is demanding that readers take not merely adequate but radical virtue – holiness – as their standard. His work is an exposition of the *vita contemplativa*, an original essay in the tradition of Richard of St Victor's *Benjamin* books or Bonaventure's *De Triplici Via*.

This didactic emphasis gives Rolle a natural entry into the exposition of his metaphysical system, since it allows him to describe those who achieve holiness, the elect. Much of the first section of *Incendium Amoris* (and the rest of the work) consists of what we can call 'model' descriptions of the elect, either as they are on earth or as they will be in heaven. These models appear in contexts which suggest their function to be didactic, but this is often little more than a screen; in practice, Rolle is far more concerned to define the elect in terms which point towards and interpret the experiences described in cap. 15 than he is to edify the reader. What I have called the 'exigencies' to which the didactic material in the work responds indeed mainly consist of the demands the business of defining the elect, in progressively more specific terms, makes on that material. Cap. 1 warns the reader against sensuality as a way of drawing a basic distinction, between *electi* who practise *caritas* and *reprobi* who practise *cupiditas*. The opening of cap. 5 warns of the danger of worldly knowledge in order to be able to introduce a more particular distinction, between those whose main concern is with *sapientia* (the elect) and those who care only for *scientia* (heretics and intellectuals, i.e. again the reprobate). Caps. 7–9 discuss tribulation in terms of a third distinction between worldly and heavenly honour, in order to distance the elect from positions of worldly power in the earthly Church, and to give Rolle the opportunity to enunciate a number of antitheses between present tribulation and final triumph. The purpose of all these discussions is the same and has little in the first instance to do with edification: it is to prepare the reader to accept the arguments of cap. 13–14, in which the solitary life emerges as by definition superior to other forms of religious life, and in which *canor, dulcor* and *fervor* are discovered to be, also by definition, the mystical experiences available to and sought by solitaries.

Many of the discussions of the elect in the first part of the work are written in a judicious and distanced style, which breaks out into praise or denunciation only when Rolle is anxious to emphasize the evangelistic purpose of his work (mainly at the ends of chapters). The aura of learning such a style creates (as in caps. 5–7, with their careful definitions of Trinitarian orthodoxy) seems intended to suggest that his concern with the elect is that of the disinterested seeker after truth, and also that his arguments have the authority that pertains to intellectual respectability. Such a treatment of the elect enables him to proceed in a stilted and piecemeal fashion which is deliberately unalarming. But this is evidently not a trouble-free process for Rolle; in one instance it even leads to a near disaster. Cap. 2 consists of an affective evocation of spiritual song, which makes an indirect claim for the high status of those who practise *canor*; in this case Rolle succeeds in shrouding direct statement not in learned but in vividly metaphorical language. However, in cap. 3, developing similar ideas in a more theoretical way, he finds that he has followed the logic of his metaphysical structure too far and too fast. In arguing that contemplatives are like the seraphim, he says that they are so taken up with the vision of God that they neglect earthly things, and are ignored by most people. They are so holy, he adds, that they do not concern themselves with performing miracles – and he backs up this remark with the comment that since sinners also perform miracles they are not even of great value.[10] The position is logical, since miracles are active works corresponding to the errands the lower orders of angels perform rather than to the contemplations of the seraphim; it is also orthodox, for the Church has always maintained that miracles are among the least important signs of sanctity. Nonetheless, saints and miracles are so closely linked in the religious imagination that to define *contemplativi* as 'saints without miracles' is to risk severing all connection in the reader's mind between them and traditional models of sanctity. Rolle apparently recognizes he has made a tactical error, for the second half of the chapter carefully contradicts all he has said. Here we are told that the holy nonetheless perform nearly all miracles – although the lower orders of angels (and active Christians) continue to be praised as God's messengers. Any pretence of logic here is sheer obfuscation.[11] Such blundering is hardly the work of a strategist who has planned his every move in advance.

Accidents aside, Rolle introduces readers to his metaphysical system by means of guarded and increasingly specific discussions of the elect. He adopts a similar means of introducing himself, eschewing all mention of his own experience (after the prologue) for the first eight chapters of the work. The idea that he is himself one of the elect is thus allowed to grow up by a process of suggestion, as we see that they, too, experience *fervor*, and as we reflect on the amount of privileged information about them that Rolle has. Only in caps. 8–11 do personal references begin to occur which make almost explicit claims for his elect status. The end of cap. 8 concerns a young man who is miraculously enabled to escape fleshly allurements and whose progress to holiness is consequently assured; as the first individual we have encountered in the work since the prologue, we naturally associate him with Rolle.[12] Caps. 9 and 11 contain a number of passages written in the first person, which consist both of formal prayers or exhortations and of casual references to Rolle's life as a hermit. The prayers are a cautious way of reintroducing first-person narrative into the work, for they are exercises in an Anselmian style of meditation, full of conventional addresses to Christ and the soul of the kind written in part for readers to appropriate to their own use.[13] Yet as the autobiographical anecdotes accumulate, all such first-person narrative comes to seem more and more closely associated with Rolle. The climax of this process occurs at the end of cap. 11, which deliberately mixes first-person reminiscence with passionate first-person exegesis of a verse from the Song of Songs, spoken in the person of an elect soul. After illustrating the need for moderation from his own experience (in a passage quoted in Chapter 1, pp. 45–46), Rolle smoothly turns the discussion into an account of the rise of a perfect soul, while in this life, to heavenly joy:

Verumtamen erubescent cum me viderint qui dixerunt me nullicubi velle morari nisi ubi delicate possem pasci. Melius enim est videre quod contempnam quam desiderare quod non videam. Ieiunium nimirum valet ad reprimenda carnalium voluptatum desideria, et ad domandam indomitam mentis petulanciam. In illo autem qui contemplacionis semitam ascendit per iubilum et ardorem amoris iam quasi extincte iacent carnales concupiscencie. Mors enim malarum affeccionum ad ipsum pertinet qui contemplacioni vacat, cuius interior homo in aliam gloriam aliamque formam iam mutatur. *Vivit ipse iam non ipse, vivit autem in se Christus* [Galatians 2.20], unde in ipsius amore liquefit et in seipso languescit, pene deficit pro dulcedine, vix subsistit pro amore. Ipsius anima est que dicit, '*Nunciate dilecto quia amore langueo* [Song of Songs 5.8], mori desidero, dissolvi cupio, transire inardesco. En morior amore! Descende Domine! Veni, mi dilecte, et leva me languore! En amo, cano, estuo, intra me ferveo! Miserere miseri, iubendo me coram te presentari!' (175.30–176.15)

[Nonetheless, those who said that I would not stay anywhere I could not dine finely, would blush when they saw me. For it is better to see what I may disdain than to desire what I do not see. Certainly fasting is useful for restraining one's desires for carnal pleasure and for controlling the wayward wantonness of one's mind. But for the person who has ascended the path of contemplation through rejoicing and through the ardour of love, carnal desires now lie as it were dead. For the death of evil desires happens to one who surrenders himself to contemplation, whose inner being is now changed into another glory and another form. *Now he lives not in himself, but Christ lives in him,* so that he melts in love for him and languishes within, almost fails because of the sweetness, can hardly live for love. This is the soul who says, '*Tell my beloved that I am sick for love,* I want to die, I long to be dissolved, I burn to pass over. Ah, I die for love! Come down, Lord! Come, my beloved, and ease my sickness! Ah, I love, I sing, I glow, I burn within! Have pity on a wretch, by commanding me to be brought before you!']

The spiritual progress described here, from fasting to inner growth and the attainment of the love of God, is much the one Rolle recounts as his own life story in cap. 15, and uses remarkably audacious language.[14] But here, although it is inevitable that we identify him with the perfect soul, the second half of the passage only refers to Rolle by juxtaposition; thus the onus for the identification falls not on him but on his readers. Such juxtapositions of first- and third-person discourse are often even more perfunctory in the rest of *Incendium Amoris*, as Rolle's attempt to distance himself from the glowing things he has to say about the elect becomes increasingly merely a gesture.

Nonetheless, the process by which Rolle identifies himself with the elect is initially at least as troublesome as the process of delineating them. The gradual drawing-together of different first-person voices in caps. 9 and 11 occurs at the same time as the status of the elect is being described with some daring. Thus the passage just quoted turns into an assertion that nobody can tell the elect what to do, since they are inspired by the Spirit, and '*The spiritual person judges everything and is judged by no one*' ('*Spiritualis omnia judicat et a nemine judicatur*', 176.26–7, 1 Corinthians 2.15). This idea that the elect are invulnerable to criticism is dimly reflected in several defensive remarks Rolle makes against his critics in these chapters (170.3–32, 175.19–33); implicitly he appears to be claiming that *no one can tell him he is wrong*. It is not surprising that the emergence of this claim sets off warning-bells in the text. In order to show he has not succumbed to spiritual pride he has to find ways of expressing his own humility. Consequently cap. 9 urges humility on the reader, and cap. 11 ends by warning that nobody should lightly presume themselves to be as holy as the *spiritualis* (176.26–27: 'Nemo autem tante presumpcionis sit quod se talem cito suspicetur'). Then in cap. 12 Rolle embarks on a humble account of how he was rescued from hell by an abundant grace, and has nothing to boast of; far from boasting, he even confesses to several sins. However, at this point, tensions latent in the text suddenly become explicit. The confession is a comic disaster. Rolle's contrary desires to demonstrate his humility and to claim that his own life has exhibited a purity characteristic of the elect become hopelessly entangled, as he belatedly attempts to retract his confession by justifying his behaviour and laying the blame elsewhere:

Verumtamen iamdudum a tribus mulieribus dignam merito reprehensionem accepi. Una me reprehendit quia cupiens corrigere insaniam earum in superfluitate et mollicie vestium ornatum illarum immoderatum nimis inspexi; que dixit quod non debui eas tam considerare ut scirem utrum essent cornute vel non, et ut mihi videtur bene me redarguit et erubescere fecit. Alia me reprehendit quia de mammis eius grossis loquebar quasi me delectarent, que ait quid ad me pertinet si essent parve vel magne, et hec similiter recte locuta est. Tercia me in ioco tangens quod minabar quasi rude eam tangere vellum (vel tetigi) dixit, 'quiesce frater' . . . Nam rediens ad meipsum gracias egi Deo meo quia per illarum verba me bonum docuit . . . non inveniar reprehensibilis coram mulieribus in hac parte. Quarta mulier cui admodum familiaris eram, non me reprehendendo sed quasi contempnendo dixit: 'Nihil habes nisi pulchrum visum et pulchrum verbum: opus nullum habes.' Et ideo melius estimo earum specialitate carere quam in earum manus incidere; que modum nesciunt tenere sive in amore sive in contemptu. Mihi autem ista contigerunt quod salutem earum procuravi, non quod in eis aliquod illicitum appetivi, cum quibus sustentacionem per aliquod tempus accepi corporalem.   (178.24–179.17)

[Still, some time ago I rightly suffered proper rebuke from three women. One reproached me because, wanting to correct their folly in the excessiveness and softness of their clothing, I looked too closely at their immoderate ornaments. She said that I ought not to look at them so closely as to know whether or not they were wearing 'horns'; and so it seemed to me she rebuked me well, and made me blush. Another reproved me because I was speaking of her large breasts as though they pleased me – she said it was none of my business if they were small or large, and she, too, spoke rightly. A third, touching me playfully because I was gesturing as though I wished to touch her rudely, or had touched her, said, 'Calm down, brother.' When I came to myself, I thanked my God for teaching me virtue through their words. May I not be found guilty in front of women henceforth! A fourth woman, with whom I was somewhat familiar, said to me not in reproof but as though in contempt, 'You're nothing but a pretty face and a pretty voice; you don't have the tools.' And so I reckon it better to go without their beauty than to fall into their hands, for they do not know how to keep within bounds either in love or contempt. And these things happened to me because I was attending to their salvation, not because I desired anything illicit from them – for it was them from whom I received bodily sustenance for some time.]

The confession is naive enough in itself, with its disclaimers ('cupiens corrigere insaniam earum') and vaguenesses ('vel tetigi'); but by its end it has been wholly taken over by self-righteousness. It is interesting that Rolle feels so strong a need to justify his actions, for his identification with the elect does not in fact require him to show he has never in his life sinned (conversion narratives indeed demand a few sins of their heroes); the difficulty he has maintaining a penitent attitude at this stage of the work must be essentially personal. This disruptive intrusion into the apologetic manœuvring of *Incendium Amoris* is suggestive of the extent to which ordinary human insecurity underlies many of Rolle's grandest assertions.[15]

Taken all in all, the first twelve chapters of *Incendium Amoris* are not notably successful in moving towards their conflicting objectives without undercutting their own efforts. The relaxed confidence with which Rolle presents himself in the prologue is badly damaged, while any moderately critical reader would have objections both to his presentation of the elect and to the way the didactic content of the chapters drifts from one topic to another. The main achievement of the section is simply to keep going for long enough to make possible the achievements of caps. 13–15. Caps. 13–14 draw out many of the themes introduced earlier, in a sustained attempt to prepare the ground for cap. 15; we approach ever closer to the personal centre of Rolle's metaphysics. The direct argument of the chapters concerns the superiority of the solitary life to both the monastic and the 'mixed' lives of the prelate (see section II of the introduction, especially pp. 10–11). For evidence, Rolle gives numerous scriptural proofs, mentions two saints who left their bishoprics to become hermits, says (in effect) that nobody without experience of the solitary life has authority to pronounce on it (179.18–29), and likens hermits to the seraphim; when hermits die, they ascend to sit with the seraphim ('subsistat cum seraphym in sede suprema', 184.32), because they have burned in love and sung the praise of God in this life (compare cap. 3). The similarity between human and angelic contemplatives is an important means by which Rolle introduces the other arguments of these chapters: that hermits leave the world to love God (which is obvious), and that their love consists of *fervor*, *dulcor* and *canor* (which is by no means so). Rolle does not give evidence for these arguments, instead writing model accounts of hermits who leave the world and find *canor*, as though the sequence were a natural one.[16] These accounts finally justify the formal introduction of the terms *fervor*, *dulcor* and *canor*, which Rolle claims he learned from his study of Scripture (184.33). At last he tells us clearly that he has had all three experiences, and that they are the ultimate expression of Christianity ('summa perfeccio christiane religionis', 185.16–17). Assertiveness and humility are balanced with extreme delicacy in the wake of this claim. Rolle states that he does not dare equate his experiences with those of the saints ('nec tamen sanctis qui in eis effulserunt me audeam adequare', 185.19–20) – capitalizing on the fact that he has just linked saintly hermits to the experience of *canor*, and so can shelter behind their superior authority. Yet he adds that we are wrong to think *moderni* cannot achieve the holiness of the apostles ('erratis enim, fratres, si putatis nunc nullos tam sanctos ut prophete vel apostoli fuerunt', 185.23–24) – and then proceeds to define *canor* and the rest as terms on which he, not any older *auctor*, scriptural or otherwise, is the principal authority ('fervorem autem *voco* ... canorem *voco* ...', 185.24, 28). This is the claim which takes us to cap. 15, where its basis is revealed in the famous account of the main events of Rolle's spiritual life; a setting has been established for a narrative in which his own decisions can be compared directly to those of the Desert Fathers (188.6–23), and in which he can assume his experience to have exemplary force for readers: 'Processum quidem [i.e. of his 'translatio ad superna'], si propolare volo, solitariam vitam predicare me oportet, nam spirans Spiritus ad hanc assequendam et amandam intencionem meam intendebat' (187.17–19: 'The course of which, if I wish to make it public, compels me to preach the solitary life, for the breathing Spirit directed my intention towards pursuing and loving this'). The chapter is lucid and compelling, somehow reading as simple personal testimony, not as a carefully prepared moment in a larger apologetic structure; it is striking how much of his metaphysics Rolle is able to include in what poses as direct reporting of experience. Even the problem of spiritual pride is cleverly evaded for the time, as Rolle finds ways of attesting to his humility in the same breath that he is claiming the most for his experience of *canor*:

Non cognitus eram ab hiis qui me cernebant, ne si scivissent me supra modum honorassent, et sic perdidissem partem floris pulcherrime et decidissem in desolacionem. Interea mirum me arripuit, eo quod assumptus essem ad tantam iocunditatem dum exul essem et quia dederat mihi Deus dona que petere nescivi nec putavi tale quid nec eciam sanctissimum in hac vita accepisse. Proinde arbitror hoc nulli datum meritis sed gratis cum voluerit Christus. (190.3–10)

[I was not perceived by those who were looking at me in case, had they known, they had honoured me beyond bounds – and so I would have lost part of the loveliest flower and fallen into desolation. Meanwhile wonder seized me that I should be raised to such joy while I was an exile, and because God had given me gifts I did not know how to seek; nor did I think that even the holiest had received such a thing in this life. For which reason, I judge that nobody is given this for merit, but is granted it by grace when Christ wishes.]

Rolle's amazement and attribution of all to the grace of God are common ways of disclaiming merit and re-establishing humility. The interesting remark is the first one: Rolle's experience was not revealed to others on account of the worldly honour it would have brought him. Not only does it show that he is still very aware of the link between proclaiming his high status and succumbing to pride; it also points forward to the next structural narrative in cap. 31, where he reports the occasion on which he at last did speak out.[17]

My analysis of Rolle's apologetic strategies in the first section of *Incendium Amoris* has focussed on his problems in combining humility with assertiveness. Rolle can claim much for the elect when he is not overtly identifying with them, but has tactical and personal difficulties with making such claims directly. Once he has done so in cap. 15, the texture of the work becomes less intricate. In terms of his apologetic strategy, Rolle has two major concerns left: to achieve a more satisfactory definition of the status of the elect, and to find a way of justifying his own assertiveness, so as to be able to discuss his highest spiritual experience, *canor*, more directly. The second section of *Incendium Amoris* thus abandons the tendency towards personal allusion found in caps. 9–15. First-person passages in this section are of a distanced, expository type, or are put into the mouths of exemplary characters: a 'devotus pauper' in cap. 16, a Loving Soul in cap. 26. Having identified himself explicitly with the elect in cap. 15, Rolle does not labour the point. What he does instead is to sketch the life of the elect many times and from a number of different perspectives, referring to them now as *humiles*, now as *contemplativi*, *recti* or *perfecti*. These model descriptions have the overt purpose of helping the reader to join the ranks of the elect; the language of spiritual guidance is used far more than in the first section of the work. Yet, as before, the apologetic direction of the chapters tends to undermine the impression they give of helpfulness; their true purpose is to define the elect in ways which distinguish them as far as possible from ordinary Christians. Indeed, this process becomes far clearer from now on, for whereas the first section makes a succession of apparently unconnected claims for the elect, these chapters attempt a more systematic argument about their nature. In view of the dangers of such an argument, it is not surprising that Rolle keeps himself for the moment in the background.[18]

The most important phase in the section's argument concerning the elect is its attempt to establish that they are sure of salvation. It is crucial to Rolle's

claim to special spiritual authority that he, and the elect of whom he is one, be
effectively beyond fear of the Judgement; only thus can they be beyond the
earthly judgement of their enemies, and freely exercise their kind of spiritual
authority. Earlier chapters have claimed that they are already saved. In
cap. 15, *canor* makes Rolle await his eternal crown with confidence ('cum
securitate me facit eternam expectare coronam', 190.29–30), like one already
confirmed in grace ('quasi in gracia confirmatus', 190.26); cap. 11 has even
stated that the elect 'non potest errare' (176.17), and cannot properly be
judged or advised by others (196.16–26). However in cap. 19 Rolle directly
addresses the issues on which the claim stands or falls:

Hic enim est amori perfectus; sed utrum iste status in amore semel habitus aliquando
posset amitti, non incongrue queri potest. Dum autem homo potest peccare, potest et
caritatem amittere. Sed non posse peccare, non est in statu vie sed patrie. Ergo omnis
homo quantumcumque perfectus est in hac vita adhuc peccare potest eciam mortaliter,
quia fomes peccati nullo viatore plene extinctus est, secundum legem communem. Si
autem aliquis talis esset qui nec concupiscere nec temptari posset, secundum hoc magis
pertineret ad statum patrie quam vie, nec esset ei multum non delinquere cum non
posset peccare. Ego, penitus ignoro si talis sit, vivens usquam in carne; quia, pro me
loquar, *Caro concupiscit adversus spiritum et spiritus adversus carnem* [Galatians
5.17]; et *Condelector legi Dei secundum interiorem hominem* [Romans 7.22], sed
nescio adhuc tam amare quod possum concupiscenciam penitus extinguere. Estimo
tamen quod unus est gradus perfecti amoris, quem quicumque attigerit, illum deinceps
numquam perdit. Aliud est enim posse perdere, aliud semper tenere quod non vult
amittere eciam si possit. Abstinent vero se perfecti quantum in se est ab omni re qua
eorum perfeccio vel posset destrui vel eciam impediri. Cum libertate arbitrii divina
gracia sunt repleti, qua assidue excitantur ad bonum amandum, loquendum, et
agendum, et a malo cordis, oris, et operis retrahuntur. Cum ergo homo ad Christum
perfecte conversus, cuncta transitoria despexerit, et se in solo Conditoris desiderio
immobiliter, ut mortalibus pro corrupcione carnis permittitur, fixerit: tunc nimirum
vires viriliter exercens, primo quasi aperto celo supernos cives oculo intellectuali
conspicit, et postea calorem suavissimum, quasi ignem ardentem sentit. Deinde mira
suavitate imbuitur, et deinceps in canore iubilo gloriatur. Hec est ergo perfecta caritas,
Quam nemo novit nisi qui accipit [Revelation 2.17], et qui accipit nunquam amittit,
dulciter vivit, secure morietur. (202.1–35)

[For this is perfection in love. But it can appropriately be asked whether this high state
of love can ever be lost, after it has once been achieved. Now while someone can sin,
he can also lose love. But the inability to sin is the condition not of a pilgrim but of one
at the fatherland. Thus everyone, however perfect he is in this life, can still commit
even mortal sin. For it is a matter of common law that the tinder of sin is not fully
extinguished in any pilgrim. But if there were anyone so perfect that he could neither
desire nor be tempted, he would thereby be closer to being at the fatherland than to
being a pilgrim, and it would be no great matter for him not to commit a fault, since he
would not be able to sin. I am utterly unsure if such a person could exist, still living in
the flesh; for, speaking for myself, *The flesh desires against the spirit and the spirit
against the flesh*; and *I delight in the law of God according to my inner being*, but I do
not yet know how to love so that I can utterly extinguish concupiscence. But I judge
that there is one grade of perfect love that whoever attains it will afterwards never lose
it. It is one thing to be able to lose a thing, it is another always to hold to that which
one does not want to lay aside, even if it were possible. But the perfect abstain, so far as

it is in them, from everything which could either destroy or even impede their perfection. Of their own freewill they are filled with divine grace, by which they are earnestly incited to good loving, speaking and doing, and are restrained from evil of heart, word and deed. So when a person, perfectly converted to Christ, despises all transitory things and establishes himself unmovingly in a single desire for the Creator (so far as fleshly corruption renders this possible for mortals), then certainly, vigorously exercising his strength, first he sees the supernal citizens with his intellectual eye, as though heaven had been opened, then he feels a very sweet heat, like fire burning, next he is imbued with wonderful sweetness, and finally he glories in joyful song. This then is perfect love, *Which nobody knows but he who receives it*; and he who receives it never lays it aside. Sweetly he lives; confidently he will die.]

Learned language is here essential to Rolle's argument, for his case hinges on a *distinctio* ('aliud . . . aliud') which is only meaningful in the context of a larger syllogistic structure. The passage is a formal *quaestio*, with its statement of an issue ('utrum'), its objections to the argument it wishes to prove and response to those objections ('estimo'), and its *auctoritates*. Indeed, Rolle is here working in a tradition of treatments of this particular question which go back to Peter Lombard's *Sententiae* and beyond.[19] Yet the passage is not an intellectually coherent treatment of the issue it raises. The *auctoritates* consist of a verse from Romans and another from Galatians, which are adduced against Rolle's conclusion but undermined in advance by the restrictive and self-consciously humble 'pro me loquar'. 'Estimo' is not a proper substitute for the scholastic 'respondeo', since no arguments support Rolle's case for the existence of the 'unus gradus perfecti amoris'. For all its parade of disin-terestedness, the *quaestio* is a manœuvre, meant to narrow, so far as appears consistent with Christian orthodoxy, the gap between the Church triumphant and those members of the Church Militant who are *perfecti*. The final part of the passage abandons the attempt to prove the argument, and returns us to the associative manner of earlier chapters. First Rolle asserts that those whose love is 'perfect' are none other than those who have undergone the passage from conversion to *canor* exemplified by his own career. Then a verse from Revelation invites us to accept two radical corollaries: that although the perfect can lay aside their charity they never do; and that such people *know who they are*. None of these claims is incoherent in the context of the rest of *Incendium Amoris*. But Rolle has not addressed any of these issues in an intellectually compelling way, any more than he has really explained why perfection should exist in this life.[20]

In caps. 9–11, discussion of the high status of the elect sets off a number of cautious remarks about the necessity of avoiding presumption and remaining humble. The claims made in cap. 19 have a similar effect. The chapter that follows is a simple exposition of prayer which brings us back to the imagery of the *incendium amoris*, and cap. 21 is a discussion of the superiority of the contemplative to the active life; both are so conventional and so beside the point that their main purpose must be to reassure the reader that nothing too outrageous has, after all, been asserted.[21] Cap. 22 then returns to the *perfecti*, giving yet another account of the ascent of the soul to *canor*, this time incorporating the new claim that the perfect can be sinless in this life by describing the way the fire of love annihilates any venial sin the perfect soul may commit; already, the new claim has been partly assimilated into the structure of Rolle's metaphysics.[22] From this point, a series of chapters introduce the idea of 'perfect love' in the context of discussions of the need to give up fleshly lusts (caps. 23–24), to read, pray and long for Christ (caps. 25–26), to practise humility (caps. 27–28), and to avoid lust and worldly power (caps. 29–30). These chapters are also part of the process of assimilation – in this case, however, of the term 'perfectus' itself, rather than of any idea that the perfect are sinless. The writing is unambitious, and Rolle often seems to be addressing himself (for no very clear reason) to readers at the beginning of the spiritual life (see especially the end of cap. 27, a simple 'respice in faciem Christi' Passion meditation).

The most cautious theme in this part of the work is that of humility, both as it is enjoined on others and as it is self-consciously practised by Rolle. Pronouncing the elect *perfecti* in cap. 19, Rolle excludes himself from their ranks, implying perfection is a condition to which he merely aspires. Again, giving a model account of spiritual ascent in cap. 22, he prefaces his account of *canor* with 'ut de privilegiatis loquar' (208.9–10: 'if I may speak about the privileged'), warning his readers not to be so presumptuous as to think themselves perfect. Later chapters also warn of pride and are increasingly concerned to define the perfect as those who are surpassingly humble. Thus in cap. 26 'perfectus amor' is identified with righteousness and humility ('recti sunt humiles', 217.18), and the 'verus amator' is represented as abjectly claiming to be outdone by everyone in hatred of sin and the world: 'Omnes me excellunt in contemptu mundi et odio peccati' (217.22–23). The model account of the ascent of the *electus* in caps. 28–29 includes the assertion that such a person is humbler than others (225.19–22), while cap. 30 warns the reader against presumption in terms which apply equally to the perfect: 'Unde et timendum nobis est dum in via sumus, et incaute nequaquam presumendum; quia nescit homo utrum odio vel amore dignus sit, aut quo fine ab hac luce recessurus' (280.18–21: 'For which reason we must be fearful while we are in this life and not be foolishly presumptuous. For no one knows whether he is worthy of hate or of love, or where he will go when he leaves this light'). This passage explicitly denies any claim that the elect can know who they are. By the end of cap. 30, the concept that the elect are 'perfect' in this life seems to have been assimilated out of existence. Whereas cap. 19 treated the *perfecti* as being conscious of their high state, and confident of their salvation, perfection is now seen to consist in consciousness of inferiority to others, and doubt as to one's eternal prospects. Such caution puts Rolle in an embarrassing position, for belief in his worth is near the heart of his enterprise in writing *Incendium Amoris*. If it is, after all, characteristic of the *perfecti* to think of themselves with such signal meekness, he should not have been making the claims for himself that he has. Far from advancing his apology for himself and the elect further, most of the second section of the work seems to retreat from the high ground it first aspires to occupy.

As the third part of *Incendium Amoris* (that which lays special emphasis on *canor*) opens, it is immediately obvious that any retreat that has occurred is temporary and tactical, *pour mieux sauter*. Cap. 31 tells the story of how Rolle, asked why he did not sing aloud at Mass, and at first unwilling to reveal the inner music that kept him silent, was eventually goaded into declaring the nature of his hidden spiritual gift:

Proinde cogitavi quidem quodammodo aliqualem ostendere responsionem, et redarguentibus omnino non disperire. Quid enim ad ipsos pertinet de vita aliorum, quorum mores in multis suam vitam excellere non ignorant? Et multo magis superiores sunt in hiis que videri non possunt. An non licet Deo quod vult facere? . . . Estimo quod ideo murmurant et detrahunt quia vellent quod alii superiores descenderent, et ipsis minoribus se in omnibus conformarent, quia putent se superiores cum merito sunt inferiores. Hinc ergo invenit animus meus audaciam ut aliquantulum aperirem musicam meam que accensit ex incendio amoris, et in qua iubilo coram Ihesum [*sic*], et pneumata resono suavissimi concentus. Porro eciam prestancius astiterunt adversum me . . . Hoc arguentes me non opinabantur, ideoque ad suam formam reducere conati sunt. Sed non potui graciam Christi deserere, et stultis hominibus, qui me interius omnino non cognoverunt, consentire. Sustinui ergo eos loqui, et feci quod faciendum erat secundum statum in quem me Dominus transferebat. Proinde propalabo gloriam Christi regracians, ut non amplius in aliis huiusmodi sic insaniant, nec assideos [*sic*] deinceps temere iudicare presumant; quia non est ex simulacione aut imaginariis quod feci suscepcionibus, ut quidam de me interpretabantur; et quibus multi seducuntur, qui se suscepisse suspicati sunt quod nunquam susceperunt. Sed in veritate venit in me invisibile gaudium, et realiter intra me concalui igne amoris, qui utique ab istis inferioribus rebus assumpsit cor meum, ut iubilans in Ihesu longe ab [exteriore] armonia in interiorem evolarem. (233.4–234.13)

[For this reason, I thought that I should somehow make some kind of an answer and not be entirely undone by my opponents. For what is their business with the lives of others, whose habits they know to be superior in many respects to their own lives – and who are much more superior in matters which cannot be seen? So is God not allowed to do anything he wants? I judge that they mutter and disparage because they want other, superior people to be brought down and conform to their own inferiority in every way, because they regard themselves as superior when actually they are inferior. And so here my soul learned daring, so that I unveiled a very little my music, which was burning up from the fire of love and in which I rejoice before Jesus and sound forth utterances of the sweetest harmony. After that they opposed me even more determinedly. My opponents did not esteem me and so tried to make me conform to their pattern. But I could not desert the grace of Christ, or agree with foolish people who did not at all understand me within. So I let them talk and did what had to be done according to the state into which God was translating me. For which reason, giving thanks, I will proclaim the glory of Christ, so that they will no longer rave about other things of this kind nor rashly presume to judge sitters ⟨contemplatives⟩. For what I have done is not based on pretence or on imaginary gifts, as some have reckoned about me – and by which many have been seduced, who think they have received things which they have never received. But an invisible joy has in truth come into me, and the fire of love has really grown warm within me, and has undoubtedly lifted my heart away from these lower things, so that, rejoicing in Christ, I have flown far from outward harmony to that which is within.]

This passage represents an extraordinary *volte face*. In complete contrast to the emphasis recent chapters have placed on self-abjection, the narrative is aggressively assertive about Rolle's superiority to those who criticize him, and is open in its claims. The warnings to fear presumption, and the whole apparatus of humility *topoi* which the elect of caps. 26–30 employed to restrain themselves, are swept aside; they apply to lesser Christians who have criticized Rolle, but not to him. At the same time as he is explaining how he had to summon *audacitas* to put these Christians right, Rolle is also being deliberately audacious towards his readers. Disdaining proofs, the end of the passage simply asserts that the experience on which his spiritual superiority is based is genuine. Confident of his high place in the Church Triumphant (whatever his lowliness in the Church Militant), he affects unconcern as to whether or not he convinces his readers. It is on them that responsibility for accepting or rejecting his assertions and his authority rests – Rolle implies by analogy that as a writer he 'does what has to be done', and is indifferent to those who would make him conform to their pattern. The final section of *Incendium Amoris* thus opens by adopting the assertive stance that Rolle might have decided upon from the start.

The suddenness with which cap. 31 breaks the pattern of abjection set by its predecessors is itself a product of the new assertiveness; Rolle does not explain in advance why the new mood is appropriate, and lays himself open to the charge of pride with ostentatious indifference. Indeed, the conceptual apparatus which allows him to be so direct in his claims is not fully worked out until later in his career, in works we will consider in the next chapter. However, the basic position of this section is that of cap. 19: the perfect are in practice without sin in this life, and rejoice in their knowledge of God and of their own salvation by singing. This position is elaborated in several directions. *Canor* now receives a more exalted definition:

Est enim angelica suavitas quam in animam accipit et eadem oda, etsi non eisdem verbis laudes Deo resonabitur. Qualis angelorum, talis est iscius concentus, etsi non tantus, nec tam perspicuus, propter carnem corruptibilem que adhuc aggravat amantem. Qui hoc experitur eciam angelica cantica expertus est, [cum sit eiusdem speciei in via et in patria]. Sonus enim ad canticum pertinet, non ad carmen quod cantatur. (237.4–11; [] from MS Dd.v.64)

[For it is an angelic sweetness and an angelic song that he has received into his soul, although he does not resound the praise of God in the same words. This harmony is the same as the harmony of the angels, although not so great, nor so clear, on account of the corruptible flesh which up until now annoys the lover. Whoever experiences this has also experienced angelic song, for they are of the same kind both in this life and in the fatherland. For the sound pertains to the song, not to the lyrics that are sung.]

Such a definition excuses contemplatives from attending fully to the Church's liturgical song, for they participate, even if not yet wholly, in the *canor* which it merely reflects. By describing the impossibility of participating in *canor* while taking part in the liturgy, caps. 31–32 differentiate the *perfecti* fundamentally from all others *in via*.

The perfect are also separated from normal patterns of Christian behaviour in other respects. In caps. 26–30, Rolle tries to protect them from the dangerous knowledge of their sanctity by endowing them with the abject humility that forms a central part of traditional monastic and eremitic definitions of holiness. In cap. 36, this humility is importantly redefined:

Verumtamen in sublimitate summa positus, sic securus est affectus ut omnino caveat negligenciam, ipsamque velut hostem pestiferum a se expellat. Solicitudinem ac timorem non amittat dum hic vivit; quia quo quis melior et Deo accepcior, eo amplius in caritate ardet, et ad instancius ac forcius operandum ea que suo statui ac vite congruunt, eciam ipsis stimulis amoris excitatur. Ac per hoc semper sollicitus est . . .

(251.10–17)

[Yet, although it is placed in the height in sublimity, the will is so secure that it is wary of every kind of negligence, and expels the same from itself like a pestilent enemy. It does not lay aside wariness and fear while it lives here. For the better and more acceptable to God someone is, the more he burns in charity, and also the more urgently and vigorously he is excited by those same goads of love to perform all the deeds which befit his state and life. And because of this he is always wary.]

Instead of denying their own status, the elect are now concerned to maintain it in order to enjoy their *canor* uninterruptedly (251.17–21). No longer are they restrained from sin by the bit of fear – although they continue to use fear in a tactical way, in order to keep themselves up to the mark – they are urged along by the goad of a love which warily keeps them to the right path. It is thus no longer necessary for Rolle to stress his humility by denigrating his own virtues; he has only to demonstrate a spiritual balance which is protected from pride by its own watchfulness. Such a change in the role of humility is fundamental to the ending of *Incendium Amoris*. Whereas the assertiveness of the rest of the work is continually being restrained by a recognition of the need for humility, here Rolle finally declares a position from which he can *legitimately* be self-assertive.[23]

The position has to be defended on two fronts. The first is rhetorical: Rolle must convince us again that he has genuinely experienced *canor*, and that his *audacitas* (233.18) is not another form of the *presumptio* (236.28–31) and *stultitia* (233.32) that characterizes his opponents; we must continue to regard him as one of the perfect. Caps. 31–32 therefore lay great stress both on the reality of Rolle's experience and on the existence of spurious experience ('ex simulacione aut imaginariis', 234.6; 'per imaginacionem', 236.23; 'non veritate sed in umbra', 236.24–25). Cap. 33 (238.23) cleverly makes the inability to mingle earthly music with *canor* into a test of the genuineness of the latter, and so 'proves' that Rolle is a true *perfectus*. Caps. 34–35 contain passionate personal devotions that are designed to show how greatly Rolle loves God. His love goes beyond the dullness of human words and wit: 'Hic deficio pre insipiencia et hebetudine ingenii'

(243.28–29); he longs for a companion to understand him fully (243.34–245.11); he begs readers not to be deceived by his exalted words, or to try to imitate them unless they, too, have experienced *fervor* and *canor*.[24] The language of these two chapters anticipates the heavy alliteration of *Melos Amoris*, as Rolle tries to wring conviction from the reader. But his most effective stroke is the story in cap. 42 (277.5), that from the time of his conversion on he wanted to sing the praises of God like a nightingale: a sentimental prophecy that is carefully prepared (notice the other nightingales in 259.33 and 273.18–20) to be irresistably believable. After this final act of self-transformation into an affective literary type (we are supposed to think both of John of Hoveden's *Philomena* and, probably, of John Pecham's *Philomela*), Rolle ends *Incendium Amoris* (apart from a brief and interestingly cautious coda, 278.22–32) with yet more assertions that what he feels is divine in origin: 'Rapitur verus amator tuus sollicitus in iubilum canori cogitatus, ut impossibile sit talem dulcedinem esse a diabolo, talem fervorem ab aliquo creato, talem canorem ab ingenio humano; in quibus si perseveravero salvus ero' (278.17–21: 'Your true and watchful lover is snatched in thought into the joy of song, in such a way that it is impossible such sweetness should be from the devil, such heat from anything made, such song from human skill; in which, if I persevere, I will be saved'). By sheer verbal virtuosity, Rolle has made it as difficult as he can to disagree.

The second front on which Rolle's newly achieved position needs to be defended is theological. Now he has declared a doctrine of *canor* to be the fundamental tenet of mystical theology, he must explain how this can be so, and give some account of his own role as a doyen of the spiritual life. Here he faces a problem of emphasis. On the one hand, he wants to present *canor* as a new doctrine and himself as its prophet; once Rolle can regard himself in such a light, he has an inbuilt justification for self-assertiveness (that prophets are by definition assertive), for building a metaphysical system around his own experience (that his life is a channel for God's truth), and even for the manipulative strategies and structure of *Incendium Amoris* (that *canor* is too high a doctrine to be stated explicitly all at once). On the other hand, just because *canor* actually is a new doctrine, it is vital to conceal that fact behind claims for its traditional status. Rolle mediates between these presentations of *canor* by distinguishing between the saints of old, who knew of *canor*, and the *moderni* who for the most part do not; he is a prophet in the sense that he is calling the world back to the spiritual ambition it has forgotten. Thus he emphasizes both his originality and his adherence to known facts when he states that he has never read any account of *canor*, although all lovers of God experience it (237.21–23: 'Ob hoc utique evenit huiusmodi amatori quod nequaquam in aliquorum doctorum scriptis inveni aut reperi expressum'). Again, he uses a distinction between learned and infused knowledge to claim that he has been inspired by the Spirit to proclaim his message boldly; but he also emphasizes his continuity with the Fathers by insisting that the Spirit once inspired them in the same way:

Et inde [i.e. 'in igneum celum assumptus', 240.15] accepit sapienciam et subtilitatem, ut sciret loqui inter locullentos et audaciter preferret quod dicendum duxit, quamvis idiota et insipiens antea estimaretur et eciam existeret. Sed docti per adquisitam sapienciam non infusam, et inflati argumentacionibus implicitis, in ipso dedignantur dicentes: 'Ubi didicit? A quo doctore audivit?' Non arbitrantur ab interiori doctore amatores eternitatis edoceri, ut eloquencius loquerentur quam ipsi ab hominibus docti qui omni tempore, pro vanis honoribus studuerunt. Si autem antiquitus Spiritus Sanctus plures inspiravit, cur eciam non nunc assumeret amantes ad gloriam Domini speculandam, cum ipsis prioribus moderni approbati non sunt inequales?

(240.17–31)

[And then, assumed into the fiery heaven, ⟨the lover⟩ received wisdom and subtlety, so that he knew how to speak among the chatterers and put forward boldly whatever he thought it necessary to say, although previously he was regarded as stupid and feeble, and perhaps even was so. But those taught by acquired not infused wisdom and swollen up with intricate arguments mock, saying: 'Where did he learn? Which doctor has he heard?' They do not reckon that lovers of eternity are taught by an inner doctor, so that they can speak more eloquently than those who were taught by people who have all the time been studying for futile honours. But if the Holy Spirit inspired many in days of old, why should he not now also raise lovers up to see the glory of God, since moderns have been approved as the equals of these their predecessors?]

(This passage is also notable as the only attempt *Incendium Amoris* makes to provide a theological justification for its own audacious eloquence; as such it is the harbinger of many things to come.) In cap. 34 he uses prophetic language to lament that few can now be found who practise *canor* (243.6), further bolstering his status as representative of a bygone holiness; by cap. 36 he is even putting words into the mouths of earlier lovers of God (248.18). The last part of *Incendium Amoris* sees him turning himself into a prophetic interpreter of a kind of hidden tradition, which takes its validity from its historical origins among the saints of the past (perhaps mainly the Desert Fathers) and its claim to continuing divine inspiration.

In the terms which it so elaborately moves towards, *Incendium Amoris* thus succeeds in establishing its author as an *auctor* of the greatest importance, and its message about the nature of divine love as fundamental to revealed Christianity. The apologetic structure of the work, it now appears, is self-supporting. Rolle's experience of *canor* is what makes his whole account of the spiritual life plausible; yet it is the success with which he expounds that experience theologically, and, still more, the conviction inherent in his account of it, that can make it believable. *Experientia* can become the basis for *auctoritas* because of Rolle's increasing ability to defend and to explain that experience, but above all because of his ability to recreate it verbally. This structure places tremendous emphasis on eloquence, for readers must decide on the work's authority mainly on the basis of the conviction it produces in them, which must by the nature of the case be a matter more of the will than the reason. It is not surprising, then, that the last chapters of *Incendium Amoris* initiate a movement in many of Rolle's later works towards elaborate and impassioned rhetorical writing. It has been obvious from the start that the work attempts not only to convert readers to God, but to convert them to accepting the doctrine of *canor* and their author's authority to pronounce on it. Yet by the end this fact has been articulated in a way which turns the sleight of hand of the opening into the affective didactic appeals of the three chapters of the work's peroration. By the end of *Incendium Amoris* evangelistic and apologetic modes have partly been fused, and Rolle's desires to declare his own sanctity, to praise *canor* and to lead others to God are beginning to be in tune with one another.

6

Contemplative life, *Dulcor: Super Psalmum Vicesimum, Super Canticum Canticorum, Contra Amatores Mundi*

The last section of *Incendium Amoris* presents us with an apparently fully confident Rolle, who has resolved the problems surrounding his subject-matter and his presentation of himself, and who would therefore seem to be in the proper position to begin exercising his newly asserted spiritual authority. An obvious way of doing this would be to return to writing works with some of the didactic clarity of *Judica Me*, works which would attempt to propagate his mystical experiences in a systematic manner, with an attention to the needs of readers such as *Incendium Amoris* itself too frequently fails to display. However, if my reconstruction of Rolle's career is correct, what actually happens is just the opposite: in the works to be discussed in this and the next chapter, the issue of spiritual authority, rather than being taken for granted, assumes ever greater prominence – while, at the same time, Rolle's writing manages to become even less responsive to his readers' need for practical edification. These apparently puzzling developments reflect the fact that there are actually numerous questions which *Incendium Amoris* has not remotely resolved: How can *canor* guarantee the spiritual security of the *perfecti*? How do Rolle's mystical experiences relate to the importantly different ones described by his own *auctoritates*? Why should readers take his eloquence as proof that his experiences are genuine? In order to address these and other difficulties, the progressive revelation from *fervor* to *dulcor* to *canor* around which *Incendium Amoris* is structured (see pp. 121–122) must continue. In this chapter we will investigate the part of this process that Rolle apparently associated with the imagery of *dulcor*: a group of works which attempt to modulate the fervent stridencies of *Incendium Amoris* into language of a sweet and holy daring, and which in their turn prepare for the sonorous climax of Rollean self-revelation, *Melos Amoris*.

I

The most conventional work of the group is *Super Psalmum Vicesimum*: an exposition of a psalm about kingship which analyses the whole as a statement about the saints. Like many of Rolle's works, it is a structural hybrid. It shares some of the characteristics of his full Psalter commentaries (for example in the way it responsibly explains every phrase in its text), but is far more discursive in its glossing, and is ten times the length of its equivalent in *Latin Psalter*.[1] In other respects it resembles a sermon. The work's opening, which sets up the dramatic introduction of the first verse of the psalm, '*Domine, in virtute tua letabitur rex*' (1.18–19), is a formal exordium, while the exposition of this verse develops the idea of kingship in ways which clearly suggest the 'divisions' of a text popular in academic preaching.[2] There is also a good deal of more emotional and evangelistic writing: passages of rhapsodic or didactic address to God or the reader which suggest other kinds of sermon. The self-conscious eloquence of the last third of *Incendium Amoris* is thus in evidence from the start.

The work quickly sets out its main themes and method of procedure:

Cum omnes psalmi dulces sint et delectabiles, iste psalmus de gloria regis precipue loquitur, consequenter insinuans quod nullus in Domino letabitur sine regimine, nec aliquis recte regitur nisi Deo rectore. Describit ergo Propheta sanctorum gaudium et tormentum impiorum. Delectabuntur namque omnes iusti et sancti in explanatione huius psalmi. Mali vero valde deterreri poterunt, qui se non bene sed male egisse meminerunt.   (1.20–2.2)

[While all the psalms are sweet and delectable, this psalm speaks especially about the glory of the king, consequently implying that nobody will rejoice in the Lord without government, and no one is rightly governed except by God the governor. Thus the prophet delineates the joy of the saints and the torment of the unrighteous. And so the just and the saints will delight in the explication of this psalm; but the evil, who will recollect that they have not done good but evil, may be strongly deterred.]

Like the psalm, the exposition concerns government, a term which applies at once to self-government, to the divine government under which the elect live and to the evil inversion of that government practised by earthly rulers. For all the conceptual formality of the way in which Rolle sets about making these distinctions – for example, by discussing kingship under several heads, identifying true 'kings' (in a skilfully argued oxymoron) with *pauperes* (2.8), and earthly authorities with hypocrisy (3.2) – he expects the work to evoke an affective response: delight from the saints (in places he gives vent to his own delight as a member of the elect), fear from the wicked (who are vilified in much of the work, especially in its last pages). *Super Psalmum Vicesimum* thus has many of the preoccupations of the rest of Rolle's writings. It treats the virtues of the elect and the vices of the damned, building model accounts of both in much the style of *Incendium Amoris*, and depicting the separation of the one from the other in terms similar to those found in *Judica Me*. Yet it does have particular and important things to say. The focus of the work's treatment of the theme of government is the question of how the perfect safeguard their spiritual status. In dealing with this question, the work develops several of the issues that emerge near the end of *Incendium Amoris*: spiritual confidence and assertiveness, vigilance and humility, perfection and the saint's experience of *canor*. Rolle shuttles between stressing the humility and lowliness of the *sancti* and expatiating on their glories, sometimes doing both things at once. The opening of the work quotes Christ's words in John

15.5 ('*Without me you can do nothing*'), and notes: 'Non utique in nostris viribus presumimus confidere, sed in Deo precipue credimus ... Illi, inquam, totum tribuimus, a quo nimirum totum habeamus' (1.11–13: 'Indeed we do not presume to trust in our own strengths, but we trust especially in God; to him, I say, we render everything, from whom truly we have everything'). This is partly a way of introducing verse 1 of the psalm as meaning 'The king will rejoice not in his own strength but in God's', and is a gesture of humility on Rolle's part as he sets out to write. But the words also embody two claims: that the perfect fully recognize their dependence on God and are thus innocent of presumption; and that these truths apply to Rolle. In quoting Psalm 84.9 ('*May I hear what God the Lord speaks in me*', see 1.10), after stating that 'we await grace confidently from our Creator' (see 1.9–10), Rolle is actually saying that his words will be divinely inspired because of his spiritual status.[3] In this respect, the passage prepares to introduce the other meaning of the first verse of Psalm 20, which he refers to as 'daring' ('tam audacter', 2.4): 'The king will rejoice in the possession of godlike strength.' The chief importance of *Super Psalmum Vicesimum* is the way it manages to assert both meanings of this and subsequent verses in the same work.

As well as being a pauper who serves Christ (2.20–21), the king governs four kingdoms: the world through his poverty, the flesh through temperance, the devil through humility and heaven through love (4.10–14). Since he has fully conquered his kingdoms and trusts in God continually ('iugiter', 4.21) he is not frightened of Satan, for his rule over his kingdoms is stable, his salvation certain:

Sane rex populum suum stabilivit qui se totum ad amandum Deum tribuit. Populum istius regis non homines terre, sed cogitationes anime vocamus, que tunc recte reguntur quando omnes ad gloriam Dei mancipantur. Itaque rex in amore Dei se totum regens, et super universorum vitiorum maculas potenter regnans, merito in virtute divina letari perhibetur qui inimicos Christi ut fortis miles expugnare conabatur. A Deo nimirum et ipse rectus est, et sine ipso vincere non potest. (5.6–12)

[Certainly a king has established his subjects who has given himself completely to loving God. We do not call earthly people this king's subjects, but rather thoughts of the soul, which are rightly ruled when they are all made over to the glory of God. Thus the king, ruling himself completely in the love of God, and reigning powerfully over the stains of all vices, is rightly shown to rejoice in divine strength, since he strove to fight off the enemies of Christ, like a strong soldier. Certainly he also is ruled by God ⟨or he is righteous from God⟩, and cannot conquer without him.]

This sounds straightforward; it seems typical of Rolle's usual extremism only in its forcefulness (adverbs like 'potenter' or 'secure' carry a heavy weight of implicit assertion at this stage of the argument). However, as this opening statement is drawn out, the stability of the king is less and less treated as the product of his renunciation of world, flesh and devil, and is increasingly identified with his conquest of the fourth kingdom, that of heaven, by passionate love. This process eventually takes Rolle's view of the elect a clear stage further than in the last part of *Incendium Amoris*.

Dulcor: Super Psalmum Vicesimum

The development of the argument is swift. The king is raised through love to embrace the eternal king (5.21), and to rejoice according to the measure of his love (5.22–6.1); God gives him his heart's desire, including *fervor, dulcor* and *canor* (6.25–7.4), and full knowledge of the Creator (7.3–4: 'plenam Conditoris cognitionem'). In accordance with verse 2, *'The king has given God the desires of his heart'* (6.17), he is said to have set ('stabilivit', 7.5) not his 'cogitationes anime', but his love in God. In accordance with verse 3, *'For you came before him in the blessings of sweetness'* (7.11), this act of establishment is quickly said to be God's doing before it is humanity's. But the dependence of the saints on God and their inherent merit are still being stressed alternately; the second half of the verse, *'You have placed on his head a crown of precious stones'* (8.10–11), introduces the claim that Christ's soldier deserves his crown for continually (8.19) contemplating him: 'Meruit igitur miles Christi coronam' (8.20). This brings us to the high point of the work's portrayal of the saints, its exposition of verse 6, *'Great is his glory in your salvation; you will bestow glory and great beauty on him'* (11.25–12.1), partly in the form of an encomium of love:

O Amor quam laudabilis es, quam amabilis, quam sine pari! . . . In hoc autem ostendis te valentem, potentem, dominantem . . . Tu solus es qui iuste remunerari non potes nisi in gloria divine visionis . . . O Amor quantum vales qui, dum immensa opera prophetie et miracula a facie Christi fugiendo delitescunt, tu solus in curiam eterni regis cum Christo duce intrare non formidas, sed et gloriose susciperis et cum magno honore ad sedem scandere iuberis. Multi Christum videbunt in humanitate, sed soli amatores Christi cernent in Deitatis dulcore . . . Penetratur amoris iaculo et audacter dicat: *Amore langueo* [Song of Songs 2.5]. Succenditur medullitus igne Spiritus Sancti, ut merito canat Propheta: *Magna est gloria eius in salutari Dei.* (12.8–13.3)

[O Love, how praiseworthy you are, how lovely, how incomparable! And in this you declare yourself effective, potent, dominating. You alone are he who cannot justly be rewarded except in the glory of the sight of God. O Love how powerful you are, you who alone do not fear to enter the court of the eternal king, with Christ leading – while huge works of prophecy and miracles, fleeing, skulk away from the face of Christ – but are gloriously received and are commanded to ascend the seat with great honour. Many will see Christ in his human nature, but only lovers of Christ will gaze upon him in the sweetness of his divinity. He is pierced by the spear of love and may boldly say: *I languish for love.* He is burned up from within by the fire of the Holy Spirit, so that the prophet can rightly sing: *Great is his glory in the salvation of God.*]

The passage resembles Rolle's account of his own ascent to the court of God in cap. 35 of *Incendium Amoris*, except that on this occasion 'Amor' is the protagonist. 'Amor' is a metaphor at once for the lovers of God and for the Holy Spirit who lifts them up to God;[4] hence it suggests that the saints are raised to God by divine inspiration and possession. Until this point in the work, such concepts have been invoked as much to stress the lowliness of the saints as to proclaim their importance. But here they enable Rolle to build the work's earlier contention, that the king is passively secure of salvation ('established', 'stable'), into a more aggressive account of the potency of the *perfecti*; the love inspiring them is 'valentem, potentem, dominantem',

145

fearless ('non formidas'), making them speak boldly of their love-longing, and distinguishing them fundamentally from the rest of humanity.

As the passage proceeds, the security of the saints, with regard to their salvation and to the criticism they receive from their enemies, becomes further identified with their ability to love God and practise *canor* in this fearless way. First, we are told that the soul's vigilance in keeping God continually in mind enables it to withstand tribulation:

Huiusmodi anima tanto gaudio undique suffulta non sentit iniurias, gaudet ad opprobria, ridet ad maledicta, quia quam sola Conditoris memoria delectat, nulla mundi molestia seu miseria ab amore perturbat. Iustus enim de iure non dicitur qui memoriam Dei a se, dum vigilat, dilabi sinere non veretur.   (13.20–24)

[A soul of this kind, supported on all sides by so much joy, does not feel injury, rejoices in opprobrium, laughs at slander, because no worldly harm or wretchedness disturbs from love the one who delights only in the memory of the Creator. For he is not lawfully called just who does not fear to allow the memory of God to melt away from him while he is awake.]

This idea is common in Passion meditation and can also be found in works of affective mysticism: a constant dwelling on the memory of Jesus Christ is salvific, because it keeps the meditator from being distracted and turned to sin.[5] Here, however, the idea develops beyond the commonplace to become a specific validation of the eremitic life, which redefines the theme of 'government' and introduces a new element into Rolle's portrayal of *canor*. Rolle begs Christ to dwell in his memory 'while I am awake' (16.10) and to be there sweetly and, again, continually ('iugiter', 'continuo'; 16.9, 12). The imagery here connects the memory of Christ with *dulcor*, as *Incendium Amoris* has also done (see 190.12–14). Yet in the commentary on part of the next verse – '*And in the mercy of the most High he will not be moved*' (16.22) – the continual memory of Christ comes to be associated with *canor* itself. We are told that the psalmist is not afraid to speak this verse, but through it daringly affirms the stability of saints ('Psalmista loqui non trepidat . . . audacter affirmat', 16.21, 22). The words 'non commovebitur' naturally lead to a discussion of the virtues of sitting (compare, e.g., *Incendium Amoris*, cap. 14), which in turn introduces the subject of the perfect life:

Non mireris igitur si iugiter sedere potuit qui celestium gaudiorum consolamine tam suaviter inebriatus fuit. Sedendo enim canit et iubilat ac superni amoris suavitate crebro rapitur et, in eternorum contemplatione stabilitus, mirabiliter iocundatur . . . Moveri non potest quia in Deo perfecte radicatus est.   (19.8–13)

[So do not be surprised if he was able to sit continually, who was so sweetly inebriated by the consolation of heavenly joy. For sitting he sings and rejoices, and is repeatedly snatched up by the sweetness of supernal love, and becomes marvellously merry, established in the contemplation of things eternal. He cannot be moved, because he is perfectly rooted in God.]

For all its resemblance to earlier accounts of the perfect life here and in *Incendium Amoris*, words like 'iugiter' and 'crebro' suggest the presence of a new claim, which will be fully articulated in *Super Canticum Canticorum*:

that the spiritual security of contemplatives rests in what is, in effect, a *permanent state* of mystical joy, for only in that state are they 'perfecte radicatus' in Christ. In *Incendium Amoris*, the view that the saints must maintain their humility through self-abasement is replaced by the assertion that on the contrary they are conscious of their virtue, and hold on to it vigilantly in order not to lose their perfect love. *Super Psalmum Vicesimum* builds on this view, at the same time as it lays new stress on the fearlessness that characterizes *canor*, by reinterpreting vigilance – the immovability of the contemplative – as an aspect of mystical experience in itself. This reinterpretation disassociates Rolle's *perfecti* still further from the world and from sin: hence, it would seem, the fearlessness of their approach to God and imperturbability in the face of criticism (16.23–25).[6]

In arguing that the self-government which marks the 'kingly' elect is not merely the basis on which a passionate love of God is built, but is itself that love, *Super Psalmum Vicesimum* propounds an oxymoron: that stability consists in 'being snatched up to God', in the passionate movement of the souls of 'sitters' towards their heavenly home. This oxymoron will appear in various forms in Rolle's later works, where the continual nature of mystical experience is expressed more forcibly. It buttresses his view that the perfect life is the solitary life, and helps him to justify his self-assertiveness as the exemplar of that life. Like the upside-down tree in canto XXXII of *Purgatorio*, the saints are rooted in heaven and thus have their own standards of behaviour; they are not afraid to risk opprobrium for seeming to be presumptuous and are not susceptible to spiritual pride. Perhaps in celebration of this view, the first-person passages in *Super Psalmum Vicesimum* are particularly unapologetic. In two passages ('O Sancte Spiritus . . .', 10.14–25; 'O Jesu bone . . .', 16.4–20) Rolle gives examples of the longing *canor* he sings as one of the saints; after the second passage he comments that the singer is the 'rex' who is worthy of such glory (16.21, 22), referring unabashedly to himself. He seems to be imitating the psalmist, to whom he refers several times as 'daring', and whom he views as in a position parallel to his own; both are perfected souls divinely inspired to write about their spiritual states.[7] This view of his role will become more explicit in the rest of this chapter.

II

Super Canticum Canticorum is a lengthy exposition of the first two-and-a-half verses of the Song of Songs, divided into two main sections or seven shorter ones: '*Osculetur me osculo oris sui / quia meliora sunt ubera tua vino, / fragrancia unguentis optimis. // Oleum effusum nomen tuum; / ideo adolescentulae dilexerunt te nimis. / Trahe me post te, / curremus in odore unguentorum tuorum.*'[8] The work somewhat resembles *Super Psalmum Vicesimum* in its structure. There are the by now familiar blends of elements drawn from the writing of commentaries with others which make us feel we are reading a particularly highly wrought sermon, and of formal structural

147

devices with rhapsodic, digressive writing. The work's exordium (1.1–3.25) looks like a formal discussion of the question, 'Set quomodo audebit eciam perfecta Christi amatrix anima a tanto rege eterno osculum petere?' (1.9–11: 'But how will even the perfected soul and lover of Christ dare to ask a kiss from so great an eternal king?'). Yet in spite of a rash of conjunctions ('autem . . . sed . . . quippe . . . sed . . . verum . . . et . . . igitur', p. 1) and a formal 'objection' ('Novi utique quod *Honor regis iudicium diligit*', 2.15–16, Psalm 98.4), we search in vain for a developing argument; a digression on feminine headwear ('pompose muliercule in tortis crinibus', 2.5) and a longer one on Rolle's wandering (2.25–3.25) swamp the discussion, the first half of which concludes in a confessedly 'shameless' way: 'Set quoniam amor pudore non confunditur, opprobrio non reicitur, racione non vincitur, quin pocius omnia novit vincere, iterum clamo, cogito, deprecor, *Osculetur me osculo oris sui*' (2.16–19: 'But because love is not confounded by shame, not repelled by opprobrium, not conquered by reason, but, rather, knows how to conquer all things, again I cry out, I think, I pray, *Let him kiss me with the kiss of his mouth*').[9] Although many passages are more formally organized than this, a similar phenomenon is evident in the work's overall structure. Each of its seven sections deals with its text as a separate entity, in the manner of a postil like *Super Mulierem Fortem* – each section being a fantasia-like exposition, or series of expositions, which need not have organized conceptual links with its predecessor or successor. By contrast with *Super Psalmum Vicesimum* (in which Rolle expounds the text as a developing argument and does not divide his exposition into discrete sections), the work for the most part therefore has no organized evolution of ideas; there is some progress between sections of the work, especially in the *Exposicio super Secundum Versiculum*, but far more mere sensation of progress. Yet at the beginning and end of sections, Rolle seems anxious to persuade us that he is after all constructing an overall argument; transitions are consciously smooth, while at significant moments he refers backwards or forwards to link one section with another (see the play on 'trahere' at the opening of the '*Curremus*' section, 65.18ff.). As in *Judica Me*, the parts of this seemingly haphazard work are carefully linked; as with *Incendium Amoris*, Bernard's *Sermones super Cantica Canticorum* may have provided Rolle with a model for this structure.

The major unifying feature of the work is its imagery, which naturally reflects the extreme sensuality of the text; the work is full of bodies, touch and taste: kisses, mouths, breasts, wine, fragrance, ointments, oil, odour – in short, the terminology of *dulcor*. As the opening statement after the *exordium* makes clear, *Super Canticum Canticorum* is Rolle's most sustained attempt to write a work that revolves around *dulcor*:

Osculetur me osculo oris sui. In hiis verbis, devota anima fervorem querit eterne dileccionis, dulcedinem superne contemplacionis, solucionem corruptibilis carnis et unionem dilecti invisibilis. Fervor utique divini amoris speculacionis preit dulcorem, quia nisi Christum quis recte diligit, proculdubio in canore celestis contemplacionis non iubilabit. Contemplativa vero suavitas mortis precedit desiderium, quia tunc cum

Dulcor: Super Canticum Canticorum

gaudio morimur quando delicias eterni amoris canentes, solam in Deo delectacionem
contemplamur.   (3.26–4.8)

[*Let him kiss me with the kiss of his mouth.* In these words the devout soul seeks the
heat of eternal love, the sweetness of heavenly contemplation, the dissolution of the
corruptible flesh and union with the invisible beloved. Certainly the heat of divine
love comes before the sweetness of sight ⟨of God⟩, for unless somebody loves Christ
properly he will certainly not rejoice in the song of celestial contemplation. On the
other hand, contemplative sweetness precedes the desire for death, for we die joyfully
when, as we sing the delights of eternal love, we contemplate only the delight of God.]

Yet even while announcing his subject, Rolle is quick to point out that *dulcor*
cannot be discussed in isolation; by placing it in the context of the mystical
experiences that lead up to it, and of those to which it in turn leads, he
demonstrates simultaneously that his text is particularly about sweetness and
that it proclaims the whole course of the spiritual life. This proves true of
Super Canticum Canticorum as a whole. As we would expect, it is much
concerned with *canor* as well as *dulcor*, and continues the process of staking
out claims for the *electi* that we have observed in *Incendium Amoris* and
Super Psalmum Vicesimum; it is this feature of the work that I will discuss
shortly. But at some points the terminology of *dulcor* is used to introduce
material more relevant to neophytes than mature contemplatives. Much of
the section expounding the clause '*Oleum effusum nomen tuum*' (37.8–48.20)
is about the Virgin, the Virgin Birth and the Holy Name of Jesus – topics
accessible to popular devotion that it deals with in a pictorial and decidedly
popular way. Although the following passage of poetic evangelism alludes to
the Rollean theme of solitude, it is unusually conventional in its content and
in its highly concrete style; the emphasis on penitence and weeping itself
shows that it is written for beginners:[10]

Circuivi per diviciarum cupidinem et non inveni Ihesum. Ambulavi per deliciarum
voraginem et non inveni Ihesum. Cucurri per carnis lasciviam et non inveni Ihesum.
Sedi cum multitudine gaudencium et non inveni Ihesum. In hiis omnibus, quesivi
Ihesum et non inveni illum, quia innotuit michi per suam graciam quod non invenitur
in terra suaviter vivencium. Diverti ergo per aliam viam et circuivi per paupertatem; et
inveni Ihesum pauperem in mundo natum, in presepio positum, et pannis involutum.
Ambulavi per asperorum toleranciam; et inveni Ihesum itinere fatigatum, fame, siti,
frigore afflictum, opprobriis et contumeliis saturatum. Sedebam solus, faciens me
solitarium; et inveni Ihesum in deserto ieiunantem, in monte solum orantem. Cucurri
per penam et penitenciam; et inveni Ihesum ligatum, flagellatum, vulneratum, felle
potatum, cruci affixum, in cruce pendentem, in cruce morientem. Ergo, Ihesu non
invenitur in divitibus, set in pauperibus; non in deliciosis, set in penitentibus; non in
lascivis et gaudentibus, set in amaris et flentibus; non in multitudine, set in solitudine.
                                                                              (45.5–22)[11]

[I went about through Desire of Riches, and I did not find Jesus. I walked through the
Abyss of Delights, and I did not find Jesus. I ran through Lust of the Flesh, and I did
not find Jesus. I sat with a crowd of revellers, and I did not find Jesus. In all these
places, I sought Jesus and did not find him; for by his grace he signified to me that he
was not to be found on earth living softly. So I turned aside by another way, and went

149

about through Poverty; and I found Jesus born a pauper into the world, laid in a manger, and wrapped in swaddling bands. I walked through the Endurance of Bitternesses; and I found Jesus tired from the journey, hungry, thirsty, weakened by cold, made weary by abuses and insults. I was sitting alone, making myself solitary; and I found Jesus fasting in the desert, praying alone on the mountain. I ran through Suffering and Penitence; and I found Jesus bound, scourged, wounded, given gall to drink, nailed to the cross – hanging on the cross – dying on the cross. So Jesus is not found among the rich but with the poor; not in the midst of the sleek but the penitent; not among the lustful and the revellers but the bitter and the weeping; not in the crowd, but in solitude.]

Several other parts of *Super Canticum Canticorum* expound their texts in this simple affective language. In these cases, the immediate explanation is usually that Rolle is following exegetical tradition; the '*Oleum effusum nomen tuum*' section discusses the Virgin Birth and deals with its subject-matter evangelistically because 'oil poured out' is generally associated with the Incarnation and with the preaching of the gospel.[12] This is perhaps a sign of Rolle's responsibility to his text and his role as a commentator. Yet it is incongruous to find him writing in so popular a vein in a commentary which – whatever its affiliations with preaching – cannot have been intended for popular consumption; part of a subsequent section, expounding the clause '*Trahe me post te*' (52.25ff.), is a theological discussion of the parts played respectively by God and the soul in the soul's mystical ascent, a subject of a quite different order. Although *dulcor* is always the most flexibly treated of Rolle's mystical experiences, this is particularly the case in *Super Canticum Canticorum*, where the language of sweetness is applied to almost all the topics the commentary raises in connection with its text.

For all this, the main subject of *Super Canticum Canticorum* is the saints (with their inevitable sidekicks, the *reprobi*) and their mystical experience. Let us look first at the work's most articulate account of the saints, which occurs in its last section and is itself a culmination of themes introduced in the two sections it follows. In the first of these, the exposition of '*Ideo adolescentule dilexerunt te nimis*' (48.20–55.24) focusses on 'nimis' in drawing a picture of the violence of love; love is wonderfully impetuous, exceeding all bounds, is singular, highest, ever growing, never comprehending God's full majesty (50.12–51.1). In the second, the clause '*Trahe me post te*' (55.24–65.17) is expounded as concerned with love as the 'root' which draws humanity to God; Rolle plays learnedly with the paradox that while God draws the soul to him, the soul also draws near to God of her own free will, and is responsible for her own progress: '*Coadiutores Dei sumus*' (61.6, 1 Corinthians 3.9). The final section, which comments on '*Curremus in odore unguentorum tuorum*' (65.18–80.26), reflects on some of these themes and seeks both to qualify and to support them. In the process it also takes the view of the saints articulated in *Super Psalmum Vicesimum* another stage.

The early part of the section develops an argument from 2 Timothy 4.7 ('*I have fought the good fight, I have kept the faith, I have finished the race*',

66.2–3), by claiming that the verse does not imply that Paul expected to die soon, but rather that he was securely confident of not falling back into sin (66.15–19). His confidence is founded on the fact that he has progressed beyond the stage of saying *'Trahe me'*, and is now one of those who say *'Curremus'* (66.25–26), since he runs to the divine embrace even when he is not being drawn or called (67.8–10). This exposition is then linked to Rolle's claim that mystical experience can be continual, which he here expounds much more carefully than hitherto, insisting that God's lovers can experience his sweetness all the time. Although 'plurimi sanctorum' who have written of the glories of the love of God assert that divine joy rarely comes to God's lovers in this life, we are told they are wrong; if the elect always desire to embrace Christ, how can it be said that Christ does not want to embrace them even more eagerly? Whoever always seeks love will always rejoice in it (67.10–68.8). With considerable daring, this passage openly contradicts other mystical writers who argue that permanent union with God cannot be achieved in this life – i.e. almost all orthodox Christian writers on the spiritual life. It does so by the simple expedient of taking the devotional commonplace that one should think of and desire Christ continually (see n. 5), and then claiming that Christ is so generous a lover, and the perfect soul is so pure, that for such a soul desiring Christ and embracing him are in effect one and the same thing.[13] This forcible dislocation of affective (and apophatic) mystical traditions, which is clearly motivated by the need to find a basis on which to rest his claim for the spiritual security of the *perfecti*, is among the most original and aggressive manœuvres in Rolle's career to this point.[14]

After this crucial moment, Rolle hastens to define the group to whom his claim applies, by identifying them with the seraphim, who burn with love for God (68.15). So fervent are the *perfecti* that their nature is transformed ('transmutatur', 69.17), and they are wholly united with Christ, and can say: *'I live, yet now not I but Christ lives in me'* (69.17–18, Galatians 2.20). Such souls seem 'deified' ('quodammodo deificatum videatur', 69.20), and thus enjoy God not rarely but continuously (69.20–70.1); as so often, Rolle weaves his newest theme into a model account of the perfect, presenting it in many lights, arguing it from all angles.[15] At this point, a modification of the imagery of the previous sections occurs. Where they presented the perfect soul's love for God as violent and without order, here we are told that there are 'orders' of God's lovers on earth ('plures sunt gradus amoris Dei', 70.7), matching the orders of angels (compare *Incendium Amoris*, cap. 3). The most perfect ('perfectissimi', 70.10) have arrived at a state in which they are like the seraphim, and their condition is again described in terms of continuous mystical joy:

Nos namque dum solum Conditorem nostrum toto corde nostro, cunctis aliis curis postpositis et oblitis, indesinenter infatigabiliterque concupiscimus, calore eterne lucis obumbrati, usque ad canorum iubilum, Christo rapiente, gaudentes evolamus. Et quia canticus iste eterni amoris non raptim, non momentanee, set continue adest nobis, nulla adversitate, nulla prosperitate concutitur; non raro set continue gratulamur. $(72.4-11)^{16}$

[For while we unceasingly and indefatigably desire our Creator alone with all our hearts, all other cares put away and forgotten, we fly up rejoicing, overshadowed by the heat of the light eternal, snatched away by Christ, to the joyfulness of song. And because this song of eternal love is not with us hurriedly and momentarily, but continually, we are not shaken by any adversity or prosperity; we rejoice not rarely but continually.]

Here, at last, *canor* itself is unmistakably claimed to be, at least potentially, a continuous experience, while Rolle declares (through his use of first-person verb and pronoun forms) that he is himself one of the *perfectissimi*. Qualifications are at once added: *canor* is not present when the saints are eating, sleeping, or being disturbed by earthly noise and people (72.11–14), and it is not so full or satisfying as it will be after death (72.9–12; compare *Incendium Amoris*, caps. 31–33). Yet words of caution are quickly swamped by a lengthy oration in praise of love, which adapts and summarizes images from the last three sections, in arguing that to find Jesus is still to seek him, to have him still to desire him:

O bone Ihesu, dulce est michi adherere tibi, tecum enim non timeo tormenta. Sine te vero nescio ubi invenire potero solacia. Tu es michi gracia me preveniens. Tu es michi delectacio me ducens, et tu es michi gloria me suscipiens . . . Quid ultra ergo quererem, cum te omne bonum haberem? Igitur habeo te et non quero praeter te. Quid est hoc? Hoc solum quero quod habeo, nec aliquid quero quod non habeo! Quomodo ergo saciabor si non sufficit michi quod habeo, quia nil aliud volo? Sufficit utique michi meus Ihesus. Set ita suave, ita dulce est gaudium, quod quantumcumque accepero adhuc non saciatum invenio desiderium meum. Saciabor autem cum apparuerit gloria eius. Set non sic saciabor, quemadmodum saciatus est fastidiosus qui ventrem dolet nec sic erit desiderium vacuum quemadmodum ieiunantis guttur esurit. Immo, quia divina gloria delicatissima est et suavissima, ineffabilis et incomprehensibilis, amans semper saciabitur et saciatus semper amare desiderabit.   (73.17–74.8)

[O good Jesus, it is sweet for me to cling to you, for with you I do not fear torments – but without you I do not know where I will be able to find comfort. For me you are grace going before me. For me you are delight leading me on, and for me you are glory receiving me. So what more should I seek, when I have you, who are everything good? Therefore I have you and I seek nothing except you. What is this? I seek only the thing that I have, and I do not seek anything that I do not have! How then will I be satisfied, if what I have is not enough for me, since I want nothing else? Jesus, you see, is enough for me. But so delightful, so sweet is joy, that however much I have received so far, I do not find my desire satisfied. I will be satisfied when his glory is manifested; but I will not be satisfied in the same way as is the squeamish person who grieves for his stomach, nor will my desire be empty as a starving man's gullet is hungry. Indeed, because the divine glory is very tender and very sweet, ineffable and incomprehensible, the lover will always be satisfied, and, being satisfied, will always desire to love.]

The violent love of the saints on earth becomes a more decorous, but still passionate, mingling of ecstasy and desire which will not, after all, change its essential character – only, it seems, its proportions – after death; Rolle is again concerned to minimize the differences between the living saints and their glorified predecessors.[17] The work ends with a series of confident prayers and short accounts of the progress of the saint – like so many verbal fanfares, forming an extended and grandiloquent peroration.[18]

In this account of the last section of *Super Canticum Canticorum* I have kept close to the course of Rolle's exposition, for this section demonstrates at its best the lyrical style of biblical exposition which characterizes the whole work, and which achieves its apotheosis in *Melos Amoris*. Earlier I suggested that the beginnings of Rollean rhapsody are to be found in the last chapters of *Incendium Amoris*, and argued that its purpose is as much to convince readers that Rolle's experience of divine love is genuine as to evangelize them. Such is surely the case here, too. Rolle quotes Paul, and takes a reasoned stance on the claim that mystical experience is continual; but this claim is still unlikely to convince, unless readers accept that he himself rejoices continually in divine love. Thus, near the beginning of this section, he overtly makes his experience of God's love the grounds on which to challenge the authority of 'plurimi sanctorum' who disagree with him:

Hoc verum scio quod qui eius memoriam iugiter retinet, et in amore eius iugiter gaudet. Ego igitur, solitarius heremita, dictus inter amatores Christi minimus [1 Corinthians 15.9], de amore loquar vobis interim prout michi dederit Deus. Set forte timeo, quia, quamquam loqui nescio, tamen tacere non queo. Quamobrem amore coactus, non alienum set quod ipse novi, loquor, quoniam non ab homine nec a carne et sanguine neque vero a me ipso habui, set a Christo [John 1.13]; et per Christum sapienciam apprehendi. (68.8–15)

[I know this to be true: that whoever keeps a continual memory of ⟨Christ⟩ also rejoices continually in his love. Therefore let me, a solitary hermit, said to be least among the lovers of Christ, nonetheless speak to you of love as far as God gives me to do. But I am very afraid, because while I do not know how to speak, I am unable to be silent. For this reason, urged by love, I will speak not of a strange matter but of what I know, since I have not had it from any human being, nor from flesh and blood, nor yet from myself, but from Christ; and through Christ I have laid hold of wisdom.]

In this passage the advantages of claiming that the perfect's experience of God's love is continuous become apparent; not only do *amor* and *canor* make the *perfectissimi* secure, they urge them, moment by moment, to speak, and guarantee the authenticity of what they say.[19] Although Rolle's claim forces him to challenge the opinions of his fellow-contemplatives, it also provides him with the necessary weaponry for doing so, for it makes this 'least of lovers' divinely inspired in a way that those who have achieved only rare and momentary union with God are by definition not. If love is what inspires the perfect to write, and their own experience of love ('quod ipse novi') is the subject about which they write, then the more love, the more inspiration; the logic of the argument (like the assumption on which it is based, that the more one desires to embrace Christ the more one does so) really is as crudely mathematical as this. Yet in making the argument point at himself, Rolle has to rely not on logic but on eloquence to fill the gap between his knowledge of his own experience and his readers' ignorance of the perfect life and of the full extent of his sanctity. Thus, as he relegates those who have not written of continual union to a place below the highest, he places heavy emphasis on the loquacity he has just denied possessing: 'Cumque vero aliquando perfecti, aliquando perfecciores, aliquando perfectissimi de caritate Dei scribere satagunt; constant profecto quia illi sermonem sapiencie excellencius ac iocundius proferunt, qui sapienciam increatam ardencius amaverunt' (70.23–71.1: 'But whenever sometimes the perfect, sometimes the more perfect, sometimes the most perfect strive to write about the love of God, it is surely agreed that those who love uncreated wisdom more ardently will produce words of wisdom more excellently and delightfully'). This seems to leave the reader with the task of distinguishing between perfect, more perfect and most perfect according to their respective 'excellence' and 'delightfulness' – that is, according to how elevated and joyful a spiritual experience they communicate, or create. On one level, this statement makes explicit Rolle's awareness that the success of his elaborate invention of his own authority depends on how far he can convince individual readers of his sanctity. Hence he implies that all the *sancti* need to be tested in the same way, and makes it clear that he has a direct incentive for developing his rhetorical skills as elaborately as possible: that he needs to be judged more excellent and delightful than 'plurimi sanctorum' who state that God cannot be embraced continually, if he is to carry his point about the *perfectissimi*. But on another level the reader is not being given any such arbitrating role, for Rolle now believes that he can be confident of his powers of persuasion. Having just claimed (and knowing the claim to be true) that he is divinely and perpetually inspired by an *Amor* who (as in John of Hoveden's *Philomena*) is at once Holy Spirit and Muse, and who thus simultaneously guarantees his sanctity and his literary virtuosity, he has good grounds for thinking that his eloquence will carry conviction. On this level, a reader's role is merely to succumb to the power of his words. The combination of these different attitudes to the reader, and hence to his own language, brings Rolle to the threshold of the position adopted in *Melos Amoris*, in which he can claim to be pre-eminently perfect simply because he is pre-eminently eloquent, but must at the same time strive for greater and greater eloquence in order to demonstrate his perfection.[20]

In the last section of *Super Canticum Canticorum*, Rolle displays not only the fervour of his love but also its boldness, making statements which imply a remarkably high view of his own status. This quality of *audacitas* is also an essential characteristic of the lovers of God as they are described in the first part of the work, for it is only through a bold fearlessness that they can embrace Christ and ignore the world's jibings. Rolle has made this point many times before, from *Incendium Amoris* on. But the *Exposicio super primum versiculum* does not only restate; it also develops the concept of fearlessness in a startlingly fearless new direction. Early in the first section of the work, Rolle proves the contemplative life to be superior to the active ('Verum est ergo quod Veritas ait, *Maria optimam partem elegit*', Luke 10.42, 7.7–8), but adds that it is important to be careful in arguing with actives who think otherwise, since they may be driven to spiritual pride by their own obduracy; he urges a lofty indifference to their cavils, unless they go too far and have to be denounced (7.19–8.2). Shortly after this (shifting his ground considerably), he addresses the question of why it is appropriate that the saints not only be confident but be so openly:

Hinc ergo devota mens suavitatem quesiti osculi presenciens se totam ad diligendum Deum offerre non desinit; et, omnibus mundi vanitatibus postpositis et oblitis, ad perfectam vite sanctitatem Christo ductore venit. Unde et ait, *Custodi animam meam quoniam sanctus sum* [Psalm 85.2]. Hec autem sanctitas non est in signis et labore corporis, set in virtutibus anime Deum veraciter diligentis. Unde et nonnullis mirum videtur quod audeat aliquis, eciam excellens quamvis sit, inter homines se sanctum dicere, cum apostoli dicebant se peccatum habere. Set hoc cito solvitur, si veritas pensatur: Paulus namque in uno loco dixit se *minimum apostolorum et non dignum vocari apostolum* [1 Corinthians 15.9]; alias dicebat se *pre omnibus laborasse* [1 Corinthians 15.10] et *bonum certamen certasse et fidem servasse* [2 Timothy 4.7]. Proculdubio sanctus fuit qui fidem servavit; et qui plus laborans apostolorum se dixit minimum, profecto veram habuit humilitatem. Sic ergo sancti ad laudem Conditoris de seipsis bonum coguntur proferre, quatinus vera humilitas semper maneat in intencione. Debemus autem cum quesiti fuerimus veritatem dicere, non mendacia loqui pro humilitate; non sic lingua nostra humilitatem appetat, ut veritatem relinquat. Vera autem aliquando tacere possumus, set falsa dicere vel mentiri non debemus. Non igitur ex arrogancia aut ex superbia loquimur set misericordiam Dei ac bonitatem eius in nobis attestamur. Quia secura spe et certa divine dileccionis cor nostrum sustollitur, ad exterius agendum et loquendum divinitus roboratur. Cum enim eterni amoris deliciis intra nos affluimus, fatemur verum quia tacere nescimus. Inde scriptum est: *Fluminis impetus letificat civitatem Dei* [Psalm 45.5]. Quemadmodum igitur nos magna et sublimia vobis eterna securitate nunciare cernitis, ita et vos ut eadem possitis facere fortiter et sine ficcione laboretis.　　　　(14.2–15.6)

[Hence the devout mind, anticipating the sweetness of the desired kiss, does not cease to offer itself totally to the love of God, and, after putting behind and forgetting all worldly vanities, comes, by the guidance of Christ, to perfect sanctity of life. For which reason it says *Guard my soul, for I am holy*. But this sanctity is not in signs and bodily labour, but in the virtues of the soul who truly loves God. For which reason it seems extraordinary to some people that anyone, however excellent he might be, should dare to affirm among people that he is holy, since the apostles used to say that they had sin. But this is quickly solved, if the truth is considered: for in one place Paul affirmed himself *the least of the apostles and not worthy to be called an apostle*; elsewhere he said he had *worked harder than others* and *had fought the good fight and kept the faith*. Without doubt he who kept the faith was holy; and he who, while working the most, said he was the least of the apostles, certainly had true humility. In the same way, therefore, the saints are compelled to reveal their own goodness for the praise of the Creator, since true humility always remains in their thought. But we ought, when we are asked, to speak truth, and not utter lies for the sake of humility; our speech should not strive so eagerly for humility as to relinquish the truth. We can sometimes be silent about true things, but we should not say false things or tell lies. We do not, then, speak out of pride or out of arrogance, but we witness the mercy of

God and his goodness in ourselves. Because our heart is raised up by hope, which is secure and certain of divine love, it is divinely strengthened to do and speak outwardly. For, when we are flowing within ourselves with the delights of eternal love, we confess the truth because we do not know how to be silent. On account of which it is written: *The force of the river makes glad the city of God.* In the same way, therefore, that you see us, in eternal security, announce great and lofty things to you, so you, too, should labour bravely and without feigning so that you can do the same.]

This passage makes a useful commentary on Rolle's self-presentation in the last part of *Super Canticum Canticorum* and in all his works from cap. 31 of *Incendium Amoris* on. He admits that for the saints to assert their sanctity 'inter homines' is problematic, but insists this is not a spiritual problem but merely one of self-presentation – for, at their most assertive, the saints are humble. (The *distinctio* between what we might call *humilitas in lingua* and 'humilitas in intencione' on which this argument turns itself shows how far Rolle has come since the beginning of *Incendium Amoris*.) He justifies the frankness of the saints about their own perfection in three ways: it glorifies God and leads others to him; it is *veritas*, which is more important than humility of speech; and it is forced on them by the vigour of their love ('coguntur proferre', 'tacere nescimus'). Thus the theme of divine coercion (a near relation to that of divine inspiration, see n. 19) is almost directly applied to Rolle's own self-referential, apologetic discourse, which is stated bluntly to be for the praise of God, and to be – the truth.

We have seen Rolle taking advantage of the position he works out here when arguing with his fellow-contemplatives in the last section of *Super Canticum Canticorum*. He does so even more directly, again in the language of truth and humility, in a parallel argument in the second section of the work, where he explains in pugnacious detail why the solitary life is a more elevated form of contemplative life than the coenobitic (25.22–29.14). Like that between active, contemplative and 'mixed' lives, the controversy between monks and hermits finds an inevitable place in Rolle's works as soon as he begins to claim a pre-eminent position for solitaries as the *perfecti* of the Church (see the introduction, section II). The substance of his case for hermits is the argument of cap. 31 of *Incendium Amoris*, that solitude is necessary for the practice of *canor*. This argument has special force in a work that defines perfection as continual rejoicing in God, and is conducted with much reference to love as more important than obedience. In deference to this principle, Rolle insists that love is the yardstick of perfection wherever it is found – although it is solitaries who love the most (26.26–27.7). But the content of his argument is of less importance than its tone and structure. He cites Anselm (see Arnould 1937a) as a representative of monks (ostensibly here against secular priests, not solitaries):

Presumpsit, autem, Anselmus docere monachos ideo eos plus quam aliquis secularis Deum diligere, quia fructum et arborem Deo volebant sub abbate offerre. Set profecto consequencia illa improbabitur quando veritas aperitur. Nam ibi videtur Anselmus magis blandiens monachis, quam veritatem sequens ... Unde et suum ordinem approbare cernitur cum illum solum, quasi aliis ad comparacionem eius relictis, laudare conatur. Et in hoc, quippe, probatur humilitatem amittere, quando se quia obendienciarius est ceteris digniorem non timet acclamare, presertim cum Veritas dicat: *Regnum Dei intra vos est* [Luke 17.21].   (25.22–6; 27.11–15)

[But Anselm presumed to teach that on that account ⟨i.e. the acknowledged holiness of some monks⟩ monks love God more than any secular, because they wished to offer the fruit and tree ⟨i.e. of charity⟩ to God under an abbot. But certainly that conclusion will be disproved when the truth is uncovered. For at that point Anselm seems more to be flattering monks than following truth. Thus he is also seen to approve his own order when he tries to praise only it, as if the others are left behind in comparison with it. And in this, to be sure, he is shown to lay aside humility – when he does not fear to acclaim himself worthier than others because he is a monk: especially since Truth says *The kingdom of God is within you.*]

Anselm's case is thoroughly undercut by the imputation of presumption and self-aggrandizement; he is at odds with *veritas*, who is identified with Christ, and, having the worst of both worlds, lays aside his humility in proclaiming something false. Rolle pleads that the reader recognize the truth, depicting the life of *canor* in some fine short passages and stating that he knows he is right: 'Ego Ricardus, utique solitarius heremita vocatus, hoc quod novi assero' (26.17–18). His knowledge of this matter, unlike Anselm's, is one with truth. This claim is taken provocatively far at the climax of the argument:

Hinc liquet veritas, quod ille, quiscumque sit, cuiuscumque ordinis sive secularis sive monachus sive solitarius, in divino amore ardencius rapitur, qui in canora iubilacione celica resonante simphonia suavius eterna contemplatur. Hec, utique, scribo non derogans cuiquam, sed scrutans veritatem; humilitatem non amittens, set verum prout potui loquens. Sic enim humilem me esse cuperem, quatinus veritatem relinquere non auderem. Unde de humili dicitur: *Humilem spiritum suscipiet gloria* [Proverbs 29.23]. De veraci vero: *Domine, quis habitabit in tabernaculo tuo?* Et respondetur: *Qui loquitur veritatem in corde suo, qui non egit dolum in lingua sua* [Psalm 14.1, 3]. Si quis forsitan verbis meis contradicere non timuerit, primum rogo ut seipsum diligenter consideret et qualis sit soliciter discuciat, si igne Spiritu Sancti cor suum senciat inardescere, et mentem suam divini amoris delicias canendo videat iubilare. Si quis vero hoc in se invenire poterit, michi nequaquam aliquando contrarius erit. Alius, autem, qui se habere putat quod non habet quamvis eciam scolas disputancium usque ad nomen magisterii frequentavit non me set ipsum reprobat, dum in hoc sapientem se ostendere nititur quod prorsus ignorat . . . Illa ergo que supra conversacionem vite vestre sunt scripta a sanccioribus non debetis reprehendere, set in quantum potestis humiliter imitari. Nec dicatis, 'Nos coram Deo maximum meritum habebimus', quia sic arrogancia mentitores totum amittetis. Qui enim boni sunt et vere Deum diligentes nullatenus sic loquuntur set seipsos pocius infimos reputant, ut in tempore iudicii superius ascendant. Mementote, ergo, quod non tantum valet altum sapere quam timere.   (28.7–29.14)

[Hence the truth is plain that he, whoever he may be and of whatever order, whether a secular or a monk or a solitary, is seized more ardently into divine love who contemplates eternity more sweetly resounding in tuneful jubilation with the heavenly symphony. Now I write this not criticizing anyone, but looking to the truth; not laying aside humility, but speaking the truth so far as I can. For I would wish to be humble only to the extent that I do not dare to abandon truth. With respect to which, it says of the humble: *Glory will sustain the humble spirit*. But of the truthful: *Lord, who will dwell in your tabernacle?* And it is answered: *He who speaks the truth in his heart, who does not speak deceit with his tongue*. If anyone perhaps is not afraid to contradict my words, I ask him first that he consider himself diligently and ponder carefully what kind of a person he is, whether he feels his heart burn with the fire of the Holy Spirit and sees his mind rejoice in singing the delights of divine love. But if anyone finds this in himself, he will never in any way be opposed to me in anything. But another, who thinks himself to have what he has not, however much he frequents schools of disputation all the way to the title of M.A., reproves not me but himself, since he tries to show himself wise in this matter in which he is wholly ignorant. So you should not criticize things which are written by holier people than yourselves about the manner of your life, but should humbly imitate so far as you can. Do not say, 'We will have the greatest merit before God', for as liars you will lose all by such arrogance. For those who are good and love God truly never speak thus, but rather consider themselves to be the least, so that they go up highest at the time of Judgement. Remember, then, that it is not so important to have lofty wisdom as to be fearful.]

Although the shape of his argument partly conceals the fact, Rolle is in exactly Anselm's position of resolutely approving his own order ('sive secularis sive monachus sive solitarius' is a paper concession, given the context of the statement). However, he insists that he lays aside only the appearance of humility, not its essence, in proclaiming the truth; the use of the phrase 'humilitatem non amittens' intentionally recalls the fact that earlier Anselm 'probatur humilitatem amittere'. That Rolle here uses his *experientia* as a basis for challenging a specified *auctor* is startling but logical in view of the way we have seen the saints 'urged by truth'. More startling – if still logical – is the way the passage tries to compel readers to accept its argument or face damning charges of spiritual pride and ignorance. Rolle is now so confident of the source of his inspiration, and so unabashed in proclaiming it, that he is prepared not only to argue his case, to cite Scripture, and to woo readers with his eloquence, but also to bludgeon them with assertions of his own canonical status. It is as though he identifies so closely with the text of which he is the commentator that he regards himself as sharing fully in its *auctoritas*.

Concluding this study of *Super Canticum Canticorum*, a work which we have seen is of real importance in Rolle's development, it is worth reminding ourselves of the obvious, by noting that the process of 'self-canonization' that I have traced from its origins in *Incendium Amoris* is not at all a common one – that its manifestations in this work are on the contrary quite extraordinary. In *Incendium Amoris*, Rolle introduces readers to a set of mystical experiences which he is aware have never been described before, and claims that they are of universal importance. In this work they have become essentially the only valid form of truly elevated mysticism, all others being relegated to the realm of the 'less perfect'. Moreover, they have grown in stature, so that they create a divide between those possessed of them and those who are not; the former are divinely inspired to the extent that their pronouncements are *per se* valid, testable only by others whose experience of God's love is of similar or greater intensity. Not only has Rolle argued himself into this position theoretically – and with more cogency than I have had space to give him credit for – he has overtly adopted a confident view of his own sanctity in his writing, and has even managed, after a fashion, to justify the fearlessness and aggression of his own language. Thus he has apparently put himself beyond the reach of anybody who might disagree, while articulating his mystical theology in ever more provocative ways. It is a feat of *audacitas* that retains its power to impress and to shock.

III

The elect are those who violently love God; the violence of their love compels them to cry out; those who cry out most loudly and most eloquently are those who love most continually. Here we have a recipe not only for exalting Rolle's sanctity, but for defining his literary output explicitly in terms of evangelism: for how else will the eloquence of the lover of God be measured except by its effectiveness in drawing others towards the same love? As I said earlier, Rolle is (with reason) confident of his rhetorical prowess. Nonetheless, a train of thought somewhat like the above seems to influence the direction of the works he wrote in this period of his career, moving him away from his dubiously successful attempts at pastoral writing in *Judica Me* towards the radical and simplified didacticism characteristic of evangelism. *Super Canticum Canticorum* indeed builds the evangelistic impulse into its model of the elect, at the opening of its final section:

Curremus in odore unguentorum tuorum. Ecce, fratres, mira amatoris Christi instancia! Dum *trahi* postulat [Song of Songs 1.2] et, quasi adhuc se impotentem ire per se dicens, in ipso desiderio perseverat, donec iam non solum letus est quia quemadmodum optavit trahitur, verum eciam alios secum admonens iam currere delectatur. (65.18–23)

[*Let us run in the odour of your ointments*. See, brothers, the wonderful importunity of the lover of Christ! She still desires to be *drawn*, and, speaking as though hitherto she has been incapable of proceeding by herself, perseveres in the same desire, until now, not only is she joyful because she is drawn just as she desires, but she also delights in admonishing others to run with her.]

In true evangelistic style, *Super Canticum Canticorum* ends by admonishing those who will not run in the odour of the ointments which Rolle has placed on such lavish verbal display; such people are running, too, but away from God, snuffing the sordid scents of carnal unguents as they go: 'Servus vero mundi in carnalibus unguentis . . . currere satagit' (78.19–21). An evangelistic mode enables him to return with renewed confidence to a simple, anagogical picture of a world already divided into opposing camps: those of the lovers of the world and of the lovers of God, both now seen not merely as running their ordained races to an eternal destiny, but as fighting one another on the way, so precisely opposed are their interests: 'Sic denique inter se adversantur amatores Dei et delectores mundi quia quod alter diligit alius odit' (78.12–14). Both kinds of lovers, in this final picture, cry out with delight at the sweet smell of heavenly, or carnal, joy ('Mundi amatores dulce et iocundum clamitant', 78.8–9); the world is turned into a place in which everyone, good and evil, seeks to give expression to their true or spurious delight, and attempts to persuade others to want to share in it.

This is the context for which the *Liber de Amore Dei contra Amatores Mundi* was written. A work of specifically evangelistic intent, it focusses to an even greater extent than is usual for Rolle on the division between *electi* and *reprobi*, taking full advantage of the satirical opportunities the latter's sins offer. It is written pugnaciously, in a style which excludes *ab initio* all but the readers who are ready to be convinced and converted, and so to show that they are of the elect. Yet it also treats these readers to some of the most lyrical writing in Rolle's works. Its overriding fiction, perhaps derived from the ending of *Super Canticum Canticorum* – that the world is the scene of a metaphysical contest between the lovers of God and of the world – allows Rolle full use both of the images of kingship that are so important in *Super Psalmum Vicesimum*, and those of sexual love which pervade *Super Canticum Canticorum*. While it is full of all his usual themes, couched in an alliterative high style similar to that of the last part of *Incendium Amoris*, it thus has the added verbal and dramatic interest of a courtly setting, being presented as an account of two competing male aristocracies, one secular, one spiritual, and of the way in which each acts out its version of courtly love: 'Habent igitur celestis amor et secularis sectatores suos, sed inter se continue decertant, quis illorum amatum suum amplius diligat, cum alter ad Christum alter ad mundum tanto ambitu suspirat' (3.27–30: 'Thus both heavenly and earthly love have their followers. But they contend continually with one another about which one loves his beloved more, as one sighs for Christ, the other for the world, [each] with so much ambition'). Like *Super Psalmum Vicesimum* and *Super Canticum Canticorum*, it thus emphasizes the imagery of *dulcor* more than that of *fervor* or *canor*.[21]

The fight in which the two sides are continually engaged is in practice more assumed than discussed, for any mention of how the reprobate persecute the lovers of God tends to be interrupted by assurances that the latter are indifferent to their enemies (3.130–140, 4.202–206). The lovers of God fight sin in themselves (3.118–129), the reprobate fight death (4.163–216) and persecute the elect, but for the most part the two sides seem to ignore one another – naturally enough, for the lovers of the world have turned from Christ, while those of Christ have turned from the world, and both sides regard the other as negligible. Nonetheless, the concept of competition is fundamental to the work, for in writing it Rolle apparently sees himself as engaged in a battle of eloquence in which he must strive to outdo the achievements (summed up in the phrase 'tanto ambitu') of secular love literature. The courtliness of the work's imagery is hence in competitive emulation of the literature of *fine amour*, while Rolle's habitual emphasis on eloquence finds a somewhat different basis.[22] In the last section of *Super Canticum Canticorum*, he attempts to surpass the ardour of his fellow-contemplatives in order to prove his status as one of the *perfectissimi*; here he must merely make spiritual love more attractive than sexual, and pour scorn on the worldly in response to their persecutions of the saints.

Much of *Contra Amatores Mundi* thus has a simplicity and clarity of purpose which none of the works I have discussed so far possess. In so far as it is a work of evangelism, it is an extroverted declaration of an already complete system of ideas and feelings, and does not contain the process of development through articulation that I have traced in *Incendium Amoris*, *Super Psalmum Vicesimum* and *Super Canticum Canticorum*. Only two passages deal with real difficulties, and although one of them takes up most of a chapter, both read like digressions from the work's main themes. At the same time, the work includes in its model accounts of the elect many of the themes that come into prominence in the two commentaries I have just discussed: the spiritual security of the elect; self-government and a continual enjoyment of divine love as a basis for that security; boldness as the main feature of that love; truth as a principle that is sometimes more important even than the need to be seen to be humble; the inferiority of monks as contemplatives (5.70–71). It accordingly seems likely that the work was written later than both *Super Psalmum Vicesimum* and *Super Canticum Canticorum* (see Excursus 1).

Manuscript copies of *Contra Amatores Mundi* divide it into either six or seven sections, usually unnumbered, and containing no explanatory rubrics; seven-section copies divide in two what the six-section copies regard as the work's first section (see Theiner 1968, pp. 42–62). There are literary grounds both for and against making such a division. It occurs at a suitable moment, for it follows a resounding peroration (1.118), and deliberately introduces a change of direction, and apparently a beginning, with fighting words: 'Iam linguis detractorum amputatis, electus Christi seipsum studeat dirigere, et quomodo Deum recte diligat curet audire' (2.1–3: 'Now the tongues of the detractors have been cut out, let the elect of Christ learn to set himself in order, and take care to hear how he may rightly love God'). The section that precedes this division is in four linked parts, which seem to form a kind of prologue. The first part consists of a passage condemning wordly insanity ('mundanorum insania', 1.1); in the second Rolle announces that 'we' (the saints?) have tried to expose the errors of the worldly and to preach truth in order to help the godly, and praises 'uncreated wisdom' ('sapiencia increata', 1.28) as the force that converts and makes secure the elect (1.22–25);[23] the third is a model account of the rise of the elect to the spiritual height; and the fourth returns us to the reprobate by remarking on their persecutions and how ineffective these are. All of this is presumably what is hoped will silence the reprobate, and has a satisfying arch-like shape to it. On the other hand, the second section of the seven-section copies also resembles a prologue. Much of this is an account of the chosen soul's progress to God, of a kind that abounds throughout Rolle's works. However, this one is unusually brief; the ascent to God is treated as so inevitable a matter that even at its earlier stages Rolle praises the lover of God with the fulsomeness he formerly reserved for the perfected soul: at the very beginning the soul assaults the enemy 'constans et fortis'(2.6), and quickly achieves *fervor* (2.28–29), while there is no question of her falling away. This triumphal progress is intended to show the world's inability to harm the saints, and leads to a confessional passage which recalls the prologue and cap. 15 of *Incendium Amoris*. Rolle tells his spiritual history briefly, concluding with *canor*: 'Mirabar quippe quod aliquis mortalium aliquando ad tantam melodiam caperetur, sed iam vere scivi per experimentum quod vera est dileccio apud Deum' (2.82–84: 'Certainly I was amazed that any mortal should ever be seized up to so great a melody, but now I know truly, by experience, that true love is with God'). This also looks like introductory material, intended to silence detractors and establish Rolle's credentials for writing.

What Theiner's base manuscript calls 'Capitulum Tercium' should thus be regarded as a first chapter, following an usually shaped prologue in two parts.[24] Appropriately, it begins with a statement that defines Rolle's purposes in writing:

Dum autem constet plurimos in gazofilacium Domini cum paupercula vidua [Mark 12.43] dona nimirum magna posuisse quia magni et divites qui ponunt, ego utique de paupertate et parvitate mea hoc quod habeo et sencio sine invidia et contencione pono. Arbitror ergo melius sentire humiliter quam ambulare *in magnis et in mirabilibus super me* [Psalm 130.1]. De eterna igitur dileccione tractare ad confusionem et despeccionem amoris temporalis compellor; immo et delector. Nam et hoc conscienciam meam a morsu immortalis vermis prorsus liberat et celesti dulcedine affectum suaviter obumbrat. Glorior utique in vocem caritatis prorumpere; plane etenim delectabile est quod amoris sapore permanet respersum. Quippe et universitas mundialis creature Dei, videlicet intellectivi spiritus necnon et angelici, diligere diligique appetit; et motiva cordis intencio quodammodo semper in amatum tendit.

(3.1–17)

[Now although it is true that many have placed gifts undeniably great in the Lord's treasury, alongside ⟨that of⟩ the wretchedly poor widow, since they are great and rich who give, I truly give from my poverty and insignificance this that I have and feel, without envy or contention. For I reckon it better to feel humbly than to walk *in great matters and wonders that are above me*. Therefore I am constrained to treat of eternal love to the confusion and contempt of temporal love – and in fact I am delighted to do so. For this also frees my conscience entirely from the bite of the immortal serpent, and overshadows my will delightfully with heavenly sweetness. I glory to break forth in the voice of charity; for truly a thing is fully delightful which remains sprinkled with the scent of love. For the whole of God's worldly creation – that is to say intellective beings and also angels – desires to love and to be loved, and the motive purpose of the heart also in some manner always strives towards a loved object.]

This passage gives an oddly confused sense of the source of Rolle's authority as a writer, for the language of inspiration ('compellor', 'prorumpere') occurs

beside more modest terms ('tractare', 'arbitror'); the claims he articulates in
Super Canticum Canticorum are here, but are veiled.[25] The mock-humility of
this opening *captatio benevolentiae* – the poor widow's gift was of course the
best, and Rolle's *paupertas* is a sign of his holiness – is also couched in
unusually mannered language; Rolle's words will be bitter for secular lovers,
but will cover him with sweetness and be sprinkled with the scent of love.
Since this language is immediately juxtaposed with a technical account of the
function of love as a power of the soul, it seems that Rolle is out to impress as
well as to appear modest.

Cap. 3 is an account of the soul's ascent to God, preceded by a discussion
of the superiority of heavenly love to earthly, and by this personal appeal:

Hucusque decepti iuvenes, vel modo saltem amare addiscite; sed pocius quem non
amastis deinceps amate. Venite mecum; audite dileccionem; amare concupiscite; sed
eternum qui vivificat, non temporalem qui occidit, amorem gustate. Quoniam adhuc
et ego iuvenis amator, tamen mirabilis, quia dilectam meam continue cogito, et ab eius
amplexibus non recedo.   (3.69–75)

[O young men who until now have been deceived, now at least learn to love; but
instead love him whom you have not loved before. Come with me; hear of love; desire
to love – but taste eternal love which gives life, not temporal love which kills. For I,
too, am a young lover – though a wonderful one, since I think continually of my love,
and I do not withdraw from her embraces.]

This passage perhaps explains the modest restraint of the chapter's opening,
for here Rolle poses not as the formidable *perfectissimus*, but as one young
lover among many, who is distinguished only by his prowess in never leaving
the embrace of his beloved, and who seeks to woo *iuvenes* away from their
sensuality into more satisfying forms of passion. The appeal is artificial, for
Rolle cannot truly expect to win over devotees of *fine amour* so simply, given
his deep disgust at those who have already in any way succumbed to fleshly
desires; but this accords with the conscious literariness of much of the work.
The love to which Rolle is summoning the *iuvenes* quickly reveals itself to be
the same process of ordering the soul and ascending to *canor* he expounds
everywhere, although here with more than usual reference to the courtly
activities of sex and warfare. As in cap. 2, the account is also one of an
automatic victory rather than of a difficult spiritual battle. Deploying
battalions of adverbs, Rolle has the soul reaching joy 'speedily' by thirsting
'violently'; shunning evil 'wholly', suffering trials, but overcoming enemies
'manfully'; conquering kingdoms, destroying castles, building her own;
returning a conqueress to her own land (3.104–122). It is unclear for much of
this account which stage of the spiritual life is under discussion, but it seems
that the confidence which Rolle attributes to mature lovers is now associated
with spiritual beginners, once they have 'truly' undertaken reformation of
life. Perhaps he considers such confidence appropriate to, and likely to be
appreciated by, *iuvenes*.

Cap. 4 takes up with the 'amatrix Christi' (4.1) where cap. 3 left her, at the
summit of the contemplative life ('ad culmen contemplative vite', 4.2). It at

once completes the model account begun in cap. 3, and initiates the discussion of the 'culmen' of contemplation that occupies cap. 5. It also shares with caps. 5–6 two slightly unexpected emphases, on images of light and dark, and on the related theme of death; while its opening resembles other passages of Rolle, he rarely describes mystical ecstasy with such attention to visual images (Christ as the 'sol iusticie', 16–17, 58), or focusses so seriously on the way *canor* released the soul from fear of death (see 62–86, but compare *Incendium Amoris*, cap. 16). Perhaps these themes are meant for *iuvenes* who were once secular lovers contemplating their mistresses in a *hortus conclusus*, from which time and death were fictionally excluded (*Roman de la Rose* 339–406); other parts of cap. 4 also seem designed for such readers, contrasting *canor* not with the liturgy (as in *Incendium Amoris*, cap. 31) but with the secular music beloved by active Christians, and ending with an attack on 'Babylonians' (163), who attend to their bodies by honouring doctors, but ignore the spirit and descend terrified into death and darkness.

However, one passage turns from the matter in hand to consider Rolle's literary method and message in a manner which is not at all evangelistic:

Morimur ergo in gaudio qui in amore vivimus . . . Sed caveat sibi lector quia hec verba communiter in persona omnium non dicuntur qui Christiano nomine censentur, sed in illorum persona qui sic sine ficcione et sine presumpcione de se senciunt qualiter in hoc volumine scripta legunt. Nam in plerisque opusculis meis sic soleo facere, nequando aliis alta scribens de me ipso videar desperare . . . Cogor autem hec isto modo dicere, ne quod aliis scribo me iudicent caruisse; vero *Nemo* hominum hoc donum *novit, nisi qui accepit* [Revelation 2.17]. Pauci ergo sunt, vel nulli qui illud referunt, quia forsitan illud nescierunt, si autem habuerint sed et aliis predicare nec verbo nec exemplo voluerunt. Estimo hoc ab eis ideo fieri, quia putabant tam gloriosum munus omnibus communiter non debere conferri; unde apostolus ait quia *raptus in* tercium celum, *audivit archana* Dei, *que non licet homini loqui* [2 Corinthians 12.2–4]. Sed vere necesse fuit ut apostolo multa revelarentur per quem et per cuius doctrinam ecclesia contra hereticos et scismaticos stabiliter fundaretur, que pluribus sanctis forsitan et nobis necesse non est revelari, cum iam ecclesia Deo concedente et agente contra venenatam doctrinam undique sit munita. Sive ergo sic fuerit, sive aliter, ad laudem Dei et profectum Christanorum, illud et verbo et exemplo conor ostendere quomodo et sine modo in eius amore michi donavit Christus iubilare. Sed quidem si iam cogitarem tacere subito venit in me ut cogar narrare; urgenti igitur caritati quis resistere audeat, aut pulsanti Deo quis assurgere contradicat? Amantes itaque eciam aliis amorem predicare studiumus, nam et nobis hoc valde utile est, quia tanto ardencius et suavius in amore capimur, quanto libencius hoc quod capere potuimus aliis predicamus.   (4.84–92, 118–140)

[So we who live in love die in joy. But let the reader beware, for such words are not spoken communally, in the person of all who reckon themselves Christians, but in the person of those who without lying and without presumption observe in themselves whatever they read written in this volume. For in most of my little works I make a habit of doing this, in case I should seem to despair for myself while writing high things for others. But I am compelled to speak in this way, in case people think that I lack the thing that I write of for others; yet *No one knows this gift unless he has received it*. So there are few or none who relate it, possibly because they have not known it, but, if they have, because they still did not want to preach it to others by word or example. I think they acted thus because they thought that so glorious a gift should not be conferred on everyone communally. So the apostle says that, *caught up into the third heaven, he heard divine secrets which it is not granted people to speak.* But indeed it was necessary that much should be revealed to the apostle, through whom and by whose teaching the Church would be solidly grounded against heretics and schismatics, which perhaps need not be revealed to more saints and to us, since now the Church is strengthened on all sides against poisonous teaching by the gift and the work of God. Whether it was for this reason or another, I am trying, by word and example, for the praise of God and the advancement of Christianity, to show by what means and how measurelessly Christ has granted it to me to rejoice in his love. But if indeed I thought to be silent, suddenly it comes to me, so that I am compelled to explain. For who would dare to resist when urged by charity? Or when God demanded, who would refuse to rise up? Therefore we lovers have studied to preach also to others of his love; for this is also extremely useful for us, because we are seized the more ardently and sweetly in love the more gladly we preach to others about what we have been able to receive.]

This passage is split in two by an important discussion of *canor* (quoted in Excursus I, item 4), which is similar to that in caps. 31–33 of *Incendium Amoris*; indeed, both here and in cap. 5 there are frequent reminders of the later chapters of that work. The passage begins with Rolle justifying his use of first-person plural forms ('verba communiter'), and warning readers against applying his words too readily to themselves (compare *Incendium Amoris* 247.20–36); he adds that he has to speak 'isto modo' in order to be credible, since the gift of which he writes '*Nemo . . . novit nisi qui accepit*'. This touches on Rolle's whole problem with verifiability in an unusually sensitive way: it seems he is concerned lest he recreate his own experience too convincingly, giving his readers delusions of grandeur. However, the main discussion which this justification prefaces initially seems unrelated to it. The issue is double-horned: the fact that almost nobody but himself ('pauci vel nulli', a worried little phrase) has written about *canor* must either be because hardly anyone, including even the saints, has experienced it, or because those who have have thought the matter too high for their readers. Rolle uneasily ignores the first possibility, but has to justify his own loquacity by redefining the silence of his predecessors as like Paul's over the 'archana Dei'; this, he argues, was a special case which cannot be used in evidence against him, since he is not revealing, and does not even know, 'secrets'. This is unsatisfactory, since it defends Rolle only against the imputation that he is failing to imitate Paul's silence; it does not explain why previous lovers of God have chosen to keep silent about *canor*, as though, contrary to Rolle's assertion, it *is* one of the 'archana Dei'. Nonetheless, he reasserts that he engages in teaching others about *canor* 'et verbo et exemplo', then mentions other grounds for 'preaching': that God and the inner promptings of the soul demand it; and that it is useful for the preacher as well as for others. The idea that *canor* is too high a matter to be shared is left hanging.

What is behind this worried and inconclusive digression? Rolle seems to be facing two problems here, one to do with evangelism, the other with the uniqueness of his mystical system. In *Incendium Amoris* the fact that his writing centres on personal experience gives such satisfaction that he asserts exultantly that he has never found accounts of *canor* written or discussed (237.21–23, 240.17–31); he compensates for the impossibility of verifying his statements about *canor* from the *auctores* by referring to his own *experientia* for proof. In the aggressive context of *Super Canticum Canticorum*, he takes a similar stance by distinguishing the *perfectissimi* – a group of which he is the only named member – from 'most of the saints' who write of love; again, rather than summoning to his aid accounts of experiences analogous to spiritual song, he relies on his own eloquence to argue the importance of (and to demonstrate the existence in his own life of) a continuous experience of *canor*. The effect these works have is to imply – although of course he never says this – that if nobody but Rolle has had the experience of continuous *canor*, this must be because he is pre-eminent as a lover of God, and has gone further than anyone else. But at this point in *Contra Amatores Mundi*, the disadvantages of his splendid isolation are close to the surface, for he is near admitting that the uniqueness of his doctrine of *canor* casts doubt on its truth, and that he is thus compelled to assert it in a forceful way even though he fears this may be reprehensible. Why might it be so? Because it may be that his experience of *canor should* be treated as one of the 'archana', which does not speak to the real spiritual needs of his readers, and may even, indeed, put them in spiritual danger. *Super Canticum Canticorum* treats evangelism as manifesting the boldness of the lovers of God. But here, in writing a work of evangelism, Rolle briefly becomes aware of complexities and pastoral responsibilities, and questions the very basis on which his career of audacious eloquence is founded.

Considered negatively, this digression could thus be described as a momentary loss of nerve. Considered positively, it is a meditation, of uncharacteristic self-honesty, on what Rolle now calls 'preaching' – on evangelism – and the relationship between evangelism and spiritual boldness. The moment of honesty, or fear, soon passes. The end of the digression shelves the whole question of responsibility by changing the assumptions on which Rolle's argument is based. Suddenly it becomes unforgivably bold to resist the promptings of God and fail to preach, however high the matter (we are back to the view that the saints' writing is inspired); preaching is redefined in terms of its usefulness to the speaker; and Rolle takes refuge again in 'verba communiter', representing all the lovers of God as silent no longer, but speaking from the heart as he does.

However, the digression has left a mark, for one of the issues it raises, that of the uniqueness of Rolle's mystical experience, reappears in cap. 5 in the form of a long defence of his definitions of holiness and mystical experience against two possible contenders: the notion that the summit of the spiritual life lies in penitential tears rather than in love and joy (which Rolle deals with in 5.19–53, in a discussion closely related to one in *Incendium Amoris*, cap. 40); and the claim that a perfect vision of God is possible in this life (which occupies him from 5.182 to 5.325, and makes much use of the images of light and dark introduced in cap. 4). Rolle's defensiveness is evident in many features of his writing in this chapter. As though in response to the digression in cap. 4, his arguments are backed up by biblical *auctoritates*, and appear to rely relatively little on his own experience. Where he does describe it, he reinterprets it in a way which brings it as close as possible to the inexpressible vision of Paul:

Verum fateor vires meas succumbere nitens loqui de eterno amore, quia verbis exprimére nequeo quantum de divine dileccionis suavitate in mente concupio; lingua deficit; cogitacio non sufficit, nam omnem humanum superat intellectum. Aperui os meum ad Deum meum, et infusa est in me tanta iocunditas ut meipsum obliviscerer; nec sensi ubi fui, Dei solius memorans: vel ad celum raptus fui vel ad me melos celicum condescendit. (5.182–189)

[In truth, I confess that my powers fail in trying to speak of eternal love, because I cannot confess in words how much of the sweetness of divine delight I long for in my mind. Speech fails, thought does not suffice, for it is above all human intellect. I opened my mouth to my God, and such joyfulness was poured into me that I forgot myself. I did not know where I was, remembering God alone. Either I was rapt into heaven, or the heavenly song descended upon me.]

The 'vel . . . vel' of the last sentence recalls Paul's '*Sive in corpore nescio, sive extra corpus nescio*' (2 Corinthians 12.2). *Incendium Amoris*, cap. 15 makes it clear that Rolle's gift of *canor* did 'descend from heaven', rather than lifting him there (189.21–25), and cap. 37 of the same work (254.26–255.14) argues that his own experience of rapture *in corpore* (in which the senses are not suspended) is superior to the *excessus mentis* he alludes to here. This passage is thus inconsistent, as well as disingenuous, in the way it rewrites Rolle's standard account of how he received *canor* in terms which aim to turn it into an equivalent of Paul's experience. Having failed in cap. 4 to defend his own audacity satisfactorily against Paul's reticence, he now makes out that his preaching of *canor* is actually equally reticent, incapable of capturing anything of a profoundly ineffable experience. Other references to himself are equally defensive. He twice begs the reader not to regard him as presumptuous for referring to himself (5.38–40, 402–408) and, while he alludes to his uniqueness as a practitioner of *canor*, he does so indirectly, by lamenting that he can find nobody else who loves God as he does (5.90–171; compare *Incendium Amoris*, cap. 34). His discussion of the vision of God, which argues that an unclouded vision is not possible in this life, is laborious and diffident. Rolle relies yet again on Paul, who did not claim actually to see God in the third heaven (5.246–258), and builds a case from 2 Corinthians 12 for regarding the purifying and glorifying qualities of *canor* as superior to those of what he insists is *aenigmatica* not *perfecta visio* – at one point even apparently treating *canor* as the same as *perfecta visio*. Even after this formal-looking argument, he takes shelter from his critics by stating that he is insignificant compared to the Fathers, and implying that absolute truth is as hidden in this life as the vision of God, in a passage that seems to be another reflection on the gulf between his own accounts of *canor* and the experiences described by other mystics.[26] Here we are far from the certainties of *Super Canticum Canticorum* as to the nature of *veritas*. Yet we are even further from real self-doubt or from concessions. The last part of the chapter follows much the course of the digression in cap. 4, shelving the discussion and arguing for exactly his original claim, that *canor* is the highest form of mystical experience, and that it can be continual (5.326–401, especially 339–358). In the light of this ending, it is clear that he does not truly face the problems of the relationship between *canor* and other forms of mystical experience, or of the uniqueness of his own testimony to *canor*; he cares about these issues only in so far as they can be used against his own position. Not surprisingly, the chapter's final disclaimer is actually a reassertion that *audacitas* is an appropriate quality for a lover of God to display:

Sed admoneo pium lectorem, ne me aut arrogantem aut superbum iudicet, ubi ardua et incognita me loquentem videt. Non enim propter me loquor, sed propter gloriam et laudem Dei, et lectorum utilitatem. Nam et ipsi si eternum regem veraciter cupiunt diligere, hec et maiora forsitan post modicum audebunt enarrare. Igitur, quamvis lector in se hec omnia non senciat, tamen non contempnat nec diffidat. (5.402–407)

[But I admonish the pious reader not to judge me arrogant or proud where he sees me speaking of hard and unknown things: I do not speak for my own sake, but for the glory and praise of God and the benefit of readers. For if they truly desire to love the eternal king, perhaps they, too, will be bold to tell of these and greater things after a little while. Therefore although the reader may not feel all these things in himself, let him not despise or distrust them on that account.]

At the end of caps. 4–5 of *Contra Amatores Mundi*, we are as unclear as before as to the relationship between *canor* and other forms of mystical experience, and the problem of the uniqueness of Rolle's experience is still unresolved.

Cap. 5 keeps up a pretence that its purpose is primarily didactic, not apologetic; but the characteristic manner of *Contra Amatores Mundi* does not resume until cap. 6, where the discussion returns to the topic abandoned in cap. 4, fear of death. This fear is reintroduced by means of a striking anecdote in which Rolle confesses to having been superstitiously terrified by the death of a patroness, and meditates on the vileness of the death of the body (6.1–60). The rest of the chapter focusses on the same themes, discussing the false boldness of carnal lovers who do not fear death but ought to, the true boldness of holy lovers who fear neither death nor earthly tribulation (6.80–110), and the dangers associated with carnality and with women. There is much of the language of social status that dominates cap. 3; Rolle was evidently conscious of needing to reassert his original intention in this work, of writing 'de amore Dei contra amatores mundi'.

So much is also true of cap. 7. This final chapter begins with an appeal to 'pudice virgines' (7.1), which parallels the appeal to *iuvenes* in cap. 3 and serves to introduce warnings about the perils of womankind especially useful to these *iuvenes* (7.61–65). There follows an account of the distinguished part

love will play at the Last Judgement, where it will serve as a yardstick for all
the virtues, and privilege its followers, the 'sancti amatores Dei' (7.107),
above all others (7.90–201). Here Rolle is able to slip in one final reflection on
the relationship between mystical love and preaching:

Qui bene agit et bene predicat meritum habebit secundum magnitudinem caritatis sue,
cum aureola que est decencia quedam premii, et debetur doctoribus sanctis, virginibus
puris, et martiribus iustis; quia causa facit martirem, humilitas virginem Deo
placentem, et sanctitas ordinat doctorem. Qui vero iustus et sanctus est, sed non
docet, nec summa nec minima nunciat, premium sorcietur prout magis vel minus
amore ardebat. (7.113–121)

[Whoever acts well and preaches well will acquire merit according to the greatness of
his charity, with the aureole which adds lustre to the reward and is earned by holy
teachers, pure virgins and just martyrs; for the cause makes a martyr pleasing to God,
humility a virgin, and holiness ordains the teacher. Yet whoever is just and holy but
does not teach, nor proclaims greater nor lesser things, will be allotted a reward
according to the more or the less he burns in love.]

This passage introduces a new element into Rolle's thoughts about his own
evangelistic activity by implying that he is now hoping to be accorded a
preacher's *aureola* as well as the supreme heavenly reward due him because of
his love; he has more to say about this in *Melos Amoris*. It also has the effect of
separating the activities of loving God and proclaiming that love – a move that
is perhaps intended as a belated justification of the assertion in cap. 4 that
many have experienced *canor* yet kept silent about it, but which is odd at the
end of a work that is openly built on an equation of love with evangelistic
eloquence. As so often, the oddity is not noticed, or is swept aside by the
mounting eloquence of the work's peroration: one last model account of the
elect, which is designed to move towards a splendid series of encomia of love,
as blatantly decisive as the end of a Beethoven symphony. Love is singular,
chaste and holy; vehement, blazing, strong and ravishing; spontaneous,
forceful, shameless, inextinguishable; inseparable, insatiable, insuperable,
violent, impetuous; excellent, incomparable, powerful, ravishing God to
humanity and drawing humanity to God; making people into contemplatives
and covering their sins (7.253–300).

All this is ending on a note both safe and impressive. The language of much
of this ending is borrowed from Bernard, Hugh and Richard of St Victor, and
from Rolle's own earlier works.[27] In any case, almost any claim can freely be
applied to the abstraction *Amor* without any theological statement seeming
to be made; the effect of this passage is principally poetic, a virtuoso feat of
amplificatio with little actual meaning. At the same time, throughout much of
Contra Amatores Mundi, *Super Psalmum Vicesimum* and *Super Canticum
Canticorum*, we have found these same epithets applied to the saints who are
inspired by love, as well as to the Holy Spirit, who is love, and who inspires
the saints to ascend to God and preach truth to the Church. Since in these
works Rolle writes explicitly as a saint, inspired by the Holy Spirit to
proclaim truths about sanctity, most of these epithets are also applicable to

the works themselves, in all their passionate rhetorical and theological audacity. Love is Rolle's aggressive, fearless Muse, which sings in this peroration of its own glory, daring and prowess, in ravishing God to the reader, the reader to God. The matter and manner of the work are revealed as one thing: both are love – violent, exciting, remorselessly self-referential. Only in *Melos Amoris* will this unity be taken still further, to the point where this prophet of *canor* is inevitably heading: to a fusion of mystical theory with rhetoric, in which the passionate words to which Love inspires the saint in his praise of the joy of continual *canor* cease merely to represent mystical experience, and instead actually become it.

7

Contemplative life, *Canor: Melos Amoris*

As Rolle approached the writing of *Melos Amoris*, perhaps during the mid-1340s (see Excursus I), he must have felt that he was reaching the climax of his career as an *auctor*. The hard labour of establishing the importance of his chosen *materia*, and of resolving in a satisfactory way the awkward relationship between extolling it and extolling himself, had been more or less completed by the end of *Incendium Amoris*. The secondary but still vital tasks of defining the full significance of *canor*, as a continual enjoyment of God which guarantees the spiritual security of its recipient, and then of defending that definition against the major *auctoritates* of the mystical life (the 'plurimi sanctorum'), had also been accomplished: first on a small scale in *Super Psalmum Vicesimum*, then in audaciously extended form in *Super Canticum Canticorum* and *Contra Amatores Mundi*. What had begun as an almost insuperable problem of persuading readers that his unique experiences were real and God-given had become a rich opportunity to exult in the greatness of the gifts that had been bestowed on him, with a divinely inspired eloquence that was itself one of those gifts and which could not fail to convince. The way forward was clear. The crowning stage in the long process of revelation must be a celebration of *canor*, matching but also transcending all he had written from the perspectives of *fervor* and *dulcor*: a work, then, which would cover much of the same ground, but in a manner that would reveal yet more of the *archana Dei* known only to the *perfectissimi*, and in a style of unimagined grandeur. The work would be a supreme challenge both to his literary powers and to his spiritual balance, testing again and again the boundaries between aureate eloquence and empty bombast, holy audacity and deadly presumption. Yet, secure in his continual intimacy with the source of all sanctity and eloquence, he must have been supremely confident that he could succeed.

As we shall see in this chapter, the actual situation that emerges in the course of *Melos Amoris* is rather more complicated than the expectations I have just speculatively outlined. In many ways Rolle certainly did succeed; the work achieves almost all it sets out to do, triumphantly recapitulating the themes we have watched developing in the course of the previous chapters, and doing so with a breathtaking eloquence and daring. But by the time we reach its end we are aware, I think, that the victory is in part a Pyrrhic one – for the work's very success unexpectedly reveals basic structural flaws in

Rolle's self-conception as an authoritative writer on the spiritual life. Put differently, the tensions that lie only just beneath the surface of *Super Canticum Canticorum* and *Contra Amatores Mundi* are inexorably exposed by their appearance in a work whose whole purpose is to celebrate, with crystalline brilliance, the harmonious perfection of the saints and the impotence of all that threatens them. What makes this process of exposure both so fascinating and in the event so productive is that Rolle becomes aware of it himself, and is thus able to turn the final part of *Melos Amoris* into a preliminary response to it. The result is a scramble to reorganize and reinterpret, to address long ignored questions and demote long-dominant themes, which by the work's end has transformed what began as a confident culmination into the first steps of yet another new and important phase of Rolle's career.[1]

I

Viewing *Melos Amoris* from a distance, with a clarity of focus it is well-nigh impossible to maintain at closer quarters, the work already seems like a kaleidoscope, in which every idea, image and structure we have encountered in Rolle's earlier works appears, divorced from its old context, part now of a luminous, shifting pattern whose strange beauty holds ear and eye even while the mind slides off in confusion. It is as if the jumbling of kinds of writing and modes of address that initially makes reading *Incendium Amoris* so annoying has been patterned until it becomes a formal principle; indeed, the sense that we are reading a transfigured version of *Incendium Amoris* is stronger and more frequent here even that it was in *Contra Amatores Mundi*, from the work's title to its opening (which does for *canor* what its earlier equivalent does for *fervor*), to its habit of shuffling between third-person discourse and autobiography, to one of its final chapters (55), where Rolle's youthful fantasy about singing his life away like a nightingale makes an unexpected reappearance. Rolle also thought of the two works in similar generic terms, dividing *Melos Amoris* into a prologue (cap. 1) and fifty-seven probably unnumbered sections (caps. 2–58), and referring to it in *Super Lectiones Mortuorum* as a *liber* ('Liber de Perfeccione et Gloria Sanctorum').[2] However, *Incendium Amoris* is not the only work it resembles and transforms. *Melos Amoris* also uses the oratorical style of biblical exposition familiar from works such as *Super Canticum Canticorum*, this time commenting on a diversity of favourite texts (mostly from the Song of Songs and the Psalms) in a rhapsodic manner referred to either as preaching ('pulcriorem quam potero predicare', 4.11) or as *postillating*: 'De gloria et perfeccione sanctorum precellencium postillas proferam que piis placeant' (15.6–7: 'I will proffer postils that may please the pious about the glory and perfection of pre-eminent saints'), Rolle announces, in outlining his intentions in writing (see Arnould 1957, p. xvii, n. 2). One's lasting and overwhelming impression is, indeed, of the work as a vast essay in the self-conscious eloquence which has been Rolle's dominant note from cap. 31 of *Incendium Amoris* on, but whose significance is not fully articulated until the final section of *Super Canticum Canticorum*: an essay, moreover, in which a single stylistic feature, alliteration, has become the governing principle, and a single subject, *canor*, has come to have precedence over all others. The style of *Melos Amoris* is astonishing: long, apparently rambling sentences held together by strings of alliterating words, with a strong rhythmic pattern which has been seen as an attempt to create a Latin version of alliterative English verse (the tradition of alliterative English prose, to which Rolle himself was to make notable contributions, is a more likely model).[3] *Contra Amatores Mundi*, we noted, has a quality of literariness to it, part of a fiction that it is written in competition with secular love literature; here, where the poetic, aural features of language are totally dominant, that quality is omnipresent – a continual reminder of the poetic, aural and continual experience of *canor* the work celebrates. If *Melos Amoris* takes *Incendium Amoris* as a structural model on which to play many of its dazzling variations and elaborations, the eloquence with which it does this owes more to the group of works associated with Rolle's experience of *dulcor*.

Yet on a closer inspection, one of these works, *Super Canticum Canticorum*, proves to have an even more intimate relationship with *Melos Amoris* – both stylistically and structurally – than any of this so far implies. Both Allen (pp. 82, 244) and Arnould (pp. lxvii–lxxi) have pointed out that the two works share common preoccupations and even some material, discussing the relative merits of hermits and monks in closely similar ways, playing elaborately with the idea of 'ordered love' (especially in their later sections), and often sounding strikingly similar to one another.[4] But the most significant use of *Super Canticum Canticorum* in *Melos Amoris* is a series of direct borrowings early in the work, which are far more extensive than has been noticed; for, after the prologue (cap. 1), the next ten chapters of *Melos Amoris* constitute a huge expansion of the first pages of *Super Canticum Canticorum* (1.1 to *circa* 10.13). At the beginning and end of this group of chapters, it is not always possible to discern the process of borrowing clearly; most of cap. 2 is only generally dependent on its predecessor (compare 1.1–2.15), and in caps. 9, 10a and 12–13 there is a gradual fading-out of direct borrowing. But for the most part *Melos Amoris* expands its source systematically, working through the text literally line by line, omitting little and almost always keeping to the original order. The text of *Super Canticum Canticorum* is woven into the narrative and sentence structure of *Melos Amoris*, and is not marked off in any way. Sometimes passages are included unmodified; sometimes phrases are expanded or qualified in brief interpolations which keep the sentence structure and general sense of the original; sometimes, on the other hand, they are worked into sentences which express different ideas from their point of departure; and sometimes passages of *Melos Amoris* are verbally independent of *Super Canticum Canticorum*, while commenting on it indirectly. There are explanations, modifications, amplifications, rhetorical arabesques of all kinds, but all the material in this large group of chapters operates within parameters defined by the argument of *Super Canticum Canticorum*.[5] Thus (see [1]) cap. 2 uses only the opening sentence of its source directly, but follows its contours throughout, moving from the 'daring' holy kiss to wicked earthly ones and back, and making of its fairly simple original a grand opening statement of the theme not this time of *dulcor* but of *canor*. Cap. 4 (see [3]) can be seen as an exposition of Psalm 38.13 ('*I am a pilgrim and a stranger*'), which cap. 3 (10.18, see [2]) has repeated from *Super Canticum Canticorum*; using the next phrases from the latter as its base, cap. 4 develops a discussion of the 'fatherland', contrasting the wanderings of *electi* and *reprobi* with much play on the themes of motion and stillness, tumult and quiet. In cap. 5 Rolle's statement of his intentions in writing (15.6–9, see [4]) relays the first passage of serious exposition in *Super Canticum Canticorum* ('In hiis verbis' etc.; 3.26–4.3); *Melos Amoris* follows the structure of its source by implying (not very helpfully) that it, too, is beginning detailed biblical exposition after four presumably introductory chapters. Chapter 7 (see [6]) weaves a passage of *Super Canticum Canticorum* into a postil on Song of Songs 1.4 ('*I am black but comely*') – though the passage has little relevance to the text it is made to comment on. In short, this group of chapters can be seen as having any conceptual coherence only in the light of its relationship to *Super Canticum Canticorum*. In spite of the implied presence of *Incendium Amoris* behind many of its features, it seems, remarkably, that *Melos Amoris* started out largely as a conscious expansion of this, Rolle's most audacious earlier work.

The early chapters of *Melos Amoris* cannot be regarded as a retraction, a conceptual revision or even an explanation of their source; they add some theological discussion, a great deal of rhetorical colouring, and scores of references to *canor*, but do not, at least on the surface, contribute to what Rolle has said already (and with far greater clarity). Probably one of the purposes *Super Canticum Canticorum* served was pragmatic; Rolle might easily have felt the need to follow a pre-existing thread of argument as a means of steadying himself while becoming used to the technical difficulties of writing his new work. But the most important thing the relationship between the two works shows is that Rolle was both conscious of and serious about the process of progressive, self-transcending revelation whose course I have been outlining over the last two chapters. In *Melos Amoris* the language and literary structures associated with *dulcor*, like those associated with *fervor*, really are systematically swept up to a new level of eloquence, as though in a literary enactment of Rolle's first experience of *canor*, when sweetness was swept up into joyful song, and what was previously said could from then on be sung (*Incendium Amoris* 189.11–18). If we want to understand what this, Rolle's supreme technical achievement, was written for, it follows that we must turn our attention to examining the precise relationship *Melos Amoris* articulates between itself and the mystical experience of *canor*.

The fullest explanation of this relationship is provided by the work's
prologue (cap. 1), which I quote here in full and discuss in detail:

Amor utique audacem efficit animum, quem arripit ab imis dum eterni Auctoris
incendium amicam inflammat et suscipit in sublimitatem supra sophiam secularem ut
non senciat nisi sanctitatem. Urget igitur amoris habundancia ut audeam aperire
eloquium ad informacionem aliorum, ostendens altitudinem amancium ardentissime
iusticiamque iubilancium iocunde in Iesu ac charitatem canenecium in conformitate
celica, necnon et claritatem conscienciarum capacium increati caloris et delectacionis
indeficientis; quatinus quisque, comperiens quomodo Conditor iuvenculum *In
germen gesserit iudicii* [Jeremiah 33.15], non dicat deinceps quia non dignatur Deus
indulcorare homines in hoc mundo nec magnificare modernos in melliphona multitudine sicut solebat sanctos qui antiquitus ambulabant. Denique devociores in degustacione divine dulcedinis non degebant, a tempore quo inciperent humiles experiri
amoris electuarium, quam adhuc ducuntur a desolacione ad domum Dominatoris; et
non finientur funditus hec fastigia a filiis fidelium donec *Effundatur phiala in flumen
Eufraten et siccentur aque eius ut preparetur via regibus venientibus ab ortu solis*
[Revelation 16.12].
    Siquidem supervenit spiritus spirans a Patre pietatis, et subito submisit ut in
solitudinem me separarem a solacio seculari. Deinde mentem tam mirifice mutavit a
merore in melos, quod metuo monstrare munus et multiplicare magnificenciam, ne
multiloquium me minuerit. Attamen inter hec alii in habitu obendienciariorum michi
apparuerunt in argumentis quod ardencius amant quam aliquis inter eos non
assumptus, et maioris meriti coram Maiestate mittunt munificenciam. Quippe non
cognoverunt quomodo cucurri et a contenciosa conticui collocucione, contineri
cupiens in hoc quod Conditor michi copulavit. Non contradicat quis, nisi sit draco qui
debiles devorare desudat, quod continuans propter charitatem in solitudine sedere
capietur in cantacionem, non corporalem, sed profecto in spiritu pulcriorem quam
potero predicare; qua carere constat cum multis morantes, immo utique omnes qui
non habent animum ut ab universis abcedant.
    Ergo hoc aspicitur quod anachorite honorifice assumentur, cum non habeant
applaudentes eis inter argumentantes, quia amplius uruntur igne amoris et carmen
charissimum canunt in corde. Non doleo si Dalida demoniis dampnetur que ducta
deliciis ditatos decepit; et, rixas reprehendens, durius non dico dum mentes mortalibus nequiunt nudari: *Omnes astabimus ante tribunal* tranquillimi Tutoris *qui iudicat
iustissime* [Psalm 9.5], iniurias non gerens, nam iocundos in iubilo superius sublevabit;
ibi absque ambiguo apparebit quis audacter intuens inter amantes oculos Auctoris
alciorem accipiet habitacionem in aula eterna cum angelis olimpi. Numquid non
reverencius resident in regno qui hic gracia repleti in requie revera Regis reficiuntur,
quam qui sic non solantur in celica sophia? Equabunt enim gloriam gracie, quia
amantibus ardencius grandior erit gloria coram Glorificante. Liquide loquor; non
timeo temptantes, nam tales in turbine trucidabuntur. Silere non scio; sic charitas me
cogit, ut cuncti cognoscant quia capax consisto cantabilis clamoris et sonum suscipio
celicum insignem, dum discedere dilexi a divitum dolore et sancte subsistere solitarie
sedendo, canens et calidus ac iubilans ingenter.   (3.1–5.3)

[Indeed Love makes the mind daring which he draws from the depths, while the
eternal Author's fire inflames the beloved and sustains her in sublimity superior to
secular sophistry, so she senses nothing except sanctity. Thus the abundance of love
urges me to dare to unveil eloquence for the informing of others: declaring the
greatness of those who love most ardently and the justice of those who jubilate
joyfully in Jesus, as well as the charity of those who chant in conformity with the

175

celestial, and likewise the clarity of those whose consciences are capacious enough for uncreated incandescence and undying delectation: so that no one, understanding how the Creator has brought forth the young man *As a branch to execute Judgement*, will subsequently say that God does not deign to dulcify people on this earth, or that he does not magnify the moderns in a mellifluous multitude, just as he used to the saints who lived long ago. Indeed, from the time at which the humble began to experience the electuary of love, persons more devout in the degustation of divine *dulcor* have not lived than ⟨those who⟩ are still led from misery to the mansion of the Master; and this culmination will not be completely closed to the sons of the faithful until *The phial is poured out into the river Euphrates and its water is dried up, so that a way may be prepared for the kings coming from the rising of the sun.*

Now a spirit sighing from the paternal piety swept over me and suddenly submerged me, so that I separated myself in solitude from secular solace. Then he changed my mind most miraculously from misery to melody, yet in such a way that I fear to declare the gift and to multiply magnificence lest loquacity lessen me. However, amidst this ⟨solitude⟩ some have appeared to me in the habit of monks, with arguments that they love more ardently than anyone not accepted amidst them, and lay munificence with more merit before the Majesty. In fact they did not know by what way I hastened and how I kept silent, away from contentious colloquy, desiring to be contained in that ⟨canor⟩ which the Creator co-ordinated for me. Let nobody deny (unless he be a dragon who strives to swallow the strengthless) that one who continues to sit in solitude for the sake of charity will be seized, not by a bodily singing, but surely by ⟨a singing⟩ in the spirit lovelier than I will be able to preach, which it is manifest that those dwelling with the many will lack; indeed all ⟨lack *canor*⟩ who have not the courage to break away from everyone.

Thus in this it is evident that, while they may not have applauders among the argumentative, anchorites will be honourably assumed because they burn more in the fire of love, and sing the sweetest song in their hearts. I do not grieve if Dalida is damned with demons, who, diverted by delights, has deceived the rich; and, ⟨while⟩ rebuking disputes, ⟨nonetheless⟩ I do not speak more harshly, since minds cannot be manifested to mortals. *All will stand before the tribunal* of the most tranquil Tutor, who *judges very justly*, not promoting injuries, for he will raise up the jocund higher in jubilation. There it will appear without ambiguity who (among the lovers daringly looking at the eyes of the Author) will receive a higher habitation in the eternal hall with Olympian angels. For will they not reside with more reverence in the realm who here, replete with grace, are really refreshed in the Ruler's rest, than those who are not consoled in celestial wisdom? For they will equal the glory of grace, because the more ardently they have loved, the greater will be their glory before the Glorifier.

I speak clearly; I am not disturbed by seducers, for such will be slaughtered in the storm. I do not know how to be silent; so charity constrains me that everyone may recognize how I continue capable of the canorous clamour, and sustain the standard of the celestial sound, since I delighted to desert the dolour of the rich and to stay sitting in saintly solitude, singing and warmed and vastly jubilant.]

This opening takes us back to the beginning of *Super Psalmum Vicesimum*, where Rolle implies that as preacher and saint he is confident of divine inspiration. But here he expresses more than mere confidence that the requisite inspiration will be forthcoming. The chapter actually enacts the process whereby Love (i.e. the Holy Spirit) inspires him with *audacitas* and constrains him to proclaim the truth about the nature of love from his own experience. Rolle purports to make good his claims even while he is making them; indeed, the very fact of making the claims makes them good. 'Love makes the soul bold',[6] we are informed, and are at once presented with an *exemplum*: Rolle's present boldness in beginning to speak 'ad informacionem aliorum' (that is, with assumed authority over his readers, but also for their benefit, not out of boastfulness). What is his subject? First he is to write of *fervor*, *dulcor* and particularly *canor*, and second he is to do so in order to make it *impossible to deny* that moderns can equal the ancients 'in degustacione divine dulcedinis': this by boldly retelling the experience of the 'iuvenculum', himself.[7] The chapter at once sets out to sketch the work's principal *exemplum*, by recounting Rolle's spiritual autobiography, in an unusual form. The Holy Spirit drove him into the desert and led him 'a merore in melos'; this is an abbreviation of *Incendium Amoris*, cap. 15. As in the same chapter (190.3–6), the Spirit's inspiration leaves him fearing to declare his experience – although here the present tense ('metuo') suggests this is a continuing predicament. The situation has been brought to a crisis by the criticisms made of him by certain monks, who do not understand the nature of his life and his need to avoid dispute; we are close to cap. 31 of *Incendium Amoris*, where Rolle is asked why he will not sing in church. But where that work recounts how he dared to answer his detractors, here he implies he remained silent ('a contenciosa conticui collocucione'). Thus the outspoken 'non contradicat quis' is presented as the first, unanswerable response that he gives monks: that his love is greater than theirs, greater than he can say. The next few sentences draw one moral: that what is not understood by the world is self-evident to hermits and will be manifested at the Judgement. But the conclusion of the chapter returns to its opening by promising a manifestation of the truth now, through Rolle's liquid words as they are drawn from him by the urgings of Love; for now, because of the inspiration he receives from the Spirit, he no longer fears those who kept him silent ('non timeo temptantes'). Only now is the transition from *meror* to *melos* complete, because only now is *metus* conquered. In other words, the prologue to *Melos Amoris* depicts Rolle's spiritual progress as culminating in itself. Here, as he writes, his fear is swept aside for the first time by the Spirit who inspired his career – and who is revealed as the Muse who inspires him to proclaim the truth about what he has achieved. The chapter is a self-referential account of its own origins, which retrospectively interprets everything he has written as a product of the fear he has only now learnt fully to master. This is self-transcendence with a vengeance.

We have encountered something of this self-reflexive quality in a number of the works discussed in the last two chapters, if never in so explicit a form. But it is most consistently evident in the work which was probably Rolle's first exercise in a rhetorical 'high' style, *Canticum Amoris*. Like *Melos Amoris*, this is a poem written under the guidance of a muse – either the poem's subject, the Virgin, or the poet's love for her, which causes him to write the poem in praise of her. As a written representation of an oral activity (praise) the poem continuously comments on what it is doing; indeed it consists of such comments. *Canticum Amoris* shares this reflexivity with one of the works that probably influenced it, John of Hoveden's *Philomena*, a poem which is structured as a series of instructions to its muse, Love, to write itself. The same reflexivity is characteristic of *Melos Amoris*. While this work is concerned with the exemplary quality of all of Rolle's spiritual life, its main subject is his experience of a special form of praise, *canor*. But in this prologue, he does not write of *canor* so much as dramatize the process whereby writing becomes possible: a process of inspiration and an endowment of *audacitas* by the same Spirit who has long endowed him with the ability and *audacitas* to practise the *canor* about which he is now to write. This dramatization, besides being highly conscious of language as such ('aperire eloquium', 'silere non scio'), is in poetic form; the chapter is written in the highest of styles. Clearly this is because, like Rolle's other 'Song of Love', *Melos Amoris* aims to represent *canor* verbally. Just as the depictions of praise in *Canticum Amoris* actually are praise, so the language in which Rolle announces his new, daring readiness to talk about *canor* actually is (is a form of, is equivalent to) *canor*. In so far as the rest of *Melos Amoris* shares the characteristics of its first chapter, the work is literally self-referential: it both is and is about *canor*. Hence the display of eloquence 'ad informacionem aliorum' that cap. 1 promises occurs on two levels: one conceptual, as the reader takes in 'information' about *canor*; the other affective, as the reader participates in (is 'informed' by) *canor*, through response to the alliterative eloquence the work 'unveils'. *Melos Amoris* indeed operates more importantly as an affective ecstasy in celebration of *canor* than as a conceptual account of it. The aspects of the work which we can describe as akin to commentary or treatise tend to be swamped by the poetic, evangelistic verve by means of which Rolle reproduces the violent, passionate, continuous, audacious nature of heavenly song. Like the love *canor* celebrates, *Melos Amoris* is a work of 'ordo sine ordine'; diffuse, and impossible to follow conceptually, it nonetheless presents the reader with a remarkable experience of an affective verbal order, of a mannerist, meticulous but highly emotional construct. The work is unrelenting and lengthy enough to reproduce the continuousness of *canor*; its style is daring enough to be an embodiment of the *audacitas* of *canor*; its impenetrability and stylistic elevation are verbal equivalents of the high spiritual state which *canor* represents and difficulties which attaining it involve; even the place the work occupies as the culmination of a phase of Rolle's career is equivalent to the place of *canor* at the *culmen* of the spiritual life. *Melos Amoris* translates every aspect of Rolle's spiritual experience of *canor* into a literary construct, in order to provide the reader with a rhetorical version or simulacrum of that experience.

It seems to me that this unique application of Rolle's experience of *canor* to the 'poetics' of *Melos Amoris* is the key to the distinctiveness of the work. Nowhere else is he so confidently clear of the significance of his own writing. This use of *canor* can nonetheless hardly be called surprising; in relation to Rolle's career as a whole it has rather the character of an inevitable climax. To recapitulate: the previous two chapters have shown how the growth of Rolle's audacity as a thinker and an individual is matched by a conscious shift of focus in his writings from *fervor* to *dulcor* to *canor*. *Incendium Amoris* contains the whole process, as a tripartite structure which imitates the structure of Rolle's mystical ascent (but retains an imagistic focus on *fervor*). *Super Canticum Canticorum*, *Super Psalmum Vicesimum* and *Contra Amatores Mundi*, all of which have the imagery of *dulcor* as their focus, take Rolle's thought and his personal audacity several stages beyond *Incendium Amoris*. Whatever their supposed focus, at their more daring all of these works are necessarily concerned with *canor*, which is much the most distinctive and important of Rolle's experiences, and on which all his claims to special status turn. At moments of particular audacity, especially where Rolle testifies to the truth of his claims for *canor* by insisting on their truth in his own life (e.g. *Incendium Amoris*, cap. 31 and the last section of *Super Canticum Canticorum*), we have seen that he relies heavily on assertion and eloquence to convince the reader. Assertion bludgeons the reader with the fact of Rolle's authority. Eloquence woos the reader into according him more authority, by making his testimony credible, bridging the gap between the reader and Rolle's experience of *canor* by recreating both the experience and Rolle's conviction of its genuineness. Yet not only are assertion and eloquence prominent in discussions of *canor* in works like *Super Canticum Canticorum*; they are characteristic of *canor* itself. The *perfectissimus* is assertive and eloquent because of the loving fearlessness that he has acquired in communion with God. In *Incendium Amoris* and the group of works that follow it, Rolle's choice of verbal weapons is thus already especially appropriate, and suggests an intention to imitate the experience of *canor*.

Rolle's 'verbal weapons' of assertion and eloquence play essentially the same roles in *Melos Amoris*. Once he moves from works that focus on *dulcor* and writes from the perspective of his climactic mystical experience, he is able to capitalize on the fact that *canor* is a verbal, communicative state of soul; thereby he systematizes his use of eloquence without fundamentally reinterpreting the concept. Here eloquence becomes explicitly his method and message: a manifestation of assertive daring, and at the same time the major part of what is daringly asserted. Cap. 1 claims that his spiritual life culminates in the eloquence it celebrates; by treating his eloquence as a proof of his perfection, it makes good the claim of *Super Canticum Canticorum* that the *perfectissimi* can be identified as those who write most eloquently about love. But in *Melos Amoris*, where *canor* is both mystical experience and rhetorical construct, this claim works the other way around, too: Rolle treats the fact of his perfection as proof that his eloquence will be efficacious, and asserts it to be impossible that the godly reader will not be convinced. Cap. 1 sets out to write 'quatinus quisque ... non dicat deinceps' that spiritual perfection is not possible; it refuses to let the reader disagree that hermits are superior to monks ('non contradicat quis'), unless the reader be one of the damned. At some points in the work, notably in caps. 47–48 where Rolle is syllogizing about monks, hermits and preachers, he takes a less aggressive stance and appeals to the reader for support (155.14) or admits that he does not expect total agreement (149.6–26); here, as in one place in cap. 1, he is willing to defer vindication until the Judgement, when the truth will appear 'absque ambiguo' (4.21–22). But as a whole the work insists that its assertions are true by definition: 'If I were lying, I would not merit the marvellous melody, nor to be purified' (54.24–26: 'Si mencior . . . mirificum non merear melos neque mundari'); because he *has* merited these things, at no point *can* he be wrong. The frequency of phrases like 'audeo hoc dicere' (18.22), 'audet annunciare' (39.31, 80.5, 136.30), 'audeo asserere' (57.31, 74.2), 'hoc quod novi nuncio . . . et hoc audeo annuere' (145.31, 35), hence does not here imply that the work is written against the tooth-and-nail opposition of *detractores*, for *Melos Amoris* is too confident of its power to worry about them. Rather, assertiveness has itself become part of a *canor* which rejoices in its own temerity – has been stylized into a trope in the service of Rollean eloquence, which insists that it must convince by dint of its own inspired virtuosity. Thus *Melos Amoris* differs from its predecessors not because Rolle's thinking has changed, but because the imagery of *canor* gives him the opportunity to write from a better articulated sense of the status of his words.

II

What else can we make of the way in which *Melos Amoris* represents itself as equivalent to *canor*? Clearly the claim is meant to give the work total authority by continually presenting the reader with verbal evidence for its inspiration: oxymorons like 'the text is inspiration' or 'the text is authority' follow from the idea that the text is *canor*. Such a claim seems to place Rolle's authority on surer ground than the mere hope of convincing through eloquence, however forcibly that hope is expressed. It also allows him to bring several other devices for claiming authority into a coherent relationship with one another: hence, indeed, the harmonious heterogeneity of the work's structure. *Super Psalmum Vicesimum* and *Super Canticum Canticorum* make explicit what is implicit in the biblical allusions of *Incendium Amoris*, that the Scriptures are a major source not only of Rolle's phraseology and ideas but of his claim to be right. These works depend on the assumption that to expound Scripture is to expound his own thought, and, indeed, to transfer the authority of the biblical text to its exposition. Such indistinct but potent ideas find a coherent place in the postils of *Melos Amoris*, which at once expound and are *canor*. The Spirit who inspired Scripture breathes *canor* into the saints, so that they can 'penetrate' the heavenly kingdom (47.16); Scripture thus naturally speaks of *canor*, while those who have experienced it are equally naturally the only ones who can 'penetrate' the hidden meaning of Scripture and expound all it says of *canor* with *sapientia* not mere *scientia*:

Sive forte iam frendent falsi fideles et in factis firmatis effundunt furorem; invidia uruntur quia lucide loquor; torquere temptantes tranquillum non tangunt, fruor tam fortiter fervore Factoris. Putabant quod non potui pure predicare nec sapere ut ceteri qui sancte subsistebant. Sed sciant simpliciter quod Auctorem amavi qui animum ardore olimpi implevit ut proferam precipue sermones amoris, Scripturam scrutans que latet carnales. (117.4–11)

[If perchance the false faithful now grind their fangs and pour forth fury at proven facts, they burn with envy because I speak lucidly. Trying to trouble ⟨my⟩ tranquillity they do not touch ⟨it⟩, so strongly do I savour the Maker's heat. They thought that I could not preach nor be wise purely, like the others who sustained life in holiness. But let them understand simply that I loved the Author, who filled my soul with Olympian ardour so that I would be especially able to bring forth sermons of love, scrutinizing the Scriptures which are hidden from the carnal.]

This passage suggests both that Rolle's love makes him an authority on the mysteries of Scripture, and that God endowed him with *fervor* so that he would be able to speak 'sermones amoris', not merely live in solitary holiness. 'Sermones amoris' is a deliberately ambiguous phrase, referring to his teachings and writings as though they were a form of *canor*; the effect of Rolle's divine inspiration extends beyond his study of the Scriptures, to the sermons of love (or 'loving sermons') by means of which he expounds what he learns.[8]

Behind this ambiguity lies another important claim, which extends our sense of the way in which the text of *Melos Amoris* 'is' *canor*, and which is new to this work; for the effect of the passage as a whole is to suggest that God's purpose in endowing Rolle with *canor* was to make public ('predicare . . . sermones') truths about divine love. This idea is obviously very much in tune with what Rolle says in cap. 1, and indeed with the work's treatment of the public proclamation of his experiences as an integral and culminating part of his life as a *perfectissimus*. But if we start to consider some of its implications, they are, I think, rather unexpected. Chapter 6 shows how Rolle's invariable enthusiasm for preaching (initially an incongruous element of his eremitic vocation) is slowly integrated into his model of the perfect life. *Super Canticum Canticorum* expounds the strange idea that eloquence is of itself a proof of holiness; *Contra Amatores Mundi* likewise asserts that evangelism and sanctity are interconnected – though it runs into such problems with this claim that Rolle finds himself saying at once that love forces the saint to speak out, and that the lovers of God do not always choose to preach or teach. The first chapter of *Melos Amoris*, ignoring these difficulties, ties holiness and preaching together as irrevocably as it can by implying that Rolle's decision to speak out about his *canor* actually initiates a new stage of his spiritual life; and here we read that God's main reason for endowing Rolle with fervent love was to bring about this new stage. In all this, we seem to have moved a long way from Rolle's first exposition of *canor* (in cap. 15 of *Incendium Amoris*) as a private culmination of the solitary life which, since it is a participation in the heavenly song, is in the fullest sense its own reward and justification. In fact we have apparently reached a position in which either *canor* is no longer treated as the highest stage of the spiritual life at all, or else is thought of as consisting, in its highest form, in its own proclamation to the world – in which case Rolle must have thought of the actual text of *Melos Amoris* as not metaphorically but literally a form of mystical experience, a form superior to the ineffable ecstasy he once regarded as *canor*. This is all both puzzling and inchoate, but seems somewhat reminiscent of the fourth of Richard of St Victor's 'grades of violent love', in which the soul, unable fully to reach its heavenly goal while in this life, turns back to the world in anguished self-sacrifice, to help others to love. Rolle is implicitly critical of this idea in *Super Canticum Canticorum* (see Chapter 6, n. 17), for Richard's painful and 'insatiable' love is foreign to his way of thinking; and *Melos Amoris* gives no indication that it is the product of an anguished turning-away from the goal of full union with God – on the contrary. Yet it is hard to avoid concluding that in some way Rolle is here attempting to fuse his experience of *canor*, which he can only achieve in continuous form as a solitary, with Richard's or some other version of the 'mixed' life, in which contemplation is combined with an active desire to save the souls of others.[9]

The notion that there is a stage of the spiritual life beyond even *canor* (or in which *canor* becomes something else) is never expounded systematically in *Melos Amoris*, nor in Rolle's late works. It is there in his increasingly rare reflections on his own writing; but it does not become fully a part of his model accounts of the *perfectissimi*. There are several things that might explain this: that Rolle is still worried that most saints have chosen not to preach *canor*; that for all the bravado of *Melos Amoris* he is unsure of the relationship *canor* has to its proclamation; that he is also unsure of the relationship between contemplative and 'mixed' lives; that 'mixed' life was not a well-defined concept in the Middle Ages; and that once he begins to take the idea really seriously, in his last works (to be discussed in the next two chapters), he also stops making many self-referential remarks about sainthood. Perhaps for all these reasons, a certain vagueness creeps in to these last stages of the processes of Rolle's self-canonization as an *auctor*. Yet there is a certain amount of discussion of what seems to be the 'mixed' life in *Melos Amoris*, enough to give a sense of the direction in which his thoughts were tending as he wrote the work – in particular, one key passage in cap. 48 dealing with the topic of preaching, which changes the direction of the whole work, presenting us with a view of Rolle's ministry as a teacher substantially different from anything we have so far encountered. Since this passage is almost the last reflection on his own situation that he gives us, it is worth extended quotation and discussion:

Hec qui intelligit que pagina panguntur, infirmum me agnoscens et mortuum mundo coram causantibus aliqualiter excuset. Racionem nam reddidi, si intime attendis, cur interius me tenui, non visitans villanos, fugiendo a festis psallencium sonore. Hic heremus non horret ardenter amanti; solus suscipiet quo coniuctus carebit; viator vacillat, quiescens calescit charitate cremante carbone succenso. Predicator perfectus pueros parturit ad pacem portandam, et capiet coronas quia captivos convertit coram Cuntipotente, dum *evellit et destruit, edificat et plantat* [Jeremiah 1.10]; immobilis manens in dileccione divina profecto percipiet diadema decoris et reverenter in regno cum rectis residebit. Sed errant nunc undique miseros mittentes qui oracula ignorant clause Scripture et integrum non habent Altissimo amorem; ac prohibent precipuos proferre sermonem, et alios admittunt qui a Deo non mittuntur: nesciunt nimirum nodum nudare, nec ut solvant signacula a Spiritu spirantur . . . heremitas abiciunt et horrent cum ipsis bonos esse et conscios. Audire hos nolunt: quicquid homo dixerit quod laude sit dignum semper ad malum interpretantur; quamquam iam sciant summa secreta et necessaria noverint humane saluti quomodoque nitor in nobili nectetur [?], utique cum ipsis acceptabiles non erunt. Revera respondeant coram Regnante qualiter constituunt de cunctis quid agunt: si non indifferenter officium ab omnibus hoc accipiatur, cur pocius non eligunt quos Deus inspirat et mittit in mundo ut multi meliorentur? . . . Predictantes profecto, veraciter si vivant, piissimo Patri non parum placebunt. Sed solitudinem qui sustinet continue quiescens et in amoris Auctoris desideriis deductus, *unum* [see Luke 10.42] accipiet quo plane precellat, quod alii eciam alti in orbe ignorant . . . Multi nimirum plures sunt qui sciunt verbum Dei predicare quam qui senciunt in se ipsis sonum eterne laudis et archanum angelice armonie. Et ista duo raro vel nunquam in eodem inveniuntur. Nam qui officium suscipit predicacionis circuit per civitates, villas et castella. Qui autem amore contemplacionis rapitur solus sedendo quiescere iugiter delectatur. Itaque bonum est predicatorem esse, pro salute animarum discurrere, movere, fatigari. Sed melius est, securius est, suavius contemplatorem esse, eternam suavitatem presentire, delicias canere eterni amoris et in laudem rapi Conditoris per infusionem canoris iubilei. Si quis autem utrumque potuerit adipisci, tanto laudabilior erit; sed hoc non continget nisi prius efficeretur contemplator quam predicator. Et procul dubio cum divine charitatis dulcedo mentem absorbuerit, caro deficit et ulterius iam ad exteriores labores sustinendas fortis non erit. Doceat, exhortetur, suadeat omnes ad charitatem, ut vivant in concordia et castitate, in mansuetudine et paciencia. Studeat quoque, si habeat intellectum Scripturarum et videat Spiritum Sanctum se inflammantem, hec et alia plura scribere que in publico non potest predicare. Set nemo qui salutem suam amat, nisi sit doctus a Deo et indicia cognoscit interne inspiracionis, tractare presumat de sacris Scripturis; alioquin errabit, nocens sibi et aliis. Qui enim gaudere desiderit de excellencia magni nominis, amicum Dei se prius faciat, ne forte efficiatur magister erroris. Humiles, obedientes, casti, mites, pacientes et precipue in amore ferventes hoc donum accipiunt, qui non suam gloriam sed divinam querunt.   (152.6–154.19)

[He who understands these things written in this book, seeing me sickly and dead to the world, may somewhat excuse me before my accusers. For I have rendered a reason, if you attend closely, why I held myself within, not visiting villeins, fleeing from feasts and the sound of singing. This desert is not dreadful to the ardent lover; alone he can experience what he will lack in company; as a traveller he totters ⟨but⟩ in quiet he kindles with consuming charity ⟨like a⟩ burning coal. Perfected as a preacher, he brings forth boys to bear peace, and will capture crowns in the presence of the Omnipotent for converting captives, since he *plucks up and destroys, he builds and he plants*; certainly, remaining immobile in divine love he will receive a decorous diadem and will reverently reside in the realm with the righteous. But now they ⟨prelates, see 152.24⟩ err, sending everywhere wretches who are ignorant of the secrets of the Scriptures, and who do not have a sound love for the Highest. They prohibit the pre-eminent ones from proferring sermons, and allow others who are not sent by God. Certainly these ⟨preachers⟩ do not know how to lay bare the knot ⟨the hidden sense of Scripture⟩, nor are they inspired by the Spirit to solve the significations. They cast aside hermits and hate to be good and wise with them; they do not want to hear them. Whatever a man says that should be worthy of praise, they always interpret it for the worst; although they ⟨hermits⟩ now know high secrets and understand things necessary for the salvation of mankind, and in what manner brightness will be knit in the noble one, they will certainly not be acceptable among them ⟨prelates⟩. Truly, they will answer before the Ruler as to how they regulate everything that they do: if their office is not treated indifferently by everyone, why do they not more readily choose those whom God inspires, and send them into the world so that many may be bettered? Indeed, those who preach, if they live truly, will please the most merciful Father in a manner not minimal. But he who sustains solitude, living in continual quiet and focussed inwards in desires for the Author's love, will receive *one thing* by which he plainly excels, which others, even the great in the world, do not know. Certainly there are very many more who know how to preach the word of God than who feel in themselves the sound of eternal praise and the secret of angelic harmony. And these two things are rarely or never found in the same person. For he who undertakes the office of preaching travels through cities, towns and castles. But he who is seized by the love of contemplation delights to be quiet alone in continual sitting. Therefore it is good to be a preacher, to run about, to move, to become tired for the salvation of souls; but it is better, it is more secure, it is sweeter to be a contemplative, to feel in advance the eternal sweetness, to sing the delights of eternal love and to be snatched in the praise of the Creator by the infusion of song in jubilation. However, whoever can obtain both will be the more praiseworthy – yet this will not occur unless someone becomes a contemplative before becoming a preacher. And without doubt, when the sweetness of divine charity absorbs the mind, the flesh fails and will no longer be strong enough to sustain external labours. He ⟨i.e. someone who has 'obtained both'⟩ should teach, exhort, persuade everyone to charity, that they may live in concord and chastity, in obedience and patience. He should also be eager, if he has understanding of the Scriptures and sees the Holy Spirit inflaming him, to write these and many other things which he cannot preach in public. But nobody who loves his own salvation, unless he is taught by God and recognizes the signs of inner inspiration, should presume to treat of the sacred Scriptures, or he will err, harming both himself and others. For whoever desires to rejoice in the excellence of the great name must first make himself a friend of God, lest perchance he be made the master of error. The humble, the obedient, the chaste, the merciful, the patient, and above all the fervent in love receive this gift, who seek it not for their glory but for the divine.]

This passage forms part of Rolle's defence of the solitary life from those who claim the coenobitic life to be superior; the dozen or so sentences which conclude the chapter (following what is quoted here) praise the solitary life and the opportunities it provides for experiencing *canor*, while the first half of the chapter likewise goes over and over the same thoroughly familiar ground.[10] Thus, although much of what I have quoted (and most of what I have omitted) deals with the inadequacies of prelates and preachers, the topic is structurally subordinate to another theme, the role of the contemplative in proclaiming the truth.[11] This theme is developed as follows: the solitary contemplative, secure in his desert, has the capacity to 'bring forth boys' (make converts), preaching with such effect that he will win a crown (the *aureola* reserved for preachers) for his efforts. Yet in practice he cannot preach, for prelates 'send wretches' out to spread the Gospel, forbidding hermits from exercising what would be a more zealous and effective ministry, and even persecuting them, so indifferent are they to the truth (*Melos Amoris* is the only work in which Rolle expressly states that he ought to be allowed to preach, and overtly criticizes his ecclesiastical superiors). There follows a harsh passage on the subject of bad preaching. Then, taking up the theme of the solitary as preacher in a new way (as though initiating the *contra* section of a *quaestio*), Rolle admits that there are good preachers, extols contemplative life as superior to that of the itinerant evangelist, but says that both can be combined to form an even higher state if contemplation is given priority. This is a surprising admission, contradicting an earlier discussion in *Incendium Amoris* (cap. 21, see pp. 15–16), and apparently implying that there is a way of life above the eremitic: that of the contemplative (friar or monk) who is allowed to preach. Out of this (as in the *respondeo* section of a *quaestio*) comes what is in effect a *distinctio*. True, there is 'active' preaching (of the kind involving hard journeys and much contact with cities), but the true solitary contemplative, burned up in the fire of love, is too weak for this; his task, rather, is teaching, exhortation and the writing of biblical commentaries and other works (referred to in the phrase 'alia plura') as the inspiration of the Holy Spirit directs. This conclusion skilfully protects the privileged status of solitaries, while allowing them to participate as fully as Rolle is in fact allowed to in the office of preaching, and to have a share in its prestige and reward.[12]

Here then, after many hundreds of pages of writing and rewriting a narrow range of ideas, Rolle at last comes near to enunciating a straightforward and plausible statement of what he thinks his place within the structure of the Church Militant to be: a practitioner of the only form of 'mixed' life which can truly combine the height of contemplative ecstasy with the service of others. The formulation is similar, though I think not related, to that made in the *Consuetudines* of the Carthusian order, which refers to 'preaching the word of God with our hands' (i.e. by writing and by transcribing the works of others – see p. 15); like Guigo, Rolle is anxious to play down rather than stress the technical distinction between preaching and teaching, and for the same reason: to ensure that hermits are seen and see themselves as having a vital part to play in the evangelistic and didactic offices of the Church. A good deal is changed by the newly matter-of-fact way in which he does this. In particular, the assertive language of 'holy audacity' vital to most of *Melos Amoris*, in which the proclamation of *canor* is treated as its own apotheosis, seems suddenly to have no clear place. It is not rejected; indeed the need for divine inspiration continues to be strongly stressed. But this version of Rolle's career as a writer (for it is obvious that yet again he is talking about himself here) no longer endows the elevation of his own mystical experience with the overriding importance it has had until now. Instead of singing aloud of the excellence and glory of the pre-eminent saints, which is what Rolle has said he is doing in writing *Melos Amoris*, the practitioner of the 'mixed' life is seen as occupied with more ordinary and useful things: exhorting others to charity, concord and obedience, or expounding the Scriptures. In other words, this passage offers a way out of the remorseless self-referentiality which has been the keynote of his writing from *Incendium Amoris* on, and which reaches its climax in *Melos Amoris* itself. It seems that at long last Rolle is ready to turn from the tasks of demonstrating his sanctity and proclaiming his authority, and to begin actually to exercise his spiritual authority in a practical way for the benefit of others. If my reading of the passage is correct, it thus represents one of the major turning-points in his career.

Rolle's new self-conception as a practitioner of the 'mixed' life has an immediate effect. Although I have read this discussion of preaching as no more than another opportunity for him to talk about himself, it would be easy to defend the passage as a fairly coherent piece of didactic writing, which displays (rather as the second part of *Judica Me* does) a genuine concern for the office of the preacher, and offers advice to the Church at large on how that office should be perceived and fulfilled. The final ten chapters of *Melos Amoris* continue to be heavily alliterative and much concerned with *canor* and the saints; yet there is a perceptible effort to structure the discussion in a clearer way, to teach as well as to declaim. For example, although Rolle has written of 'ordered love' on many previous occasions, cap. 50 is the only place in his works in which he tells us what the priorities of such a love ought to be: that God is to be loved first, then our own soul, our body, friends and patrons, and finally our enemies.[13] These chapters are also more intelligible and helpful as biblical commentary than the rest of *Melos Amoris*. Caps. 49–55 comment in a relatively systematic way on two verses of the Song of Songs (here the postil form of the work is for once quite evident), and caps. 56–58, which end the work with a discussion of the 'glory' of the saints, construct this as a narrative account of the Last Judgement and the rewards accorded the saved, which consists largely of the quotation and careful analysis of relevant biblical passages. There are, finally, more overt signs that Rolle is reflecting on his new role as a proponent of the 'mixed' life. For example, there are further references to writing as a natural and important activity for 'the saints', such as the apostrophe to *caritas* in cap. 50, which states that love 'sustains the sitter, makes the silent one rejoice . . . sweetens the mediator, feeds the contemplator, enriches the singer, teaches the writer' (160.28–31: 'Sustinet sedentem, letificat tacentem . . . indulcorat meditan-tem, pascit contemplantem, impinguat canentem, docet scribentem') – impli-citly giving the activity of writing a place at the very summit of the spiritual life. Again, near the end of the work, after attacking heretics who ignore or disbelieve the Scriptures, yet have the temerity to believe that they will judge the world with Christ at the Last Day, Rolle steps back to explain the didactic purpose of his vehement descriptions of the terrible fate of the damned:

Preterea, numquid non scribo pro tua salvacione? Tam districtum iudicium sencies tu quantum ego. *Corpus meum castigo et in servitutem redigo, ne aliis predicans reprobus efficiar* [1 Corinthians 9.27]. Si ergo timeo, quare non timeres et tu, presertim cum *Deo equalis sit cura de omnibus* [Wisdom 6.8]? Aut quid proderit michi si homines dampnentur? Numquid ego dampno malos, vel pocius eorum malicia? Scribimus igitur non ut dampnentur, sed *ut magis convertantur et vivant* [Ezekiel 18.23] et salventur; pronunciantur eis terrores inferni et stricta iudicia Dei ut ea caveant, non ut in illis cadant. (184.26–35)

[Besides, am I not writing for your salvation? You will experience just as strict a judgement as I will. *I chastize my body and keep it in servitude lest while preaching to others I myself become reprobate.* So if I am afraid, why are you not afraid, too, especially since God *will take the same care of everyone?* And how does it help me if people are damned? Do I condemn the wicked, or is it more their own malice? So we write not so that they may be damned but *so that more may be converted and live* and be saved; the terrors of hell and the strict judgement of God are proclaimed so that they may fear them, not so that they fall into them.]

This satirist's apologia acts as a much-needed gloss on the occasions where Rolle, in writing of the damnation of the wicked and the joy it will evoke among the saints in heaven, has seemed to begin his rejoicing prematurely, and to look forward to the damnation of fellow-Christians. It also embodies a change of attitude which will become important in what was probably his next work, *Super Lectiones Mortuorum*: in his anxiety to make his experience relevant to his readers, and in spite of his vaunted spiritual security, he is prepared to state that he, too, fears the Judgement. The theme of security and the harshness of satire returns at the end of the work: 'Amorem et odium utrumque ostendi, et puer nunc propero ad finem felicem; nam pene perfudi gressus gravantes, ut calcans contagium in cantico consummer. Charitatem charissimam cunctis commendo, Amen' (191.29–32: 'I have set forth both love and hate, and now, a boy, I hasten to a happy end; for I have quite bestrewn the weary ways, so that, trampling contagion, I may be consumed in song. I commend loveliest love to all, Amen'). Yet for most of these final chapters we are clearly in the presence of a new voice, a new self-conception.

III

Incendium Amoris, the work which initiates what has proved from my present perspective the most significant phases of Rolle's career, points forward to developments of which he can only have been dimly aware when he wrote it. In the same way as the work evolves from *fervor* to *dulcor* to *canor*, from an attitude of anxiety to one of audacity, so the works which follow evolve, each pointing forward to the next in an increasingly triumphant progress that culminates in the strange symphony which is *Melos Amoris*. Here, we might think, with this brilliant verbal translation of the majestic song of the perfect in heaven, Rolle's career as a writer could rest, while he 'hastened to his happy end'. Yet far from bringing his career to its close, this culmination turns out also to be a beginning, as the last part of the work points us beyond the subject and language of saintly *canor* to present us with a suddenly clarified perception of the solitary saint's role as an inspired didactic writer. Before turning, in the last two chapters of this book, to the works to which this aspect of *Melos Amoris* points, I wish to reflect on why this unexpected new beginning is necessary – or, rather, why Rolle considers it so.

Rolle's own view of his introduction of a version of the 'mixed' life into the last section of *Melos Amoris*, and of the new phase of his career that it initiates, was presumably that here, as so often before, he was only making explicit what he had long implied, and had in fact practised in all his writings. There is a good deal of justification for such a claim. The desire to preach and teach, and the imagery and structures of preaching, have been evident in his writing from the beginning. The idea that *canor* leads to the verbal eloquence associated with preaching is implied as early as cap. 31 of *Incendium Amoris*, and from *Super Canticum Canticorum* on forms an overt part of a model of the holy life, in which the most perfect are seen as those who preach the word of God most eloquently and effectively. As we saw, this model leads naturally to a new emphasis on the proclamation of *canor* as an act of evangelism; *Contra Amatores Mundi* seeks to woo secular lovers to the love of God, while *Melos Amoris*, more assertively, sets out to make unbelief in the power and reality of *canor* impossible, and thus in principle to convert all who are not actively obdurate. All these works (as well as the earlier commentaries) also engage strenuously in the interpretation of Scripture. Moreover, as we will see, there is considerable stylistic continuity between them and the works written under the influence of Rolle's idea of the 'mixed' life, particularly *Super Lectiones Mortuorum*. For example, like *Melos Amoris*, many passages of these last works are clearly intended as divinely inspired expressions of *canor*; many also borrow ideas, images, even long passages of prose verbatim from the earlier works. Rolle had good reason to claim that, however late in his career the formulation came, he had in fact been a practitioner of the 'mixed' life from the start – thus that by introducing it explicitly at this stage he was not embarking on a radically new venture.

This is all well and good. However, we have already seen signs that the articulation of Rolle's view of 'mixed' life does mark a radical departure, for it changes vital features of his subject-matter, tone, self-presentation and relationship with his readers. Unlike the rest of the work, the last chapters of *Melos Amoris* are no longer concerned exclusively with the 'glory of the saints' and the proclamation of *canor*, but with the need to save the lost and to exhort the Church to virtue. Faced with the urgency of these tasks, Rolle no longer presents himself as a *de facto* member of the Church Triumphant, but also as a Christian preacher whose life, however elevated, is subject to the same contingencies as those of his readers. Again, unlike the rest of the work, in which didacticism is wholly engulfed by eloquence, many parts of these last chapters are comparatively clear, readable, and practical – and this is true to a far greater extent of the works which Rolle embarked on when he finished *Melos Amoris*. The evolution of Rolle's style from the beginning of *Incendium Amoris* to that of *Melos Amoris* is one long crescendo, in which the aural and affective qualities of his writing become ever more dominant. If there is a smooth transition between the assertive, endlessly self-reflexive writing of most of *Melos Amoris* and the tone of the last chapters and of Rolle's subsequent works, it seems odd that these latter should read so differently from their increasingly bizarre predecessors.

If there is a real discontinuity, then, what is it and why is it there? My answer to both questions inheres in what has been the leitmotif of much of this book: the fact that the pressure impelling the works between *Incendium Amoris* and *Melos Amoris* towards their increasingly florid eloquence is not in reality Rolle's desire to convert the world, but his need to assert his supreme holiness. Holding that eloquence is a proof of holiness and that divine inspiration makes him supremely eloquent, he turns to evangelism not primarily as a practical task but as a literary mode which shows off his verbal skills to their best advantage; hence the odd abstraction from the world of real sin and repentance discernible in *Contra Amatores Mundi*. *Melos Amoris* gives the theme and practice of eloquence another turn of the screw by identifying its own words with *canor* itself, so that in theory even to read the work is to participate in Rolle's experience, and be converted to belief in fervent love and the sanctity of the author. But this notion is even more distant from reality, even more clearly a literary fiction. It is, after all, just possible to imagine someone being converted by reading *Contra Amatores Mundi*; the idea that any sinner would repent of anything after reading *Melos Amoris* other than the sheer folly of doing so is simply not plausible. In most of this work, all the things that give Rolle's didacticism its vigour – his warmth, the specificity of his mysticism, even his insistence on his own audacity – have become parts of an esoteric rhetorical fantasy which, while it is magnificent in its passionate unreadability, no longer makes any practical contact with the idea that it is supposed to be of use to the world. Thus, if we step outside the structure of ideas that Rolle builds (with its suave assumptions that rhetorical intensity equals evangelistic effectiveness, that self-aggrandizement equals usefulness) to contemplate this edifice from the outside, we have to admit that *Melos Amoris* is not in a proper sense a work of 'preaching' at all, but a literary show-piece which for the most part merely poses as a work of didacticism.

These remarks may seem too exasperated and subjective to be received with anything other than suspicion. However, there are objective grounds for claiming that Rolle's writing lost sight of the needs of its readers even as it became more declamatory: the relatively few copies that survive of the more grandiloquent works. While there are over forty copies of *Incendium Amoris* (plus extracts, compilations and an English translation), nearly thirty of part or all of *Super Canticum Canticorum* (most forming part of the compilation *Oleum Effusum*), and nineteen of *Contra Amatores Mundi*, there are only ten of *Melos Amoris*, excluding one fragment and the single copy of the 'Carmen Prosaicum' (see n. 3). Most of these, moreover, are found in large collections of Rolle's works intended for connoisseurs of his thought[14] – and if the lack of marginalia and underlinings in these manuscripts is a reliable indicator, even these do not seem to have been much read.[15] Unlike most of his work,

Melos Amoris seldom appears in extracts of compilations (see Allen, pp. 115–116); unusually, Rolle apparently does not even borrow from it himself. By contrast, the Latin works he wrote after *Melos Amoris* and as a conscious practitioner of 'mixed' life, *Super Lectiones Mortuorum* and *Emendatio Vitae*, are among his most popular, the former surviving in over forty manuscripts (as well as an 'incinabule'), the latter in over a hundred, and in several English translations – while two of the English works, the *English Psalter* and *The Form of Living*, also survive, more or less complete, in over thirty and over forty manuscripts respectively. Given Rolle's great popularity in the late Middle Ages (and for all the vast creative energy he put into the work), medieval readers seem to have shown impressively little interest in *Melos Amoris*. Thus it is proper to suggest that at this climax of his career Rolle came close to declaiming himself into an absurd position: one in which he would be assured of his absolute and all-encompassing authority, but have hardly any prospective audience on which to exercise it.

In spite of the fact that it often seems like one enormous peroration, *Melos Amoris* could not, then, have marked a fitting end to Rolle's writing career as he conceived this, because neither it nor the works immediately preceding it could possibly achieve their stated goal of proclaiming the truth to 'all', since in effect they address themselves to a successively smaller and smaller readership. For Rolle to have stopped with *Melos Amoris* would in fact have meant admitting that he was an essentially marginal figure, a mere virtuoso of the spiritual life, whose assertiveness and contrived rhetorical brilliance were little more than ends in themselves – devotional entertainment for himself and the few others with the learning and taste to enjoy them. Admittedly, it is true that he could have decided to be content with such a place. After all, his early poem *Canticum Amoris* unselfconsciously belongs to the category of 'devotional entertainment', expressing his joy and longing at the thought of the Virgin in a way intended to please her, assuage his own desire, and move readers to feel as he does. Moreover, as we saw (pp. 105–109), this poem is an exercise in an established mode of devotional writing, exemplified in the poetry of John of Hoveden, whose verse is as richly convoluted, self-conscious and audacious as Rolle's prose in *Melos Amoris*, and whose attempts to praise God in an epic style which aspires to be at once pleasing and worthy of its subject cannot be dismissed as frivolous, even if they are not in any obvious sense 'useful'. It would be possible to construct a defence of *Melos Amoris* as a brilliant development of this kind of writing, in which an elevated style and elevated subject-matter are fused into a single act of praise with such skill that the work's lack of didactic realism and popular appeal are irrelevant. Yet in the last chapters of the work (and the late works they anticipate) Rolle is apparently not happy with such a defence himself, in view of the way he scrambles to re-establish contact with his readers and with an effective didactic style. It seems as though he becomes aware of the increasing tendency towards unreality of his project (at least when this is considered not as praise but as teaching or evangelism), and is anxious to counteract it.

Convinced as he is of the reality of his mystical experiences, of their importance for all as the 'highest perfection of the Christian religion' (*Incendium Amoris* 185.16–17), and consequently of his own importance, he is evidently not prepared merely to exercise a largely notional authority over an elite audience. Instead, having in his own eyes established the bases of that authority by amply demonstrating his own sanctity, his next priority is to exercise it for the good of the world by adapting the style and content of his message to the needs of a wider and better-defined readership – for his effectiveness will be a final proof of his status as a saintly modern *auctor*. Thus in the last phase of his career, the apologetic, the didactic and the evangelistic finally come together in reality, as Rolle moves on from the overt self-aggrandizement of *Melos Amoris* and the rest, and begins to do in earnest what to a large extent he has been doing only fictionally until this point: to teach the world about the overwhelming power of love.

PART IV

8

'Mixed' life: *Super Lectiones Mortuorum* and *Emendatio Vitae*

There is a tendency in most of what has been said about Rolle in this century to assume that a great gulf is fixed between the writer of *Melos Amoris* and that of *Emendatio Vitae* and the English works (usually thought of as the main products of his 'late' period). The relative moderation of these latter is taken as evidence that towards the end of his life Rolle underwent a psychological or spiritual change, achieving at long last a measure of maturity and humility, and expressing himself in ways which not only avoid but seem actively to abhor his earlier stridencies. As Excursus 1 shows, Allen's chronology of his works was largely based on this principle, placing *Melos Amoris* and *Emendatio Vitae* as far apart as possible in date of composition, and positing a slow 'mellowing' of his personality to account for what she viewed as the increasing simplicity of his style. Arnould's edition of *Melos Amoris*, claiming (correctly) that the work must have been written towards the end of Rolle's life, made a brave attempt to establish it as the climax of a mystic's progress; but his best-qualified reviewer, Eric Colledge (*Medium Aevum* 27 (1958), p. 204), would have none of it, seeing the relationship between *Melos Amoris* and the last works (as Knowles was also to do (1961, p. 52)) only in terms of contrast: 'One turns with relief to the simple spontaneity of the vernacular treatises, finding more of Everlasting Wisdom in the candid brevities of *Ego Dormio* or *The Form of Living* than in the repetitive asperities of [*Melos Amoris*].' Colledge is as clearly right in describing the modern reader's response to the English epistles as one of 'relief' as he is wrong in ascribing 'simple spontaneity' to these works, which are as artful as anything Rolle wrote. Yet we have already seen that the actual situation is more complicated than Colledge allowed: that while there are discontinuities of style, authorial self-presentation and subject-matter between *Melos Amoris* and the works that follow it, there are also ways in which the former, especially in its final stages, anticipates the late works. Although the previous chapter focusses on the discontinuities between the main part of *Melos Amoris* and the ideal of eremitic 'mixed' life which it articulates towards its close, there is still an obvious sense in which the late works which these final chapters herald represent a culmination of the theme of preaching which first emerges in *Super Canticum Canticorum*. As for psychological changes in Rolle, there must have been some, simply because writing *Emendatio Vitae* would affect anyone differently from writing *Melos*

Amoris – but these are mainly beyond our reach. All we can assert is that there are no signs that his overriding desire to canonize himself as a modern *auctor* was in any way displaced in the last works he wrote. True, he seems to have argued himself into a much greater self-confidence, and has certainly 'resolved the tone of address in his prose writings' in a new and important way (as Rosamund Allen argues in an astute article, 1984, p. 29); but such a resolution, while it may be a product of a new 'emotional maturity' (ibid., p. 28), survives for us as a literary, not a psychological, phenomenon.

These two final chapters, like their five predecessors, thus investigate the strategies of a writer one of whose primary concerns is still with how he is regarded by his readers and the world at large, and who remains near stage centre even in these, his most self-assured writings. Nonetheless, the analyses in these chapters have their own distinctive focus. My accounts of *Judica Me* and *Incendium Amoris* try to show how the apologetic emphasis of Rolle's career emerges out of a more or less conventional didacticism; they accordingly offer two readings of these works, first as significantly flawed essays in didactic writing, second as increasingly articulate attempts at self-apology. In the four works which follow *Incendium Amoris*, from *Super Psalmum Vicesimum* to *Melos Amoris*, the apologetic theme is so dominant that my analyses can glance only in passing at the many ways in which these works are still concerned with the instruction of the reader. Only here, looking at the last phases of Rolle's career, is it feasible to discuss apology and didacticism at once – for only here are the conflicting strains resolved into one another. This chapter and its successor, then, try to show how the works they deal with achieve this harmonious effect of contributing at the same time to Rolle's self-presentation and to the spiritual lives of potential or actual readers. They also try to show how Rolle sets out to achieve another kind of resolution, between the idiosyncrasies of his own mystical system and the broader tradition of affective devotion and mysticism from which that system first emerges. Lastly, putting these themes together, they argue that by the time he finished his final work, *The Form of Living*, just before his death in 1349, he had shaped his career into a form that could give him real confidence that posterity would think of him as he thought of himself: as an authoritative 'modern master' of the spiritual life.

I

The 'late work' which most resembles *Melos Amoris*, and which I think was written immediately after its completion, is *Super Lectiones Mortuorum*, a passionately engaged verse-by-verse commentary on the nine readings from Job which form the *lectiones* of the Office for the Dead.[1] In harmony with the text on which it comments, the work is a long meditation or expository sermon in a penitential vein, dealing with God's anger at sin, his chastisement of the just as well as the unjust, the need to have contempt for the body and the brevity of its life, and similar topics. Such *materia* aligns the work more closely with *Super Threnos* than with the works discussed in the last three chapters; for whereas these seem to treat penitential themes (except those associated with the damned) as beneath them, here, as Moyes notes (1988, vol. 1, pp. 103–104), even the references to *fervor, dulcor* and *canor* which do find their way into the work are diluted by the somber language Rolle derives from his text and from the classics of penitential literature: Innocent III's *De Miseria Condicionis Humanae*, pseudo-Bernard's *Meditationes Piissimae* and the *Speculum Peccatoris*.[2] Yet while *Melos Amoris* and *Super Lectiones Mortuorum* belong to different genres and deal with different subjects – one with the sublimities of the *perfectissimi*, the other with the universal facts of sin and death and the theme of *contemptus mundi* – the works are in some respects similar enough to be regarded as companion-pieces: as if, after postillating his prophetic way through expositions of favourite verses of David's Psalms and Solomon's Song, Rolle turned to another style of Old Testament *canor*, the mournful chantings of Job the just, in an attempt to show how flexible the concept, and consequently his own writing, could be.[3] Thus, although the work's opening was probably on one level contrived with the precise purpose of offering as striking as possible a contrast to that of *Melos Amoris* ('Amor utique audacem effect animam'), it is still surely to be read as an attempt to adapt the singing style of that work to the 'mixed' life's concern with the condition of fallen humanity as a whole:

Parce michi, Domine, nichil enim sunt dies mei [Job 7.16]. Exprimitur autem in his verbis humane condicionis instabilitas que non habet in hac miserabili valle *manentem mansionem* [Hebrews 13.14]; sed peribit potestas a principibus perversis, et ferientur procul dubio in profundissimas flammas infernorum, ludusque omnium hominum lasciviorum cito labitur in lamentacionem denique, quia divicie divitum cum tabernaculis tyrannorum infra breve tempus terminabuntur. Hoc itaque annuncio vobis qui in transitoria dulcedine delectamini et in istis terrenis diviciis abundare anhelatis, quod de gaudio vestro dolorem hababatis, videntes quod evanescunt universa que sub sole adquisistis: ludus vester in luctum vertitur et prosperitas vestra in tormentum commutatur . . . Sed quomodo *sunt dies* nostri *nichil*, cum unicuique nostrum dies videntur multi, longi et laboriosi? Ergo noli errare, noli decipi, noli presentes dies tibi multas promittere: nichil sunt, nulli sunt audeo dicere . . . Ergo divites decipiuntur, luxuriosi illaqueantur; omnes, temporalibus bonis dediti, carnalibus curis obfuscati, hamo hostis capti, strangulantur. Hinc postulo, deposco, flagito, rogo: *Parce michi Domine*, ut non periam cum pravis, non condempnor cum iniquis . . . (124.1–125.11)

[*Spare me, Lord, for my days are as nothing.* In these words are expressed the instability of the human condition, which does not have in this vale of anguish any *abiding estate*; rather, power will pass from perverse princes, and they without doubt will be thrust into the thickest flames of hell, and the laughter of all the lascivious will then lapse at once in lamentation, because the riches of the affluent and the temples of tyrants will within a short time come to an end. Therefore I announce this to you who delight in a transitory sweetness and long to abound in these earthly riches: that you will have sorrow from your joy, seeing that everything which you gather together under the sun will vanish; your play will turn into pain and your prosperity be changed into torment. Yet how are *our days nothing*, when our days seem to each of us many, long and laborious? But do not be mistaken, do not be deceived, do not promise yourself many present days: they are nothing, there are none, I dare to say.

Thus the rich are deceived, the voluptuous are ensnared; all devoted to transitory things, overshadowed by carnal cares, caught by the enemy's talons, will be strangled. Here I demand, I beg, I implore, I ask: *Spare me, Lord*, so I may not perish with the depraved, not be condemned with the wicked.]

Structurally, this sermon-like opening is modelled on that of *Super Canticum Canticorum*, from the proclamatory introduction of a *thema*, to its repetition as a question, to the citing of *prothemata* (three verses with 'dies' in them, 125.3–7), to the 'begging' reintroduction of the *thema*; 'postulo, deposco, flagito,' is clearly based on *Super Canticum Canticorum* 2.18–19 (itself from Bernard, see Chapter 6, n. 9): 'Iterum clamo, cogito, deprecor, *Osculetur me osculo oris sui.*' Yet stylistically the passage recalls *Melos Amoris*, being heavily alliterative and ostentatious in its assumption of a prophetic voice which constantly identifies its own utterances as unanswerable truth. 'Annuncio vobis . . . audeo dicere': the whole work is full of such expressions of inspired daring, much like the ones sprinkled through *Melos Amoris*, but here used for denouncements of sinners and expressions of penitence, not bold statements about the elect. Thankfully, the expositions do not also maintain the remorseless alliteration of *Melos Amoris* (this would be impossible in a work engaged so seriously in the interpretation of Scripture), reserving this device for climaxes, and elsewhere employing an expository language which strives for the clarity and intensity of Anselmian meditation and is dense in biblical quotation and allusion. Nonetheless, it seems likely that Rolle's conscious intention in writing this exposition was to represent *canor* in the same sense *Melos Amoris* does, this time in a work which would proclaim a more widely applicable message, and be written in a medium that would attract a much larger audience. *Canor* is now being used to teach the way to the joyful heavenly feast, as well as being a participation in it.

Super Lectiones Mortuorum is thus a production of Rolle's newly articulated desire to be of spiritual benefit to his readers, and to address not only mystical specialists like himself but the Church as a whole. In these terms the work is an enormous success, a *tour de force* of didactic exposition which constitutes Rolle's most important breakthrough since he found his bold and winsome narrative voice in *Incendium Amoris*. So much is clear, even before we look at the work itself, from the evidence of its bibliographic history, as this has been assembled by Moyes. Several points are of interest here. First, the work was among Rolle's most popular; surviving complete in forty-two manuscripts, and in several more in extracts, it was the first of his works to be printed, and the only one (other than *Super Threnos*) to appear in print on its own (in Theoderic Rood's Oxford edition of 1483, and again in Bernard Rembolt's Paris edition of 1510) before modern times.[4] Second, it proved popular with the readers in whom Rolle was probably most interested, the secular clergy who exercised the ministry of preaching denied to him, through whom, and only through whom, he could truly hope to speak to the whole Church; Moyes shows that the work appears in a number of clerical wills from the diocese of York (vol. 1, pp. 75–76; vol. 2, p. 115), and that several of the surviving manuscripts (e.g. MSS Bodley 52, 315 and Lat. Th. 11) were owned or copied by members of the secular clergy. There is nothing in the work (as with *Judica Me*) to imply that it was written only for this group, but its many allusions to priests (e.g. 200.5, 230.7–8, 231.5–232.2, 251.10–252.15) and the fact that it offers a mass of material suitable for preaching suggest that Rolle had the secular clergy especially in mind.[5] Third, the work was intellectually respectable, as is witnessed by the number of copies associated with Oxford or owned by Oxford men, and by Rood's edition of the work – the title page of which claims (justifiably) that the commentary 'glosses very precisely the historical not less than the tropological and anagogical meanings for the use of students' ('qui non minus hystoriam quam tropologiam et anagogiam ad studentium utilitatem exactissime annotavit'; Moyes, vol. 1, pp. 77–78; vol. 2, p. 118). Lastly, many of the manuscripts in which it occurs are not otherwise associated with Rolle – this in contrast to the way *Melos Amoris* almost always appears in manuscripts solely dedicated to his writings (see Chapter 7, n. 14) – and in these manuscripts it is in varied and often distinguished company. Thus in MS Bodley 525 it appears with pseudo-Bernard's *Meditationes Piissimae* and a *vita* of Paul the first hermit; in Laud Lat. 94 it is part of a sermon-collection; in Magdalen 6 it is part of a miscellaneous scholarly collection that includes Holcot's commentary on the Book of Wisdom; in New College 93 it follows a copy of Paul's epistles and sermons by Bede, Gregory and Augustine; in St John's College, Oxford 147 it opens a collection of saints' *vitae*; and in Dd.iv.54 we find it with *Emendatio Vitae* and part of *The Form of Living* alongside the *De Miseria Condicionis Humanae*, pseudo-Bernard's *Meditationes*, and treatises on temptation and its remedies from the *Speculum Spiritualium* (vol. 2, pp. 1–51). There are few signs that the work was known on the Continent before the sixteenth century (Moyes, vol. 1, pp. 70–72); but in England it was evidently considered an important contribution to the canon of penitential and expository literature, and was read by an array of educated people, some of whom may not otherwise have known Rolle's work.

The success of *Super Lectiones Mortuorum* can be accounted for in a general way by comparing it with Rolle's own earlier commentaries. After his first exercises, which stay close both to the text on which he is commenting and to the text of the *Glossa Ordinaria* which he is imitating, Rolle slowly takes wing as a lyrical expositor of lyrical texts; these he increasingly expounds, from *Super Magnificat* on, with sole reference to the *verus amator Christi*, showing less and less interest in the interpretations given in the *Glossa*. *Super Psalmum Vicesimum* is self-consciously original in its presentation of the 'king' in that psalm as the *perfectus*, and *Super Canticum Canticorum*, though it follows tradition in interpreting the Song of Songs mystically, insists on a highly idiosyncratic version of the text's mystical message. With the possible exception of the Psalter commentaries, *Super Lectiones Mortuorum* is, then, the first commentary since *Super Apocalypsim* or *Super Threnos* to focus on what Rolle deems the Holy Spirit to say through the text about and for the benefit of ordinary Christians, as well as the *perfecti*; moreover, it is the only commentary he wrote to do this without being based on an authoritative earlier gloss (see Clark 1986, pp. 180–183). It is true that to an extent the clarity and independence of the work simply show how much Rolle learned from writing *Super Canticum Canticorum* and *Super Psalmum Vicesimum*. Thus the way in which *Super Lectiones Mortuorum* emphasizes the structure of the text at moments of transition is clearly a development of the attempts *Super Canticum Canticorum* makes in the same direction.[6] The work also imitates *Super Canticum Canticorum* by formally subordinating the text on which it comments to its glosses. Where most of *Super Threnos* or *Super Apocalypsim* could be presented on the page in the manner of a gloss – as sets of marginal notes surrounding the texts on which they comment – Rolle's exposition here follows *Super Canticum Canticorum* in the way it weaves Job's words, the other biblical texts they evoke and his own comments into a seamless expository narrative. Yet in spite of these instances of indebtedness, *Super Lectiones Mortuorum* is unique in combining the passionate, declamatory voice of the commentaries immediately preceding it with the lucid verse-by-verse exposition of a text which remains the real focus of the proceedings – and in managing this combination with a dexterous sophistication which adds to, rather than detracting from, the impression of a weighty moral seriousness he intends to create. It is not surprising that, notwithstanding even the popularity of the *English Psalter*, it should have been the most widely read of all Rolle's biblical expositions.

So much for the success and originality of *Super Lectiones Mortuorum* in general: how do these qualities emerge in detail? A complete answer to this question would involve a vast range of rhetorical and expository strategies and kinds of subject-matter, for in spite of having what seems to us the narrow label 'penitential' attached to it, this is among the most varied of Rolle's works. Here, however, our account of the particular quality of the expository voice in this work – its passion, clarity, sophistication and responsiveness to the text – must confine itself to the analysis of a single extended passage. I have chosen the following extract from *Lectio* III:

Pelle et carnibus vestisti me ossibus et nervis compegisti et cetera [Job 10.11]. Hec ad litteram potent manifeste intuente. *Pelle et carnibus*, id est, corpore vestisti me, vestimentum vero anime est corpus. Unde in Ysaia: *Vestimentum mixtum sanguine erit in combustione, et cibus ignis* [Isaiah 9.5], id est, corpus sceleribus et immundicia peccati pollutum *erit in combustione et cibus ignis* infernalis; istud autem fit quando homo moritur et anima egreditur ac siquis a vestibus suis exuatur. Cupiens igitur iustus vir magnificare Deum et flectere ipsum ad faciendum cum eo misericordiam beneficia que ei exibuit recolit, et quantum ad corpus et quantum ad animam pertinet evidenter ponit: *Pelle et carnibus vestisti me et cetera.* Hec corporis sunt; et statim subigit de anima: *Vitam et misericordiam tribuisti michi* [Job 10.12] – vitam spiritualem eciam et corporalem tribuis et misericordiam qua salvor largiris. Inde vero scribitur: *Vivens vivens ipse confitebitur tibi* [Isaiah 38.19]; vivens corpore, vivens gracia et caritate ipse confitebitur tibi, id est, laudabit te, quia *non infernus confitebitur tibi, neque mors laudabit te; et non expectabunt qui descendunt in lacum veritatem tuam* [Isaiah 38.18]. Dicit ergo fidelis anima ab hac luce transiens: 'O domine Ihesu Christe, creator et redemptor meus, bene fecisti michi. *Pelle et carnibus vestisti me et cetera*, id est, spirituali fortitudine et non ficta humilitate conglutinasti me tibi, ut in societate superna tecum eternaliter subsistam, videndo te *facie ad faciem* [1 Corinthians 12.13], in deliciis divinitatis tue saciatus, quod est gaudium plenum perfectum et consummatum.' Sine ossibus robur in homine non est, ergo per illa ossa quibus viciis et voluptatibus resistit quis fortitudo interior recte intelligitur. Per nervos autem habemus liniamenta membrorum, ut in iuncturas movere et stare, sedere et ambulare possimus, per quos igitur humilitatem designare non incongrue videmus; nam sine humilitate nec in unitatem caritatis coniungimur, nec recte movemur, nec in mandatis Dei stamus, nec in bona vita sedemus, et bene non ambulamus sed erramus. Dum ergo devota mens in desideriis celestibus suspenditur, ossibus et nervis fortitudine et humilitate conpaginatur; et inde fit quod suavitate consciencie purgate in se iugiter retinet, cui vitam et misericordiam eterna magestas prebet. Unde sequitur: *Vitam et misericordiam tribuisti michi* [Job 10.11], id est, teipsum qui solus vera et eterna vita es, quam qui habet per graciam securus est, quia gloriam angelicam introibit; et misericordiam tribuis quia me *ab omnibus malis liberas* [Matthew 6.13], et inter sanctos et electos tuos sedem perhennis requiei concedis sortiri. (184.1–185.20)

[*You have clothed me with skin and flesh, and fastened me together with bones and sinews etc.* These words can obviously be understood in the literal sense. *Skin and flesh*: i.e. you have clothed me in a body, since the body is the soul's clothing. Thus in Isaiah: *Clothing mixed with blood will be in the burning and be food for the fire*, i.e. the body of the sinner polluted by wickedness and uncleanness *will be in the burning and be food* for the infernal *fire*; for the same thing happens when a person dies and the soul comes forth as when somebody strips off his clothing. Thus the just man, desiring to glorify God and to move him to have mercy on him, calls to mind the benefits he has bestowed on him, and clearly describes what pertains to the body, what to the soul: *You have clothed me with skin and flesh etc.* These are of the body; and he at once adds, of the soul: *You have bestowed on me life and mercy* – you bestow spiritual life even as fleshly life, and you grant the mercy by which I am saved. So it is written: *Living, living, he will trust in you*; living in body, living by grace and charity, he will trust in you, i.e. he will praise you, since *Hell will not trust in you, nor death praise you; and those who go down into the pit do not await your truth*. And so the faithful soul, passing away from this light, says: 'O lord Jesus Christ, my creator and redeemer, you have done well by me. *You have clothed me in skin and flesh etc.* (i.e. you have cemented me to you with spiritual fortitude and unfeigned humility) so that I may live with you for ever in the community of heaven, seeing you *face to face*, replete in the delights of your divinity, because joy is full, perfect and consummate.' There is no strength in someone without bones; thus the inner fortitude by which one resists vices and indulgences is properly understood by these bones. Through our sinews we derive the shape of our limbs, so that we can move and stand, sit and walk as one entity; therefore it does not seem odd to denote humility by them, since without humility we are neither knit together in the unity of love, nor do we move aright, nor stand in the commandments of God, nor sit in the good life, and we do not walk well but go astray. So when the devout mind is lifted up in celestial desires, it is knit together by bones and sinews, fortitude and humility; and thus it is that he to whom the eternal majesty offers life and mercy holds himself together continually with the sweetness of a purified conscience. And so it goes on: *You have bestowed on me life and mercy*, i.e. yourself, you who alone are life true and eternal, which whoever has by grace is secure, because he will enter the angelic glory; and you bestow mercy since you *free me from all ills* and are willing to grant me a seat among your saints and elect in perpetual rest.]

This passage immediately follows a prolonged discussion of the corruption of the earthly bodies of the elect after death (179.14–184.2), and is largely independent of earlier commentaries, sharing with the *Glossa Ordinaria* only the interpretation of 'bones and sinews' as 'fortitude and humility' (see PL 113, col. 786). It offers several interpretations of parts of the verse, constructing out of the whole a single, albeit criss-crossing, narrative. First the words of the text are explicated in the literal sense, with the aid of a verse of Isaiah which is used to account for the image of the body as clothing, and which briefly reminds us of the fate of the bodies of the damned. Then the speaker of the verse, the *iustus vir* who is figured by Job himself, is described as trying to win mercy by reminding God of the good things he has bestowed, bodily and spiritual. Isaiah is brought in for clarification, and to reinforce the speech of the *iustus vir* by calling to God's attention that those who live in body and spirit glorify him in ways those who are damned do not. There follows a passage of direct speech by a *fidelis anima* at the point of death. This looks like a dramatization of Job's and Isaiah's words in the abject form in which they have so far been expounded; in fact, though, it breaks new ground by suddenly shifting to a tropological reading of the verse, in which God is seen endowing the faithful with the necessary fortitude and humility to attain salvation, and in which he thus no longer needs to be reminded of his goodness, but can be addressed with joy and gratitude. The heavy alliteration and sonority of this short speech are succeeded by a more matter-of-fact pair of sentences, in which the new moral interpretation of the verse is justified in retrospect and a warning note sounded about the need for humility; but this soon gives way to an optimistic restatement of the idea that a *devota mens* who longs for God has, and keeps, the virtues and purity needed to attain eternal life and the vision of God. Just as the literal 'bones and sinews' in the text are interpreted morally, so the moral terms 'life and mercy' are now interpreted anagogically, as referring to God himself. The passage can thus end with the speaker, who has been identified in turn as the penitential *iustus vir*, as the justified *fidelis anima* and as the spiritually secure *devota mens*, taking a place in the saints' everlasting rest. What this relatively brief exposition offers, then, is a linked series of interpretations, which are demanding morally, intellectually and emotionally, and which bring out the meaning of two verses as they apply both to the whole course of the spiritual life and to the whole spectrum of the elect – from those who fear damnation to those who are secure of salvation. Its usefulness lies in its clarity, its moral earnestness, perhaps in the ease with which a priestly reader could adapt it as a sermon outline (it provides theme, antitheme and divisions). Most important, though, is the fact that rather than focussing entirely on the perfect and the reprobate it attempts to bring out what the Holy Spirit intends the verses to say to the whole Church, giving a complete reading of the text from which everyone, potentially, could benefit.

'Mixed' life: Super Lectiones Mortuorum

I hope this example of Rolle's procedures in *Super Lectiones Mortuorum* is adequate to show first that this work is unlike his earlier expositions, second that it is a conscious manifestation of the teaching role he accords himself in the last chapters of *Melos Amoris*. But we should also note that this passage, in common with the work as a whole, is suggestive of a quite particular view of the kind of teaching it is proper for hermits to engage in. Cap. 48 of *Melos Amoris*, where the idea of an eremitic 'mixed' life is first articulated, introduces it as part of a digression on preaching, and does not draw clear distinctions between the ways in which the secular clergy address parishioners in their charge and those in which solitaries address the Church, except to say that the latter write rather than speak. Yet it is obvious that Rolle is not likely to take much interest in the mundane, pragmatic and simple kinds of teaching appropriate for the lowliest members of the Church; indeed, *Super Lectiones Mortuorum* proves that he has something different in mind. What Rolle means by preaching in this work, and to a large extent in even the most practical of his other late works, involves the exposition of a text or structure of ideas in loftily general didactic terms. The *utilitas* of the work, lauded by Theoderic Rood, is not a matter of its engagement in the predicament of Christian individuals, any more than it is a matter of its articulation of a balanced view of the penitential themes with which it deals; it lies, rather, in the skill of the exposition itself, and in the affective end to which the exposition is directed. The work casts its net more effectively in the direction of sinners than the nominally evangelistic *Contra Amatores Mundi*. Yet, for all its expository complexity, its didacticism is no more than a sophisticated version of what the first part of *Judica Me* describes as 'encouraging the good and terrifying the wicked' (4.20–21). This can be superbly effective in its way; the work's denunciations of sin, for example, can still elicit twinges of self-disgust and fear (see, e.g., 248.13). But these passages, like most of the work, are informative only in the inspirational sense that they remind us forcibly how much God abhors sin; they do not provide us with a plan of action to help us recognize and flee sin. Even in *Emendatio Vitae* and *The Form of Living*, which are greatly more practical and programmatic than *Super Lectiones Mortuorum*, Rolle seems to assume either that such a plan is too obvious to need describing, or that his readers know it already. His teaching ministry remains somewhat aloof and spiritually aristocratic: he leaves the details to those who are still engaged in the world in a way he is not.

This aspect of Rolle's practice as an eremitic preacher is important when we return to our starting-point, the notion that *Super Lectiones Mortuorum* is a divinely inspired expression of *canor*, and examine how the work makes such a claim for itself; for it is no part of his programme as a practitioner of 'mixed' life that we should forget the divine source of all he says. In many earlier works which make this claim, the urgent audacity of Rolle's assertiveness derails his attempts to write in ways which are of spiritual *utilitas* to readers, forcing him, as we have seen, on to ever more esoteric and self-concerned ground. Here, however, he avoids this difficulty, not by retreating into the background, but by taking a stance as a prophetic mediator between text and reader, who amplifies Job's words, and whose self-conscious verbal gestures contribute considerably to the excitement, hence the inspirational effectiveness, of the work. The text, in its interpreted form, is full of voices – voices of the damned, the sinner, the penitent, the saved, the just. Rolle, of course, distances himself from the first of these, but dramatizes the others in long passages of first-person commentary, such as his amplification of Job 7.20a, '*Peccavi*': 'Ergo statuam me coram me et arguam meipsum, condempnans culpam meam; scrubator vitam meam ab infancia mea purgans *renes meos et cor meum* [Psalm 26.2] . . .' (142.20–143.2: 'So I will judge myself before myself, and accuse myself, condemning my sin; I will consider my life from my childhood, purging *my loins and my heart*'). In these passages, as in some of the last chapters of *Melos Amoris*, Rolle is anxious to humble himself, to stress the solidarity rather than the gulf between the *perfectissimi* and ordinary Christians. In other passages, his prophetic role is expressed in more assertive ways. I have noted that *Super Lectiones Mortuorum* is as full of expressions of ostentatious narratorial daring as *Melos Amoris* – and it is true that the prefacing of any remark with 'audeo annunciare' or 'dico' does much to keep readers excitedly aware of a modern voice speaking, meaning, and thus revitalizing long-established penitential themes. But in this work Rolle also employs more complex devices for remaining in the forefront: in particular, he finds ways of stressing the difficulty of his expository task, the need for inspiration if he is to continue, and the certainty that he is inspired when he does. The passages in which he does this form a vital and often effective part of his overall didactic stance, with its grandiose concern for the universal rather than the particular, at the same time as serving to remind us that we are in the presence of a modern *auctor* to whom it behoves us to listen. Hence they are as relevant to the pastoral function of *Super Lectiones Mortuorum* as they are to its place in Rolle's programme of self-canonization as an authority.

The first passage in which Rolle comes to stage centre as a commentator occurs in his exposition of the second verse of *lectio* I, '*Quid est homo quia magnificas eum?*' (Job 7.17, 131.9: '*What is man that you magnify him?*'), at the point where he turns from a penitential reading ('Man is earth, ash and dust', 130.14) to a mystical one ('Of what sort is the man you magnify?'):

Qualis aut quantus est vellem noscere; si dignatus fueris servo tuo ostendere satagam aliis revelare; sed angustus sum valde in visceribus meis; amplifica me in misericordia et in miseracionibus tuis . . . Nempe conor *eructare verbum bonum* [Psalm 45.1], spargere eloquium tuum, ut cognoscant homines quid ille homo sit *quem tu magnificas*, ne quisquam frustra se extollat . . . Vere scio quod si non habeam a te quod quero, nullicubi inveniam illud; ergo si dederis dulce lumen oculorum meorum, ambulans non devio, loquens non erro, tacens non decipior, sedens in otium non laboro, vivens non illaqueor, moriens non tormentor.   (131.9–132.3)

[I want to know of what kind or how great he is; if you deign to show this to your servant, I will make it my business to reveal it to others. But I am strongly constrained in my vitals; in your mercy and compassion, enlarge me. Surely I try *to give out good words*, to scatter forth your eloquence, so that people may know what the man *whom you magnify* is like – lest someone should glorify himself in vain. Truly I know that if I do not have what I want from you, I will find it nowhere; so, if you will grant a sweet light for my eyes, while I walk I will not stray, while I speak not err, while I am silent not be deceived, while I am sitting at rest not work, while I live not be ensnared, when I die not be tormented.]

The passage develops from being a prayer for understanding of a particular point (and implicitly of the whole text on which he is to comment) into an appeal for divine inspiration in Rolle's entire life. The tone of the prayer is in accord with the humbly penitential attitude the work as a whole takes towards God; where *Melos Amoris*, with its stress on the idea that Rolle's *canor* is continuous, only shows us poetic inspiration in full flood, here we are allowed to see the expositor having to wait on a Holy Spirit who blows where he wills. Yet this makes little difference, for we are prevented from harbouring any doubts that Rolle's petition has succeeded by his immediate answer to Job's question – '[Homo] est autem mundus, iustus, pius, castus . . .' (132.5–6) – and by the freedom he then takes to ask further questions: 'Non solum miramur, *Quid sit homo quia magnificas eum*, sed eciam querimus ut sciamus vel ad *quid apponis erga eum cor tuum?*' (Job 7.17, 132.16–18: 'We do not only wonder, *What is man that you magnify him*, but we also seek to know why *you set your heart on him?*'). Clearly the 'enlargement' he begged for has occurred. The spirit of the two works may be quite different, but in this appeal *Super Lectiones Mortuorum* celebrates the process of its own inspiration with almost as much *audacitas* as does *Melos Amoris*.

There are a number of similar passages in the work. In one, Rolle asks for the prayers of the 'holy elders' to protect him from error: 'O sancti seniores orate pro me iuvene, ut non errem in hac exposicione' (169.4–5). Faced with a difficult text, he refuses to follow other commentaries but enlists the help of all the Church Fathers to pray for him – preferring to have earlier *auctores* provide him with inspiration from their seats in heaven than to subject himself to what they wrote while on earth. In another, Rolle claims that a verse is so hard that almost nobody can expound it, but that he can declare what has been revealed to him (254.15–20). At the beginning of the last *lectio* he states that he is unwilling to continue, so harsh is the subject-matter, but that he is constrained to speak lest he be found silent or ignorant (274.7–9). Finally, in many manuscripts, the work ends with a verse signature (surely authentic), which seems intended to round off this series of reminders of Rolle's inspiration:

> Talentum traditum timens subffodere fimum,
> Sit pueris pabulum, hoc semen spargit opimum;
> Dilexit heremum, sonuit sibi cantus amorum,
> Quem geris in iubilum, tu, Christe corona Ricardum.
> Amen. Explicit. (283.3–8)

[Fearing lest he bury his God-given gift in earth,
He scatters this rich seed – may it be food for youth.
He loved the desert, for himself he sang his song of love,
Which you manifest in joy, O Christ; crown Richard above.]

Like Milton, Rolle is not prepared to conceal his 'one talent which is death to hide' (Sonnet XIX, see Matthew 25.18), when he can instead be the sower, some of whose seed falls on good ground and multiplies (Matthew 13.23; compare the close of *Melos Amoris*, quoted on p. 187).

Super Lectiones Mortuorum thus keeps before our eyes a view of its own authority which has as little as possible to do with its highly traditional subject-matter, as much as possible with its literary independence and direct reliance on God. For all the care Rolle brings to his exposition of Job's words, he implicitly lays claim to an authority which is of the same kind as that inhering in his text – at least in the sense that he aims to produce a final and definitive interpretation of that text. It is not surprising, then, that at one point in the work he should feel the need to address the question of his status as a commentator more directly than he can do in the cut and thrust of exposition – and it is with a look at the passage in which he does this that my analysis of this work ends. The passage is introduced as a digression from Rolle's exposition of Job 13.25, which argues that God damns the wicked in a mood not of anger but of indifferent scorn:

Propter quod nec ego timeo hereticos aut invidos qui forsitan insurgent contra me dicentes aut me in exposicione errasse, aut sacra verba congruenter non tractasse, non acceptantes quia modernus sum. Sed profecto qui bonos modernos reprobat, hesternos non laudat. Non enim est Deus modo minoris bonitatis quam fuit in primitiva ecclesia, quia adhuc electos suos ad amorem eternitatis desiderandum preparat et quos vult celesti scientia sapienciaque divina inspirat. Verum sciatis quia episcopus non sum neque prelatus neque rector Ecclesie; tamen solicitus sum pro Ecclesia Dei, si possem aliquo bono modo quicquam facere vel scribere quo Ecclesiam Christi augmentum capiat in divina dilectione. Sum utique solitarius intencione et heremite propositum arripui, atque mutata tunica soli Deo vacare concupivi; quamobrem forsitan quia pauper sum et non reputatus inter magistratus mundi, parvipenditis verba que loquor vobis. Sed si me contempnitis, quod parvum reputo, hoc unum sciatis: quia nunquam Deus nec pape nec episcopo nec alicui alio cuiusquam status fuerit, singulari Virgine excepta, de gloria eterni amoris in hac vita illam prerogativam tribuit quam vero solitario et eminenti denegavit. Unde qui arguere contendunt communem vitam plus valere quam heremiticam, si considerent instanciam exterioris operis non affluentiam interne contemplacionis, nimirum decipere probantur; quia dum austeriori penitencie heremita se subicit, atque et cum hoc in canorum iubilum Christo amante surgit. Quis audeat aliquem hic preponere, et quamvis mortuos suscitaverit, et maxima opera fecerit, quem Deus in tanto amoris sui misterio dignatur collocare? Sed querite de hac materia in Libello de Vita Heremitarum et etiam in Libro de Perfeccione et Gloria Sanctorum, quia ibi invenietis de eminencia sanctitatis. (195.15–197.10)

[On account of which ⟨the fact that God will damn the wicked⟩ I fear neither heretics nor the envious who will perhaps rise up against me, saying either that I erred in exposition or that I did not treat the holy words properly, not accepting me because I am a modern. But certainly he who rejects the good moderns will not praise the good people of antiquity. For God is not now of less goodness than he was in the earliest time of the Church, since he still prepares his elect to desire love of eternity, and inspires whom he will with celestial knowledge and divine wisdom. Know truly that I am not a bishop, nor a prelate, nor a rector of the Church; but I am concerned for the Church of God, if I may in any way do or write something good, by which the Church of Christ may lay hold of an increase in the divine sweetness. In fact I am a solitary by intention and took to the way of life of a hermit, and after changing my dress desired only to be alone with God. On which account, perhaps, because I am a poor man and not of repute among the magistrates of the world, you may despise the words I say to you. But if you condemn me, which I reckon a small thing, know this one thing: that God never bestowed on Pope or on bishop or on anyone else, whatever their status was (with the single exception of the Virgin), that privilege of the glory of eternal love in this life which even to the eminent and solitary he denied. Thus those who try to argue that the communal life is more worthy than the eremitic, if they consider the zeal of external works, not the richness of internal contemplation, are proved indubitably to be deceived; for while the hermit submits himself to a greater austerity of penance, he also rises up with Christ as lover in the jubilation of song. Who dares to set anyone – even if he raises the dead and does the greatest works – over the one whom God has deemed worthy to establish in so great a mystery of his love? But look for this subject in the Book of the Eremitic Life, and also in the Book of the Perfection and Glory of the Saints, for there you may discover about the eminence of sanctity.]

All the points Rolle puts forward here are familiar from his earlier works. His opening statement, that moderns have the potential to be as holy and as truly inspired as the ancients (the Church Fathers) is the principal subject announced by the first chapter of *Melos Amoris* ('De Perfeccione et Gloria Sanctorum', see Chapter 7, n. 2); his view of the solitary life emerges in *Incendium Amoris* (perhaps 'De Vita Heremitarum', see Chapter 1, n. 21). Only his insistence that solicitude for the Church is his motive in writing, and the way in which he finally shrugs off the whole subject, are particularly characteristic of the phase of his career I have labelled as the eremitic 'mixed' life. My analysis of *Super Lectiones Mortuorum* as an expression of that phase has treated the work as an independent and self-sufficient piece of inspired exposition, which has progressed beyond the apologetic exigences of the works it follows. It is interesting that at this one point Rolle should have felt the need to refer us back to the arguments of those works, and even to mention two of the works themselves, as if to steady himself, and to remind us of the apologetic structure by which his generally confident performance here is sustained.

II

Super Lectiones Mortuorum represents an attempt to uphold Rolle's view of his divine inspiration, as propagated by *Melos Amoris*, while drastically changing his subject-matter. It is self-conscious about its own eloquence, and about the originality of its expositions of the details of the biblical text, but is for the most part correspondingly unoriginal in the penitential message it proclaims. Although there are references in the work to virtually all the elements of Rolle's mystical system, these are so unemphatic as to have little impact on the conventionality of the work's universal call to repentance.[7] By writing this work, Rolle clearly signals his intention of realigning himself both with his readers and with the mainstream of religious literature, from which his earlier writings emerge with such distinctiveness.

This intention clearly underlies the form, style and content of what was probably Rolle's last Latin work, *Emendatio Vitae*. Yet as we turn to this, by far his most popular and still his most readable achievement, it is at once striking how much it differs from *Super Lectiones Mortuorum* in the ways in which it sets about realizing this same double realignment. Gone is the prophetic voice, the overt claim to inspiration, the audacity, much of the stylistic elevation; gone is the uncharacteristic emphasis on penitential themes. Here instead is a voice which speaks mostly in the *stylo humilis* Augustine recommends to preachers (*De Doctrina Christiana* IV; see Copeland 1984), warmly personal but no longer overtly autobiographical, undeniably inspiring without ever alluding to the sources of its own inspiration; here, too, is Rolle's mystical system, which has again become his major focus, but which is described with a new clarity and respect for what other writers have said. Unlike *Super Lectiones Mortuorum*, the work can claim to be genuinely original in its structure, which is not that of Rolle's earlier *libri* and is only generally reminiscent of spiritual writings by anyone else; yet far from making any such claim, parts of the work are borrowed from several sources, including Rolle's own earlier writings, and the whole seems designed to give the impression that it is little more than a collection of spiritual commonplaces. In short, *Emendatio Vitae* is as clearly an expression of the priorities of the 'mixed' life as is *Super Lectiones Mortuorum*, but one which has been made to an intriguingly different recipe.

As we saw in Chapter 2 (which gives a partial account of the work as its means of entry into the structure of Rolle's thought), the form of *Emendatio Vitae*, like that of many mystical works, is the same as the form of the ascent to God it describes, from conversion to contemplation:

Hic est Libellus De Emendatione Vite, sive De Regula Vivendi, et distinguitur in xii capitulis: primo, de conversione; secundo, de contemptu mundi; tercio, de paupertate; quarto, de institucione vite; quinto, de tribulacione; sexto, de paciencia; septimo, de oracione; ottavo, de meditacione; nono, de leccione; decimo, de puritate mentis; undecimo, de amore Dei; duodecimo, de contemplacione.   (MS Dd.v.64, f. 1r.)

[This is the Book of the Amending of Life, or of the Form of Living, and it is divided into twelve chapters: the first about conversion; the second about contempt for the world; the third about poverty; the fourth about organizing one's life; the fifth about tribulation; the sixth about patience; the seventh about prayer; the eighth about meditation; the ninth about reading; the tenth about purity of mind; the eleventh about the love of God; the twelfth about contemplation.]

This description was omitted by Faber in his 1536 edition of the work, but is in almost all the manuscripts (either as a prologue or as an epilogue), and is certainly authentic, as are the titles and numbers of the chapters when they appear again in the body of the work.[8] Where Rolle's three earlier *libri* consist of probably unnumbered (and certainly untitled) sections, here each chapter has a specific and specified place in an overall scheme. The obvious numerical symbolism involved (twelve chapters discernibly subdivided into four groups of three),[9] as with the nine orders of angels in *Ego Dormio* and the trios of 'violent love' in several of the late works, contributes to the authority of the scheme, but also to its mnemonic clarity and hence practical value. The spiritual ascent itemized here is, of course, based on Rolle's own life, as well as on the model accounts of the way to God he develops out of his own experience in earlier works. There is indeed a surprising amount of auto-biographical material to be found between the lines of the work. Even the ordering of the chapters makes best sense when we think of them as stages in a hermit's progress: conversion, flight from the world, embracing of poverty, establishment in a rule of life, persecution and the acquisition of patience in the face of it, performance of spiritual exercises, final arrival at purity of soul, the love of God, and the graces of contemplation. But this hidden self-referentiality is developed into a picture of the spiritual life which has been abstracted and generalized for non-eremitic readers more fully than in any of Rolle's other works; for the principal material for each chapter or group of chapters is drawn from one or another part of the great pool of common-places about the spiritual life, and is not obviously tied to the experience of any one individual. By thus combining established autobiographical themes with equally established religious commonplaces, *Emendatio Vitae* achieves a fusion of the personal and the general which must have gone far towards making it one of the most successful works of spiritual guidance ever written in England. Behind the scenes, but in a move which is crucial for the way we read Rolle's earlier works in retrospect, it also achieves an apologetic goal which can properly be described in two ways: as showing how Rolle's spiritual life, on which he has expended so much ink and praise, fits into a wider pattern and is not the idiosyncratic thing it has seemed; and as generalizing that life, so that it becomes itself the pattern for all who aspire to holiness to follow, whether or not they aspire to the solitary life. Yet again, though nowhere so tellingly as here, Rolle has set himself up as 'the glass of fashion, the mould of form, th'observed of all observers' (*Hamlet* III.i.152–153).

Before looking at parts of the work in more detail, what help does the manuscript tradition give us in interpreting *Emendatio Vitae*? I have already alluded to the work's great success: 110 manuscript copies, in Latin and in seven distinct English translations, still survive (Allen, pp. 230–245; Moyes 1988, vol. 1, p. 19, n. 100). It was printed in 1510 (in Paris, at the end of an edition of the popular compilation *Speculum Spiritualium*, which itself contains quotations from the work), in 1533 (in Antwerp), and in Faber's Cologne edition of Rolle's works in 1535 and 1536; it features in other compilations, including the *De Excellentia Contemplationis* and the vernacular

Richard Rolle and the invention of authority

treatises *Disce Mori* and the much-copied *Pore Caitif* (Allen, p. 243, Brady 1981). As with *Super Lectiones Mortuorum*, the wide distribution of the work and the variety of contexts in which it appears in manuscripts amply support this general picture: it, too, is found as the only work of Rolle's beside sermons, e.g. those attributed to Augustine in MS Bodley 43; with theological treatises, e.g. the *Compendium Theologicae Veritatis* in Bodley 456, and Hugh of St Victor's great *De Sacramentis* (in a thirteenth-century copy) in Hatton 26; with the pastoral letters of Peter of Blois, in Trinity College, Cambridge 17; and with academic biblical expositions by John Waldeby and Grosseteste, as well as with *Super Lectiones Mortuorum*, in Royal 7.E.ii. In manuscripts produced in England it also occurs very regularly alongside the other great ascetic and devotional works which were similarly written for a wide audience: St Edmund Rich's *Speculum Ecclesie* (e.g. Bodley 54, Hatton 26, Ff.v.36, BL Add. 16170), the pseudo-Bonaventuran *Stimulus Amoris* (e.g. Magdalen 71) and *Meditationes Vitae Christi* (e.g. Bodley 61, Ff.v.36, Trinity College, Cambridge 17), pseudo-Bernard's *Meditationes Piissimae* (e.g. Bodley 61, Harley 275), the *Speculum Peccatoris* (e.g. Hatton 26, Ff.v.36, Harley 5938), Innocent III's *De Miseria Condicionis Humanae* (e.g. Harley 275 and 5938). The English translations of the work are to be found with Rolle's English works in manuscripts which contain relatively specialized devotional or mystical material (e.g. Ff.v.40, Lansdowne 455), but also in Edinburgh University 93, a codified compendium of the Ten Commandments, the gifts of the Spirit and other basic religious topics. Faced with a work which had so wide-ranging an appeal, a superficial survey of the manuscripts such as this can indicate no more than that we need to focus our attention on the features of *Emendatio Vitae* which were deemed to have made it suitable for virtually anyone, lay or learned, to read.

Each chapter of *Emendatio Vitae* has its own tone and mode of procedure, and the length, style, and structure is different in each case. This makes it hard to generalize about the work's strategies from particular examples, but is an integral feature of a book which embodies a spiritual ladder up which the reader is supposed to ascend – for the reader's development is both mirrored and encouraged by the shifts from one kind of writing to another, from the penitential opening to the mystical climax in caps. 11–12. Most of the chapters do, however, have features in common. With the exception of cap. 5, all of them are structured around a single word or phrase, usually corresponding to the chapter's title; in differing degrees, they return to this word or phrase as to a keynote, rather as one of Rolle's extended commentaries returns to phrases of its text. Most of them provide at least one definition of this word or phrase, often couched as a question: 'Quid enim est conversio ad Deum nisi aversio a mundo?' (cap. 1, f. 135r. 21–22); 'Contemnere mundum est cuncta temporalia et transitoria sine amore illorum per hanc vitam transire' (cap. 2, f. 135v. 25–26); 'Quid enim est paupertas nisi . . . ' (cap. 3, f. 136r. 26); 'Est autem charitas virtutum nobilissima, excellentissima et suavissima quam amatum cum amato coniungere scimus' (cap. 11, f. 140v. 21–22); 'Si quaeretur quid sit contemplatio, difficile est diffinire' (cap. 12, f. 141r. 27). The way chapters elaborate these definitions, e.g. by giving definitions of vices corresponding to the virtue in question (as in the play on 'conversio' and 'aversio' in the first passage quoted below) also resembles Rolle's practice as a commentator; the structure 'Quid enim est . . . nisi' is used in *Super Lectiones Mortuorum* (e.g. 202.9–10) as a means of defining a phrase. But the most significant generic affiliation suggested by the work's habit of defining and circling around the key words it uses as its chapter titles is with a form Rolle has not previously attempted (although see *Judica B1* 18.14–20, p. 81): the compendium. Rolle knew (and may use in cap. 4 of *Emendatio Vitae*, as he does elsewhere) the *Compendium Theologicae Veritatis* by Hugh of Strasbourg; he may also have been aware of Bonaventure's *Breviloquium*, another essay in the form. Both these works attempt to summarize the science of theology in a series of short chapters each of which deals with a particular topic. The prefaces to both works, like the dedication in some manuscripts of *Emendatio Vitae* (see n. 8), emphasize that their authors aspire at once to brevity and to summary completeness. Bonaventure explains that he wishes to write 'breve in summa . . . de veritate theologiae', touching only on what is most important; Hugh, that he has collected his short compendium from the writings of great theologians, shunning prolixity, the mother of disgust.[10] Bonaventure (like Rolle) begins with a list of chapters, dividing his work into a symbolically significant, and memorable, number of parts.[11] As with *Emendatio Vitae*, many of Hugh's chapters contain multiple definitions of a key word. For example, Book v, cap. xxiii is entitled 'De Caritate', and lists one definition of the word by Paul, another from Prosper of Aquitaine's (i.e. Julius Pomerius's) *De Vita Contemplativa*, and four from Peter Lombard's *Sententiae* iii, including 'Quid est charitas? Vita copulans amantem cum amato', which Rolle also gives. Of course there are large differences between *Emendatio Vitae* and both these much longer compendia. Yet within the confines of his chosen subject, and the affective modes appropriate to that subject, Rolle does very much what Hugh or Bonaventure does: he collects together the most important ideas connected with a topic – sometimes, like Hugh, compiling them from existing writings, more often formulating them, like Bonaventure, in original but pregnantly general *sententiae* – and places them in an organized framework. The status of *Emendatio Vitae* as a compendium of affective generalizations about the life of holiness is a major cause of its widespread popularity.

The first chapter of the work provides good illustrations of many of the points I have just made. I quote about the first half of the chapter:

Ne tardes converti ad Dominum et ne differas de die in diem [Ecclesiasticus 5.8]. Nam subito rapit miseros inclementia mortis inopinatae et devorat acerbitas poenarum. Nec a nobis numerari possunt quot mundanos praesumptio decepit. Magnum enim peccatum est in Dei misericordia confidere et a peccato non cessare, aestimando

Richard Rolle and the invention of authority

tantam esse Dei misericordiam ut nec iustam peccatoribus velit inferre poenam. *Ergo dum dies est operamini: venit nox quando nemo poterit operari* [John 9.4]. Lucem vel praesentem diem vocat vitam in qua a bonis operibus cessare nunquam debemus, scientes quod mors nobis incerta est. Noctem mortem appellat, in qua ligantur membra, privantur sensus, et iam aliquid salutiferum operari non possumus, sed secundum opera nostra gaudium recepturi sumus vel tormentum. In puncto vivimus, imo minus puncto, quia si totum tempus nostrum aeternitati comparetur nihil est. Quomodo non sine gravissima damnatione vitam nostram in amore vanitatum consumimus, et tota die ociosi stamus [Matthew 20.3]? *Converte ergo nos Domine* negligentes et impoenitentes *et convertemur ad te* [Lamentations 5.21]. Sana nos Domine et sanabimur [Jeremiah 17.14]. Multi enim sanantur sed corrumpunt vulnera eorum et putrescunt, quia hodie ad Deum conversi, cras autem a Deo sunt aversi, hodie poenitentes, cras ad pristina mala redeuntes. De talibus dictum est: *Curavimus Babylonem et non est sanata* [Jeremiah 51.9], quia ad Christum non est vere conversa. Quid enim est conversio ad Deum nisi aversio a mundo, a peccato, a diabolo, et a carne? Quid est adversio a Deo nisi conversio ad bonum commutabile, ad delectabilem speciem creaturarum, ad opera diaboli, ad voluptates carnis et mundi? Non enim incessu pedum ad Deum convertimur sed mutatione affectuum et morum. Conversio itaque sit ad Deum dum aciem mentis nostrae in Christum dirigimus, et eius consilia atque mandata incessanter cogitamus ut a nobis impleantur, et ubicumque fuerimus, perrexerimus, vel sederimus timor Dei a corde nostro non recedat. Non loquor de timore qui poenam habet, sed de illo qui est in charitate, quo reverentiam exhibemus praesentiae tantae maiestatis, et semper timemus ne Christum in modico offendamus. Sic quidem dispositi ad Deum recte convertimur a mundo quia avertimur. Averti autem a mundo nihil aliud est quam omnes delectationes postponere et amaritudines eius pro Christo libenter sustinere, et dare oblivioni omnes occupationes inutiles et negotia secularia; quatinus animus noster in toto ad Deum conversus ad omnia que in mundo sunt, amanda vel quaerenda medullitus moriatur.

(f. 135r. 1–35)

[*Do not be slow to be turned to the Lord, and do not put it off day after day.* For the harshness of death unlooked for suddenly seizes the wretched, and the bitterness of torment devours them. Nor can it be numbered by us how often presumption has ensnared the worldly. For it is a great sin to trust in the mercy of God and not to leave off sinning, reckoning God's mercy to be so great that he will not want to impose a just punishment on sinners. *So while the day is here, let us work; the night comes, when no one can work.* 'Light' or 'the present day' is what he calls life, in which we should never leave off doing good works, knowing that the time of our death is unknown. 'Night' is what he calls death, in which our limbs are tied, our senses blocked; and now we cannot perform any saving works, but are to receive, according to our works, joy or torment. We live in a moment – yes, in less than a moment, for if all our lifetime is compared to eternity it is nothing. How may we not without the deepest damnation consume our life in the love of vanities, and stand all the day in idleness? So *Turn us, Lord*, neglectful and impenitent, *and we will be turned to you.* Heal us and we will be healed. For many are healed, but their wounds decay and putrefy, since turned to God today, tomorrow they are turned away from God – penitent today, tomorrow gone back to their original wickedness. Of such people it is said: *We have treated Babylon and she is not healed*, because she is not truly turned to Christ. For what is turning to God except turning from the world, from sin, from the devil, and from the flesh? What is turning away from God except turning to changeable good, to the pleasing appearance of things that are made, to the works of the devil, to the indulgences of the flesh and the world? For we are not turned to God

212

by moving our feet but by changing our desires and behaviour. Therefore turning towards God is when we direct the keenness of our minds into Christ, and think constantly of his counsels and commandments, so that we may fulfil them; and wherever we are, wherever we go about, wherever we sit, the fear of God does not leave our hearts. I do not speak of the fear which is associated with punishment but of that which is in charity, by which we manifest reverence before the presence of so much majesty, and have constant fear in case we offend Christ in any little thing. So disposed, we are truly turned to God because truly turned away from the world. But to be turned away from the world is nothing else than to put behind us all its pleasures, and to suffer its bitterness freely for Christ, and to give all useless occupations and worldly business to forgetfulness. So far as our soul is turned to God in all, it is dead, deep within, to loving and seeking everything that is in the world.]

After a series of works beginning dramatically in the first person (*Judica Me, Incendium Amoris, Super Canticum Canticorum, Melos Amoris, Super Lectiones Mortuorum*), *Emendatio Vitae* opens with an earnest second-person exhortation, establishing the mode of address that is dominant throughout; until cap. 11, almost all the first-person pronouns and verbs are plural, identifying the speaker with whichever stage of the spiritual life he is expounding. We might consider the list of chapters before this opening as a brief prologue, but even so the work begins in a much more matter-of-fact way than Rolle has so far allowed himself, with none of the paraphernalia of *exordia*, voices declaring, intoning, asserting and the other self-reflexive tricks of his rhetorical high style. This voice merely speaks, starting with the most basic but also the most critical point the work makes – do not fail to turn to God – and stating matters with all the bluntness and apparent lack of artifice characteristic of the *stylo humilis*. As a whole, the passage has the apothegmatic quality of Chaucer's *Balade de Bon Conseyl* (e.g. 1–4: 'Flee fro the prees and dwelle with soothfastnesse; / Suffise thyn owene thing though it be smal; / For hoord hath hate and climbing tikelnesse; / Prees hath envye and wele blent overal'). Each statement stands on its own as a *sententia* requiring consideration; most seem to say much the same thing. Yet each follows from its predecessor and forms a necessary link to its successor; not only is there a clear overall argument, the position of any two sentences in the structure cannot be reversed without incongruity. The Latin is simpler than any Rolle has written since *Judica Me*. The ideas expressed are also simple, and none could be denied or qualified within the medieval Christian frame of reference. Rolle has found a new and deeply compelling way of identifying his own utterances with divine truth.

The chapter circles around the exhortation to 'turn', which sounds like a bell in sentence after sentence. But it also gradually evolves a picture of what this involves, by developing the distinctions between *conversio* and *aversio* mentioned above, indicating what worldly snares make conversion hard, and describing false conversion (with an *exemplum* of its dire consequences). As it goes, it develops an important claim, which has been implied earlier (by Rolle's insistence that fear of God should be reverent, not abject), and which places the penitential language of the chapter into the framework of the rest of

Emendatio Vitae: the claim that it is only love for Christ, not the fear of hell in a mind yet cold ('frigidam mentem', f. 135v. 4), which is strong enough to make conversion from the allurements of this life permanent. Thus a penitential attitude alone cannot be enough, and the reader must go on to the more advanced states described in later chapters. To reinforce this idea, Rolle even gives one of several anticipatory glimpses in the work of the lover of God, whom the world sees as downtrodden but who flees from vice, is lifted up into Christ, and rejoices in him (f. 135r. 49–v. 2). Finally the chapter addresses itself, in the third person, to the 'novi conversi' (f. 135v. 16) who have heeded its words, telling them to avoid occasions of sin and, sighing for the love of God, to despise the world – which, it concludes, is the next topic to be dealt with (f. 135v. 23–24).[12] If this chapter is partly a compendium of generalized *sententiae* about conversion, it is also a systematic attempt to urge a particular response.

Caps. 2 and 3 (*De Contemptu Mundi* and *De Paupertate*) are also penitential in subject. Cap. 2 defines *contemptus mundi*, offers meditative material to help the reader achieve it, including two addresses to the soul ('O misera anima, quid in mundo quaeris?' f. 135v. 37; 'O carnalis amator, quid in carne reperis?' f. 135v. 53), and ends with some miscellaneous thoughts for readers to develop for themselves: 'Ad contemptum mundi ipse mundus nos compellit ... Et alia sunt quae movere nos possunt ad contemptum mundi, videlicet mutabilitas temporis, brevitas vitae presentis, certa mortis expectatio ... veritas futurorum gaudiorum' (f. 136r. 1, 6–8: 'Even the world urges us to have contempt for the world. And there are other things that move us to have contempt for the world, that is, the changeableness of the times, the shortness of this life, the certain expectation of death, the truth of future joys'). Cap. 3 is more complex, for with the topic of poverty arises, for the first time, a potential conflict between the eremitic, autobiographical model of the religious life on which *Emendatio Vitae* is based and the needs of a general audience. Rolle has easily advocated conversion and contempt for the world without implying that his readers should retire into the wilderness; here, however, he has to give the contemplative ideal of poverty a more radical reinterpretation. Thus although the chapter first sets out this ideal straightforwardly – perfection consists in giving up all for Christ – it soon moves to an interpretation of poverty suitable to readers whom it assumes cannot do this: 'Tu vero intelligens quae dicta sunt, per aliam viam accipias paupertatem; cum dicit *Vade et vende* [Luke 18.23] nota immutationem affectuum et cogitationum ut qui prius superbus fuerat iam humilis deveniat' (f. 136r. 17–20: 'But you, understanding what is said, take the idea of poverty in another way. When it says *Go and sell*, think of the exchange of desires and thoughts, so that he who was proud before now becomes humble'). As in *Judica Me* (see pp. 91–92), poverty here becomes an inner attitude, detached from the external act of giving up all and applicable to everybody.[13] Yet unlike *Judica Me*, the chapter does not let the matter rest here:

Dicunt enim quidam, 'Omnia relinquere non possumus, infirmi sumus, necessaria nobis oportet retinere unde vivamus'; et hoc est licitum. Sed minus valent quam angustam paupertatem et miseriam sustinere pro Deo non audent. Possunt tamen ad culmen virtutum per gratiam Dei attingere, et ad contemplationem supernorum se levare, si occupationes et negotia saecularia deserant, et ad orandum et meditandum indefesse assurgant, atque ea quae habent non amando possideant, et possidendo relinquant. (f. 136r. 50–v. 1)

[For some say, 'We cannot relinquish everything, we are weak, we must keep with us the necessaries by which we live'; and this is allowed. But it is less a matter of not being able than of not daring to suffer harsh poverty and wretchedness for God. Still, they can by the grace of God attain to the summit of the virtues and can lift themselves to contemplation of things above, if they abandon worldly occupations and business, and rise up indefatigably in prayer and meditation, and possess the things they have without loving them, and in possessing them relinquish them.]

Rolle distinguishes the way of life of those who do not give up everything as less audacious than that of perfect poverty, but also says clearly and for the first time that such a life – susceptible to disturbance as it must inevitably be – is compatible with perfection and contemplation. This vital concession, which is the one he cannot bring himself to make in *Judica Me*, and which he writes *Super Lectiones Mortuorum* without even mentioning, is of inestimable importance both for *Emendatio Vitae* and for Rolle's status as an *auctor* who aspires to teach the whole world.

The full significance of the concession that is made here does not become clear until caps. 10–12. Before then Rolle must adapt the intermediate stages of his spiritual life to the needs of his readers; but this process does not prove difficult, and requires little comment – indeed, a single example will suffice. Cap. 4, *De Institutione Vitae*, deals with the organization of the religious life in such general terms that its dictates would apply as well to the laity as to solitaries. The chapter begins with lists – first of sins of thought, word and deed, then of things which counteract these sins – which may be indebted to the *Compendium Theologicae Veritatis*,[14] and rounds them off with a passage taken from Rolle's own *Latin Psalter* comparing those who follow virtue to a *'tree planted by the waters'* (Psalm 1.3).[15] It then moves to an account of *disciplina*, which covers some of the same ground as earlier chapters (f. 137r. 3–7), and develops at length an anti-penitential discussion of the danger of excessive abstinence (7–38), emphasizing not an ascetic view of discipline but an affective one centred around the continual memory of Christ (38 to end).[16] As with caps. 5–6 (*De Tribulatione Patienter Sustinenda* and *De Patientia*), both of which deal with diabolic temptation and the persecution of the true Christian by the world, and as with caps. 7–9 (*De Oratio*, *De Meditatio* and *De Lectio*), which discuss three basic spiritual exercises, the particular axes Rolle has to grind here are instantly adaptable to the general reader. But with cap. 10, *De Puritate Mentis*, we reach material which is more problematic. In order to be capable of any form of the experiences which are the goal of Rolle's version of the spiritual life, his non-eremitic readers must attain to a state of freedom from all but venial sin, and hence also of spiritual security, such as he first describes in cap. 19 of *Incendium Amoris* (see pp. 133–134). How far does he really consider they can do this, without first completely abandoning the world as he has? The chapter does not answer this question, but it does develop its argument with illuminating caution. At its boldest it explains that the purified soul is so filled with the fire of love that even venial sins are soon consumed (see Chapter 5, n. 22), and that in this state the soul can attain to a 'melos coelicum' in which 'potest homo cognoscere quod sit in charitate, et in illa quam nunquam amittet' (f. 139v. 50: 'Someone can know he is in charity – and in the kind which is never set aside'). But it carefully introduces this claim with reflections on the inevitability of sin in this life taken from Proverbs and Job, and qualifies the word 'purity' in its very first sentence: 'Per hos novem gradus praetactos ad puritatem mentis ascenditur qua videtur Deus: puritatem, dico, quae in via haberi potest' (f. 139v. 29–30: 'By the nine steps mentioned here one ascends to the purity of mind in which God can be seen – to that purity, I mean, which can be had in this life'). After its brief mention of *canor*, it also concludes with a rare confession of personal sinfulness on Rolle's own part: 'Parco hic aliquid loqui amplius, quia valde miser mihi videor. Nam saepe caro mea affligitur et tentatur' (f. 139v. 53–140r. 1: 'I do not say anything more on this occasion, since I seem to myself most wretched. For my flesh is often afflicted and tempted'). Rolle does extend to his readers the possibility that they may reach a degree of purity, but thinks it appropriate they should retain some of the self-abjection that he cast aside himself in cap. 31 of *Incendium Amoris*; they are not to imitate the *audacitas* with which he has often spoken to God and the world. As in *Super Lectiones Mortuorum*, he thus identifies as his own attitude the humility he wants his readers to have.

Cap. 10 performs a balancing act, preaching purity and the knowledge of one's own salvation, but simultaneously advocating (and demonstrating) a continuing attitude of humility and self-abjection. Caps. 11–12, *De Amore* and *De Contemplatione*, which constitute the climax of *Emendatio Vitae*, offer a similar spectacle, in that they seem to hold out to the reader the prospect of sharing in the life of the *perfectus*, while at the same time redefining and simplifying Rolle's characteristic view of that life. Both chapters are largely compilations, drawn partly from Rolle's own earlier works, partly from Richard of St Victor's *De Quattuor Gradibus Violentae Caritatis* and probably other works.[17] Cap. 11 begins (f. 140r. 3–24) with effusive prayers to the persons of the Trinity, which mingle Rolle's characteristic imagery of *fervor*, *dulcor* and *canor* with references to the soul's ascent that use the visual imagery favoured by apophatic mystics: God as the uncircumscribed 'dulce lumen' who endows the purified soul who looks upon him with 'claritate increata' (see [1–2]). Evidently Rolle is trying to assimilate his experience to a wider mystical tradition. The prayers are exercises, not effusions; cap. 10 ends by stating that everything in the last two chapters is written 'ad vestram utilitatem', and the prayers are followed by instructions as to their use: 'In his et huiusmodi meditationibus delecteris ut quoque ad medullam amoris ascendas, (Dd.v.64, f. 11v.; see Faber f. 140r. 24–26: 'Delight in these and similar meditations so that you also may ascend to the essence of love'). What I think we expect after this opening is a discussion of the 'medulla amoris' couched in the language of *fervor* and *dulcor* – for in almost all his other works, Rolle's treatment of the theme of love is specifically associated with his own mystical experiences. But what we get instead is an account of three grades of love, *amor insuperabilis*, *inseparabilis* and *singularis*, which refers to these experiences only in passing, and which is mainly taken from Richard of St Victor. There is a certain appropriateness to the idea of the 'gradus amoris' themselves in a work which consists of the 'grades' of the holy life, and Rolle has made use of individual elements of Richard's terminology many times before (see, e.g., Chapter 6, nn. 14 and 27). Yet it is strange to find him structuring part of his discussion of love around a set of terms which have no clear relation to his own experience, and thus no clear place in the model of spiritual ascent articulated by *Emendatio Vitae*. Stranger still is the way Rolle then proceeds to modify part of Richard's analysis. At first he follows Richard, sometimes distantly, sometimes closely, borrowing phrases and ideas, and adding a mere flavour of his own mystical imagery, as where he says of Jesus 'Cuius memoria quasi musicum melos in convivio vini' (f. 140r. 52–53).[18] But at one point he directly contradicts Richard by the simple expedient of adding negatives to his source. Where Richard writes that the singular lover longs for God so violently that his flesh fails and his heart is consumed ('corpore deficit et corde tabescit', 137.7–8), Rolle states that this lover does *not* fail in his body, nor does his heart weaken ('constanter persistere in corpore non deficit, nec corde tabescit', f. 140v. 3–4); on the contrary, such a lover continues to feel greater and greater love as long as he lives: 'Et quanto amplius in illo sic vivit tanto magis amore succenditur, et ei sublimior efficitur' (f. 140v. 4–5). This idea becomes the leitmotif of the second half of cap. 11, which mingles exposition and effusion (mostly taken from *Super Canticum Canticorum* and *Contra Amatores Mundi* (see [3–6])), and which is designed to show that, as it says, 'the lover of Christ is neither subservient to a rule nor desires to reach a particular stage, but directs his love towards God more and more burningly and joyfully' ('Amator Christi in amando nec ordinem servat nec gradum cupit ... plus et plus ardentius et iucundius Deum amare intendit', f. 140v. 41–43). In imitation of this process, the chapter itself finds more and more passionate epithets for love, culminating with the magnificent peroration of *Contra Amatores Mundi* (see [6]). The grades of love return near the end ('O amor inseparabilis, o amor singularis', f. 141r. 5), but they seem to be introduced into cap. 11 largely in order to be transcended by kinds of love so passionate as to resist categorization.

What are we to make of this? Rolle is both assimilating his experience to the categories developed by Richard of St Victor and showing how those categories do not encompass the reality of love as he sees it. No doubt the latter has much to do with his rejection of the fourth of Richard's grades of love, *amor insatiabilis* (see Chapter 6, n. 17), and his unease over the Ovidian association of love with pain which is a vital element of *De Quattuor Gradibus Violentae Caritatis*. But why, then, adapt Richard's structure at all, especially since its relationship with Rolle's experience of love is so vague? I suggest that it is useful largely for this very reason: that it enables Rolle to write passionately about love, in language which easily incorporates the images of heat, sweetness and song that he elsewhere uses to describe his own mystical experiences, without making these experiences the basis for his accounts. He has both an apologetic and a pastoral reason for wanting to do this. The apologetic reason is that he is thereby able to claim Richard as at least a partial ally, and to suggest more convincingly that his own mystical experience is not after all unique. The pastoral reason is that he wants to write about fervent love for the benefit of those who may never, he believes, attain the experiences of *fervor* and *dulcor*, but who thereby need all the more to be moved to a longing for love and a sense of love by his passionate words. The passages from his own earlier works, by means of which he first introduces Richard's grades of love, only to diverge from Richard into his own account of love as 'plus et plus ardentius', are for the most part highly affective evocations of and invocations to love; while they all belong to the stage of his career in which the primary affiliation of his writing is with his experience of *dulcor*, they could all be taken, in their original contexts, as instances of his desire to create verbal equivalents of *canor*. In their new positions in cap. 11 of *Emendatio Vitae*, they do imply that Rolle is singing his way through his introduction to love; but they do not in any organized way teach the reader to attain to *canor*, or, indeed, to *fervor* and *dulcor*. From the reader's point of view, the imagery of heat, sweetness and song in this chapter is affective, not mystical, vaguely and conventionally evocative of the higher transports of love, not parts of a systematic spiritual ascent. Rolle subordinates his usual mystical *schema* to a structure adapted form Richard of St Victor because, in spite of the assurances he made in cap. 3, he is still concerned to preserve a distinction between his own experiences as a saintly solitary and those to which many at least of his readers can realistically hope to attain.

Rolle's decision in *Emendatio Vitae* to separate his discussions of what he normally regards as inevitably linked topics, *amor* and *contemplatio*, is a sign of his desire to provide material for the use of an array of readers: those who will follow him to the summit of perfection, but equally those who will not. After writing mainly for the benefit of the latter throughout cap. 11, he can turn, in the final chapter of the work, to an exposition of his most elevated contemplative experience, *canor*, which he must have meant for a much smaller audience. Cap. 12 is completely different in tone from its predecessor, for instead of an exclamatory evocation of a passionate love which irresistibly and perpetually augments itself, it gives us the most serious and sustained exposition of Rolle's views about contemplation to be found in any of his works. Indeed, as is clear from its opening, Rolle's agenda in this

chapter is not merely to help particular readers to share in the saintly
pleasures of *canor*, but to place *canor* itself into some kind of a relation with
other versions of mystical experience:

Contemplatio, vel vita contemplativa, habet tres partes, scilicet lectionem, orationem
et meditationem. In lectione loquitur nobis Deus. In oratione loquimur nos Deo . . .
[*more definitions*] . . . Si quaeratur quid sit contemplatio, difficile est diffinire. Dicunt
quidam quod vita contemplativa nihil aliud est quam rerum latentium futurarumque
notitia, sive vocatio ab omnibus occupationibus mundi, sive divinarum studium
literarum. Alii dicunt quod contemplatio est perspicatia in sapientiae spectacula, cum
admiratione suspensa. Alii dicunt quod contemplatio est libera et perspicax animi
intuitus ad vires perspicandas circumquaque diffusus. Alii dicunt, et bene, quod
contemplatio est supernorum iubilus. Alii dicunt, et optime, quod contemplatio est
per sublevantis mentis iubilum mors carnalium affectionum. Mihi videtur quod
contemplatio sit iubilus divini amoris, suscepta in mente suavitate laudis angelicae.
Haec est iubilatio quae finis est orationis perfecte et devotionis summae in via . . . Et
est actus iste consummativus omnium actuum.   (f. 141r. 17–38)

[Contemplation, or the contemplative life, has three parts, that is, reading, prayer and
meditation. In reading, God speaks to us. In prayer, we speak to God. If one asks what
contemplation is, it is hard to define. Some say that the contemplative life is nothing
other than the knowledge of things hidden and to come; or else, being called from all
worldly occupations; or else, the study of divine letters. Others say that contemplation is a clear gaze into the wonders of wisdom, while one is rapt with amazement.
Others say that contemplation is a free and clear-sighted intuition of the soul when its
faculties of perception are spread out on every side. Others say, and well, that
contemplation is supernal jubilation. Others say, and best, that contemplation is the
death of carnal affections through the jubilation of the uplifted mind. It seems to me
that contemplation is the jubilation of divine love, received into the mind with the
sweetness of angelic praise. This is jubilation, which is the goal of perfect prayer and
the summit of devotion while we are *in via*. And this act is the consummation of all
acts.]

If this opening is not taken from an existing compilation, it is a conscious and
impressive display of Rolle's mystical learning. Having formally divided
contemplation into three parts and defined these,[19] he proceeds to give a
number of definitions of contemplation itself, taken from the most celebrated
auctores of the contemplative life: Prosper of Aquitaine (Julius Pomerius),
and Hugh and Richard of St Victor.[20] Beginning with the definitions furthest
from his own, Rolle gradually moves towards those congenial to him, before
finally stating his own view that contemplation is *canor* (see [7]): a gesture
which has the effect of inscribing his mystical experience into the authoritative tradition of writing about contemplation the passage evokes, as its latest,
but by no means its least significant, member. Thus the passage achieves in
miniature what the entire work (indeed, Rolle's entire career) attempts: to
enshrine his account of the spiritual life as a legitimate addition to the canon
of writing on the subject, and to enrol him as a member of an elite club of
contemplative *auctores*. The rest of the chapter develops from this introduction into a long amplification of Rolle's own statement about contemplation, which, significantly, carefully avoids engaging in arguments with the

other authorities he has cited. The chapter confronts rival views of contemplation only in the sense that it repeats two passages from *Contra Amatores Mundi*, one on the deficiencies of 'mentalis visio' for those still *in via* (see Chapter 6, n. 26), the other on the low place in the contemplative life occupied by penitential tears, and borrows conventional sentences from two passages in *Super Canticum Canticorum*, one about contemplation as work, the others about the superiority of contemplative to active life (see [8–9]). In this cautious discussion, Rolle also avoids making any statement about who can achieve contemplation as he defines it. On the one hand we are presented with a model of spiritual ascent (f. 141r. 45–v. 12), which interiorizes the concept of poverty in the way Rolle has already done in cap. 3; this suggests that those who do not relinquish their all may still be able to contemplate God. Near the end of the work, on the other hand, the contemplative is redefined as a lover of solitude ('Omnis vero vir contemplativus solitudinem diligit', f. 141v. 51–52), and the solitary life is commended as the highest (f. 141v. 53–142r. 2), in a passage which also makes reference to the 'mixed' life.[21] We are clearly meant to think well of the eremitic vocation, and to associate *canor* with solitude. But whatever Rolle's private views may be about the availability of *canor* to those who do not live in solitude, he still holds it up in this chapter as the final goal for all who amend their lives according to the pattern he has laid down. Without exactly conceding any of the positions he has taken in earlier works, he is thereby able to bring to its conclusion what has been the special project of *Emendatio Vitae*: the process of representing his eremitic and mystical experiences as a model which has an immediate pastoral relevance for everyone.

With the end of *Emendatio Vitae* we have also come to the end of Rolle's career as a writer of Latin: a career which, whatever else one might say about it, bestowed to posterity one of the most distinctive of all medieval Latin voices. Of all the works we have considered in this and the last five chapters, *Emendatio Vitae* is the most painstakingly controlled in its style and content, the most carefully balanced in its use of his personal spiritual development as a framework for others to structure their lives around. In no other work does he confront so calmly the problems arising from some features of his mystical system; avoiding both the aggressive competitiveness with which *Super Canticum Canticorum* outfaces rival views of mystical rapture and the anxiety with which *Contra Amatores Mundi* looks for signs that the *canor* it describes is not unique, he is most successful in mediating between his own picture of spiritual truth and the other traditions he evokes. The early chapters, with their reliance on the penitential language of *contemptus mundi*, skilfully steer the reader away from a negatively ascetic and towards a positive and affective understanding of the spiritual life. Cap. 11 makes Richard of St Victor an ally even while it corrects him on a major issue, and cap. 12 presents an array of views about contemplation among which *canor* is placed as merely a *primus inter pares*, as Rolle redefines as colleagues the mystical writers he has previously treated, when he has noticed them at all, as rivals. The measured way in which these last realignments are effected also makes a contribution to the work's pastoral appeal to the reader, for here Rolle's awareness of other views allows him to state his own position with clarity without impelling him to extremes. Thus he can describe *canor* without even mentioning his belief that for the tiny group he calls the *perfectissimi* it is a permanent state, and he even avoids his usually categorical limitation of his experience to those who live in solitude. It seems that he has at last freed himself from the constraints of his own defensiveness, and can move at ease inside the framework of his own thought without being continually deflected by one or another apologetic exigency. *Emendatio Vitae* is a triumphant result of the new definition of the eremitic writer's function in the Church produced at the end of *Melos Amoris*, an entirely successful product of Rolle's attempt to live his own kind of 'mixed' life.

9

'Mixed' life: the English works

I

It is not certain at what point in his complex and carefully organized career as a writer of Latin commentaries and *libri* Rolle first turned to the medium of English. Apart from one short personal piece (*Ghostly Gladness*), all his English works – epistles, Passion meditations, commentaries, prose pieces and lyrics – are best seen as varieties of pastoral writing, belonging most naturally to what I have called the 'mixed' life phase of his career: that is, to the last few years of his life. However, while it is clear that *The Commandment* and *The Form of Living* were products of this period, and most likely that the *English Psalter* was, too, it may be that a few of the English works were composed earlier, while he was engaged on the series of apologetic writings which began with *Incendium Amoris* and reached its climax with *Melos Amoris*. Though this can doubtless neither be proved nor disproved, it is worth stressing at the outset for two reasons. First, modern interest in Rolle's 'supreme place in the history of English prose' (Chambers 1932, p. ci) – which largely rests on the fact that during the century and a half after his death his works 'attracted a larger audience than [those of] any previous writer in the language' (Alford 1984, p. 38) – has often led to the assumption that in turning to English he must have felt he had found his true *métier*, and so have in effect rejected Latin; Allen, for example, can state blandly: 'It is likely that when once Rolle began to write English, he wrote little more Latin' (p. 186). But this is to view his choice of the vernacular in an anachronistic and sentimental light; for it is Latin, not English, that must be seen as his natural medium of expression, in which all the major literary and personal struggles of his career had to be played out. In the first half of the fourteenth century the spiritual *auctoritas* to which many of his works lay such aggressive claim was only available to a writer of Latin; the canon of *auctores*, ancient and modern, was, and was long to remain, a Latin canon. To write pastoral works in the vernacular was one thing; to be thought of as having made a definitive contribution to the Church's mystical theology was quite another. Had Rolle not died soon after completing *The Form of Living*, he would surely have gone on writing in Latin, both out of his desire to make such a contribution and out of a sense of duty to the secular clergy, for whom *Super Lectiones Mortuorum* and *Emendatio Vitae* seem primarily to have

222

been written, and through whom he saw himself as addressing the whole Church of Christ. It is often, no doubt rightly, argued that Rolle's English works provided much of the impetus behind the flood of prose works of instruction in the vernacular which began to appear in quantity towards the end of the fourteenth century, and found an ever wider audience during the fifteenth (see, e.g., Hughes 1988, chapter 2 *passim*). Yet when he wrote them, it must have seemed that he was addressing a narrower, not a wider, section of the Church than in his Latin writings; given how small the fourteenth-century audience for a work like *Ancrene Wisse* seems to have been, he is not likely to have anticipated the scale of their popularity, or to have realized that they would make so important a contribution to his reputation.[1]

This brings me to my second, and closely related, reason for stressing the possibility that Rolle could have written some of his English works in tandem with even the most aggressive phases of his Latin career: that the former belong to an area of his literary activity which is in important ways separate from the exigencies which drove that career. After *Judica Me*, which was written on request, the Latin works succeed one another according to what seems their own internal logic, responding to the pressure of Rolle's needs, not in the first instance to those of a determinable audience; even the works following *Melos Amoris*, which pointedly stress their own *utilitas*, do so in a grandly general way which seldom gives one cause to suspect that their tone of address or content has been modulated to suit a particular individual. The English works were born out of an equal concern to be of use, and also tend to a generalized form of didacticism, but they do seem, at least in most instances, to have been composed for a specific situation or person, and thus to be in effect occasional pieces, rather than bricks in the tower of Rolle's authority. *The Form of Living* was not meant as the personal monument it is sometimes taken to be, but as an epistolary treatise to help a close friend settle into her anchorage. The Passion meditations are the products not of an inner compulsion but of the fact that somebody had need of them. The same is also true of most of the lyrics and prose pieces, and certainly of the other epistles. Even the *English Psalter*, an ambitious work which must have taken a year or more to complete, probably began as a response to Margaret Kirkeby's desire to understand the doctrine behind the spiritual songs she was to spend so much of her life, as nun and anchoress, chanting. It is true that the occasional status of the English works could not prevent them from contributing to Rolle's self-portrait as a spiritual authority, and he must himself have seen an intimate link between his Latin ministry to the whole Church and his English one to a few individuals. In acting as 'spiritual director' to the recipients of his epistles, he perhaps thought he was exercising an eremitic equivalent of a priestly teaching office, to complement the way many of his Latin works engage in an eremitic version of the priestly office of preaching. Yet in spite of the ways in which we could see his English works as offshoots of his Latin ones, their special quality is most fully explained in a different set of terms – terms which, in view of the aggressively public manner in which he conducts his Latin career, may strike some as oddly personal. For what gives many of the English works an atmosphere distinct from those of all Rolle's Latin writings is their status as the literary products of a particular, and it would seem to him precious, area of his life: his intimate friendships with and concern for women.

To this point in the present study, we have had the opportunity to note only the unfortunate aspects of Rolle's interactions with women: the way feminine susceptibility to what was clearly his physical beauty helped create a picture of him as a *girovagus* (pp. 45–50); or his signal failure to efface this picture in *Incendium Amoris*, cap. 12, in which he pretends to confess a few trivial sins involving women, only at once to deny his instrumentality (pp. 129–130). However, even if the story of his cure of Margaret Kirkeby (by making her sleep on his shoulder) had not survived for us in the *Officium* (*lectio viija*), we would still have material for a more positive view. On at least two occasions in his Latin works, Rolle writes about his relations with women in a manner which suggests he is trying to define what he knows is an unusual and personal stance. Cap. 39 of *Incendium Amoris*, a discussion of *amicitia* with no clear relevance to the treatments of *canor* surrounding it, seems to have been written largely for the sake of its reflections on friendship between men and women. The subject of spiritual friendship has been raised in a strange passage at the end of cap. 34, where Rolle declares his longing for someone with whom he could share his mystical experiences (244.34–245.37). Cap. 39, which takes up this theme in a more abstract tone, states bluntly that 'vix aut raro invenitur fidus amicus' (263.4–5), implying the search for true friendship to be a difficult one. Yet it at once goes on to consider as a likely candidate a variety of friendship which is generally treated with a good deal of suspicion in the literature of *amicitia* (see Patterson 1987, pp. 142–144), that between the sexes. Rolle concedes that such friendship is dangerous – 'inter viros et mulieres amicicia sit periculosa' (263.12) – since it can easily lead to sexual sin. But he also insists that love between men and women occurs naturally (not sinfully) even among the holy, because it was instituted by God from the beginning as a fundamental human attribute: 'Est et quedam naturalis dileccio viri ad mulierem et mulieris ad virum, qua nullus caret nec eciam sanctus, secundum naturam a Deo primo institutam' (263.28–30). There is a good deal more, but Rolle's underlying concern here seems fairly clearly to be his desire to find (or justify having found) a woman to play, as it were, Clare to his Francis.[2] This passage needs to be read alongside a very different one in cap. 43 of *Melos Amoris*, in which he answers those who have criticized him for his involvement with women (particularly young secular women) and have drawn prurient conclusions as to its nature. Here there is no hint of the loving equality of *amicitia*. Rolle states that his relationship with these women is that of a teacher ('Loquebar cum feminis de fide Factoris', 132.22–23) who has remained holy in all his dealings with them ('Sed sciant simpliciter quod sanctus subsisto', 132.28). He goes on to explain:

Nam hec est intencio qua sic pergebam, ut omnes addiscerent Auctorem amare
vanaque relinquerent et recia ruine . . . et virgines viverent a viciis colantes ad vitam,
vota Regi rectissime non reprobe reddentes. Profecto plurisque et hoc predicavi ut
amico mundano non macularentur . . . castis et pie deinceps degentes gestiant de iure
in Iesu iubilare quem solum suscipiant amicum et sponsum . . . Hec si non creditis,
querite que dixi; interrogare potestis qui me audierunt.

(132.34–133.14; compare *Super Canticum Canticorum* 22.2–11)

[For this is the reason that I proceeded in this way: so that they might all learn to love
the Author, and leave vain things and ruinous snares behind . . . and live as virgins,
fleeing from vices into life, fulfilling their vows to the King most truly, not falsely.
And certainly I preached this to many: that they should not soil themselves with an
earthly friend . . . that at once, becoming chaste and pure, they should burn to rejoice
lawfully in Jesus, whom only they should take as friend and spouse . . . If you do not
believe this, ask what it is I have said – you can talk to those who have listened to me.]

Rolle closes the discussion by warning readers not to regard his engagement
with women as something to imitate, implying that God has bestowed on him
a special grace which frees him from the fear of succumbing to carnal love
(133.19–134.10); 'Non accipe exemplum ex hoc quod narravi, nescisti
namque quod dedit michi Deus: eiecit me in ignem et exuri non permisit'
(133.26–28). Taken as a whole the passage claims that Rolle, with his unusual
resistance to carnal temptation, exercises a divinely appointed apostleship to
women, and has a special role to play in persuading them to the life of
perfection.

Except in that they justify a misunderstandable aspect of Rolle's life, the
arguments of these passages do not constitute an important part of his claim
to spiritual authority in the form in which this is articulated in the rest of his
Latin writing. As a would-be modern *auctor*, with a special interest in
contemplation but also a mission to incite everyone to fervent love, he is in
principle concerned as much with women as with men throughout his works.
But as he makes his case in Latin to a potential readership which is essentially
one of celibate males, it is hardly surprising that this fact generally goes
unmarked, and that little stress is laid on his private belief that he has a
particular ministry to women – let alone that he makes them his friends.
Indeed, even though the passages which I have discussed are clearly exceptions
to this rule, they both betray, through a kind of verbal shuffling of the feet, a
peculiar sense of authorial awkwardness. Yet the same passages provide us
with our key to many of the English works – for it is the special achievement
of these works to be demonstrations of the authority which *Melos Amoris*
claims Rolle has over women, at the same time as evoking a tenderness very
like the *amicitia* described in *Incendium Amoris*. Rolle's greatest predecessor
as a writer of English works of instruction for women, the author of *Ancrene
Wisse*, achieves his own highly individual combination of intimacy and
authority by means, first, of a detailed engagement in the lives of his readers,
second, of a judiciously exercised tone of absolute command in which his role
as priestly representative of the Church and of Christ comes to the fore. Rolle
can imitate neither half of this recipe, for his teaching is largely unconcerned

with day-to-day life, and he is not in a position to assume the institutional authority of the priest commanding his readers to obedience. What he does instead – to generalize about a situation which is very varied in practice – is typically to charm the reader with the affective force of his personality as a youthful lover of Christ, bathing the fervent love he is always commending in the glow of his own magnetism. Watching him do this, one is sometimes reminded of gestures made by his Latin works, which express or anticipate his concept of the eremitic 'mixed' life: the moment in *Contra Amatores Mundi* where Rolle says to his audience of youthful worldly lovers, 'Quoniam adhuc et ego iuvenis amator, tamen mirabilis, quia dilectam meam continue cogito, et ab eius amplexibus non recedo' (3.73–75: 'For I, too, have hitherto been a youthful lover, though a miraculous one, since I think continually of my beloved, and do not draw back from her embraces'); or the way the narrative voice in *Emendatio Vitae* draws readers step by step up the spiritual ladder with it, rather than (as in so many of the Latin works) merely shouting encouragement from the top. One is reminded even more of the dazzling narrative persona of *Incendium Amoris*, trying to make his way in the world by a sort of literary mesmerism, or of the prototype of that persona, the yearning lover of the Virgin in *Canticum Amoris*. Yet in spite of these continuities between the modes of Rolle's self-presentation in the Latin works and in the English, we shall see that just as the English works as a whole have a distinctive place in his career, so also his talent for making a pleasing and personal impact on the reader often emerges in these works in highly distinctive ways.

II

The English work in which Rolle's sense of intimacy with a female reader and his belief in his divinely appointed mission to women both emerge most clearly is *Ego Dormio*, a brief epistolary homily on the stages of spiritual perfection which MS Dd.v.64 states was 'scriptus cuidam moniali de ʒedingham' (f.29r., *English Writings*, p. 72). The work is an exposition of 'þre degrees of loue' (66), which correspond first to the nine orders of angels (16–19), second to the active, the coenobitic and the solitary lives, and third to interior states associated with those lives: that of the *mediocriter boni*, whose spirituality is mainly negative, centred on avoidance of mortal sin; of serious aspirants towards perfection, who are striving to root out venial as well as mortal sin, and to follow Christ in virginity and poverty; and of the *perfecti*, who have received some or all of the mystical gifts of Sight into Heaven, *fervor*, *dulcor* and *canor*. This division parallels the common distinction between the purgative, illuminative and unitive states found in Bonaventure's *De Triplici Via*, and is used here as yet another way of articulating Rolle's own spiritual career, like the twelve 'gradus' which make up *Emendatio Vitae*. It is also closely similar to a threefold division Rolle adopts from Peter Lombard in his account of the structure of the Psalter: 'Alswa þis boke is distyngid in thris fyfty psalmes, in þe whilk thre statis of cristin mannys religion is sygnifyd: þe first in penance, þe toþer in rightwisnes, þe thrid in louynge of endles lyfe' (*English Psalter*, p. 4). As Jennings points out (1975, p. 199), the one triadic division to which that in *Ego Dormio* has no relation is the one with which it is most often compared (e.g. by Allen, p. 251): that of the degrees of inseparable, insuperable and singular love, taken over by *The Commandment* and *The Form of Living* from *Emendatio Vitae*. A belief that the degrees of love in *Ego Dormio* are a primitive version of those found in the other epistles has led to an assumption not only that *Ego Dormio* is the earliest of the epistles, which is probably true, but also that its teachings are the most basic, which is not. *Ego Dormio* does not contain detailed discussion of mystical love such as we find in *The Form of Living*; yet its account of the third degree of love has the clearest references to Rolle's system of mystical experiences in any of the English works, and urges its reader to strive for *fervor*, *dulcor* and *canor* in a way which implies real confidence in her ability to achieve them. As we shall see, if any of the epistles is confined to basic teaching, it is *The Commandment*.

One consequence of regarding *Ego Dormio* as the most rudimentary of the epistles is that it begins to seem an unsuitable work to have been written for a nun, in spite of the rubric in MS Dd.v.64. Thus Allen favours the idea that the work's intended reader became a nun after it was written (p. 250), and S. J. Ogilvie-Thomson flatly rejects the rubric, stating that 'the author appears to be addressing one ignorant of any form of conventual life . . . who has yet to take the first step' (1988, p. lxvi). There are apparent signs that Ogilvie-Thomson is right. After all, the work does begin with the 'first step', the active life, and at one point seems to exhort the reader to leave this stage behind in order to embrace the contemplative life: 'Bot when þou hast wel lyved in þe comandementʒ of God, and straytly kept þe fro al deddly synnes, and paied to Crist in þat degre, bethynke þe þat þou wil more loue God, and do better with þi soule, and bicum perfite. And þan entres þou in to þe toþer degre of loue, þat is to forsake al þe world, and þi fadyre and þi modyre and al þi kyn, and folow Crist in pouert' (92–97). This passage could indeed be taken to imply that *Ego Dormio* was written for a laywoman, perhaps one seriously considering becoming a nun. Yet there are good reasons for upholding the Dd.v.64 rubric. The prologue to the work (which I discuss below) may indicate that Rolle was writing for a relative newcomer to the spiritual life, but she is clearly in some sense already an 'insider', for whom he can write of the summit of perfection: 'I wot neuer jf many men be in suche loue, for euer þe hegher þat þe lif is, þe fewer folowers hit hath here' (59–60). Moreover, the work shows little interest in the rudimentary spirituality of the active life, for the first degree of love is given less than thirty lines (65–93), and is described only in the most general terms, as though it is of little further relevance to the reader. By contrast, the second degree – closely associated and often identified with the coenobitic state – is given over a hundred (92–215), which constitute the heart of the work and contain its most detailed and practical material: warnings against over-anxiety about the spiritual welfare of friends and relations (105–117, see 55–58); discussion of the proper use of the psalms in private devotion (129–138); a description of the difficulties the reader must overcome, and a Passion meditation to assist her in doing so (150–215). Again, the account of the third degree, which takes about fifty lines (216–264) – excluding the lyric with which the work ends (265–313) – is prefaced by a warning that it may never be relevant to the reader: 'For I say nat þat þou, or another þat redeth þis, shal do hit al' (218). Yet in spite of this caution, the third degree is described in ways that emphasize its attainability for someone who has already reached the second. For one thing, Rolle does not here follow the logic of his own overall structure by insisting that reaching this degree involves becoming a solitary; instead, he merely states (much as he does in cap. 12 of *Emendatio Vitae*) that this degree 'loueth to be onely, withouten ryngen or dyn and syngynge and criynge' (224–225), carefully not specifying how total this solitude has to be. Even more strikingly, he describes what happens in the third degree in the same intimate voice he has used for the second – though not for the first – couching his account in the second person and the present tense: 'And þan þou entres in to þe þrid degre of loue . . . At þe begynnynge, when þou comest thereto, þi goostly egh is taken vp . . .' (216, 225–226). Since Rolle here refers to what is in essence a fictional 'þe' experiencing things in the present that he has stated the reader may never accomplish in the future, it seems likely he is doing something similar earlier, when he exhorts the reader to enter the second degree: using the intimate second-person present to describe an important event which is already in her past. *Ego Dormio* must have been written not for a beginner but for a reader already established in the 'second degree of love' – for a nun, not a laywoman.

So much for the work's structure and how this is articulated to address the needs of a certain kind of reader. It remains to say something about the very special tone of *Ego Dormio*. As his use of second-person present forms suggests, Rolle is concerned to bathe this work in as much intimacy as he can, affirming his sense of the reader as someone who matters in a way which is often almost fawning: 'Pan Ihesu is al þi desire, al þi delit, al þi ioy, al þi solace, al þi comfort, so þat on hym will euer be þi songe, and in hym al þi rest' (232–233). But the present tense here is also a means of affirming the reality of two other people: Christ, whose love is presented as being always available now; and Rolle himself, who is always to be heard 'speaking' the words he has written. Indeed, though the work is in theory meant to promote a single relationship – the love between reader and Christ – it is in fact almost as occupied with those between Rolle and the reader, and to an extent Rolle and Christ. There are a number of passages which directly imply this triple set of relationships, like the parenthetic, 'And thynke on me, þat I be nat foryeten in þi praiers, þat is aboutward þat þou ware dere with Crist, whose mercy me nedeth' (169–170), or the account of desire for and union with Christ, found only in the Longleat MS, and couched (uniquely in this work) in first-person plural forms: 'And I wene, fro þou or I or anoþer be broght in to þis ioy of loue, we mow nat lyue longe after as oþer men doth, bot as we lyue in loue, also we shal dey in ioy, and passe to hym þat we haue loued' (249–252). But there are two special features of *Ego Dormio* which particularly contribute to our sense of Rolle's personal presence in the work, as well as going some way towards justifying it. One is his inclusion of three lyrics, each of which is placed at the end of one of the degrees of love. The first of these, a short, impersonal piece of unrhymed alliterative verse on mutability which some manuscripts treat as prose, is a kind of declamatory prophecy spoken by Rolle. The other two are introduced respectively as a meditation and a love-song, each to be said by the reader at different times. The former, which deals with the Passion, is for daily use, and is presented as a means of ascent from the second to the third degree of love (212–215). The latter is associated with the third degree, but is set off by an introduction which implies it may be useful at an earlier stage: 'Now I write a songe of loue þat þou shalt haue delite jn when þou art louynge Ihesu Criste' (265–266). The inclusion of lyrics in a pastoral epistle, and the structural function they are given, are highly innovatory features of *Ego Dormio*; Rolle's Latin works often contain set-piece passages of poetic prose, but never in so structured a way, and the only other vernacular pastoral work I know which does something similar is *The Form of Living*. What I think he is trying to do by including them is to provide his reader not simply with a set of useful exercises (which might as well have been in prose), but with devotional material which is indelibly stamped with his own hallmark – in short, with a verbal expression of his gift of *canor*. The three degrees of love are, after all, modelled on his ascent to this supreme gift, and Allen (pp. 290–294) has shown that the second and third lyrics are indebted to his foremost account of that ascent, *Incendium Amoris*. In writing *Ego Dormio*, he is inviting his reader to follow his own progress to union with God; it seems natural he should encourage her with poems which she can not only use for herself but understand as reminders of his earlier journey, on which hers is modelled. When he introduces one of these poems with 'Now I write a songe of loue', he is indeed presenting it as a personal effusion, as well as an exercise, by focussing attention so dramatically on his own act of composition – it is a strategy reminiscent of the appeals for inspiration in *Super Lectiones Mortuorum*. Much of the affective success of the poems thus resides in the fact that the 'I' singing them in longing love to Jesus is in effect a compound of Rolle and reader. By patterning her responses on the feelings they proclaim while she recites them, the reader comes closer and closer to participating in Rolle's love for Christ. Hence *Ego Dormio* is not only a treatment of the reader's ascent to union with Christ by means of Rolle, but also to a kind of union with Rolle himself.

The last point is doomed to seem far-fetched. But by putting things in these lurid terms, I am in fact only adapting language used by Rolle himself in the passage of flamboyantly daring mystical-cum-sexual fantasy with which *Ego Dormio* begins. This prologue to the degrees of love (1–64) is the work's major statement of what I called the 'triple set of relationships' between Christ, Rolle and reader, preparing the ground for the affective interactions I have been describing, and setting them in a specific didactic and imagistic context. It also provides the most revealing comment on Rolle's sense of his own role as a writer for women to be found in any of the English works:

Ego dormio et cor meum vigilat [Songs of Songs 5.2]. The þat lust loue, hold þyn ere and hyre of loue. In þe songe of loue I fynd hit written þat I haue set at þe begennynge of my writynge: 'I slepe and my hert waketh.' Mich loue he sheweth þat neuer is wery to loue, bot euer, standynge, sittynge, goynge, or any oþer dede doynge, is euer his loue þynkynge, and oft sithe þerof dremynge. Forþi þat I loue þe, I wowe þe, þat I myght haue þe as I wold, nat to me, bot to my Lord. I will becum a messager to brynge þe to his bed þat hath mad þe and boght þe, Crist, þe kynges son of heuyn, for he wil wed þe if þou wil loue hym. He asketh þe no more bot þi loue; and my wil þou dost, if þou loue hym. Crist couaiteth þy fayrnesse in soule, þat þou gif holy þi herte, and I prech noght elles bot þat þou do his wille, and afforce þe day and night to leue al fleisshely loue, and al lykynge þat letteth the to loue Ihesu Crist verraily. For whils þi hert is holdynge to loue of any bodily thynge, þou may nat perfitly be cowpled with God.

(1–15)

The work begins by quoting the source text for the image developed in the rest of the passage, and calling for the reader's attention in somewhat the manner of a secular romance, as though Rolle is posing as a kind of minstrel. There is a note of self-conscious inspiration here familiar from many of the Latin works. Not only does *Ego Dormio* erupt into excited action, one of its first gestures is to assume the authority of the verse it quotes, by means of the slightly tortuous 'I fynd hit written þat I haue set at þe begennynge of my writynge' – in which we move smoothly from what Rolle finds written to what he writes, from the *ego* who speaks the verse to the 'I' who transcribes and repeats it. (Thus the next sentence, 'Mich loue he sheweth ...', which looks like a simple exposition of the text, is also a self-portrait, in which Rolle commends himself and his epistle in advance for the proof the latter furnishes that he 'neuer is wery to loue': hence the logic of 'Forþi þat I loue þe'.) The general image that emerges in the rest of the passage, of Christ as the bridegroom, the reader as the bride, is of course conventional both in interpretations of the Song of Songs and in devotional writing for women. *Ancrene Wisse* and the texts associated with it employ it as a key structural metaphor for the religious life; as we saw above, Rolle does the same in *Melos Amoris*, setting the sensual pleasure of earthly lust against the superior qualities of Christ as lover in a manner evidently intended to be so traditional as to deflect any criticism.[3] Here, however, he adds a further and most untraditional element, by placing himself in the centre of the picture as a mediator between the reader and Christ who is also a lover of both: 'Forþi þat I loue þe, I wowe þe, þat I myght haue þe as I wold';[4] 'my wil þou dost, if þou loue hym'. These charged images express his purpose in writing as akin to that of a sexual go-between, like Pandarus in Chaucer's *Troilus and Criseyde* (or any embodiment of the courtly figure of the *ami*, who uses his own charms to arouse a woman's love for the man he represents, before stepping aside). Thus *Ego Dormio* begins by announcing its intention to be the spiritual seduction of the reader. She is to be swept along by Rolle's carefully immediate and intimate words, by his poetic evocations of love and of Christ, and led, enraptured, to the bed of the king, who sends his beloved messenger to speak for him. She is to be moulded for heavenly love by being made to feel a passionately pure earthly love, through which, as she conforms herself to Rolle's will by patterning her inner life on the letter he writes her – a letter that follows the pattern of *his* life – she will ascend to God. Rolle sees himself and his letter as playing a part such as Beatrice plays for Dante. Nowhere else in his writings is a definition of the eremitic 'mixed' life served up for the reader in so yeasty a brew.

This intensely self-regarding variation on the imagery of bridal mysticism has several functions. First, it defines Rolle's pastoral authority in the work as different in kind from that of a priest and spiritual confessor. He writes not because it is in a formal sense his responsibility to do so, but because he has already reached a goal to which he now beckons the reader. His voice is that of an angelic messenger, or of a romanticized counterpart of another hermit, John the Baptist, making straight the way of the Lord by singing tenderly in the wilderness. Yet authoritative though this makes him, he still insists on the fact that he writes out of his own love, not only as a mouthpiece of God's. Although he has such intimate contact with the 'king' that he can bear the reader to his very bed, his message is couched not as command but allurement, and concerns not what the reader must do to gain salvation as what she may do if she wishes to gain perfection, and the love Christ reserves for the perfect. Second, on a more personal level, the way Rolle teasingly evokes a sensual relationship with his reader (only to pass her on to his Lord with words condemning carnal love) is an expression of the *amicitia* between man and woman discussed in *Incendium Amoris*, with its pleasures of joint talk and chaste touches (see 'in mutuis colloquiis et tactibus honestis', 263.33). Here, admittedly, the relationship is more one-sided, but there is no doubt that Rolle is exploiting a fondness between himself and his reader which already exists and is part of his reason for writing; later he indeed adds, 'To þe I writ þis speciali, for I hope in þe more goodnes þan in anoþer' (33), nudging her with an intimate flattery which recalls strategies some tutors use to make their students adore them and so study harder to please them. He even implies that in writing for her he is making a special effort: 'For I ne wil nat helle fro þe þat I hop may turne þe to holynesse' (67–68). Finally, these manœuvres are surely intended as proof of the assertion in *Melos Amoris* that Rolle has a special ministry to women – for it is hard to imagine a more self-conscious demonstration of how what *Incendium Amoris* calls 'natural' love between men and women can be used as an evangelistic tool, at least by someone immune to carnal temptation who has been appointed a 'messager'. I am arguing that Rolle's English writings should be seen primarily as expressions of intimacy, and not be assimilated to the structure of claims for *auctoritas* made by the Latin works. Yet it is clear that in *Ego Dormio* Rolle is very aware of the sort of authority he wields, and opens the work by, in effect, staking out a position for himself which the rest of the work can then develop. The intimacy so flirtatiously proclaimed here is thus partly a self-referential way of demonstrating what Rolle considers to be his divinely appointed function as a teacher of women.

The authorial stance Rolle takes at the opening of *Ego Dormio*, which casts so particular a light over the whole of that work, is not precisely repeated in any of the other English writings. As we shall see, the other epistles cultivate relationships with their readers in very different ways, and the same is perforce true of the *English Psalter* and of the short didactic prose pieces. However, the foregoing discussion does provide us with a point of entry into our analysis of one group of works, the independent lyrics (i.e. the seven poems by him which do not occur as part of *Ego Dormio* or *The Form of Living*).[5] This collection of affective spiritual exercises seems to have been intended for the same readers as the epistles. Several are so complex in their affective strategies that they must have been written for readers who already knew how to use them; both manuscripts in which most of them are found, Longleat 29 and Dd.v.64, present them next to copies of the epistles. Moreover, the poems themselves sometimes refer to their reader (or speaker) as female or as a religious. In 'Ihesu swet,' the speaker tells 'Ihesu, my lef, my lord, my kynge' of her soul's love-longing for him, adding 'Þou hast hit weddit with þi rynge' (vi.401–403): a reference to the wedding-rings worn by the nuns Rolle assumes will use the poem in their devotions. 'Thy ioy be euery dele' exhorts the reader to 'Forsak þe ioy of men þat þou his loue may wyn' (iv.26), and reminds her 'Thou chese hym for þe beste, he is þi wedded kynge' (iv.90). 'Al synnes shal þou hate' exhorts 'Toumble nat fro þe state þat þou hast tane þe tille' (v.3), presumably that of a nun or solitary. The poems are thus meant for readers in the second degree of love described in *Ego Dormio*. Their function, I suggest, is like that of the lyrics in that epistle: to establish the readers where they are, and in some cases to help them towards the third degree, the attainment of *fervor, dulcor* and *canor*.

The main issues I wish to raise with respect to the lyrics have been dealt with in discussing *Ego Dormio*; here I shall summarize them before proceeding to detailed points. Rolle uses poetry as a form for didactic and meditative writing because he is not a priest with an official concern for the salvation of his audience, but an eremitic lover of God, who sings mystical songs to him and who freely acts as a messenger, exhorting others to exercise their own inner freedom by striving to sing with them. Lyric verse provides him with an alluring vehicle for inviting his readers to follow not merely the commandments of God but his counsels – to embark on the way of perfection by means of love, abandoning the world and embracing Christ in the full sense implied by their status as coenobitic contemplatives. But in their song-like form, the lyrics also incarnate a message like that implicit in the lyrical prose *Melos Amoris*, or the inspired expository style of *Super Lectiones Mortuorum*: that the reader who takes the words to herself is participating (if imperfectly) in Rolle's own experience of love (*canor*), and is therefore moving closer to conformity both to Christ and to him. The lyrics are to be read at once as expressions of *canor* and as aids to the achievement of *canor*; both their message and their metre contribute to what *Incendium Amoris* calls 'ordered love' (148.7): a love patterned on Rolle's exemplary spiritual career, the climax of which is the attainment in this life of an experience of the ultimate pattern, the love-song of the blessed in heaven. For someone with Rolle's views about the spiritual life, verse seems an inevitable medium in which to call others to follow where he has gone before.

One other general point about the lyrics, which is not a necessary adjunct of their form but which provides us with further grounds for comparison with *Ego Dormio*, is that they share that work's intimacy, seeming to emanate from a similar relationship of *amicitia* between Rolle and his first readers. So much is evident even in the least complicated of the group, the brief 'Al synnes shal þou hate': a penitential piece which suggests a state of soul only a little more elevated than that evoked by the alliterative verses which end the account of the first degree of love in *Ego Dormio*. This exhortation to avoid mortal sin is remarkable chiefly for its affability. The poem moves from warnings about sin to penance, death, Judgement and an evocation of Paradise. Parts of this are dramatic and appropriately chilling:

> Now may we quake tremblynge, for dred to low lye.
> The beme bloweth at our hand, the dome is fast bye,
> The kynge cometh with his hoste for to fel his enemye,
> And al þe proud with har boste he demeth to deye. (v.13–16)

Yet the apparent severity even here is modifed by the phrase 'Now may we' (rather than, e.g., 'most þou'), while the climax announced by the first line of the next stanza – 'Me þynke hit ryngeth in myn ere: "Ded men, rise to be demed!"' (v.17) – is undercut by reassurances which seem to suggest that in practice the reader has little to fear: 'Bot hym þe deuyl may nothynge dere, that here hath Crist quemed' (v.18). The final lines further distance the reader from a sense of real danger, by contrasting 'þe wicked', who 'to helle fyre is flemed' (v.19) with the saved for whom 'That day *our* ioy shal bigyn' (v.21), and by concluding with what is evidently intended as saintly humour: 'Our setys heuyn ben wythin, *me list sit in myn*; / Loue Crist and hate syn, and so purchace thyne' (v.23–24). The life of penitence has seldom been made to sound so pleasant or so sure of success.

'Al synnes shal þou hate' shows Rolle operating in the mode he perfected in *Super Lectiones Mortuorum*, the work in which he most determinedly descends from his saintly eminence to state that he, too, fears the Judgement. Thus while the 'I' voice in the poem does issue warnings to the reader, many of these ostensibly apply equally to the speaker; there is a progression from an opening address to the reader (v.1–11), to a passage in the first-person plural (v.12–23a), to a final separation of speaker and reader, indicating that the latter's salvation lies in her own hands (v.23b–24). As Gillespie shows (1982), some of the other lyrics make a similar didactic use of varying forms of address. In 'Love is lif', for example, the 'I' voice itself has more than one function, operating partly as didactic interlocutor ('If þou wil loue as I þe say, thou may be with þe beste', i.4), partly as a focus of the reader's aspirations, as she undergoes the spiralling process of spiritual growth the poem outlines ('Ihesu, þat me lif hath lent, in to þi loue me brynge', i.21) – a process falling into a number of stages, in each of which the relationship between reader, words and the 'I' voice is again subtly different. The situation is especially complex in Longleat, which divides what Dd.v.64 treats as a single poem into two lyrics ('Love is lif' and 'I sigh and sob'), in between which is inserted the lyric that occurs just before 'Love is lif' in Dd.v.64, 'Ihesu, Goddis son'. Although one manuscript (Lambeth 853) treats all three as one poem, Ogilvie-Thomson (1988, pp. lxxxi–lxxxiv) argues that we should regard them as distinct, noting that 'Love is lif' borrows extensively from *Incendium Amoris*, whereas the other two have no known source. Yet 'I sigh and sob' ends with what is clearly meant to be a restatement of the opening stanza of 'Love is lif':

> Ihesu is loue þat lesteth ay, to hym is our langynge.
> Ihesu þe nyght turneth to day, þe ebbynge in to sprynge.
> Ihesu, þynke on vs nowe and ay, for þe we hold oure kynge.
> Ihesu, gif vs grace, as þou wel may, to loue without endynge. (iii.25–28)

> Love is lif þat lesteth ay, þer hit in Crist is feste;
> Whan wel ne wo hit chaunge may, as written hath men wisest;
> The nyght is turned in to day, the trauaille in to reste;
> If þou wil loue as I þe say, thou may be with þe beste. (i.1–4)

The second passage offers the reader instruction in applying a theological dogma to herself; the first is the confessional result of her doing so. The reader progresses from being the object of the speaker's concern to a state in which she joins with him in bestowing her love on the poem's final object, Christ; she achieves a union with the speaker like that implied in *Ego Dormio* – which in Longleat also ends its exposition in the first-person plural (249–264). If 'Love is lif' was initially written as a single poem, 'I sigh and sob' must have been intended as its companion. Thus Gillespie seems to be right in treating the triptych of lyrics in Longleat, 'Love is lif', 'Ihesu, Goddis son' and 'I sigh and sob', as movements of a single complex process, which engage the reader in the sophisticated ways he describes.

'Love is lif' and its companions work in a formal way which does not of itself require that we posit any particular relationship between reader and writer, except that the former regards the latter as an authority on ordered love; the nature of this authority, its intimacy, and its connection (via *canor*) with the medium of poetry, are all implicit. Rolle's personal presence is similarly veiled in two of the three lyrics that remain to be mentioned, 'Heyle Ihesu', a short invocation found only in Dd.v.64, and the long Passion meditation 'Ihesu swet', found in Longleat and in several other manuscripts.

Both of these (like 'Ihesu, Goddis son') are written solely in the voice of the reader, the first as an expression of the love-longing which is much emphasized in the English works ('Gyf me grace, als þou wel may, þi lufer for to be: / My langyng wendes neuer away, til þat I com til þe', 15–16), the second as a recital of the events of Christ's suffering and death which culminates in an outpouring of similar sentiments ('Ihesu, þyn ore, þou rew on me; / Whan shal my soul cum to þe? / How longe shal hit here be, / Þer I ne may þe, my lemman, se?', vi.393–396). As with the lyrics in *Ego Dormio*, these poems may have gained in affective power as a result of their association with Rolle, but there is nothing in the verse to indicate this. However, the final lyric to be discussed here, 'Thy ioy be euery dele', does make important use not merely of an abstract didactic interlocutor but of Rolle's own warm eremitic persona. This 108-line poem puts the reader through a process of spiritual reformation similar to that articulated by the 'Love is lif' lyrics. It opens with sixty lines of direct instruction: the reader must bend her energies to serving God, abandon sin, keep his commandments, seek his love in all ('In Crist couait solace, his loue chaungeth þi chere', iv.21), and think on his Passion (iv.5–6, 29–32). These stanzas are something of a jumble, and could indeed be considerably rearranged without causing any incongruity; at this point the poem seems to be working less in an affective than in a didactic mode of a largely mnemonic kind. As it continues, however, it progressively acquires both affective urgency and a narrower focus on love; thus stanza 11 instructs the reader to 'Say to hym day and nyght: "When may I negh þe nere? / Wisse me to þi right, thi melody for to hire"' (iv.43–44), and the stanzas following deal alternately with false and true loves. With stanza 17, the reader arrives at a state of true love for Christ – and it is here that her relationship with the didactic interlocutor suddenly changes:

> If þou loue, whils þou may, the kynge of mageste,
> Thi woo wendeth away, thi hele hegheth to þe,
> Thi nyght turneth to day, þi blisse mow euer be,
> When þou art as I say, I pray þe thynke on me.
>
> Our þoght shal we sette togedyre in heuyn to dwelle,
> For þer þe good ben mett, that Crist holdeth fro helle.
> When we our syn han grette, þe tythynge may we telle
> That we fro ferre hath fette the loue þat non shal felle. (iv.65–72)

After this, we return to direct instruction, with more about loving Christ backed by a somewhat warmer narrational tone: 'His loue is tristy and trewe, who-so hym louynge ware. / Sen first þat I hit knewe, hyt keped me fro kare' (iv.81–82). The end of the poem suggests that the reader is meant to have moved from the first steps in learning 'to loue þi kynge' (iv.17) mainly as a way of avoiding sin to a more passionate, disinterested love: 'Afforce þe for to feste in Crist þi couaitynge' (iv.89). Yet its real focal point, it seems to me, is in the passage quoted above, where a relationship between reader and writer which exists outside the poem briefly intrudes, as Rolle seeks to lure his reader towards loving 'the kynge of mageste' by offering his spiritual friendship if she does. Once she reaches a certain state of soul, she and he will be able to join forces in weeping for their sins and encouraging one another with stories of the love they both 'fro ferre hath fette'. Rolle is offering – at a much lower level of the spiritual life – the same *amicitia* he himself longs for in vain in cap. 34 of *Incendium Amoris*.

III

By comparison with *Ego Dormio* and the more intimate lyrics, the epistle we know as *The Commandment*[6] is distant in its tone of address. Where *Ego Dormio* opens with a daring statement of Rolle's passionate concern for the reader and makes their mutual love into a major theme, *The Commandment* begins with a careful exposition of the first great commandment (Matthew 22.37–38), which at once announces the work to be a far more formal affair. Here the relationship between writer and reader is the traditional one of teacher to pupil; any intimacy that may have existed between Rolle and the Hampole nun for whom Dd.v.64 states the work was written is excluded as inappropriate (f.34r.). Indeed, some passages are couched in a satirical mode which Rolle normally employs only in Latin, as when he denounces 'ianglers and bacbiters þat appeireth other mennes lif' (15–16), or attacks the reader's vanity: 'How may þou for shame þat art bot seruaunt with many cloþes and riche folow þi spouse and þi lord þat yed in a kyrtel, and þou trail as myche behynd þe as al þat he had on?' (101–104). In the light of such remarks, it is no surprise that the work mainly restricts itself to the second of *Ego Dormio*'s degrees of love, the coenobitic state which is also meant to be that of the aspirant to perfection, mentioning only the lesser of Rolle's mystical experiences, *fervor* and *dulcor* (178–193). Moreover, *The Commandment* is the only Rolle work of any length since his earliest expositions to contain no personal references; here, the narratorial voice assumes the institutional authority of a preacher, issuing general instructions – albeit urgent and affective ones – not inducements to spiritual growth based on Rolle's personal experience. It is a testimony to the conventionality of the work's didactic pose that while it may not have been more popular than *Ego Dormio* in the Middle Ages (fifteen manuscripts survive to thirteen of the latter), it does appear as the only Rolle work in several manuscripts (Dd.v.55, Ii.vi.40 and Trinity College, Cambridge 374), where *Ego Dormio* hardly ever occurs except with *The Form of Living*. *Mutatis mutandis*, and taking into account those of Rolle's preoccupations that do find their way into the work, a lesser colleague of the author of *Ancrene Wisse* might almost have written *The Commandment*.

The Commandment can be described as a series of set-pieces on the subject of love, linked by a common topic and a common occasion: Rolle's decision to write in a sometimes severe way to a particular nun. There is a pattern to the work – an alternation of positive and negative, abstract and practical – and it does not seem random or incomplete; but nor does it have any formal structure. This may be a result of the fact that *The Commandment* is more of a patchwork of borrowed passages and ideas, in which some of the seams are still exposed, than an original composition. Thus the exposition of Matthew 22.37 with which it opens (1–23) amplifies a few sentences of the *Compendium Theologicae Veritatis* (v, cap. 29),[7] before giving a simplified account of the degrees of love from *Emendatio Vitae* (24–41, see Excursus I, item 1.3). There follows an affective passage which exhorts the reader to choose Jesus, who contains in himself all she can desire: 'Therfor, if þe list loue any þynge, loue Ihesu Criste, þat is þe fairest, rychest and wisest . . . If þou be coueitouse after good, loue hym and þou shal haue al good . . .' (42–46). This is similar to the series of offers Christ makes in part VII of *Ancrene Wisse*, which form the basis for the first half of *The Wooing of Our Lord*, where the meditator chooses Christ since 'inwið þe ane arn alle þe þinges igedered þat eauer muhen maken ani mon luuewurði to oðer' (10–13), working her way through his beauty, wealth, largesse and other desirable male qualities. There are no exact parallels between the two works, but Rolle lists several of the same characteristics in the same order, and may have taken the *topos* either from *The Wooing* or from its fourteenth-century offshoot, *A Talking of the Love of God*. After a passage of practical instruction which seems to be original (61–81), *The Commandment* goes on to insist on the need to seek Jesus in the proper way, like Mary who found him in the temple, the shepherds who found him in a crib, the kings who found him in swaddling bands (89–100):

He saith þat he loueth ham þat loueth hym, and þay þat erly waketh to hym shal fynd hym [Proverbs 8.17]. Thou art erly wakynge oft sithes [i.e. for Prime and Matins]: whi þan fyndes þou hym nat? Certes, if þou seke hym right, þou shal fynd hym; bot euer whils þou sechest erthly ioy, þogh þou wake neuer so erly, Crist may þou nat fynd, for he is nat founden in har land þat lyveth in fleishly lustes . . . if þou seke hym verraily, þe behoueth go in to þe way of pouert and nat of riches . . . Therby vndrestond, whils þou art in pride and vanyte, þou fyndest hym nat. (84–101)

Rolle here expands a verse from Proverbs partly by means of biblical stories, partly by transforming a passage in *Super Canticum Canticorum* (45.5–22; quoted on pp. 149–150) about the soul's search for Jesus; he may also be indebted to Aelred's *De Ihesu Puero Duodenni* (see Chapter 6, n. 11). Next there is a didactic passage for which I have found no source (110–193). But the work ends with two more instances of borrowing. One is the closing exhortation to love the name of Jesus (214–224), which is adapted from *Super Canticum Canticorum* (43.8–23). The other is a consciously sinister passage designed to prevent backsliding:

Bot perauentur þou wil say, 'I may nat despise þe world. I may nat fynd in myn hert to pyne my body; and me behoueth loue my fleishly frendes, and take ease when hit cometh.' If þou be tempted with such þoghtes, I pray þe þat þou bethynke þe, fro þe begynnynge of þis world, whare þe worldes louers ben now, and whar þe louers ben of God. Certes þei wer men and wommen as we ben, and ete and dranke and laghet; and þe wreches þat loued þis world toke ese to har body, and lyued as ham lust in lykynge of har wicked wille, and lad har dayes in lust and delites; and in a poynt þai fel in to helle.

(194–202)

This wonderful *exemplum* of God's punishment on frivolity is directly taken, with small modifications which render it even more dramatic, from the pseudo-Bernardine *Meditationes Piissimae*.[8] More than half *The Commandment* proves to be closely related either to one of Rolle's earlier works, or to passages of affective meditation by other writers. In the whole of Rolle's output, only the last two chapters of *Emendatio Vitae* and (arguably) parts of *The Form of Living* share this patchwork method of composition.

The fact that *The Commandment* is largely a reworking of earlier materials with no immediate points of contact with Rolle's life no doubt adds to the tone of urgent but formal didacticism that is its hallmark. To gauge this tone, one has only to compare the quotations so far made from the work, which focus exclusively on putting didactic pressure on the reader, with what we saw of *Ego Dormio*, whose strategies are so self-regarding, so concerned to stress the personal presence, not the institutional authority, of the writer. It is all the difference between the *amicitia* described in *Incendium Amoris* and the apostleship asserted in *Melos Amoris*. Indeed, *The Commandment* says just what *Melos Amoris* claims Rolle always does say to women: it urges its reader to embrace Christ as spouse and to turn from fleshly lusts. Moreover, unlike *Ego Dormio* – which is, after all, structured around the same imagery of bridal mysticism – *The Commandment* treats its reader with all the suspicion that *Melos Amoris* implies is a vital part of Rolle's pastoral relationship with women. It is a peculiarity of *Ego Dormio* that it calls the external state of the life of a nun and the inner state of the aspirant to perfection by the same name, 'the second degree of love', assuming an identity between inner and outer as Rolle seldom does elsewhere, and portraying the spiritual life of its reader as a triumphal progress, not a sharp battle in a fallen world. *The Commandment* is far more practical. Here the fact that the reader is a nun guarantees nothing. Admittedly, she is thought worthy of accounts of the degrees of violent love, of the 'swet licour' of love that fills the hearts of those who are practised in holiness (121–127), and of the way the fire of love burns away venial sin (183–187); it is not that Rolle does not consider her a serious aspirant to perfection. But even as it excites her with these elevated topics, the work also treats her as though she is far from being secure in the spiritual life. She is exhorted to avoid mortal as well as venial sin (1–23); urged to love Christ by having him described as the fulfilment of her most worldly aspirations (42–60); reminded that he is found only through poverty and humility, not pride (82–109); and thought to be in danger of falling into the worst sin in Rolle's pantheon, hypocrisy: 'And loke wel þat þou seme nat on withouten and be anoþer within as ypocrites done, þe which ben like to a sepulcre þat is peynted richely withouten and within reten stynkynge bones. If þou haue delite in þe name of religioun, loke þat þou haue more delite in þe dede þat falleth to religion' (150–154). Even the end of the work is still warning of the danger of backsliding (194–213). We expect pastoral writers, from the author of *Ancrene Wisse* to Walter Hilton, to assume that a reader who aspires to the heights of the spiritual life still needs to be warned against the most ordinary sins and temptations. But while Rolle is not often so unappreciative of such needs as he is in *Ego Dormio*, he does not commonly mix discussions of what he considers are basic spiritual issues with accounts of *fervor*, *dulcor* and violent love. On the contrary, most of his works put extraordinary emphasis on the need to reach a state of inner purity before these elevated spiritual experiences can be looked for: hence the way in which *Emendatio Vitae* organizes its account of the spiritual life as a ladder. *The Commandment*'s mixture of descriptions of passionate love with warnings against sin thus marks something of a new departure in Rolle's presentation of the spiritual life, as well, perhaps, as a *rapprochement* with the representations of that life as a long and uncertain struggle that he would have found in almost all of the pastoral writings, English and Latin, that he encountered. Indeed, it is in this evidence of Rolle's continuing willingness to adapt his methods and message as occasion demands – in this case, we have seen, by writing an epistle of unusual conventionality – that the work's major claim to our attention lies.

We will see further signs both of Rolle's adaptability and of his growing awareness of the complexity of the spiritual life when we come to *The Form of Living*. But these phenomena are discernible in miniature in the minor English works that remain to be mentioned: the Passion meditations, and the miscellany of prose pieces which include *Ghostly Gladness* (found in Dd.v.64 and Longleat), *Desire and Delight* (found in Longleat and the famous Thornton manuscript), and *The Ten Commandments*, *The Bee*, and *The Seven Gifts of the Holy Spirit* (all found in Thornton, the last also occurring as cap. 11 of *The Form of Living* in Dd.v.64). It is impossible to know the context in which any of these works was written, and there remains a small but inexpungeable question as to whether Rolle really wrote the meditations associated with his name.[9] Anything we say about these works is thus provisional. As a whole, however, they seem to indicate Rolle's interest in contributing to all phases of the spiritual lives of his readers by providing sundry kinds of material: devotional exercises (the meditations), and expositions both of the basic structures of Christian thought (the commandments, the seven gifts) and also of areas of special interest to himself. Thus, *The Bee* presents and interprets an allegorical image of the contemplative life; *Desire and Delight* describes the state of spiritual pleasure and security which Rolle links with purity; and *Ghostly Gladness* expresses in highly personal language the mystical ecstasy that lies at the end of the spiritual journey. *Ghostly Gladness*, a minute work of alliterative prose, which Longleat places between *Desire and Delight* and the lyrics, and Dd.v.64 positions with the lyrics, is a strangely haunting account of spiritual joy clearly intended as verbal expression of *canor*; like a tiny version of *Melos Amoris*, it even makes a reflexive comment on the reasons for its composition: 'Loue maketh me to melle, and ioy [gars] me jangle' (7–8). The other works are more systematic. *Desire and Delight* describes the qualities of 'delit in Ihesu Criste' – that it is 'wondreful, pure and fast' (1–2) – explains them (2–8), then says how each is achieved: 'Thre þynges make þe delite in God hegh [= wondreful]' (9); 'Two þynges maketh our delite pure' (18); 'Forþi þe delit þat noght hath of vnordynat styrrynge . . . maketh a mannes soule in reste and sikernesse (= fast]' (22–25).[10] *The Bee* has a similar structure, moving from a bee's 'kyndis' ('Ane es þat scho es neuer ydill . . . Anothire es þat when scho flyes scho takes erthe in hyr fette . . . The thyrde es þat scho kepes clene and bryghte hire wyngeʒ', p. 193) to a moral interpretation of these qualities, then adding further information and moralities. This work is interesting for the satirical role it accords the righteous, who shun idleness by prayer, reading and good deeds, but also by 'withtakand ydill mene and schewand thaym worthy to be put fra þe ryste of heuene for þat þay will noghte trauayle here' (ibid.). It warns against over-intimate friendships in much the terms we find in *Ego Dormio* (114–117) and *The Commandment* (82–84): 'For many are þat neuer kane halde þe ordyre of lufe ynesche þaire frendys . . . for thay are so heuy in erthely frenchype þat þay may noghte flee in till þe lufe of Ihesu Criste' (ibid.; see also *Melos Amoris* 158.21–159.7). This emphasis suggests that, like the epistles, *The Bee*, with its evocation of female industry and communality, was written for a nun. Lastly, *The Seven Gifts of the Spirit* shows an equal interest in the contemplative life, viewing each gift as part of a *via contemplativa* (so that wisdom, for example, 'es forgetynge of erthely thynges and thynkynge of heuen . . . In þis gyfte schynes contemplacyone', p. 197), whereas *The Ten Commandments* emphasizes the active life, except when it describes honouring the Sabbath in 'general', 'special' and 'contemplative' terms (p. 195), making a triple division which Jennings points out is analogous to the degrees of love in *Ego Dormio* (1975). Although the predominant stress in these short pieces is on material suitable for the same audience for whom Rolle wrote the epistles and lyrics, there is thus something here for everyone.

A peculiarity of Rolle's English writings, directed in the first instance almost exclusively at their female audience, is the far greater emphasis they place on Passion meditation than do the Latin works. *Emendatio Vitae* commends such meditation only with qualifications: 'Aestimo quod hoc meditatio utilior sit omnibus aliis his qui noviter ad Christum convertuntur' (f. 139r. 10–11: 'I judge that this meditation is more useful than any other for those newly turned to Christ'). Both *Ego Dormio* (169–215) and *The Commandment* (187–193), on the contrary, commend it unreservedly at fairly advanced stages of the spiritual life, and several lyrics, notably 'Ihesu, Goddis son', 'I sigh and sob' and 'Ihesu swet', are sophisticated exercises in the genre none of which assumes the reader is a new convert. Like devotion to the Holy Name, Passion meditation is considered especially suitable for those whose spiritual lives are structured around the 'carnal' image of marriage to

Christ. Thus, while we may never be sure that it was Rolle who wrote the matter-of-fact account of the Passion attributed to him in Cotton Titus c.xix (*Meditation A*) or the impassioned narrative found in five manuscripts in two versions (*Meditation B*), there is a strong *prima facie* case for thinking that he did. The two meditations are very different in both style and purpose. *Meditation A* is evidently designed (like the Passion lyric in *Ego Dormio*) for daily use. It is written in a flat and not especially elegant style, interspersing the narrative with instructions for the recitation of Latin prayers (which can also be spoken in English, 135–137), and mentioning each episode of Christ's passion with the same formula: 'Umbethinke the than how thei toke him oute fro prisone . . . Sithen how mekeli he stode tofore Herode. Sithen how Herode sent aʒein . . . Sithen how they naked him . . .' (85–91). Here, the reader is left to do most of the work in her own imagination, the written words acting merely to remind her of what comes next in a narrative she is assumed to have interiorized already. Towards the end, the focus shifts to her life: 'I say, thou wrecched caitife, sithen thou schalt ʒiue a rekenyng of the leste thouʒte, umbithinke the how thou hast spended this day, whiche is ordened to the to spende to the loouynge of thi lord and helthe of thi soule' (147–150). The use of the same formulaic 'Umbethynke' and 'sithen' suggests a parallel which ought to exist between the reader and Christ: has she spent her day as well as he spent that of the death? *Meditation B* has a similar basic structure, the narrative being interspersed by repeated Latin prayers. But here the entire piece is a prayer, moving to and fro between gratitude for the events of Christ's death ('Swet Ihesu, I thank þe of þy deseses þat þou haddest when Iudas betraied þe', 68–69) and petitions based on those events ('Now lord Ihesu, I beseche þe kepe me of gret synnys . . . and yeve me grace to þynk euery syn grete þat on any manere wise may greue þe', 70–73). The meditation is, moreover, superbly dramatic, building up from a subdued opening, to a long and masterly series of meditations on the wounded body of Christ – how it is like the sky full of stars, a net, a dovehouse, a book, a meadow full of flowers (195–200) – to an ever more impassioned account of the *via dolorosa*, crucifixion and death of Christ (251–553), before ending with unexpected serenity, addressing not the dead Christ but the living Mary: 'Graunt me, swet lady, to haue and to hold þis passion in mynd as hertely, as studiously, in al my lif, as þou, lady, and Iohn hadden in mynd when þe peple was gone, and ye abiden stil by þe rode fote', 557–559. In the third section the narrative suddenly becomes independent of the meditator, who now sees the events rather than merely recalling them: 'Swet Ihesu, I yeld þe þankynges for al þe angyr and sorow þat þou suffred when þou bare þe cros toward þy deth; and me þynketh, lord, I se how þey led þe forth naked as a worme, turmentours about þe and armed kneghtes. Þe prese of þe peple was wondyr mych . . . A, þis is a reuthful syʒt' (307–312). Much of this section is derived from James of Milan's *Stimulus Amoris* (Allen, p. 285), and is aimed at producing an inner transformation of the meditator through compassion; at one point, she complains of her lack of response – 'I fynd no swetnesse, bot speke as a iay and nat wot what I mene; I stody in passioun, and fynd no tast' (388–389) – and the work ends with her still asking Christ for 'oo sparcle of loue, oo reuth of þy passioun' (525), and Mary to 'graunt me of þy gret grace a poynte of þy peyne, a syʒt of þy sorow, to seigh and to sorow with þe' (554–555). In Chapter 2 (p. 62) I represent this fine work as intended for the new convert who wishes to feel true sorrow for her sins and thereby begin her ascent up the spiritual ladder. However, we could also regard it as having the same transitional function as the second *Ego Dormio* lyric, moving the meditator not merely to sorrow for sin, but to the higher states of passionate love. In contrast with *Meditation A*, this work is not meant to form part of the everyday routine of a spiritual life, but to be used at particular stages, when the affective necessity arises. Like *The Commandment* (though in an utterly different style), the existence of this work suggests Rolle's growing awareness of the difficulty of the spiritual transformations that *Ego Dormio*, in company with many of the Latin works, describes so glibly. 'Afforce þe for to feste in Crist þi couaitynge', says one of the lyrics (iv.89); *Meditation B* proceeds on the assumption that this advice may, in some cases at least, be extremely hard to follow.

IV

Finally we come to the works Rolle wrote for Margaret Kirkeby, *The Form of Living* and (almost certainly) the *English Psalter*.[11] It is on these that his medieval and modern reputation as a writer of English rests; surviving complete in thirty and nearly forty manuscripts respectively, they are the most popular and important of the works discussed in this chapter. Indeed, Margaret Kirkeby deserves to be seen as a key figure in the development of English spirituality, even in the history of English prose. Her friendship with Rolle, and his sense of responsibility towards her, were not the only factor motivating his composition of what seem to have been the first major English guide to the anchoritic life since *Ancrene Wisse* and the first long biblical commentary ever written in English; the scale of both works itself implies his awareness that he was ultimately writing for a wider readership. But it remains likely that without the stimulus of this outstanding friendship, Rolle's output of English writings would have been, relatively speaking, negligible, a mere footnote to his career, not a chapter in itself.

In the present state of scholarship there is, sadly, little that can be said with confidence about the *English Psalter*. Although there have been contributions in this direction, we still lack a definitive edition.[12] In the absence of any modern edition of the *Latin Psalter*, on which the work is said to draw extensively – as well as of investigation into the possible existence of further sources – we cannot say for certain where and how Rolle diverges from the Latin commentaries he is following, and so cannot argue with conviction why he does so.[13] Hence we are not in a position to answer any of the most important questions we need to ask of the work: How original is it? When it

differs from Peter Lombard and the *Latin Psalter* does it do so systematically? How far does it constitute an adaptation of its sources for a female
vernacular readership? – and so on. For the present, then, some inadequately
supported generalizations about the place of the work in Rolle's career,
which draw mainly on an analysis of its prologue, must suffice.

The prologue to the *English Psalter* is divided into two main sections, one
an expansion of the opening of the prologue to the *Latin Psalter*, the other an
abbreviated version of that to Peter Lombard's commentary. Both of these
serve to introduce and describe the psalms, but in different ways. The first,
more affective, section takes up approximately the opening thirty lines. Here,
the psalms are presented as the source of all the experiences that for Rolle
mark the summit of the spiritual life, and of all moral virtue besides:

Grete haboundance of gastly comfort and ioy in God comes in þe hertes of þaim [þ]at
says or synges deuotly þe psalmes in louynge of Jhesu Crist; þai drope swetnes in
mannys saule and hellis delite in þaire þoghtis, and kyndils þaire willes wiþ þe fyre of
luf, makand þaim hate and brennand withinen, and faire and lufly in Cristis eghen.
And þaim þat lastes in þaire deuocioun, þai rays þaim in til contemplatyf lyf, and oft
sith in til soun and myrth of heuen. Þe sange of psalmes chases fendis, excites aungels
til oure help; it does away synne, it quemes God, it enformes perfytnes; it dos away
and distroys noy and angire of saule, and makes pees itwix body and saule; it bryngs
desire of heuen and despite of erthly thynge. Sothly þis shynand boke is a chosen sange
byfor God, als laumpe lyghtnand oure lyf, hele of a seke hert, huny til a bittire saule,
dignyte of gastly persons, tonge of priue vertus, þe whilke heldes þe proud til meknes,
and kynges til pore men makes vndire-loute, fosterand barnes wiþ hamlynes. In þaim
is so mykill fayrhed of vndirstandynge and medicyne of wordes, þat þis boke is cald
garthen closed, wel enseled, paradyse ful of all appils [Song of Songs 4.12]: now wiþ
halesome lare drouyd and stormy saules it bryngis in til clere and pesful lyf, now
amonestand to fordo synne wiþ teris, now hyghtand ioy til ryghtwis men, now
mannassand hell til wyckyd. Þe sange þat delites þe hertes and lerese þe saule is made a
voice of syngand, and wiþ aungels whaim we may noght here we menge wordis of
louynge – sa þat worthily he may trow him aliene fra verray lyf what sa has noght þe
dilatabilte of þis gyft. O wondirful suetnes, þe whilk waxis noght soure thurgh þe
corupciouns of þis warld, bot, ay lastand in þe dignyte of it, in grace of purest softnes is
waxand! All gladnes and delite of erth wanys, and at þe laste wytes til noght; bot it, þe
langere tyme it has, þe mare it is – and aldiremast agayns man ded, when luf is perfitest.

(3.1–30)

The personal impetus behind this opening – as the work's original reader
would have known – is the fact that Rolle's first experience of *canor*,
described in the famous account in cap. 15 of *Incendium Amoris*, grew out of
a recitation of the psalms. They are thus seen as a potent source both of what
is here called devotion (apparently referring to *fervor* and *dulcor*) and
ultimately of contemplation itself (i.e. *canor*), and are described (in words
adapted from the prologue to Augustine's Psalter commentary)[14] as having
an inherent and almost magical power of the kind Rolle elsewhere attributed
to the Name of Jesus (see, e.g., *The Form of Living* 612–625), to defeat Satan,
reform the soul and lead it to God. As the work of that most charming of
kings, David, written in the sensual medium of affective poetry, they partake

of the allure that Rolle himself projects in the lyrics and *Ego Dormio*, belonging to an unfallen world in which there is 'pees itwix body and saule' and 'paradyse' is still 'ful of all appils'. Most important, they are treated as written examples of *canor* in their own right. Having said that the psalms induce *canor* in someone who says them devoutly, Rolle calls the whole 'shinand book' a 'chosen sange byfor God', and gives an allusive account of how 'þe sange þat delites þe hertes . . . is made a voice of syngand'. As R. Allen points out (1988, p. 200), this odd-sounding sentence closely translates part of the prologue to the Psalter commentary by Cassiodorus, where it refers to the nocturnal singing of a monastic community.[15] But in its new context I think it must mean that for someone who truly delights in the Psalter, the psalms – a written, and from a reader's viewpoint potential, form of *canor* – turn into actual, experiential *canor*, as the noun 'sange', with its generic definite article, turns into the present participle 'syngand', the product of a single 'voice': an interpretation which again recalls the place in *Incendium Amoris* in which Rolle describes exactly this happening to him. If I am right, the last part of the passage (which may be original) is thus not only concerned with the psalms, as appears on first reading, but with *canor* in both written and experienced forms; like *amor singularis* in cap. 11 of *Emendatio Vitae*, which grows the more passionate the longer it is felt, the mystical reading of the psalms and the enjoyment of the experience which develops out of it constantly grow more delightful. It follows that even for the person who has attained to *canor*, the Psalter continues to provide material for ever more profound rejoicing; so much is indeed implied by the ecstatic style of the passage itself, which seems to represent a third kind of *canor*, Rolle's written reduction of a mystical experience which remains closely related to his reading of the psalms. The first part of the prologue is thus suffused on every level with images of *canor* – it is a song about how song turns into song – as Rolle strives to draw readers into the charmed circle of spiritual growth and delight which a life with song and psalmody at its centre offers.

The second part of the prologue presents the Psalter in a more formal way. Although this section is much shorter than Peter Lombard's discussion, it retains many of his major points and a surprising amount of the structure of the 'Type c prologue'.[16] It gives information about the book's name ('Þis boke is cald þe Psautere, þe whilk nam it has of an instrument of musyke', 3.30–32), structure ('Alswa þis boke is distyngid in thris fyfty psalmes in þe whilk thre statis of cristin mannys religion is sygnifyd', 4.3–4), use ('Þis boke of all haly writ is mast oysed in halykyrke seruys', 4.8–9), formal title and contents ('Þis scripture is cald boke of ympnes of Crist', 4.19), *materia* ('Þe matere of þis boke is Crist and his spouse, þat is haly kyrke or ilk ryghtwise mannys saule', 4.26–27), *intentio* ('Þe entent is to confourme men þat are filyd in Adam til Crist in newnes of lyf', 4.28–20), and *modus tractandi* ('Þe manere of lare is swilke: vmstunt he spekis of Crist in his Godhed, vmstunt in his manhed', 4.29–30). This passage is important to the development of English as a learned language, representing as it does one of the earliest attempts to render the structures of medieval academic commentary in the English vernacular. It is also of interest as a sign of the serious way in which Rolle wished his readers to approach his exposition of what he (like Peter Lombard) views as a supremely inspired compendium of moral and mystical theology. Where the first part of the prologue represents the Psalter as an agent of various kinds of spiritual transformations, the second is concerned with the book as an instrument of teaching and analysis.

Rolle's commitment to both views of the Psalter – as affective devotion and as moral theology – are amply confirmed by the commentary itself. The final part of the prologue explains the procedures he follows here:

> In þis werke I seke na straunge Ynglis, bot lyghtest and comonest, and swilk þat is mast lyke til þe Latin, swa þat þai þat knawes noght Latyn by þe Ynglis may com til mony Latin wordis. In þe translacioun I folow þe lettere als mykyll as I may; and þare I fynd na propire Ynglis, I folow þe wit of þe worde, swa þat þai þat sall red it þaim þare noght dred errynge. In expounynge I fologh haly doctours, for it may come in some enuyous man hand þat knawes noght what he sould say, þat will say þat I wist noght what I sayd, and swa doe harme til hym and til oþere, if he dispise þe werke þat is profytabile for hym and oþere.   (4.35–5.7)

Before embarking on the work, the reader is made aware of the strategies of translation and exposition Rolle has felt appropriate. His English is as simple as he can make it; yet his translation is also as literal as possible, in order to send the reader back to the Latin with some understanding of what it means ('errynge' here is used in both doctrinal and grammatical senses).[17] The exposition likewise follows 'haly doctours' to reassure unlearned readers who lack a detailed knowledge of Catholic orthodoxy; Rolle's concern for the effectiveness of his commentary is such that he waives his right to expound in the original, inspired manner which *Super Lectiones Mortuorum* and other expositions employ (see pp. 203–207). In practice, the commentary seems to be more original than this statement implies. For example, more than half of the long exposition of Psalm 1 is not derived from Peter Lombard, and the proportion of new material in the next fifteen psalms seems similar, unless there is another, unidentified source; my impression is that Rolle is working with Peter Lombard's commentary at his elbow, but is referring to it more than copying it.[18] By giving the credit for his exposition to 'haly doctours' Rolle is both proclaiming its theological conservatism and, on another level, institutionalizing his presentation of the Psalter as a book which places *canor* at the heart of the spiritual life.[19] But the translation is certainly literal, often amounting to a word-by-word gloss which needs restatement in proper English in the ensuing commentary; Rolle refuses to abandon the letter and resort to following 'þe wit of þe worde' if he can avoid it. Thus verse 2 of Psalm 1 – '*Sed in lege Domini voluptas eius: et in lege eius meditabitur die ac nocte*' – is transcribed, then translated – '*Bot in laghe of Lord þe will of him: and in his laghe he sall thynke day and nyght*' – but then still needs to be put into workable English: 'Hys wil is in Godis laghe . . . bot he sall thynke in hys laghe . . . day and nyght' (6.18–24). As the prologue says, this presentation, in which the translation is manifestly not self-sufficient and the commentary deals purely with the meaning of the verse, forces the reader to 'com til mony Latin wordis' by making her focus her reading around the original. For Rolle the psalms evidently must be sung and felt in Latin.

Nonetheless, the commentary does more than merely paraphrase the Latin; it also provides a full analysis of what each verse means. With Psalm 1 this involves a five-point treatment of 'blisfulhede' from 'saynt Austyne' and a similar discussion of 'man', all in explication of the phrase '*Beatus vir*' (5.16–36); a phrase-by-phrase account of verses 2–5; and, in explication of verse 6 ('*Ideo non resurgunt impii in iudicio*'), a long description from Peter Lombard of the 'foure ordirs' of souls at the Last Judgement (8.7–22). The process of assimilating this material, which demands keeping a grasp on the overall argument of the psalm while attending to numerous details, is intellectually strenuous and takes a good hour, even if one does not then make the expected transition from *lectio* to *oratio*; a reading and praying of the whole *English Psalter* would require many months. Admittedly, Rolle's commentary is both shorter and far simpler than Peter Lombard's. He omits the introductory discussions of the title, structure, *materia* and *intentio* of each psalm; he hardly ever gives alternative explanations of a passage; he omits detailed theological discussions; and he seldom cites authorities by name. Conversely he takes pains to present each psalm as the outpouring of a single voice and as having a coherent subject; Psalm 13 is spoken by 'Þe prophet, blamand þaim þat gifes þaim til all þe lust and lykynge of þaire flesch' (47.14–15), Psalm 12 preserves 'Þe voice of haly men, þat couaitis and ȝernys þe comynge of Ihesu Crist' (45.20–21), Psalm 10 is written in 'Þe voice of haly kyrke' (40.14–15), and so on. Moreover, most of the material included is homiletic, not theological, and there are frequent references to themes particular to Rolle, especially to his English writings; as well as mystical discussions of the fire of love, spiritual song and contemplation (10.17–25, 13.26–32, 14.1–5, 47.1–14), there are, for example, numerous mentions of the Name of Jesus (21.6–10, 28.10–16, 32.30–35, 90.7–11). On occasion Rolle uses a metaphorical or anecdotal mode more usual in sermons than commentaries: as when the *beatus vir* of Psalm 1.1 is described as going swiftly over the ground on which the wicked stand, 'as he þat gas on qwik grauel þat gers him synk þat standis þar on' (6.4–5); or when the sin of grumbling at providence is illustrated by a tale 'as I herd say noght lang sythen of a man of religious and of gret fame' (30.18–19). In short, the *English Psalter* is a popularization, not a genuinely scholarly commentary. Yet if we bear in mind how little access a non-Latinate English reader can have had to this kind of serious, lengthy religious work in the fourteenth century, it will be clear that this *summa* of practical theology, which doubles as an enormously laborious devotional exercise, makes unusually heavy demands on such a reader's time, intelligence and concentration.

The *English Psalter* can thus be seen as an indirect testimony to the woman at whose request it seems to have been written. Margaret Kirkeby must indeed have been remarkable to elicit such a work from the author of *Ego Dormio* and *The Commandment*: a work which leaves so much of the process of learning to the reader, demanding she master such a range of material and of interpretive skills; a work which places *canor* and the steps which lead to it so carefully in a theological and biblical context. The density and relative abstraction of the *English Psalter* is, in fact, something of a puzzle when we compare it with Rolle's epistles, lyrics and miscellaneous short works which likewise aim to teach women readers about contemplation. The opening of the prologue is couched in characteristically optimistic terms, describing the power of the psalms to transform lives and induce *canor* in their readers as though the process is partly automatic. But the commentary itself indicates that this is far from being the case; on the contrary, to achieve even the basic understanding of the Psalter that Rolle's commentary offers emerges as an arduous business. *Ego Dormio* tells its readers to 'gyf þe myche to say psalmes of þe psauter and pater noster and auees, and take nat entent þat þou say many bot þat þou say ham wel, and in al þe deuocioun þat þou may' (129–132); yet only in the *English Psalter* is it made clear how much slow and difficult *lectio* must precede this slow and affective *oratio*. Perhaps Rolle thought of his lyrics and meditation as an alternative route to the summit of the spiritual life, in which the study of moral theology had little part. After all, in *Meditation B* the speaker describes Christ's body as a book she wants 'to rede vpon . . . and somwhate to vndrestond þe swetnes of þat writynge, and to haue likynge in studious abydynge of þat redynge' (238–240). Self-transformation through meditation on Christ's death involves its own demanding forms of affective *lectio* (see Gillespie 1984 and 1987). Nonetheless, set beside the *English Psalter*, which assumes its reader may spend years 'in studious abydynge' of a different kind, so that she may sing her praises with understanding (see Psalm 46.7), the other English spiritual exercises Rolle provides begin to seem like stopgaps. They might be profitably combined with the study of the *English Psalter* (which frequently commends devotion to the Name of Jesus), and no doubt were. But it is difficult to see the lyrics or *Ego Dormio* as in themselves constituting serious attempts to lead their readers to the same level of spiritual attainment that the *English Psalter* implies. The prologue to *Incendium Amoris* states that the learned are in principle better qualified to feel fervent love than the ignorant (147.27–28: 'Quo enim scienciores sunt eo de iure apciores sint ad amandum'), while that to the *English Psalter* says that *canor* itself grows more intense the longer it is felt, and links such growth with understanding the psalms. In making material that was normally accessible only to readers of Latin available to Margaret Kirkeby (and thence to all readers of English), Rolle seems to be pointing her towards heights he does not envisage in many of his English works. Such a conclusion points up the existence of a real gap between the Latin writings and all the English ones except those written for her. It even seems possible that the structure of the *English Psalter* – the way it persists in focussing the reader on Latin verses she may only partially understand – is the product of an undeclared assumption on Rolle's part that *canor* itself is ideally a Latin experience.

The *English Psalter* pays its reader the compliment of treating her to a long series of discussions of the spiritual life which are not exclusively concerned with her own particular state, and which leave her to put them to her own use. *The Form of Living*, to the contrary, is the most carefully particularized of all Rolle's works, addressing as it does not simply an anchoress but a woman who has just become an anchoress ('Atte þe begynnynge turne þe entierly to þi lord Ihesu Crist', 267), and directing much, though by no means all, its teaching to this very specific condition. Appropriately, it is the only one of his works whose date and occasion of composition is known to us; it was written in late 1348 or early 1349, in the last months of his life, on the occasion of Margaret Kirkeby's enclosure at an anchorhold in Richmondshire (see p. 275). We also appear to have the wherewithal to deduce a good deal about the literary context in which it was presented to her: this from evidence provided by the manuscript whose outstandingly good copies of Rolle's English works I am using here, Longleat 29. Longleat, copied c. 1430–1450 in an East Midlands dialect (and recently edited almost in its entirety by Ogilvie-Thomson (1980)), contains a large collection of devotional and mystical writings in English, prominent among which we find those of Rolle, organized into a coherent series: first, the three epistles, from the longest and most advanced (*The Form of Living*) to the shortest and least so (*The Commandment*); next, the prose pieces *Desire and Delight* and *Ghostly Gladness*, and the six lyrics (ending with the Passion lyric, 'Ihesu swet'), followed by some lyrics in praise of Mary which are probably not Rolle's; finally, a fragment of *Meditation A*.[20] The series begins and ends with rubrics which treat it as a single treatise, one reading 'Tractatus Ricardi heremite ad Margaretam de Kyrkby reclusam de Vita Contemplativa' (f. 30r.), the other 'Explicit tractatus Ricardi heremite de Hampolle ad Margaretam reclusam de Kyrkby de amore Dei' (f. 58v.). These unique rubrics, which claim this series to have been written for a particular woman, and the uniformly good texts they enclose – texts that according to Ogilvie-Thomson (1988, p. lxii) may be as few as two removes from their archetypes – suggest that Longleat preserves a copy of a collection of English writings made for Margaret Kirkeby by Rolle himself, presumably when he composed and presented her with *The Form of Living*. A number of special features of the Longleat texts support this conjecture: notably the presence of a passage of *Ego Dormio* which is clearly authentic but occurs in no other manuscript, implying it is the product of an authorial revision or recopying of the work (Ogilvie-Thomson 1988, p. lxxv); and, in *The Form of Living*, the absence of the chapter divisions which are found in Dd.v.64 and other manuscripts but seem unlikely to be authentic.[21] Even the date of the manuscript, fifty years later than Dd.v.64, might be taken to suggest that the archetype from which the Rolle material descends remained in the hands of solitaries, and so was long unavailable for copying. If the 'De Vita Contemplativa' is what I think it is, *The Form of Living* was written to head a collection of all Rolle's major English works except the *English Psalter* and *Meditation B*, made for someone who was on her way to a life far both from books and Rolle.[22]

Longleat thus apparently provides us with a further notable instance of the *amicitia* that existed between Rolle and Margaret Kirkeby, which here led to his putting together his three very different epistles with some of the devotional exercises he had written at various times, all perhaps intended to supplement – and no doubt provide relief from – the rigours of the *English Psalter*. If this collection really is authorial in origin, it also brings us back to a theme introduced in discussing *The Commandment*, that of Rolle's growing awareness (in the English works probably written after *Ego Dormio*) of the complexity of the spiritual lives of his readers: the way that in practice they do not follow the pattern of unidirectional spiritual ascent he loves to trace in most of his Latin works. (The *English Psalter* could indeed have been invoked as a further variation on this theme.) For the series of works gathered in Longleat suggest a life which for a time at least is in need both of relatively simple material (*Meditation A*, several of the lyrics, parts of *The Commandment*) and of the advanced discussions found at the end of *Ego Dormio* and in the second half of *The Form of Living*. The same is true in a slightly different sense even if we consider *The Form of Living* on its own. As Excursus I (item I) shows, the epistle makes substantial use of parts of *Emendatio Vitae*, Rolle's most schematic work; the relationship the two have is closer than that between any other pair of his works except *Super Canticum Canticorum* and *Melos Amoris*.[23] Yet the first half of the work seems to be a conscious exercise in undermining any notion the reader may have that her new state as a solitary guarantees she is in, or will consistently maintain, an inner condition pertaining to any particular degree of holiness. Rolle begins by expounding 'þre wrechednesse' which can bring 'euery synful man and womman þat is bounden in dedely syn . . . vnto þe deth of helle' (1–2): 'defaut of gostly streynth', 'vse of fleisshely desires' and 'chaungynge of lestynge good for a passynge delyte' (2–11). On the face of it, an anchoress is safe from all these dangers; her heroic decision to cut herself completely off from the world would seem to demonstrate her 'gostly strength', and could properly be defined as 'chaungynge of a passynge delyte for a lestynge good', while her opportunities to indulge 'fleisshely desires' are severely limited. But rather than pointing this out, Rolle goes on to state that there is often a close link between the evidently worldly and the apparently holy: 'These wrechednes þat I of told ben nat only in worldisshe men and wommen . . . bot þei ben also in sum men þat semen in penaunce and in good lif' (18–20). This statement leads directly to the first passage taken from *Emendatio Vitae* ('For þe deuyl, þat is enemy vnto al mankynd . . .', 20–21), which here acts as a generalized declaration of what is then shown in detail: that the attempt to lead a holy life initially only intensifies the enemy's assaults, and that in a sense Margaret Kirkeby can therefore not yet be said to have 'left the world' at all. She has

begun to do so but must still remember that 'Many begynneth þe worke þat
þei neuer more mowen for to brynge to an end' (55–56). Indeed, the greatest
dangers she faces lie in the temptation to treat the anchoritic life in a 'worldly'
way, paying heed to the praise and vituperation to which her prominence
exposes her (87–96), or confusing holiness with its outward signs, such as
penance and abstinence; as in cap. 4 of *Emendatio Vitae*, Rolle gives a good
deal of attention to the need to practice discretion by not fasting too much
(48–86).

What we should possibly think of as the *exordium* of *The Form of Living*
ends by apparently dismissing the subject of diabolic temptation, and
initiating a discussion of the purity that a burning love for God can instil:
'Thou hast herd nowe a partie how þe deuyl deceyueth with his sutil craftes
vnstable and vnwise men and wommen. And if þou wilt do good consaille and
folowe holy lernynge as I hope thou wolt, þou shalt destroy his trappes and
brand in þe fire of loue al þe bondes þat he wol bynd þe with' (105–109). The
next stage of the work does indeed begin by describing the solitary life in the
glowing terms we expect from Rolle. He assures his reader he is confident
that the Holy Spirit will lead her to purity, 'So þat in a few yers þou shalt haue
more delite to be by þyn on and spek to þi loue and þi spouse Ihesu þan if þou
were lady of a thousand worldes' (128–130); alludes for the first time to the
fact that he, too, is a solitary ('Men weneth þat we haue peyn . . . bot we haue
. . . ioy and verrey delite', 130–131); and describes solitude as the ideal state
for the reception of 'reuelaciouns of þe Holy Goste', glossing these as
'Swetnesse and delyte . . . brandynge of loue and . . . ioy and melody'
(143–145). We seem to be on the threshold of the third degree of love as *Ego
Dormio* describes it. Yet for Margaret Kirkeby these delights still lie some
years in the future, for 'No man cometh to such reuelaciouns and grace þe
first day, bot þrogh longe trauaille and bisynesse to loue Ihesu Criste',
(148–149). In the present, there is work to be done, and the remainder of this
part of *The Form of Living* thus returns to much the issues Rolle has already
dealt with: temptation and the need to resist it with discretion and constant
vigilance (151–260). This new discussion is directed especially towards
solitaries and the physical manifestations of the devil (in human and angelic
form or in dreams) to which they are traditionally thought to be prone
(161–181, 203–232). Yet much of this section goes over earlier ground by
once again issuing a general warning against over-abstinence (183–202), and
by returning to the themes of the relation between outer and inner lives and
the danger of hypocrisy (233–260). It is not surprising that, like its predecessor, this section ends as though it has constituted the work's *exordium*:
'And if þou wilt do as I teche the in þis short fourme of lyvynge, I hope þrogh
þe grace of God þat, if men hold þe good, þou shalt be wel bettre' (264–266).
Rolle seems to be reverting to the device of the double prologue we saw him
employ in *Contra Amatores Mundi* (see pp. 161–162).

The first two sections of *The Form of Living* are negative in emphasis,
concerned with the need to avoid sin and to beware of various temptations.

The long third section (267–484) does offer some negative advice, but mainly consists of a series of practical and positive instructions, corresponding to (and drawing much of its material from) cap. 4 of *Emendatio Vitae*. Rolle again makes it clear he is writing for a beginner in the solitary life: the section opens with 'Atte þe begynnynge turne þe entierly to þi lord Ihesu Crist' (267), continuing by defining 'turning' in ways which recall parts of caps. 1–2 of *Emendatio Vitae*, as if the reader is only now in a position truly to turn from the world (270–309). Most of this section, however, consists of long lists of sins from the *Compendium Theologicae Veritatis* (III, caps. 30–33), followed by other lists of the ways in which sin is cleansed (*Emendatio Vitae* providing the framework for this whole discussion), and a concluding section on how our wills can be conformed to God's (323–484). Not all this material seems relevant to an anchoress; since Rolle states that part of 'satisfaccioun' for sin is to 'enfourme ham how þay shal do þat ben in poynt to perisshe' (409–410), he perhaps provides these lists partly to help Margaret Kirkeby to act as a teacher of others. But he does manage to introduce two more appeals to practise moderation by avoiding over-abstinence (310–322, 436–468), giving this theme an extraordinarily heavy exposure. Such an insistent return to material one would have thought had already been amply expounded confirms one's impression that the whole of the first half of *The Form of Living* is designed to assist Margaret Kirkeby in the difficult first few months or years of her solitary life – and thus that, in spite of the borrowings from *Emendatio Vitae*, this part of the work is not in any way structured around Rolle's usual model of spiritual ascent. The model is still alluded to, but no more than in *The Commandment* does Rolle really trust his reader to apply it to her own life without a great deal of detail he never feels the need to include in his Latin works. Indeed a major cause of the oddly repetitive structure of this part of the work may be his warm but fussy solicitude for his young spiritual charge, who, after some years under his eye at Hampole, has just taken on the full responsibility for her own spiritual destiny by moving to an anchorhold which is too far away for regular visits. Rolle returns again and again to the same issues because he is worried that she may be trying too hard, starving herself and weakening her body in a mistaken effort to imitate the lives of the Desert Fathers, when what he wants for her is not a life of mortification but of contemplation. Since he cannot be there to instruct her, he makes his point unmistakably clear, but still frets that she may succumb to the expectations that people around her have of her: 'Men þat comen to þe praise þe for þei see þi gret abstinence and for þay se þe enclosed. Bot I may nat praise þe so lightly for oght þat I se þe do withouten, bot if þi wil be conformed entierly to do Goddis wille' (460–463). Perhaps Rolle was right to worry, for in *lectio viija* of the *Officium* we learn that Margaret Kirkeby was taken ill and was only cured after he visited her. It is difficult to separate fact from legend in this story, but it does seem to help justify the view that part of *The Form of Living* is organized around a touching personal anxiety as much as it is around any more elevated or general principles.

Much of the first half of *The Form of Living* is frankly laborious, as Rolle deals with basic materials in which he has only a temporary interest. The second half begins with what reads like a sigh of relief from both writer and reader: 'Now [h]as þou herd how þou may dispose þi lyf, and reul hit to Goddis wille. Bot I wot wel þat þou desirest to hyre some special poynt of þe loue of Ihesu Criste and of contemplatif lif þe which þou hast taken þe to at mennys syȝt. As I haue grace and connynge I wil lere þe' (485–488). From this point on the whole of the work deals with passionate love, in an organized and ambitious exposition consisting of: first, an introduction, on the need to love and on love as the special preserve of solitaries (489–524), followed by an exposition of three degrees of love, expanded and adapted from cap. 11 of *Emendatio Vitae*, which in turn becomes a rhapsodic account of *canor* (525–625); second, a series of questions and answers about love – what love is (633–677), where love is (678–704), how God is to be loved (705–772), how the reader may know if she is in charity (773–818), and in what state of life God can be loved most passionately (819–893).[24] This discussion reveals the other side of Rolle's solicitude for Margaret Kirkeby, which is his desire and confidence (for all the anxiety he has expressed) that she will in time come to love God as he does. Rather as the *English Psalter* was written to initiate her into areas of thought usually available only to readers of Latin, so this part of *The Form of Living* provides her with information about the upper reaches of the spiritual life which occurs nowhere else in Rolle's English works. It gives a lengthy account of *fervor*, *dulcor* and especially *canor* (549–609); it translates theological definitions of love which the *Compendium Theologicae Veritatis* takes from Prosper of Aquitaine's (Julius Pomerius's) *De Vita Contemplativa* (633–651 and note); it adopts the daring images for divine union from the climax of Bernard's *De Diligendo Deo* (670–677 and note), and adapts a passage of *Super Canticum Canticorum* which gives a precise account of the transforming power of the name 'Jesus' (610–621, see *Super Canticum Canticorum* 43.8–44.5). In general, throughout this part of the work Rolle shows a concern that the reader gain a theological understanding of the spiritual processes in which she is engaged that is largely lacking from *Ego Dormio*, and still more from *The Commandment*. It is true that the second half of *The Form of Living* also needs to be seen as Rolle's last and greatest attempt to create a verbal equivalent of *canor* in English; this has been amply demonstrated in a fine study of the verbal patterning of the work by Lois Smedick (1979), who shows that many of the manuscripts punctuate it according to aural, not grammatical or conceptual, principles. Not only does Rolle write Margaret Kirkeby a lyric which evokes and is to be used in the degree of 'synguler loue' ('When wil þou cum to comfort me and brynge me out of care', 598–609); he composes much of this part of the work in a lyrical prose which greatly reinforces both the content of his message concerning love and the reader's sense of his own presence. Nonetheless, what is most striking here is the depth, complexity and implied respect for the reader's intelligence found in every part of this treatment of the solitary's special gift, love (494).

This point can be exemplified by comparing portions of the second half of
the epistle with the treatments of love and contemplation in the last two
chapters of *Emendatio Vitae*, a work which was never far from Rolle's mind
(or, probably, his desk) when writing *The Form of Living*. A brief discussion
of 'contemplatif lif' at the end of the epistle (861–893) echoes cap. 12 of
Emendatio Vitae in several details. As we saw earlier (pp. 218–220), Rolle's
chief preoccupation at this point in the Latin work is with setting up *canor* as
the climax of a series of definitions of contemplation by earlier *auctores* – thus
inscribing his own mystical and literary career into a long tradition which
culminates in himself. The epistle is concerned with more practical matters,
but nonetheless provides an account of the contemplative life of considerable
sophistication and clarity. Rolle presents 'two parties' of contemplative life,
the lower consisting of *lectio, meditatio* and *oratio*, the higher of *contemplatio*
much as *Emendatio Vitae* defines it:

The hegher partie of contemplacioun is biholdynge and desyre of þe þynges of heuyn,
and ioy in þe Holy Goost, þat men hath oft, þogh hit so be þat þai be nat praiynge with
þe mouth, bot only thynkynge of God and of þe fairheed of angels and holy soules. Þan
may I say þat contemplacioun is a wonderful ioy of Goddis loue, þe which ioy is a
praysynge of God þat may nat be told. And þat wondreful praisynge is in þe soule, and
for aboundance of ioy and swetnesse hit ascendeth in to þe mouth, so þat þe hert and
þe tonge accordeth in on, and body and soule ioyeth in God lyuynge.   (865–874)[25]

Rather than simply restating his personal version of divine union as *fervor,*
dulcor and *canor* (described earlier in the account of 'synguler loue'), Rolle is
anxious that Margaret Kirkeby understand the literal meaning of the Latin-
derived 'contemplacioun' as 'biholdynge'; later he reiterates 'contemplacioun
is a sight' (888). These are not just references to his gift of 'Sight into Heaven';
they correspond to many of the definitions of contemplation against which
Emendatio Vitae sets his own. Here as there *canor* is described as one among
several kinds of contemplation. (In this instance, indeed, though the passage
clearly implies *canor* to be superior to the kinds that do not involve 'praiynge
with þe mouth', it is introduced with a slightly apologetic formula – 'Þan may
I say' – as though the reader may be aware of an awkwardness in calling an
aural experience 'contemplation'.) The last sentences of the work before the
dedication, a brief account of the spiritual progress of 'a man or a womman
þat is ordeynet to contemplatif lif' (875–876), again describe the climax of that
progress partly in visual terms ('þai seth in to heuyn with har gostly eigh'),
adding the usual warning that 'perfite sight of heuyn' is not possible in this
life, but looking ahead to the perfect *vision* of God (not the perfecting of
spiritual song) in the next: 'Bot as sone as þai dey, þai ben broght bifor God,
and seth hym face to face and egh to eigh, and wonneth with hym withouten
end' (887–892). Rolle is evidently trying to achieve the same *rapprochement*
between his own and competing versions of contemplation that he attempts
at the end of *Emendatio Vitae*, in order that his reader have a proper
understanding of where his accounts of *canor* and violent love fit into
traditional views of *contemplatio*.

The treatment of *contemplatio* in *The Form of Living* is briefer and more general than the one in *Emendatio Vitae*. When we return to consider the two works' respective discussions of love, however, the situation is the other way round: the English work is longer, fuller, and theologically both more precise and more daring. I have argued that the discussion of the degrees of violent love which occupy most of cap. 11 of *Emendatio Vitae* should be seen as affective rather than mystical, suitable for those whose situations make it unlikely that they will ever achieve contemplative *canor* (pp. 216–218). But whereas *Emendatio Vitae* was written for those who are not professional contemplatives, *The Form of Living* was intended for someone whose entire life was to consist of contemplation: 'Þou . . . hast nat elles to do bot for to loue God' says Rolle to Margaret Kirkeby, predicting that she should be able to reach at least the second degree of love, 'if any may get hit' (546–548). Here the degrees of love carry far weightier meanings than do their counterparts in *Emendatio Vitae*. In particular, where the latter develops an argument that *amor singularis* never ceases to grow, illustrating its point with a potpourri of affective passages from the three works Rolle associated with *dulcor* while carefully refraining from introducing *canor*, *The Form of Living* substitutes a detailed account of the upper reaches of the spiritual life, turning for its inspiration (as do so many of the English works) to *Incendium Amoris*:

> Synguler loue is when al confort and solace is closet out of þe herte, bot of Ihesu Crist only. Oþer delite ne other ioy list hit nat, for þe swetnesse of hym in þis degre is so confortable and lestynge, his loue so brennynge and gladynge, þat he or sho þat is in þis degre may as wel feele þe fyre of loue brennynge in har soule as þou may fele þi fynger bren if þou put hit in þe fyre . . . Þan þi þoght turneth in to songe and in to melody; þan þe behoueth synge þe psalmes þat þou before said; than þou mow be longe about fewe psalmes. Than þe wil þynke þe deth swetter þan hony, for þan þou art siker to see hym þat þou louest . . . Þe soul þat is in þe þrid degre is as a brennynge fyre, and as þe nyghtgalle, þat loueth songe and melody, and failleth for mykel loue . . . Who-so hath hit, hym thinke al þe songe and þe mynstralcie of erth nat bot sorowe and woo þerto.
>
> (550–584)

Part of the success of this highly affective passage has probably always been bound up in its obvious allusions to Rolle's personal experience, in the form in which *Incendium Amoris* celebrates it: the image of the finger in the fire, which recalls the opening of the prologue; the sentence about thought turning into song, which directly translates a famous moment in cap. 15 ('cogitacio mea in canorum commutabatur . . . Deinceps usque ad canendum que prius dixeram', 189.25–190.1); the references to the honey-sweet desire for death, which are reminiscent of parts of cap. 16; and the image of the nightingale, which is borrowed from an autobiographical moment in the last chapter of the work. But as well as being exciting prose, this section of *The Form of Living* contains parts of Rolle's mystical system which we have hardly glimpsed in any of the other late works (English or Latin) that I have associated with the 'mixed' life. Here we read of the intensely private nature of *canor* and of the assurance it brings that after death 'þou art siker to see hym þat þou louest' – a point that re-emerges in the fourth question about love, which asserts that 'if any had grace þat he myght wyn in to þe þrid degre of loue . . . he wold knowe þat he ware in loue' (783–784). Here, too, we find a stronger expression of the incompatibility between earthly and heavenly song than Rolle has felt appropriate in any work since *Melos Amoris*. The only major claim that *The Form of Living* does not reiterate from Rolle's most daring mystical works is the one concerning the continual nature of *canor*. Apart from this significant omission it is clear, first, that Rolle has not changed his mind about the pre-eminence of *canor* and the solitary life since embarking on the programme of teaching initiated by *Super Lectiones Mortuorum*; second, that he considers almost his whole mystical system to be of direct pastoral relevance to his outstanding female disciple. It is true that he addresses issues more cautiously here than in the Latin works, underplaying rather than emphasizing the idiosyncratic nature of his view of contemplation as *canor*; these are lessons learned from writing *Emendatio Vitae* and *The Commandment*. Yet in *The Form of Living* as in the *English Psalter*, Margaret Kirkeby's needs and interests, and Rolle's devoted concern that they be met, act as historically important conduits for the transmission of relatively advanced mystical material from Latin into English.

When Rolle died on 30 September 1349 (the feast of St Michael and All Angels), he may have thought he still had some years to live. We can guess this from what seems to be his own annotation of cap. 15 of *Incendium Amoris* – now surviving only in MSS Bodley 861 (f. 99v.), Durham B.iv (f. 112v.), and in two citations (Allen, pp. 27–28). It reads: 'In nocte purifica-cionis beate marie virginis, dictum mihi fuit in sompnis, anno domini mccccxliii, "anni duodecim vives"' ('In the night of the purification of the Blessed Virgin Mary [2 February], in the year of our Lord 1343, there was said to me in a dream "You will live twelve years"'). Unless this note is some kind of forgery, it is likely that Rolle approached the worst of the plague years with the idea that he still had five or six years in which to continue his active teaching role in the Church Militant, and to carry out such further literary projects as his fertile mind had conceived. Yet what is striking about both his last Latin work, *Emendatio Vitae*, and his final English one, *The Form of Living*, is how fitting a conclusion they nonetheless make to a career that was both self-consciously and intricately planned – for as we have seen, they are in different ways equally successful in mediating between his unique mystical system, a wider tradition of contemplative thought, and the pastoral needs of their respective readers. As we read them, we can have no doubt that in all essential ways his self-imposed task of articulating and canonizing a structure of ideas, and of placing himself in the midst of that structure, was accomplished. In other ways, too, his affairs appear to have been perfectly in order. Apart from one incomplete early work, *Super Apocalypsim*, he left no surviving fragments behind. From the state of the surviving manuscripts (as well as from his habit of borrowing from his own work), it seems clear that he had carefully kept copies of most of his Latin writings, so that few, if any, were dispersed or lost; the evidence of MS Longleat 29 suggests that just before his death he entrusted Margaret Kirkeby with a collection of his major English ones, with a similar result. Finally, by the time of his death he must have found readers more influential than the nuns of Hampole who were convinced that his claims for himself and his writing were valid; in view of the proliferation of copies of his work in the late fourteenth and early fifteenth centuries, the seeds of his fame must have been sown during his life. For any writer who died in his early forties (see p. 278) this would be a notable achievement. For Rolle, who had at most only two decades in which to evolve a mature style out of the uncertainties of *Judica Me*, the imitativeness of the early commentaries, and the contradictions of *Incendium Amoris*, it was nothing short of remarkable.

Rolle as a late medieval *auctor*

Turning at last from this long series of analyses, and looking back to take our final view of the ground we have covered in the course of making them, the shape of Rolle's career appears in many respects as schematic as the structure of ideas around which it was built. The literary landscape across which our eye passes is patterned, at least in retrospect, with an almost obsessive neatness. Here, as we survey Rolle's works in what seems to be chronological order, is a careful progression from discussion of the active life, to a long engagement in the affairs of the contemplative life, to a final and self-conscious shift to the perspective of the 'mixed' life. There, focussing our gaze in a different way, the same progression appears as an elaborate movement from an early phase of cautious imitation, to a middle one of audaciously original inspiration, to a late one of confidently individual spiritual direction. There, too, in the smaller group of works which are at the heart of this study, from *Incendium Amoris* to *Melos Amoris*, we can see a sustained evolution from one phase of self-revelation to the next, which corresponds in some way to an imagistic development from *fervor* to *dulcor* to *canor*; perhaps this is meant to appear as the fundamental triad on the model of which all the others are constructed. A glance at some of the individual works which make up our total picture reveals equally careful rhythms, and gives some grounds for confidence that all this patterning is not merely in the eye of the beholder. The tripartite structure of *Incendium Amoris* comes into view most readily. Here again, of course, is the familiar movement from *fervor* to *dulcor* to *canor*, each section of the work focussing on one of these mystical sensations. But as if not satisfied with so simple a pattern, Rolle chose to present these sensations within a different, albeit closely related triadic framework, which consists of the accounts of crucial moments in his life with which each section opens: from his reception of both *fervor* and *dulcor* (the Prologue), to his secret attainment of *canor* (cap. 15), to its first public proclamation (cap. 31). The harmonic tension which this counterpoint sets up is resolved in *Melos Amoris* by means of another triad, again related but not the same. Cap. 1 of this work has its protagonist first driven like Christ into the desert, away from worldly misery (*meror*); next, swept up irresistably into joyful song, though still kept from speaking about his experience by fear (*metus*); finally, compelled by the urgings of the Holy Spirit to broadcast his song, in the triumphant culmination at once of his spiritual and his literary career that is the work itself (*melos*). Rolle's later works ring yet further changes on the number three, this time of a more abstract and formal kind. *Super Lectiones Mortuorum* is divided (as the text on which it comments indeed dictates) into nine sections. *Emendatio Vitae* is in twelve chapters, clearly subdivided into groups of three. *Ego Dormio* falls into three sections separated from one another by lyrics, the sections corresponding to a progress at once from active to contemplative to solitary life and from penitence to spiritual desire to the attainment of divine love. *Emendatio Vitae, The Commandment* and *The Form of Living* all borrow three of Richard of St Victor's grades of 'violent' love, superimposing them (in ways which are never fully explained) on to the triad of *fervor, dulcor* and *canor*. Even the Psalter commentaries follow Peter Lombard in dividing the Psalms into three groups of fifty, the first singing of penitence, the second of justice, the third of eternal life. In contrast, say, to Bonaventure (a writer also much preoccupied with triadic structures), Rolle does not seem especially interested in numerological symbolism; all these threes cannot be said to 'mean' anything in particular, however much they tempt one into theorizing about their interrelationships. But this accumulation of similar patterns does manage to suggest, with mesmeric forcefulness if not beauty, the divine and Triune source of all he has been, experienced and written. From our present eminence, Rolle's whole career is spread out before us like a single vast rhetorical construct, an inspired product of that process of forethought known to medieval poets and rhetoricians as the *ars inveniendi*:

> For everi wight that hath an hous to founde
> Ne renneth naught the werk for to bygynne
> With rakel hond, but he wol bide a stounde,
> And sende his hertes line out fro withine
> Aldirfirst his purpose for to wynne.
>
> (*Troilus and Criseyde* 1.1065–1069)

Thus Pandarus, meditating on the task of seducing his niece on behalf of his *ami*, in words taken from Geoffrey of Vinsauf's instructions to the poet, who cannot hope for the inspiration of the Muse unless he has first 'invented' his material, deciding its nature and scope and disposing it in its proper form in his mind before even lifting his pen (*Poetria Nova* 43–59).[1]

It is all too easy to imagine Rolle taking satisfaction in contemplating the authoritative construct that is his career, secure (unlike Troilus) in his seraphic place in the ninth sphere. But there is no reason to allow the retrospective gaze we are sharing with him here to become too transfixing. His progress to this point, and ours, has after all been a far less smooth affair than it now appears with the benefit of hindsight. As we saw in the first part of *Judica Me*, repeatedly in *Incendium Amoris*, and even in *Melos Amoris*, Rolle is often in fact far from being in control of what he is doing. *Inventio* is by definition a hidden art, manifested only through the propriety and ingenuity with which a poet's *materia* is embodied in a written work; to invent with skill is to achieve an effect of inspired order such as we have just commended in the general shape of Rolle's career, but to do so in such a way as to efface signs of the hesitation and doubt which are an inevitable part of the creative process. Rolle is brilliantly inventive, in a modern sense, in his ability to reinterpret past contradictions and uncertainties as integral parts of the larger unity of his thought – or else, failing that, at least to conceal them behind an almost impermeably rich veil of rhetorical ornament. Yet there is no hiding many of the false moves that he makes. In *Judica A*, for example, we are given far too revealing a view of how a major part of his *materia*, the praise of the eremitic life, pushes its way to the surface of his writing, in response to pressures that are irrelevant to the purposes of this particular work. Similar, though more complicated, moments of self-betrayal inevitably occur through much of *Incendium Amoris*, a work written in large part to carry out an agenda which must remain hidden from the reader, the canonization of its author. In so far as Rolle's *materia* here is his own sanctity, he is in the strange position of having to appear ignorant of what he is writing about, and so cannot seem in full control of the process of *inventio*. This situation is already difficult to describe, or to deal with, using the structures of ideas developed in the rhetorical manuals; things are made greatly worse by the fact that Rolle, as we saw, is at first deeply uneasy about his need to assert his own sanctity, and so to an extent actually conceals from *himself* what it is he is writing about (e.g., p. 125). The result is chaotic; again, his material is 'invented' as it were on the page, and we are inadvertently allowed to witness both the mechanics of his self-establishment as a saintly authority and the confusion into which these periodically throw him. On balance, during most of his work he woos us with less skill than Pandarus woos Criseyde. This is not to deny that *Incendium Amoris* achieves signal successes, especially when it manages to redefine its author's overwhelming tendency towards overt self-praise as a direct, audacious and love-inspired response to the promptings of the Holy Spirit. Once Rolle has begun to formulate a coherent theory of his divine inspiration, he can portray himself as not answerable for the egocentricity of his *materia*, since it is now God, not himself, who is in control of the process of invention. Naturally enough, then, the works following *Incendium Amoris* – *Super Psalmum Vicesimum, Super Canticum Canticorum, Contra Amatores Mundi* and finally *Melos Amoris* – are closer to being consistent and finished rhetorical productions, and display relatively few further signs of personal insecurity. The problems that gradually emerge here are not so much with the presentation of the *materia*, which is conceptually increasingly cogent and rhetorically increasingly brilliant, as with the relevance of what Rolle is saying, and the accessibility of the way he is saying it, to the large audience he wishes to influence. Yet these problems, too, are serious enough to cause considerable – and again evidently inadvertent – dislocations at a number of key moments. The drive to solidify his position as an authority on the contemplative life, by proving his mystical experiences to be both genuine and supremely elevated, causes him to dwell more and more on these experiences, and to do so in a style which is itself so elevated as to be, on occasion, virtually incomprehensible. When this new situation becomes so serious that it has to be acknowledged, as it implicitly is towards the end of *Melos Amoris*, we see our inspired *auctor* disconcerted yet again, and scurrying to find a style and subject which can seriously engage more than a handful of readers; once more the process of *inventio* has let him and his audience down. The last two Latin works, *Super Lectiones Mortuorum* and *Emendatio Vitae*, and the group of English ones associated with them, thus effect a further shift, which is at once a move forward (to the 'mixed' life) and a retreat to the kind of writing Rolle was attempting, without complete success, as early as *Judica Me*, in which spiritual *utilitas* is the principal criterion of quality. It is only with these last works that he achieves the integration of style, subject and audience that has allowed us to look back with such complacency on a career that can make retrospective sense of many (even if by no means all) of its own confusions. Impressive though all those triadic structures certainly are, powerful though his writing often is, we must keep in our minds not only the consistency of purpose that Rolle finally succeeded in attaining but also the prolonged, costly and sometimes deeply revealing struggle he engaged in on the way.

What, for us, then is the significance of Rolle's career, its successes and failures, its mixtures of pattern and confusion, verbal sophistication and intellectual naivety, pastoral concern and personal egotism? For the most part, I am anxious to leave this question to others, who will be able to formulate a wider range of responses than I am capable of doing. But more in the hope of opening up than of closing this discussion, I wish to conclude it by offering three possible answers (two positive, one much less so), and following each of them with an exploration of its implications that may prove suggestive. The first, positive answer is simply that this self-canonizing career is significant because for all its tortuous intensity it seems by and large to have achieved its goal; at least if we take sheer popularity as our measuring-stick, Rolle did indeed become an *auctoritas* on the spiritual life, self-evidently so in England, and to a lesser extent on the continent as well. This is no place to attempt even a sketch of the history of Rolle's medieval reputation, a subject which deserves a book to itself, and which has already attracted a higher quality of scholarly attention than his works have done.[2] The problem at this stage of our knowledge of the subject is the benign one that we have too much potential information: hundreds of manuscripts; a large body of early printed material; an appreciable number of compilations and other works which make use of or allude to Rolle; library catalogues, wills and other historical records, all of which need to be assessed in the light of our growing, but still tentative, understanding of late-medieval English spirituality. Until this material is assimilated, the details of Rolle's posthumous career as *auctor* will remain obscure, and we will continue to lack clear answers to many basic questions: How and why did he become (as it seems he did become) the most widely read English author of the late Middle Ages? What kind of people read him? What kind of people did not read him? What changes did his reputation undergo in the eighteen decades between his death in 1349 and the English Reformation in the late 1520s? Why, for example, in spite of their popularity, were none of his English works ever printed?[3] I would not want to exaggerate the extent of our ignorance, which has been a good deal alleviated even during the last decade. For example, Moyes has made a full investigation of the circulation of one work, *Super Lectiones Mortuorum*, in an exemplary article that points the way for similar studies of other works, and is often suggestive as to the conclusions such studies might reach (1984). In his book *Pastors and Visionaries* (1988), Jonathan Hughes has tried to trace the dissemination of Rolle's works and influence in and beyond Yorkshire, giving a vivid, though speculative, picture of his impact on a clergy and laity who were slowly moving away from a penitential spirituality towards an affective one. Yet the large gaps in this account themselves attest to how much remains to be done before we fully understand Rolle's place in the religious culture of late-medieval England.[4]

One body of evidence for Rolle's reputation which is of special interest here is the small number of apparently direct responses to his teaching found in the works of Walter Hilton, the author of *The Cloud of Unknowing*, Margery Kempe, Richard Methley, the compiler of the *De Excellentia Contemplationis*, and the anonymous Carthusian in response to whose lost attack on Rolle the hermit Thomas Bassett wrote his *Defensorium contra Oblectratores*.[5] Some of these responses, notably Hilton's in *The Scale of Perfection* and *Of Angels' Song*, have become well known for the way they seem to anticipate the dislike and suspicion of Rolle felt by many modern scholars (see, e.g., Knowles 1961, pp. 107–109). But there is more to them than this. First, all these writers take his popularity for granted, and assume in one way or another that the experiences of *fervor*, *dulcor* and *canor* are important. It is probably true, as Knowles thought, that the passages in *The Scale of Perfection* which warn against sensual devotional feelings of warmth, smell, taste and song, were partly written to temper the excitement engendered by Rolle's eloquence. Yet these passages deal with misunderstandings of *fervor*, *dulcor* and *canor*, not the experiences *per se*. Hilton also discusses *fervor* in a different style in two highly respectful chapters of the *Scale* (1, caps. 26 and 31), which carefully avoid contradicting Rolle, and indeed contain echoes of his teaching.[6] Similar echoes are heard in *Of Angels' Song*, which opens with an account of *canor* that has been written with close attention to the claims Rolle makes for it.[7] It seems that within a few decades of his death, *fervor* and *canor* have already become parts of the furniture of the mystical life. This is also apparent in the way Margery Kempe, writing in the 1430s, uses phrases from *Incendium Amoris* to describe her own sensations of inner heat (which may, indeed, have been instigated by reading that work), evoking a marginal comment in an early sixteenth-century hand, 'So s.R. hampall' (St Richard of Hampole).[8] Fifty years after Margery Kempe, in the *Refectorium Salutis* (1487), the Carthusian mystic Richard

Methley, whose devotion was full of spiritual sensations of heat and sweetness, compares his experiences with Rolle's in a manner which suggests the latter are again a crucial point of reference: 'For my life consists of love, languor, sweetness, heat, song; but not often of sensible heat, since the beloved promised me more frequent experiences of languor – just as that bountiful Richard known as "of Hampole" more often experienced heat, of whom I have never read that he was so much in languor.'[9] A century after Hilton, Methley still assumes that Rolle is the quintessential authority on *fervor*, *dulcor* and *canor*, and equally assumes that these are among the most important experiences of the spiritual life. Admittedly, Methley has relatively little to say, here or elsewhere, about *canor*; his account of this experience earlier in the work (cap. 5) suggests an awareness of Rolle in his choice of words (*clamor, canor, carmina, iubilus* etc.), but does not imply any interest in the metaphysical structures Rolle built on it. Similarly, when Margery Kempe hears the merry melody of heaven, to the disgruntlement of her husband and annoyance of her neighbours (cap. 3), there may not even be a connection with Rolle. Yet one other late-medieval writer, at least, did take *canor* and all its metaphysical implications with manifest seriousness: the anonymous compiler of a skilfully organized work on the mystical life, put together from some of the most passionate passages in Rolle's writings, and known as the *De Excellentia Contemplationis*. This work survives in five manuscripts, all being directly or indirectly connected with the fifteenth-century Carthusian foundation at Sheen or its Bridgettine sister-house at Sion (Sargent 1984b, p. 38), which are both known to have had an interest in advanced contemplative teaching. No full study has yet been undertaken, but the work is apparently a conscious attempt to force readers to take more careful notice of the most elevated elements of Rolle's thought. Its opening is taken from the prayer for spiritual union with which *Emendatio Vitae*, cap. 11 begins (see Excursus 1, item 2.1–2). But here, this devotional exercise is transformed – by the addition at its close of words not found in the source – into a prayer for the divine inspiration of the author: give me the fire, sweetness, song of your love, Rolle is made to pray, 'so I may give forth eloquent words to others *which they have not yet properly heard*' ('ut emittem aliis eloquium quod nondum apte audiverunt'; BL Add. 24661, f. 49v.). The work then plunges into the account of the continual nature of *canor* from the final section of *Super Canticum Canticorum* (see Chapter 6, n. 18, Extract 1), adding a sentence of self-justification which defends the author against charges of arrogance, and thence moving to what becomes its major statement of intent: a version of the confessional passage 'Ego igitur, solitarius heremita' (*Super Canticum Canticorum* 68.9, see p. 157), in which Rolle declares his credentials for speaking and insists he has no alternative but to do so (BL Add. 24661, f. 49v.; see Egerton 671, f. 27v.). After this *exordium*, much of the rest of the *De Excellentia Contemplationis* is derived from *Super Canticum Canticorum*, *Super Psalmum Vicesimum*, *Contra Amatores Mundi*, and possibly other works; these are woven into one another with an intricacy that suggests detailed knowledge of all of them. But what the compiler has done in this introductory sequence is in effect to father another work on Rolle, who is presented as repeating his own earlier words so that they will have more effect, in order to propagate the most audacious of his mystical claims, the continual nature of *canor*. In the circle in which this work was written, even the most extreme of Rolle's assertions were clearly thought important.[10]

Like Methley, Margery Kempe and perhaps even Hilton, the compiler of the *De Excellentia Contemplationis* apparently assumes that the experiences for which Rolle was famous can only be discussed in relation to him; although they can be shared by others, *fervor* and *canor* nonetheless 'belong' to him in a far more intimate way than, say, the 'kiss of the mouth' could be said to 'belong' to Bernard, or the stigmata to Francis. Here we see Rolle's autobiographical tendencies bearing fruit. One advantage of this situation is that his works fairly seldom suffered the minor ignominy of circulating anonymously or under someone else's name; unlike, say, William of St Thierry or Aelred of Rievaulx, Rolle's personal reputation and that of his writings seem to have been mutually supporting.[11] But the corresponding disadvantage is that it was easy for anyone who disapproved of his teaching to challenge its authority merely by expressing suspicion about its intimate ties to its author's experience. So much is clear from the only such challenge we know to have been made, between about 1390 and 1410, by an anonymous but learned Carthusian, whose words are reported in the reply which they precipitated, the *Defensorium contra Oblectratores* by an otherwise unknown hermit named Thomas Bassett.[12] The Carthusian, it seems, refuses to accept either that one of Rolle's experiences, *fervor* ('ardor divini amoris', 52), can necessarily be said to exist, or that he is under any obligation to believe that Rolle's 'spiritualia sentimenta' (205) in general are genuine; his view seems to be that one can properly only speak of 'burning' in love metaphorically, and implicitly that in claiming more Rolle is dangerously mistaken about his own level of holiness. This last point emerges through his criticism of Rolle's writings, which he also regards as dangerous, saying 'that [Rolle] was the stuff as it were of ruin and deception, since . . . he made people judges of themselves, and that [he] did not know as many people to have profited from his books as those who were wretchedly deceived by them'.[13] Such criticisms strike at the foundations of Rolle's entire authoritative edifice, which is built on an *audacitas* that allows him to judge himself spiritually secure and to proclaim this to others, since he knows his *canor* is genuine, God-given and continual. Refusing to be wooed by all Rolle's eloquence, this Carthusian in effect asks two simple questions, the very posing of which is damaging: How can Rolle know that his experiences are genuine and mean what he says they mean? And how can his readers know that he knows these things, and that what they experience is what he did? – For without this knowledge, they have no authority for judging their own experiences genuine, or for considering themselves certain of salvation. Bassett's reply is interesting largely for its defensiveness and its failure to confront the issues his opponent has raised. He makes a good case for *fervor*, citing passages from the Bible, Henry Suso, Bridget of Sweden and the *Stimulus Amoris* to confirm its real, rather than metaphorical, status. But his main defence of Rolle is that Christian charity makes it the Carthusian's duty to consider him (and those who claim to have been influenced by him) to be as they say they are – so that in voicing his suspicions the Carthusian has demonstrated no more than that he lacks charity and is thus himself in the position he claims Rolle to be in, of being the 'stuff of ruin and deception' (36–50, 205–249, 297). As an *argumentum ad hominem* this is not bad (it is just the sort of tactic Rolle himself employs), and it does succeed in highlighting the real difference between Bassett and his opponent, that the latter holds with a penitential spirituality which demands an attitude of self-abjection, while Bassett thinks of the spiritual life in the newer way, as a love-relation between God and the soul. Yet at the root of the Carthusian's attack is a pastoral concern which is in principle a charitable one, and which is similar to the concern displayed by Hilton in the passages where he warns against spurious experiences of *fervor* and *canor*. For Hilton's remarks are evidence enough that the Carthusian is justified in his anxiety about the effect of Rolle's teachings – which do in fact allow readers to move much too easily between a set of experiences he describes in mainly sensual terms, a fulsome spiritual self-confidence based on these experiences, and the expectation that his readers, too, can be as he was. Rolle himself warns of the need to read his writings with discretion (notably in cap. 5 of *Contra Amatores Mundi*, quoted by Bassett (277–280; discussed above, pp. 164–166), but gives little help in doing this; on the contrary, his ecstatic prose manifestly encourages one to throw discretion to the winds. For the Carthusian, who doubts that Rolle's experiences are genuine, this makes him a dangerous influence, and even for Hilton, who believes in them, he still needs to be read with care. Although Bassett passionately defends him, and although his supporters must have far outnumbered those who had reservations about him, it seems that Rolle's strategies as an exponent of his own brand of affective mysticism did not evoke any single or simple response in many of his medieval readers. However successful his campaign to establish his own *auctoritas* was in general, its complexities and internal inconsistencies evidently attracted the attention of some in such a way as to give them pause. Further research on his late-medieval reputation would surely unearth more signs that Rolle's status as a 'modern authority' was a fluid, rather than a fixed entity, and thus that the process whereby he invented it *ex nihilo* in the course of his career did not – as he must have hoped it would – truly end with his death.[14]

The second way in which Rolle's career is significant for us is as a model of the problems and opportunities faced by many would-be *auctores*, religious and secular, as the Middle Ages drew to a close. It was here, indeed, that I began this book, the introduction to which outlines my case for treating his 'predicament' as typical both of mystical writers and of late-medieval authors in general. In the light of the last nine chapters there is now much more that could be said about these matters, but rather than attempting to encompass an absurd amount of material, I prefer to speculate briefly on a more specific topic: on how some aspects of Rolle's career and those of the great late-medieval poets – Dante, Petrarch, Boccaccio, Chaucer, Langland and so on – might prove mutually illuminating. We have had frequent occasion to note the influence of particular poems, and more importantly of a kind of poetic self-conception, on Rolle's career, both where he overtly presents himself as an inspired singer (in *Canticum Amoris* and *Melos Amoris*) and in many other works; *Contra Amatores Mundi*, for example, makes explicit a view of the author as engaged in a rhetorical (and in essence fictional) competition with secular love-poets for the souls of its putative readers, *iuvenes*. From a perspective which views his career as that of a religious writer whose goal should be to persuade as many readers as he can towards a life of holiness, such a self-conception, for all the affective charm in which it bathes his writing, has seemed problematic. Indeed, several of my analyses have treated it with open disapproval, arguing that it encourages an elaboration of Rolle's style which divorces his writing from the actual world of human difficulty, and diminishes the didactic and evangelistic value of some of his most powerful works (see especially Chapter 7, section III). It should be clear by now why this perspective was adopted: Rolle's declared goals were of this didactic kind, and to attempt to take his works seriously as didactic entities was thus the most effective way of bringing out their latent tensions. But if we think of him instead, as he sometimes seems in practice to have thought of himself, not primarily as a didactic writer but in a broad sense as a poet, a number of phenomena we have previously had to treat as being at odds with his ostensible goals come into sharper focus. The most pertinent case in point is the main subject of this book, Rolle's quest for authority. His most inclusive way of accounting in solely didactic terms for the shape and intensity of this quest is to imply that he is imitating the process of progressive revelation found in the Scriptures. While this is in some ways an effective defence, it leaves much unexplained, perhaps most seriously the remorseless self-referentiality of the works (from *Incendium Amoris* to *Melos Amoris*) in which he gradually unveils his vision of the truth. However, if we redefine this quest for authority as one for poetic fame – for the laurel wreath – it comes suddenly to have a new clarity of purpose and a new potential source of legitimacy:

> Exegi monumentum aere perennius
> regalique situ pyramidum altius,
> quod non imber edax, non Aquilo impotens
> possit diruere aut innumerabilis
> annorum series et fuga temporum.
> Non omnis moriar multaque pars mei
> vitabit Libitinam: usque ego postera
> crescam laude recens . . .
>   . . . sume superbiam

quaesitam meritis et mihi Delphica
lauro cinge volens, Melpomene, comam.

(Horace, Carmina III.30)

[I have finished a monument more lasting than bronze and loftier than the Pyramids'
royal pile, one that no wasting rain, no furious north wind can destroy, or the
countless chain of years and the ages' flight. I shall not altogether die, but a mighty
part of me shall escape the death-goddess. On and on shall I grow, ever fresh with the
glory of after time. Accept the proud honour won by thy merits, Melpomene ⟨i.e. the
muse of tragedy⟩, and graciously crown my locks with Delphic bays.

(Translation: C.E. Bennett)]

Ever since Horace finished the last book of his *Carmina* with this magnificent
example of poetic *audacitas*, the pursuit of fame has been a legitimate part of
the Latin (and by the late Middle Ages the vernacular) poet's enterprise;
although poets, especially Christian ones, also adopted the opposite posture
of radical humility, subordinating their desire for poetic to their hope of
spiritual immortality, serious theological writers still availed themselves of
this self-glorifying way of reflecting on their achievements. Such was
particularly the case in the fourteenth century, which saw the birth of new
literary traditions and conceptions of literature, first in Italy, later in England
and elsewhere, which constitute the beginnings of what we now call the
Renaissance. A few years before Rolle went to Oxford, Dante was writing the
opening cantos of the *Paradiso*, in the first of which he prays for the
inspiration of Apollo (who for Dante here figures Christ), to help him 'come
to your beloved tree, and there crown myself with those [laurel] leaves of
which the *materia* and you will make me worthy' (125–27: 'Venir . . . mi al
tuo diletto legno, / e coronarmi allor di quelle foglie / che la materia e tu mi
farai degno'), and in the second of which he implicitly asserts his prayer has
been answered, by warning unprepared readers not to follow him across the
deep and unexplored ocean into which he is now venturing (II.1–18). In 1341,
when Rolle must have been at some point on the exhilarating road from
Incendium Amoris to *Melos Amoris*, Petrarch was crowned with laurels in
Rome, in a ceremony which had everything to do both with his personal
poetic fame and with that of modern poetry in more general terms, now
confident enough to assert its own status as equal to that of ancient writers
like Horace. Between 1351 and 1355, a few years after Rolle's death,
Boccaccio wrote his *Trattatello in laude di Dante*, which explores the
symbolism of the poet's laurel (in terms borrowed from Petrarch), and
emphasizes Dante's desire to attain it, in an argument which also sets out a
daring claim for poetry: that far from being mere fable-making, it has the
same purpose and dignity as theology. Rolle's career coincided with the
precise period in which poetry began its rise to a new consciousness of its
own eminence that has been of fundamental importance for the subsequent
evolution of European literary culture.[15]

News of the remarkable developments in literary theory and practice
which these events portended seems not to have reached England until

Chaucer visited Florence in the 1370s, and their first English embodiment, *The House of Fame*, may be as late as 1380. Nonetheless, Rolle's career as 'poet' has many points in common with those of his Italian contemporaries, especially with the poet-theologian Dante. Like both Dante and his successors, Rolle presents himself as a modern who is fully the equal to his predecessors. Just as in *Inferno*, canto IV (set in Limbo) Dante has himself welcomed into the 'bella scuola' of authoritative poets, so Rolle closes his final Latin work, *Emendatio Vitae*, by inscribing himself into the authoritative tradition of writers on contemplation (see p. 219). Like Dante, Rolle also sometimes rates himself even more highly than his colleagues. In *Inferno*, canto XXV, Dante overtly competes with two members of the 'scuola' to whom this very canto is much indebted, Lucan and Ovid, by asserting that his account of a serpentine metamorphosis outdoes both the *Metamorphoses* and the *Pharsalia* (94–99); just as aggressively, at the end of *Super Canticum Canticorum*, Rolle competes with his predecessors, most notably Bernard and Richard of St Victor, by claiming, in language which is clearly influenced by both of them, that his own version of union with God outdoes anything they have written about (see pp. 150–154 and notes). Like Dante, Rolle is intensely aware of his own originality and of the divine inspiration that sustains it; where Dante invokes a succession of muses at different stages of the *Divine Comedy*, Rolle is content with one, *amor*, but for both the true source of inspiration, who guarantees their high status as modern poets, is the Holy Spirit. In deference to their belief in their own inspiration, both are preoccupied with the internal consistency of their careers, and engage in complex processes of reinterpretation of their lives and writings in order to present them as patterned in meaningful ways. For Dante this involves writing extensive commentary on his own poetry (in the *Vita Nuova*, the *Convivio* and, if it is authentic, the *Epistle to Can Grande*) as well as the reflections on his own life we find in the *Divine Comedy*, and necessitates some skilful manœuvring to account for the inconsistencies and changes of direction in his career (see especially *Convivio*, Book III). For Rolle, as we have seen, it means interpreting and reinterpreting events in his life, creating retrospective patterns where none were before, and writing something analogous to a self-commentary in the opening chapters of *Melos Amoris*, which expand and revise the opening of *Super Canticum Canticorum* from the more elevated perspective of *canor*. Yet finally, in justification of these revisionist attempts to eliminate contradictions, the careers of both writers are in fact impelled by profound inner forces which compel a large measure of consistency, and to which both give the one name, *amor*. As is violently pointed out in canto XXX of the *Purgatorio*, Dante does not always stay faithful to the human manifestation of this force, Beatrice; but this does not detract from the single-mindedness of his career – any more than does Rolle's failure, until the last stages of his career, to integrate the various demands 'love' makes on him into a fully integrated literary style. For his medieval readers, Rolle remains the singer of 'violent love', who is as closely identified with his *materia* (devotion to the Holy Name, *fervor*, *canor*) as Dante is with Beatrice, or any other poet with his characteristic subject-matter; one can almost imagine him on a pillar in the House of Fame, 'holding up' the reputation of *canor*, as Homer and the rest hold up the fame of Troy (*House of Fame* 1464–1480). Indeed, in *Melos Amoris*, written almost explicitly in praise of its author's sanctity, Rolle achieves a total fusion with his *materia* such as we otherwise find only in Petrarch's *Rime sparse*. Just as Petrarch's *materia*, Laura, is at once a beloved woman and a symbol of the poetic fame the writer desires for himself (the laurel), and just as the poems concerning her both aspire to the laurel and in a sense constitute it, so in *Melos Amoris* Rolle's *materia*, *canor*, is simultaneously an elevated mystical experience, a symbol of the author's own elevation, and a means of proclaiming – and thereby 'inventing' – that elevation. It seems, in short, that Rolle's quest for spiritual authority closely parallels the quest for literary fame engaged in by his most sophisticated poetic contemporaries.

It would be interesting to pursue these observations in any of several directions. We might use them as the basis for further enquiry into Rolle's poetic antecedents: from where does he derive his self-conception as a kind of epic poet of *canor*? Are we to look again at John of Hoveden, at Richard of St Victor's *De Quattuor Gradibus Violentae Caritatis* (with its Ovidian echoes), or at some other undiscovered source? And, whatever they were, in what ways did consciousness of these poetic antecedents influence the first readers of his works? On the other hand, we might use them rather to point to Rolle's modernity: could it be that, some decades before Chaucer, England already had a writer in whom the kinds of consciousness we associate with the terms 'Medieval' and 'Renaissance' already intersected, as they did in Dante and his humanistic successors? If so, we may have located one reason for Rolle's popularity in the fifteenth century, the period during which English poets, in the wake of Chaucer, began seriously to imitate the self-conscious assurance and aureate eloquence of their continental forebears and contemporaries: was Rolle perhaps regarded as a consciously rhetorical writer whose modernity set him apart in important ways, and whose self-concern, like his eloquence, was actually treated as an advantage? I cannot, of course, pursue these subsidiary questions now; but whether or not they are even answerable in the form I have given them here, they indicate, merely by posing themselves, that further study of Rolle could tell us a good deal about late-medieval developments in the concept of the *auctor* and in the meaning of that key term, *auctoritas*.

It may be suspected that in comparing Rolle to Dante and Petrarch my main concern is to canonize him myself, in a pantheon not of saints and spiritual *auctores* but of major late-medieval literary figures. Up to a point, I plead guilty to this charge; somewhat to my own surprise, I am now convinced, after prolonged exposure to his writings, that Rolle deserves to be thought of as a major *auctor*, not merely for his late-medieval popularity, but for the brilliance, resourcefulness and originality of his prose, and for the grandeur of the task he set himself and successfully carried out. Yet, as on other occasions on which this book has praised Rolle, such a commendation will seem backhanded in the light of my final and sadly negative reason for regarding as significant the process of self-aggrandizement that I have been arguing in effect to constitute his career: that the study of this process is now the only way in which we can seriously engage with him as a writer. At least so far as his Latin works are concerned, Rolle seems a clear example of a writer whose time has come, but has also – and past all recovery – gone. During more than 150 years (for the many who submitted to his mesmerizing charm) he must have been deeply exciting to read: a master of daring effects, emotional and rhetorical colours, and ever-compelling subject-matter, whose words seemed inhabited by an extraordinary sense of personal presence, and whose writing opened a window on areas of experience which most could otherwise scarcely conceive. Looking through manuscripts of a work like *Incendium Amoris*, with their clusters of *nota bene*s and other more elaborate scrawls, one can catch moments of this excitement – a feeling perhaps remotely akin to the experience of many nineteenth-century readers of Carlyle or Emerson, who also made the hearts of more than one generation burn. But, as may have happened already with these more recent purveyors of inspirational ideas in stirring and grandly general prose, the power has seeped from Rolle's words as the religious culture in terms of which alone they contained any meaning has disappeared. Some of his English works, which are a little more rooted in human reality than their Latin counterparts, may retain a certain resonance – though hardly much when set beside *The Scale of Perfection* or *The Cloud of Unknowing* – while the autobiographical passages of the Latin works arouse a natural curiosity, and he is sometimes praised in a routine fashion by writers on mysticism or English prose. Yet I believe that few people still seriously turn to Rolle – as they do to other medieval English mystics and to writers of Latin prose – either for edification or for aesthetic pleasure. Why, if I am wrong, should both popular and scholarly interest in him have become so moribund immediately after the publication of Allen's *Writings Ascribed to Richard Rolle*, sixty years ago, unless as an ironic result of the establishment of the true canon of his works?

If I am not wrong and Rolle's affective fires are indeed grown ineluctably cold, it becomes doubtful whether there is any prospect even of sustaining such interest in his work as there is, for all his status as a major *auctor*. That, of course, remains to be seen; as most people who have won through to this point will understand, the immediate gratifications he offers the modern reader are few, and the art of appreciating what he does offer is a difficult one to cultivate. Yet that he merits our interest, and that his career has much to teach us if we ask the right questions of it, seems to me undeniable. The answers this book gives are only a beginning. Not only do they need to be scrutinized and sometimes no doubt challenged, they raise further and potentially much larger questions – those suggested in the last few pages and many others – the answers to which, so I believe, could take us far towards gaining an understanding of how late-medieval religious and literary culture operated. In saying this, I may be doing no more than hastening the time when my intricately circular argument for the shape of Rolle's career is found wanting. But even if this is so – indeed, especially if this is so – it would be a shame if sixty years were to go by again before the next large-scale attempt is made to comprehend this strange and impressive writer.

EXCURSUS I AND II

The chronology of Rolle's writings

This study advances a view of Rolle's career that depends on assumptions about the chronology of his works. These have partly been explained in the course of the last seven chapters, but since my chronology differs markedly from the only systematic earlier one, that of Hope Emily Allen, the matter deserves special attention, even at the risk of repetition. I begin by discussing her views, which are still regularly treated as established facts, but which are demonstrably wrong in a large number of cases.[1]

The problems with Allen's work on the chronology of Rolle's writings spring from several sources, including her desire to apply every scrap of evidence to her biography of the hermit, her confidence in her own ability to make literary texts yield biographical information, and the nature of her basic assumptions about her subject. She presents Rolle more or less as an uncouth youth who made good, taming the excess of his early enthusiasms and becoming in time a wise and moderate counsellor of others.[2] Much of the force of this portrait is derived from her view of the development of his style, which she assumes mirrors his spiritual progress. Thus in her view both *Melos Amoris* and *Super Canticum Canticorum* were written under the immediate impact of his initial experience of *canor*, and express its raw power and the extremism it at first engendered in him; Allen dislikes the Latin of these works and the Rolle that emerges from them.[3] The penitential *Super Lectiones Mortuorum* is a first reaction against the 'irresponsible subjectivity' of *Melos Amoris*, while later works show how this subjectivity was channelled; *Contra Amatores Mundi* already lacks the worst crudities of its predecessors, and *Incendium Amoris*, with its passages of analytic prose, shows signs of real maturity. Such maturity is finally reached with *Emendatio Vitae*, *The Commandment*, *Ego Dormio* and *The Form of Living*, in which Rolle's thoughts are expressed with the clarity of ripeness and experience. To this late period belong also the lyrics and other English works, in all of which Rolle's devotional enthusiasm is tempered by moderation; in her view of the last period of the hermit's life, Allen is in virtual accord with her more sentimental colleagues, Frances Comper and Geraldine Hodgson.[4]

In so far as this chronology depends on stylistic assumptions it can simply be dismissed, since, if nothing else, this book is proof that the story can equally be told the other way round. But Allen has a number of more specific arguments to back up her position (and indeed never acknowledges the weight she gives to stylistic considerations). One of these, closely related to the matter of style, is that of Rolle's terminology. Allen assumes that there was an immediate connection between Rolle's mystical experiences, his invention of a terminology to express them, and their proclamation in his writings. For example, she allocates *Judica Me* to the period before Rolle experienced spiritual song (hence, according to *Incendium Amoris*, to his early twenties) largely on the grounds that it lacks a developed use of the terms *fervor*, *dulcor* and *canor* (or their synonyms) and contains few ecstatic expressions of love;

Rolle has 'found Jesus', she says, but his love 'is still inchoate and inarticulate' (p. 109). Yet it is unlikely that he realized immediately upon receiving *canor* that it marked the climax of his contemplative career; and it is still more so that he at once found a style and a set of terms in which to express his experience, let alone that he resolved straight away to proclaim it as an exemplar for all to follow. As Daly points out (p. lii), cap. 31 of *Incendium Amoris* suggests rather that Rolle was initially silent about his gift of *canor*. There is thus no reason why the absence in *Judica Me* of the terminology of Rolle's mature writing should imply that he had not yet had the experiences on which that terminology was based. At least on these grounds, Allen's attempt to assign *Judica Me* to an early stage of Rolle's eremitic life is unacceptable, as is her whole apparatus of links between his literary and spiritual biographies.

The rest of Allen's argument for the early composition of *Judica Me* makes a good point of entry into her other methods of conjecturing the chronology of Rolle's works. Allen claims that the work's failure to mention the violent events that took place in Yorkshire in 1322 means it must have been written before then (p. 112). Subsequent scholarship has established she is wrong. The source for most of *Judica Me* was William of Pagula's *Oculus Sacerdotis*, which Boyle shows was not finished until 1326–1328 and was apparently little read before the mid-1330s.[5] Thus Rolle cannot have copied large portions of the work before 1322, and probably wrote *Judica Me* no earlier than 1330. Yet on this early dating of *Judica Me* depends not only Allen's ascription of *Melos Amoris* to 'about 1326' (and those of other works to other years) but also her dating of Rolle's birth. For the events of the earlier stages of Rolle's life we are provided with two accounts, in the *Officium* and in cap. 15 of *Incendium Amoris*. Between them these establish his conversion (that is, his donning of the hermit's robes) to have taken place at about the age of eighteen; his experience of spiritual song apparently began about four years later. Since Allen holds that Rolle wrote *Judica Me* just before he attained spiritual song (at the age of twenty-two) and just before 1322, she concludes that he was born around 1300.[6] The evidence of Boyle's studies destroys these conjectures, and we are left with no indications as to when Rolle was born.

Without such indications, we have cause to be suspicious of Allen's last major argument for the placing of *Judica Me* and three other works, *Canticum Amoris*, *Melos Amoris* and *Super Lectiones Mortuorum*: 'In four of Rolle's works he calls himself "juvenis" and these can therefore be treated together with the certainty that they were produced in the same period' (Allen, p. 89). This period she considers to be the first half of the 1320s, when Rolle was, she thinks, between about nineteen and twenty-seven; since the date of his birth has now to be regarded as uncertain, no such absolute dating is possible. But can we even place these four works as 'early' in relation to his other writings on the strength of the word 'iuvenis'? The term is used very flexibly in the Middle Ages.[7] In the *Convivio* (IV, cap. 24) Dante applies the term to the years between twenty-five and forty-five, by no means an unusual application; if the term were to be taken in this sense, it would imply that where Rolle uses it of himself he is assuring us of his maturity. In support of Allen it can be argued that Rolle sometimes uses the term to refer to young manhood. In *Melos Amoris* he uses 'iuvenis' interchangeably with 'puer' and 'adolescentulus', words which clearly denote youth. One chapter makes much use of 'iuvenis' in contrast to 'senectus' in the context of the text '*Adolescens iuxta viam suam ambulat et cum senuerit non recedet ab ea*' (96.17–18, Proverbs 22.6); here the phrase 'adolescentiam meam' clearly refers to the age of Rolle's conversion in one place (98.26, see *Incendium Amoris* 187.10–11), just as in *Judica Me* the term 'iuventus' clearly refers to his young years: '*non inutile arbitrandum est si in iuventute mea plura loca viderim*' (2.6–7). Yet even if he does not use words denoting age in the way Dante does, there is no justification for assuming his frame of reference for such words is literal. Where Rolle contrasts youth and age, his use of both terms is as artificial and as moral in intention as Dante's, and often has its basis in Scripture; the terms usually apply not to physical, but to spiritual youth. This is especially clear in the most important instance in which Allen sees auto-biographical statements being made. Following Horstmann, she thinks that the conclusion to *Melos Amoris*, 'et puer nunc propero ad finem felicem' (191.29–30), tells us directly that the author is still very young (*English Writings*, p. xxxvi). Yet at twenty-six, when Allen thought Rolle wrote this work, he would hardly be a 'puer'; the term is evidently intended as a gesture of humility, as it is when Rolle says 'tuum puerum purifica, piissime Pater' (76.5–6), to emphasize the gap between God and humanity with the metaphor of father and youthful son. Similarly, in *Contra Amatores Mundi* Rolle calls himself 'iuvenis amator', after appealing to other 'iuvenes' (3.69–74) to flee lust and turn to divine love. Here he is presenting himself as an exemplar in order to assure the reader that he knows about the delights of divine love: 'Quia dilectam meam continue cogito, et ab eius amplexibus non recedo' (3.74–75).[8] In assuming that Rolle's use of the terminology of age has a literal referent, Allen is again misled by her desire to prise biographical data out of his works.[9]

Thus, most of Allen's arguments for the chronology of Rolle's works are faulty. Yet although we do not in most cases have external evidence with which to date Rolle's works, and cannot place them in a clear relation to what we know of his life, their order of composition can to some extent be deduced from his habit of reusing or readapting his own material, and from a variety of other internal indications, of which Allen was either unaware or which she chose to ignore. This evidence suggests a picture of his literary development which differs in many respects from hers.

As Allen does point out, the clearest evidence for the date of any work by Rolle is that for the composition of *The Form of Living* in the last year of the hermit's life (1348–1349); her evidence will bear rehearsal (see Allen, pp. 256–258 and *English Writings*, pp. 82–83). The name of the recipient of *The Form of Living* is given in many manuscripts as Margaret, in Longleat 29 as 'Margareta de Kyrkby'. The copy of the *English Psalter* in Laud Misc. 286 explains that this work was also written for the recluse Margaret Kirkeby; the *Officium* (*lectio viija*) mentions 'Margareta' as a disciple of Rolle's, the copy of the *Officium* in Lincoln c.5.2 referring to her as formerly an anchoress at Anderby. There is record of an anchoress named Margaret Kirkeby leaving her enclosure at 'Laton' to go to Anderby in 1357. Allen identifies her with the 'Margaret la Boteler nun of Hampole' who was enclosed at East Layton near the end of 1348 – less than a year before Rolle's death. There seems little doubt either that this identification is correct or that it was Margaret Kirkeby for whom *The Form of Living* was written – especially since the *Officium* says that Rolle lived near Hampole in his last years. As *The Form of Living* addresses itself to a solitary it cannot have been written long before Margaret's enclosure, and thus dates from the last year of Rolle's life. This does not seem seriously open to question.[10]

The Form of Living provides an invaluable fixed point for establishing a general chronology of Rolle's works. It can be dated; it is very likely to be his last major work; and, most useful of all, a number of passages in it form parts of the intricate network of self-borrowing which link so many of his writings, and through which, I submit, it is possible to begin to piece together a chronology based on real evidence. Like *The Commandment*, *The Form of Living* derives material from *Emendatio Vitae*. *Emendatio Vitae* in turn borrows from four works, the *Latin Psalter* (see Chapter 8, n. 15), *Super Psalmum Vicesimum*, *Super Canticum Canticorum* and *Contra Amatores Mundi*. *Melos Amoris* also makes use of material from the last two of these. As items 1–4 below show, there is no doubt that these works really do share material, and in my opinion (although here readers must decide for themselves, from the passages and from my preliminary discussions of them) little question in any individual case which work is borrowing from which; this structure of relationships thus provides a fairly objective framework upon which more detailed and difficult chronological arguments can be built.

One obvious gap in the information provided by this network of borrowings concerns the chronological relationship between *Melos Amoris* and *Emendatio Vitae*. As we have seen (Chapter 7, n. 2), *Melos Amoris* is clearly referred to in *Super Lectiones Mortuorum*. This work has a good deal in common with *Melos Amoris* stylistically, but its assumptions about its own didactic role are closer to *Emendatio Vitae*. It is natural to conclude, as I do in Chapter 8, that *Super Lectiones Mortuorum* thus forms a bridge between the two works. This could be wrong, and if it is the possibility remains that *Melos Amoris* postdates *Emendatio Vitae*; my last argument that this is not so consists of my detailed discussions of the works concerned. Another gap concerns the relationships between the four works from which *Emendatio Vitae* (and in two cases, *Melos Amoris*) borrows; as things stand, they could have been written in any order, and *Super Psalmum Vicesimum* might indeed postdate *Melos Amoris* and *Super Lectiones Mortuorum*. Unfortunately, I have failed to locate the *Latin Psalter* in any more detailed way, except that it must also predate the *English Psalter*, to which it lends part of a prologue and perhaps much else (Chapter 9, n. 13); the *English Psalter*, apparently written for Margaret Kirkeby like *The Form of Living*, is clearly a late work, though it, too, cannot be located more precisely. However, the ending of *Contra Amatores Mundi* uses language which may derive from *Super Psalmum Vicesimum* and *Super Canticum Canticorum* (see Chapter 6, n. 27). Chapter 6 considers *Super Psalmum Vicesimum* as the earliest of the three, since the work's main concern is with the development of the position that *canor* can be continuous: a position which is taken further and more aggressively in *Super Canticum Canticorum* but which forms an integral and apparently uncontroversial part of Rolle's picture of the spiritual life in *Contra Amatores Mundi*. *Contra Amatores Mundi* also looks like the latest of the three because it embodies the evangelistic programme set out at the end of *Super Canticum Canticorum*. These arguments are not irrefutable, and need to be followed in some detail; yet, the fact that they are held in place by the structure of self-borrowings outlined above renders them more powerful than many theories based on internal evidence.

But how are we to locate the many works which have not yet been mentioned, *Judica Me*, *Canticum Amoris*, several English works and Latin commentaries, and above all *Incendium Amoris*? For these we are forced to rely on internal evidence which is not strongly supported by the evidence of self-borrowing. Yet, although there are difficulties here, some of them are more apparent than real. For example, few readers who compare the naive passage of self-defence from *Judica Me* quoted on p. 48 with any demonstrably mature work by Rolle will be in any doubt that the former is, as Allen thought, an early work; the prose is short-winded, and Rolle was to think of much better and more theological justifications for his actions than those he gives here. It is also significant that *Judica Me* does not contain even a suggestion of the terminology of *fervor*, *dulcor* and *canor*, omnipresent in all the works from *Super Psalmum Vicesimum* to *The Form of Living*. Finally, most of the work is taken without alteration from a source, whereas even the most imitative of the demonstrably mature works, the *English Psalter*, transforms what it borrows. The final two grounds for assigning *Judica Me* to an early stage of Rolle's career apply equally well to many of the commentaries. *Super Psalmum Vicesimum* opens by stating that Rolle does not intend to borrow material from others (see Chapter 6, n. 3), initiating a mode of consciously original exposition which recurs in both *Super Canticum Canticorum* and *Super Lectiones Mortuorum*, and is acknowledged (by being overtly renounced, see p. 245) even in the *English Psalter*. Those commentaries which do derive directly from standard glosses are therefore likely to be early works, all the more when (like *Judica Me*) they contain no references to Rolle's mystical terminology; those which do contain such references may postdate *Judica Me*. *Super Symbolum Apostolorum*, *Super Symbolum S. Athanasii*, *Super Orationem Dominicam* are in the first category, and may well predate *Judica Me*. Clearly in the second category is *Super Apocalypsim*, which refers to *fervor* and *dulcor*, and trembles on the brink of mentioning *canor* (see p. 101); less clearly here is *Super Threnos*, which is about *canor* in the sense that it forms part of Rolle's concerted attempt to write commentaries on all the biblical songs, but which does not refer to it. This leaves *Super Magnificat* and *Super Mulierem Fortem*, which are original expositions (the first of them states this openly, see p. 103), but neither of which introduces mystical terminology into its portrait of the contemplative. I suspect these belong to the period of *Super Apocalypsim* (and perhaps *Super Threnos*), during which Rolle was (as cap. 31 of *Incendium Amoris* explains) keeping silent about his gift of *canor*, while trying to find ways of expressing it indirectly or rhapsodically. This is also where *Canticum Amoris* fits best, since this work does employ the terminology of *fervor*, *dulcor* and *canor*, but displaces it by applying it to Rolle's relationship with the Virgin. My evidence is far from conclusive here – indeed, one or other of these guesses is probably wrong – but these works also seem to postdate *Judica Me*.

Incendium Amoris is interestingly absent from the network of borrowings which link so many of the Latin works, but has considerable influence on some of the English ones, the lyrics (see Allen pp. 287–306) – including two in *Ego Dormio* – and a passage of *The Form of Living* (see p. 254); is it, then, a late work, as Allen thinks? In my view it is not. External evidence here is slender and complex. Allen argues that a note, dated 1343, in which Rolle apparently describes a premonition of his death in the margin of cap. 15 of his copy of *Incendium Amoris*, suggests he was writing the work at the time (Allen, pp. 228–229; see pp. 255–256). But in fact it more easily suggests the opposite: that Rolle is recording his vision in a marginal note to a work which he has come to regard as his major autobiographical statement, and which has thus been complete for some years (see also Clark 1986, p. 196). This implies that *Incendium Amoris* was finished before 1343. Again, cap. 4 of *Contra Amatores Mundi* justifies Rolle's use of first-person plural forms ('verba communiter') in his accounts of the saints, saying he uses them in 'plerisque opusculis mei' (4.90–92) in order to show that he does not despair of his own sanctity (see pp. 164–165). But the only work which clearly predates *Contra Amatores Mundi* and makes much use of 'verba communiter' is *Super Canticum Canticorum*; almost all of *Super Psalmum Vicesimum* is written in the third person, and the early commentaries and *Judica Me* do not contain first-person passages in which Rolle identifies with the saints. Thus 'plerisque', which surely refers to more than one earlier work, is a puzzle, unless we assume Rolle is also thinking of *Incendium Amoris*. These are hardly conclusive arguments. However, internal evidence firmly points to the location of *Incendium Amoris* after *Super Apocalypsim* and before *Super Psalmum Vicesimum* and its successors – for *Incendium Amoris* contains the systematic exposition of Rolle's mystical experiences of the kind *Super Apocalypsim* avoids making, but which his later works assume, to the extent that they are scarcely comprehensible without *Incendium Amoris* (see Theiner 1968, p. 40). The work is self-conscious about its status as Rolle's first explicit statement of the doctrine of *fervor*, *dulcor* and *canor*. It begins with a deliberately startling account of his first experience of *fervor*, goes on to describe his acquisition of all three experiences (in cap. 15, an account the ground of which has been carefully prepared), and opens its final section (in cap. 31) by explaining the reasons for which he decided no longer to conceal his participation in heavenly song, in spite of the threat to his humility that declaring himself involves. Chapter 5 argues that in the process it evolves positions about the sanctity of its author and about his mystical system on which *Super Psalmum Vicesimum* and later works build. This evidence may not convince the sceptical, especially anyone deeply committed to Allen's reading of Rolle's career, with which I am here in total opposition. But to show that I am wrong would involve a large-scale rewriting of most of the material presented in this book.

For the reasons given above, then, my case for the chronology of Rolle's career (some parts of which, it must be remembered, are much stronger than others) can be summarized as follows. (1) Early Works: (a) *Judica Me*, with *Super Symbolum Apostolorum*, *Super Symbolum S. Athanasii* and *Super Orationem Dominicam*; (b) *Super Apocalypsim*, with *Super Threnos* (?), *Super Magnificat*, *Super Mulierem Fortem* and *Canticum Amoris*; (2) Middle Works, in the order given: *Incendium Amoris*, *Super Psalmum Vicesimum*, *Super Canticum Canticorum*, *Contra Amatores Mundi*, *Melos Amoris*; (3) Late Works, also in the order given: *Super Lectiones Mortuorum*, *Emendatio Vitae*, *The Commandment*, *The Form of Living*, with the *English Psalter* also postdating *Melos Amoris* (?), and *Ego Dormio*, with the short English works, postdating at least *Super Canticum Canticorum*. The missing work here is the *Latin Psalter*, which would fit into the period just before *Incendium Amoris* and *Super Psalmum Vicesimum*, but also fairly well among the late works, before *Emendatio Vitae*; I only suspect that it belongs to the earlier period.

Finally, a word about dates. None of those given by Allen, except that for *The Form of Living*, is based on any viable evidence. In particular we saw that *Judica Me* must have been written perhaps a decade after the date she gives, 1322, while *Incendium Amoris* is likely to have been written before 1343. Two points can be deduced. One is that since *Judica Me* is an early work, the whole of Rolle's career as a writer took place in the 1330s and 1340s, over a period of little (if any) more than twenty years – rather than thirty, as Allen and others have assumed. The other is that he was probably born some years after the date which has usually been accepted, 1300. We think he became a hermit at about the age of twenty, and it is hard to imagine him refraining from putting pen to parchment for a full decade, or keeping silent about his mystical experience for even longer. A birth-date of around 1305–1310 is likely to be nearer the mark, and Rolle was probably nearer forty than fifty when he died, still easily a *iuvenis* according to most of the medieval divisions of human life. I think this fits the evidence of his writing: so excited an exponent of contemplation might be expected to have a fast-paced and relatively brief career.

II

In the following section, source-passages appear before those which are considered to borrow from them. The italicization of the latter indicates only the closest examples of indebtedness. Each item begins with my reasons for deciding which of the works is borrowing from which.

Item 1: Emendatio Vitae as source for The Commandment and The Form of Living

[(1) *The Form of Living* was written in the last year of Rolle's life and is thus unlikely to have preceded *Emendatio Vitae*. (2) In passage 3 *The Form of Living* includes catalogues taken from the *Compendium Theologicae Veritatis* (here mostly omitted). These must be interpolated into a complex structure of divisions and subdivisions borrowed from *Emendatio Vitae*, for it is hard to see how the latter could extract its clear exposition of the same topics from the resulting chaos of details. (3) Adaptation of English material for a Latin work is much less common than the opposite process.]

Excursus I: The chronology of Rolle's writings

1. (Emendatio Vitae, ff. 137v. 53–138r. 3)

Cum diabolus viderit unum hominem ex mille ad Deum perfecte converti, Christi vestigia imitari, presentia despicere, sola invisibilia quaerere et amare, perfectam poenitentiam assumere, ab omni contagione mentis et corporis se purgare, mille fraudes pugnandi reparat ut ipsum ab amore Dei ad amorem mundi ducat et iterum sordibus scelerum polluat, ut saltem libidinosis cogitationibus Deo suo odibilem reddat.

(Form of Living, 20–28)

For þe deuyl, þat is enemy vnto al mankynd, *whan he seth a man* or a womman *amonge a þousand turne ham holy to God,* and forsake al þe vanite and þe richesse þat men þat loueth þe world coueiteth, *and seche þe ioy lestynge, a thousand wiles he hath in what manere he may deceyue ham.* And whan he may nat brynge ham in to sych synnes þe which myght make al wondre on ham þat knewe ham, he begileth many so priuely þat þai can nat oft tymes fele þe trape þat hath take ham.

2. (Emendatio Vitae, f. 135r. 14–17)

In puncto vivimus: imo minus puncto, quia si totum tempus nostrum aeternitati comparetur, nihil est. Quomodo non sine gravissima damnatione vitam nostram in amore vanitatum consumimus, et tota die ociosi stamus.

(Form of Living, 281–283)

For we lyve bot in a poynt, þat is þe lest þynge þat may be, and sothly oure lif is lasse þan a poynt if we likene hit to þe lif þat lesteth euer.

3. (Emendatio Vitae, f. 136v. 6–32)

Ut homo ad honorem Dei, ad commodum suum, et ad utilitatem proximi recte dirigatur, quatuor occurrunt dicenda. Primo quae sint quae coinquinant hominem: et sunt tria peccata vel tria genera peccatorum, scilicet peccata cogitationis, oris et operis. Cogitatione peccat quis, quando aliquid contra Deum cogitat; si cor suum non occupet laude et amore Dei; si illud diversis cogitationibus abstrahi et mundo vagari permittat. Ore peccat quis multis modis: quando mentitur, quando periurat, quando detrahit, quando errorem siquis ignorans defendit, quando stultiloquia aut turpiloquia aut vana et ociosa profert. Opere peccat quis multis modis luxuriando, lubrice tangendo, osculando, voluntarie se polluendo vel procurando vel sustinendo, vel sine maxima necessitate qua se credit posse perire, furando vel percutiendo, et aliis modis consimilibus. Secundo quae sunt quae mundificant hominem, et sunt tria: scilicet contritio cogitationibus, expulsio omnis affectionis quae non pertinet ad laudem et honorem Dei et amorem eius; confessio oris, quae debet esse tempestiva, nuda et integra; satisfaccio operis, quae habet tres partes, scilicet ieiunium quia peccat contra seipsum, orationem quia peccat contra Deum, elemosynam quia peccat contra proximum. Non tamen dico quod de bonis alienis faciat elemosynam, sed restitutat, quia non dimittitur peccatum nisi restituatur ablatum. Tertio quae sunt quae munditiam cordis servant, et sunt tria: scilicet vigil Dei meditatio, ut nullum tempus sit in quo de Deo non cogitet, excepto somno qui est omnibus communis; solicitudo custodiae sensuum exteriorum, ut gustus et olfactus, auditus, visio, tactus, sub freno disciplinae sapienter arceantur; et honesta occupatio, ut legendo, aut aliquid de Deo loquendo, aut scribendo aut aliquid utile agendo. Similiter quae observant munditiam oris, scilicet loquendi praemeditatio, cavere multiloquia, mendacii detestatio. Item munditiam operis tria conservant: scilicet alimentorum moderatio, pravae societatis declinatio, et iugis mortis meditatio. Quarto quae ad conformitatem divinae voluntatis nos illiciunt, et sunt tria: scilicet creaturarum exemplaritas, quae attenditur per considerationem; Dei familiaritas, quae attenditur per orationem et meditationem; et regni coelestis iucunditas, quae admodum sentitur per contemplationem.

(Form of Living, 323–484 (extracts))
Wherfore, þat þou be right disposed, both for þi soule and þi body, þou shalt vndrestond foure þynges. *The first is what thynge fileth a man. That other, what maketh hym clene. The þrid, what holdeth hym in clennesse. The fourth, what þynge draweth hym for ordeyne his wille al to Goddis will.* For þe first, *witte þou þat we synneth in þre thynges þat maken vs foule: þat is with herte, mouth, and dede. The synnes of oure herte ben þese* . . . [A catalogue of sins.] *Synnes of þe mouth ben these* . . . [A catalogue of sins.] *Synnes in deede ben these* . . . [A catalogue of sins.] *The thynges þat clenseth vs of þat filthede ben þre*, ayeyns þay þre manere of synnes. Þe first is *sorowe of hert* ayeynes þe synnes of thoght . . . The tother is *shrift of mouth* agayn þe syn of mouth: *and þat shal be hasted withouten delayynge, naked withouten excusynge, and entier without departynge* . . . The þrid is *satisfaccioun, þat hath þre parties, fastynge, prier, and almysdede* . . . *For þe þrid þynge, þou shalt witte þat clennesse behoueth be kept* in hert, in mouth, and in werk. *Clennesse of herte þre þynges kepeth. Oon is wakynge thoght and stabil of God. Anoþer, bisynes to kepe þi fyve wittes,* so þat al þe stirrynges wickid of ham be closed out of þi fleisshe. *The þrid is honest occupacioun* and profitable. *Also clennesse of mouth* kepeth þre þynges. *Oon is that þou bethynke þe befoor ar þou speeke. Anoþer, þat þou be nat of mych speche bot of litelle* . . . [A passage on speech.] *Clennesse of werke þre thynges kepeth. Oon is assiduel þoght of þe deethe,* for þe wise man seith 'Bethynk þe on þi last endynge, and þou shal nat syn.' *Anoþer is, fle fro il felewshipe* . . . Þe þrid is *temperaunce and discrecioun in mete and drynke* . . . [A passage on moderation.] *For to draw vs þat we confourme our wille to Goddis wille, þer ben þre þynges. On is ensample of holy men* and wommen, þe which was ententif nyght and day to serue God and dred hym and loue hym; and if we folow ham in erth, we mowe be with ham in heuyn. *Anoþer, þe goodnesse of our lord God* . . . The þrid is þe wondre ioy of þe kyngdome of heuyn . . . [A passage on the joys of heaven.]

4. (Emendatio Vitae, f. 140r. 24–50)
In his et huiusmodi meditationibus ut quandoque ad medullam amoris ascendas, in quibus ab uno ad alium proficit qui eligitur ad amorem, te iugiter exerceas. Amor autem animam amantem non in se manere sinit, sed extra se rapit ad amatum, ut magis sit ibi anima ubi diligit, quam ubi corpus est, quod per illam sentit et vivit. Sunt quidem tres gradus amoris Christi. Primus gradus vocatur insuperabilis, secundus inseparabilis, tertius singularis. Tunc quippe amor est insuperabilis, quando nulla affectione alia potest superari, et quando libenter propter Christum omnia impedimenta abiicit, omnes tentationes, et omnia carnalia desideria extinguit, quando propter Christum omnia angusta patienter patitur, et nulla delectatione vel blandimento superatur. Facilis est amanti labor omnis, nec melius vincit quis laborem, quam per amorem. Amor inseparabilis est, quando iam vehementi dilectione succensa mens, atque Christo inseparabili cogitatione adhaerens nullo quidem momento ipsum a memoria recedere permittit, sed quasi in corde ligaretur, ipsum cogitat, et ad ipsum suspirat, eius amore se teneri clamat, ut compedem mortalitatis exolvat et ad ipsum quem solum desiderat perducatur: et maxime hoc nomen Iesu tantum honorat et diligit, quod in ipsius mente iugitur recumbit. Cum ergo amor Christi in corde dilectoris Dei et mundi contemptoris in tantum excreverit, ut ab alio amore separari non poterit, summus dicitur. Cum autem illum cogitando nulla occasione illum obliviscendo Christo inseparabiliter inhaeret, inseparabilis et sempiternus nuncupatur. Et quis amore isto amor maior vel altior esse potest, si summus et sempiternus est?

Sed adhuc restat tertius gradus quod dicitur singularis. Aliud est enim solum esse, et aliud summum esse: sicut aliud est semper praesidens esse, et aliud consortem non admittere. Possumus enim multos socios habere, et tamen per omnibus superiorem locum tenere; si alienam consolationem quaris vel recipis quam Dei tui, et si forte summe diligis, non tamen singulariter. Vides ergo quanta magnitudo supereminentiae ad excrescendum supersit ut iam summus et solus esse possit. Ad singularem ergo gradum amor ascendit, quando omnem consolationem, praeter unam quod est in Iesu, excludit: quoniam nihil praeter Iesum sibi sufficere poterit.

(Commandment, 24–36; see Form of Living, 525–564 for parallels)
And þat þou may wyn to þe swetnesse of Goddis loue, I set here þre degrees of loue, in þe which þou be euer wyxynge. *The fyrst degre is cald insuperabile, þe toþer inseperabile, þe þryd synguler. Thi loue is insuperabile when no þynge may ouercum hyt*; þat is neþer wel ne wo, ese ne anguys, loue of fleishe ne lykynge of þis world, bot euer hit lesteth in good thoght, if hit ware tempted gretly, and hit hateth al syn *so þat no thynge may quenche þat loue. Thi loue es inseparabile when al þi þoghtes and willes ben gedered togeddre and festned holely in Ihesu Criste, so þat þou may no tyme foryet hym, bot euer þou þynkest on hym*, and forþi hit is cald inseperabile, for hit may nat be departed fro þe þoght of Ihesu Crist. *Thi loue is synguler when al þi delite is in Ihesu Crist*, and *in non oper thynge fyndeth ioy and comfort*.

Item 2: Super Psalmum Vicesimum, Super Canticum Canticorum, Contra Amatores Mundi as sources for Emendatio Vitae

[(1) While it is possible that Rolle should have found the last two chapters of *Emendatio Vitae* so rich that he used parts of them again on several other occasions, it is unlikely that he should have done so without ever borrowing any passage twice. (2) Two of the works which share material with *Emendatio Vitae* also do so with *Melos Amoris*; in the case of *Super Canticum Canticorum* there can be no doubt that *Melos Amoris* is the source. It is more natural to assume that Rolle borrowed from the same two works on two occasions, than that he wrote *Emendatio Vitae*, then *Super Canticum Canticorum* and *Contra Amatores Mundi*, and only after them *Melos Amoris*. (3) *Emendatio Vitae* is a structured account of the contemplative life written in a carefully moderate style, without autobiographical content, and in the form of a compendium; the other three are highly affective, in two cases autobiographical. Since the material they share with *Emendatio Vitae* is also of this affective kind, it is more likely to have originated with them than with *Emendatio Vitae*.]

1. (Super Psalmum Vicesimum, 16.4–8)
O Jesu bone, quis michi det ut sentiam te, infunde te in visceribus anime mee! Veni in cor meum et inebria illud dulcore tuo. Reple mentem meam fervore amoris tui ut, omnia mala obliviscens, te solum complectar; certe tunc gaudebo. Amodo ne recedas a me quia sola tui presentia michi solatium est, sola tui absentia me tristem relinquit.

(Emendatio Vitae, 140r. 3–16)
Dulce lumen et delectabile, quod es Conditor meus incircumscriptus, illustra faciem meam et aciem oculorum meorum interiorum claritate increata et mentem meam: ut medullitus ab immunditiis mundata ac mirificata muneribus, agiliter evolet in altitudinem: amoenissimi amoris tui sapore succende, quatinus sedeam et quiescam, et in te Iesu iubilans superna quoque suavitate quasi raptus incendens, invisibilium quoque speculatione stabilitus, nunquam nisi divinitus delecter. O amor aeterne, inflamma animum meum ad amandum Deum, ut non ardeat in me nisi ad amplexus eius. *O bone Iesu, quis mihi det ut sentiam te* in me, qui nunc sentiri et non videri

281

potes, *infunde te visceribus animae mee. Veni in cor meum et reple illud dulcedine tua praeclarissima, inebria mentem meam ferventi vino dilectionis dulcisonae, ut omnia mala omnesque circumscriptas visiones, illusorias imagines obliviscens, ac te solum contemplans,* exultem et iubilem in Deo Iesu meo. *Amodo dulcissime Domine, non discedas a me* iugiter manens mecum in tua dulcedine, *quia sola tua praesentia mihi solatium est, et sola tua absentia tristem me relinquit.*

2. (Super Psalmum Vicesimum, 10.14–22)

O Sancte Spiritus, veni et rape me tibi! Et bene sanctus nuncuparis qui omnes cum quibus manere dignatus es sanctos facis! Amor diceris et vere es qui semper tuos ad amorem accendis. Deus meus es tu; doce me facere voluntatem tuam. Ure igne tuo renes meos et cor meum; ardeat ignis ille in altari tuo. Veni, precor te, O dulcis gloria! Veni, dulcedo suavissima! Veni dilecte mi! Tota consolatio mea, anime mee languenti pro te salubri ac dulcifluo fervore illabere; igne tuo penetralia cordis mei incende; et intima queque tua luce illustrando, mellifluo eterni amoris iubilo universa mentis et corporis depasce.

(Emendatio Vitae, f. 140r. 16–24)

O Sancte Spiritus, qui spiras ubi vis, *veni in me, rape me tibi,* naturam quam creasti donis inuncta mellifluis: ut in tuo delicata absorpta gaudio, despiciat et abiiciat omne quod est in hoc mundo, spiritalia charismata te largiente percipiat, et per canorum iubilum tendens in incircumscriptum lumen amore sancto tota liquefiat. *Ure igne tuo renes meos et cor meum, qui in altari tuo ardebit in aeternum. Veni, precor te, O suavis et vera gloria. Veni dulcedo desideratissima, veni dilecte mi, qui es bona consolatio mea, animae languenti pro te et ad te dulcifluo ardore illabere, calore tuo penetrabilia cordis mei incende, et intima quoque luce tua illuminando, mellifluo amoris iubilo cuncta pro raptu mentis et corporis depasce.*

3. (Super Canticum Canticorum, 42.3–25)

Nescio orare, nescio meditari nisi resonante Ihesu nomine. Non sapio gaudium quod Ihesu non est mixtum. Quocumque fuero, ubicumque sedero, quicquid egero, memoria nominis Ihesu a mente mea non recedit ... Devicit me eternus amor, non ut me occidat, set ut vivificet. Attamen, vulneravit me ut mederetur; transfixit cor meum ut medullitus sanetur. Et iam victus, succumbo; vix vivo pre gaudio. Pene morior, quia non sufficio in carne corruptibili tante maiestatis perferre tam affluentem suavitatem ... Cor totum in desiderio Ihesu defixum in igne amoris convertitur, et dulcore deitatis funditus absorbetur. Hinc, O bone Ihesu, miserere miseri; ostende te languenti; medere vulnerato. Si veneris, sanus sum. Infirmum me non sencio, nisi languens amore tuo.

(Emendatio Vitae, f. 140v. 9–18)

O anima mea desine ab amore saeculi, et tota liquesce in amorem Christi: ut semper tibi sit dulce et suave de Christo legere, loqui, scribere, ipsum cogitare et orare, ipsum incessanter laudare. Anima mea sibi devotam Deus te videre desiderat, ad te ex longinquo clamat, in te ardet, amore tuo languet. *Devicisti enim me, o amor indeficiens, vulnerasti me, perennis dulcedo et pulchritudo: et iam victus et vulneratus succumbo, vix vivo prae gaudio et pene morior, quia non sufficio in carne corruptibili tantem maiestatis perferre suavitatem. Totum enim cor in desiderio Iesu defixum, et in amoris ardorem convertitur, et in illam gloriam atque formam absorbetur. Hinc o bone Iesu miserere miseri, ostende te languenti, medere sauciato. Infirmum me non sentio, nisi languentem amore tui.*

4. (Super Canticum Canticorum, 35.14–36.8)
Est itaque caritas virtutum perfectissima, nobilissima et suavissima, quam iste
sanctus possidere meruit qui, de virtute in virtutem transiens, usque ad summam
pervenit. Istam virtutem amantem cum amato scimus coniungere, id est, Christum
cum electa anima perenniter copulare. Reformat autem in nobis caritas summe trinitatis ymaginem, et creaturam creatori facit esse simillimam. O donum caritatis
qua[ntum] vales pre omnibus quod solum supremum gradum tibi vendicas cum
angelis, quanto enim quis de te in via plus accipit, tanto in patria sublimior et glorio-
sior erit. O singulare caritatis gaudium, quod tuos ligas vinculis, supra mundialia
quaque usque ad celestia rapis! Qui te non habet in terris, iacet quicquid habet; qui
autem in te toto posse letari nititur, supra terrena cito levatur. O cara caritas, quam
bona es, que sola coram conditore apparere non formidas! Tu audacter intras in
cubiculum eterni regis; tu sola Christum rapere non vereris. Ipse est quem quesisti;
ipse est quem amasti. Tuus Christus est; tene illum. Non potest te non suscipere cui
soli desiderasti obedire. Sine te, prorsus nulla Christo placent opera. Ergo tua est
sedes celica; tua est societas angelica; tua est sanctitas mirifica; tua est visio Dei glori-
fica; tua est vita sine fine permansura.

(Emendatio Vitae, f. 140v. 20–34)
Est autem charitas virtutum nobilissima excellentissima et suavissima, quam amatum
cum amato coniungere scimus, id est Christum cum electa anima perpetuo copulare.
Reformat enim in nobis summae trinitatis imaginem, etiam creaturam creatori facit
simillimam. O donum amoris, quantum valet prae omnibus, qui supremum gradum
sibi vendicat cum angelis. Quanto enim quis in via de amore plus accipit, tanto in
patria maior et sublimior erit. O singulare gaudium aeterni amoris, quod suos ligans
nexibus virtutum supra mundalia quaeque ad coelestia ipsos rapit. O charitas chara,
qui te non habet, in terra iacet quicquid habet. Qui vero in te laetari nititur supra
terrena statim elevatur. Tu audacter intras cubiculum aeterni regis, tu sola Christum
rapere non vereris. Ipse est quem quesisti, quem amasti. Tuus Christus Iesus est, tene
illum, quia non potest te non suscipere, cui soli desiderasti obedire. O charitas, sine te
nulla prorsus placent opera. Tu omnia facis sapida, tu es sedes coelica, societas angel-
ica, sanctitas mirifica, visio beatifica et vita sine fine mansura. O sancta charitas,
quam suavis es et confortabilis, quae fractum redintegras, restituis ruinam, servum
liberas, angelis hominem aequiperas, sedentes et quiescentes sublevas, levatos
indulcoras.

5. (Super Canticum Canticorum, 49.2–10; 50.19–51.4)
Est itaque verus amor, castus, sanctus, voluntarius, amatum pro seipso non pro suis
amans, in amato se totum figens, nil extra se querens, de se contentus, flagrans,
estuans, ex amato inardescens, vehemens, se in se ligans, impetuosus miro modo,
omnem modum excedens, ad solum amatum se extendens, cuncta alia contempnens
set et obliviscens, in amato canens, illum cogitans, illum incessanter meminens,
ascendens desiderio, pergens in amato, ruens in amplexibus, absortus in osculis,
totus liquescens igne ardentis amoris . . . Servat, autem, verus amator Christi nec
modum, nec gradum, nec ordinem in amore, quia in hac presenti vita, qua[ntum]-
cumque fervens et gaudens et iubilans in divino amore fuerit, adhuc plus et plus
ardencius et iocundius Deum amare intendit. Eciam si hic in eternum posset vivere,
non putaret se aliquando stare, et ulterius in amore non proficere posse, aut non cre-
scere, set pocius quanto diucius viveret, tanto in amore amplius ardet. Hoc, profecto,
liquet quia Deus infinite magnitudinis, inexcogitabilis bonitatis, innumerabilis dulcedinis, omni create nature incomprehensibilis, numquam ab aliqua creatura com-
prehendi potuit, quemadmodum in se eternus existit.

(Emendatio Vitae, f. 140v. 34–47)
In hoc statu vel gradu amoris *est amor castus, sanctus et voluntarius. Amatum amans pro seipso non pro suis et se totum in amato figens, nihil extra ipsum quaerens, de seipso contentus, flagrans, aestuans, vehemens, illum in se ligans, impetuosus miro modo, omnem modum excedens, ad solum amatum se extendens, cuncta alia contempnens et oblivescens, in amato iubilans, ipsum cogitans, ipsum incessanter reminiscens, ardens in desiderio, ruens in dilecto, pergens in amplexibus, absorptus in osculis, totus liquefactus in igne amoris. Itaque vero Christi amator in amando nec ordinem servat, nec gradum cupit, quia in presenti vita quantumcunque fervens et iubilans in divino amore fuerit, adhuc plus et plus ardentius et iucundius Deum amare intendit, et si posset hic semper vivere, non putaret se aliquando stare et ulterius in amore proficere non posse: sed potius quanto diutius viveret, tanto in amore amplius arderet. Deus enim infinitae magnitudinis et inexcogitabilis bonitatis et innumerabilis dulcedinis omni creatae naturae incomprehensibilis, nunquam a nobis compehendi ita poterit, quemadmodum in se aeternus existit.*

6. (Contra Amatores Mundi, 7.296–303)
Tu es sapor condiens; tu es odor redolens; tu es dulcor placens. O amor gloriosus qui solus facis homines gloriosos! Tu viros contemplativos efficis; tu ianuam celi aperis; tu Deum ostendis visibilem; tuque abscondis multitudinem omnium peccatorum. Te laudo, te predico, per quem mundum vinco, per quem iubilo, per quem salvus fio; illabere michi in tua dulcedine. Te mecum et meis commendo sine fine. Amen.

(Emendatio Vitae, f. 141r. 10–16)
O clara charitas, veni in me et rape me in te, sic ut praesenter coram te Conditore. *Tu enim es sapor condiens, odor redolens, dulcor placens,* fervor purificans, consolatio sine fine manens. *Tu viros contemplativos efficis, ianuam coeli aperis,* ora accusantium claudis, *Deum ostendis visibilem, et multitudinem abscondis peccatorum. Te enim laudamus, te deprecamur, per quam mundum vincimus, per quam iubilamus, per quam scalam coeli ascendimus, illabere mihi, et in tua dulcedine te mecum et meis commendo sine fine, Amen.*

7. (Super Canticum Canticorum, 26.24–26)
Hinc, ergo, colligitur quod contemplatio est iubilus divini amoris, suscepto in mente sono celice melodie vel cantico laudis eterne.

(Emendatio Vitae, f. 141r. 34–35)
Mihi videtur *quod contemplatio sit iubilus divini amoris, suscepta in mente suavitate laudis angelicae.*

8. (Contra Amatores Mundi, 5.192–199)
Mentalis visio sursum capitur, celestia non terrena contemplantur. Est autem hec enigmatica visio et speculativa, non clara et perspicua, quia dum per fidem currimus eciam per speculum et in enigmate videmus. Unde scribitur in psalmo quia tenebre non obscurabuntur a te, et nox sicut dies illuminabitur; sicut tenebre eius, ita et lumen eius.

(Emendatio Vitae, f. 141v. 12–17)
Mentalis enim visio sursum rapitur, et coelestia contemplatur per visionem aenigmaticam, per speculativam, non claram et perspicuam. Quia dum per fidem currimus, per speculum in enigmate videmus. Si enim oculus intellectualis nititur in lucem spiritualem contemplari, illud lumen ut in se est non videt, sentit tamen se ibi fuisse, dum

saporem et fervorem incircumscripti luminis secrete retinet. *Unde Psal. Sicut tenebrae eius, ita lumen eius.*

9. *(Contra Amatores Mundi, 5.19–30, 41–42, 151–158)*
Hinc in veritate comperi quod sanctitas non est in rugitu cordis aut in lacrimis, sed in suavitate perfecte caritatis. Hec enim ordinat mentem, disponit recte penitentem, et conscienciam facit regulatam. Multi enim in lacrimis liquefacti postea nichilominus in malum declinaverunt, sed nullus unquam in eterno amore veraciter gaudens iterum mundanis sollicitudinibus se polluit. Flere autem et gemere sunt noviter conversorum et incipiencium, sed iubilare et canere non sunt nisi perfectorum. Qui adhuc ergo, quamvis longo tempore penituit, conscienciam de reatu suo mordentem sentit, sciat sine dubio quia perfectam penitenciam nondum egit. Fuerunt michi lacrime mee panes die ac nocte . . . Considerabam sane quod nisi prius flere amavissem ad illud canorum solacium non pervenissem . . . Hec utique contemplacionis dulcedo laboribus immensis adquiritur. Immo verius dono Dei datur, sed profecto a primo sancto usque hodie nec unus veraciter contemplacione eterni amoris usque ad canorum iubilum rapi potuit, qui antea omnem mundi vanitatem vere non reliquit, et cum hoc in iugi meditacione devotaque oracione ac multo spirituali exercitatus labore fuit.

(Super Canticum Canticorum, 6.22–7.2; 9.15–17)
Labor utique est contemplacio, set dulcis, desiderabilis et suavis; laborantem letificat, non aggravat. Hoc nullus nisi gaudens perfruitur. Non dum adest set quando abest laborans fatigatur. O bonus labor ad quem mortales languent! O mira laboris exercitacio, quam precipue sedentes ascendunt! . . . Requiritur utique necessario ut magnam mentis et corporis quietem capat, qui igne Sancti Spiritus veraciter inflammaricurat.

(Super Canticum Canticorum, 26.26–27.7)
Cum ergo constat vitam contemplativam digniorem esse et magis meritoriam quam activa vita, et omnes viros contemplacionis solitudinem amantes et precipue in amore divino ferventes, liquet profecto quod, non monachi vel alii, quicumque ad congregacionem collecti, summi sunt aut maxime Deum diligunt, set solitarii, contemplacione sublimati, qui pro magno eterni amoris gaudio, quod senciunt, in solitudine sedere incessanter concupiscunt.

(Emendatio Vitae, ff. 141v. 28–142r. 2)
Hinc patet quod sanctitas non est in rugitu oris, aut in lachrymis, aut in exterioribus actibus, sed in suavitate perfectae charitatis et supernae contemplationis. Multi enim in lachrymas liquefacti sunt, et postea in malum declinaverunt. Sed nullus unquam mundanis solicitudinibus se polluit, postquam aeterno amore veraciter exultaverit. Flere et gemere, est iam noviter conversorum et incipientium et proficientium; sed iubilare et in contemplationem exire, non est nisi perfectorum. Igitur quamvis longo tempore qui adhuc cum reatu suo conscientiam sentit, sciat quod perfectam poenitentiam nondum egit. Interim sint lachrymae panes die ac nocte, quia prius fletibus ac suspiriis se afficiat, ad dulcedinem contemplationis se pervenire non posse cognoscat. Contemplativa suavitas non nisi laboribus adquiritur immensis. Sed cum inerrabili laetitia possidetur, imo non est meritum, sed Dei donum: tamen a principio usque hodie nec unus in contemplationem amoris aeterni rapi potuit, nisi qui ante omnem mundi vanitatem perfecte reliquit. Insuper salubri meditatione, devota quoque oratione, ipsum exerceri oportet, priusquam in contemplationem coelestium veraciter pervenerit. Laboriosa est contemplatio, sed dulcis, desiderabilis et suavis, laborantem laetificat non aggravat; hac nullus nisi gaudens perfruitur, non quando venit, sed quando recedit fatigatur. O bonus labor ad mortales per quem se dirigunt. O nobilis ac

mira excercitatio, per quam perfectius agunt. Requiritur enim ut magnam mentis et corporis quietem capiat, quem ignis Sancti Spiritus veraciter inflammat. Multi enim sunt nescientes sabbatizare in mente neque scientes vanas et inutiles cogitationes expellere, ut in Psalmo praecepitur: Vacate et videte, quoniam ego sum Deus. Vacantes enim non possunt impleri corpore sed vagantes corde non merentur gustare et videre quam suavis est Dominus, id est, quam dulcis sit altitudo contemplationis. Omnis vero vir contemplativus solitudinem diligit, ut eo ferventius et liberius quo a nullo impeditur, in suis affectibus exercere se possit. *Cum enim constet vitam contemplativam digniorem esse ac magis meritoriam quam activam vitam, et omnes contemplativos instinctu Dei amantes solitudinem* et propter contemplationis dulcedinem *in amore sunt praecipue ferventes, liquet utique quod solitarii dono contemplationis summi sunt ad perfectionem maximi.*

Item 3: Super Canticum Canticorum as a source for Melos Amoris, caps. 2–13

[The series of postils in caps. 2–13 of *Melos Amoris* treat several subjects with little systematization, whereas the part of *Super Canticum Canticorum* from which *Melos Amoris* borrows is one of Rolle's more coherent pieces of writing. Every phrase of many passages of *Super Canticum Canticorum* recurs in *Melos Amoris* in the same order, but as parts of longer discussions which do not necessarily treat the same topic, or preserve the original sentence structures. Moreover, *Melos Amoris* is more heavily alliterative when it is not quoting *Super Canticum Canticorum* than when it is, and often adds allusions to *canor* to passages dealing with *dulcor*. It is inconceivable that the shorter, more coherent work can have been created from the less alliterative phrases and sentences of the longer and less coherent one, without there being even any alterations in the order.]

1. Super Canticum Canticorum, 1.1–2.15; Melos Amoris, cap. 2 (5.4–8.32)

(Super Canticum Canticorum, 1.3–5)
Suspirantis anime deliciis eternorum, vox in orbe terrarum clare intonat, Osculetur me, inquit, osculo oris sui. Dilecta utique a dilecto petit osculum.

(Melos Amoris, 5.4–13)
Languentis limpide spiritus spirati ad speciem perhennem vox vitalis in aura amoris auribus intrinsecus *perspicue* proclamet que *intonat in orbe terrarum,* quamquam lubricos lateat leticia scrutinii Scripture. *Ait* itaque anima anhelans eterno Auctori nam amore affluens amplexibus ardet: *Osculetur me osculo oris sui.* Amor utique sine frigore fervens fortissime festinat frui, qui fovet quia quasi violencia vehitur, et inverecunda amatrix iugiter se gerit ut capiat Conditorem. Aperte igitur osculum exposcitur in exordio Cantici charitatis, ut denotet quia, depulso dolore, *dilecte cum dilecto coniunccio consequatur.*

2. Super Canticum Canticorum, 2.15–26a; Melos Amoris, cap. 3 (9.1–10.26)

(Super Canticum Canticorum, 2.15–19a)
Novi utique quod honor regis iudicium diligit. Set quoniam amor pudore non confunditur, opprobrio non reicitur, racione non vincitur, quin pocius omnia novit vincere, iterum clamo, cogito, deprecor, Osculetur me osculo oris sui.

(Melos Amoris, 9.1–9)
Inter hec autem quamquam quidem *non ignorem quod honor regis iudicium diligit,* amor implens, habundans ac affluens ad canendum amorosum canticum me cogit prorumpere et *iterum orando ac deprecando postulare: Osculetur me osculo oris sui.*

Excursus I: The chronology of Rolle's writings

Hinc itaque liquet quia amatrix ardens amato inheret usquequaque; que *pudore non confunditur, obprobrio non reicitur, nec quidem modo aut mensura stabilitur; quin pocius novit omnia vincere* et audacter inverecunda secreta summi Regis parata penetrare.

(Super Canticum Canticorum, 2.19b–26a)
Longum michi videtur quod dilectus moratur; longus utique est incolatus meus, quia amore langueo. Inquilinus mundi, sedem in celo concupisco. Set que est expectacio mea? Nonne dominus et substancia mea apud ipsum est? Mori itaque langueo et vitam paciter suffero; quia, quamquam cum angelis pocius quam cum hominibus lucem videre cuperem, voluntatem tamen Dei letanter expectarem. Peregrinus igitur ego sum et advena sicut omnes patres mei.

(Melos Amoris, 10.3–18)
Quamobrem, dum differtur concupitum, augetur desiderium et *videtur longa que brevis est dilecti mora. Utique incolatus meus prolongatus est, quia amore langueo: mundi quippe inquilinus ad celestem sedem suspiro, sed que est expectacio nostra? Nonne dominus Iesus, et substancia nostra apud ipsum est?* Itaque *langor meus* pro visione vite invisibilis letabundum me moriturum duceret et *vitam nimirum paciencia* interius inspirata *equanimiter sustinet,* dum mens mirifico munere madefacta in divina dileccione iugiter sanctificari suadet. *Quamquam igitur angelorum pocius lumen lucens veraciter sine varietate quam hominum,* a nobis noctis caligine separato, intueri *cupio,* non meam *tamen voluntatem* sequi sarcinor, sed *divinam utique ordinatam* letanter expecto, quoniam *itaque advena ego sum apud te et peregrinus sicut omnes patres mei.*

3. Super Canticum Canticorum, 2.26b–3.25; Melos Amoris, cap. 4 (10.27–15.2)

(Super Canticum Canticorum, 2.26b–3.12a)
... dum in hac presenti miseria; nec mansionem manentem habeo nec inquiro. Nempe, quemadmodum Caim vagus et profugus factus fuit pro culpa fratricidii super terram, ita et ego in hoc exilio incerte sedis de loco ad locum transeo ut eternam consequar hereditatem. Cernimus autem quod tam electi quam reprobi corporaliter vagi et profugi nonnuncquam fiunt. Set in hoc differunt quia electi quocumque in corpore transferantur, in celo iugiter intencionem ponunt. Unde et illud discursus incommodum electis meritum exaggerat, quod tamen populus vel saltem aliquis presumptor iniquus dampnum esse anime iudicare non formidat. Omnis enim verus Christi electus quietem mentis et corporis continuam appetit; unde tunc maxime tribulatur quando discurrit.

(Melos Amoris, 11.26–12.13)
Corporalem namque *in hac miseria nec mansionem habeo nec manentem inquiro.* Distractus denique per adversa, vana non capiens commoda carensque carnali cupidine, eterni amoris tantummodo concipio consolacionem. *Quemadmodum quippe Caym vagus et profugus factus fuit super terram pro facinore fratricidii, ita et ego in hoc exilio incerte sedis fio: de loco ad locum transeo,* donec Omnipotens dignetur servum suum dirigere *ut deinceps iam non indigeam circumquaque transmigrare. Scimus autem quod non solum reprobi, verum eciam electi, nonnunquam secundum corpus vagi et profugi sunt. Sed profecto hii inter se vehementer differunt: quia electi Christi, quocumque moveantur in corpore, in celestibus perfruendis gaudiis mentis intentionem non cessant collocare.* Super fundamentum illud infallibile quod positum est, Christus Iesus, edificant aurum et argentum et lapides preciosos quibus nimirum percipientibus premia structura paratur fulgida. *Unde et labor discursus* pro divina dileccione vel compulsione violenta in immobilibus mente *meritum exaggerat quod*

287

plerumque populus aut presumptor improvidus anime detrimentum iudicare non formidat. Verus namque et ardens amator Dei quietem mentis et corporis continuam esse appetit, quia maxime tribulatur quando discurrit.

(Super Canticum Canticorum, 3.12b–25)
Reprobi vero in gestu corporis figuram ostendunt mentis. Quemadmodum circumquaque discurrere vix aliquando desinunt, ita et in corde instabiles existunt. Et cum vana presentis vite solacia inardescunt cernere, eciam in eorum gaudio cordis radicem non timent plantare. Tales vero peregrini apud Deum non sunt, set pocius apud diabolum, quia mundum amantes cum mundo pereunt. Neque hic manentem habentes civitatem, neque futuram celestis patrie inquirunt. Hi vitam cupiunt quam sciunt se non posse assequi; merito hinc expulsi mortem inveniunt, a qua nuncquam poterunt abduci. Ve peregrinis qui magno labore in via fatigantur, et tamen ad patriam pervenire non tendunt, ubi eternam requiem possiderent. Non sufficit eis malam vitam agere, nisi illam eciam sub habitu paupertatis studeant palliare.

(Melos Amoris, 12.29–13.2; 13.18–30; 14.28–15.2)
Nimirum namque stabilitus status in suavitate celica fremitum fugit funestorum et, cingulo se cingens solitario, affluencia armonie angelice se sentit solidatum. Deinde, delectatus dulcore desideratissimo, quamvis corpus per plura transferat, nunquam tamen ab interno sapore ieiunat. *Reprobi vero in gestu corporis figuram ostendunt mentis: quemadmodum autem circumquaque discurrere non desinunt, ita et in corde instabiles fiunt*: Peccatum peccavit Ierusalem; propterea instabilis facta est . . . Etenim quidem *cum inardescunt vana presentis vite gaudia cernere, eciam in illorum solaciis radicem cordis non timent plantare. Hii et hiis similes apud Deum peregrinos se non efficiunt, sed pocius apud diabolum* ad quem properant, nam *mundum amantes cum mundo pereunt neque hic manentem habentes civitatem neque futuram concupiscunt*; perdunt namque pariter celestem et terrenam et tormentis tacti tartarorum ignem induunt infernalem. In presentis periculosis ponderibus *vitam vellent videre* perhenniter quam profecto *sciunt se non posse consequi: merito hinc expulsi et morsi monstris immortalibus, mortem inveniunt a qua non poterunt abduci. Ve viventibus in viciis et vacuis a virtutibus . . . Ve peregrinis qui* ad pascua peccatorum per portenta putredinis parantur properare: *magno nimirum labore languescunt* in lusibus sine lucro, viam non veritatis vadentes et *fatigati* falsariis in furtis offendunt famam, *ad curiam canencium coram Conditore non tendentes* transduci, pastum peregrinacionis perite sine precio perdiderunt et, vitam vendentes pro vilissima voluptate, avide assumunt carmen captivitatis. Execrabiles utique in operibus eradicantur sine reversione a sapore celico, quia *non sufficit* sanguisugis non solum *vitam virus evomentem ducere nisi eciam illam*, ut peiores fiant et teneros ad tormentum traiciant, *sub habitu alieno studeant palliare.*

4. *Super Canticum Canticorum, 3.26–4.5; Melos Amoris, cap. 5 (15.3–16.20)*

(Super Canticum Canticorum, 3.26–4.3)
Osculetur me osculo oris sui. In hiis verbis, devota anima fervorem querit eterne dileccionis, dulcedinem superne contemplacionis, solucionem corruptibilis carnis et unionem dilecti invisibilis. Fervor utique divini amoris speculacionis preit dulcorem, quia nisi Christum quis recte diligit, proculdubio in canore celestis contemplacionis non iubilabit.

(Melos Amoris, 15.29–16.6)
Itaque aiebat in exordio oraculum amancium: *Osculetur me osculo oris sui.* Hec verba vitalem virorem iocundamque iubilacionem emanant, in quibus eciam mistica et mirifica memorantur. Deo namque *dilecta anima* et devocione dulcorata dummodo

divulgata *fervorem querit eterni amoris, dulcedinem* discit *sancte contemplacionis, solucionem cupit carnis corruptibilis et in unionem* anhelat *Dilecti invisibilis.* Clamat ergo amando et clamando amat, capere cupiens consolacionem et degustatam dulcedinem petens perfici et dona desiderata perimpleri: Osculetur me osculo oris sui. *Ardor autem divine dileccionis primus est ut prebeatur speculacionis species. Nimirum nisi qui Christum recte diligit in canore contemplacionis non iubilabit.*

5. *Super Canticum Canticorum, 4.6–5.4; Melos Amoris, cap. 6 (16.21–18.34)*

(Super Canticum Canticorum, 4.6–5.4)
Contemplativa vera suavitas mortis precedit desiderium, quia tunc cum gaudio morimur quando delicias eterni amoris canentes solam in Deo delectacionem contemplamur. Foras enim mittitur omnis transitorie cupidinis delectacio, dum igne Sancti Spiritus veraciter inardescimus, et eternitatis gloriam incessanter desideramus. Qui autem adheret Deo, ut ait apostolus, unus spiritus est cum eo. Unde et in hoc nostrum consistit gaudium, cum Deus in nobis habitat, ut nos in eo vivamus. Qui autem putat se per ipsum vivere, frustra se sublimans, non cessat ad nichilum devenire. Eternus quippe Conditor tali modo omnem creaturam ab inicio constituit, ut eciam sine ipso nec aliquid agere valebit. Vera igitur consolacio humane menti nequaquam aliquando illabitur, nisi ille per graciam suam menti assit qui eam tante bonitatis capacem fecit. Quid est ergo quod habent seculares desideriorumque carnalium amatores? Ecce enim ita vehementer et infatigabiliter terrenis voluptatibus se saciant, ac si in eis felicitatem et perpetuam vitam cognoscerent. Ita autem carnalis consolacio non est vera, set vana; non eterna, set momentanea; non laude digna, set detestanda. Insuper et nec est continua, que dolore tristique labore sepe est respersa. Venenum cum melle miscetur, et letam gloriam luctus comitatur. Illa profecto delectacio vera est et sempiterna, que ab indeficiente vite fonte emanat, quam creator, non creatura, prestat, que non tam carnem quam mentem letificat, que nobiscum iugiter perdurat . . .

(Melos Amoris, 17.9–28, 34–18.28)
Unde dissolvi desidero ut ducar ad dilectum; *nam contemplativa suavitas desiderium mortis* mandat in mentibus, et patrie quam percipiemus *precedit premium, quia tunc cum gaudio,* in gracia gravidi, *ab hoc mundo morimur, quando iam delicias dileccionis divine in canora cogitantes contemplacione,* adventum glorie magni Dei parati prestolamur. *Foras festinanter emittitur omnis utique depravacio deceptorie delectacionis,* et captivi, quondam carnali concupiscencie conglutinati, quaciuntur a cordium curiositate, *dum igne Sancti Spiritus incipiunt inardescere et eternitatis gloriam indefesse desiderare.* Afflati inde affabiliter dulcore divinitus dato, non libet ludos lingere lubricos humanitus oblatos, sed aspirantes apte ad aspectum angelorum, lucem laudant faciem confortantem, sicque suscepti in sanctorum solaciis propius procedentes splendore solis superni interius incalescunt. *Qui enim adheret Deo unus spiritus est cum eo. Igitur in hoc nostrum consistit gaudium cum Deus in nobis habitat et nos in eo:* virtutis vigore veraciter vivimus, quatinus cupientes charitatem canere, eciam et melos mellifluum ad alta ambulantes audiamus . . . Superbus enim insaniam sapiens severitatis sentenciam senciet et, quia *putavit quod per semetipsum in potenciis pergere potuit, frustra sublimatus, ad nichilum devenit. Quippe eternus Conditor eo modo ab inicio omnem creaturam constituit ut sine ipso nec aliquid agere nec quidem vivere aut esse valebit:* quanto magis in pietate aut potestate non perficitur si non intelligit quod hoc ab Omnipotente habuerit, in cuius dominio cuncta constituent. Quamobrem *vera consolacio racionabili creature concupiscenda nequaquam alicui aliquando illabitur, nisi ille* Opifex omnium menti mortalium, *per graciam* et gratitudinem *affuerit qui eam bonitatis beate capacem creavit. Habent* attamen *seculi* sapientes *solacium quod suspirant,* per quod postea supplicium suscipiunt et sectatores siquidem venenatarum

voluptatum capiunt callide quod cupiunt consolamen. Etenim *infatigabiliter* faciunt ut *desideriis dampnabilis delectacionis* tam sufficienter *se sacient acsi* in illis oblectamentis aures obturantibus ab amore Dei felicitatem futuram integre invenirent. Sed nimirum nodati necis nexibus in dolosa dulcedine decipiuntur, *nam vera non est, sed vana, non eterna sed momentanea, non laude digna sed detestanda; insuper et cum brevi termino consumitur,* patet quia nec continuis complexibus gratulatur. Vanitas namque virorum non vere vivencium et mollicies mulierum morula retibus respersa ruinosis in lacum liquefient languido labore cum lite lanceata. Exinde aspicitur ut oportunitati adhereamus ad amandum Auctorem, quia lugubris non laudabitur lenitas; *nam mors cum melle miscetur et gloriancium carnaliter casus curam comitatur. Illa ergo desiderabilis delectacio vera est que veraciter vivificat, que a fonte invisibilis vite eternaliter emanat, quam prestat Conditor non creatura, que mentem non ventrem letificat,* et cum viris in virtutibus vivacitate vigilantibus perpetue *perdurat.*

6. *Super Canticum Canticorum, 5.4–11; Melos Amoris, cap. 7 (19.1–21.36)*

(Super Canticum Canticorum, 5.4–11)
... quam fidelis anima sciciens clamat, Osculetur me osculo oris sui. Divinum osculum eterni amoris suave est solacium. Dum enim mens nostra amore Christi intime rapitur, Deus pater dulcore filii sui illam quasi osculatur. Rapimur autem amore invisibili conditoris nostri, cum omnia que exteriora sunt penitus obliviscimur, et ad sola interna – scilicet divina – querenda, sapienda, contemplanda, celitus sublevamur.

(Melos Amoris, 20.14–24)
Sic quoque latibula languencium amore Altissimi penetrabuntur puritate perfecta, et pacificam mentem plenissima species dulcedine debriabit *quam devota anima siciens clamat,* charitate concepta: *Osculetur me osculo oris sui. Divinum itaque osculum est solacium sentire eterni amoris. Dum enim mens dileccione Dei recte rapitur, Deus Pater ore suavitatis Filii sui illam quasi osculatur. Capimur autem ad contemplacionem sonantibus epulis insignitam amore ardentissimo vite invisibilis, cum omnia exteriora prorsus obliviscimur et ad sola interna, divina scilicet, querenda, sapienda, speculanda, divinitus sublevamur ...*

7. *Super Canticum Canticorum, 5.11–7.13; Melos Amoris, cap. 8 (22.1–25.18)*

(Super Canticum Canticorum, 5.11–23)
Hinc corda nostra estu eterne lucis incipiunt calefieri et dulcore divino suaviter obumbrari, ut nos ignis superni caloris ab estu male cupidinis refrigeret, ne nos adversarius noster tamquam leo rugiens per temptamenta sua blanda vel aspera devoraret. In hoc autem intelligimus quia incircumscriptum lumen verum est et eternum; nam, cum mentes nostras illuminat, quanto ab illo calore medullitus exurimur, tanto suavius cum Deo gloriamur. Non autem quemadmodum sol iste materialis, qui se diu considerantes pene excecat; set proculdubio, qui illum solem celestis patrie cum desiderio et diligencia non respicit, sine fine cecus erit. Eternum utique illud lumen indubitanter cognoscimus quia quanto diucius in hac vita vivimus, tanto illud veracius sentimus.

(Melos Amoris, 22.5–22)
Intendamus ergo integro intellectu Omnipotentis amore incendi et recte refutare reliquias reproborum; *hinc etenim corda nostra estu eterne lucis incipiunt calefieri et dulcore divino suaviter obumbrari, ut iam ignis superni fervor a calore captivantis cupidinis nos refrigeret, ne adversarius noster, tanquam leo rugiens, per temptamenta sua blanda vel aspera nos devoret. In hoc autem intelligimus quia illud lumen*

incircumscriptum est verum et eternum dum mentes nostras illuminat quia, quanto ab illo splendore medullitus magis exurimur, tanto suavius in Christo gratulamur. Non utique quemadmodum iste sol materialis qui diu se considerantes excecat, sed sine dubio qui illum solem celestis patrie cum desiderio et diligencia non respicit, sine fine cecus erit. Eternam itaque lumen incunctanter illam [= illum?] cognoscimus, quia quo diucius in hac vita virtutibus vestiti et a viciis vacui vivimus visibiles, eo ipso veracius et subtilius illam [= illud?] interiorem hominem inflammantem sentimus.

(*Super Canticum Canticorum, 5.23–6.9*)
O quam suave est gaudium ab omni istius seculi solacio prorsus despici, et internis divine lucis deliciis in mente penetrari! O quam dulce et delectabile est canticum eterni amoris canere, et celica resonante melodia contemplando iubilare! Impinguat autem animam mellifluus ardor caritatis, nec ad ocium sinit illam dilabi, quin pocius eam ad exercendam se iugiter in virtutibus rapere nititur; ut, postpositis omnibus, in Christo continue delectetur. Hec utique vita est angelica veracius quam humana, sic in carne vivere et nullum delectacionem nisi divinam in animo sentire. Set et contemplativa vita convenienter dicitur; ut sic inter homines habitet, quod nichilominus eterni amoris gaudio interius rapiatur.

(*Melos Amoris, 22.27–23.19*)
O quam suave est gaudium ab omnibus istius seculi solaciis prorsus de[spici] et interius eterni splendoris incendiis perfecte penetrari, quatinus cor concipiens consolacionem spiritalis cantici supra mortalium multitudinem regimine racionis se rapiat et in deliciis Deitatis delectatus in canticum charissimum laudans liquefiat! O quam dulce et delectabile est, immo delectabilius quam excogitare possumus, consolatorium canticum eterni amoris canere et, celica resonante cithara, contemplando iubilare! Decidit desolacio et mesticia foris mittitur, dum mens moratur in melodia et migrat in montem mellifluum manantem. Impinguat autem animam dulcor dulcifluus dileccionis et ardor amabilis audacem facit animum ac infert ad intuitum internorum, et collectum in charitatem continue ad sublimem sumit sanctitatem. Nec eum unquam ad ocium sinit dilabi, quin pocius, ut exerceatur in virtutibus rapere nititur ut, postpositis perturbacionibus populorum, in Deo iugiter delectetur. Hec utique vita sanctissima est quam nonnisi summi sorciuntur, angelica veracius est quam humana, tam virtuose et vigilanter in carne corruptibili vivere quod nullam delectacionem nisi divinam in anima sciat sentire. Hinc itaque et contemplativa vita congrue et convenienter dicitur cum quis inter homines sic habitet quod nichilominus sonum in se suscipiat celicum supernumque aspiciat apertum ostium et eterni amoris incendiis interius se senciat raptum.

(*Super Canticum Canticorum, 6.9–7.1*)
Non ergo contemplatores celestis iubili ociosi sunt, ut nonnulli estimant, qui, ita esse asserentes, vim contemplacionis superne penitus ignorare probantur; quin pocius nonnunquam contigit, quod qui pluribus exterioris operacionis negociis coram hominibus instare cernitur, coram Deo ociosius maxime videatur. Parum enim prodest corporalis exercitatio, ubi mens, a divinis cogitandis distracta, in fallibilium mundi rerum fantasmatibus non metuit discurrere, et oculum cordis ab intencione spiritualis gustus permittit evagare. Amodo igitur non audeant laborantes corporaliter, eciam quamvis iuste, viro vero contemplativo in labore maiorem, set nec equalem se ostendere; quoniam quanto anima corpore est excellencior, tanto labor spiritus laudabilior est quam labor corporalis. Labor utique est contemplacio, set dulcis, desiderabilis et suavis; laborantem letificat, non aggravat. Hoc nullus nisi gaudens perfruitur. Non dum adest, set quando abest, laborans fatigatur. O bonus labor ad quem mortales languent! O mira laboris exercitacio, quam precipue sedentes ascendunt!

(Melos Amoris, 23.33–24.13)
Nimirum namque *nonnunquam contingit quod plerique qui pluribus exterioris operacionis implicacionibus instare cernuntur coram hominibus, ociosi maxime videantur in oculis divinis. Parum autem prodest corporalis exercitacio ubi mens, a celestibus cogitandis distracta, in fantasmatibus fallibilium mundanarum rerum non metuit discurrere et oculum cordis ab intencione spiritalis gaudii gustus permittit evagare. Quanto ergo anima dignior corpore et excellencior creditur, tanto labor spiritus quam labor corporis melior esse et fructuosior probatur. Est utique contemplacio labor, sed dulcis, desiderabilis et suavis: laborantem letificat, non gravat. Hoc nullus nisi gaudens perfruitur; non quando assumitur, sed quando perditur, laborans fatigatur;* letatur quis si talis amica advenit, lugebit si recedit. Hec est Rachel pulcra facie et venusto aspectu, quam Iacob in tantum dilexit quod pro illa spacium septem annorum parum putavit. *O bonus labor, per quem laborem ad quod ministerium mortales languent! O mira laboriosa occupacio quam precipue quiescentes agunt!*

(Super Canticum Canticorum, 7.1–13; 7.1–3, 9–10a are omitted in Melos Amoris)
O quam igitur delectabile est ab omnibus prorsus istius seculi desideriis divinitus eripi et eterni amoris delicias canendo contemplari! Iste, exterius non operans, splendore eterne lucis perfunditur. Ille, multum agens, ab illo gaudio longe propulsatur. Quid tamen prodest ei, quia multa exterius videtur agere; aut obest illi alteri, quia divina dulcedo eum intus non cessat ligare? Verum est ergo, quod veritas ait, Maria optimam partem elegit. Non intumescant activi amplius, quia in exterioribus rebus mira et magna cernuntur agere; ecce enim, qui nichil nisi Christum diligere nititur, eciam a Christo omnibus prefertur. Credimus enim nichil quomodo amor apud Deum potest accipi; nec tam opus quam voluntas reputari.

(Melos Amoris, 24.31–25.1; 25.15–18)
Alter exterius non operans, sed diligendo Deum in contemplacione quiescens, *splendore superni luminis perfunditur; alter, multum in exterioribus agens, ab illo adhuc gaudio longe separatur. Sed, queso, quid prodest ei si magna et multa videtur agere, aut alteri obest quia eum intus divina dileccio dignatur ligare? Verum profecto est quod Veritas ait: Maria optimam partem elegit ... Ecce iam que nichil nisi Christum diligere nititur a Christo omnibus prefertur: putamus enim quod non potest quicquam quo modo amor apud Deum accipi nec tam opus quam voluntas reputari.*

8. *Super Canticum Canticorum, 7.13–10.13; Melos Amoris, caps. 9–12 (25.19–37.37)*

(Super Canticum Canticorum, 7.13–8.16) has little undeniable influence on *Melos Amoris* caps. 9–10a (25.19–29.35), although there is a similarity of subject-matter and enough parallelism to suggest that it is still a source. Both texts move from the subject of povery to that of judgement, quoting *'Iudicabunt naciones et dominabuntur populis'* (Wisdom 3.7). With caps. 10b–12, *Melos Amoris* returns to direct quotation of *Super Canticum Canticorum,* but at ever wider intervals, and with phrasing ever less reminiscent of its source.)

(Super Canticum Canticorum, 8.16–9.11 – 8.25–9.4 appearing only indistinctly)
O nequissima presumpcio, peccatores contra iustum arguere et eternis ignibus cruciandos virum sanctum diffamare! Detractores Deo odibiles, ut quid frustra dilectis Christi derogare non metuitis, quos iam, velut agnos inter lupos, aspicere potestis? Plane ostenditis vos miseros, cum non parum videtur vobis Christum non diligere, nisi eciam illum in sanctis suis studeatis impugnare. Recte ergo propheta, culpabilem mundane vanitatis amatorum vitam intuens, ait: Quaquam in ymagine ambulet homo, tamen frustra conturbatur. Utique in vanum conturbantur qui circa ea locucione, cogitacione et opere soliciti et afflicti esse non renuunt, a quibus tamen non

gaudium, sed tormentum adquirunt. Deinceps igitur, ponite custodiam ori vestro, ne, dum in verba malicie corda vestra declinare tenditis, ab eterno iudice dampnacionis sentenciam senciatis. Set et mentes vestras ab immundis et iniquis cogitacionibus purgare nitimini; quatinus animus divina et celestia cogitans, tanto velocius ac securius ad sempiterna gaudia infatigabiliter properet, quanto in carnis sapiencia nec in mundo pomposa gloria penitus non gaudet. Cumque vero omnia que visibilia sunt mundi vana predia pro invisibilibus celi gaudiis libenter postponimus, ad eterni amoris suavitatem gaudentes avolamus.

(Melos Amoris, 30.6–18; 31.18–34)
Sed hec nimirum presumpcio nequissima predicatur, cum peccator impurus iustum iniuste redarguit et ignibus eternis cruciandus sanctum Dei diffamare non pertimescit. Putet plane peccator impaciens quia iuste in iudicio iudicabitur et ab illo quem in hoc mundo despexerat et cui iniurias irrogaverat peremptus punietur. *Detractores Deo odibiles, ut quid frustra dilectis Dei derogatis quos velut agnos inter lupos videtis? Prorsus perversos et sine pietate vosmetipsos ostenditis, cum non parum vobis videtur Christum non diligere nisi ipsum et in servis suis studeatis impugnare. Recte ergo redarguit propheta perversos, secundum aliam litteram que legitur: Quamquam in imagine ambulet homo, tamen frustra conturbatur* . . . Sed et vos, miseri, qui adhuc manetis sine mansuetudine, mementote, antequam moriamini in malis quibus mancipati estis, *mentes ab immundiciis mundare medullitus et cogitaciones carnales non capere nec cupidinem corporalium comportare, quatinus, purificato pectore, animus, in alta ascendens et divina diligere dignumducens, tanto cicius ac securius ad sempiterna solacia se sublevet quanto in seculari sapiencia nec in pomposa carnis petulancia penitus non gaudebat,* et, quia cogitat anhelans ultra omnem exteriorem altitudinem utcumque Conditorem cognoscere, volet ad vicinos Vivificantis et efficax efficietur assumi in archana que absconduntur. *Verum cum, venantes in virtutibus comparabili constancia, vanitates visibilium prediorum pro invisibilis veritatis precepto perpetuo perfecteque postponimus, devote diligentes absque ambiguitate, ad saporem celestis suavitatis ab insipido scelerosoque solacio ad eternum amorem ardenter aspicientes, per transitum a terrenis tute transmigramus.,*

(Super Canticum Canticorum, 9.11–17)
Inde nobis Christus incipit dulcescere, et, paulatim in nobis presencie sue dulcedinem ostendens, eo ipso nos ab omnibus istius vite concupiscenciis celitus abstrahit, quo in eius amoris solacio nos magis succendit. Requiritur utique necessario ut magnam mentis et corporis quietem capiat, qui igne Sancti Spiritus veraciter inflammari curat.

(Melos Amoris, 32.23–29; 33.10–12; 34.1–3)
Unde et, ex quo assumpsit animam ad amandum, denique *deinceps dulcessit in dilectis dulcor Divinitatis,* mulcens merencium mentes ne desperacione delerentur et, *paulatim* proficiens in parvulis pauperibus pietate plenis, perlibandum se ocium odientibus amicabiliter *ostendit,* ut eciam intra tramites tempestatis tranquillitas traducatur et turbo temporalitatis ad eternitatem tendentibus terminetur . . . Quippe quo Conditor custodiens castos, in eterni amoris incendium hos erigit eo subtilius incendit et *abstrahit* ab illicitis, cadente *concupiscencia* carnali . . . *Requiritur* recte regibus quo reficiuntur dulcedine divina, ne reprobis ruant a regno, ut *magnam mentis et corporis quietem capiant. Sic quidem eos invisibilis ignis amoris incendia inflammant* . . .

Item 4: *Contra Amatores Mundi* as a source for *Melos Amoris*

[This part of *Melos Amoris* (cap. 47) is about the relative merits of eremitic and coenobitic lives. Rolle quotes a passage from *Contra Amatores Mundi* which deals with the related question of the merits of eremitic and active lives, making it relevant to its new context by adding a sentence which helpfully begins with the phrase 'et hoc audeo annuere' (most MSS read 'annectere').]

(Contra Amatores Mundi, 4.102–19)
Nam omnis melodia mundialis, omnisque corporalis musica instrumentis organicis machinata, quantumcumque activis seu secularibus viris negociis implicatis placuerint, contemplativis vero desiderabilia non erunt. Immo fugiunt corporalem audire sonitum, quia in se contemplativi viri iam sonum susceperunt celestem. Activi vero in exterioribus gaudent canticis, nos contemplacione divina succensi in sono epulantis terrena transvolamus; illi nostrum nesciunt, nos illorum nesciamus gaudium, quia dum intra nos celestias delicias sonora voce iubilantes canimus, nimirum ab omnibus psallentibus et loquentibus segregari affectamus. Alioquin iam desinimus canere, atque ab illa invisibilis gaudii affluencia cessare, ut dum ab illis corporaliter perstrepentibus non fugimus, veraciter discamus quia nemo unquam in amore Dei gaudere potuit, qui prius vana istius mundi solacia non dereliquit. Cogor autem hec isto modo dicere, ne quod aliis scribo me iudicent caruisse.

(Melos Amoris, 145.30–146.2; 146.29–38)
Nimirum hoc quod novi nuncio. *Nam omnis mundialis melodia, omnis corporalis musica instrumentis organicis machinata, quantumcumque activis viris et secularibus negociis implicatis placuerint, sanctis profecto contemplativis desiderabilia non erunt. Immo et hoc audeo annuere quia fervore fruentes dulciflue dileccionis fremitum fugiunt et,* canoro capti iubilo, eciam psallencium solempnia audiunt inviti; utpote qui *iam sonum susceperant celicum, clamori corporali ulterius non concordant . . . Activi in exterioribus exultant organis. Nos contemplacione Creatoris succensi suaviter in sono epulantis terrena transvolamus. Illi nostrum nesciunt gaudium; nos illorum neupma nequimus, quia dum intra nos delicias divinas sonora voce iubilantes canimus, ab omnibus profecto psallentibus et loquentibus cupimus segregari. Alioquin iam desinimus canere atque ab illa invisibilis melodie affluencia cessamus ut dum ab illis corporaliter perstrepentibus non fugimus, veraciter discamus quia nemo unquam in amore Dei gaudere potuit nisi qui vana istius mundi solacia recte reliquit.*

Rolle's reading and the reliability of the *Officium*

Chapter 1 avoids addressing the issue of how far the account of Rolle's life provided by the *Officium* is reliable. My concern there is with showing that his life did not correspond to saintly and eremitic norms, however much it is presented in terms of those norms by the compilers of the *Officium* or by Rolle. In such a context it makes small difference who is doing the normalizing, since it is in the interests of all parties – the compilers, Rolle as he lives out his life, and Rolle as he writes about it – to make as saintly a thing as possible out of the raw material. Indeed, this community of interests is what gives one most confidence in the work's reliability. We can surely take for granted that Rolle did in fact become a hermit without ecclesiastical licence, that he did move his cell and change his patron, that he was criticized on that account, and that he remained in canon law an eremitic 'irregular'; nobody anxious to have him canonized would invent or imply these biographical details unless they were unavoidable facts.

Yet the literary and formalizing tendencies evident in the *Officium* have certainly distorted Rolle's biography as well as laying it open, even once we have distinguished between what the text says and what Horstmann and his successors say it says. Occasionally this shows up in a specific detail. For example, the first two *lectiones* of the *Officium* have their protagonist rushing – oddly but symbolically garbed – into the wilderness, arriving at the Daltons, and preaching a sermon in the church they attend, on the Feast of the Assumption. Steele (1979, p. 59) points out that this is a highly appropriate occasion for Rolle to preach his one recorded sermon, because the gospel for the day is Luke 10.38–42, the story of Martha and Mary, and sermons preached on this day expound the relationship between the active and contemplative lives. Thus according to the *Officium*, Rolle left home on the vigil of a feast commemorating the superiority of contemplative to active life, and at once availed himself of an opportunity to expound his decision for the spiritual benefit of others. This looks suspiciously neat. There is, in a sense, a literary imagination at work in anybody's decision to move from active to contemplative life, since such a decision is based not only on a human exemplar but on a particular structure of understanding. But can this same literary imagination really lie behind the whole of the *Officium*'s account: both the impulsive energy of the protagonist's flight into the wilderness, and the care that goes into his clothing and the timing of his action? Can this all be the work of a self-conscious young man who is imitating St Francis and behaving in carefully symbolic ways, rather than being the product of retrospective interpretation? Given the half-century that separates the tale and the telling, it seems most unlikely.

On its own, this observation is trivial, and brings us back to a point that has already been well made in Alford's 1976 article (as in Noetinger's 1926 article), and that ought not, perhaps, to have been necessary to make at all: that the *Officium* is not an eye-witness account or biography, but a work written for religious (and I would add apologetic) purposes. Yet the scope of the observation can be considerably enlarged. If the *Officium* simplifies Rolle's conversion from the world into a partial re-enactment of a scene from Bonaventure's *Legenda S. Francisci*, how much else does it invent? Can we take its account of Rolle's departure from university at the age of eighteen as a historical record – or should we regard it as a fictional dramatization of his rejection of *scientia* for *sapientia*, which prepares the way for the conversion story that follows? Perhaps Rolle stayed longer at Oxford, and became a hermit much older. Doubt begins to qualify our acceptance of all the *Officium* says, except where there is corroboration from another source, or where the facts it reveals make it harder, not easier, for the compilers to present Rolle in a positive light.

It would be easy to overstate this case; after all, there must be a real relationship between the presentation of Rolle in the *Officium* and his actual life and personality, if only because the compilers rely heavily on *Incendium Amoris*, and produce what is in many ways so ingenuous an account. But there is one area in which the *Officium*, read in conjunction with some of Rolle's own apparently autobiographical remarks, has consistently proved misleading: in presenting him as an anti-intellectual with little interest in, and little access to, books. We see him abandoning an academic career, living with secular patrons, teaching women religious, and writing – but never reading, talking to learned people, or taking any kind of intellectual stance. This is arguing from omission, but the effect may be deliberate, for it broadens the analogy with the *Legenda S. Francisci* and other lives of simple saints. It also follows Rolle's self-presentation. His accounts of himself invite us to view him as an indigent, outcast by secular patrons and religious for his desire to love God rather than conform and live with others. He claims to be taught by the Holy Spirit, and assumes his enemies will think of him as ill-educated (*Incendium Amoris*, cap. 33); sometimes he seems to regard his enemies as primarily the learned, in a schematic opposition of *scientia* and *sapientia* (*Incendium Amoris*, caps. 5–7). These pictures of the wandering hermit – wretched in the world's eyes, joyful in the sight of God, living in pious ignorance far from places of learning – cannot be accurate reflections of his external circumstances. So much becomes clear if we consider his career in relation not to his own remarks about it but to what is implied by the kinds of works he wrote and the ways in which he apparently wrote them. The picture we get of his life from this perspective looks very different from anything the *Officium* or Rolle himself give us.

Rolle wrote hundreds of pages of careful Latin and English prose; he thus had a steady supply of parchment or paper, which could not necessarily be obtained easily, and was far from cheap. More than half of what he wrote is derived from a source. He must have had long-term access to at least one commentary on the Psalter for his *Latin Psalter* and *English Psalter*; to a glossed Bible for *Super Threnos* and similar works, to Anselm of Laon's commentary on the Apocalypse for *Super Apocalypsim*, and probably to another volume for his liturgical commentaries; to William of Pagula's *Oculus Sacerdotis*, which is the source for most of *Judica Me*, and which he must have seen soon after its completion; to the *Compendium Theologicae Veritatis*, which he uses in *Incendium Amoris* (a fairly early work) and extensively in *The Commandment* and *The Form of Living* (late works); and to his own earlier works, a number of which he borrows from extensively and accurately. All these sources must have been in front of him as he wrote – and writing two complete Psalter commentaries must have occupied two distinct and lengthy periods of time. There are also a number of works which he saw at some stage, but need not have had available to him for a long period. Richard of St Victor's *De Quattuor Gradibus Violentae Caritatis* is an important presence behind many of his works, as is Bernard's *De Diligendo Deo*, and to a lesser extent Hugh of St Victor's *De Laude Caritatis* and the hymn *Dulcis Ihesu Memoria*, which he perhaps knew by heart. He knew John of Hoveden's *Philomena*, and no doubt other devotional Latin poems; he knew Aelred's *De Spirituali Amicitia* or something like it, and perhaps the *De Ihesu Puero Duodecenni*, and had read

Excursus II: *Rolle's reading and the* Officium

Bernard's *Sermones Super Cantica Canticorum*, the pseudo-Bernardine *Meditationes Piissimae* and James of Milan's *Stimulus Amoris*, from all of which he borrows directly. He knew how to write a commentary that would be widely read in a university milieu (*Super Lectiones Mortuorum*), and how to construct a *quaestio*; indeed, he had studied *quaestiones* on the relations of active to contemplative and coenobitic to solitary lives, and on the different kinds of rapture. He knew how to construct a theme-sermon, and was experienced in penitential, ascetic and several other modes of writing. He must have known some alliterative English prose and was versed in Latin traditions of anti-feminine satire. He was a remarkably accomplished writer of affective Latin prose, and a trained rhetorician with some knowledge of secular Latin poetry – very likely acquired at Oxford. This vague list is not even the result of a systematic search; I am convinced that a full study of Rolle's sources and literary affiliations would reveal his specific indebtedness to numerous other works.

As it stands, this roster does not make Rolle a 'learned' writer. But it does make the picture of him we have inherited from Horstmann, Allen, Rolle himself and the compilers of the *Officium* look implausible. For one thing, there is no room in his eremitical rucksack for all the books he has to carry. For another, secular patrons like the Daltons would not have owned glossed Bibles or the writings of Hugh of Strasbourg; nor can we imagine them taking much interest in Rolle's vast writing projects. In the light of the evidence provided by his writings, I think we have to add the following suppositions to our picture of his life:

(1) Rolle's university career may well have been a longer and more serious one than the *Officium* allows. His earliest works, probably commentaries, show him to have self-confidence and the necessary skills as a writer. Derivative though they are they suggest his desire to articulate a theological position, for his own and others' benefit; this is the attitude of someone who thinks of himself as educated, and who assumes that others will regard him in the same light, in spite of all he says about his lack of learning. If he did not acquire this view of himself at Oxford, he must have undergone some kind of further education between going down and writing his first works.

(2) Most of Rolle's eremitic career must have been a fairly stable affair, for all his talk of wandering, and much of it must have been lived within reach of a library – belonging to a cathedral, a monastery or canonry, or a secular priest with a university training and a good income. He did, in that case, enjoy good as well as bad relations with clerics, and had intellectual companionship with people who regarded him as an educated man who could suitably use and perhaps borrow books. These people must have known what he wrote. He was also in a position to keep copies of his own writings near at hand, and to refer to them again at will. He evidently cared very much for their preservation, and left them in suitable hands at his death.

(3) Rolle's writing career must then have been a less isolated phenomenon than it looks. We know that *Judica Me* and some late works were written for specific people; other works must also have been written in the expectation that they would find readers, and not merely as subjective and undirected exercises in devotional or apologetic effusion. Assuming that he had no financial resources of his own – as he often states – somebody must have provided the wherewithal for his work, and thus presumably took an interest in it. In effect, Rolle must have had a clerical patron or patrons in addition to the secular patron mentioned in the *Officium*.

(4) There is, of course, little we can say with certainty about Rolle's clerical patronage; there is no telling even whether his 'patrons', 'readers' and

'disciples' were the same people. Two points, however, are worth making. First, Rolle had access to a good deal of material written in Yorkshire or by Yorkshiremen – works by Aelred, John of Hoveden and William of Pagula. His educated acquaintances thus included people with an interest in local religious writing. The second point depends on the truth of two claims: Boyle's that William of Pagula's *Oculus Sacerdotis* was not widely read in the first years after its completion in 1326–1328 (Boyle 1955, pp. 105–106), and mine that *Judica Me* must have been written early in Rolle's career, and thus within a few years of 1328. If both claims are true, Rolle's use of *Oculus Sacerdotis* is a sign that whoever owned the copy he used had strong connections with the south of England and probably with Oxford. William of Pagula was vicar of a Salisbury parish near Windsor Forest, but studied at Oxford and may have done much of his writing there. It has been argued (by Gillespie 1981, p. 95) that lengthy and sophisticated manuals such as *Oculus Sacerdotis* were written largely for university graduates, rather than ordinary parish priests. Oxford is thus a likely centre for the distribution of the work, and the most likely source of a copy that reached Rolle in the north of England within a few years. Perhaps Rolle knew an Oxford graduate with an interest in pastoral writing, and had at least an indirect link with the university some years after leaving it.

All this has more ifs and perhapses than one would like; but it does seem to provide a picture of the background to Rolle's writing career coherent enough for us to use them to amplify the impressions he and his would-be canonizers have given. This career must have had a close relationship with the literary and religious interests of one or more 'educated clerics', who provided Rolle with books and perhaps writing materials, and who may have constituted the immediate audience for most of his Latin works. If these clerics had Oxford connections, they were able to appreciate Rolle's virtuoso handling of different literary modes – satire, various kinds of commentary, literary sermons and exercises in many different prose styles – and could understand his uncommonly wide vocabulary. Some of them must also be assumed to have liked what he wrote – a taste for Rolle seems compatible with one for John of Hoveden and the *De Quattuor Gradibus Violentae Caritatis*.

This frustratingly shadowy background of clerical readers and patrons is, then, the most important of the things that we can deduce the *Officium* leaves out of its account of Rolle's life, just as Rolle leaves them out of his own autobiographical remarks. There was presumably no cause to mention them in works written to edify, and they do tend to complicate the picture both the *Officium* and Rolle like to present of his life and works as the direct products of divine inspiration, and as proclaiming a sapiential rather than learned spiritual message. Their absence from the work need not further undermine our sense of the reliability of the *Officium*.

Notes

1 One vital element in late-medieval discussions of perfection, the concept of perfect poverty, is not discussed here, since Rolle's references to the concept seem self-explanatory, untouched by the bitter thirteenth- and fourteenth-century controversies over its meaning.

2 No detailed study of the active and contemplative lives has appeared in print, the fullest being pp. 225–325 of Cuthbert Butler's *Western Mysticism* (1927), which deals with Augustine, Gregory and Bernard; Clark 1979 is a useful shorter study. For this outline I have mostly drawn on Francis Steele's outstandingly helpful thesis on the active life (1979), with some reference to Christopher Pankhurst's thesis on all three lives (1976).

3 See, e.g., Butler 1927, pp. 236–242 (citing Augustine's *Confessiones*, the *De Civitate Dei*, etc.), and pp. 253–273 (citing Gregory's *Regula Pastoralis*, *Moralia in Job* and *Homilia in Ezechiel*); see also Steele 1979, chapter 3.

4 Clark 1979, pp. 260–261 quotes a passage of Bede's *Homilia* where this rigid way of distinguishing active and contemplative lives is already evident.

5 Caps. 16–23 of this work also provide a detailed analysis of the Martha and Mary story, which (as Hodgson's notes show) makes extensive use of Augustine's sermons and are typical of the tradition I am here describing.

6 *Utrum Vita Solitaria Sit Perfectior Vita Viventium in Congregatione*: the title of one of three *quaestiones* edited in Oliger 1934 on which the present account is based. Two are anonymous, one is from Aquinas, *Summa Theologica* II.ii., q. 188, art. 8. The three occur together in two MSS, Magdalen 141 and Cotton Junius A.IX (both c. 1400, (?) Carthusian), the Oxford MS also containing other works on the solitary life, including the Latin translation of Hilton's *Scale of Perfection* and Petrarch's *De Vita Solitaria*.

7 I follow Steele (1979), Pankhurst (1976) and others in using the term 'mixed', albeit in quotation marks. The term was not widely used in the Middle Ages, but the concept was nonetheless a real one. The alternatives to the term are even less satisfactory: Robertson and Huppé's 'prelatical' (1957, pp. 236–237) is an ugly modern coinage, and other possibilities, such as 'vita ex utraque composita', amount to lengthy periphrases for 'mixed'.

8 Steele 1979, chapter 4, shows that Augustine and Gregory were regarded as the great authorities on the 'lives' in the late Middle Ages. The triadic model of active–contemplative–'mixed' lives could be plotted on to the binary model of Martha–Mary by grammatical casuistry: commentators argued (as in cap. 21 of *The Cloud of Unknowing*, and examples in Steele, p. 242) that Mary can only be said to have the 'best' part if there is a 'good' and a 'better' one as well; thus Luke 10 is concerned with three states of life, not two.

9 Chapter 9 of Pantin 1955 (pp. 189–219) is still a useful introduction to this

material, and, for the preaching that resulted, Owst 1926. For vernacular manuals see Gillespie 1981, with its bibliography. The present discussion of preaching also makes use of Leclerq 1946, Gillespie 1980 and Minnis 1986.

10 The passage is translated from a Latin compilation called *Cibus Anime*, which makes a good deal of use of Rolle; see Gillespie 1981 (pp. 188–245) and 1983 for a discussion of this work and its sources.

11 Hugh distinguishes between the act of preaching and its office, in a passage borrowed from Aquinas (VII, cap. 31, see *Summa Theologica* III, q. 96, art. 7): 'Nec est dicendum, ut quidam voluerunt, quod haec aureola debeatur tantummodo illis quibus competit praedicare ex officio, et docere; sed quibuscumque exercentibus licite actum istum. Praelatis autem non debetur haec aureola, quamvis habeant officium praedicandi, nisi et actu praedicent, quia aureola non debetur habitui, sed actui pugnae.' While the qualification is important, so is the tendency which it seeks to correct, of thinking of preachers as worthy of an aureole *ex officio*.

12 The twists and turns in Aquinas's argument are good evidence of how shadowy the concept of the 'mixed' life remained. Aquinas does not mention it as such, arguing that 'Life is adequately divided into active and contemplative' (q. 179, art. 2), and that the contemplative life is of more merit than the active (q. 182, arts. 1–2), but that, in spite of this, perfection resides more fully in prelates than in religious. However, this ruling applies only to bishops; archdeacons and priests are not so perfect as bishops, since they can change their state (q. 184, art. 6), and religious are accordingly more perfect than priests (art. 8) – this with many qualifications. The idea of the 'mixed' life seems to operate in the interstices of all these arguments, as a powerful pressure the source of which is never fully articulated. It comes closest to the surface in q. 188, art. 6, which distinguishes between two forms of the active life, the higher of which, consisting of teaching and preaching, is better than simple contemplation, since it proceeds from the fullness of contemplation.

13 Hence the progress of Piers from plowman (active) to pilgrim (contemplative) to Pope ('mixed'); see also Conscience's speech in C XXI, which associates Dobest with Christ's bestowal of authority on the Church (183–190). Derek Pearsall's note on C x.78–98, in his edition of *Piers Plowman* C, is doubtful about this reading of Do-wel, Do-bet and Do-best, citing an article by S.S. Hussey (1956), which shows that 'Do-best' does not correspond to Hilton's 'medled' life, as had been claimed. This is true, but as T.P. Dunning pointed out in the same year, Hilton's treatment of 'medled' life is untraditional, and conventional references to the concept treat it as the exercise rather of prelatical authority (see pp. 232–237). The very fact that Langland calls Do-best a bishop suggests that he is trying to evoke the idea of 'mixed' life. (For an opposing view, see Godden 1990, pp. 20–21 etc.)

14 See also his Latin *Epistola ad Quemdam Seculo Renunciare Volentem* (*Latin Writings*, vol. 2, pp. 249–298), which has much in common with *Mixed Life*.

15 This appeal to the idea that 'actives' underestimate contemplatives because they do not understand them is common both in Rolle and in writing on the lives; see, e.g., *Summa Theologica* II.ii, q. 188, art. 8, reply obj. 4.

16 Early readers of *Incendium Amoris* clearly saw cap. 13 as a contribution to the debate about the lives, for in several MSS (e.g. Emmanuel 35, Dd.v.64) it bears the introductory rubric: 'Quod vita solitaria seu heremitica vitam communem et mixtam precellit' (179).

17 One of the best accounts of the rise of affective spirituality outlined in this paragraph is still Woolf's study of Middle English lyrics (1968). For the devotion

to the Holy Name, see Wilmart 1943, Cabusset 1952 and Moyes 1984 (pp. 89–92); for an account of the Middle English material alluded to in this paragraph, see Sargent 1981; for a survey of the influence of twelfth-century writers on the late Middle Ages, see Constable 1971.

18 In these two paragraphs I am indebted to David Carlson's scrupulously structuralist thesis on 'Structural similarities between the literatures of mysticism and *fin' amors*', which looks at the relationship between Richard of St Victor's and Rolle's 'grades of love' in a way which has also influenced my reading of Hugh (chapter 3). I am not aware of any other scholarly treatments of the tradition of writing about 'violent' love outlined here, except in surveys such as Rousselet 1908, though it influenced writers as diverse as Dante, Hadewijch and John of Hoveden, and makes an early appearance in Middle English at the end of part VII of *Ancrene Wisse* (ff. 110b–111a); but see the survey of twelfth-century writers in Ghellinck 1954.

I. INTERPRETING ROLLE'S LIFE

1 I accept Allen's verdict on all the works she considers to be Rolle's except for the treatise *De Dei Misericordia*, which has been convincingly reattributed to the Augustinian Friar John Waldeby (Hackett 1956, pp. 464–466). I include tentatively one work she lists as doubtful, in spite of its appearance in two large MS collections and several printed editions of Rolle's works, the commentary *Super Symbolum S. Athanasii* (p. 312). The rest of Allen's *dubia* can be dismissed; they seem to have been included out of deference to Carl Horstmann and other scholars, and for the most part in the absence of any evidence for Rolle's authorship. (For the authorship of the Passion meditations, see further Chapter 9, n. 9.)

2 Among the more important examples of medieval recasting of Rolle are: a short version of *Incendium Amoris*; several collections of extracts from that work; abbreviations of *Melos Amoris* and *Super Canticum Canticorum*; a compilation from *Super Canticum Canticorum* and *Incendium Amoris* known as *Oleum Effusum*; a compilation from *Emendatio Vitae, Super Canticum Canticorum, Super Psalmum Vicesimum* and probably other works called *De Excellentia Contemplationis*; and another compilation of passages in praise of the Holy Name in MS Kk.vi.20 (edited by Esposito 1982). Some of his works were translated into English (*Incendium Amoris*, part of *Super Canticum Canticorum*, and *Emendatio Vitae* at least seven times); some of his English works (two of the epistles) were rendered into Latin. Among the works attributed to Rolle were *The Prick of Conscience*, William Flete's *De Remediis*, and the anonymous *Contemplacyons of the Drede and Loue of God*.

3 The earliest firmly datable MS copy of a work by Rolle of which I am aware (BL Add. 34763) is as late as 1384, thirty-five years after his death (Allen, pp. 46 and 236). Allen gives an index of MSS (pp. 563–567), to which should be added several discoveries summarized by Moyes (1984, p. 97, n. 15). Allen also gives an account of early printed editions (pp. 9–14), the last six of which are Continental. One of them, Johann Faber's edition of *Emendatio Vitae* and a number of other works (Cologne 1535; there was an expanded edition in 1536) was reprinted as part of vol. 15 of de la Bigne's *Magna Bibliotheca Veterum Patrum* in 1622, and in vol. 26 of its reprint (Cologne 1654) and final expansion (*Maxima Bibliotheca Veterum Patrum*; Lyons 1677 and Cologne 1694). 1694 was the last year any work of Rolle's was printed until EETS published *Hampole's English Prose Treatises*, edited by G.G. Perry (and containing little real Rolle) in 1866.

4 The *Officium* is as circumstantial as a saint's life. (One version of the *Officium*,

found in MS Uppsala c.621, edited by Lindkvist in 1917, indeed consists only of the biographical *lectiones*, presumably for reading as a *Vita Sancti Ricardi Heremitae.*) Vauchez (1981, pp. 111–112, n. 36), notes that Offices of this type were written for private reading and (in spite of the *Officium*'s opening disclaimer) for unofficial public worship. However, with *miracula* included in two of the four MSS, it seems likely that the work was also meant to play a part in an attempt (for which it is our only evidence) to have Rolle canonized. This possibility (borne out by the work's occasional lapses into apologetic) forces us to be cautious in treating its accounts as historically accurate. Still, the work abounds in details (people and places) which suggest its outline to be factual, and confirm Allen's hypothesis that it originated from a source close to Rolle himself (Allen, pp. 51, 517). For further discussion, see Excursus II.

5 For drawings of Rolle, see the (seventeenth-century) frontispiece to MS Laud Misc. 528 and the illustration in BL Add. 37049's copy of *The Desert of Religion* (ff. 52v., 37r.), reproduced by Freemantle (1911, p. 164), along with a depiction of Rolle from the frontispiece to Wynkyn de Worde's edition of *Contemplacyons of the Drede and Loue of God* (1506); a scrawl in Cambridge Mm.v.37, f. 21r. may also depict Rolle. Annotations referring to Rolle by name occur in MS Dd.v.64's copy of *Incendium Amoris*, beside the autobiographical narratives in caps. 15 and 31.

6 *Oleum Effusum* survives in ten MSS in Latin, four in English (Allen, pp. 67–68), and consists of two autobiographical passages of *Incendium Amoris* (caps. 12 and 15, with part of the didactic cap. 8), a fragment of pseudo-Anselm, and the last four sections of *Super Canticum Canticorum*. Cap. 15 of *Incendium Amoris* is found between sections IV and V of *Super Canticum Canticorum* in MSS Jesus College Cambridge 46, ff. 100v.–103v., Harley 5235, ff. 13v.–14v. and several early printed editions, and appears alone in Arundel 507, f. 49v.

7 Hilton's treatise *Of Angels' Song* apparently warns the reader away from too simple an understanding of Rolle's concept of *canor* (Clark 1978). Perhaps a problem arose when material on the subject that Rolle had written in Latin became available to uneducated enthusiasts – e.g. in two independent English translations of the *Enconium Nominis Ihesu* (part of section IV of *Super Canticum Canticorum*) in MSS Harley 1022, f. 62 and Trinity College Dublin 155, or in the form in which it was included in the popular tract *Pore Caitif* (see Allen, pp. 68, 406, Brady 1983). Rolle's imaginative appeal is also evident in the cult of the Holy Name. Moyes 1984, discussing annotations in several Rolle MSS in which the Holy Name is mentioned (e.g. Kk.vi.20, Magdalen 71, Bodleian th. d. 15, Lyell 38), concludes: 'In the eyes of some medieval readers, the mere repetition of the word "Ihesu" in the context of a Rolle work evoked a response denied to the same words in another writer's work' (p. 91).

8 For a more general study of Rolle scholarship, see Moyes 1988, chapter 1, 'The critical position', which comes to similar conclusions as I do here.

9 Of these three writers, only Underhill shows any interest in Rolle. The first modern champion of Rolle as a mystic was R.H. Benson, whose anthology *The Book of the Love of Jesus* (1909) is a selection of modernizations from Horstmann. Interest in Rolle stemmed both from this collection and from a new historical concern with medieval devotion – manifested in the publication of R.M. Clay's *Hermits and Anchorites of England* in 1914, and two years later of F.D. Darwin's *English Mediaeval Recluse*. Rolle was naturally a focus of such a concern, the more so since Horstmann presented many characteristics of late-medieval English devotion – devotion to the Passion and the Holy Name, and a mood of spiritual extravagance – as deriving directly from him; he thus came to be seen as the

foremost representative of the spirituality of his time. The truth of Horstmann's view was widely accepted, for Allen's seminal article, 'The mystical lyrics of the *Manuel des Péchiez*' (*Romanic Review*, 9, 1918), challenges it as though it is the established scholarly position.

10 In addition to these secondary studies, Rolle's real and spurious English works were much published between 1910 and 1930, in modernized versions and in slim, attractive volumes, always with biographical introductions. They provided a devout Catholic and Anglo-Catholic readership with material that could be considered at once charmingly simple and esoteric. See especially G. Hodgson 1910, 1923, 1929a, Comper 1916 and Heseltine 1930.

11 See, e.g., Pepler 1948, 1958, 1959; Womack 1961, Wright 1963, Jennings 1975, Russell 1978. Womack champions the quality of Rolle's mystical experience; other scholars are dubious or condescending (Knowles 1961, pp. 53–54 especially so). The problem for devout modern readers of at least Rolle's Latin works is that he is shocking as often as he is edifying; yet the natural reaction to this state of affairs, to deny him the status of an important mystic, makes it impossible to read him at all, for his whole output is posited on the assumption of his high spiritual status. Besides this, a tendency to assume first that Rolle's English works depict his own spiritual state rather than being written to the needs of his audience, second that mystical experience always follows the patterns set by the sixteenth-century Spanish mystics, seems to me to vitiate most of these studies.

12 Noetinger's outstanding work on Rolle is his French translation of *Incendium Amoris* (1928), the introduction to which builds on the article here discussed. His view of Rolle remains influential, in some respects nearly as much as Allen's; it is particularly evident in the work of other French-speaking scholars – Renaudin (1945, 1957), Madon (1950), Arnould (1957), Marzac (1968), Vandenbroucke (1971) – who all tend to assume that Rolle was learned, saintly and at worst eccentric in a typically English way.

13 Allen's treatment of Noetinger's argument was at first rather uncertain (see Allen, pp. 490–500); but in a letter to *The Times Literary Supplement* (17 March 1932; Allen 1932a) she decides against Rolle's priestly status. This letter was answered by George Heseltine, the first modern English translator of *Incendium Amoris* (1932b; 14 April 1932), who reiterates Noetinger's views. Allen soon counterattacked (1932b; 14 July) and has much the better of the exchange.

14 Flight from parents is often mentioned as part of the abandonment of worldly obligations in the *Vitae Patrum* (which Rolle certainly knew). See, e.g., the *Vitae* of Pachomius (caps. 3–4) and Simeon Stylites (cap. 1; PL 73, cols. 232–233, 325–326); the latter abandons his father's sheep to talk to a holy man, to whom he is soon saying 'Tu es pater meus et mater mea'.

15 Francis seeks solitude immediately after leaving his father, and is given a poor tunic by a friend in Gubbio (cap. 2). Parallels between the narratives may reflect the traditional nature of both rather than the influence of the *Legenda* on the *Officium* or of Francis on Rolle; the circumstantial details involved in each are different, and Moyes challenges a critical tradition of comparing Rolle and Francis, implying that it is too vague to be useful (1988, vol. 1, p. 10). But I think it possible that the compilers of the *Officium* were at least trying to capture the tone of the narratives of Francis.

16 See further Clay 1914, pp. 85–90, and V. Davis 1985, p. 207. Versions of such offices survive in pontificals from Exeter and York (Clay, pp. 86, 94); at least four others refer to the benediction of hermits or their garments.

17 The *Legenda* is, by contrast, concerned to stress to the point of fiction the ecclesiastical involvement in Francis's change of garb; Bonaventure has the bishop

(and later the Pope) clothe him with his new garments. In Giotto's Assisi fresco of Francis's 'renunciation', taken out of the *Legenda*, the saint stands in a baptismal posture on the right of the painting, in front of a group of ecclesiastics, and opposite his father, who likewise stands in front of a group of citizens: an arrangement which stresses both the symbolic and institutional significance of the event.

18 Rolle uses the phrase 'singulare propositum' to allude either to his own experience or to the eremitic life in general (e.g., *Judica Me* 15.22–16.16, *Incendium Amoris* 180.14–15), and calls monks 'obedienciarii' in caps. 47–48 of *Melos Amoris*, where he is critical of the type of holiness that depends on obedience to a vow. For Rolle the hermit is distinctive since his life is freely undertaken, and is responsible only to God. The phrase 'singulare propositum' is also found in the *Regula Heremitarum* where it is quoted from an unidentified sermon by St Maximinus (pp. 299–300). The *Regula* in turn may derive the reference from cap. 72 of Peter the Cantor's *Verbum Abbreviatum* (*Commendatio Solitudinis Loci*), which records an item from 'Maximinus episcopus' that describes the 'singulare propositum' of anchorites (PL 205, col. 215). But the word 'propositum' also occurs in Peter Damian's discussion of hermits in the *De Contemptu Saeculi* (cap. 24, PL 144, col. 277), and was widely current as a word for designating any formal religious undertaking not bound by a vow. The Oxford *Regula* (cap. iv, p. 313) states that the hermit makes a vow of poverty and chastity to God, but not to anyone else, unless he wishes to make a vow to his bishop and live 'secundum consilium suum'.

19 The place of hermits in medieval English society awaits the detailed analysis given anchorites in Anne Warren's book *Anchorites and their Patrons* (1985). (References to recent research on hermits can be gleaned from the articles in W.J. Sheils 1985.) It is clear from Warren's analysis (especially chapter 3) that bishops and their delegates took care to ensure that an anchorite had proper financial backing and spiritual commitment before being allowed to submit to the rigours of enclosure. Yet entry into the anchoritic life involved the taking of vows, being deprived of most of the means of getting food and clothing, and adopting a defined pattern of behaviour. While at its most rigorous the eremitic life may have resembled the anchoritic, its structure was not so defined, and it seems that bishops did not exercise the authority over hermits, or take on the responsibilities towards them, that they did with respect to anchorites. In a striking passage of *Piers Plowman* C (ix.187–281), Langland complains that bishops are doing nothing to curb the spread of hermits who live idly and do not attend Mass or live to a rule; these hermits do not render due obedience to the Church (219–239), and the responsibility for their existence lies heavily on the episcopate (255–281). According to the *Dictionnaire de droit canonique* article on 'Ermites' (vol. 5, cols. 413–429), such complaints were common in the fifteenth century, indirectly leading to post-Tridentine attempts to achieve a better definition of the place of hermits, and to place them under a rule.

20 For the Monk of Farne see Farmer 1957; for discussion of the author of *The Cloud of Unknowing* see P. Hodgson, 1982, pp. ix–xii, and for Hilton's eremitism *Latin Writings*, vol. 1, pp. 69, 103–105. Hilton's move away from life as a hermit into a community seems as indicative of his mature view of the hermit's life as is his epistle *On the Mixed Life*. Malcolm Godden suggests we add Langland to the list of eremitic writers (1984, pp. 162–163), as a *girovagus* in the tradition of one of Helen Waddell's 'wandering scholars'. Yet while the wandering hermit is undoubtedly one of Will's roles, and may have been one of Langland's, it seems doubtful that a serious medieval religious writer would consistently have thought

of himself as a *girovagus*. Godden's case depends on a parallel with Rolle, whom he portrays as more or less a self-declared *girovagus*, using Allen's reconstruction of Rolle's career as evidence. The rest of this chapter shows why this is inappropriate.

21 The *Regula* survives in two substantially different Latin versions (a longer 'Cambridge' one from Mm.vi.17, ff. 70v.–76v., a shorter 'Oxford' one from Rawlinson c.72, ff. 166v.–169v.), and three English MSS which ascribe the rule to Pope Celestine (Sloane 1584, ff. 89r.–95v., BL Add. 34193, ff. 131 *et seq.*, Bristol 6, ff. 137r.–140r.). In spite of the support the editor of the Latin versions of the *Regula* gives (Oliger 1928, pp. 162–165), Allen's development of Horstmann's theory that the *Regula* is the 'Libellus de Vita Eremitarum', mentioned in *Super Lectiones Mortuorum* (196.19, quoted on pp. 206–207) as one of Rolle's own works, is baseless. (See Horstmann 1895–1896, vol. 2, p. xxxvii; Allen, pp. 324–329 lists the *Regula* under *dubia*, but shows a good deal of enthusiasm for the idea that Rolle might have written it; Warren 1985, pp. 297–298 has given the theory further currency.) This *libellus* is clearly not a formal Rule at all, since it is mentioned – in the same breath as the 'Liber de Perfeccione et Gloria Sanctorum', i.e. *Melos Amoris* (see Chapter 7, n. 2) – as helpful for those who want to read about how contemplatives are more fervent, and sing to God more freely, than those in active life. Rolle is most likely to be referring to *Incendium Amoris*. Allen cites the *Regula*'s use of the phrase 'singulare propositum', and its teaching about the independence of hermits – that they 'should offer obedience to God alone' (Oliger 1928, p. 304), a remark on which she builds a theory about Rolle's heretical leanings (pp. 331–335). But as we have seen (n. 18), the phrase 'singulare propositum' is commonplace. Moreover, hermits are often described as owing obedience only to God; the *Dictionnaire de droit canonique* (vol. 5, cols. 417ff.) shows that their position was defined in just these terms in medieval canon law. There are no grounds for thinking Rolle wrote this work.

22 For a useful discussion of this topic, see the *Dictionnaire de droit canonique*'s article on 'Stabilité monastique' (vol. 7, cols. 1078–1086); the distinction it makes between *stabilitas loci* and *stabilitas morum* is fundamental to the following discussion, and to all Rolle's allusions to the concept.

23 For *girovagi*, see, e.g., Damian's description of wandering hermits in *De Contemptu Saeculi* (PL 144, cols. 271–276), and Payen Bolotin's satirical poem (twelfth century) 'De Falsis Heremitis qui Vagando Discurrant' (edited by Leclerq 1958). The verb of motion 'discurrere' sums up the restless worldly energy which characterizes this group; it occurs in the *Regula*, frequently in Damian and Bolotin, and finds a Middle English equivalent in the Prologue to *Piers Plowman*, where 'Bidders and beggers *fast about 3ede*' (C 41). This Prologue, like much else in *Piers Plowman*, is full of the motifs of anti-girovagal satire: the wandering Will in his hermit's garb is a typical *girovagus*, all too like the heaps of beggars and hermits described in 41–55 as greedy and idle womanizers, who have dressed in eremitic garb for cynical reasons; set against these false contemplatives are true hermits and anchorites who 'holdeth hem in here celles' (30) – see further Bloomfield 1961, pp. 24, 67–71, Godden 1984. The history of anti-girovagal satire is complicated by the fact that in the thirteenth and fourteenth centuries it was annexed to the purposes of anti-fraternal satire (Szittya 1977); but, as the *Regula* and the Prologue to *Piers Plowman* witness, it was still applied to hermits.

24 By claiming to conform to those around him, so as to avoid appearing holier than he is, Rolle draws on St Paul's assertion that he '*became all things to all men*' (1 Corinthians 9.22), and more directly on a tradition of monastic writing against 'singularity' in matters of fasting, prayer or vigil (see, e.g., Bernard, *Sermones super Cantica Canticorum* 19.7). But this tradition was meant to apply to monks, friars

or nuns living with others of their kind, not to a hermit eating with secular patrons. The *Regula Heremitarum* (Oxford version, caps. 6 and 13) envisages that hermits will eat alone in their cells, unless they have to travel (cap. 11), when they must eat what they are given – as Patience does in Conscience's house in *Piers Plowman* (C xv), where he is fed with coarse food 'at a syde-table' (42), which I take it is what Rolle means here by 'communiter et duriori modo'. Rolle implies that he was sometimes fed in this way, but that on occasion he dined at the table of the families under whose patronage he was living, more in the style of a family chaplain than a hermit. See also *Melos Amoris*, caps. 42–43, especially 130.6ff.

25 Rolle could have claimed, with e.g. William of St Thierry's *Epistola Aurea* (XXII) as his authority, that meditation and writing were themselves forms of manual labour, and were more suitable for the contemplative than harder physical work. But his works do not discuss these, or any other, activities as manual labour. One passage of the *Officium* makes great claims for Rolle's asceticism in other areas; it has him punishing his body with many fasts and vigils, repudiating all softness in his clothing or bedding, living in a small and bare cell (*lectio quinta*: 'Maceravit carnem suam multis ieiuniis, crebris vigiliis, insistendo singultibus atque suspiriis, deserens omnem strati molliciem, scamnum durum habens pro lecto, brevem casellam pro domo . . . '). This does not fit the situation suggested by *Incendium Amoris*; perhaps the compilers of the *Officium* – like the annotations in MS Vienna 4483, which make much of Rolle's austerities (ff. 136v.–137r.; Allen, pp. 42–43) – were trying to make their protagonist conform to type, or referring to austerities he practised at the beginning of his career.

26 Although I have here focussed on Rolle's relationship with his patrons, there is evidence that an important group who propagated stories about him were monks. Cap. 31 of *Incendium Amoris* and cap. 1 of *Melos Amoris* state that he had to defend himself against monks who thought he should share their way of life (which in their estimation was superior to his) and that he tried unavailingly to answer them by explaining, for the first time, about his gift of *canor*. Both chapters are of crucial importance to Rolle's self-definition as a writer, since they act as his justification for proclaiming publicly a mystical experience which he initially thinks of as private; thus they are evidently accounts of an incident which was also crucial. It seems from the aggressive tone of the chapters and of Rolle's remarks about monks everywhere that the issue was unresolved, and that he regarded some monks frankly as enemies; see especially *Melos Amoris*, cap. 46, where we find the trenchant remark 'Odium et invidiam tantam non inveni nec habui inter omnes mortales sicut sustinui ab hiis qui se dicebant discipulos Iesu Christi' (143.29–31). The precise form of the hate and envy Rolle has suffered is never made clear, but it seems reasonable to suppose that the persecuting monks may have been in the front line of those accusing him of being a *girovagus*: an accusation which would have stung all the more coming from that particular quarter.

27 'Pax est in cella nil exterius ubi bella. / Si pacem queris tunc rarius egredieris. / Dina, Cain, Corus, Esau, Iuda, Semeyis / Egressum vobis ostendunt periculosum' (*Regula*, p. 301). Wandering friars are constantly identified with Cain in anti-fraternal satire: see examples given in Szittya 1977, p. 312.

28 Rolle's use of 'discursus', and, at 3.14, 'circumquaque discurrere', provide further evidence that he is here thinking of *girovagi*; see n. 23.

2. THE STRUCTURE OF ROLLE'S THOUGHT

1 Allen, pp. 66–68 lists Latin and English MSS of the *Enconium* (the fourth section of *Super Canticum Canticorum*); the texts found in two of the latter are printed in

Horstmann 1895–1896, vol. 1, pp. 186–191. There is a compilation of passages from Rolle's work concerned with Jesus in the fifteenth-century MS Kk.vi.20, ff. 11r.–26v., called *Orationes Excerpte de Diversis Tractatibus quos Composuit Beatus Ricardus Heremita ad Honorem Nominis Ihesu* (edited by Esposito 1982); see Moyes 1988, vol. 1, pp. 83–86.

2 Here Rolle may be following *Compendium Theologicae Veritatis* VII, caps. 26–28, which, however, lists the *dotes animae* as *cognitio, dilectio, comprehensio*; the *dotes corporis* are the same as in Rolle's list. For other lists of the attributes of the saved compare Aquinas's *Summa Theologica* III, q. 95, arts. 1, 5, *Prick of Conscience* 7813ff., and *Speculum Ecclesie*, sections 87–88. *Judica Me* 69.4–6 provides its own, shorter list.

3 Aquinas's *Summa Theologica* III, qq. 97–98, similarly makes much of the remorse felt by the damned (q. 97, art. 2), of their belated repentance for sin (q. 98, art. 2), and of the torment they experience seeing the blessed in joy, or, after the Judgement (when such sight is lost – see *Compendium Theologicae Veritatis* VII, cap. 22), remembering that sight (q. 98, art. 9).

4 The description of those elect who will judge others at the Judgement as *pauperes* is standard: Aquinas's *Summa Theologica* III, q. 89, art. 2, argues that Matthew 19.28, which gives the apostles a hand in the Judgement, applies to all the *pauperes*. *Compendium Theologicae Veritatis* also writes of a group of the elect who will judge others and not be judged themselves (VII, cap. 19).

5 See also *Super Canticum Canticorum* 11.24–12.4. Saintly rejoicing in the damnation of the evil is not mentioned in *Compendium Theologicae Veritatis*, but is part of a usual picture of the Judgement: see, e.g., *Summa Theologica* III, q. 94, arts. 1–3, and Innocent III's *De Miseria Condicionis Humane* 3.4.

6 Rolle is probably following either *Compendium Theologicae Veritatis* VII, cap. 19 ('Ordines quatuor erunt in judicio . . . ') or Lombard's gloss on Psalm 1.6 (which Rolle translates directly in *English Psalter* 8).

7 *Judica Me* 1.10 uses both phrases, the second of which can also be found in, e.g., Lombard's *Sententiae* IV, dist. xlv, 5 (entitled *Quibus Suffragiis Iuvabuntur Mediocriter Boni qui in Fine Reperientur*).

8 Rolle here alludes formally to the doctrine of prevenient grace, which states that even humanity's desire for grace is the product of grace; see, e.g., Lombard's *Sententiae* II, dist. xxvi, where much of the terminology of this passage of *Super Psalmum Vicesimum* can be found.

9 See cap. 36 of Guigo II's *Liber de Exercitio Cellae*, entitled *De Opere Manuum* (PL 153, cols. 880–883), where Benedict's injunction against idleness is used to introduce the subject of writing as manual work (col. 883).

10 Rolle alludes here to 1 Timothy, 4.8– '*Nam corporalis exercitatio ad modicum utilis est, pietas autem ad omnia utilis est*' – misquoting a verse which is commonly used by monastic writers to counter too great an emphasis on outer works; see, e.g., Bernard's *Sermones super Cantica Canticorum* 33.10. By citing this verse in support of its argument that contemplatives avoid *otiositas* not by working with the hands but by engaging in the sweet labour of contemplation, Rolle is reinterpreting the Benedictine concept of *labor*.

11 Womack 1961, pp. 104–111 rightly discusses Rolle's attitude to food and drink in terms of the monastic concept of *discretio*, citing in particular a discourse by Abbot Moses in Cassian's *Collationes* (II, PL 49, cols. 523–558, especially 549ff.). Rolle could have found discussions of conformity and discretion similar to his own in the *Meditationes Vitae Christi*, cap. 44, a study of poverty which draws heavily on Bernard and on William of St Thierry's *Epistola Aurea*. What is distinctive about his treatment is his emphasis on avoiding over-abstinence and corresponding lack

of interest in the danger of over-indulgence; see, e.g., *The Form of Living* 45–86, in which three lines are given to the former, nearly forty to the latter.

12 Contrast, e.g., Hilton's *Scale of Perfection*, with its intricate treatments of the variety of problems afflicting contemplatives (e.g. 1, caps. 36–40).

13 'Orationes sive meditationes quae subscriptae sunt, quoniam ad excitandum mentem ad Dei amorem vel timorem, seu ad suimet discussionem editae sunt, non sunt legendae in tumultu, sed in quiete . . . Nec debet intendere lector ut quamlibet earum totam perlegat, sed quantum sentit sibi Deo adiuvante valere ad accendendum affectum orandi, vel quantum illum delectat' (3.2–4, 5–8). Directly or indirectly this passage lies behind Rolle's devotional and private (i.e. non-liturgical) use of the triad *lectio, meditatio, oratio*.

14 Contrast the elaborate treatment of prayer and meditation in Book 1 of *The Scale of Perfection*, caps. 24–36.

15 Compare *Contra Amatores Mundi* 4.120–122: 'Pauci ergo sunt vel nulli quid illud [canor] referunt, quia forsitan illud nescierunt, si autem habuerint sed et aliis predicare nec verbo nec exemplo voluerunt.'

16 Pseudo-Anselm's gloss on this verse runs: '*Et ecce ostium apertum in coelo*, scilicet, clausura Scripturarum quae est via ad vitam, vel obscuritas coelestium mysteriorum, vel in his qui coelum sunt' (PL 162, col. 1517).

17 *Compendium Theologicae Veritatis* II, cap. 14 describes the Seraphim as distinguished by their fervent love: 'Proprium est Seraphim ardere et alios ad incendium divini amoris promovere.' For the analogy between the Seraphim and contemplatives see Bernard's *Sermones super Cantica Canticorum* 19.5.

3. ACTIVE LIFE: *JUDICA ME* AS APOLOGETIC PASTORAL

1 An article which draws on parts of this chapter (as well as on a portion of the material presented in Chapter 1), has been published in the volume *De Cella in Seculum*, edited by Michael Sargent (Watson 1989a).

2 For accounts of the pastoral manual as a genre, see Pantin 1955, chapter 9 and Boyle 1974. For the author, date, structure and purpose of *Oculus Sacerdotis*, see Boyle 1955. Daly's edition of *Judica Me* prints the parts of *Oculus Sacerdotis* which the work borrows; it is otherwise unedited.

3 Most of the sixteen MSS of *Judica Me* contain abridgements of the work, which omit one or more of its parts in a number of different ways (see Daly 1984, p. xxvi for a breakdown). There are five MSS of the complete work.

4 The verse makes an appropriate beginning for a work which is to be concerned with the priestly office, because (in the Sarum rite) Psalm 42 is recited by the priest before Mass (perhaps because verse 4 begins '*et introibo ad altare Dei*'). Thus in *Piers Plowman* B XI.284, Trajan quotes verse 1 as part of an appeal to priests to practise purity.

5 For the structure of the university sermon, see Robert of Basevorn's *Forma Praedicandi* and Ross 1940, pp. xliii–li. As in many of Rolle's works, this structure is not applied in any systematic way.

6 Margaret F. Nims provides the following definitions of these figures (1967, pp. 103–106): '*membrum* [colon]: two, or preferably three, succinct clauses, each complete in itself, but joined to express a total meaning'; '*exclamatio* [apostrophe]: an expression of grief or indignation, addressed to a person, place, or object'; '*contentio* [antithesis]: a statement built on contraries'; '*dissolutio* or *dissolutum* [asyndeton]: a concise series of clauses without connectives'; '*traductio*: (a) use of words with the same sound, but with different meaning or function; or (b) repetition of a single word, preferably in different cases'; '*conclusio*: a brief

argument deducing the necessary consequences of what has been said and done'. She defines as follows the two figures mentioned in the next paragraph: '*similiter cadens* [homoeoptoton]: two or more words with the same case ending, within one sentence'; '*similiter desinens* [homoeoteleuton]: two or more indeclinable words with the same endings, within one sentence'.

7 Rolle here avails himself of a number of common Judgement *topoi*. The first part of this quotation is a version of a famous passage in Anselm's *Meditatio* 1: 'O angustiae! Hinc erunt accusantia peccata, inde terrena iustitia; subtus patens horridum chaos inferni, desuper iratus iudex; intus urens conscientia, foris ardens mundus' (72–74). Rolle's adaptation removes many of the spatial metaphors, has world, flesh and devil accusing the reprobate (see 4.7–10 where the elect are said to be protected from these forces), and throws the elect into the imbroglio, rather than having them sitting above with Christ, the *Judex iratus*, where, theologically, they ought to be.

8 Parts of *Judica A* – especially those which employ plural verb and pronoun forms – also seem to have been intended to provide the priestly reader with preaching material, but this is clearly a secondary, not a primary, purpose.

9 With this opening, which uses many of the standard *topoi* of the dedicatory prologue, compare, e.g., that of Bernard's *De Gradibus Humilitatis et Superbiae* (a work also written on request), which describes the conflict that took place in Bernard, while he tried to decide whether or not to write, between his fear of pride on the one hand and his love for the work's intended recipient on the other, humbly submitting the result to be criticized as necessary by the reader (16.2–17). In characteristic contrast to Bernard, Rolle's internal debate is fought not between fear of pride and love, but between love and 'the envy of the malicious', while the dedicatee is not expected to use his discretion in judging it, but in deciding who else to show it to.

10 For the four causes, see the description of the 'Aristotelian prologue' in Minnis 1984, pp. 28–29; elsewhere, Minnis (1979a, especially pp. 387–390) discusses conventional disclaimers made by *compilatores* in their prologues, citing, e.g., Vincent of Beauvais's *Speculum Maius*. As Rouse 1979, pp. 40–42 notes, emphasis on *utilitas* characterizes all kinds of late-medieval pastoral works. The phrases 'vestro statui profutura' and 'ad utilitatem legencium' are thus also conventional; indeed, *utilitas* was another topic covered both by the 'Aristotelian Prologue' and by the more informal epistolary prologue.

11 Arnould takes Allen to task for assuming the phrase 'nondum in publico predicando cogor dicere' really means 'not allowed to preach in public' (Arnould 1957, p. ix, n. 11, citing Allen pp. 101, 108). I think Allen is right, and that Rolle is using the word 'cogor' to imply that he awaits an inner compulsion to preach (compare *Contra Amatores Mundi* 4.135–136) – disingenuously, since in fact he cannot do so simply because, not being in orders, he lacks an ecclesiastical licence.

12 Thus *Judica Me* makes no use of the *Pars Sinistra* of *Oculus Sacerdotis*, a treatise on sacramental theology, and in discussing confession omits all mention of absolution, the moment at which the sacrament becomes efficacious. The list of penitential canons, detailing the sins which priests or bishops are not competent to absolve – a feature that distinguishes *Pars Oculi* from other penitential manuals – is excluded from *B2* (except at 66.5–12), and the main concerns of *Dextera Pars* are omitted from *B1*: 'the vernacular form of baptism; the use of the baptismal form in case of danger or death . . . the variety of forms in which homicide can occur . . . a list of . . . excommunications . . . to which people are liable *ipso facto*' (Boyle 1955, pp. 88–89).

13 Here and subsequently in this chapter, angled brackets indicate Rolle's additions

to his source. The additions here make it absolutely clear that Rolle is writing a single work not a 'collection of tracts'.

14 Rolle's basic amplification of Lamentations 2.19 is traditional; see, e.g., part v of *Ancrene Wisse* (f. 87a.23–28). Another interesting change made to *Pars Oculi* occurs where the latter, following requirements laid down in the Pecham Syllabus (see Boyle 1955, pp. 84–90), enjoins the preaching of a pre-Lent sermon expounding the Creed and the need to make Confession. Ignoring this, *Judica B2* substitutes sermons on Christ's temptation in the wilderness and Paul's encomium to love in 1 Corinthians 13 (34.1–8; see Daly, p. 117, nn. 10–11 for the liturgical appropriateness of these topics), adding that the effectiveness of a preacher's expositions will depend on the measure of his divine inspiration: 'Et debetis exponere eis evangelia et epistolas prout vobis Deus dederit scienciam et noticiam celestem secretorum' (34.8–9). Again, the emphasis on the inner life and on direct didacticism is clear.

15 For Rolle's possible sources in these 'theological' passages, see Chapter 2, nn. 2 and 6. The account given here of the *dotes animae et corporis* of the elect acts as a counterpart to the account in *Judica A* of the way the reprobate are successively deprived of their earthly *dotes*: 'gloria vertitur in dolorem . . .' (7.19–22); compare sections 87–89 of the *Speculum Ecclesie*, which contain a schematic juxtaposition of the *dotes* with the state of the reprobate. The account given here of the quadripartite division of souls provides theological background to remarks about the *electi* at the Judgement in *Judica A* (e.g. 6.16–17.2), as well as to the distinction *A* draws later between the *pauperes* and the *pusilli fideles* (to be discussed below).

16 Such fluidity is demonstrated by the fact that *Oculus Sacerdotis* itself, as well as having a large professional readership, was owned by laymen for their own edification (see the evidence amassed in Boyle 1956, vol. 2).

17 Two of the three citations from the Psalms here are clarified by Rolle's commentaries. *Latin Psalter* comments on Psalm 42.1: 'Loquitur hic vir sanctus, volens separari mente in praesenti hic ab iniquis, et socio in futuro. Unde quia non timet iuditium, orat ut veniat et iudicetur securus de aeterno premio' (pp. 195–196). This is similar to parts of Peter Lombard's gloss (PL 191, cols. 423–424), except that the latter makes the Psalm refer to the Church's thirst for righteousness, not an individual's. *English Psalter* comments on Psalm 109.1–2: '*When I was in anguys of syn, I cryed til my Lord, þat he wild delyuere me; and he herd me*, settand me in greis of steghynge. Bot when a man is in will to do wele, þan he has many ianglers, bakbiters, and flaterers; agayns þaim he praies . . . *Lord, delyuer my saule fra wickid lippis, and fra swikil tunge*. *Wickid lippis* ere þa þat eggis men to lefe þaire penaunce and goed purpose; *swikil tunge* is þat vndire colour of goed counsaile bryngis til syn' (p. 437). Again, this is close to phrases in Peter Lombard's gloss (PL 191, cols. 1133–1134).

4. CONTEMPLATIVE LIFE, 'SEEING INTO HEAVEN': COMMENTARIES AND CANTICUM AMORIS

1 My view that these are minor works receives a kind of confirmation from the fact that the members of this miscellaneous group were among the less frequently copied of Rolle's works during the Middle Ages. *Super Symbolum Athanasii* survives in two MSS (Allen, p. 312), *Super Symbolum Apostolorum* in seven (pp. 157–158), *Super Orationem Dominicam*, the most popular of the group, in eleven (pp. 155–156), *Super Apocalypsim* in three (pp. 152–53), *Super Threnos* in three (p. 150), *Super Mulierem Fortem* in five (p. 159), *Super Magnificat* in four (p. 192), *Canticum Amoris* in two (p. 90) – compare figures for the overtly

mystical works given on pp. 189–190 below. Yet several of these works fared better than Rolle's mystical treatises in the era of printing. Four of them (all but the last three and the incomplete *Super Apocalypsim*) were printed by Faber in 1536; some found their way into de la Bigne's seventeenth-century editions (see Chapter 1, n. 3), while *Super Threnos* was printed separately at Paris in 1542 (Allen, p. 151). These four works thus appeared in print alongside *Super Psalmum Vicesimum*, *Super Lectiones Mortuorum* and *Emendatio Vitae* (as well as short portions of *Super Canticum Canticorum* and *Incendium Amoris*), and helped establish Rolle's post-medieval reputation, with its emphasis on his most sober and conventional writing. As we shall see, there is a real link between these early works and those Faber printed from Rolle's last period.

2 The sources for *Super Symbolum Athanasii* are discussed by Ommaney 1897, pp. 250ff., who shows the work to differ in few details from one or another of its predecessors. Parts of *Super Orationem Dominicam* are derived from the commentary on Matthew, cap. 6 in the *Glossa Ordinaria*, although there may be a second source as well. Both *Super Threnos* and *Super Apocalypsim* make much use of the *Glossa Ordinaria*; however, as Clark 1986, p. 166 notes, *Super Threnos* is closer to the *Glossa* than *Super Apocalypsim* – which has a second, more important source, a standard commentary by pseudo-Anselm of Laon, and which also contains much original writing.

3 Compare pseudo-Anselm, whom Rolle is here copying closely, but who lacks any sense of drama: '*Et ideo posuit dexteram suam,* id est auxilium suum vel spem confortantem *super me,* id est ultra vires humanitatis, *dicens* id est commovens me per Scripturas: *Noli timere* pro me pati tribulationem . . . ' (PL 162, col. 1506). Rolle's effect is partly created by the affective figure *interpretatio* ('misericordie et auxilii atque proteccionis', repeating the same sense in different words) and the phrase 'possem pati et vellem sufferre', which is both *interpretatio* and *correctio* (the substitution of a word by one more suitable). Such repetitive figures feature prominently in the more affective portions of *Super Apocalypsim*.

4 Rolle might also have found the exotic visual imagery of Revelation too distant from his own mystical experience for him to be able to complete the commentary. There is a curious alternation in the work between long passages in which pseudo-Anselm or the *Glossa Ordinaria* are transcribed with few alterations and comments on verses are brief, and occasional digressions in which Rolle's mature mystical doctrine, as it occurs in *Incendium Amoris*, is nearly, but never quite fully, expounded; see, e.g., a second exposition of the phrase '*Ostium apertum*' (148.39–150.15). It could be that he was developing preoccupations with mystical themes while writing the work, and found it less and less suitable as a vehicle for them. However, while all three MSS of the work end in mid-sentence and with the same phrase, it remains possible that the ending of the work was merely lost.

5 Raby (1929, pp. xxiv–xxvi) notes that *Incendium Amoris* 259.19–260.2 is a paraphrase of *Philomena*, stanzas 464–474. The passage is a fanciful poetic catalogue of the fallacious delights of the world – the nightingale mooing louder than a cow ('philomenam magis vacca mugientem', 259.33) etc.; Rolle is looking for effective ways of closing his work. Raby (1929, pp. xxv–xxvi, n. 5) also suggests that *Meditation B* borrows from *Philomena*, and from another long Hoveden poem, the *Cythara*; as Moyes 1988, vol. 1, p. 51, n. 138, notes, the evidence could also point to a borrowing from Hoveden's own *Canticum Amoris*. Although I have not been able to find more examples of Rolle's overt indebtedness to Hoveden, I suspect the latter was an important influence on works like *Contra Amatores Mundi* and *Melos Amoris*.

6 For example, *Philomena* consists of 1,131 four-line stanzas of meditation on the

doings of its hero (who is also its muse), *Amor*, as exemplified in the incarnation, life, death and resurrection of Christ. The incidents and characters in this narrative give rise in turn to elaborate musings, not dissimilar in tone or function to the florid arias which make up the bulk of J.S. Bach's two major Passions. The poetry is very fine if one has (as many medieval readers did have) a taste for *amplificatio* and for startling imagery; it is also (perhaps deliberately, see next note) very hard to read.

7 *Canticum Amoris* contains many difficult readings and ambiguities which should be born in mind throughout the ensuing discussion; I do not present this strained translation as in any sense definitive. As George Rigg has suggested to me, the poetry may be deliberately difficult because it is meant to be read slowly and with an appreciation of its complexities, in an aesthetic equivalent of *ruminatio*. I would like to thank him, and Claire Fanger, for the help they have given me with the intricacies of this poem.

8 Walter of Wimborne's *Marie Carmina*, which owes its own debt to Hoveden (or perhaps *vice versa*), and has some points of contact with *Canticum Amoris*, including much highly mannered and mystical language, was nonetheless considered by its author inoffensive enough to be dedicated to his schoolboys: 'Hoc opus pueris legendum offero' (stanza 643).

9 In spite of the predominance of first-person forms in both works, neither Walter of Wimborne's *Marie Carmina* nor the *Philomena* has a narrator with a distinguishable personality, both merely being the sum of the rhetorical flourishes which exploit the personal voice. *Canticum Amoris* is not only restrained in language by comparison with the other poems, it is short and has a single and consistent subject and method of treatment: the Virgin seen as a spiritually sexual object. Although it, too, relies heavily on catalogues and on repetition, it is more clearly structured than its predecessors.

10 *Philomena* is written as a series of instructions to Love to write, so that each stanza (many of which begin with the instruction 'scribe') is seen to write itself; this is, of course, a variation on a common epic convention. *Marie Carmina* begins with a lengthy disquisition on the impossibility of singing Mary's praise, in which she is eventually seen dictating the work to Walter as to a nervous scribe. Both earlier works share the extensive alliteration found in *Canticum Amoris*.

5. CONTEMPLATIVE LIFE, *FERVOR*: *INCENDIUM AMORIS*

1 *Incendium Amoris* survives in over forty MSS, mostly in one of two forms: Rolle's original version, and a 'short text' from which about half the work has been cut (Allen pp. 209–225; Deanesley's edition allows one to reconstruct the 'short text', which betrays no obvious principles of selection). Two MSS also contain a fifteenth-century English translation by Richard Misyn. Latin and English texts have been edited, modernized or translated seven times in the last hundred years (see Lagorio and Bradley 1981, items 262, 264, 266, 269, 271, 324, and del Mastro 1981), making *Incendium Amoris* far Rolle's most popular Latin work in modern times. Remarkably, the present chapter is, however, the first attempt at a literary analysis of the work.

2 Rolle's narrative persona is an outstanding original achievement. Yet it may in part be indebted to his reading of early Cistercian literature, Bernard's *Sermones super Cantica Canticorum* and works like the *De Gradibus Humilitatis et Superbiae* and Aelred's *De Spirituali Amicitia*. Bernard's written sermons carefully evoke an oral context, presenting the preacher in many different lights – as voice of God, abbot, mystic – but always maintaining the tone of warm intimacy appropriate to

someone addressing brothers who are fundamentally his equals. We find the same tone in the dedicatory prologues to many Cistercian treatises, in which the writer submits his work to the correction of the reader, sometimes revealing uncertainties about his fitness for his task that are seldom mentioned in the body of the work. Aelred and Bernard are able to present themselves with such immediacy because they are writing, in the first instance, for a small circle of Cistercian colleagues. Rolle's achievement is to extend a similarly intimate tone to cover his own far less well-defined readership, and to adapt it to an eremitic persona.

3 Rolle may also have intended to remind readers of Lamentations 1.13 (*'De excelso misit ignem in ossibus meis'*), and of the opening of the *De Quattuor Gradibus Violentae Caritatis*, a clear influence here: 'Magna vis dilectionis miranda virtus caritatis ... supra hos tamen omnes dilectionis gradus est amor ille ardens et fervens qui cor penetrat et affectum inflammat, animamque ipsam eiusque medullitus transfigurat' (127.8–14; see also 131.11–13).

4 Modern television and door-to-door evangelists well understand the power of 'personal testimony' over an audience, a power which resides precisely in its irrefutability and its initial disconnection from its listeners, who identify with the narrative before realizing that it makes demands on them also. It has often been pointed out (e.g. by Sargent 1981, pp. 176–182) that the reservations later writers, like Hilton, had about Rolle centre on just the physicality he most notably expresses here; *The Scale of Perfection* I, caps. 26 and 31 indeed seem to be glosses on this passage. Yet it would be a mistake to deduce from Hilton's modifications of Rolle that the boldly physical terms used here are inherently suspect and must have attracted criticism from his first readers; it is likely that they became questionable only when Rolle's reputation as an *auctoritas* on the spiritual life became an accomplished fact, and readers had begun trying to use this passage as a model for their own spiritual lives.

5 MSS of *Incendium Amoris* use so many numbering systems for chapters that it seems likely none are authentic. Some (e.g. Caius 140, Royal 5.c.III, Rawlinson A.389) have no numbers; others (Emmanuel 35, Dd.v.64, Bodley 66) have a prologue and forty-two chapters, or (like Harley 275 and Bodley 861) no prologue and forty-three chapters. Dd.v.64 divides its forty-two chapters into two books (breaking at cap. 31); Misyn's translation also starts a new book at cap. 31, but numbers it as cap. 1 of Book II – a system also alluded to in a short-text MS, Laud 528 and in the *Officium* (*lectio iv*), which, however, refers to cap. 15 as 'capitulo tercio decimo' of 'libro suo primo'. Chapter headings of the type printed by Deanesley are found only in three Latin MSS (her two base MSS and Bodley 66) and in Misyn's translation (though there are at least two other sets of headings in Continental MSS, one found in Ghent 291, the other in Metz 361; see Allen, pp. 219–220); most are so inappropriate to the contents of the chapters they can hardly be Rolle's. Nonetheless, all MSS of the whole work that I have seen break chapters or sections in the same places, and I take these breaks to be genuine; many are clearly indicated in the text itself.

6 The *Orationes sive Meditationes*, like *Incendium Amoris*, is divided into sections with their own coherence, each of which is short enough to be read at a sitting and is structured according to an affective, not a conceptual, logic. Parts of *Incendium Amoris* may directly imitate Anselm's didactic soliloquies, as where Rolle uses the Anselmian term 'homuncio' in denouncing human pride (222.9, see, e.g., *Meditatio* 2.44), or where he writes an address to his own soul (169.16–20).

7 See, e.g., cap. 11, which explains that the elect soul sings because his heart is on fire ('et hoc [canor] nimirum accidit, dum canentis cor igne celico funditus exuritur', 174.10–12) – a statement which ignores the fact that *canor* is a separate, and higher,

gift. All the first fifteen chapters of *Incendium Amoris* (except for 6, 7 and 12) refer to *fervor*, usually in a prominent place near the beginning or end of the chapter.

8 A comparison of the language of this part of *Incendium Amoris* with that of *Super Canticum Canticorum*, a work dominated by the imagery of *dulcor*, shows many similarities. In *Super Canticum Canticorum*, the *amore langueo* theme forms an important part of Rolle's discussion of the name of Jesus (41.12ff., see especially 42.18ff.), and Jesus's name is linked to *dulcor* by the imagery of the verse which evokes that discussion – '*Oleum effusum nomen tuum*' (Song of Songs 1.3). The *amore langueo* theme is also developed in caps. 16–17 of *Incendium Amoris*, in intense language full of images of touch and taste; moreover, one of the few allusions to the name of Jesus in the work comes in cap. 15, where Rolle tells readers that devotion to that name is a prerequisite for experiencing *canor* (190.11–13): a subordination of *canor* to a devotion associated with *dulcor* which perhaps has a structural function. Cap. 26 of *Incendium Amoris* is an exposition of the first verse of the Song of Songs, asking for the delightfulness of Christ's kiss, and again mentioning his sweetest name: '*Osculetur me*, inquit, *osculo oris sui*, scilicet, delectet me unione Filii sui. Ideo enim *amore langueo* ... eius nomen dulcissimum in mente mea retentum canens cogitabo' (216.8–15).

9 Some MSS of *Incendium Amoris* treat cap. 31 as the beginning of 'Book II' (see n. 5). Noetinger 1928 (p. 100) suggests that cap. 15 ends the first part of the work, and that the subject of the new part (caps. 15–30) is charity.

10 'Contemplativi viri qui excellenter uruntur amore eternitatis quemadmodum quidem superiores existunt in ardore amenissimo et preamabili amoris eterni, ita ut nunquam aut rarissime exeunt in externis ministeriis, neque dignitatem prela-cionis et honoris accipiunt ... Enitatur enim in hoc ecclesia angelicam ierarchiam, in qua superni angeli ad exteriora non mittuntur, Deo iugiter assistentes ... Habet igitur electus quisque statum suum a Deo preordinatum. Dum iste ad prelacionem eligitur, ille soli Deo vacare conatur; et ad hoc ipsum Deus interius elevat, ut omnes exteriores occupaciones pretermittat. Tales denique sanctissimi sunt, et tamen ab hominibus minores estimantur, qui rarius egrediunt ad miracula fac-ienda, eo quod solummodo interioribus manent ... Non enim omnes sancti faciunt vel fecerunt miracula eciam nec in vita nec post mortem, neque omnes reprobi vel in vita vel post mortem miraculis caruerunt' (153.1–28). For the association between the orders of angels and those of humanity, see, e.g., *De Claustro Animae* (by Hugh of Folieto, attributed to Hugh of St Victor, PL 176, cols. 1164–1166); for (diabolical) miracles performed by the wicked, see the authorities mustered by Aquinas, *Summa Theologica* I, q. 110 (Noetinger 1928, pp. 20, 24).

11 '*Nam et* sepe contingit quod mediocriter boni et minus perfecti miracula faciunt, *et* plerumque *eciam* summi ab hiis in celestibus sedibus coram vultum Dei constituti penitus quiescant, habentes utique merita sua inter summas choras angelorum. *Quia et* festum sancti Michaelis celebratur specialiter, et tamen unus de supremo ordine angelorum esse non creditur. *Quidam et* conversi ad Deum et penitenciam agentes, seculariaque negocia deserentes, gaudent in cogitacione sua, si ipsorum nomen post mortem suam apud posteros honoretur. *Ad hoc quidem* respectum non habebit fidelis servum Christi, ne totum perdat quod operatur' (154.4–15). The italicized words show Rolle attempting to make contradictions into a smoothly flowing logical argument.

12 The young man's history closely resembles Rolle's, who often speaks of himself as tempted, as this *iuvenis* is, by flattery, beautiful women, and affluence (166.23–24; compare, e.g., the opening of cap. 15). The implication that Rolle is the *iuvenis* is particularly potent in view of the fact that the passage purports to present him as an

exemplum of the dangers of the flesh (ending with the command 'Ideoque non tangas lubrice', 167.7–8), while actually stressing a different idea: that surviving fleshly temptation makes the elect soul holier, and implicitly that only ordinary Christians need fear temptation. Rolle is alluding to the remarkable way in which the elect, and himself, differ from the common herd. (See also Noetinger 1928, p. 41.)

13 'O bone Ihesu, hic flagella, hic seca, hic percute, hic ure, immo facias de me quicquid placeat bonitati tue, dummodo in futuro malum non habeam, sed tuam amorem sensiam hic et in eternum' (168.8–11); 'O anima mea, inter omnia qui contingunt devocione delectata, lauda Dominum, laudando sencias dulcissona et canendo degustes mellita. *Quia laudabo Dominum in vita mea*, sive tribulor sive prosperor, sive opprobrium sive honorem accipio, *Psallam Deo meo quamdiu fuero* [Psalm 103.33]' (169.16–20).

14 The words from 'cuius interior homo in aliam gloriam aliamque formam iam mutatur' to 'vix subsistit pro amore' deliberately evoke radical passages from Bernard's *De Diligendo Deo* (x.28) and Richard's *De Quattuor Gradibus Violentae Caritatis* (38–39), the first describing the fourth degree of love (which Bernard sees as unattainable in this life except in brief moments), the second, which itself draws heavily on Bernard, describing the third degree of violent love (in which the soul finds herself almost united with God before falling back with sorrow into the fourth degree, where she attends to the needs of her neighbours). Rolle reverts to this language in the last section of *Super Canticum Canticorum* (see pp. 150–154 and notes), where, like here, he uses it in a more radical way than either of his sources by applying it to experiences which can be fully enjoyed in this life. The passages from Bernard and Richard are quoted in full in Chapter 6, n. 18; Richard's language is heavily redolent of Rolle's experiences of *fervor* and *dulcor* (see n. 3).

15 Rosamund Allen (1988, pp. 24–25) points out that as cap. 12 of *Incendium Amoris* circulated as part of the *Oleum Effusum* compilation, it must have been well thought of in the Middle Ages, and suggests that Rolle intended this final passage to be a wryly humorous self-caricature. This implies a kinder reading than mine, but still one in which Rolle is avoiding the issue: his expressed intention to confess his sins.

16 Behind Rolle's manœuvre lurks a logical fallacy to which he often has recourse: 'Those who experience *canor* are generally solitaries (185.2–3); therefore the purpose of being a solitary is to experience *canor* (181.17–182.2).' The fallacy is somewhat veiled by the way that, until the second half of cap. 14, *canor, dulcor* and *fervor* do not inevitably refer specifically to mystical experiences, but can be taken as metaphors for holy love of any kind.

17 See the chapter's ending, in which he demands to be imitated and at the same time denies that he wishes to be praised: 'Ecce fratres, narravi vobis quomodo perveni ad incendium amoris: non ut me laudetis sed Deum meum glorificetis, a quo accepi quicquid bonum habui, ut et vos, cogitantes quod cuncta sub sole vanitas, ad imitandum non ad detrahendum incitemini' (191.11–15). This conclusion also misrepresents the subject of the chapter, which is not the 'incendium amoris' but Rolle's reception of *canor*: another sign that *canor* is being kept in reserve until the final third of the work.

18 The more distant tone of these chapters is partly achieved by borrowing from sources which deal with affective material in a formal way. One such source on which Rolle clearly draws here is Hugh of Strasbourg's *Compendium Theologicae Veritatis*; part of cap. 17 (195.5ff.), and the opening of cap. 18, use phrases and sentences from Book v, caps. 23, 25 and 27 of that work. For example, Rolle writes:

'Caritas regina virtutum, stella pulcherrima, decor est anime que hec omnia facit in anima: scilicet, vulnerat eam, languidam facit . . . cuius actus ordinatus et habitus venustus est' (197.27–30). *Compendium Theologicae Veritatis*, citing Richard of St Victor's *In Psalmum XLIV*, has: 'Charitas excellit alias virtutes in multis . . . Secundo in speciali dignitate; Richardus: Charitas est regina virtutum . . . Quarto in speciositate, quia est planeta Veneris . . . sic etiam pulchritudo animae est ex decenti ordinatione actuum, et habitu venusto: hoc autem facit charitas in anima, cujus actus ordinatus est, et venustus habitus' (cap. 27; also compare the last part of cap. 25 with *Incendium Amoris* 196.18ff.).

19 See *Sententiae* III, dist. xxxi (*Si Caritas Semel Habita Amittatur*). Peter Lombard's sources here include Hugh of St Victor's *De Sacramentis* II.13.11 (*Utrum Charitas Semel Habita Amittatur*, PL 176, col. 539); his answer differs from Hugh's, but is similar to Rolle's: 'Quae semel habita non amittitur; exordia vero caritatis aliquando crescunt, aliquando deficiunt . . . Sed dum habetur, non sinit habentem criminaliter peccare' (9–10). The comments on this passage by Alexander of Hales may also have influenced Rolle; part of Alexander's argument against the proposition is strikingly reminiscent of *Incendium Amoris*: 'Sed hoc non est quia aliquis habens caritatem non possit amittere eam; sed quoniam ipsa potest esse et in patria et in via' (*Glossa in Quatuor Libros Sententiarum Petri Lombardi*, pp. 364–365). (For the opposite view, see Aquinas, *Summa Theologica* II.ii, q. 24, art. 11.)

20 Rolle's use of the term *perfectus* reflects common theological practice: see, e.g., Aquinas, *Summa Theologica* II.ii, q. 184, which states (with qualifications) that perfection in this life is possible; for a survey, see the article 'Perfection' in the *Dictionnaire de spiritualité*, vol. 12a, cols. 1074–1136. For Rolle, the word is clearly tinged by Peter Damian's claim that the eremitic life is the *vita perfectorum* (see cols. 1123–1124), as well as by the account in 1 John 4.18 of *'perfecta caritas'*, which *'foras mittit timorem'*. But what he means by the term, that the *perfecti* are saved souls who, aware of their gift of *canor*, are also aware their salvation is certain, is radical. Bernard and Richard of St Victor both shy away from considering what the perfect think of themselves, even though their mystical systems clearly imply that souls who attain their higher stages are destined for salvation; Peter Lombard's *Sententiae* similarly avoids saying whether anyone can know they have the true *caritas* which cannot be lost. Aquinas (*Summa Theologica* I, q. 112, art. 5) does discuss the matter, stating that it is only possible to know one will continue in a state of grace by divine revelation. Rolle's position seems to be orthodox (Clark 1983, pp. 114–115), but it is daring, and the fact that he introduces the term *perfectus* so late in the work suggests he was aware of this.

21 Cap. 20 begins, with fine disingenuity, 'Ad hanc mentem stabilitatem adquirendam et retinendam, iugis oracio multum adiuvat' (203.1–2), as though the *quaestio* at the end of cap. 19 has had, after all, merely a pastoral function; 'spiritual security' all at once becomes *stabilitas mentis*.

22 'Et tamen iste perfectus amor non facit ut homo omnino non peccet, sed ne aliquod peccatum in ipse duret quod non statim igne amoris adnihiletur' (208.20–22). Here Rolle may have been indebted to *Compendium Theologicae Veritatis* VI, cap. 24, where charity is described as one of the things that diminish the effect of venial sin: 'Notandum etiam quod tam fervens potest esse motus charitatis in Deum quod omnia peccata venialia consumat, etiam sine actuali cogitatione ipsorum.' The idea may originate with William of St Thierry (Bell 1983, pp. 191–193); it recurs in modified form in Hilton's revisionist account of the fire of love in *The Scale of Perfection* I, cap. 31.

23 Hugh of St Victor's *De Sacramentis* II.13 provides a useful commentary on Rolle's

thought here, being in substantial agreement with him over the effect charity has on the will: 'Quanto magis crescit charitas tanto magis crescit voluntas; quanto magis crescit voluntas tanto magis decrescit necessitas. Et jam perfecte charitate amat ad reverentiam voluntarius; non timet ad poenam fortiorem invitus' (PL 176, col. 527). Hugh's next chapter develops this statement into an analysis of four kinds of fear, from servile to filial, the last of which is born of a burning love, and is to be desired and not shunned: 'Hunc sequitur timor filialis qui ex succedente charitate nascitur, ut ipsum timere nihil aliud sit quam degustatum in charitate bonum jam nolle amittere' (col. 528). This seems closely equivalent to what Rolle calls 'solicitudo' in the passage just quoted. However, Hugh goes on to say that servile fear is always necessary in this life, and here Rolle is in disagreement so far as the perfect are concerned. Compare the discussion of tears in cap. 40, which relegates them to the beginning of the spiritual life, in spite of 'doctors who assert that the perfect should weep' (270.11), and sets up a direct opposition between sorrow for sin and the fire of love: a frontal attack on traditions of penitential spirituality which see a life of abject asceticism as the nearest thing to perfection possible on earth.

24 247.19–21: 'Audite, obsecro, amici mei, nemo vos seducat. Hec et huiusmodi alloquia in conspectu Creatoris eructantur ex incendio amoris, et non audet aliquis alienus ab immensa dileccione talia tractare.' This warning is similar to that made at the opening of *The Cloud of Unknowing*, which attempts to confine that work's readership to those who are 'in þe autorite of charite' (1.22). But Rolle's warning is oddly undirected – is he merely saying that 'imperfect' readers should not get too excited by his prose? Again, his primary emphasis seems to be on stressing the gulf between his own, 'perfect', prayers, and those of the common Christian.

6. CONTEMPLATIVE LIFE, *DULCOR: SUPER PSALMUM VICESIMUM, SUPER CANTICUM CANTICORUM, CONTRA AMATORES MUNDI*

1 Both *Super Psalmum Vicesimum* and *Latin Psalter* diverge widely from Peter Lombard's gloss (PL 191, cols. 219–225; see Clark 1986, p. 175), which reads Psalm 20 as an account of Christ's two natures (as does *English Psalter*); apart from this, the two works also seem unrelated to one another.

2 'Rex itaque dicitur vel quia regit vel quia regnat; immo plenius dicatur et quia regit et quia regnat. Sed rex de quo sanctus propheta loqui conatur, quid est quod regit, et super quo regnat, quia tam audacter asserit: *In virtute Domine letabitur?*' (2.2–5). These questions provide two divisions of the word 'rex'; later, two more are added, with the help of a verse from the gospels: 'Sed unde rex et ubi regnat, cum Christus dicat non solum pro se, sed etiam pro membris suis: *Regnum meum non est de hoc mundo* [John 18.36]?' (4.6–7). The four questions (*quid, super quo, unde* and *ubi*) are related to the 'topics' defined by classical rhetoric as the *ars inveniendi* – the process of deciding what needs to be said about a subject (see Cicero's *Topica*, especially XXI.82, and the *Rhetorica ad Herennium* II). But they also resemble one kind of sermon *distinctiones* (see Rouse 1979, pp. 66–67); for example, Peter Comestor's sermon on Psalm 81.8 (in Bonnes 1945–1946, pp. 211–215) asks 'quis est iste qui stetit et ubi stetit et ad quid stetit?'

3 See also the assertion 'aliena non diripimus' (1.9), which I think should be translated 'we do not plagiarize from others', and taken as a declaration of Rolle's intention to expound Psalm 20 in an original way, as an inspired *auctor*. Compare the opening of *Super Magnificat* (see p. 103).

4 In an earlier passage, Rolle has identified the Holy Spirit with love in order to prepare for the deliberate ambiguity here: 'O Sancte Spiritus, veni et rape me tibi!

... Amor diceris et vere es qui semper tuos ad amorem accendis' (10.14, 16). The identification is, of course, traditional.

5 See, e.g., *Meditationes Vitae Christi*, the prologue; *Stimulus Amoris* I, cap. I, and II, cap. 4 (entitled *Qualiter Homo Ordinet Cogitationes Suas ad Deum, ita quod Deum Semper Habeat in Corde*); Richard of St Victor's account, in *De Quattuor Gradibus Violentae Caritatis*, of the way love (in the *primus gradus*) comes gradually to occupy the heart (131.17–27); and these lines in the hymn *Dulcis Ihesu Memoria*: 'Amor tuus continuus, / Mihi languor assiduus', and 'Hic amor ardet iugiter' (stanzas xx and xxvii). Against this tradition, Aquinas (*Summa Theologica* II.ii, q. 24, art. 8) argues that continual love of God is impossible in this life, that charity can therefore be lost even by someone who truly has it (art. 11), and thus that spiritual security cannot be achieved in this life (see Chapter 5, n. 19): an argument that is most suggestive of the high stakes for which Rolle is playing here.

6 The claim that *canor* can be a continuous experience is distantly anticipated in the last chapters of *Incendium Amoris* (see 247.37 and 267.1–17), but is never clearly stated; the words 'hic [canor] permanet usque ad finem' in cap. 15 (190.19–21) seem to imply only that *canor* will undergo no further developments (after all, the work begins by stating clearly that even *fervor* cannot always be maintained; 146.14–15). As my argument here implies, Rolle's doctrine of continuous *canor* seems to have its roots in the idea of continual meditation on and prayer to Christ (see previous note), rather as *canor* itself has its roots in the spiritual exercises of *meditatio* and *oratio* (see pp. 68, 70).

7 For David as a *figura* of Christ and hence of the perfect man, see Minnis 1984, pp. 88–92. If David is also taken to be the *rex* in a psalm written by himself (as implicitly here and explicitly in Aquinas's commentary on the psalm; see Minnis, pp. 89–90), Psalm 20 turns into a piece of writing quite as audacious and self-referential as Rolle's commentary upon it.

8 The verses are given in the form in which they appear in MS Trinity College, Dublin 153, as edited by Murray. In the Trinity MS and others, the major division in the text is marked by Rolle quoting the whole text he has expounded (Song of Songs 1.1–2), followed by 'Explicit exposicio super primum versiculum canticum canticorum' (37.6–7); the *explicit* at the end of the work runs 'Explicit exposicio super secundum versiculum Canticum Canticorum secundum Ricardum' (80.24–26). The shorter sections are not marked in the Trinity MS (as they are, for example, in MS Corpus Christi, Oxford 193), but are easily discernible. These sections are also subdivided, Rolle expounding each clause several times and quoting the clause (or the phrase on which he wishes to focus) at the beginning of each exposition. The work proved as easy as *Judica Me* to copy in sections, and there are only four surviving MSS which contain the whole work (or once did), the other ten MSS (not counting fourteen MSS of the compilation *Oleum Effusum*) containing a variety of combinations of sections (Allen, pp. 64–68).

9 Some of this passage is directly taken from Bernard's *Sermones in Cantica Canticorum* 9.2 (the Bride's speech about the Bridegroom): '"Non quiesco", ait, "nisi *Osculetur me osculo oris sui* ... Non sum ingrata, sed amo ... Nec ignoro quia *Honor regis iudicium diligit*; sed praeceps amor, nec iudicium praestolatur, nec consilio temperatur, nec pudore frenatur, nec rationis subicitur. Rogo, supplico, flagito: *Osculetur me osculo oris sui*."'

10 See *Incendium Amoris*, cap. 41 and *Contra Amatores Mundi* 5.19ff., especially 25–27: 'Flere autem et gemere sunt noviter conversorum et incipiencium, sed iubilare et canere non sunt nisi perfectorum.'

11 This fine passage is perhaps an amplification of Song of Songs 3.1 ('*In lectulo meo per noctes quesivi quem diligit anima mea, quaesivi illum et non inveni*'), as well as

of two New Testament analogues of this verse, Mary Magdalene's search for Christ in the garden (John 20.11–18), and Mary's and Joseph's search for him in Jerusalem (Luke 2.43–46). Rolle may also owe a debt to Aelred's meditation on this latter incident in the *De Ihesu Puero Duodenni*, on which he seems to be drawing in *The Commandment* (82–109, see p. 237): 'O dulcis puer, ubi eras? ubi latebaris? quo uterabaris hospitio? quorum fruebaris consortio? . . .' (1.1.28–30).

12 See the exposition in the *Glossa Ordinaria* (PL 113, col. 1120): 'Nomen Jesu venit in mundum, et statim praedicatur.' Rolle borrows this statement, adding his own sensual variation, at 41.15: 'Nomen Ihesu venit in mundum et statim adoratur oleum effusum.'

13 Contrast, e.g., the account of the intense frustration even the *perfecti* experience when awaiting the coming of God, in Book IV of Richard of St Victor's *Benjamin Major* (caps. 10–16).

14 The passage is quoted (as Extract 1) in n. 18 below, in juxtaposition with Bernard's *De Diligendo Deo* x.27–28, to which it clearly alludes. Bernard and Richard of St Victor seem to be the main writers comprehended by the phrase 'plurimi sanctorum', and hence to be Rolle's main targets, here and in the pages that follow (see next notes); both are certain that union with God cannot be permanent in this life (see also Butler 1927, pp. 148–157). In implicitly singling out these writers for criticism, Rolle is launching a major offensive on the founding fathers of the affective mystical tradition in which his own career is set (see the introduction, pp. 18–22), and doing so in the context of a work which is full of echoes of both Bernard and Richard. For example, the two sections before this final one are clearly indebted to *Sermones super Cantica Canticorum* 21–22, and manifestly draw both on the famous opening sentence of *De Diligendo Deo* ('Causa diligendi Deum, Deus est; modus, sine modo diligere') – see, e.g., 'omnem modum excedens' (49.6), 'modus . . . sine modo, gradus sine gradu, ordo sine ordine' (61.18) – and on Richard's *De Quattuor Gradibus Violentae Caritatis* – see, e.g., 'melius dicitur hic dileccio summa quia singularis, et singularis quia summa' etc. (50.12–13; compare Richard 135.6–18). Indeed, even in this final section, where Rolle is in disagreement with Bernard and Richard, he borrows their terminology, only then to use it to attack their position.

15 This passage is quoted (as Extract 2) in n. 18 below, and again alludes to Bernard and Richard, this time adapting their language for Rolle's ends, largely to buttress his argument with a display of self-consciously daring mystical terminology. Deification is mentioned only once by Bernard and rarely by Richard, and although the term was current among the Rhineland mystics (see Underhill 1911, pp. 420–423) it has radical associations (see the article 'Divinisation' in the *Dictionnaire de spiritualité*, vol. 4, cols. 1370–1459, especially 1432–1445). (Compare *Melos Amoris* 43.22 and context.)

16 Again, Rolle's language alludes to Bernard ('non raptim, non momentanee, set continue . . . non raro set continue gratulamur'; see n. 18).

17 In the light of other allusions to Bernard and Richard in this section, this passage is probably an attempt to redefine Richard's fourth grade of love, *amor insatiabilis*, in terms acceptable to Rolle's mysticism. Richard's 'insatiable love' occurs when the soul recognizes that it cannot attain its desire in this life, but turns back to the world in anguished charity (44–47). Against this, Rolle argues that although he, too, continues to desire, he already has what he desires, and is thus 'satisfied'. This argument, which depends on an earlier (and particularly glib) claim that to desire Christ is to have him (68.7–9), effectively neutralizes the whole idea of 'insatiability', turning it into a mere rhetorical counter.

18 For part of this conclusion, which is yet again dependent on Bernard's and Richard's imagery for much of its effect, see Extract 3. This note gives passages in which Rolle's indebtedness to (and disagreement with) Bernard and Richard are clearest (1–3), and their sources in *De Diligendo Deo* x.27–28 and *De Quattuor Gradibus Violentae Caritatis* (4–5). Particular parallels are suggested by italicization.

(1) 'Set, ut plurimi sanctorum qui de amore Dei gloriosa conscripserunt asserunt, non potest quis in carne habitans corruptibili nisi *raro* in illa dulcedine *affici*, et non nisi *raptim et momentanee* tam suaviter *debriari* . . . Quomodo ergo cum nos ad eum venimus hoc a nobis abstrahit quod si cencies cuperemus, quando nec *vix* cupimus *semel* dare non recusaret? . . . Qui ergo eius amorem semper quereret, semper gaudium inveniret' (67.13–17, 68.2–8).

(2) 'Solo eternitatis amore delectatur quorum cor in igne amoris divini *liquefactum* in contemplacione Deo vicinius rapitur, et eterna absortum dulcedine, *in alia gloria in alia forma* totum *transmutatur* ut iam dicat cum apostolo: Vivo ego iam non ego; vivit vero in me Christus. Nimirum illud cor est quasi ignis splendidus, eterno amore funditus ignitus, ut iam non hoc quod fuit cernitur, set pocius quodammodo *deificatum* videatur. Si quis autem sic supernis dulcoribus *inebriaretur*, proculdubio nequaquam assereret quod anima Deo dilecta aut *raro* in contemplacione raperetur, aut propter gravedinem carnis raro amoris gaudium degustaret, nec diceret quod nisi *raptim et momentanee* rapitur, set pocius quod pene continue in amplexibus immoratur' (69.14–70.1).

(3) 'Sicut ergo ignis carbonem vivum *in suam formam* redigit et a forma carbonis mortui *penitus deficere* facit, ut iam totus carbo *videatur* et tamen *manet substancia* carbonis, ita eterni amoris ignis animam tangens et penetrans paulatim in ea proficit, donec illam manentem tamen substancia *in suam formam suamque gloriam plene mutaverit*. Carbo vivus *similis est igni*; qui non vivus terre erat similis; et anima amore repleta Dei representat similitudinem que non amans ymaginem portabat terrenam' (80.11–18).

(4) (Bernard): 'Quando huiuscemodi experitur affectum, ut divino *debriatus* amore animus, oblitus sui, factusque sibi ipsi tamquam vas perditum, totus pergat in Deum et, adhaerens Deo, unus cum eo spiritus fiat . . . Beatum dixerim et sanctum, cui tale aliquid in hac mortali vita *raro* interdum, aut vel *semel*, et hoc ipsum *raptim atque unius vix momenti spatio*, experiri donatum est . . . Sic affici, *deificari* est. Quomodo stilla aquae modica, multo infusa vino, *deficere* a se tota videtur, dum et saporem vini induit et colorem, et quomodo ferrum ignitum et candens *igni simillimum fit*, pristina propriaque exutum forma, et quomodo solis luce perfusus aer in eamdem transformatur luminis claritatem, adeo ut non tam illuminatus quam ipsum lumen esse videatur, sic omnem tunc in sanctis humanum affectionem quodam ineffabili modo necesse erit a semetipsa *liquescere*, atque in Dei *penitus transfundi* voluntatem. Alioquin quomodo omnia in omnibus erit Deus, si in homine de homine quidquam supererit? *Manebit quidem substantia*, sed *in alia forma, alia gloria* aliaque potentia.'

(5) (Richard, see Extracts 2 and 3 only): 'Cum enim ferrum ignem projicitur, tam nigrum quam frigidum procul dubio primo videtur. Sed dum in ignis incendio moram facit, *paulatim* incalescit, paulatim nigredinem deponit,

sensimque incandescens paulatim in ignis similitudinem trahit, donec tandem totum *liquefiat* et a seipso *plene deficiat* et *in aliam* penitus qualitatem transeat' (167.18–23). See also *'penitus deficit'*, 'tota *in aliam gloriam* transit' etc. (167.26–27, 15).

19 By saying he is 'urged by love', Rolle is laying a claim to divine inspiration which recurs in several later works (see, e.g., *Contra Amatores Mundi* 4.135–137 and *Melos Amoris* 3.1–5, quoted on pp. 164 and 175). *Amor* is the Holy Spirit, as well as the effect of the Spirit's workings in Rolle's soul, and thus lies behind both his outpourings of unheard *canor* and his literary production. Rolle's phraseology may be indebted to 2 Corinthians 5.14 ('*Caritas enim Christi urget nos*'), and to the first words of the *De Quattuor Gradibus Violentae Caritatis*: 'Urget caritas de caritate loqui' (127.1). Although the claim is clearly meant literally, and is thus audacious, the terms in which it is expressed are commonplace: compare, e.g., the opening of the *Tractatus ad Severinum de Gradibus Caritatis* (PL 196, col. 1195), or any portion of John of Hoveden's *Philomena*, the whole of which is sung, in epic style, by *amor* as muse.

20 The implications of Rolle's discussion of eloquence in the last section of *Super Canticum Canticorum* can be seen as deeply ironic when one applies them to Bernard and Richard. On the one hand, his case is (1) that since they deny the possibility of continuous mystical experience they must have been less perfect than himself; (2) that since this is so, they must have written of their experience with less eloquence than he does of his. On the other hand, as we have seen (n. 18), Rolle's display of eloquence in this section is substantially indebted to them, especially at the points where he is describing the summit of the spiritual life. To adapt Harold Bloom's language (in *The Anxiety of Influence*, 1973), Rolle is engaged here in an Oedipal struggle for superiority over his own literary 'fathers'; it is not, perhaps, surprising that he chooses not to mention them directly.

21 It is the language of *dulcor* that tends to be employed at moments of structural significance. See, e.g., the opening of cap. 1 ('delectacionem . . . mellifui dulcoris haustum . . . immundicie sapore . . . dulcedinem . . . gustum . . . fastidit . . . languet', 1.5–16), those of caps. 3 and 5, and the close of the work, with its encomia of love ('tu es sapor condiens; tu es odor redolens; tu es dulcor placens', 7.296–297). All parts of Rolle's writings which deal with love in sexual terms make heavy use of the imagery of *dulcor*.

22 *Contra Amatores Mundi* does not state explicitly that it is written as a saint's answer to secular love-literature. But much of it is concerned with winning *iuvenes* from the wrong to the right kind of love, and, at least in caps. 3 and 6, both are discussed in courtly terms: see, e.g., 3.78–80, where Rolle admits his social inferiority to his loved one; 3.83 and 3.132, where the idleness associated with *fine amour* (embodied in Oiseuse, porteress of Deduit's garden in the *Roman de la Rose*) is contrasted with the vigorous activity demanded of the lovers of God; and 6.80–110, where the bravery of knights going into battle is unfavourably compared with the boldness of the saints. The idea of earthly love having *sectatores* is also courtly. More generally (and often using biblical language to achieve this effect), the work seems irradiated by a glamour, a consciousness of charm, which Rolle appears to think is necessary to outdo the verbal charm of secular love.

23 *Sapientia* is regularly treated as the beloved object in this work: a feminine noun designating God is needed to stand in as an *amica pulchra* to set against secular mistresses (compare *Super Canticum Canticorum* 22.20–21).

24 Compare the Prologue and passus 1 of *Piers Plowman*, which could be seen as another such two-part prologue: one introducing the scene on which the poem's narrative is to be played out (tower, dungeon, field full of folk), the other the moral

and theological axes within which its argument is to be plotted. The first vision proper begins at the opening of passus II.

25 'A morsu immortalis vermis' recalls the opening of *Super Psalmum Vicesimum*, where Rolle rejoices in being free of the jaws of the wicked dragon ('a faucibus maledicti draconis liberatos', 1.6–7), as part of his claim to be spiritually secure and hence authoritative. Here the same claim is veiled by the implication that such security will be a consequence of having written, not a basis for authority in setting out to do so.

26 See 'Sed aliter sunt qui aliter dicunt' etc. (5.244). The passage, like a similar discussion of two kinds of *raptus* in *Incendium Amoris*, cap. 37 (254.26ff.), may be indebted to his reading of *quaestiones* on visions, such as q. 68 of Alexander of Hales's *Quaestiones Disputatae Antequam Esset Frater*, entitled *De Raptu Pauli*, which defines rapture and its relation to other mystical experiences. It also seems likely, though I have not found clear evidence, that here (as perhaps in the *Incendium Amoris* chapter) Rolle is confronting a particular mystical work from the affective pseudo-Dionysian tradition, and attempting to argue that *canor* is a higher experience than all those offered by speculative contemplation (rapture, *excessus mentis*, etc.), *at the same time* as using the technical language and imagery of this tradition to bolster the prestige of *canor* (*Contra Amatores Mundi* has far more of such language than any of Rolle's other works). If there is such a work behind this chapter, it may well be Richard of St Victor's *Benjamin Major*, which makes much use of the language of rapture, of the idea of heavenly *archana*, and so on. At at least one point, when Rolle denies the possibility of 'visio . . . clara et perspicua', he is probably alluding to the famous definition of contemplation ('Contemplatio est perspicatia in sapientiae spectacula') in *Benjamin Major* I, cap. 4; he quotes this sentence directly in *Emendatio Vitae* (see p. 219 and Chapter 8, n. 20). What is puzzling is that Richard, indeed any orthodox spiritual writer, would agree with Rolle that God cannot be fully apprehended in this life; hardly anyone held the opinions Rolle attributes to 'aliter'. It seems the chapter may deliberately travesty speculative contemplative thought by pretending to engage it on ground it does not seek to occupy – thus making it possible for Rolle to imply that the speculative mystical experience is nothing more than a form of his own lowest experience, Sight into Heaven (5.298–310).

27 As at the end of *Super Canticum Canticorum*, Rolle borrows from the *De Diligendo Deo* (1) and the *De Quattuor Gradibus Violentae Caritatis* (2); he also apparently adapts phrases from Hugh of St Victor's *De Laude Caritatis* (3), and his own *Super Psalmum Vicesimum* (4) and *Super Canticum Canticorum* (5).

> (1) *Rolle*: 'Igitur vere amas Deum propter ipsum Deum et nichil aliud, nec eciam teipsum nisi propter Deum . . .' (7.279–281); *Bernard*: 'Hic vere diligit Deum propter Deum, et non propter seipsum . . . Iste est tertius amoris gradus . . . Felix qui meruit ad quartum usque pertingere, quatenus nec seipsum diligat homo nisi propter Deum' (27). (7.245–250 also recalls elements of both the Bernard and Richard passages quoted in n. 18: especially 'nostra interior natura in aliam gloriam aliamque potenciam tota liquefiat'.)
>
> (2) *Rolle*: 'O amor inseparabilis et insaciabilis, insuperabilis, violentus et impetuosus!' (7.274–275); *Richard*: 'amor insuperabilis . . . inseparabilis . . . singularis . . . insatiabilis' (143.22–24).
>
> (3) *Rolle*: 'Deum rapis ad hominem et hominem trahis ad Deum. Agis utiliter, curris velociter, et pervenis feliciter' (7.290–293); *Hugh*: 'O bona caritas, per quam Deum diligimus, Deum eligimus, ad Deum currimus,

ad Deum pervenimus . . . Tu Deum ad hominem deducis, tu hominem ad Deum dirigis' (PL 176, col. 974).

(4) *Contra Amatores Mundi*: 'Dum mira et magna agentes a facie Christi fugiunt, tu solus intrepidus ante tribunal Christi audacter astabis' (7.293–295); *Super Psalmum Vicesimum*: 'O amor quantum vales qui, dum immensa opera prophetie et miracula a facie Christi fugiendo delitescunt, tu solus in curiam eterni regis cum Christo duce intrare non formidas, sed et gloriose susciperis et cum magno honore ad sedem scandere iubileris' (12.15–19).

(5) *Contra Amatores Mundi*: 'Est itaque in hoc gradu summus, singularis, castus atque sanctus. O amor vehemens, flagrans, fortis, rapiens . . .' (7.252–254); *Super Canticum Canticorum*: 'Est itaque verus amor, castus, sanctus . . . flagrans, estuans, ex amato inardescens, vehemens . . .' (49.2–5).

7. CONTEMPLATIVE LIFE, *CANOR: MELOS AMORIS*

1 An article based on the same material as part of this chapter has been published in *The Medieval Translator*, edited by Roger Ellis (Watson 1989b).

2 'Querite de hac materia . . . in libro de perfeccione et gloria sanctorum' (196.19–20), referring to, e.g., *Melos Amoris* 15.6–7 (quoted below); see also 141.1, 145.7, 180.2–6. See Allen, pp. 136–137 and Moyes 1984, pp. 81 and 96, n. 3; *pace* Arnould 1957, p. lxvii, whose claim that *Melos Amoris* is not this 'Liber' – because *Super Lectiones Mortuorum* in which the latter is mentioned is less 'spiritually advanced' than *Melos Amoris* and must therefore be earlier – is clearly indefensible.

3 See Liegey 1957, an edition of a group of extracts from *Melos Amoris* found in MS Douai 396, and there entitled the 'Carmen Prosaicum', which can, with difficulty, be made to fit a Middle English four-stress alliterative pattern. Liegey's claim that *Melos Amoris* should thus be seen as alternating prose and verse has been taken up by de Ford (1980, 1986). No convincing evidence of this thesis has yet been adduced, and the consistency with which the MSS treat the work as prose, and the title 'Carmen Prosaicum' itself, make the hypothesis more than doubtful. For a general study of the work's style, see Liegey 1954.

4 *Melos Amoris* discusses hermits and monks in cap. 47; see *Super Canticum Canticorum* 23–29, and, for one passage (quoted in Excursus 1, item 4), cap. 4 of *Contra Amatores Mundi*. In the account of ordered love in caps. 48–52 of *Melos Amoris*, we find language like this, which is clearly related to *Super Canticum Canticorum* 48–49, as well as to the peroration of *Contra Amatores Mundi*: 'Ergo optimus est ordo charitatis quando est sine ordine; gloriosus est gradus amoris qui est sine gradu, et laudabilis modus sine modo . . . amor noster in Deum sit flagrans, vehemens, estuans, impetuosus, invincibilis, inseparabilis, singularis, totum hominem ad se trahens, in se ipso transformans, totum in eius servitutem redigens' (159.25–160.3).

5 The relevant passages from both works are set out in Excursus 1, item 3, to which the numbers 1–8 which identify the passages below refer.

6 This opening remark is related to stanza xiv of *Dulcis Ihesu Memoria*: 'Cum digne loqui nequeam, / De te tamen non sileam: / Amor facit ut audeam, / Cum solum de te gaudeam' (Wilmart 1943, pp. 149–150). Both works also echo *Metamorphoses* 4.96, 'Audacem faciebat Amor' (i.e. Thisbe), listed as no. 1684 of Walther's *Proverbia Sententiaeque*.

7 Notice how the deference Rolle expresses towards the Fathers in *Contra Amatores*

Mundi (5.311–325) is replaced by competitiveness. The passage is apparently based on *Incendium Amoris* 240.27–31: 'Si autem antiquitus Spiritus Sanctus plures inspiravit: cur eciam non nunc assumeret amantes ad gloriam Domini speculandam, cum ipsis prioribus moderni approbati non sunt inequales?'

8 The phrase 'sermones amoris' also seems designed to evoke the titles of some of Rolle's own works: *Canticum Amoris, Incendium Amoris, Liber de Amore Dei contra Amatores Mundi, Melos Amoris.*

9 For conceptual background to these paragraphs, see the introduction, especially pp. 11–15, an account of medieval ideas of the 'mixed' life.

10 The chapter as a whole immediately follows the *quaestio* on the solitary life which takes up cap. 47, where Rolle writes against those who think the coenobitic life superior to the eremitic. This *quaestio* is in its turn the climax of a group of chapters which goes back at least as far as cap. 40 (and might be considered to go back to cap. 35) of which *canor* is increasingly the focus, and which is a sustained definition and defence of the solitary life.

11 This topic forms an integral part of all Rolle's attempts to elevate the solitary life above the monastic, such as *Incendium Amoris*, caps. 31–33 (which this passage frequently recalls) and the attack on Anselm in *Super Canticum Canticorum* (of which *Melos Amoris* makes much use in the previous chapter, 47). Indeed, to a large extent Rolle's theory that *canor* is inspiration seems to have grown out of his (real or fictitious) arguments with monks.

12 Note that by this stage of the argument the fact these 'alia plura' must be written not preached has been assigned a spiritual cause (the debilitating affect of violent love) which reflects well on solitaries, and is no longer admitted to have anything to do with ecclesiastical legislation preventing secular hermits like Rolle from preaching. Yet while love is often seen as debilitating by medieval mystics (see, e.g., *De Quattuor Gradibus Violentae Caritatis* 137.4–8), it seldom is by Rolle, who often writes that travelling and noise impede *fervor* and *canor* but nowhere else that the reverse is also true; in *Emendatio Vitae*, indeed, he directly contradicts Richard's statement that love makes the flesh fail (see pp. 217–218). It would seem that the concept of 'mixed' life arrived at in this passage involved a certain amount of conceptual juggling on Rolle's part.

13 This passage may be based on Peter Lombard's *Sententiae* III, dist. xxix, cap. 1 (*De Ordine Diligendi: Qui Prius, Qui Post*), or a commentary thereon.

14 The work occurs in MSS Bodley 861, Corpus Christi, Oxford 193, Emmanuel 35, Sloane 2275, Hereford Cathedral O.VIII.1, Lincoln Cathedral c.5.2 and in Trier 685 (fragmentary); all of these are large collections of Rolle's Latin works, many with aspirations to completeness. In St John's College, Cambridge 23, it is found with *Incendium Amoris* and *Judica Me*, in Uppsala c.1 with *Incendium Amoris*; only in Lincoln College 89 and Trinity College, Dublin 159 does it appear as the sole Rolle work. (See Allen, pp. 114–115.)

15 I have not surveyed *Melos* MSS systematically, but according to Allen (pp. 114–115) only Lincoln College 89 has more than the odd note. This is borne out by my observations, and is in marked contrast to MSS of *Incendium Amoris* and *Super Canticum Canticorum* which (as Allen also attests) tend to be enthusiastically annotated. However, MS Dd.v.64 preserves part of an alphabetical list of 'verba difficilia per diversos doctores exposita que continentur in libro qui vocatur melum R. heremite' (f. 84), which suggests that at least some readers tried to make sense of the work.

8. 'MIXED' LIFE: *SUPER LECTIONES MORTUORUM* AND *EMENDATIO VITAE*

1 My analysis of this work has been much expedited and sometimes influenced by the fine edition and study by Malcolm Moyes (1988); unless otherwise indicated, references to Moyes in this chapter are to this edition.

2 See Moyes, vol. 1, p. 93 and Allen pp. 353–354; for Rolle's knowledge of the *Meditationes Piissimae*, see Chapter 9, pp. 237–238 and n. 8.

3 In the late Middle Ages, the Office for the Dead was usually appended to the Psalter, and was, of course, sung rather than spoken; thus its *lectiones* might naturally be seen as a form of song (Moyes 1984, p. 97, n. 9).

4 Strictly speaking the work does not appear on its own in these editions, being followed in both cases by a brief 'chaser', a 'Sermo beati Augustini de misericordia et pia oracione pro defunctis'.

5 Compare, however, the statement in 230.19–231.3 of the need for everyone, seculars and contemplatives, to practise 'mixed' life as Christ's soldiers, repelling the enemy's darts not only from their own breasts but from those of others: 'Milites quippe Christi sacerdotes et religiosi, heremite et monachi ... esse deberent, qui non solum a seipsis hostilia iacula repellere, verum eciam ab aliorum cordibus in quantum poterint niterentur auferre'.

6 Compare, e.g., the opening of *Lectio* II (156.1–6) with that of the final section of *Super Canticum Canticorum* (65.18–22). See also the beginning of *Lectio* VI, which quotes its text (Job 14.13), then breaks out with a fine inversion of the *felix culpa* motif: 'O infelix culpa et dirus lapsus primi parentis nostri ...' (222.6–7).

7 Rolle's principal ideas can only be reconstructed from the work by putting together scattered sentences and short passages the significance of which is unclear unless one is familiar with his earlier works. Thus for a model account of the ascent of the chosen soul to *fervor*, see 226.13–227.2; for the importance of ardent love, 204.3–5; for the possibility of continual *fervor*, 176.17–20; for continual desire leading to sure salvation, 236.20–237.6; for spiritual security, see 143.11–20; for the idea that love once had is never lost, 183.12–15; for the heavenly rejoicing of the elect while on earth, 186.1–187.2; for the perfection and holy daring of the *amator Christi*, 201.10–203.3. (Most of these passages also refer to *canor*, but I have found no references to the claim that *canor* itself can be continual.)

8 The dedication which occurs in five MSS (though only twice with a name included, in MSS Bodley 16 and Shrewsbury 25) may also be genuine: 'Ecce, Willelme, formam vivendi paucis verbis descripsi quam si sequi volueris proculdubio ad magnam perfectionem attingeris ...' (quoted in Allen, p. 231). However, Allen's identification of 'William' with a Dr William Stopes, who is mentioned in the marginalia of MS Vienna 4483 as 'valde intimus socius huius Rychardi' (f. 134; Allen, p. 41), is unconvincing; the same marginal note implies that Stopes was a monk or friar (at his death he is 'vocatis fratribus'), and *Emendatio Vitae*, as we will see, can hardly have been written in the first instance for a member of a religious house.

9 Caps. 1–3 are penitential in subject-matter; caps. 4–6 all deal with self-discipline and what threatens it – put another way, with sin and temptation, and how to deal with them; caps. 7–9 concern the exercises of *oratio, lectio, meditatio*; and caps. 10–12 describe the culmination of the spiritual life.

10 The work opens: 'Veritatis theologicae sublimitas, cum sit superni splendoris radius illuminans intellectum, et regalium deliciarum convivium, reficiens affectum, de magnorum theologorum scriptis breve Compendium colligere dignum duxi: quo et evitetur mater fastidii prolixitas, et tamen ad investigandum plura via detur et occasio sapienti.'

11 Bonaventure's preface ends: 'Ut autem sequentia clarius elucescant, titulos particulares capitulorum praemittere curavi, ad faciliorem memoriam, et lucidiorem contuitum dicendorum, quae septem partitionibus, et septuaginta duobus capitulis, distinguuntur.' Seventy-two is six times twelve.

12 The transitions between one chapter of this work and the next are all most skilfully devised to articulate the various relationships between the different stages of the argument, as well as simply to keep one reading. Some chapters, such as 3 and 12, begin unannounced. Others are treated as an 'ascent' from one stage to the next, as at the end of cap. 3: 'Dum ergo considerant altiora quae non attingunt, de minoribus non praesumant: sed humilibus consentant, ut ad institutionem vitae sic ascendere mereantur, de qua consequenter sequitur' (f. 136v. 3–5, compare the end of cap. 4). Cap. 5, *De Tribulatione*, ends by stating that suffering 'patientia nos docebit' (f. 138r. 17), introducing cap. 6, *De Patientia*. Cap. 7, *De Oratione*, begins by referring back to the previous two chapters – 'Si in tribulatione vel tentatione positus fueris, mox ad orationem curras' (f. 138v. 21) – and ends by pointing forward to cap. 8, *De Meditatio*; here, indeed, the local logic of the work causes the spiritual exercises *lectio*, *meditatio* and *oratio* to be treated in the reverse of their normal order. Finally, cap. 10, which is the chief structural hinge in the work, begins by summing up all that has gone before as 'hos novem gradus praetactos' (f. 193v. 29) and ends by introducing the final two chapters (f. 140r. 1–2, see below).

13 It is this passage which makes it clear that Rolle is writing *Emendatio Vitae* with non-eremitic and non-contemplative readers specifically in mind. As with *Judica Me* and *Super Lectiones Mortuorum*, the work's intended audience was thus probably the secular clergy – and, through them, everyone else.

14 A long passage in *The Form of Living* is structured around the first part of this chapter (see Excursus 1, item 1.2), but intersperses additional lists from *Compendium Theologicae Veritatis* III, caps. 30–33 (see Ogilvie-Thomson's notes to 329–398). *Emendatio Vitae* may be less immediately indebted to the same source, or may be taken from another treatment of the vices and virtues.

15 'Itaque in hunc modum ad vivendum vir Dei institutus, erit *tanquam lignum quod plantatum est secus decursus aquarum* in fluentiam gratiarum, ut semper virescat in virtute et numquam arescat vitii ariditate, quod *fructum* in bona terra, in bona opera in exemplum et bona data in subsidium *dabit* ad honorem Dei, non vendendo pro inani gloria, *in tempore suo*, contra singulares qui dant exempla ieiunandi quando est tempus comendendi et econtra, et contra avaros qui dant fructus qui aut putridi sunt, aut differunt usque ad mortem' (*Emendatio Vitae*, f. 136v. 32–38). Compare '*Et ideo erit tanquam lignum*, id est aliis erit utilis, non solum sic, *quod plantatum est* a Deo *secus decursus aquarum*, id est fluenta scripturarum, *quod fructum suum*, id est bona opera in exemplum, et bona data in subsidium *dabit* ad honorem Dei, non vendet pro inani gloria *in tempore suo*, contra singularitates quae dant exempla ieiunandi quando est tempus comedendi et econverso, et contra avaros qui fructus dant quando putridi sunt, vel differunt dare' (*Latin Psalter*, Psalm 1.3, 12.10–18; not derived from Lombard's commentary).

16 Faber's edition, f. 137v. 6–51 interpolates (before the last sentence of the original chapter) a long passage consisting of most of cap. 4 and part of cap. 5 of *Incendium Amoris*.

17 For Rolle's self-borrowing in these two chapters, and for much of the chapters themselves, see Excursus 1, item 2.1–8, to which numbers in square brackets in this and the next paragraphs refer.

18 Rolle writes that 'amor est insuperabilis quando nulla affectione alia potest

superari' (f. 140r. 30), Richard that 'insuperabilis est qui alii affectui non cedit' (143.228); Rolle that 'amor inseparabilis est quando iam vehementi dilectione succensa mens, atque Christo inseparabili cogitatione adhaerens, nullo quidem momento ipsum a memoria recedere permittit, sed quasi in corde ligaretur' (f. 140r. 34–36), Richard that 'insuperabilis qui a memoria numquam recedit' (143.28–145.1), and 'secundus [gradus est] ille quam ligat' (133.7); Rolle that 'ad singularem ergo gradum amor ascendit, quando omnem consolationem, praeter unam quod est Iesu, excludit: quoniam nihil propter Iesum sibi sufficere poterit' (f. 140r. 49–50), Richard that 'ad tertium itaque jam violentie gradum amor ascendit quando omnem alium affectum excludit, quando nichil preter unum vel propter unum diligit' (135.19–21). *Emendatio Vitae*, f. 140r. 44–v. 6 is based especially closely on *De Quattuor Gradibus Violentae Caritatis* 135.13–137.18.

19 The division of contemplation into three parts occurs in Aquinas, *Summa Theologica* II.ii, q. 180, art. 3, where it is derived from Hugh of St Victor. The definitions also seem to be standard. Bonaventure writes 'In lectio spiritualiter [Deus] loquitur nobiscum' (comment on Psalm 1; *Works*, vol. 9, p. 158). Alexander of Hales, *Glossa in Sententiarum III*, dist. xvii, 24.1, has 'Oratio est pius animae affectus in Deum directus'; compare 'Est autem oratio purus mentis affectus in Deum directus' (f. 141r. 21).

20 Identified by Allen, p. 341. The first definition ('rerum latentium') is from Julius Pomerius, *De Vita Contemplativa* I, cap. 13 (PL 59, col. 429); the next two are from Richard of St Victor, *Benjamin Major* I, cap. 4 (PL 196, col. 67), though the second ('libera et perspicax') first appears in Hugh of St Victor (PL 175, col. 175; 176, col. 879). The last two are untraced, though a definition similar to one ('per sublevantis mentis iubilum') appears in Rolle's English piece *The Seven Gifts of the Holy Spirit*, where it is attributed to Augustine: 'In þis gyfte [Wisdom] schynes contemplacyone, þat es, saynt Austyne says, a gastely dede of fleschely affecyones thurghe þe Ioy of a raysede thoghte' (p. 197).

21 See f. 142r. 2–5: 'Et si forte aliqui sint in eo statu quod et contemplativae vitae culmen arripiunt, et tamen praedicationis officium implere non desistunt, isti solitarios licet in contemplatione summos et solis divinis intentos, non necessitate proximorum, in hoc superant, quod caeteris operibus aureolam propter suam praedicationem merentur.' Compare *Contra Amatores Mundi* 7.113–123, and *Melos Amoris*, cap. 48.

9. 'MIXED' LIFE: THE ENGLISH WORKS

1 We have no evidence to suggest that any single individual or group produced a substantial body of Middle English devotional prose between about the 1230s, when *Ancrene Wisse*, and the *Katherine*- and *Wooing*-groups, were completed, and the 1340s, the decade in which Rolle's English works were written. *Ancrene Wisse* and the works associated with it survive in English in less than a dozen manuscripts.

2 The best discussion of this chapter of *Incendium Amoris* is in Moyes 1988, vol. 1, pp. 56–68, which has useful references to more general studies of the theme of *amicitia*, and explores the relationship between the chapter and Aelred's *De Spirituali Amicitia*. A complicating factor is that the words for 'friend' in *Incendium Amoris* often refer especially to patrons (see 196.31–197.26); when Rolle writes of living with his friend 'in mutuis colloquiis et tactibus honestis, grataque cohabitacione' (263.33–34), he is evidently concerned with the problems and proprieties not of female friendship in general but of life with a female patron in particular. Nonetheless, the fact that he discusses such a relationship in the language of *amicitia* seems significant in itself.

3 For a discussion of this metaphor in Middle English literature, see Riehle 1981, chapter 3. Two at least of the anchoritic works, *The Wooing of Our Lord* and *Hali Meiðhad*, are dominated by the idea that an anchoress chooses Christ instead of an earthly lover, and the same concept is near the centre of all three of the saints' passions, *Katherine*, *Margaret* and *Juliana*.

4 For the sexual sense of 'haue' implied here, see *The Ten Commandments* (196): 'The sexte commandment es: "thou sall be na lichoure", þat es, thow sall haue na man or womane bot þat þou has takene in fourme of haly kyrke.'

5 For the purposes of this chapter, I am taking a relatively conservative approach to the canon of Rolle's lyrics, including only the six poems from MS Longleat 29 printed in Ogilvie-Thomson's edition of the English works (which includes 'Ihesu swet', at least some of which may be Rolle's, but excludes the three Marian lyrics that follow it in the MS), and the one clearly Rollean poem in MS Dd.v.64 which is not in Longleat.

6 The titles of both *Ego Dormio* and *The Commandment* derive from Horstmann.

7 'In al oure hert: þat is, in al our vndrestongynge, witouten errynge. In al our soule: þat is, in al oure wille, withouten syggynge ayeyne. In al our thoght: þat is, þat we thynke on hym withouten foryetynge' (2–5). Compare: 'Diligendus est Deus *toto corde* id est, intellectu sine errore; *tota anima*, id est, voluntate sine contrarietate; *tota mente*, id est, memoria sine oblivione' (v, cap. 29, see also III, caps. 12—13).

8 'Si vero dicis, "Durus est hic sermo; non possum mundum spernere, et carnem meam odio habere", dic mihi: ubi sunt amatores mundi, qui ante pauca tempora nobiscum erant? Nihil ex eis remansit, nisi cineres et vermes. Attende diligenter quid sunt vel quid fuerunt. Homines fuerunt sicut tu: comederent, biberunt, riserunt, duxerunt in bonis dies suos; et in puncto ad inferna descenderunt' (Job 21.13; PL 184, col. 491).

9 Allen includes two versions of *Meditation B* in her list of Rolle's works, because all but one of the manuscripts attribute them to him; but she admits that neither is unmistakably authentic, like most of his works. Some critics, notably Morgan (1953) and Ogilvie-Thomson (1988), doubt the attribution: in the first case because Morgan tries to show that the work has an Anglo-Norman source, and a complicated prehistory she thinks incompatible with Rolle's authorship; in the second mainly because the work does not circulate with his other English writings (p. xciv). The last consideration is the more powerful. The sources of the two versions of *Meditation B* require further study, and Morgan gives no good reasons why Rolle should not have compiled material on the Passion from existing sources. But how likely is it that he composed a work of some stylistic virtuosity, like *Meditation B*, without introducing his own mystical imagery, and without apparently keeping a copy alongside those of his other English works? I suggest that it is entirely possible he did this, especially if he was adapting a source rather than creating a work *ex nihilo*, and if he was writing for a specific individual. A parallel is *Meditation A*, a work not known by Allen when *Writings Ascribed* was published, which survives in MS Cotton Titus C.XIX (where it was discovered by Francis Wormald in 1935), and in fragmentary form as the last of the series of Rolle works in Longleat. As Ogilvie-Thomson says (p. xlix), the Longleat fragment goes far to establishing this work as authentic. But here again, there are no traces of Rolle's style or characteristic concerns, and the work does not otherwise circulate with his other English writings; on the face of it *Meditation B*, which is highly affective and uses material from *Stimulus Amoris* and probably from the poetry of John of Hoveden (Moyes 1988, vol. 1, p. 51), is the more akin to Rolle's other writing. In the light of the manuscript attributions, with their rare use of Rolle's

surname (the authority of which is challenged most unconvincingly by Ogilvie-Thomson, p. 213), it seems to me we have to continue to regard at least the longer version of *Meditation B* as probably authentic.

10 The structure is a much-simplified version of that of an academic sermon, with the opening statement standing in for a biblical text, which is then divided into parts, each of which is dealt with in turn by means of further divisions. Compare *The Form of Living* 633–772.

11 A verse prologue to the copy of the *English Psalter* in MS Laud Misc. 286 states that Rolle 'Glosed þe sauter þat sues here in englysch tong sykerly / At a worthy recluse prayer, cald dame Merget kyrkyby' (see Bramley's edition, p. 2). There is no reason to doubt this is true; it is unlikely Rolle would have written so laborious a work in English without some specific impetus.

12 The only complete edition is by Bramley (1884), who uses a good base MS (University College 64) but provides only a few alternate readings from less than a third of the surviving MSS; his semi-diplomatic text is also hard to follow, which has reinforced an erroneous impression that the *English Psalter* is ill-written. Recently Cavallerano (1976), Newton (1976), Callanan (1977), Carney (1980) and Rodriguez (1980) have edited parts of the *English Psalter* in a series of Fordham University dissertations, which encompass Psalms 1–105, except for *lacunae* from 16–30 and 76–90. The series is useful for the textual variants it provides, but even if it is ever completed will need a good deal of work before it can replace Bramley. The major study is by Dorothy Everett (1922–1923), who groups the MSS into three categories, one 'uninterpolated', the others variously 'interpolated', one with orthodox commentary, the other with material clearly Wyklifite in inspiration. Her arguments are impressive and convincing, but we should not assume, as all the editors of the Fordham series do, that her work is definitive; it seems at least worth considering the possibility, for example, that the first 'interpolated' version contains Rollean material omitted from the 'uninterpolated' one.

13 The influence of Peter Lombard on Rolle's commentaries was established by Middendorf in 1888 (in a study which considerably overstates the degree of Rolle's dependence). The influence of the *Latin Psalter* on the *English Psalter* is on occasion obvious (e.g. in the prologue), but has not been demonstrated in detail. Few of the parallel passages Allen quotes (pp. 179–185) show a clear relation between the two, and many of the instances which might be given are simply a result of the dependence of both works on Peter Lombard; the parallels pointed out by Everett (1922, pp. 226–227) between the two comments on the six Old Testament canticles may also merely indicate a shared source. In a few places (see, e.g., Psalm 1.1) the *English Psalter* contains matter attributed to an authority which is not in Peter Lombard; this suggests that Rolle may have drawn on one or more further sources. Both G. Hodgson (1926, pp. 151–188) and Rodriguez (1980, pp. xxii–xxxvi) claim a direct relationship between Rolle's commentary and Augustine's (which forms Peter Lombard's own major source), but I remain dubious.

14 Compare: 'Psalmus tranquillitas animorum est . . . adducens in concordiam discrepantes . . . charitas Psalmus instaurat . . . Psalmus daemones fugat, angelos ad adjutorum invitat' (PL 36, col. 64). Since other parts of this passage are borrowed from another source (see next note), it is likely that Rolle was drawing on some kind of compendium of comments on the Psalter.

15 Compare: 'Cantus qui aures oblectat et animas instruit, fit vox una psallentium, et cum angelis Dei, quos audire non possumus, laudum verba miscemus . . .' (PL 70, col. 10). The whole passage from 'Sothly, þis shynand boke' is from the same source, and is translated equally closely.

16 For a discussion of this kind of prologue, its origins in the eleventh century and supersession in academic circles (by the 'Aristotelian' prologue) in the thirteenth, see Minnis 1984, pp. 19–28, and 40ff.

17 For comment on Rolle's strategies and their relation to those of other medieval biblical translators, see Ellis 1982, especially pp. 29–30.

18 For other recent comments on the extent and nature of Rolle's borrowing from Peter Lombard, see Newton 1976, pp. xli–xlvi and Cavallerano 1976, pp. l–lxii. After the first few dozen psalms, and as Rolle's commentary grows less and less detailed, his dependence on Peter Lombard seems to increase.

19 Note, however, that the 'haly doctours' do give Rolle a good deal of help in this endeavour, expounding many of the references to song in the Psalter with what look like discussions of *canor*. See, for example, the comment on Psalm 150.5, literally translated from Peter Lombard: '*Omnis spiritus laudet Dominum* . . . Pis ioiynge is wondirful louynge of God, þat cummys noght bot out of þe saule. And for he will þat all be vndirstandyn gastly, he loukis his boke in a cunabil end: "Ilke a spirit, aungels and mannys, louys þe Lord", whaim I loue. For he is noght forto loue bot gastly . . . In þere instrumentis þat he neuens is perffecioun of all musyke, for blast is in þe trumpe, pouste in þe harpe and in chymys voice in croude, in þe whilke instrumentis of musyke gastly melody is bitakynd, þat mare is persayfid with pure thoght þan with eryn of body. Forþi "Ilke a spirt lou[y]e þe Lord!"' (493.13–36).

20 The fragment is meaningless on its own, probably indicating that the whole meditation was originally present in the MS form from which the Longleat scribe was copying, but that the bulk of it had been lost by the time the copy was made. (This explanation implies that the conclusion of *Meditation A* in MS Cotton Titus C.XIX, which addresses a 'dere brothere in Ihesu' (170–174), did not form an original part of the work.) The three Marian lyrics (edited in Ogilvie-Thomson 1974) show no signs of Rolle's authorship, but could have been adapted by him for Margaret Kirkeby's use; *The Form of Living* tells her to 'haille oft Mary, boþ day and nyght' (621), placing this devotional duty alongside that of the devotion to the Name of Jesus.

21 Neither Allen nor Ogilvie-Thomson indicates which MSS contain chapter divisions; all those I have seen do so, and they must have found their way into the textual tradition of the work very early. Nonetheless, while they are mostly logically placed (except for cap. 11, see n. 24) and may preserve some kind of divisions in the original text (probably paragraph marks) they seem to me to interrupt the flow of the epistle, and to imply an external structure of a kind we find in *Emendatio Vitae* but which is absent here. The major transitions in the work (105, 261–266, 485–488, 626–632) are clear without formal divisions, since they are all introduced by 'now': 'Thou has herd nowe', 'Now maist þou see', 'Now as þou herd', 'Bot now may þou ask'.

22 In this paragraph I am developing ideas which are occasionally alluded to, but never systematically advanced, in Ogilvie-Thomson's edition of the English works. Ogilvie-Thomson directs her energies towards claiming that the Longleat rubrics should supersede those in Dd.v.64, since the former imply that all three epistles were written for Margaret Kirkeby, where the latter dedicates *Ego Dormio* to a nun of Yedingham, *The Commandment* to an unspecified Hampole nun (see especially pp. lxvi–lxvii, lxxx). This emphasis diffuses the significance of the Longleat rubrics, which lies in the fact that they apply to a collection, not to individual works – for if we take this fact seriously, there is no competition between the two sets of rubrics, one identifying the individuals to whom Rolle originally addressed the epistles, the other the woman for whom he collected them into a single volume.

23 Even the title Rolle gives in referring to the work as 'þis short fourme of lyvynge' (264–265) translates the equally general subtitle of *Emendatio Vitae*, which in most MSS is called 'Emendatio vitae sive de regula vivendi'.

24 The MSS with chapter divisions break this fifth question in two at 836, creating a final chapter on the active and contemplative lives which seems irrelevant when cut off from the question to which it belongs. Especially in combination with the spurious interpolation of *The Seven Gifts of the Holy Spirit* in MS Dd.v.64 at this point, this artificial division has tended to obscure the organizational clarity of this part of the work.

25 The first sentence is indebted to *Emendatio Vitae*, cap. 8, 'Quidam etiam meditantur de gloria bonorum angelorum et sanctarum animarum ad Christum exultantium; et haec meditatio ad contemplationem pertinet' (f. 193r. 18–20). The last seems related to the statement Rolle borrows from Augustine in the prologue to the *English Psalter*, about the way psalmody 'Makes pees itwix body and saule' (see above and n. 14).

EPILOGUE

1 For the complexities of the concept of *inventio*, see Curtius 1948, pp. 68–71, and the article *Invention* in the *Princeton Encyclopedia of Poetry and Poetics*, pp. 401–402. Geoffrey of Vinsauf is drawing on Cicero's treatise *De Inventione*, the pseudo-Ciceronian *Rhetorica ad Herennium*, and a number of other works. For a discussion of Rolle and rhetorical theory (particularly the levels of style), see the useful article by Rita Copeland (1984).

2 Some basic information is given in Chapter 1, pp. 31–34 and notes. For the circulation of Rolle's works, see especially Doyle 1953, 1981, Sargent 1976 and further items cited below; for versions, translations and adaptations of Rolle's works, see Amassian 1979, Arntz 1981, Brady 1980, 1981, 1983, Gillespie 1983; for medieval responses to Rolle, see items cited below.

3 Wynkyn de Worde printed in 1506 the *Contemplacyons of the Drede and Loue of God*, and in 1508 *The Remedy Ayenst the Troubles of Temptacyons* (reprinted 1519). The latter contains brief extracts from *The Form of Living*; the former describes the 'three degrees of love' from the same work, and the degrees of love from *Ego Dormio*, but deliberately focusses its attention on lower stages of the spiritual life (see n. 14). De Worde seems to have been happier to have Rolle's name on his title pages than to print his genuine works.

4 Hughes's book is an ambitious attempt to draw together various strands of the scholarly study of late-medieval religiosity in the north of England; he looks at devotional, mystical and theological writing, episcopal, diocesan and parish records, wills, and a good deal besides, and makes large claims for the influence Rolle and a few others wielded. Unfortunately, his picture of Rolle is distorted by guesswork, inaccuracies, and over-reliance on Allen. For example: p. 82, Rolle did not 'translate Aelred of Rievaulx's *Rule for Recluses*' (nor does Allen say he did); pp. 83–86 first accept Allen's datings of Rolle's works, then correctly challenge her dating of *Judica Me* to 1322 (n. 36), but after this continue to describe his supposed patrons as if this date was correct (hence most of the speculation on p. 86 is invalid); pp. 90, 93, the *Officium* does not say that Rolle wrote *libelli* for his 'neighbours' in a geographical but a theological sense – thus the reference is not to his English works in particular, nor to his interest in edifying his patrons; p. 90, there is no sign that the Psalter bequeathed by Joan Walkyngham in 1346 is Rolle's; pp. 107–108, the account of the scribe of MS Bodley 861 as a north country hermit wandering Richmondshire looking for MSS of Rolle's works is

pure fantasy; p. 119, so, too, is the idea of Rolle using *Judica Me* as a confession manual in the Scrope household; pp. 220–226, an account of the Yorkshire clergy controlling the circulation of Rolle's works is intriguing but must be treated with caution, especially with respect to MS Emmanuel 35 (on which, *pace* n. 64, Sargent is probably right, Hughes wrong); and so on. Almost every reference to Rolle is problematic. There is, it should be said, much of interest in this book; but, sadly, what it most clearly demonstrates is that we are not yet in a position to make the synthesis it attempts – at least with respect to Rolle.

5 For the Hilton passages which are generally taken to refer to Rolle's teaching, see *Scale of Perfection*, I, caps. 10–13, 26, 31; (doubtfully) II, 29–30; and *Of Angels' Song* (probably but not certainly by Hilton), which apparently warns against over-literalistic interpretations of *canor*. Parts of the digression in *The Cloud of Unknowing* devoted to false contemplatives (caps. 45–56) are also taken to refer to experiences modelled on *fervor*; see especially 47.33–41 and 58.26–31. (For discussion see Sargent 1981.)

6 Cap. 26, which discusses the 'fire of love', argues it to be spiritual, not a physical sensation, but concedes that the workings of the soul may cause a sensation of bodily heat; this seems to be a gesture towards the prologue to *Incendium Amoris*, which describes *fervor* as 'vere non imaginarie, quasi sensibile', but also 'ex interiori ... non ... a carne' (see pp. 113–115). Cap. 31 speaks of how *fervor* would be unendurable to soul and body if it were not sometimes withdrawn, and warns those who experience it against taxing their bodies with penance; the prologue to *Incendium Amoris* similarly states that prolonged exposure to *fervor* would cause the soul to quit the body, while many passages of Rolle's works warn against harsh penance.

7 The work is clearly an attempt to place *canor* in a theological perspective which differs markedly from Rolle's. As well as warning against self-created experiences of pseudo-*canor*, it distinguishes between true angels' song and other kinds of song, such as the soul's praise of the Holy Name. In itself, this is not more than a clarification of the confusing shifts of meaning *canor* undergoes in Rolle, especially in *Super Canticum Canticorum*, which may well be the main work Hilton has in mind (see pp. 180–181, whose discussion of the Holy Name may be indebted to the section of *Super Canticum Canticorum* which circulated under the name *Enconium Nominis Ihesu*). The work's opening, which describes angels' song with great care, acknowledges that the gift is given only to the *perfecti* who burn in the fire of love, but takes issue with Rolle over its ultimate importance and to an extent over the form it takes: it is a valuable gift, but it is not the sovereign joy of the soul, and is clearly not conceived of as a continual experience. Nonetheless, the most striking thing about the work is how much it concedes; *canor* emerges unchallenged in most respects, and Hilton ends by deferring to the superior experience of anyone else who 'sauour be grace þe contrarye here-to', leaving one free to accept Rolle's more adventurous interpretations of *canor* if one wishes.

8 'Also owr Lord 3af hir an-oþer tokne, þe whech enduryd a-bowtyn xvj 3er, & it encresyd euyr mor & mor, & þat was a flawme of fyer – wondir hoot & delectabyl & ryth comfortabyl, nowt wastyng but euyr incresyng – of lowe [probably = *love*, not *flame, pace* Meech and Allen]; for, thow þe wedyr wer neuyr so colde, sche felt þe hete brennyng in hir brest & at hir hert, as verily as a man schuld felyn þe material fyer 3yf he put hys hand or hys finger þerin' (188.26–33). Compare *Incendium Amoris*, prologue, 'Sed sicut si digitus in igne poneretur fervorem ...' (quoted on pp. 113–115). For Margery Kempe's knowledge of this work, see 39.24, 143.28, 154.11.

9 'Nam vita mea consistit in amore, languore, fervore, canore; rarius tamen in

sensibili fervore, quia dilectus michi promisit quod frequencius in languore, sicut et ille almus Ricardus, dictus "de Hampol", frequencius in calore, de quo non legi quod tam frequens fuerit in languore' (cap. 12).

10 As Allen recognized (pp. 320–324), there is a small chance that the *De Excellentia Contemplationis* actually is what it purports to be, a compilation made by Rolle himself; we know he reused earlier material when it suited him (see Excursus 1), and *Super Canticum Canticorum*, *Super Psalmum Vicesimum* and *Contra Amatores Mundi*, all of which make appearances in this work, were among his favourite repositories of passages for later plundering. At this stage, I have two strong, though not conclusive, reasons for thinking the work is not his. One is the connection of all the MSS with Sheen and Sion, which suggests fifteenth-century Carthusian authorship. The other is that the work does not, so far as I have been able to find, contain any passages of more than a few phrases which do not occur in one of Rolle's genuine works; this fails to fit the pattern of self-borrowing he follows in *Emendatio Vitae* and especially *Melos Amoris*, where a good deal is changed or added. Particularly in a work which begins by praying for divine inspiration, as this does, it is hard to imagine Rolle staying so close to his own earlier words.

11 See the mass of material on MSS ascriptions in Allen, whose success in establishing the canon of Rolle's works was much facilitated by the fact that few of them are ever attributed to any other writer. The works of William of St Thierry usually circulated under the name of Bernard, both during and after the Middle Ages; those of Aelred which attained some popularity, such as the *De Institutis Inclusarum*, generally circulated anonymously.

12 *Pace* Allen, pp. 527–528 and Hughes 1988, pp. 90 etc., there seems no reason to identify this Bassett with the Norwich hermit of the same name, who died in 1435; nor is there evidence for the date Hughes assigns the *Defensorium* (1405; p. 90 but see p. 217). The *Defensorium* survives in only one MS, Uppsala c.621, copied in England by the Bridgettine monk, Katallus Thorberni, some time between 1408 and 1421 (see Taavitsainen 1990, p. 58, drawing on an unpublished paper by Monica Hedlund); the MS also contains other works of Rolle, and a version of the *Officium* revised for non-English readers (Allen, pp. 53–54). The presence of these works in Sweden, and of two MSS of the *De Excellentia Contemplationis* (Uppsala c.17 and c.631), seems to suggest an attempt by the Bridgettine nuns of Sion or their Sheen mentors to spread the Rolle cult beyond the borders of England, and also implies that Rolle's supporters in the Carthusian order were more influential than his detractors.

13 'Preterea quo ad hoc quod dixisti de prefato venerabili Ricardo, cuius memoria in benediccione est, vicilicet quod fuit materia quasi ruine et decepcionis, quia, ut tibi videbatur, fecit homines iudices sui, et quod tu non nosti tot homines in libris eius profecisse, quot in eis miserabiliter decepti sunt' (250–254).

14 One of many places to look for evidence of such 'fluidity' would be the *Contemplacyons of the Drede and Loue of God*, which opens with an exposition of Rolle's degrees of love for the benefit of those who have not heard of them, but quickly moves on to less elevated matter, on the grounds that few in these corrupt times can aspire to such contemplative heights (see also n. 3). This in itself suggests that Rolle is an *auctor* of whom ordinary Christians ought to be aware but will hardly be likely to read and follow. Yet the 'corrupt times' *topos* is also used to distinguish the holy men of the past from Rolle, who is described (as the main person referred to by the phrase 'other ful holy men of ryght late tyme') as no longer able to match their austerity, in spite of being 'vysyted by the grace of god with a passynge swetenes of the loue of cryste', but as having had to take his

'lyuelode as feblenesse of man asketh now in our dayes' (p. 74) – a reference to his emphasis on eating and drinking what was needful. Saintly *auctoritas*, it seems, is not what it was; the moderns, for all Rolle's protestations, do not compare with the ancients. But if this is so, why does the writer begin with Rolle at all? A proper study might provide insights into a work which already manifests an intriguingly complicated attitude to Rolle.

15 For this paragraph see, e.g., Curtius 1948, especially chapters 12 and 17, and Minnis and Scott's *Medieval Literary Theory and Criticism* (1988), chapters 9 and 10 (both written with the assistance of David Wallace).

EXCURSUS I

1 Porter (1929), Liegey (1954), Murray (1958), Marzac (1968), Daly (1984), Lagorio (1987), and Hughes (1988, pp. 82ff.) all treat most or all of Allen's conjectured chronology in this way, while Lagorio and Bradley organize the Rolle chapter of their bibliography around it (1981, pp. 53, 60). Dissenting views about single works (notably *Melos Amoris*) are expressed by Arnould (1957, pp. lxv–lxvii), de Ford (1980), and most effectively by Clark (1986), whose analysis agrees in many respects with mine, and repays careful reading (see also R. Allen 1988, pp. 41–50).

2 Allen's portrait of Rolle emerges most clearly in the introduction to *English Writings* (pp. ix–lxiv), in which she wrote for a more general audience than that of *Writings Ascribed* (but see Allen, pp. 1–8).

3 Allen's chronology of Rolle's work is greatly influenced by Horstmann, although her dislike of these early works is her own. In *Writings Ascribed* she refers to *Melos Amoris* as 'a childish excursion into barbarism' (p. 306), while in *English Writings* she muses that it 'may express some sort of tragic interval in the author's youth, an intensely, almost insanely, egocentric period, when his mood flowed out naturally into strident language, and his desire for alliteration and rhetoric overcame all restraints of idiom and right measure' (pp. xxxv–xxxvi). The equation of rhetoric with egocentricity is a characteristic stylistic judgement; it becomes explicable when one reflects that Manly's famous lecture 'Chaucer and the rhetoricians', with its not dissimilar assumptions about the nature of rhetoric, was given only the year before Allen's work appeared in 1927.

4 The order Allen argues for and in large measure assumes is as follows: (1) Early Period: Miscellaneous biblical commentaries, *Judica Me*, *Canticum Amoris*; slightly later *Melos Amoris*, then *Super Lectiones Mortuorum*; fairly early *Latin Psalter*. (2) Middle Period: *Super Canticum Canticorum*, somewhat later *Contra Amatores Mundi*, then *Incendium Amoris*, most of which was written by 1343; *English Psalter* at about the same date. (3) Late Period: *Emendatio Vitae*, all the other English works. She does not concern herself with the period of composition of some of the biblical commentaries (including *Super Canticum Canticorum*, *Super Mulierem Fortem* and *Super Magnificat*).

5 See Boyle 1955, pp. 105–106. *Pars Oculi* of *Oculus Sacerdotis* (of which *Judica Me* makes extensive use) quotes from a commentary which was finished in 1326, but does not refer to Mepham's provincial constitutions of 1328.

6 According to Allen, *Judica Me* cannot have been written long before 1322, since Rolle must have been younger than his first patron, Thomas de Neville, who was born in 1292. Scholars generally place Rolle's birth at *c.* 1300 as a result of this tenuous and inaccurate argument (but Arnould, pp. lxv–lxvii, is more cautious). It is the sole basis for Marzac's claim that 'beaucoup d'incipit des manuscrits de Richard Rolle situent sa naissance aux environs de 1300' (p. 17); there are no such manuscripts.

334

7 Ghellinck (1948) gives various upper and lower limits for terms such as 'puer', 'adolescentus' and 'iuvenis'. For example, Isidore regards 'pueritia' as extending from the ages of 7 to 14, 'adolescentia' from 14 to 28 and 'iuventia' from 28 to 49; other writers also associate 'iuventus' with the 30s and 50s. Burrow (1986) is sceptical about the possibility of drawing specific conclusions from any of these terms, given the numbers of competing systems for dividing human life available to medieval writers.

8 Allen's case is not helped by her missing this instance of the word's use, for she plausibly argues that *Contra Amatores Mundi* is a fairly mature work.

9 Allen is not alone in her attempt to make 'iuvenis' yield biographical information. Arnould (p. xxiii, n. 8), Noetinger (1926, p. 15, n. 2) and Horstmann (vol. 2, p. xix, n. 1) all wrestle with the term with the same end in view.

10 *Pace* Hughes 1988, p. 85, n. 35, who challenges Allen's identification of Margaret le Boteler, by pointing out the difficulty of telescoping the events described in *lectio viija* of the *Officium* – in which Margaret, already an anchoress, is healed by Rolle and only attacked again by the same disease 'some years later', on the very day he dies – into the last ten months of his life. But the *Officium* is probably revising history here in order to present the healing of Margaret as a miracle; Rolle's powers would not seem nearly so impressive if the narrative admitted they were efficacious for only a few months. To deny the identification between Margaret le Boteler and Margaret Kirkeby necessitates an impossibly complex scenario, in which two Hampole nuns called Margaret are enclosed at far-off East Layton within a few years, Margaret le Boteler in 1348, Margaret Kirkeby in time to live there and leave in 1357 for Anderby, having first been an anchoress (somewhere else near Richmond) for some time before Rolle's death in 1349. Anchoresses moved seldom, and only with a good deal of bureaucratic difficulty.

Bibliography

TABLE OF MANUSCRIPTS

This table lists manuscripts in the form cited in the text, giving their location where necessary. For most, see also Allen (especially pp. 563–567), and/or Moyes 1988, vol. 2, pp. 1–121.

Arundel 507 (BL)
BL Add. 16170
BL Add. 24661
BL Add. 34193
BL Add. 34763
BL Add. 37049
BL Add. 37790
Bodleian th. d. 15
Bodley 16
Bodley 43
Bodley 52
Bodley 54
Bodley 61
Bodley 66
Bodley 315
Bodley 456
Bodley 525
Bodley 861
Bristol 6 (Bristol Reference Library)
Burney 356 (BL)
Burney 359 (BL)
Caius 140 (Cambridge, Caius and Gonville College)
Corpus Christi, Oxford, 193
Cotton Junius A.ix (BL)
Cotton Titus c.xix (BL)
Dd.iv.54 (CUL)
Dd.v.55 (CUL)
Dd.v.64 (CUL)
Douai 396 (France, Douai, Bib. de la ville)
Douce 107 (Bodley)
Durham b.iv (Durham Cathedral)
Edinburgh University 93
Emmanuel 35 (Cambridge, Emmanuel College)
Ff.v.36 (CUL)
Ff.v.40 (CUL)
Ghent 291 (Belgium, Ghent, Bib. de la ville)
Harley 106 (BL)

Harley 275 (BL)
Harley 1022 (BL)
Harley 5235 (BL)
Harley 5938 (BL)
Hatton 26 (Bodley)
Hereford Cathedral o.viii
Hereford Cathedral p.i.9
Ii.vi.40 (CUL)
Kk.vi.20 (CUL)
Jesus College, Cambridge 46
Lansdowne 455 (BL)
Lat. Th. 11 (Bodley)
Laud Lat. 94
Laud Misc. 111 (Bodley)
Laud Misc. 202 (Bodley)
Laud Misc. 286 (Bodley)
Laud Misc. 528 (Bodley)
Lincoln c.5.2 (Lincoln Cathedral)
Lincoln College 89 (Oxford)
Longleat 29 (Longleat House)
Lyell 38 (Bodley)
Magdalen 6 (Oxford, Magdalen College)
Magdalen 71 (Oxford, Magdalen College)
Magdalen 141 (Oxford, Magdalen College)
Metz 361 (France, Metz, Bib. de la ville)
Mm.v.37 (CUL)
Mm.vi.17 (CUL)
New College 93 (Oxford)
New College 292 (Oxford)
Ohio State University Latin MS 1
Rawlinson A.389 (Bodley)
Rawlinson c.72 (Bodley)
Rawlinson c.269 (Bodley)
Rawlinson c.397 (Bodley)
Royal 5.c.iii (BL)
Royal 5.E.ii (BL)
Royal 5.F.vii (BL)
Royal 7.Eii
Shrewsbury School 25
Sloane 1584 (BL)
Sloane 2275 (BL)
St John's College, Cambridge 23
St John's College, Oxford 147
Stowe 38 (BL)
Thornton (Lincoln Cathedral)
Trier 685 (West Germany, Stadtbibl.)
Trinity College, Cambridge 17
Trinity College, Cambridge 374
Trinity College, Dublin 153
Trinity College, Dublin 155
Trinity College, Dublin 159
University College 64 (Oxford)
Uppsala c.1 (Sweden, Uppsala University)

Bibliography

Uppsala c.17 (Sweden, Uppsala University)
Uppsala c.621 (Sweden, Uppsala University)
Uppsala c.631 (Sweden, Uppsala University)
Vienna 4483 (Vienna, National Library)

PRIMARY AND SECONDARY SOURCES

All citations in the text are included here, except for those medieval authors and works which are mentioned only in passing, if these are easily available (e.g. in PL), or if my information about them is taken directly from a secondary source cited in the text. Where more than one edition of a work is listed, the one to which citations refer is delineated by (*).

Aelred. *Aelredi Rievallensis Opera Ascetica*, ed. A. Hoste and C.H. Talbot. *Corpus Christianorum, Continuatio Medievalis*, 1 (1971).
    De Institutis Inclusarum. In *Opera Omnia*, vol. 1, pp. 637–682.
    De Jesu Puero Duodenni. In *Opera Omnia*, vol. 1, pp. 249–278.
    De Spirituali Amicitia. In *Opera Omnia*, vol. 1, pp. 287–350.
Alexander of Hales. *Glossa in Quatuor Libros Sententiarum Petri Lombardi*. 4 vols. Bibliotheca Franciscana Scholastica Medii Aevi, vols. 17–25. Quaracchi, Collegio S. Bonaventurae (1951–1957).
    Quaestiones Disputatae Antequam Essem Frater. 3 vols. Bibliotheca Franciscana Scholastica Medii Aevi, vols. 16–18. Quaracchi, Collegio S. Bonaventurae (1960).
Alford, John (1973). Biblical *imitatio* in the writings of Richard Rolle. *Journal of English Literary History*, 40, pp. 1–23.
    (1976). The biblical identity of Richard Rolle. *Fourteenth-Century English Mystics Newsletter*, 2/4, pp. 21–25.
    (1984). Richard Rolle and related works. *In* Edwards 1984, pp. 34–60.
Allen, Hope Emily (1910). *The Authorship of 'The Prick of Conscience'*. Radcliffe College Monographs, 15 Boston and New York, Ginn and Co.
    (1918). The mystical lyrics of the *Manual des Péchiez*. *Romanic Review*, 9, pp. 154–193.
    (1927). *Writings Ascribed to Richard Rolle, Hermit of Hampole, and Materials for his Biography*. Modern Language Association Monograph Series, 3. New York, D.C. Heath and Co.
    ed. (1931). *English Writings of Richard Rolle, Hermit of Hampole*. Oxford, Clarendon Press.
    (1932a). New manuscripts of Richard Rolle. *The Times Literary Supplement*, 31, p. 202.
    (1932b). Richard Rolle. *The Times Literary Supplement*, 31, p. 516.
Allen, Rosamund (1984). 'Singular Lufe': Richard Rolle and the grammar of spiritual ascent. *In* Glasscoe 1984, pp. 28–54.
    trans. (1988). *Richard Rolle: The English Works*. The Classics of Western Spirituality. Mahwah, Paulist Press.
Amassian, Margaret G. (1979). The Rolle material in Bradfer-Lawrence MS 10 and its relationships to other Rolle manuscripts. *Manuscripta*, 23, pp. 67–78.
Ancrene Wisse. *The English Text of the Ancrene Riwle: Ancrene Wisse (Cambridge, Corpus Christi College MS 402)*, ed. J.R.R. Tolkien. EETS (os), 249 (1962).
Anselm. *Orationes sive Meditationes*. In *S. Anselmi Opera Omnia*, vol. 3, pp. 5–91, ed. F.S. Schmitt. 6 vols. Edinburgh, Nelson (1946).
(pseudo)-Anselm of Laon. *Enarrationes in Apocalypsim*. *In* PL 162, cols. 1499–1586.

Bibliography

Arnould, E.J.F. (1937a). Richard Rolle and a bishop: a vindication. *Bulletin of the John Rylands Library*, 21, pp. 55–77.
  (1937b). On Richard Rolle's patrons: a new reading. *Medium Aevum*, 6, pp. 122–124.
  (1939). Richard Rolle and the Sorbonne. *Bulletin of the John Rylands Library*, 23, pp. 68–101.
  ed. (1957). *See* Rolle, Richard, *Melos Amoris*.
  (1960). Richard Rolle of Hampole. *The Month*, n.s. 23, pp. 13–25.
Arntz, Mary Luke, ed. (1981). *Richard Rolle and Þe Holy Boke Gratia Dei: An Edition with Commentary*. Salzburg Studies in English Literature: Elizabethan and Renaissance Studies, 92: 2. Salzburg, Institut für Anglistik und Amerikanistik.
Ayto, John and Barratt, Alexandra, eds. (1984). *Aelred of Rievaulx's 'De Institutione Inclusarum': Two English Versions*. EETS (os), 287.
Bassett, Thomas. *Defensorium contra Oblectratores eiusdem Ricardi quod composuit Thomas Basseth sancte memorie*. In Allen 1927, pp. 529–537.
  Defensorium contra Oblectratores eiusdem Ricardi quod composuit Thomas Basseth sancte memorie. In Sargent 1981, pp. 188–205. (*)
Bell, David (1983). *The Image and Likeness: The Augustinian Spirituality of William of St Thierry*. Cistercian Studies Series, no. 78. Kalamazoo, Cistercian Publications.
Benedictine Rule. The Rule of St Benedict: The Abingdon Copy (Cambridge, Corpus Christi College MS 57), ed. John Chamberlin. Toronto Medieval Latin Texts, 13. Toronto, Centre for Medieval Studies (1982).
Benson, R.H. (1906). *Richard Raynal, Solitary*. London, Pitman.
  (1909). *A Book of the Love of Jesus*. London, Pitman.
Bernard of Clairvaux. *Sancti Bernardi Opera*, ed. J. Leclerq, C.H. Talbot, H.M. Rochais. Vols. 1– . Rome, Editiones Cistercienses (1957–).
  De Diligendo Deo. In *Sancti Bernardi Opera*, vol. 3, pp. 119–154 (1963).
  De Gradibus Humilitatis et Superbiae. In *Sancti Bernardi Opera*, vol. 3, pp. 1–59 (1963).
  Sermones super Cantica Canticorum. In *Sancti Bernardi Opera*, vols. 1–2 (1957–1958).
(pseudo)-Bernard. See *Meditationes Piissimae*.
de la Bigne, Marguerin, ed. (1622, 1654). *Magna Bibliotheca Veterum Patrum*, vol. 15. Cologne.
  ed. (1677, 1694). *Maxima Bibliotheca Veterum Patrum*, vol. 26. Lyons, Cologne.
Bloom, Harold (1973). *The Anxiety of Influence: A Theory of Poetry*. New York, Oxford University Press.
Bloomfield, Morton W. (1961). *Piers Plowman as a Fourteenth-Century Apocalypse*. New Brunswick, N.J., Rutgers University Press.
Bonaventure. *Opera Omnia Sancti Bonaventurae*, ed. A.C. Peltier. 15 vols. Paris, Vives (1864–1871).
  Omnia Opera Sancti Bonaventurae. 10 vols. Quaracchi, Collegio S. Bonaventurae (1882–1892). (*)
  Breviloquium. In *Omnia Opera*, vol. 5, pp. 199–291.
  Itinerarium Mentis in Deum. In *Omnia Opera*, vol. 5, pp. 293–316.
  Legenda S. Francisci. In *Omnia Opera*, vol. 8, pp. 504–576.
  In Librum Quartum Sententiarum. In *Omnia Opera*, vols. 1–4.
pseudo-Bonaventure. *See* James of Milan, *Stimulus Amoris*; and see *Meditationes Vitae Christi*.
Bonnes, J.P. (1945–1946). Un des plus grands prédicateurs du XIIe siècle: Geoffrey de Loroux, dit Geoffrey Babion. *Revue Benedictine*, 56, pp. 174–215.

Bibliography

Book of Vices and Virtues, ed. W. Nelson Francis. EETS (os), 217 (1942).

Boyle, Leonard (1955). The *Oculus Sacerdotis* and some other works of William of Pagula. *Transactions of the Royal Historical Society*, 5th Series, 5, pp. 81–110.

(1956). A study of the works attributed to William of Pagula. 2 vols. Dissertation, Oxford University.

Brady, Sister Mary Teresa, ed. (1954). See *Pore Caitif*.

(1980). Rolle's *Form of Living* and *The Pore Caitif*. *Traditio*, 36, pp. 426–435.

(1981). The seynt and his boke: Rolle's *Emendatio Vitae* and *The Pore Caitif*. *Mystics Quarterly*, 7, pp. 20–31.

(1983). Rolle and the pattern of tracts in *The Pore Caitif*. *Traditio*, 39, pp. 456–465.

Bradley, Ritamary (1981). See Lagorio, Valerie Marie.

Burrow, John (1986). *The Ages of Man: A Study in Medieval Writing and Thought*. Oxford, Clarendon Press.

Butler, Cuthbert (1927). *Western Mysticism: The Teaching of SS Augustine, Gregory and Bernard on Contemplation and the Contemplative Life: Neglected Chapters in the History of Religion*. 2nd ed. London, Constable.

Bynum, Caroline Walker (1987). *Holy Feast and Holy Fast: The Religious Significance of Food to Medieval Women*. The New Historicism: Studies in Cultural Poetics. Berkeley, California University Press.

Cabusset, André (1952). La Dévotion au nom de Jésus dans l'église d'occident. *La Vie Spirituelle*, 86, pp. 46–69.

Callanan, Marion, ed. (1977). See Rolle, Richard, *English Psalter*.

Cantor, Peter. See Peter Cantor.

Carlson, David Richard (1983). Structural similarities between the literatures of mysticism and *fin' amors*. Dissertation. University of Toronto.

Carney, Ellen, ed. (1980). See Rolle, Richard, *English Psalter*.

Cassian. *Collationes*. *In* PL 49.

Cavallerano, Jerry D., ed. (1976). See Rolle, Richard, *English Psalter*.

Chambers, R.W. (1932). Introduction to *Nicholas Harpsfield: The Life and Death of Sir Thomas More*, ed. E.V. Hitchcock and R.W. Chambers. EETS (os), 186. (Reprinted in part as *On the Continuity of English Prose from Alfred to More and His School*, EETS [os], 191A.)

Charland, Th.-M. (1936). *Artes Praedicandi: Contribution à l'histoire de la rhétorique au moyen âge*. Publications de l'Institut d'Etudes Médiévales d'Ottawa, 7. Paris, Vrin.

Chaucer, Geoffrey. *Works*, ed. F.N. Robinson. 2nd ed. Boston, Houghton Mifflin (1957).

Christina of Markyate. *The Life of Christina of Markyate, a Twelfth-Century Recluse*, ed. C.H. Talbot. Oxford: Clarendon Press (1959).

Cicero, *De Inventione*. In *De Inventione, De Optimo Genere Oratorum, Topica*, ed. H.M. Hubbell. The Loeb Classical Library. London, Heinemann (1959).

Cicero, attrib. See *Rhetorica ad Herennium*.

Clark, J.P.H. (1978). Walter Hilton and 'liberty of spirit'. *Downside Review*, 96, pp. 61–78.

(1979). Action and contemplation in Walter Hilton. *Downside Review*, 97, pp. 258–274.

(1983). Richard Rolle, a theological re-assessment. *Downside Review*, 101, pp. 15–29.

(1986). Richard Rolle as biblical commentator. *Downside Review*, 104, pp. 165–213.

Clay, Rotha M. (1914). *The Hermits and Anchorites of England*. London, Methuen.

The Cloud of Unknowing and Related Treatises, ed. Phyllis Hodgson. *Analecta Cartusiana*, 3 (1982).

Bibliography

Colledge, Edmund (1956). *Epistola Solitarii ad Reges*: Alphonse of Pecha as organizer of Birgittine and Urbanist propaganda. *Mediaeval Studies*, 17, pp. 19–49.

Colledge, Eric (1958). Review of Arnould 1957. *Medium Aevum*, 27, p. 204.

Compendium Theologicae Veritatis. See Hugh of Strasbourg.

Comper, Frances M.M., ed. (1916). *Contemplations of the Dread and Love of God*. London, Washbourne.

—— (1928). *The Life of Richard Rolle, Together with an Edition of his English Lyrics*. London, Dent.

Constable, Giles (1971). Twelfth-century spirituality and the late Middle Ages. *Medieval and Renaissance Studies*, 5, pp. 27–60.

Contemplacyons of the Drede and Loue of God. London, Wynkyn de Worde (1506). (Reprinted in Horstmann 1895–1896, vol. 2, pp. 72–105. (*))

Copeland, Rita (1984). Richard Rolle and the rhetorical theory of the levels of style. *In* Glasscoe 1984, pp. 55–80.

Curtius, Ernst Robert (1948). *European Literature and the Latin Middle Ages*. London, Routledge and Kegan Paul. (Originally published in German. English ed. published 1953).

Daly, John Philip (1984). *See* Rolle, Richard, *Judica Me*.

Damian, Peter. *See* Peter Damian.

Dante Alighieri. *Vita Nuova*, ed. Fredi Chiappelli. Milan, Mursia (1965).

—— *Il Convivio*, ed. Maria Simonelli. Bologna, Riccardo Patrona (1966).

—— *The Divine Comedy*, ed. Charles S. Singleton. 6 vols. Princeton University Press (1977).

—— *Epistle to Can Grande*. In *Opere Minori*, vol. 2, Pier Vincenzo Mengaldo, pp. 598–643. Milano, La Letteratura Italiana, Storia e Testi (1981).

Darwin, Francis D. (1916). *The English Mediaeval Recluse*. 2nd ed. London, SPCK (1944).

Davis, Virginia (1985). The rule of St Paul, the first hermit, in late-medieval England. *In* Sheils 1985, pp. 203–214.

Davlin, Mary (1981). *Kynde knowyng* as a Middle English equivalent for 'wisdom' in *Piers Plowman* B. *Medium Aevum*, 50, pp. 5–17.

Deanesley, Margaret (1915). *See* Rolle, Richard, *Incendium Amoris*.

Denis, Leopold, ed. and trans. (1927). *Du Péché à l'amour divin ou l'Amendment du pécheur*. Editions de la Vie Spirituelle. Paris, Declée.

Dictionnaire de droit canonique, ed. R. Naz *et al.* 7 vols. Paris, Librairie Letonzey (1935–1965).

Dictionnaire de spiritualité, ascétique et mystique. In progress (12 vols. so far published). Paris, Beauchesne (1932–).

Disce Mori. Compilation of Rolle, Hilton . . . Unprinted.

Dolan, James C. (1968). See *Super Psalmum Vicesimum*.

Doyle, Ian (1953). A survey of the origins and circulation of theological writings in English in the fourteenth, fifteenth and early sixteenth century. Dissertation, Cambridge University.

—— (1981). Carthusian participation in the movement of works of Richard Rolle between England and the other parts of Europe in the fourteenth and fifteenth centuries. *Analecta Cartusiana*, 55/2, pp. 157–166.

Dulcis Ihesu Memoria. In Wilmart 1943.

Dunning, T.P. (1956). The structure of the B-text of *Piers Plowman*. *Review of English Studies*, n.s. 7, pp. 225–237.

Edmund of Abingdon. *Speculum Religiosorum* and *Speculum Ecclesie*, ed. Helen P. Forshaw. Auctores Britannici Medii Aevii, III. London, Published for The British Academy by Oxford University Press (1973).

Bibliography

Edwards, A.S.G., ed. (1984). *Middle English Prose: A Critical Guide to Major Authors and Genres*. New Brunswick, N.J., Rutgers University Press.

Ellis, Roger (1982). The choices of the translator in the late Middle English period. *In* Glasscoe 1982, pp. 18–46.

Elwyn, Verier (1930). *Richard Rolle, A Christian Sannyasi*. The Baktas of the World, no. 3. Madras, Christian Literature Society for India.

Esposito, Lisa, ed. (1982). *Orationes Excerpte de Diversis Tractatibus quos Composuit Beatus Ricardus Heremita ad Honorem Nominis Ihesu*, edited from Cambridge University Library MS Kk.vi.20. Dissertation, University of York.

Everett, Dorothy (1922–1923). The Middle English prose Psalter. *Modern Language Review*, 17, pp. 217–27, 337–50; 18, pp. 381–393.

De Excellentia Contemplationis. See Rolle, Richard.

Faber, Johann, ed. (1535). *D. Ricardi Pampolitani Eremitae . . . de Emendatio Peccatoris Opusculum . . .*, Cologne, apud Melchiorem Novesianum. (*See* Allen, pp. 12–13.)

— ed. (1536). *D. Richardi Pampolitani Anglosaxonis Eremitae . . . in Psalterium Davidicum . . .*, Cologne, ex officina Melchioris Novesiani. (*See* Allen, pp. 13–14; Moyes 1988, vol. 2, p. 120.)

Farmer, Hugh (1957). The meditations of the monk of Farne. *Analecta Monastica*, 4, pp. 141–245.

— (1961). *The Meditations of a Fourteenth-Century Monk, Translated by a Benedictine of Stambrook*. London, Darton, Longmann and Todd.

de Ford, Sarah (1980). Mystical union in the *Melos Amoris* of Richard Rolle. *In* Glasscoe 1980, pp. 173–201.

— (1986). The use and function of alliteration in the *Melos Amoris* of Richard Rolle. *Mystics Quarterly*, 12, pp. 59–66.

Freemantle, W.T. (1911). *A Bibliography of Sheffield and Vicinity*, Section 1 (to the end of 1700). Sheffield, Pawson and Brailsford.

Geoffrey of Vinsauf. *Poetria Nova*, trans. Margaret F. Nims. Toronto, Pontifical Institute of Mediaeval Studies (1967).

— *Poetria Nova*, ed. Edmond Faral. *Les Arts poétiques du XIIe et du XIIIe siècle: recherches et documents sur la technique littéraire du moyen âge*. Paris, H. Champion (1962).

Gerald of Liège. *Quinque Incitamenta ad Deum Amandum Ardenter*, ed. A. Wilmart. *Analecta Reginensia* (1933), pp. 181–247.

Ghellinck, J. de (1948). Iuventus, Gravitas, Senectus. In *Studia Mediaevalia in Honorem admodum Reverendi Patris Raymundi Josephi Martin*, pp. 39–59. Bruges.

— (1954). *L'Essor de la littérature latine au XIIe siècle*. Museum Lessianum. Section Historique, 4–5. Brussels, Desclée de Brouwer.

Gillespie, Vincent (1980). *Doctrina* and *predicacio*: the design and function of some pastoral manuals. *Leeds Studies in English*, n. s. 11, pp. 36–50.

— (1981). The literary form of the Middle English pastoral manual with particular reference to the *Speculum Christiani* and some related texts. Dissertation, Oxford University.

— (1982). Mystic's foot: Rolle and affectivity. *In* Glasscoe 1982, pp. 199–230.

— (1983). The *Cibus Anime*, book 3: a guide for contemplatives? *Analecta Cartusiana*, 35: 3, pp. 90–119.

— (1984). *Lukynge in haly bukes: lectio* in some late medieval spiritual miscellanies. *Analecta Cartusiana*, 106, pp. 1–27.

— (1987). Strange images of death: the Passion in later medieval English devotional and mystical writing. *Analecta Cartusiana*, 117, pp. 111–159.

Bibliography

Glasscoe, Marion, ed. (1980). *The Medieval Mystical Tradition in England: Papers Read at the Exeter Symposium, July 1980.* Exeter University Press.

ed. (1982). *The Medieval Mystical Tradition in England: Papers Read at Dartington Hall, July 1982.* Exeter University Press.

ed. (1984). *The Medieval Mystical Tradition in England: Papers Read at Dartington Hall, July 1984.* Cambridge, Brewer.

Glossa Ordinaria. In PL 113–114.

Godden, Malcolm (1984). Plowmen and hermits in *Piers Plowman. Review of English Studies*, n.s. 35, pp. 129–163.

(1990). *The Making of Piers Plowman.* London: Longman.

Saint Godfric. *See* Reginald of Durham.

Guigo I. *Consuetudines. In* PL 153, cols. 631–760.

Guigo II. *Liber de Exercitio Cellae. In* PL 153, cols. 799–884.

Hackett B. (1956). The spiritual life of the Augustinian friars in the fourteenth century. In *Sanctus Augustinus Spiritualis Vitae Magister.* Settimana Internazionale di Spiritualità Agostiniana. Rome (1956).

Hadewijch. *The Complete Works*, trans. Columba Hart. The Classics of Western Spirituality. Mahwah, Paulist Press (1980).

Hali Meiðhad, ed. Bella Millett. EETS (os), 284 (1982).

Hardwick, J.C. (1916–1917). A medieval anti-scholastic. *Modern Churchman*, 6, pp. 251–255.

Heseltine, George C. (1930). *Selected Works of Richard Rolle.* London, Longmans, Green and Co.

(1932a). Richard Rolle. *The Times Literary Supplement*, 31, p. 271.

(1932b). *Great Yorkshiremen.* London, Longmans, Green and Co.

Hilton, Walter. *Walter Hilton's Latin Writings*, ed. John P.H. Clark and Cheryl Taylor. 2 vols. in *Analecta Cartusiana*, 124 (1987).

Of Angels' Song. In Horstmann 1895–1896, vol. 1, pp. 175–182.

On the Mixed Life, ed. Sarah Ogilvie-Thomson. Salzburg Studies in English Literature: Elizabethan and Renaissance Studies, 92: 18. Salzburg, Institut für Anglistik und Amerikanistik (1986).

The Scale of Perfection, ed. Evelyn Underhill. London, Watkins (1923).

Hodgson, Geraldine, ed. (1910). *The Form of Living and Other Prose Treatises of Richard Rolle of Hampole.* London, Baker.

ed. (1923). *Some Minor Works of Richard Rolle with the Privity of the Passion by S. Bonaventura.* London, Watkins.

(1926). *The Sanity of Mysticism: A Study of Richard Rolle.* London, Faith Press.

ed. (1929a). *Richard Rolle's Version of the Penitential Psalms.* London, Faith Press.

ed. (1929b). *Rolle and 'Our Daily Work'.* London, Faith Press.

Hodgson, Phyllis (1982). See *Cloud of Unknowing.*

Horace. *Carmina. In Odes and Epodes*, ed. and trans. C.E. Bennett. Loeb Classical Library. London, Heinemann (1914).

Horstmann, Carl, ed. (1895–1896). *Yorkshire Writers: Richard Rolle of Hampole, an English Father of the Church, and His Followers.* 2 vols. London, Swan Sonnenschein & Co.

von Hügel, Friedrich (1909). *The Mystical Element in Religion.* 2 vols. London, Dent.

Hugh of Folieto. *De Claustro Animae. In* PL 175, 1017–1184.

Hugh of St Victor. *De Laude Caritatis. In* PL 176, cols. 968–976.

De Sacramentis Christianae Fidei. In PL 176, cols. 173–617.

Hugh of Strasbourg. *Compendium Theologicae Veritatis. In* Bonaventure, *Opera Omnia* (ed. Peltier), vol. 8, pp. 60–246.

343

Hughes, Jonathan (1988). *Pastors and Visionaries: Religion and Secular Life in Late-Medieval Yorkshire.* Woodbridge, Boydell.
Hussey, S.S. (1956). Langland, Hilton and the three lives. *Review of English Studies,* n.s. 7, pp. 132–150.
Innocent III. *De Miseria Condicionis Humane,* ed. Robert E. Lewis. The Chaucer Library. Athens, University of Georgia Press (1978).
James of Milan. *Stimulus Amoris. In* Bonaventure, *Opera Omnia* (ed. Peltier), vol. 12, pp. 631–703.
James, S.B. (1941). Richard Rolle, Englishman. *Christian Reivew,* n.s. 20, pp. 31–44.
——— (1949). Medieval individualist. *New Catholic World,* 169, pp. 440–445.
James William (1902). *The Varieties of Religious Experience.* Gifford Lectures. London, Longmans, Green and Co.
Jennings, Margaret (1975). Richard Rolle and the three degrees of love. *Downside Review,* 93, pp. 193–200.
John of Ford. *Life of Wulfric of Hazlebury,* ed. Maurice Bell. Somerset Record Society, 47 (1933).
John of Hoveden. *Philomena,* ed. Clemens Blume. Hymnologische Beiträge. Leipzig, Reisland (1930).
——— *Poems,* ed. F.J.E. Raby. Surtees Society, 154. Durham (1929).
John Pecham. *Philomela. In* Bonaventure, *Opera Omnia* (ed. Peltier), vol. 12, pp. 162–166.
Jolliffe, P.S. (1974). *A Check-List of Middle English Prose Writings of Spiritual Guidance.* Toronto, Pontifical Institute of Mediaeval Studies.
Julian of Norwich. *A Revelation of Love.* Published as *A Book of Showings to the Anchoress Julian of Norwich,* ed. Edmund Colledge and James Walsh. 2 vols. Studies and Texts, 35. Toronto, Pontifical Institute of Mediaeval Studies (1978).
Kempe, Margery. *The Book of Margery Kempe,* ed. Sanford B. Meech and Hope Emily Allen. EETS (os), 212 (1940).
Knowles, David (1961). *The English Mystical Tradition.* London, Burns and Oates.
Lagorio, Valerie (1987). Mystics, English. *The Dictionary of the Middle Ages,* vol. 7. New York, Scribner.
Lagorio, Valerie Marie, and Bradley, Ritamary (1981). *The Fourteenth-Century English Mystics: A Comprehensive Annotated Bibliography.* New York, Garland.
Langland, William. *Piers Plowman,* ed. Walter W. Skeat. 2 vols. Oxford University Press (1886). [References to A and B only are to this edition.]
——— *Piers Plowman, by William Langland: An Edition of the C-Text,* ed. Derek Pearsall. York Medieval Texts. London, Arnold (1978).
Leclerq, Jean (1946). Le Magistère du prédicateur au xiiie siècle. *Archives d'histoire doctrinale et littéraire du moyen âge,* 21, pp. 105–147.
——— ed. (1958). Le Poème de Payen Bolotin contre les faux ermites. *Revue Bénédictine,* 68, pp. 52–84.
Lehmann, Max (1936). *Untersuchungen zur mystischen Terminologie Richard Rolles.* Jena, Gustav Neuenhahn.
Liegey, Gabriel (1954). The rhetorical aspects of Richard Rolle's *Melum Contemplativorum.* Dissertation, Columbia University.
——— ed. (1956). *See* Rolle, Richard, *Canticum Amoris.*
——— ed. (1957). *See* Rolle, Richard, 'Carmen Prosaicum'.
Lindkvist, Harald, ed. *Richard Rolle's Meditatio de Passione Domini According to MS Uppsala C.494.* Uppsala, Akademiska Bokhandeln, 1917. (An Appendix on pp. 73ff. contains a version of the *Officium* in Uppsala c.621.)

Bibliography

Lochrie, Karma (1986). *The Book of Margery Kempe*: the marginal woman's quest for literary authority. *Journal of Medieval and Renaissance Studies*, 16, pp. 33–55.

Lombard, Peter. *See* Peter Lombard.

Love, Nicholas. *The Mirrour of the Blessyd Lyf of Jesu Christ*, ed. Lawrence F. Powell. Oxford, Clarendon Press (1908).

Madigan, Mary F. (1982). *The Passio Domini Theme in the Works of Richard Rolle: His Personal Contribution in its Religious, Cultural, and Literary Context.* Salzburg Studies in English Literature: Elizabethan and Renaissance Studies, 79. Salzburg, Institut für Anglistik und Amerikanistik.

Madon, Y., ed. (1950). Le *Commentaire* de Richard Rolle sur les premiers versets du *Cantique des Cantiques. Mélanges des Sciences Religieuses*, 7, pp. 311–325. (Part of *Super Canticum Canticorum.*)

Manly, John M. (1926). Chaucer and the rhetoricians. Warton Lecture on Poetry. *Proceedings of the British Academy*, 12, pp. 95–113.

Marzac, Nicole (1968). *Richard Rolle de Hampole 1300–1349: Vie et œuvres suiviés du Tractatus super Apocalypsim.* Paris, Librairie Philosophique J. Vrin.

del Mastro, M.L., trans. (1981). *The Fire of Love and the Mending of Life, by Richard Rolle.* New York, Doubleday.

Meadows, George D. (1928). The father of English mysticism: Richard Rolle of Hampole, 1290–1349. *New Catholic World*, 126, pp. 456–460.

Meditationes Piissimae. In PL 184, cols. 485–508.

Meditationes Vitae Christi. In Bonaventure, *Opera Omnia* (ed. Peltier), vol. 12, pp. 509–630.

Methley, Richard. *Refectorium Salutis*, ed. James Hogg. *Analecta Cartusiana*, 55.1, pp. 203–238 (1981). (See also *Analecta Cartusiana*, 64.2, a facsimile of MS Trinity College, Cambridge 0.2.56.)

    To Hew Heremyte a Pystyl of Solytary Lyfe Nowadays, ed. James Hogg. *Analecta Cartusiana*, 31 (1977), pp. 91–119.

Middendorf, Heinrich (1888). *Studien zu Richard Rolle von Hampole unter besonderer Berücksichtigung seiner Psalmkommentar.* Magdeburg: Friese und Fuhrmann.

Minnis, A.J. (1977). Discussions of 'authorial role' and 'literary form' in late-medieval scriptural exegesis. *Beiträge zur Geschichte der deutschen Sprache und Literatur*, 99, pp. 37–65.

    (1979a). Late-medieval discussion of *compilatio* and the role of the *compilator. Beiträge zur Geschichte der deutschen Sprache und Literatur*, 101, pp. 385–421.

    (1979b). Literary theory in the discussions of *formae tractandi* by medieval theologians. *New Literary History*, 11, pp. 133–46.

    (1984/1988) *Medieval Theory of Authorship: Scholastic Literary Attitudes in the Later Middle Ages.* 1st ed. London, Scolar Press. 2nd ed. Aldershot, Wildwood House.

    (1986). Chaucer's pardoner and the 'office of preacher'. In *Intellectuals and Writers in Fourteenth-Century Europe: The J.A.W. Bennett Memorial Lectures, Perugia, 1984*, ed. Piero Boitani and Anna Torti. Tübingen, Günter Narr Verlag.

Minnis, A.J. and Scott, A.B., eds., with the assistance of Wallace, David (1988). *Medieval Literary Theory and Criticism*, c. 1100–c. 1375: The Commentary Tradition. Oxford, Clarendon.

Misyn, Richard. *See* Rolle, Richard, *Incendium Amoris.*

Moorman, F.W. (1914). Richard Rolle, the Yorkshire mystic. *Transactions of the Yorkshire Dialect Society*, 3, pp. 89–106.

Monk of Farne. See Farmer, Hugh.

Moyes, Malcolm (1984). The manuscripts and early printed editions of Richard

Rolle's *Expositio super Novem Lectiones Mortuorum*. In Glasscoe 1984, pp. 81–103.

ed. (1988). *Richard Rolle's Expositio super Novem Lectiones Mortuorum: An Introduction and Contribution Towards a Critical Edition*. 2 vols. Salzburg Studies in English Literature: Elizabethan and Renaissance Studies, 92: 12. Salzburg, Institut für Anglistik und Amerikanistik.

Murray, Elizabeth, ed. (1958). See *Super Canticum Canticorum*.

Newton, Sandra, ed. (1976). See Rolle, Richard, *English Psalter*.

Nims, Margaret F., trans. (1967). See Geoffrey of Vinsauf.

Noetinger, Maurice (1926). The biography of Richard Rolle. *The Month*, 147, pp. 22–30.

ed. and trans. (1928). *Le Feu d'amour, le modèle de la vie parfaite, le Pater, par Richard Rolle l'ermite de Hampole*. Collection Mystiques Anglais. Tours, Maison Alfred Mâme.

The Officium et Miracula of Richard Rolle of Hampole, ed. Reginald M. Woolley. London, SPCK (1919).

Ogilvie-Thomson, S.J., ed. (1980). An edition of the English works in MS Longleat 29, excluding *The Parson's Tale*. Dissertation, Oxford University.

ed. (1988). *Richard Rolle: Prose and Verse*. EETS (os), 293.

Oliger, P.L., ed. (1928). Regulae tres reclusorum et eremitarum angliae saec. xiii–xiv. *Antonianum*, 3, pp. 151–190 and 299–320.

ed. (1934). Regula reclusorum angliae et quaestiones tres de vita solitaria saec. xiii–xiv. *Antonianum*, 9, pp. 37–84 and 243–268.

Ommaney, George Druce Wynne (1897). *Early History of the Athanasian Creed*. London, Rivingtons.

Owst, Gerald R. (1926). *Preaching in Medieval England*. Cambridge University Press.

Pankhurst, Christopher Keith (1976). The active life, the contemplative life and the mixed life. Dissertation, York University.

Pantin, W.A. (1955). *The English Church in the Fourteenth Century*. Cambridge University Press.

Patch, Howard R. (1928). Richard Rolle, hermit and mystic. *American Church Monthly*, 28, pp. 32–38, 108–114.

(1929). Review of Allen (*Writings Ascribed*). *Speculum*, 4, pp. 469–471.

Patterson, Lee (1987). *Negotiating the Past*. Madison, University of Wisconsin Press.

Payen Bolotin. See Leclerq 1958.

Pepler, Conrad (1948). Love of the world. *Life of the Spirit*, 2, pp. 540–546.

(1958). *The English Religious Heritage*. London, Blackfriars Publications.

(1959). English spiritual writers III: Richard Rolle. *Christian Review*, 44, pp. 78–89.

Perry, G.G., ed. (1966). *English Prose Treatises of Richard Rolle of Hampole*. EETS (os), 20.

Peter the Cantor. *Verbum Abbreviatum*. In PL 205, cols. 23–370.

Peter Damian. *De Contemptu Saeculi*. In PL 145, cols. 251–292.

Vita Sancti Romualdi. In PL 144, cols. 953–1008.

Peter Lombard. *Sententiae in IV Libris Distinctae*. 3 vols. Spicilegium Bonaventurianum, vol. 4 and 5, Grottaferrata (Romae), Editiones Collegii S. Bonaventurae ad Claras Aquas (1971–1981).

Commentarium in Psalmos. In PL 191, cols. 61–1296.

Petrarch, Francesco. *Rime sparse*. In *Petrarch's Lyric Poems: The 'Rime sparse' and Other Lyrics*, ed. and trans. Robert M. Durling. Cambridge, Mass., Harvard University Press (1976).

Bibliography

Piers Plowman. See Langland, William.

Pomerius, Julius. *De Vita Contemplativa. In* PL 59, cols. 415–520.

The Pore Caitif, ed. Sister Mary Teresa Brady. Dissertation, Fordham University (1954).

Porete, Marguerite. *Speculum Simplicium Animarum / Le Mirouer des simples ames,* ed. P. Verdeyen and Romana Guarnieri. Corpus Christianorum, Continuatio Medievalis, 69 (1986).

Porter, Mary Louise (1929). *See* Rolle, Richard, *Latin Psalter.*

The Pricke of Conscience, ed. Richard Morris. The Philosophical Society. Berlin, A. Asher (1863).

Princeton Encyclopedia of Poetry and Poetics, ed. Alex Preminger etc. 2nd ed. Princeton, Princeton University Press (1974).

Raby, F.J.E., ed. (1929). *See* John of Hoveden, *Poems.*

Reginald of Durham. *Libellus de Vita et Miraculis S. Godfrici,* ed. J. Stevenson. Surtees Society, 20 (1845).

Regula Heremitarum. In Oliger 1928, pp. 299–320.

The Remedy Ayenst the Troubles of Temptacyons. London,Wynkyn de Worde (1508).

Renaudin Paul (1938). Le Dénouement de l'amour dans la vie de Richard Rolle. *La Vie Spirituelle,* 61, pp. 143–162.

— (1940). Richard Rolle, poète de l'amour divin. *La Vie Spirituelle,* 62, pp. 65–80.

— (1945). *Quatre mystiques anglais.* Paris, Editions du Cerf.

— ed. (1957). *Mystiques anglais: Richard Rolle, Juliane de Norwich, Le Nuage de l'inconnaissance, Walter Hilton.* Paris, Aubier.

Rhetorica Ad Herennium, ed. Harry Caplan. In *[Cicero] Ad C. Herennium de Ratione Dicendi.* The Loeb Classical Library. London, Heinemann (1968).

Richard of St Victor. *Benjamin Major. In* PL 196, cols. 64–192.

Benjamin Major. In PL 196, cols. 1–64.

De Quattuor Gradibus Violentae Caritatis. Textes Philosophiques du Moyen Age, 3. Paris, Librairie Philosophique J. Vrin (1955).

Riehle, Wolfgang (1981). *The Midddle English Mystics.* London, Routledge, Kegan and Paul 1981. (First published in German, 1977.)

Robert of Basevorn. *Forma Praedicandi. In* Charland 1936, pp. 233–323.

Robert of Knaresborough. *Vita [Recentior] Sancti Roberti iuxta Knaresburgum,* ed. Paul Grosjem. *Analecta Bollandiana,* 57 (1939), pp. 364–400.

Robertson, D.W. and Huppé, B.F. (1957). *Piers Plowman and Scriptural Tradition.* Princeton University Press.

Rodriquez, Zane José, ed. (1980). *See* Rolle, Richard, *English Psalter.*

Rolle, Richard. *The Bee. In English Writings,* pp. 54–56.

Canticum Amoris, ed. Gabriel Liegey (1956). In *Traditio,* 12, pp. 369–91.

'Carmen Prosaicum', ed. Gabriel Liegey (1957). In *Medieval Studies,* 19, pp. 15–36.

The Commandment. In Ogilvie-Thomson 1988, pp. 34–39.

Contra Amatores Mundi, ed. Paul F. Theiner. Berkeley, University of California Press (1968).

De Excellentia Contemplationis. Unprinted compilation of several Rolle works.

Desire and Delight. In Ogilvie-Thomson 1988, p. 40.

Ego Dormio. In Ogilvie-Thomson 1988, pp. 26–33.

Emendatio Vitae. See Speculum Spiritualium. Rolle, Richard. *Emendatio Vitae. In* Faber 1536, ff. 135r.–142v. (*)

Enconium Nominis Ihesu. Part of *Super Canticum Canticorum.* ME translation in Horstmann 1895–1896, vol. 1, pp. 186–191.

English Psalter, ed. H.R. Bramley. *The Psalter or Psalms of David and Certain*

Bibliography

Canticles, with a Translation and Exposition in English by Richard Rolle of Hampole. Oxford, Clarendon Press (1884). (*)

English Psalter, Prologue through Psalm 15, ed. Sandra Newton. Dissertation, Fordham University (1976).

English Psalter, Psalms 31–45, ed. Jerry D. Cavallerano. Dissertation, Fordham University (1976).

English Psalter, Psalms 46–60, ed. Marion Callanan. Dissertation, Fordham University (1977).

English Psalter, Psalms 61–75 (with an introductory essay on Rolle and the tradition of psalm commentary), ed. Zane José Rodriguez. Dissertation, Fordham University (1980).

English Psalter, Psalms 91–105 (with an introductory essay on Rolle's style), ed. Ellen Carney. Dissertation, Fordham University (1980).

The Form of Living. In Ogilvie-Thomson 1988, pp. 1–25.

Ghostly Gladness. In Ogilvie-Thomson 1988, p. 41.

Incendium Amoris, ed. Margaret Deanesley. Manchester University Press (1915). (*)

Incendium Amoris, trans. Richard Misyn, ed. Ralph Harvey. *The Fire of Love and the Mending of Life or The Rule of Living of Richard Rolle.* EETS (os), 106 (1896).

Judica Me Deus, ed. John Philip Daly. Elizabethan and Renaissance Studies, 92: 14. Salzburg, Institut für Anglistik und Amerikanistik (1984). (Unrevised version of Dissertation, North Carolina University, 1961.)

Latin Psalter. ed. Mary Louise Porter (from Faber 1536 without reference to the MSS). *Latin Commentary on the Psalms.* Dissertation, Cornell University (1929).

Liber de Amore Dei contra Amatores Mundi. See *Contra Amatores Mundi.*

Lyrics. In Ogilvie-Thomson 1988, pp. 42–63.

Meditation A. In Ogilvie-Thomson 1988, pp. 64–68.

Meditation B. In Ogilvie-Thomson 1988, pp. 69–83.

Melos Amoris, ed. E.J.F. Arnould. Oxford, Blackwell (1957).

Oleum Effusum. A compilation from *Incendium Amoris* and *Super Canticum Canticorum.* Unprinted.

The Seven Gifts of the Holy Spirit. In Horstmann 1895–1896, vol. 1, pp. 196–197.

Super Apocalypsim. In Marzac 1968, pp. 118–173.

Super Canticum Canticorum, ed. Elizabeth Murray. Dissertation, Fordham University (1958).

Super Magnificat. Unprinted. *See* Allen, pp. 192–193. Quotations are from MS BL Add. 24661.

Super Mulierem Fortem. Unprinted. See Allen, pp. 159–160. Quotations are from MS Emmanuel 35.

Super Lectiones Mortuorum. Published as *Explanationes in Job.* Oxford, Theoderic Rood (?1483). (*See* Moyes 1988, vol. 2, pp. 118–119.)

Super Lectiones Mortuorum. Published as *Explanationes in Job.* Paris, Bernard Rembolt (1510). (*See* Moyes 1988, vol. 2, pp. 119–120.)

Super Lectiones Mortuorum. In Moyes 1988, vol. 2, pp. 124–283. (*)

Super Orationem Dominicam. In Faber 1536, ff. 145v.–146v.

Super Psalmum Vicesimum, ed. James C. Dolan. Dissertation, University of Illinois (1968). Published (in revised edition) by Edward Mellon Press (Lewiston, 1991); references are to thesis edition.

Super Symbolum Apostolorum. In Faber 1536, ff. 136v.–140v.

Rolle, Richard (?) *Super Symbolum Athanasii. In* Faber 1536, ff. 141v.–153r.

Bibliography

Super Threnos Jeremiae. In Faber 1536, ff. 123r.–129v.

Ten Commandments. In Horstmann 1895–1896, vol. 1, pp. 195–196.

Ross, Woodburn O., ed. (1940). *Middle English Sermons.* EETS (os), 209.

Rouse, Richard H. and Mary A. (1979). *Preachers, Florilegia and Sermons: Studies on the Manipulus Florum of Thomas of Ireland.* Studies and Texts, 47. Toronto, Pontifical Institute of Mediaeval Studies.

Rousselet, P. (1908). Pour le problème de l'amour au moyen âge. *Beiträge zur Geschichte der Philosophie (und Theologie) des Mittelalters,* ed. C. Baeumker, 6. Münster.

Russell, Kenneth C. (1978). Reading Richard Rolle. *Spirituality Today,* 30, pp. 65–80.

Ruusbroec. *The Spiritual Espousals,* trans. James A. Wiseman. The Classics of Western Spirituality. Mahwah, Paulist Press (1985).

Rygiel, Dennis (1978). Structures and style in Rolle's *The Form of Living. Fourteenth-Century English Mystics Newsletter,* 4/1, pp. 6–15.

Sargent, Michael (1976). The transmission by the English Carthusians of some late-medieval spiritual writings. *The Journal of Ecclesiastical History,* 27, pp. 225–240.

——— (1981). Contemporary criticism of Richard Rolle. *Analecta Cartusiana,* 55: 1, pp. 160–205.

——— (1984a). Minor devotional writings. *In* Edwards 1984, pp. 147–175.

——— (1984b). *James Grenehalgh as Textual Critic.* 2 vols. *Analecta Cartusiana,* 85.

——— (1988). Richard Rolle, Sorbonnist? *Medium Aevum,* 57, pp. 284–289.

Sawyer, Michael E. (1978). *A Bibliographical Index of Five English Mystics.* Pittsburgh, Barbour Library, Pittsburgh Theological Seminary.

Sheils, W.J., (ed.) (1985). *Monks, Hermits and the Ascetic Tradition.* Ecclesiastical History Society: Studies in Church History, vol. 22. Oxford, Blackwell.

Smedick, Lois (1979). Parallelism and pointing in Rolle's rhythmical style. *Mediaeval Studies,* 41, pp. 404–467.

Speculum Christiani, ed. Gustav Holmstedt. EETS (os), 182 (1933).

Speculum Ecclesie. See Edmund of Abingdon.

Speculum Peccatoris. In PL 40, cols. 983–992.

Speculum Spiritualium . . . Additur Insuper et Opusculum Ricardi Hampole de Emendatione Vite . . . Paris, Wolfgang Hopilius (1510). (Mystical compilation which includes passages of Rolle. *See* Allen, pp. 11–12.)

Steele, Francis J. (1979). Definitions and depictions of the active life in Middle English literature of the thirteenth, fourteenth and fifteenth centuries, including special reference to *Piers Plowman.* Dissertation, Oxford University.

Stimulus Amoris. See James of Milan.

Stock, Brian (1983). *The Implications of Literacy: Written Language and Models of Interpretation in the Eleventh and Twelfth Centuries.* Princeton University Press.

Szittya, Penn R. (1977). The anti-fraternal tradition in Middle English literature. *Speculum,* 52, pp. 287–313.

Taavitsainen, Irma (1990). Ave Maria: a meditation connected with Richard Rolle in Uppsala MS 17.c.XVII. *Neuphilologische Mitteilungen,* 91, pp. 57–66.

A Talking of the Love of God, ed. M. Salvina Westra. The Hague, Nijhoff (1950).

Theiner, Paul F. ed. (1968). *See* Rolle, Richard, *Contra Amatores Mundi.*

Thomas Aquinas. *Summa Theologica.* In *Opera Omnia,* ed. T.M. Zagliara. Rome, Ad Sanctae Sabinae, Ex Typographia Polyglotta. Vols. 4–12 (1888–1906).

Tractatus ad Severinum de Gradibus Caritatis. In PL 196, cols. 1195–1208.

Underhill, Evelyn (1911). *Mysticism: A Study in the Nature and Development of Man's Spiritual Consciousness.* London, Methuen.

Vandenbroucke, Francois, Les Moniales des Wisques, eds. (1971). *Le Chant d'Amour (Melos Amoris)*. 2 vols. Paris, Editions du Cerf.

Vauchez, André (1981). *La Sainteté en Occident aux derniers siècles du moyen âge, d'après les procès de canonization et les documents hagiographiques*. Rome, Ecole Française.

Vices and Virtues. See *Book of Vices and Virtues*.

Vitae Patrum. In PL 73–74.

Walter of Wimborne. *Marie Carminis*. In *The Poems of Walter of Wimborne*, ed. A.G. Rigg. Studies and Texts, 42. Toronto, Pontifical Institute of Mediaeval Studies (1978).

Walther, Hans (1963). *Proverbia Sententiaeque Latinitatis Medii Aevi*. Carmina Medii Aevi Posterioris Latina, 11/1. Göttingen, Vandenhoeck and Ruprecht.

Warren, Ann K. (1985). *Anchorites and their Patrons in Medieval England*. Berkeley, University of California Press.

Watson, Nicholas (1989a). Richard Rolle as elitist and popularist: the case of *Judica Me*. In *De Cella in Seculum: Religious and Secular Life and Devotion in Late-Medieval England*, ed. Michael G. Sargent, pp. 123–144. Cambridge, Brewer.

(1989b). Translation and self-canonization in Richard Rolle's *Melos Amoris*. In *The Medieval Translator: The Theory and Practice of Translation in the Middle Ages*, ed. Roger Ellis, pp. 167–180. Cambridge, Brewer.

Watts, H.G. (1916). Richard Rolle of Hampole. *New Catholic World*, 103, pp. 798–804.

The Wooing of Our Lord, ed. W. Meredith Thomson. EETS (os), 241 (1958).

Wenzel, Siegfried (1986). *Preachers, Poets and the Early English Lyric*. Princeton University Press.

William of Pagula. *Oculus Sacerdotis*. Unprinted. See Boyle 1955, 1956.

William of St Thierry. *Epistola Aurea*. In *Lettre aux frères du Mont-Dieu*, ed. R. Thomas. 2 vols. Pain de Citeaux 33–34. Chambarand (1968).

Wilmart, A. (1932). *Auteurs spirituels et textes dévots du moyen âge latin*. Reprinted by Etudes Augustiniennes (1971).

(1943). Le 'jubilus' sur le nom de Jésus dit de Saint Bernard. *Ephemerides Liturgicae*, 57, pp. 1–285.

Womack, Sam J., Jr. (1961). The *jubilus* theme in the later writings of Richard Rolle. Dissertation, Duke University.

Woolf, Rosamond (1968). *The English Religious Lyric in the Middle Ages*. Oxford, Clarendon Press.

Wormald, Francis, ed. (1935). *De Passione Secundum Ricardum* (possibly a new work by Richard Rolle). *Laudate*, 13, pp. 37–48.

Wright, Gilbert G. (1963). The definition of love in Richard Rolle of Hampole. Dissertation, University of Wisconsin.

Wulfric of Hazlebury. *See* John of Ford.

Index

abstinence, 45–6, 63, 249–51, 305–6
nn. 24–5, 333–4 n. 14
active life, 9–10, 92–3, 103, 134, 155,
299 nn. 2, 4, 300 n. 15 (*see also*
contemplative life, Martha and
Mary, 'mixed' life, priests, secular)
Aelred, 18, 55, 263, 298, 333 n. 11; *De
Ihesu Puero Duodenni*, 237, 296,
318–19 n. 11; *De Institutis
Inclusarum*, 44, 62, 331–2 n. 4; *De
Spirituali Amicitia*, 117, 296,
312–13 n. 2, 327 n. 2
'Al synnes shal þou hate', 232, 233
Alexander of Hales, 122; *Glossa
in Sententiarum*, 316 n. 25, 327
n. 19; *Quaestiones Disputatae*, 322
n. 26
Alford, John, 39–40, 52, 77, 99, 222, 295
Allen, Hope Emily, xiii, 34–8 *passim*,
43, 195, 222, 227, 229, 269, 273–5,
297, 301 n. 1, 303 n. 13, 305 n. 21,
309 n. 11, 328–9 n. 9, 331–2 n. 4,
334–5 nn. 1–8
Allen, Rosamund, 196, 244, 315 n. 15,
334 n. 1
amicitia, 224–5, 231, 235–6, 249, 327
n. 2
'ancients', the, 25, 140, 175, 205, 323–4
n. 7 (see also *moderni*)
Ancrene Wisse, 62, 63, 223, 225, 230, 236,
237, 239, 242, 310 n. 14, 327 n. 1
angels, 71, 127, 137, 151, 162, 226, 314
nn. 10–11 (*see also* seraphim)
Anselm, 38, 156–8, 198, 324 n. 11;
Orationes sive Meditationes, 18, 65,
120, 122, 308 n. 13, 309 n. 7, 313
n. 6
Anselm of Laon, pseudo-, 68, 296, 308
n. 16, 311 nn. 2–4
Apostle, the, *see* Paul
Aquinas, Thomas, 318 n. 7; *Summa*

Theologica, 12–13, 14, 15–16, 299
n. 6, 300 nn. 11–12, 15, 307
nn. 2–5, 314 n. 10, 316 nn. 19–20,
327 n. 19
Arnould, E. J., 35, 37–40, 52, 195, 309
n. 11, 323 n. 2, 335 n. 9
assertion, 117, 131–2, 137–9, 155–9,
175–6, 179 (see also *audacitas*,
eloquence)
audacitas 136–8, 154, 158–9, 175–6, 178,
266, 323 n. 6 (*see also* assertion)
Augustine, 10, 11, 14, 208, 243, 299
n. 3, 327 n. 20, 329 nn. 13–14, 331
n. 24
aureoles, 12, 17, 169, 184, 300 n. 11, 327
n. 21
authority, 1–27 (*see also* assertion,
eloquence, *experientia*, preaching)

Bassett, *Defensorium*, 261, 263–4, 333
nn. 12–13
Bee, the, 239, 240
Benedict St, see *Benedictine Rule*
Benedictine Rule, 10, 45, 62
Bernard, 18, 55, 66, 72, 169, 198, 263,
267, 307–8 n. 11, 316 n. 20, 321
n. 20; *De Diligendo Deo*, 19–20,
117, 252, 296, 315 n. 14, 319–21
nn. 14–18, 322–3 n. 27; *De
Gradibus Humilitatis et Superbiae*,
117, 309 n. 9, 312–13 n. 2;
*Sermones super Cantica
Canticorum*, 19, 20, 69, 122, 148,
297, 305–6 n. 24, 307 n. 10, 308
n. 17, 312–13 n. 2, 318 n. 9, 319
n. 14
Bernard, pseudo-, *Meditationes
Piissimae*, 55, 197, 199, 210, 237–8,
297, 325 n. 2, 328 n. 8
Bible, *see under separate books and*
Scripture

351

Index